books**online**

Read this book online today:

With SAP PRESS BooksOnline we offer you online access to knowledge from the leading SAP experts. Whether you use it as a beneficial supplement or as an alternative to the printed book, with SAP PRESS BooksOnline you can:

- Access your book anywhere, at any time. All you need is an Internet connection.
- Perform full text searches on your book and on the entire SAP PRESS library.
- Build your own personalized SAP library.

The SAP PRESS customer advantage:

Register this book today at *www.sap-press.com* and obtain exclusive free trial access to its online version. If you like it (and we think you will), you can choose to purchase permanent, unrestricted access to the online edition at a very special price!

Here's how to get started:

1. Visit *www.sap-press.com*.
2. Click on the link for SAP PRESS BooksOnline and login (or create an account).
3. Enter your free trial license key, shown below in the corner of the page.
4. Try out your online book with full, unrestricted access for a limited time!

Your personal free trial **license key**
for this online book is: **5cpt-kb8g-n9qd-37ew**

Dear Reader,

I'm sure you know this situation: You commit to something, and only when you're long past the point of no return, you realize what that project you've signed up for actually demands.

There are a couple of resources out there—printed or in HTML format, for free or on sale—that claim to be a "reference" for SAP transaction codes. But in fact, none of them does the job. When Venki, Martin, Norman, and myself held the first phone conference to discuss the idea of finally delivering something that deserves that name, we ended in a cheerful mood: "Let's do this!"

Well, we did it: The authors researched endless amounts of codes, talked to numerous colleagues, weighed the importance of hundreds of transactions to decide whether to include them in this book or not, and finally explained what all these transactions do. And I, their editor, encouraged them to dig into modules they usually don't work with, pointed out the deadlines, and badgered them with questions and requests for clarifications.

I think I may speak for all of us when saying: We're a little exhausted. But we're also happy, because we delivered a book that we think is unique and that we're sure the readers will find a useful guide in their daily work with the system.

We appreciate your business, and welcome your feedback. Your comments and suggestions are the most useful tools to help us improve our books for you, the reader. We encourage you to visit our website at *www.sap-press.com* and share your feedback about this work.

Thank you for purchasing a book from SAP PRESS!

Florian Zimniak
Publishing Director, SAP PRESS
Galileo Press
Boston, MA
florian.zimniak@galileo-press.com
www.sap-press.com

 **PRESS**

SAP PRESS is a joint initiative of SAP and Galileo Press. The know-how offered by SAP specialists combined with the expertise of the Galileo Press publishing house offers the reader expert books in the field. SAP PRESS features first-hand information and expert advice, and provides useful skills for professional decision-making.

SAP PRESS offers a variety of books on technical and business related topics for the SAP user. For further information, please visit our website: *www.sap-press.com*.

Heinz Forsthuber, Jörg Siebert
SAP ERP Financials User's Guide
2010, 593 pp., hardcover
ISBN 978-1-59229-190-8

Janet Salmon
Controlling with SAP—Practical Guide
2012, 582 pp., hardcover
ISBN 978-1-59229-392-6

Martin Murray
Materials Management with SAP ERP:
Functionality and Technical Configuration
3rd edition 2011, 666 pp., hardcover
ISBN 978-1-59229-358-2

Martin Murray
Warehouse Management with SAP ERP:
Functionality and Technical Configuration
2nd edition 2012, app. 600 pp., hardcover
ISBN 978-1-59229-409-1

Matt Chudy, Luis Castedo
Sales and Distribution in SAP ERP—Practical Guide
2011, 406 pp., hardcover
ISBN 978-1-59229-347-6

Venki Krishnamoorthy, Martin Murray, and Norman Reynolds

SAP® Transaction Codes

Your Quick Reference to Transactions in SAP® ERP

Bonn • Boston

Galileo Press is named after the Italian physicist, mathematician and philosopher Galileo Galilei (1564–1642). He is known as one of the founders of modern science and an advocate of our contemporary, heliocentric worldview. His words *Eppur si muove* (And yet it moves) have become legendary. The Galileo Press logo depicts Jupiter orbited by the four Galilean moons, which were discovered by Galileo in 1610.

Editor Florian Zimniak
Copyeditor Pamela Siska
Cover Design Janina Conrady
Photo Credit Janina Conrady
Layout Design Kelly O'Callaghan
Production Kelly O'Callaghan
Typesetting Publishers' Design and Production Services, Inc.
Printed and bound in Canada

ISBN 978-1-59229-374-2

© 2012 by Galileo Press Inc., Boston (MA)

1st edition 2012

Library of Congress Cataloging-in-Publication Data
Krishnamoorthy, Venki.
SAP transaction codes : your quick reference to T-codes
in SAP ERP / Venki Krishnamoorthy, Martin Murray,
Norman Reynolds. — 1st ed.
p. cm.
Includes index.
ISBN-13: 978-1-59229-374-2
ISBN-10: 1-59229-374-3
1. SAP ERP. 2. Business—Computer programs.
I. Murray, Martin, 1964- II. Reynolds, Norman. III. Title.
HF5548.4.R2K76 2012
658'.0553—dc23
2011027425

FSC
www.fsc.org
MIX
Paper from
responsible sources
FSC® C011825

Contents

Introduction

The functionality of the SAP Business Suite is broken down into more than sixteen thousand individual transactions. Transaction codes (or t-codes) provide an easy way to access this functionality and to accomplish a specific task. By entering the code for a transaction in the command field of the SAP GUI, you can easily navigate to the exact transaction you need without taking the detour via the menu structure of SAP Easy Access. Thus, transaction codes save you valuable time.

This book aims to provide you with a reference for the most commonly used business transactions in SAP ERP. It lists the codes in alphabetical order, including their short text, and gives an explanation as to which functionality the individual transaction provides and what input it requires.

It would be a enormous task to list and explain every one of the sixteen thousand delivered transactions and it is doubtful whether such a book would be helpful or easy to navigate for the reader. Therefore, based on our experience in projects and that of our colleagues, we focus on the most commonly used functional transactions in the following modules of SAP ERP 6.0 Enhancement Pack 4:

- ▶ Financial Accounting
- ▶ Controlling
- ▶ Inventory Management
- ▶ Materials Management
- ▶ Warehouse Management
- ▶ Production Planning
- ▶ Sales and Distribution
- ▶ Plant Maintenance
- ▶ Quality Management
- ▶ Project System
- ▶ Human Capital Management
- ▶ Basis System

Many of these transactions can be accessed by following the menu path in SAP Easy Access or in the IMG (configuration transactions). It is a common practice to bookmark the commonly used transactions as favorites in SAP Easy Access.

Target Audience

This book is written for professionals—including business users, power users, administrators, and SAP consultants—interested in learning about SAP transaction codes and how they can be used in implementing and using SAP solutions. Whether you need a refresher on a transaction in "your" module that you have not used in a while or you want to understand a transaction in a module that you usually do not work in, this book is for you.

Navigating this Book

We organized the transactions based on the modules where they are used. Transaction codes such as SQ01, which are commonly used across all modules, are covered in the Basis System chapter. Within each chapter, the transactions are sorted by their code, in the following order:

▶ Symbols: ., -, _, /

▶ Numbers: 0 – 9

▶ Letters: A – Z

You can search for a particular transaction code by simply browsing the specific module chapter, but the book's extensive index provides you with several more search options:

▶ You can search by transaction code. This is useful if you are not sure which module a specific code belongs to.

▶ You can search by transaction short text. This helps if you know the exact short text but not the code of a specific transaction.

▶ You can search by functionality. If you are looking for a transaction that provides a specific functionality but you know neither the transaction code nor the short text, try searching the index by activity keywords.

Many SAP users are still working with Releases 4.x and SAP ERP 5.0, and some of the transactions became obsolete in SAP ERP 6.0 EhP 4. For such transactions, we specify what the alternative transaction code is.

In SAP ERP, sometimes more than one transaction code is available to execute a particular functionality. In such circumstances, we mention all the various transaction codes.

Here is a quick look at what will be covered in each chapter:

Chapter 1 explains transaction codes in the **Financial Accounting** module, including the following sub modules: Asset Management, General Ledger, Accounts Receivable, Accounts Payable, and Cash and Funds Management. This chapter does not include many treasury or financial supply chain management transactions. The transactions included in the book are intended to meet the organization's external/ legal reporting requirements and control the consistent and structured process for recording financial transactions.

Chapter 2 includes the most common transactions in the following sub modules in the **Controlling** module: Cost and Profit Center Accounting, Internal Order and Product Cost Planning, and Cost Object Controlling and Profitability Analysis. The transactions is this chapter are intended to meet an organization's business requirements for internal and management reporting. The Controlling sub modules and associated transactions facilitate controlling master data, resource planning, recording actual business transactions, and flexible reports and reporting tools.

Chapter 3 explains the transactions associated with **Inventory Management** functionality. The chapter includes transactions for inventory movements, physical inventory, material documents, inventory analysis, and inventory reporting.

Chapter 4 includes the most common transactions in the **Materials Management** module. The chapter includes descriptions for transactions in a number of areas such as material master data, vendor master data, purchasing functionality, invoicing, and creating message outputs.

Chapter 5 explains the transactions associated with the **Warehouse Management** module. The chapter includes descriptions for transactions across the warehouse management component such as warehouse master data, transfer requirements, transfer orders, cycle counting, storage unit management, hazardous materials, and warehouse reporting.

Chapter 6 includes the most common transactions in the **Production Planning** module. The chapter includes descriptions of production planning transactions such as master data, product costing, MRP, forecasting, production orders, process orders, capacity leveling, and Kanban.

Chapter 7 explains the transactions in the **Sales and Distribution** module for major components such as master data for business partners and pricing, sales management (which includes quotes, contracts and sales orders), and shipping and billing. These transactions are intended to meet the business requirements for the sales and distribution of materials and services as part of the supply chain process. For example, the process may start with an organization taking a quote, contract or sales order with automatic checking of inventory levels and production/procurement lead times. Follow-on transactions may result in a delivery document being created to control the shipping process, such as transportation planning and goods issue, and this may also result in recognizing revenue and billing the customer.

Chapter 8 presents transaction codes used in **Plant Maintenance**. For example, the chapter explains transaction codes that can be used to create a Bill of Materials (BOM) or to replace work centers in task lists. Commonly used reports and analyses are explained as well.

Chapter 9 explains transaction codes used in **Quality Management**. In this chapter, we focus on transactions used to create objects related to Quality Management. Usually, you can use these transaction codes to edit or to display these objects as well. (Of course, there are individual transaction codes available to edit and to display these objects.) We also explain transaction codes that can be used to generate reports related to Quality Management.

Chapter 10 presents transactions in the **Projects Systems** module, including Structuring Projects, Planning and Controlling Costs/Revenues, Managing Resources/Materials, Confirming Tasks, Simulating Project Plans and Managing Project Progress/Reporting. Transactions in this chapter are intended to control all tasks in project execution, which requires an organizational form that is specific to the project and that is shared by all departments involved. The projects system transactions typically represent the internal processes of a company, where project goals can be described and activities can be structured.

Chapter 11 provides transaction codes related to **Human Capital Management**. Unlike the rest of the chapters, the HCM chapter has several subsections, organized by functional area, namely Organizational Management, Personnel Administration, Benefits, Time Management, Personnel Development, Enterprise Compensation Management (ECM), SAP Learning Solution (LSO), Travel Management, Performance Management, Succession Management, and Payroll. For transaction codes related to Payroll, we have explained transaction codes that are related to a US Payroll.

In a US Payroll-related transaction code, if you replace the country code 10 with the code designated for your country (for example, 08 for Great Britain), you can obtain the transaction code for your country.

Chapter 12 presents transaction codes related to the **Basis System**. This chapter has the greatest number of transaction codes that are obsolete in EhP 4. We included those transactions to benefit users of SAP systems versions 4.x and ERP 5.0. If a transaction code is obsolete, we specify what the new transaction code is and we mention the relevant SAP Notes as well.

Short Text for Transactions

The short texts for the transactions used in this book were derived from table TSTC. You can access table TSTC using transaction SE16 (Data Browser). Enter the transaction for which you wish to derive the short text in the field TCODE, and click EXECUTE. The short text is displayed as a report output.

Transaction Integration

For new users, it is worth pointing out that SAP is a fully integrated system with optimal processing of all business transactions. Business processes are connected and can replace many segmented structures within a cross-functional organization. Business objects (such as the use of master data) control the flow of data throughout the process. For example, inventory quantities are automatically kept in sync with the flow of values in Financial Accounting. Data collected and posted from external systems such as electronic bank statements also use the same master data (e.g., customers/bank accounts) and posting rules to meet business requirements. This facilitates consistency and synchronization of distributed data.

An example of this integration can be realized in the supply chain process. This process may start with a sales order being received and posted in Order Management, which can then be planned and manufactured by determining the quantity and timing of materials required through a Material Requirements Planning (MRP) run. The MRP run results in either a planned and then production order for production or a purchase requisition for materials to be received in inventory. Logistics can track the movement of goods throughout the supply chain. Simultaneously, Financial Accounting is tracking the values of the goods, verifying the inventory receipt, and issuing a vendor payment. The delivery of the goods according to the

Sales and Operations Plan initiates the customer invoice and the customer payment is received in Financial Accounting.

Copy Model

In SAP, you can create an object by copying an existing object or using an existing object as a reference. This method is commonly referred to as "Copy Model." When you create an object using copy model, the system will automatically generate a new object ID and will copy all the characteristics or specifications of the existing object into the new object. You can change the required characteristics or specifications and then press ENTER to complete the creation of the new object.

While describing the transactions related to CREATE OBJECT, we also describe how to create a new object by copy model. In some transactions, the copy functionality is available as an icon in the menu bar.

Acknowledgments

Venki Krishnamoorthy

This project draws inspiration from the effort and support of many individuals. Without these friends and colleagues, this book would not have been possible. Thank you to my friends at Galileo Press for your guidance, patience, and support. I would especially like to thank Florian Zimniak, who made this book possible. Florian suggested this book's title, helped form this authoring team, and encouraged me to get the words onto the page (once again!).

I would like to say a big "thank you" to my co-authors Martin Murray and Norman Reynolds for their dedication and participation in this project. Their personal sacrifices have ensured that this project is a success, and I have greatly enjoyed being part of this team.

I owe the utmost gratitude to my family, who supported me during the writing of this book. Thank you for your love and patience throughout this project.

I would like to thank my managers Dan Stein, Paul Blaney, and Peter Barby for their support in making this project a reality.

I wish to thank Wayne Harmon, Ercument Ozdemir, Dave MacArthur, Sandeep Bahra, Fernando Altamirano, Greg Newman, Phil Ross, Vittal Agirishetti, Yasmine Abdallah, Sandip Shah, Mohit Singh, Gaye Sopp, and Debbie Moses. Based on their implementation experience, these colleagues suggested the transactions to be included in this book. They also dedicated countless hours to reviewing the chapters and to providing valuable feedback. Without their dedication, this project would not have become a reality.

I hope you find this book informative and easy to read. I hope this book provides new perspectives, introduces you to transactions that you have never used before, and explains practical usage of transactions, as you embark on your SAP implementations.

Norman Reynolds

I would like to say thank you to Florian Zimniak and the team at Galileo Press for giving me the opportunity to write this book and for their support in making the whole process as smooth as possible.

I would also like to thank my co-authors Martin Murray and Venki Krishnamoorthy. They were a pleasure to work with and I greatly enjoyed being part of the team.

Lastly, I would like to express my thanks to my wonderful family, Caroline, Jay and Sascha, for their support and encouragement in completing this book. They are truly inspirational.

We hope that this book gives you information that will help you maximize your use of the transaction codes available in SAP. We hope that you can use the knowledge you gain from reading this book to develop your skills and to help your company benefit from using SAP.

1   Financial Accounting (FI)

AB01   Create an Asset Transaction

This transaction is used for posting a general asset transaction. An asset number, company code, sub number, document date, posting date, posting period, and transaction type are required. The transaction type will determine the general ledger entries. Enter an amount of the asset posting, the asset value date and, optionally, any text to complete the posting.

AB02   Documents for Asset (Change)

This transaction is used to change existing asset accounting documents. There are only a few fields that can be changed once an asset accounting document has been posted, for example, the text and assignment fields at the line item level. The asset value date can also be changed, but this does not automatically re-determine the depreciation start date (this can be done only by changing the asset master).

AB03   Documents for Asset (Display)

Use this transaction to display asset accounting documents. The important field to recognize is the transaction type, which controls the classification of the transaction and the integration into the general ledger.

AB08   Documents for Asset (Reverse)

This transaction is used to reverse asset accounting documents due to an error. The default selection criteria will be the company code and asset number. Additional selection criteria may be utilized using dynamic selection functionality. Once the asset accounting document is displayed, the reverse document transaction can then be executed.

ABAA   Unplanned Depreciation

Use this transition if an asset requires depreciation outside of the automatically calculated ordinary depreciation. Select the asset number, company code, document date, posting date, and posting period. The default transaction type is 640 (unplanned depreciation on prior-year acquisitions), which can be changed to 650 (unplanned depreciation on current-year acquisitions). On the next screen enter the amount of unplanned depreciation and post to all the asset depreciation areas.

ABAON   Enter Asset Transaction: Asset Sale without Customer

Use this transaction to sell an asset without recording an accounts receivable with the customer (Transaction F-92 can be used for an asset retirement with revenue with a customer). Upon posting, the acquisition value accumulated depreciation is reversed, a gain/loss on the sale is recorded, and a clearing account is posted with the proceeds from the sale in a subsequent general ledger entry. Enter the asset number, document date, asset value date. Then, optionally, partial amounts can be entered and posted, as opposed to retiring the whole asset.

ABAVN   Enter Asset Transaction: Asset Retirement by Scrapping

Use this transaction when an asset is to be scrapped without receiving any revenue for the disposed asset. Upon posting the acquisition value, accumulated depreciation is reversed and a gain/loss on the disposal is recorded. The partial retirement of an asset can also be recorded. Enter the asset number, document date, asset value date. Then optionally, partial amounts can be entered and posted to, as opposed to scrapping the whole asset.

ABAW   Balance Sheet Revaluation

Use this transaction to perform a one-time revaluation of a fixed asset to reflect the effects of inflation. Some countries require this valuation to be separately identified in depreciation area 20 (historical). Enter company code, asset number, document date, posting date, transaction type (800-post revaluation gross) and then revaluation date and revaluation amount.

ABGF   Credit Memo in Year after Invoice

This transaction is used to post a credit to asset acquisition and production costs. Use this transaction to post the offsetting entry to an offset account, which has to be subsequently cleared with the external vendor invoice. Transaction type 160 is used to post the credit in prior years. Note that prior year depreciation is manually corrected using a write up before the credit memo can be posted.

ABGL   Credit Memo in Year of Invoice

This transaction is used to post a credit to the asset acquisition and production cost. Use this transaction to post the offsetting entry to an offset account, which has to be subsequently cleared with the external vendor invoice. Transaction type 105 is used to post the credit in the current year.

ABMA   Manual Depreciation

Use this transaction to manually calculate and post depreciation. Using a special depreciation key, MANU, this transaction may be used where there is an unexpected permanent reduction in the asset's net worth or there is a special tax depreciation that is only partially taken into account. Transaction ABAA, unplanned depreciation, is more commonly used when additional depreciation calculation and posting is required.

ABNAN   Enter Asset Transaction: Post-Capitalization

This transaction is used to subsequently correct the acquisition and cost value of the fixed asset. For example, an expenditure was neglected when capitalizing the fixed asset that is linked to the assembly of the asset in a fiscal year that is now closed. Post-capitalization is posted to the asset using standard transaction type 400.

ABNE   Subsequent Revenue

Use this transaction to post revenue to a retired asset, for asset reporting purposes. Note that there is no integration with the general ledger or controlling, so any entry made using this transaction must also be made in the general ledger and controlling module.

ABNK   Subsequent Costs

Use this transaction to post costs to a retired asset, for asset reporting purposes. Note that there is no integration with the general ledger or controlling, so any entry made using this transaction must also be made in the general ledger and controlling module.

ABSO	Miscellaneous Transactions

This transaction can be used with most asset transaction types but is not commonly used because other transaction codes, designed with a specific business objective in mind, have been developed, for example, posting an asset retirement or unplanned depreciation.

ABST2	Reconcile. Program FI-AA <-> G/L: List of Accounts Showing Differences

This transaction selects asset summary records, totals the values at the company code and business area level, and writes the values to table EWUFIAASUM. This table is then read and reconciled with the asset accounting general ledger accounts. This transaction should be used before year end closing.

ABT1N	Enter Asset Transaction: Intercompany Asset Transfer

Use this transaction to transfer a fixed asset between two company codes. The retirement and acquisition values are posted in one step. A transfer variant is selected in customizing, which is used by this transaction for the postings. The transfer variant will consider the legal structure of the company codes, the transfer method (i.e., gross, net, new value), sending/target company code depreciation areas and field contents of the sending target asset master. Note that if a manual entry to a depreciation area is required, use transaction ABT1.

ABUMN	Enter Asset Transaction: Transfer within Company Code

Use this transaction if organizational changes are required for the asset, for example, reclassification of the asset class or profit center. This transaction can also be used to settle an asset under construction managed at a summary level. To facilitate the transfer, a new asset can be created, or a new asset can be generated from the transaction. Standard transaction types 300, 310, 320, and 330 determine the capitalization start date and depreciation start date of the receiving asset.

ABZE	Acquisition from In-house Production

This transaction is used to post acquisition cost to an asset. The default posting key is 70 and transaction type is 110, with the default offsetting account proposed, set up in customizing.

ABZON	Enter Asset Transaction: Acquis. W/Autom. Offsetting Entry

This transaction can be used where the acquisition value is posted before the receipt of an invoice from a vendor. The acquisition value is posted to the asset, and an offsetting entry is automatically posted and requires clearing upon the subsequent receipt of a vendor invoice.

ABZP	Acquisition from Affiliated Company

Use this transaction to post acquisition costs from one company code to another company code within a group company. The default transaction type is 150, which is linked, via customizing, to consolidation transaction type 125.

ABZU	Write-up

Use this transaction to make a subsequent change to the value of an asset, e.g., reversal of accumulated depreciation and increase the value of the asset. A write-up will increase the planned depreciation when used with a depreciation method based on the net book value. The transaction type will differ depending on the depreciation type used. Standard transaction type 700 is used.

AFAB — Depreciation Posting Run

Planned depreciation is not posted to the general ledger until this transaction has been executed. When posting depreciation in update mode, the program must be run in background. Depreciation is posted for each depreciation area, but only the standard delivered depreciation area 01 (book depreciation area) posts to the general ledger.

AFAR — Recalculate Depreciation

This transaction can be used to recalculate the planned annual depreciation for a large number of fixed assets if, for example, the depreciation keys have been changed in configuration. Note that it is not possible to recalculate depreciation for prior closed fiscal years.

AFBP — Log of Posting Run

This transaction is used to access the posting log for posting depreciation via transaction AFAB, the depreciation posting run. The log will display the list of assets posted to and the summarized posting by account assignment.

AIAB — Settlement AuC

This transaction is used to create the distribution of costs for the settlement of an asset under construction (AUC) managed at a line item level. Costs collected for an AUC can be managed at a summary level. In this case, the settlement is performed when the AUC is complete, using transaction ABUMN. Use transaction AIAB to specify, at the line item level, what the settlement receiving objects are (e.g., FXA is an asset, CTR is a cost center)

and the % of the AUC cost that will be settled to the respective receiving objects.

AIBU — AuC Settlement

This transaction is used for the settlement of an asset under construction (AUC) managed at a line item level. The distribution rule is created via transaction AIAB. If the asset under construction is managed at a summary level, it can be settled once or several times using transaction ABUMN.

AIST — Reversal of Settlement of AuC

Use this transaction to reverse the settlement of an asset under construction using transaction AIBU. The last settlement is reversed, so if you want to reverse the settlement before the most recent settlement then you must reverse the last settlements first, i.e., in chronological order.

AJAB — Year-end Closing Asset Accounting

This transaction is used to close the fiscal year. Enter the company code and fiscal year to close. After this transaction has been executed, postings or value changes can no longer be made in asset accounting. This transaction must be run before transaction AJRW can be successfully executed.

AJRW — Asset Fiscal Year Change

Use this transaction to open the new fiscal year. Enter the company code and new fiscal year. Note that the transaction has to be run for the whole company code and will carry over asset values from the previous year to the current year. Run this transaction after the previous year has been closed, i.e., after transaction AJAB.

AR01   Asset Balances

This transaction is a report on asset balances in a depreciation area. It can be used in conjunction with transaction AR31 in order to make mass changes to assets via a worklist. The following values are displayed: cumulative acquisition value at the beginning of the fiscal year, accumulated depreciation and the planned book value at the end of the reporting year. After the report has been run, create and save the worklist and then execute the worklist via transaction AR31.

AR11   Investment Support

This transaction reports on all assets with at least one investment support key. If required, you can have SAP directly post the support amounts determined. The transaction types for the posting are determined from the investment support measure.

AR31   Edit Worklist

This transaction, in conjunction with transaction AR01 can be used to make mass changes to assets. Process the worklist created using transaction AR01.

AS01   Create Asset

This transaction creates an asset master record. A company code and an asset class are required. The asset class will determine the default values in the general asset master data section and the depreciation area section. There is also an option to create multiple similar assets at one time. The asset class will structure the asset in terms of the number assignment, the general ledger postings, and terms of depreciation, e.g., useful life of the asset, etc.

AS02   Change Asset

Use this transaction to change an asset master record. The asset class will determine the values available to change in the general asset master data section and the depreciation area section.

AS03   Display Asset

Use this transaction to display an asset master record. The asset class will determine the values displayed in the general asset master data section and the depreciation area section.

AS04   Changes Asset

Use this transaction code to report all changes to the asset master. Enter the company code, and asset number. There is the option to select the sub number, depreciation area, changed by user ID, and changed from date. There is also the option to select from a specific date, time, and the individual making the change. The report output will display the fields changed with the option to drill down and display the old field, new field, and date changed.

AS05   Block Asset

Use this transaction to block an asset. Enter the asset number, sub number (if any), and company code to block any further acquisition values being posted to the asset.

AS06   Delete Asset

Use this transaction if the asset has no value and does not need to remain in SAP. Enter the asset number, sub number (if any), and company code. Then on the next screen, set the radio button to physically delete the asset from SAP.

AS11	Create Sub Number

Use this transaction to sub divide the main asset in order to, for example, value the asset or account for the costs separately. The sub number is assigned sequentially starting with the number 1. Furthermore, it is possible to account for subsequent acquisition of an asset separately by year of acquisition using the sub number. This can be a requirement if the indicator ACQUISITION ONLY IN THE YEAR OF CAPITALIZATION is set in the depreciation key.

AS22	Create Group Asset

Use this transaction if there is a need to manage and depreciate an asset at a higher level than the individual asset, for instance, in the US, according to the Asset Depreciation Range (ADR) system. The group asset is maintained in the same way as an individual asset except that a specific depreciation area is assigned. To assign an individual asset to a group asset, you can use transaction AS01 and then within the specific deprecation area, assign the asset the group asset number.

AS23	Display Group Asset

This transaction is used to display the group asset master, which has the same views as an individual asset except it includes a specific depreciation area which groups assets for the calculation and posting of depreciation.

AS25	Block Group Asset

Use this transaction to block postings to a group asset. Use transaction AS05 to block postings to individual assets.

AUN0	Analysis of an Asset and Its Environment: Data Collect. and Analysis

This report displays the environment of an asset (master data, annual values, line items, control parameters) in order to facilitate the analysis of problems that might arise.

AUVA	Incomplete Assets – Detail List

This transaction reports on asset master records based on a completeness indicator. The following indicators are possible:

- 0—Asset is complete (all required asset master fields have been maintained)
- 1—Asset is incomplete but can be posted
- 2—Asset is incomplete and cannot be posted (essential fields needed for posting are missing)
- 3—Asset is incomplete (cst ctr, int.order, activ.type missing)
- 4—Asset is incomplete (investment account assignment missing)

AW01N	Asset Explorer

This transaction can be used to display asset values including acquisition and production costs and depreciation. In the header section, enter a company code, asset number, sub number (if any) and fiscal year. The overview section enables an analysis of planned asset value and posted values, with the ability to tab through the depreciation areas. There are many ways to explore the value of an asset using this reporting tool, for example, viewing the depreciation calculation and drilling down to the general ledger posting.

BPC1	Create Business Partner

Use this transaction to create a business partner in order to conduct treasury transactions. For example, to invest a liquidity surplus, you must first create a financial institution as a business partner, in order to conclude the investment. The business partner can be an organization, natural person, or collective partner. The grouping field will determine the business partner numbering, and the role category will determine the functions that can be performed with the business partner, such as paying bank, borrower, and ultimate borrower.

BPC2	Change Business Partner

Use this transaction to change the business partner used for treasury transactions. The fields that can be changed will be determined by the role category of the business partner.

BPC3	Display Business Partner

This transaction is used to display the business partner created for treasury transactions. There are three main areas of the master data: central data (name, address, bank details, etc.), general data (role data, credit standing, tax data, etc.) and company code data (account information, payment data, dunning data, etc.).

BPC4	Create Business Partner from Customer

Use this transaction to create a business partner from a customer master record that already exists in FI. Enter the grouping and role category as you would with transaction BPC1 and the customer master number. The business partner related data is then transferred.

BPC5	Change Business Partner with Customer Reference

This transaction can be used to change a business partner by linking a customer master data that already exists in FI. Enter the

business partner number, the role category, and the customer number.

BPCD	Change Documents (Business Partner)

This transaction reports the log of change documents associated with changes made to the business partner master data. The date changed, user ID of the individual making the change and the old/new field contents are reported.

CRF1	Payment Cards: Read, Display, Check, Save Incoming File

This transaction imports into SAP the inbound file of a payment card company with the data records of the individual card transactions for the process PAYMENT CARD PROCESSING in Financial Accounting. The data file must be in data format CRFLATFILE, and all fields, including the amount fields, in character format. From the data of the inbound file, the program creates a payment card file that can be saved. In doing so, the data records are converted in such a way that FI account documents can be generated from them. Enter card type and the location of the inbound file.

CRF2	Payment Cards: Delete Saved File

Use this transaction to delete the file saved when executing transaction CRF1. Enter year, period, card type, and card file number.

CRF3	Payment Cards: Display File, Create Postings, Edit Log

Use this transaction to generate financial postings from the payment card data file generated using transaction CRF1. Enter year, period, card type, and card file number. Check the CREATE ACCOUNTING DOCUMENTS box to generate the financial postings.

| F.03 | Financial Accounting Comparative Analysis |

This transaction reconciles posted financial transaction documents with the totals tables/ application indexes in accounts payable, accounts receivable, and the general ledger. Differences in the application indexes can be caused by changing the LINE ITEM DISPLAY setting in the G/L account. For more information, see OSS note 31875. SAP recommends that the transaction be run for closed periods and in background.

| F.05 | Foreign Currency Valuation |

Use this transaction to revalue open items that have been posted in a foreign currency or have a balance sheet general ledger account that is managed in a foreign currency. The valuation can be carried out in the local currency or a parallel local currency (i.e., group currency). The result of the valuations can be stored per valuated document and posted to adjustment accounts and P&L accounts.

| F.07 | Carry Forward Receivables/Payables |

This transaction calculates and carries forward the financial balance for vendors and customers from the previous year to the new fiscal year as part of the year end closing process. When posting into a previous year, the system carries forward the balance automatically, regardless of whether the program has been executed. SAP recommends that the program be run at the beginning of the new fiscal year.

| F.08 | G/L: Account Balances |

Use this transaction to report general ledger balances by account, company code, chart of accounts, reporting period(s), business area, and currency. The report displays, by general ledger account, business area and currency, the balance carried forward, credit totals per reporting period, debit totals per reporting period, and accumulated balance. Totals for all company codes are displayed at the end of the report.

| F.09 | G/L: Account List |

Use this transaction to display a list of general ledger accounts. Selection criteria include chart of accounts, company code, and various details on the general ledger master record such as account control and cash management indicators.

| F.10 | Chart of Accounts |

Use this report to display a list of general ledger accounts that may or may not be set up as master records at the company code level. The output displays a list of general ledger accounts and the description of each account. Also by double-clicking the general ledger account, the user is taken to transaction FSP0 which displays the general ledger account at the chart of accounts level including the description of the account and a profit and loss or balances sheet indicator.

| F.13 | Automatic Clearing |

This transaction is used to clear open items automatically in the general ledger, customer or vendor accounts. Table V_TF123 is maintained to set the criteria used to clear open items. Selection criteria when executing the transaction include company code, fiscal year, assignment, document number, posting date and selection range of accounts. The transaction can be executed in test mode before posting the clearing in update mode.

F.14 Create Posting Documents from Recurring Documents

This transaction is used to post recurring documents created using transaction FBD1. Company code, document number, and fiscal year can be selected as well as general selection criteria. A settlement period is required and a run schedule, which determines the posting period, can be used. The transaction creates a batch input session, which posts the financial documents and updates the recurring reference document in the header.

F.15 Recurring Entry Documents

Use this transaction to display recurring documents created using transaction FBD1. The output displays documents that are to be posted in a particular time period. Furthermore, the list displays documents that have not been posted and will be posted during the next run of the recurring entry program, i.e., F.14.

F.19 Analyze GR/IR Clearing Accounts and Display Acquisition Tax

This transaction analyzes the goods receipt/invoice receipt (GR/IR) clearing accounts at a specified key date and generates adjustment postings if necessary. The general ledger account requires an adjustment in order to display correctly in the balance sheet: goods delivered but not invoiced, and goods invoiced but not delivered. In some countries, the input tax on goods delivered but not paid for can also be deducted.

F.1A Grouping Customer/Vendor Master Records

This transaction enables you to group customers and vendors into intervals of a particular size or into a particular number

of intervals. You can then use the information, for example, when creating variants for balance confirmation programs if you would like to schedule several jobs in parallel in the background.

F.20 Customer List

Use this transaction to display a list of customers. Selection criteria include customer, company code, and many of the data sets on the customer master record.

F.21 List of Customer Line Items

This transaction is used to report customer line items in accounts receivable. Selection criteria include customer, company code, and many of the data sets on the customer master record. There are various ways to format the report layout; however, if drill down capability is required, then use transaction FBL5N.

F.22 Customer Evaluation with OI Sorted List

This transaction is used to report open customer line items in accounts receivables on a key date. The accounts receivable balance can be grouped into accounts receivable days outstanding. Up to five groupings may be selected.

F.23 Customer Balances in Local Currency

Use this transaction to report on customer balances that are displayed for particular months. Various formatting options are available, but there is no drill-down capability to the actual lines items. Use transaction FBL5N for drill-down capability.

F.24   Calculate Interest on Arrears

This transaction calculates interest on open customer line items that have not been paid or were paid too late. A letter is generated at a chosen level of detail, such as the interest rate used and the line items selected. Postings are automatically generated to the customer account and the interest received/paid account. There are three variants of this transaction: F.2A without open items, F.2B with open items, and F.2C without postings.

F.25   Bill of Exchange List

Use this transaction to view the bill of exchange list, which is a subsidiary ledger containing all the essential data of incoming bill of exchange receivables. The day of expiration of the bill of exchange and the address data of the issuer are included in this list. The list contains all open bills of exchange as of a key date, and depending on the selection parameter, also displays cleared bills of exchange.

F.26   Customer Interest Scale

This transaction is used to calculate interest on the balance on a customer's account. Use this transaction, for example, to calculate interest on the staff loan accounts managed in accounts receivable. Select the customer account, company code, calculation period and an interest indicator. The interest indicator contains control settings for the interest calculation, such as the interest rate. Use transaction F.24 to calculate interest on customer open items in arrears.

F.27   Periodic Account Statements

Use this transaction to generate account statements or open items lists for customers manually. Customers are selected via a customer master setting and the table for financial statement correspondence requests is updated. In a second step the correspondence request is printed out. Account statements can also automatically be printed periodically, without a request having been made, if the customer has a corresponding key for this in the master record.

F.28   SD, FI: Recreation of Credit Data after Organizational Changes

This transaction is used to recreate credit control data after organizational changes such as, assignment of the credit control area, currency of the credit control area and risk class in the customer master. On the FI side if, for example, the classification of a difference reason, as a disputed item or on-disputed item was changed, this program also needs to be executed. The program reads all open items and determines the new amount in the credit control area currency and correct credit control area. On the SD side, the report updates credit data (credit control area, credit account, credit currency, credit value, risk class) in sales documents.

F.31   Credit Overview

This transaction reports on a customer's credit data. Selection criteria for the report include credit account, credit control area as well as other credit master record data. Output from the report can include address data, credit limit, account balance and special general ledger balance of each customer in the list, dunning data, days in arrears and open items.

F.32   Customers with Missing Credit Data

This transaction checks on missing credit data. For example, checks for any missing central data of the credit master or missing credit control data. Furthermore the report will also check if there are any company codes that do not refer to credit control data. Output from the report will display missing credit data statistics.

F.35   Credit Master Sheet

The credit master sheet is used to display and print the customer master data of an individual account, which is needed in the area of credit management. It is also possible to call this report from the accounts receivable line item display and account analysis transactions. The following output is displayed: address data, credit limit, account balance, payment history on a control area level, days in arrears and open items. Transaction S_ALR_87012218 can also be used.

F.38   Deferred Tax Transfer

Use this transaction when deferring taxes on sales and purchases. Normally, tax on sales and purchases is reported when an invoice is issued. The tax payable amount is calculated as the balance of the input and output taxes and cleared in the subsequent period. The tax for some transactions, such as services, can be deducted only on settlement. This is common in France (output and input tax) and Italy (input tax). This transaction will transfer the deferred tax posting to the regular tax account upon payment for the services.

F.40   Vendor List

Use this transaction to display a list of vendors. Selection criteria include customer, company code and many of the data sets on the customer master record.

F.41   List of Vendor Line Items

This transaction is used to report vendor line items in accounts payable. Selection criteria include vendor, company code and many of the data sets on the vendor master record. There are various ways to format the report layout; however, if drill-down capability is required, then use transaction FBL1N.

F.42   Vendor Balances in Local Currency

Use this transaction to report on vendor balances, which are displayed for particular months. Various formatting options are available, but there is no drill-down capability to the actual lines items. Use transaction FBL1N for drill-down capability.

F.44   Vendor Interest Scale

This transaction is used to calculate interest on the balance on a vendor account. Select the vendor account, company code, calculation period, and an interest calculation indicator. The interest indicator contains the control settings for the interest calculation, such as the interest rate. Use transaction F.47 to calculate interest on vendor open items overdue.

F.47   Calculate Interest on Arrears

This transaction calculates interest on vendor open items that have not been paid or were paid too late. A letter is generated at a chosen level of detail, such as the interest rate used and the line items selected. Postings are automatically generated to the vendor account and interest received/paid account. There are three variants for this transactions namely, F.4A without open items, F.4B with open items and F.4C without postings.

F.50   Profit and Loss Adjustment

Use this transaction in conjunction with the classic general ledger. The transaction is used to distribute cash discounts and/or exchange rate differences to the appropriate profit centers, business areas, profitability segments or other coding block assignments when a default assignment is made. The system uses the account assignments of the offsetting entries in the initial document to calculate the distribution.

F.51   General Ledger Line Items

This transaction is used to report general ledger line items. The selection criteria include general ledger account, company code and many of the data sets on the general ledger master record. There are various ways to format the report layout; however, if drill-down capability is required, then use transaction FBL3N.

F.52   G/L Account Interest Scale

This transaction is used to calculate interest on a balance in the general ledger. Select the general ledger account, company code, calculation period, and an interest calculation indicator. The interest indicator contains the control settings for the interest calculation, such as the interest rate.

F.53   Account Assignment Manual

Use this transaction to report the long text for each G/L account. Selection can be made via the chart of accounts, the company code or a combination of these specifications. You can add the key word in the G/L account assignment manually by using the selection parameters.

F.56   Delete Reference Documents

Use this transaction to delete either reference documents (doc type D) or sample documents (doc type M) or both. The deletion indicator must be set on the document before the deletion can take effect. There is also a test run indicator.

F.58   Open Item Account Balance Audit Trail from the Document File

This transaction reports on transactions concerning customer accounts, vendor accounts, and G/L accounts that are managed on an open item basis. Output can be configured and manipulated using ABAP List Viewer.

F.5D   Calculate Balance Sheet Adjustment

Use this transaction in conjunction with the classic general ledger. The transaction is used to distribute accounts payable, accounts receivable, taxes, cash discounts and valuated exchanges rate differences in open items, to the appropriate profit center or business area. The system uses the account assignments of the offsetting entries in the initial document to calculate the distribution.

F.5E   Post Balance Sheet Adjustment

Use this transaction to post the adjustments calculated in transaction F.5D. Enter the company code, key date of open items (payables and receivables) and a lower date limit for tax (posting date up to which no tax distribution takes place because, for instance, the tax return has already taken place). Also, there are selection options for actual postings to take place and log generation. Follow-up transactions are also available to display the log (transaction F.5F) and re-determine the adjustment accounts if they were to be changed in configuration.

F.64	Maintain Correspondence Requests

This transaction is used to create a correspondence request such as a statement of an account that can be delivered to a customer. Enter the correspondence code, the company code, and the master data type, for example D for customers and open item account. Once the correspondence has been generated, a preview button can be selected, and then the preview may be printed. The follow-on transactions, F.61 (print internal documents), F.62 (print requests) and F.63 (delete requests), may also be used to control the print function.

F.80	Mass Reversal of Documents

Use this transaction to make mass reversals of financial posting documents. Selection includes company code, document number, fiscal year and account type. The posting date is today's date by default but must be within the current posting period. All documents selected in test mode are not reversed. Use transaction FB08 for a single financial document.

F.81	Reverse Accrual/ Deferral Documents

This transaction is used to reverse the accrual posting made using transaction FBS1. The reverse posting date is specified in the accrual document. The transaction can be run in test or update mode.

F.97	Application Tree Report Selection General Ledger

Use this transaction to access a grouping of reports or functions in the general ledger area. The tree display can be customized using transaction SE43N.

F.98	Application Tree Report Selection Vendors

Use this transaction to access a grouping of reports or functions in the vendor/accounts payable area. The tree display can be customized using transaction SE43N.

F.99	Application Tree Report Selection Customers

Use this transaction to access a grouping of reports or functions in the customer/accounts receivable area. The tree display can be customized using transaction SE43N.

F-01	Enter Sample Document Header Data

This transaction creates a sample document that can be used as a reference when posting a financial document. Sample documents have a separate number range and do not update transaction figures. The sample document can be transferred to an actual posting document, but you cannot make any changes at time of entry.

F-02	Enter G/L Account Posting: Header Data

Use this transaction to post a general ledger transaction. The default document type can be customized and there are also numerous entry options available via transaction FB00. Select company code, posting date, document date, currency, document header text and then enter line items and post.

F-03	Clear G/L Account: Header Data

Use this transaction to process open items on a general ledger account. This process is not initiated by another event and requires the appropriate credits and debits to exist on the general ledger account to enable clearing. This transaction differs from a Post with Clearing transaction (transaction F-04) in that you do not need to enter a document header: simply match existing open items and clear from one account.

F-04	Post with Clearing: Header Data

Use this transaction to post and clear debits and credits from across multiple general accounts/open items. The posting header data is entered followed by the offset account and amount. Then open items can be chosen, processed and saved with a unique clearing number and date. This process will allow the user to select multiple open items and select debit and credit amounts for clearing against each other. Transaction FB05 can also be used.

F-05	Post Foreign Currency Valn: Header Data

This transaction is used to post manual revaluation adjustments as a result of a foreign currency valuation but this can also be done automatically using transaction F.05.

F-06	Post Incoming Payments: Header Data

Use this transaction to post and clear open line items. This transaction is similar to F-30 but specifically used for processing incoming payments. Enter the document header data, the bank posting data to which the offset posting will be cleared and then select the customer or vendor account(s). Then activate and save the open items to be cleared, which will generate a unique clearing number and date.

F-07	Post Outgoing Payments: Header Data

Use this transaction to post and clear open line items. This transaction is similar to F-30 but specifically used for processing outgoing payments. Enter the document header data, the bank posting data to which the offset posting will be cleared and then select the customer or vendor account(s), Then activate and save the open items to be cleared, which will generate a unique clearing number and date.

F-19	Reverse Statistical Posting: Header Data

Use this transaction to reverse a statistical posting that can be made to a special general ledger account. For example, to reverse a bill of exchange liability once the due date for recourse has passed.

F-20	Reverse Bill Liability: Header Data

Use this transaction to clear bills of exchange receivables on the customer account, the special G/L account and the contingent liability account after the expiration date and the country-specific protest period has elapsed. Thus there is no longer any recourse liability (bill of exchange liability).

F-21	Enter Transfer Posting: Header Data

Use this transaction to transfer a value from one customer to (usually) another customer. The posting keys will determine which type of sub ledger or general ledger account can be posted to. Since this transfer happens without clearing, you run this transaction without selecting open items and therefore the amount you are transferring is not dependent on any prior postings to that customer. Editing options can be maintained via transaction FB00.

F-22 | Enter Customer Invoice: Header Data

Use this transaction to post a manual customer invoice directly in the finance module as opposed to an invoice originating in the sales and distribution module. The document type and posting keys will determine which type of sub ledger or general ledger can be posted to. Since the invoice posts without clearing you run this transaction without selecting open items and therefore the amount you are posting is not dependent on any prior postings to that customer. Editing options can be maintained via transaction FB00.

F-23 | Return Bill of Exchange Pmt Request: Header Data

This transaction is used to reverse a bill of exchange request posted using transaction FBW1. Bill of exchange requests are special bills of exchange receivables that are issued not by the customer but by you. Bill of exchange payment requests are sent to the customer for acceptance, so use this transaction if the request is not accepted. These transactions are common in Italy, France, and Spain.

F-25 | Reverse Check/Bill of Exchange: Header Data

Use this transaction to clear bills of exchange receivables on a customer account, special G/L account and the contingent liability account after the expiration date and the country-specific protest period has elapsed. Therefore, there is no longer any recourse liability (bill of exchange liability). Transaction F-20 also performs the same function but has additional functionality, for example, processing failed payments.

F-26 | Incoming Payments Fast Entry: Header Data

This transaction can be used to process customer receipts by rapidly entering payments and clearing documents. Types of transactions include manual deposits, manually entering wire transfers or advice of credit (payments to credit the customer's account).

F-27 | Enter Customer Credit Memo: Header Data

Use this transaction to post a manual customer credit memo directly in the finance module as opposed to a credit memo originating in the sales and distribution module. The document type and posting keys will determine which type of sub ledger or general ledger can be posted to. Since the invoice posts without clearing, you run this transaction without selecting open items and therefore the amount you are posting is not dependent on any prior postings to that customer. Editing options can be maintained via transaction FB00.

F-28 | Post Incoming Payments: Header Data

This transaction posts an incoming payment to a customer account and clears the open item. Enter the clearing document header (bank information and customer information), select a clearing transaction, choose open items you want to clear, process the items selected and post the clearing document. You also have the option to post additional line items as part of the clearing process. This posting is not integrated with the sales and distribution module.

F-29 | Post Customer Down Payment: Header Data

Use this transaction to record a down payment received from a customer. A down payment can be recorded with or without a down payment request (a down payment request is a noted line item on the customer account that can be recorded via transaction F-37). A down payment is recorded, via a special general ledger indicator, to a general ledger account other than accounts receivable and then is cleared against the customer invoice using transaction F-39.

F-30	Post with Clearing: Header Data

Use this transaction to post and clear debits and credits from across multiple customer accounts. The posting header data is entered followed by the offset posting account and amount. Open items can be chosen, processed and saved with a unique clearing number and date. This process will allow the user to select multiple open items and select debit and credit amounts for clearing against each other.

F-31	Post Outgoing Payments: Header Data

Use this transaction to create a debit to a customer account. Enter the clearing document header (bank information and customer information), select a clearing transaction, choose open items you want to clear, process the items selected and post the clearing document. You also have the option to post additional line items as part of the clearing process. This posting is not integrated with the sales and distribution module and is used, for example, if a manual credit refund is needed.

F-32	Clear Customer: Header Data

Use this transaction to process open items on a customer's account. This process is not initiated by another event and requires the appropriate credits and debits to exist on the customer account to enable clearing.

Customer account clearing differs from a Post with Clearing transaction (transaction F-30) or a Post with Payment transaction (transaction F-28) in that you do not need to enter a document header: simply match existing open items, and you can only clear open items from one account.

F-33	Post Bill of Exchange Usage: Header Data

Use this transaction to record the deposit of the bill of exchange at the bank. A bill of exchange can be discounted at a bank in advance of its due date (discounting). The bank buys the bill of exchange from you. Since it does not receive the amount until the date recorded on the bill, it charges you interest (discount) to cover the period between receiving the bill of exchange and its eventual payment. Some form of handling charge is also usually levied. The accounting entries are debit bank account, credit bill of exchange contingent liability account and debit bank charges/discount. Use transaction F-20 to reverse contingent liability.

F-34	Post Collection: Header Data

Use this transaction if a bill of exchange is either presented to your customer for payment on the due date, or is deposited at a bank shortly before the due date for collection. The bank usually charges a collection fee for this service. The accounting entries are debit bank account, credit bill of exchange contingent liability account and debit bank charges/discount. Use transaction F-20 to reverse the contingent liability.

F-35	Post Forfaiting: Header Data

Use this transaction if you sell your bill of exchange receivable abroad (forfaiting). When you use the bill in this way (otherwise known as non-recourse financing of receivables) you are, upon the sale of the bill, freed from any liability to recourse. The accounting entries are debit bank account, credit bill of exchange contingent liability account and debit bank charges/discount. Use transaction F-20 to reverse the contingent liability.

F-36	Bill of Exchange Payment: Header Data

Use this transaction to record the acceptance by the customer of a bill of exchange. The posting will transfer the open accounts receivable to a bill of exchange receivable account, via a special general ledger indicator. The outstanding receivable can still be displayed as part of the customer's open line item list.

F-37	Customer Down Payment Request: Header Data

This transaction is used to post a down payment request, which is a noted item on a customer's account and does not update the general ledger balances. The down payment request is posted to a special general ledger account that can be viewed in accounts receivable line item display as a noted item. A customer down payment request can be used by the dunning program to remind a customer of a down payment due.

F-38	Enter Statistical Posting: Header Data

Use this transaction to post a noted special general ledger posting, for example, letters of credit or performance guarantee for a customer. The offset posting is to the same general ledger account, which makes this a statistical posting that is not displayed in the financial statement version. Use transaction F-19 to reverse a statistical posting.

F-39	Clear Customer Down Payment: Header Data

This transaction is used to clear a customer down payment manually against a customer's invoice manually. Use the customer's invoice as a reference to clear the special general ledger account and record the accounts receivable. The customer down payment can also be cleared automatically using the payment program.

F-40	Bill of Exchange Payment: Header Data

This transaction is used to transfer an open accounts payable item to a bill of exchange payable account via a special general ledger indicator. The outstanding payable can still be displayed as part of the vendor's open items line item list.

F-41	Enter Vendor Credit Memo: Header Data

Use this transaction to post a manual vendor credit memo directly in the finance module, as opposed to originating in logistics invoice verification. The document type and posting key will determine which type of sub ledger or general ledger account can be posted to. Since the invoice posts without clearing, you run this transaction without selecting open items and therefore the amount you are posting is not dependent on any prior postings to that vendor. Editing options can be maintained via transaction FB00.

F-42	Enter Transfer Posting: Header Data

Use this transaction to transfer a value from one account to another. The posting keys will determine which type of sub ledger or general ledger account can be posted to. Since this transfer happens without clearing, you run this transaction without selecting open items and therefore the amount you are transferring is not dependent on any prior postings to that account. Editing options can be maintained via transaction FB00.

| F-43 | Enter Vendor Invoice: Header Data |

Use this transaction to post a manual vendor invoice directly in the finance module as opposed to an invoice originating via logistics invoice verification. The document type and posting keys will determine which type of sub ledger or general ledger can be posted to. Since the invoice posts without clearing, you run this transaction without selecting open items and therefore the amount you are posting is not dependent on any prior postings to that vendor. Editing options can be maintained via transaction FB00.

| F-44 | Clear Vendor: Header Data |

Use this transaction to process open items on a vendor account. This process is not initiated by another event and requires the appropriate credits and debits to exist on the vendor account to enable clearing. This vendor account clearing transaction differs from a Post with Clearing transaction (transaction F-52) in that you do not need to enter a document header: simply match existing open items, and you can only clear open items from one account.

| F-47 | Down Payment Request: Header Data |

This transaction is used to post a down payment request for advances to vendors. The posting is a noted item on a vendor account and does not update the general ledger balances. The down payment request is posted to a special general ledger account that can be viewed in accounts payable line item display as a noted item. A vendor check can be printed and posted using transaction F-58

in reference to a vendor's down payment request.

| F-48 | Post Vendor Down Payment: Header Data |

Use this transaction to record a down payment made to a vendor. A down payment can be recorded with or without a down payment request (a down payment requested is a noted line item on the vendor account that can be recorded via transaction F-47). A down payment is recorded, via a special general ledger indicator, to a general ledger account other than the accounts payable account and then is cleared against the vendor invoice using transaction F-54.

| F-49 | Customer Noted Item |

Use this transaction to post a noted item on a customer's account using a special general ledger account. A special general ledger account can be configured to not update account balances. This is also the case with a down payment request and bill of exchange payment request.

| F-51 | Post with Clearing: Header Data |

Use this transaction to post and clear debits and credits from across multiple vendor accounts. The posting header data is entered followed by the offset posting account and amount. Open items can be chosen, processed and saved with a unique clearing number and date. This process will allow the user to select multiple open items and select debit and credit amounts for clearing against each other.

| F-52 | Post Incoming Payments: Header Data |

This transaction posts an incoming payment to a vendor account and clears the open item, for example, to clear a credit memo. Enter the clearing document header (bank information and customer information), select a clearing transaction, choose open items you want to clear, process the items selected and post the clearing document. You also have the option to post additional line items as part of the clearing process. This posting is not integrated with the materials management purchasing module.

F-53	Post Outgoing Payments: Header Data

Use this transaction to post checks that have been created manually to pay a vendor (i.e., perhaps typed or hand-written checks). A check will not be generated in SAP but the vendor and cash accounts will be updated appropriately. Enter the clearing document header (bank information and vendor information), chose the open items you want to clear, process the items selected and post the clearing document. For automatic accounts payable payments, use transaction F110.

F-54	Clear Vendor Down Payment: Header Data

This transaction is used to clear a vendor down payment manually against a vendor's invoice. Use the vendor's invoice as a reference to clear the special general ledger account and record the accounts payable entry. The vendor down payment can also be cleared automatically using the payment program via transaction F110.

F-55	Enter Statistical Posting: Header Data

Use this transaction to create a noted special general ledger posting, for example, letters of credit or performance guarantees for vendors. The offset posting is to the same general ledger account, which means these statistical postings are not displayed in the financial

statement version. Use transaction F-19 to reverse a statistical posting.

F-56	Reverse Statistical Posting: Header Data

Use this transaction to reverse a statistical posting made with transaction F-55. Select the same vendor name and alternative reconciliation account used when posting via transaction F-55.

F-57	Vendor Noted Item: Header Data

Use this transaction to post a noted item on a vendor's account using a special general ledger account. A special general ledger account can be configured not to update account balances. This is also the case with down payment requests and bills of exchange payment requests.

F-58	Payment with Printout: Header Data

Use this transaction to post and printout checks where no open items exist to clear, for example, advance payments to vendors. Payments can be made with or without reference to a payment request from transaction F-47 or F-59.

F-59	Payment Request

Use this transaction to process payment requests where there are no open items to clear. This transaction is used mostly in the treasury module, for example, where a business partner is a bank. Payment requests can be entered via transaction F-59 and then paid via transaction F111. Note that for each payment request a clearing account is required per company code in customizing.

F-62	Change View "Currency Exchange Rates": Overview

This transaction is used to change foreign currency exchange rates. The exchange rates are arranged based on exchange rate types. Generally, the amounts posted in foreign currencies are translated using exchange rate type M (standard translation at the average rate) to the local currency.

F-63	Park Document: Document Header Vendor Invoice

Use this transaction to enter and store (park) incomplete vendor invoices without carrying out extensive entry checks, such as the document being in balance. Parked documents can be completed, checked and then posted at a later date, if necessary by a different individual, using transaction FBV0. Parked documents can be processed online for reporting purposes from the moment they are parked. Transaction FV60, which is a single entry screen can, also be used.

F-64	Park Document: Document Header Customer Invoice

Use this transaction to enter and store (park) incomplete customer invoices without carrying out extensive entry checks, such as the document being in balance. Parked documents can be completed, checked and then posted at a later date, if necessary by a different individual, using transaction FBV0. Parked documents can be evaluated online for reporting purposes from the moment they are parked. Transaction FV70, which is a single entry screen can, also be used.

F-65	Park Document: Document Header General Ledger

Use this transaction to enter and store (park) incomplete general ledger postings without carrying out extensive entry checks, such

as the document being in balance. Parked documents can be completed, checked and then posted at a later date, if necessary by a different individual, using transaction FBV0. Parked documents can be processed online for reporting purposes from the moment they are parked. Transaction FV50, which is a single entry screen, can also be used.

F-66	Park Document: Document Header Vendor Credit Memo

Use this transaction to enter and store (park) incomplete vendor credit memos without carrying out extensive entry checks, such as the document being in balance. Parked documents can be completed, checked and then posted at a later date, if necessary by a different individual, using transaction FBV0. Parked documents can be evaluated online for reporting purposes from the moment they are parked. Transaction FV65, which is a single entry screen, can also be used.

F-67	Park Document: Document Header Customer Credit Memo

Use this transaction to enter and store (park) incomplete customer credit memos without carrying out extensive entry checks. Parked documents can be completed, checked and then posted at a later date, if necessary by a different individual, using transaction FBV0. Parked documents can be evaluated for reporting purposes from the moment they are parked. Transaction FV75, which is a single entry screen, can also be used.

F-90	Acquisition from Purchase w. Vendor

Use this transaction to post an acquisition value or credit memo to an asset as a result of a purchase from a vendor. This transaction is integrated with accounts payable. An invoice is posted to an accounts payable vendor account and the offsetting entry is posted to the acquisition value of the asset. Use transaction ABZON where the acquisition value is posted before the receipt of an invoice from the vendor.

F-91	Asset Acquis. Posted w/ Clearing Acct: Header Data

Use this transaction to post an acquisition value or credit memo to an asset, but, as opposed to transaction F.90, the offset account is a clearing account. This transaction is integrated with the general ledger. In this scenario, a vendor invoice or accumulated costs would be processed manually and posted to the offset account.

F-92	Asset Retire. frm Sale w/ Customer: Header Data

Use this transaction to sell an asset and record an account receivable with a customer. (Transaction ABAON can be used for an asset retirement with revenue without customer.) Upon posting, the acquisition value and accumulated depreciation are reversed, a gain/loss on the sale is recorded and the customer accounts receivable posted. Enter the asset number, document date, asset value date, and then, optionally, partial amounts can be entered and posted as opposed to retiring the whole asset.

F110	Parameters for Automatic Payment

This transaction is used for the automatic processing of open accounts payable. Select a run date and identification ID. Then input selection parameters including posting date, document entered up to date, company code, method of payment (e.g., C for check). Selection can be narrowed further by vendor/customer account and free selection. Defaults can be defined for the payment medium in customizing. Once selections have

been saved, the program can be executed and payments generated. Furthermore, a log can be printed via transaction F110S.

F111	Automatic Payment Transactions for Payment Requests

Use this transaction to process an automatic payment request from a general ledger account. This transaction is used mostly in the treasury module, for example, where the business partner is a bank. Payment requests can be entered via transaction F-59. Note that for each payment request, a clearing account is required per company code in customizing.

F150	Dunning

This transaction is used to print dunning letters to, for example, customers who have an account in arrears. Enter a run data and identification ID. Enter parameters such as documents posted up to date, dunning date, company code and customers/vendors. Execute the program, check the log for any errors and then print out dunning letters.

FB00	Accounting Editing Options

This transaction is used to set user defined options for financial postings, open item management and displaying line items. For example, the foreign currency posting options can be suppressed when posting financial transactions and when clearing open items or an open item listing can be displayed as initially inactive when clearing.

FB01	Post Document: Header Data

Use this transaction for general financial postings. The document type will determine the type of financial posting, for example a general ledger posting or vendor invoice. Posting keys will determine whether a general ledger or sub ledger account is posted to.

FB01L	General Posting for Ledger Group: Header Data

This transaction is used to post a general ledger entry utilizing the new general ledger functionality. The new general ledger facilitates parallel accounting whereby a posting to a non leading ledger group can be made that satisfies local GAAP reporting requirements but does not affect the group GAAP reporting requirements.

FB02	Change Document

Use this transaction to change a posted finance document. A limited number of fields can be changed such as the text and assignment field. A list of documents can also be viewed by clicking the DOCUMENT LIST icon.

FB03	Display Document

This transaction is used to display a posted finance document. A list of documents can also be viewed by clicking the DOCUMENT LIST icon.

FB04	Document Changes

Use this transaction to display changes to a posted finance document. There is a period option but this relates to just one document; however, multiple document selection is possible by clicking ENVIRONMENT • MULTIPLE DISPLAY.

FB05	Post with Clearing: Header Data

Use this transaction to post and clear debits and credits from across multiple general accounts/open items. The posting header data is entered followed by the offset posting account and amount. Then open items can be chosen, processed and saved with a unique clearing number and date. This process will allow the user to select multiple open items and select debit and credit amounts for clearing against each other. Transaction F-04 can also be used.

FB08	Reverse Document: Header Data

Use this transaction to make a reversal of financial posting documents. Select the document number to be reversed, company code and fiscal year and the reason for reversal. The posting date defaults to today's date but must be within an open posting period. Use transaction F.80 for multiple financial document reversals.

FB09	Change Line Items

Use this transaction to change a posted finance document at the line item level. A limited number of fields can be changed such as the text and assignment field. A list of documents can also be created by clicking the DOCUMENT LIST icon. Also, there is the option to select just asset, customer, vendor or general ledger line items only.

FB09D	Display Line Items

This transaction is used to display posted finance documents at the line item level. A list of documents can also be created by clicking the DOCUMENT LIST icon. Also, there is the option to select just asset, customer, vendor or general ledger line items only.

FB11	Post Held Document: Header Data

Use this transaction to post a previously held financial document. Using the financial posting document transaction, for example, FB50, it is possible to hold an incomplete document, which SAP assigns a temporary document number. Enter the temporary document number and complete the document and then post. It is also possible to recall the temporary document number from the document posting transaction, FB50.

| **FB12** | Request Correspondence |

Use this transaction to create a correspondence request such as a customer's request for an ad hoc account statement or an internal document. The follow-on transaction code, F-64, will maintain the contents of the correspondence and printout.

| **FB13** | Release Line Item |

Use this transaction to post or reject a posted document/line item for payment that has been created, for example, with an incoming invoice using workflow.

| **FB50** | Enter G/L Account Document: Company Code XXXX |

Use this transaction for general financial postings. The document type will determine the type of financial posting, for example, a general ledger posting or vendor invoice. As opposed to transaction FB01, the posting keys are predefined in that postings can only be made to general ledger accounts via posting key 40 or 50.

| **FB50L** | Enter G/L Acct Document for Ledger Group |

This transaction is used to post a general ledger entry utilizing the new general ledger functionality. The new general ledger facilitates parallel accounting whereby a posting to a non leading ledger group can be made that satisfies local GAAP reporting requirements but does not affect the group GAAP reporting requirements.

| **FB60** | Enter Vendor Invoice: Company Code XXXX |

Use this transaction to post a vendor invoice. Both transactions FB60 and F-43 accommodate the same business requirement; however, this transaction enables the posting to be made on a single entry screen. Also, the posting keys are predefined making the entry easier. This transaction is not integrated with materials management invoice verification, so posting is to the finance module only.

| **FB65** | Enter Vendor Credit Memo: Company Code XXXX |

Use this transaction to post a vendor credit memo. Both transactions FB65 and F-41 accommodate the same business requirement; however, this transaction enables the posting to be made on a single entry screen. Also, the posting keys are predefined making the entry easier. This transaction is not integrated with materials management invoice verification, so posting is to the finance module only.

| **FB70** | Enter Customer Invoice: Company Code XXXX |

Use this transaction to post a customer invoice. Both transactions FB70 and F-22 accommodate the same business requirement; however, this transaction enables the posting to be made on a single entry screen. Also, the posting keys are predefined making the entry easier. This transaction is not integrated with the sales and distribution billing module, so posting is to the finance module only.

| **FB75** | Enter Customer Credit Memo: Company Code XXXX |

Use this transaction to post a customer credit memo. Both transactions FB75 and F-27 accommodate the same business requirement;

however, this transaction enables the posting to be made on a single entry screen. Also, the posting keys are predefined making the entry easier. This transaction is not integrated with the sales and distribution billing module, so posting is to the finance module only.

FBCJ	Cash Journal XXX
	Company Code XXX

Use this transaction to post cash receipts and payments. This transaction is facilitated by a single entry screen that can be saved and posted to the general ledger at a later date. Various periodic displays can be viewed and printed.

FBD1	Enter Recurring Entry:
	Header Data

This transaction is used to create a financial posting on a recurring basis. The static amount is posted on a periodic basis by executing transaction F.14. The posting can be made using a specific interval as defined by the recurring document or a run schedule that can be created in customizing and used across many recurring documents.

FBD2	Change Recurring Document

Use this transaction to change the posting amounts or dates on a recurring document created using transaction FBD1. A list of recurring documents can be displayed by clicking the DOCUMENT LIST icon.

FBD3	Display Recurring Document

Use this transaction to display a recurring document created by transaction FBD1. A list of recurring documents can be displayed by clicking the DOCUMENT LIST icon.

FBD4	Recurring Document Changes

This transaction is used to display changes that have been made to a recurring document using transaction FBD2. There is an option to select from a specific date, time and the user ID of the individual having made the change.

FBD5	Realize Recurring
	Entry: Header Data

This transaction is used to change the parameters of a recurring entry created using transaction FBD1, for example, the next run date. This transaction can also post at the same time.

FBE1	Create Payment Advice

Use this transaction to record a payment advice note from a business partner manually. The payment advice note can be used to record the payment details including payment amount, payment date and reference details about the payment. On the initial screen the payment advice note number can be assigned internally or externally.

FBE2	Change Payment Advice

Use this transaction to change a payment advice note created using transaction FBE1. A list of payment advice documents can be displayed by clicking the DOCUMENT LIST icon.

FBE3	Display Payment Advice

Use this transaction to display a payment advice note created using transaction FBE1. A list of payment advice documents can be displayed by clicking the DOCUMENT LIST icon.

FBE6   Delete Payment Advice

Use this transaction to delete a payment advice note created using transaction FBE1. A list of payment advice documents can be displayed by clicking the DOCUMENT LIST icon.

FBL1N   Vendor Line Item Display

This transaction is used to report open/closed vendor line items in accounts payable on key dates. Selection criteria include vendor, company code and many of the data sets on the vendor master record. Drill-down capability into the actual vendor document is available, as are various list formatting options. Alternatively, transaction F.41 can be used, but this report does not have drill-down capability.

FBL3N   G/L Account Line Item Display

Use this transaction to report open/closed vendor line items in accounts payable on key dates. Selection criteria include general ledger account, company code and many of the data sets on the general ledger master record. Drill-down capability into the actual vendor document is available, as are various formatting options. Alternatively, transaction F.09 can be used, but this report does not have drill-down capability.

FBL5N   Customer Line Item Display

This transaction is used to report open/closed customer line items in accounts receivable on key dates. Selection criteria include customer, company code and many of the data sets on the customer master record. Drill-down capability into the actual customer document is available as are various list formatting options. Alternatively, transaction F.20 can be used but this report, does not have drill-down capability.

FBM2   Change Sample Document

Use this transaction to change a sample document created using transaction F-01. A limited number of fields can be changed, for example, line item text and assignment, depending on customizing. Sample documents can be used as a reference when posting a financial document. Sample documents have a separate number range and do not update transaction figures.

FBM3   Display Sample Document

This transaction is used to display a sample document, which can be used as a reference when posting a financial document. Sample documents have a separate number range and do not update transaction figures.

FBM4   Sample Document Changes

This transaction is used to display changes to a sample document. There is an option to select from a specific date, time and user ID of the individual making the change. Sample documents can be used as a reference when posting a financial document. Sample documents have a separate number range and do not update transaction figures.

FBME   SAP Easy Access Banks

Use this transaction to gain easy access to all relevant banking transactions.

FBR1   Post with Reference Document: Header Data

This transaction is used to post a financial document using a previously posted finance document as a reference. Sample documents may also be used as a reference. This transaction can also be accessed via the regular financial posting transaction, for example, FB50, FB60 and FB70.

FBRA   Reset Cleared Items

Use this transaction to reset previously cleared items. Enter the clearing document, company code and fiscal year of the clearing posting. When resetting clearing postings, the clearing data is removed from the line items. This process will be utilized, for example, for opening misapplied payments or reversing/reissuing credit refunds.

FBRC   Reverse Clearing with Payment Card Data

Use this transaction to reset previously cleared items using the payment card functionality. Enter the clearing document, company code, fiscal year and payment card item number of the clearing posting. When resetting clearing postings, the clearing data is removed from the line items and reversal data, where it existed, is removed from the document header.

FBS1   Enter Accrual/Deferral Doc.: Header Data

Use this transaction to create an accrual posting. Selection is the same as a regular financial posting with the addition of a posting reversal reason and reverse posting date. Transaction F.81 can be executed on a periodic basis to reverse the posting made by this transaction.

FBU8   Reverse Cross-Company Code Transaction: Header Data

This transaction is used to reverse an intercompany financial posting. When intercompany postings are processed, two financial documents are created (one in each company code) but they are linked via a cross-company reference number. Using this transaction and the reference number, both documents can be reversed at the same time.

FBV0   Post Parked Document

This transaction is used to post a previously parked/stored document using FV50. Parked documents can be completed, checked and then posted at a later date, if necessary by a different individual. Parked documents can be posted either individually or via a list. To post several parked documents via a list, the system issues a list of parked documents for you to choose from. From this list, you can then carry out any necessary post processing to the parked document such as missing information/cost accounting assignment.

FBV2   Change Parked Document

Use this transaction to change a parked document. Changing a parked document is broken up into two transaction codes: FBV2 and FBV4. To change line item details use transaction code FBV2, while transaction code FBV4 is used to change header details.

FBV3   Display Parked Document

This transaction is used to display a parked document. Parked documents may be displayed individually or via a list.

FBV4   Change Parked Document (Header)

Use this transaction to change a parked document. Changing a parked document is broken up into two transaction codes: FBV2 and FBV4. To change line item details, use transaction code FBV2, while transaction code FBV4 is used to change header details.

FBV5   Document Changes of Parked Document

This transaction will allow the user to view the changes in a parked document. The user ID of the individual making the change and the date of the change can also be viewed.

FBV6   Reject Parked Document

This transaction can be used in conjunction with workflow whereby a parked document can be routed to an approver and, using this transaction, the approver can reject the document. The rejected document is then routed back to the originator for processing. The document number or list of documents can be processed.

FBW1   Enter Bill of Exchange Payment Request: Header Data

Use this transaction to post special bills of exchange receivables that are not issued by the customer but by you. Bill of exchange payment requests are sent to the customer for acceptance, and bank bills are passed directly to a bank for financing. Bank bills are subject to a general agreement with the customer whereby the customer's acceptance is not required. Both payment procedures are common in Italy, France, and Spain.

FBW2   Post Bill of Exch. acc. to Pmt Request: Header Data

This transaction is used to post a bill of exchange in accordance with the bill of exchange request posted using transaction FBW2.

FBW5   Customer Check/Bill of Exchange: Header Data

Use this transaction to post a check/bill of exchange in accounts receivable, which is sometimes referred to as a reverse bill of exchange. The customer pays an invoice by sending both a check and a reverse bill of exchange on which you are entered as the drawer. Once the due date and any country-specific protest period have elapsed, you cancel the liability.

FBW6   Vendor Check/Bill of Exchange

Use this transaction to post a check/bill of exchange in accounts payable. You pay an invoice with a check and at the same time you send a bill of exchange to your vendor. The vendor is recorded on the bill of exchange as the drawer, and your company code is entered as the drawee. Your vendor returns the bill of exchange to you signed, enabling you to pass it on for bill of exchange usage.

FBZ0   Payment Proposal

This transaction is used to create a proposal list to be used in a payment run. Enter proposal date, proposal ID, paying and sending company code. Then enter the proposal parameters and, if required, display/edit the proposal list. Transaction F110 can be used to create both the proposal list and the payment run but these functions can be split up to accommodate a segregation of duties using this transaction.

FBZ5   Print Form for Payment Document

Use this transaction to reprint a check.

FBZ8   Display Payment Run

Use this transaction to display the payment run results. Enter proposal date, proposal ID, paying and sending company code. Transaction F110 can be used to create, execute and display a payment run but this transaction may be used for segregation of duties purposes.

FCH1   Display Check Information

Use this transaction to display check information via the check number. From the check information display you can view the check recipient and check issuer as well as branching to display the corresponding payment and invoice documents.

FCH2   Payment Document Checks

Use this transaction to display check information via the payment document number. From the check information display you can view the check recipient and check issuer as well as branching to display the corresponding payment and invoice documents.

FCH3   Void Checks Not Used

This transaction is used to void checks before the print run has been executed. Checks may be voided if they have been accidentally damaged, stolen or rendered unused for any reason. Input the check numbers and the void reason code and then click CHECK and then VOID.

FCH4   Renumber Checks

Use this transaction to renumber checks, for example, where a trail printout used more numbers than anticipated. This would lead to numbers of used checks not corresponding to the check numbers determined in the print run. Select the paying company code, house bank, account ID, check lot number range from/to, void reason code and then enter the first check number in the renumbering sequence and click RENUMBER.

FCH5   Create Check Information

This transaction is used for checks that have been issued manually and you want to link the payment document and the check. A separate number range for manually created checks is recommended. Allocate a payment document number to the check number and, if you want to input additional information, such as the name of the payee, click ENTER, enter the data and save.

FCH6   Change Check Information/ Cash Check

Use this transaction to enter brief information about a check, such as the check recipient, as well as the date the check was cashed. If you are processing manual checks, you can correct the data saved.

FCH7   Reprint Check

This transaction is used when a check goes missing or is rendered unusable for any reason and requires reprinting. The original check is voided and a new check is reprinted.

FCH8   Cancel Check Payment

Use this transaction to reverse all cleared items after a check has been printed. This may be required if an incorrect check was selected to be paid. The check in question will be marked as void, the payment document reversed and the invoice set to open status ready for payment again.

FCH9   Void Issued Checks

Use this transaction to void checks after the print run has been executed. For example, checks that are not required because cash payment has been chosen instead of a check. To void printed checks, enter the check number and void reason code and click CHECK and VOID.

FCHD   Delete Check Information on Payment Run

Use this transaction where the print program crashed, i.e., where the print management file is incomplete. Because there is no way verifying whether the data so far created is consistent, the only option is to delete the check information on the payment run. Enter the payment run in question and click EXECUTE. In addition, you must delete the print management print jobs that were generated.

FCHE — Delete Check Information on Voided Checks

This transaction is used to delete information stored for unused checks that were incorrectly voided. Enter the paying company code and the relevant check numbers.

FCHF — Delete Information on Checks Created Manually

Use this transaction to delete information about a manually created check. This may be required if an incorrect check number was entered or check payment was unexpectedly not made.

FCHG — Reset Check Information Data

This transaction is used if an issued check was mistakenly voided. The data can be reset, including check number and void reason code, etc. so that the check can become valid again and be cashed by the recipient.

FCHI — Check Lots

This transaction is used to maintain check lots. A check lot contains a check number range and is used so that the check number in SAP corresponds to the printed check number. The print program uses the number range to link the check with the payment. Choose CREATE, enter the lot number, the check number range and the next lot number, click ENTER and then enter a short description of the check lot. The text will facilitate the assignment of the check lot to a user ID or printer.

FCHK — SAP Easy Access Check Management

Use this transaction for easy access to the check management transaction codes. Alternatively, these transactions can also be accessed when executing the payment program via transaction F110.

FCHN — Check Register

This transaction is the standard report for displaying the check register. The report gives an overview of the check information, for example, house bank issuing the check, check numbers issued, vendor or account number for which the check was created and outgoing payment document number.

FCHR — Online Cashed Checks

Use this transaction to clear checks that have been cashed. If you receive the list of cashed checks in electronic form, you can import the list into SAP using program RFEBCK00. But if the bank sends the information in list form, then you can use this transaction to transfer the data. This transaction also clears the outgoing checks account and updates the bank account.

FCHX — Check Extract Creation

This transaction is used to create a file containing data on checks issued to a certain house bank, more commonly known as a positive pay file. The bank can then use this file to detect any errors in incoming checks. Converting the data into a format required by the house bank may require running a custom developed program that supports the particular bank's format.

FD01 — Customer Create

This transaction is used to create general and company code views of the customer master record. Customer master fields that are either optional or required fields, as determined by the account group, can be maintained. Use transaction XD01 to create the sales areas of the customer master for business partners, such as sold-to, ship-to, payer and bill-to.

FD02   Customer Change

This transaction is used to change the customer master record general and company code level data. Customer master data fields that are either optional or required, as determined by the account group will be available to change. Use transaction XD02 to change the sales area data for business partners such as sold-to, ship-to, payer and bill-to.

FD03   Customer Display

This transaction is used to display the customer master general and company code level data only. To view the sales area data for business partners, such as sold-to, ship-to, payer and bill-to use transaction code XD03.

FD04   Customer Account Changes

Use this transaction code to report changes to the customer master general and company code level data. The report is by customer and company code. There is an option to select from a specific date, time and the user ID of the individual making the change. The report output will display the fields changed with the option to drill down and display the old field, new field value and date changed. Use transaction XD04 to view changes at the sales area data level.

FD05   Customer Block/Unblock

This transaction is used to block the customer master from using various transactions such as processing financial transactions. Use transaction XD05 to block/unblock at the sales area level.

FD06   Customer Flag for Deletion

Use this transaction to flag a customer master for deletion. The deletion flag can be set by company code or all company codes. Furthermore, the deletion flag can be set at the general area data and general area data including selected company code area data. The deletion flag will ensure that the customer cannot be used in transactional processing and can be included in the archiving process. Use transaction XD06 to flag the customer at the sales area level.

FD08   Customer Confirm Change

This transaction is used when the DUAL MASTER DATA CONTROL functionality has been activated and you want to confirm the change to a sensitive field for a single customer. Certain fields can be flagged as sensitive fields, which will require a second user, using this transaction, to confirm the change. Creating or changing sensitive fields can block a vendor or customer (in the case of paying credit memos) from payment until the changes to the master record have been confirmed using this transaction.

FD09   Display/Confirm Critical Customer Changes

This transaction is used when the DUAL MASTER DATA CONTROL functionality has been activated and you want to confirm the change to a sensitive field for a list of customers. Certain fields can be flagged as sensitive fields, which will require a second user, using this transaction, to confirm the change. Creating or changing sensitive fields can block a vendor or customer (in the case of paying credit memos) from payment until the changes to the master record have been confirmed using this transaction.

FD10N Customer Balance Display

Use this transaction to display a customer account balance. The account balance will show the opening balance (which is the carry forward balance from last year), total transactions per posting period broken down by debits and credits, balance per posting period and accumulated account balance. In addition to the above balances, the system displays the gross sales/purchases per period for each account. The balances from special G/L account transactions are also included in an account balance. The drill-down function enables the display of line items that make up the account balance.

FD10NA Customer Balance Display with Worklist

Use this transaction to display a customer account balance with a worklist. A worklist allows you to display a range of customers. The account balance will show the opening balance (which is the carry forward balance from last year), total transactions per posting period broken down by debits and credits, balance per posting period and accumulated account balance. In addition to the above balances, the system displays the gross sales/purchases per period for each account. The balances from special G/L account transactions are also included in the account balance. The drill-down function enables the display of the line items that make up the account balance.

FD11 Customer: Initial Screen Account Analysis

This transaction is used to perform an analysis of a customer or group of customers. In addition to displaying customer account balances and line items (i.e., transaction FD10N) the account analysis function can also display data related to days in arrears, net/cash discount overview, payment history, and credit history. This report provides the ability to drill down to document level detail, select various views/layouts for the report, and customize the layout and the data presented.

FD15 Transfer Customer Master Data from Source Company Code

This transaction is used to transfer customer master data maintained in a source company code to other target company codes. Due to run time considerations there is a selection option to select only those customers for whom company code dependent data has changed since a specific date. Only data fields that are ready for input may be transferred, so it is recommended that the field control be the same. Execute the program in direct transfer mode and a batch input session is created and ready for processing. Customer master data can be written to a sequential file and processed via transaction FD16.

FD16 Transfer Customer Changes: Receive

Use this transaction to transfer customer master data to an external system. Once transaction FD15 has been executed to create a sequential file this transaction can be used to import the data and create a batch input session.

FD24 Credit Management Changes

Use this transaction to report any changes made to credit management master data for all accounts. This report will show the old to new field change, the date and user ID of the individual having made the change.

FD32 Customer Credit Management Change

This transaction is used to change a customer's credit master. Fields that can be changed, for example, include the customer's overall credit limit for all credit control areas, individual credit limit within a credit control area, the currency in which the customer's credit information will be managed and risk category.

FD33	Customer Credit Management Display

Use this transaction to display the following data for a customer in a credit control area:

► Receivables from sales (unless they are marked as disputed items)

► Receivables from special G/L transactions, which are marked as credit limit-relevant (for example, down payments)

► Order value (consisting of open orders, deliveries and billing documents)

► Total liabilities (sum of the rest)

When you post a customer invoice, the system automatically adds the amount to the existing receivables or to receivables from a special G/L transaction, depending on the posting key involved. When the customer incoming payment is posted, the appropriate amount is subtracted from the existing receivables.

FD10	Execute Drill-Down Report

This transaction is used to execute a drill-down report for customer account financial reporting. This type of interactive report allows drill-down capability from a basic list. You also have the option to switch the order in which the drill down occurs. Use transaction FDI1 to create the report.

FDI1	Create Drill-Down Report

Use this transaction to create a drill-down report in customer account financial reporting. This type of interactive report allows drill-down capability from a basic list. You can define default values when creating a report and navigation options for the drill-down list display.

FDI2	Change Report: Settings

Use this transaction to change a customer account financial report. This type of interactive report allows drill down capability from a basic list. You can define default values when creating a report and navigation options for the drill-down list display.

FDI3	Display Report: Settings

Use this transaction to display the settings of a customer account financial drill-down report. This type of interactive report allows drill-down capability from a basic list. You can define default values when creating a report and navigation options for which a drill-down list can be displayed.

FDI4	Report Painter: Create Form

This transaction is used to create a form for a customer account financial drill-down reporting. In a form you define the content and formal structure, which is displayed in the report in the detail list. Here you determine the characteristics and key figures, which you want to display in the report.

FDI5	Report Painter: Change Form

Use this transaction to change the settings of a form used in a customer account financial drill-down report. In a form you define the content and formal structure, which is displayed in the report in the detail list. Here you determine the characteristics and key figures, which you want to display in the report.

FDI6	Report Painter: Display Form

Use this transaction to display the settings of a form used in a customer account financial drill-down report. In a form you define the content and formal structure, which is displayed in the report in the detail list.

FEBA   Edit Bank Statement

Use this transaction to manually post process a bank statement entered either automatically or manually because it is not always possible to clear all items automatically. Enter the application, company code, house bank, account ID and statement number. Double-click the bank details to display the statements for the bank. A green checkmark next to the statement indicates that the postings were processed without errors. A red cross next to the statement indicates that the account statement contains items that could not be posted. You have to post process these items

FEBP   Post Electronic Bank Statement

This transaction is used if, for any reason, the posting that is generated from transaction FF.5 fails. This may occur, for example, if a user is working in a bank statement using transaction FEBA when transaction FF.5 is being executed. Normally, transaction FF.5 will import the electronic bank statement and generate the financial postings.

FF.5   Select Program: Import Electronic Bank Statement

This transaction is used to import an electronic bank statement. This transaction allows the user to select the relevant program used by the bank statement format. The process is ideally automated whereby the banks are polled for prior-day statements. SAP makes a G/L entry to move the transactions from the G/L clearing accounts into the master bank G/L accounts. The import of electronic bank statements is aimed at a daily bank reconciliation process.

FF.6   Select Program: Display Electronic Bank Statement

Use this transaction to print the bank statement after import. You must enter a company code, house bank ID and account ID. If you do not enter a statement date or a statement number, you receive a printout of all the bank statements for this bank account.

FF_3   Cashed Checks per Bank Account

This transaction is used to report on the following data:

▶ The average period outstanding for checks already cashed

▶ The average period outstanding for checks not yet cashed

▶ The number and amount total of checks currently outstanding

The program can be used as an alternative to determining the difference between the planned cash outflow and the actual cashing date. To do this, you must select the option DEVIATION FROM PLANNING DATE.

FF_4   Outstanding Checks Analysis per G/L Account and Vendor

Use this transaction to evaluate the outstanding period, i.e., the difference between cashing date and posting date, for each G/L account managed on an open-item basis for each vendor. To do this, you can select the date relevant for cashing the check. When you select the value date, it is taken from the check debit-line items. If the value date is not entered, the corresponding bank line items are taken to determine the value date. If several check debits exist for a clearing procedure and the value or document date of the check debit is used as the reference date, then the system tries to assign the check posting to the check debit by comparing the amount and the currency. The document creation dates are also compared (the check debit cannot lie before the check posting). If no assignment can be determined, the checks are ignored and they are not included in the calculation of the period outstanding.

You can place the average outstanding period calculated for each vendor into a batch input session. The report then checks whether the existing figure in the vendor master record field CHECK CASHING TIME equals the one calculated. If this is not the case, the field is updated when the session is processed.

| FF63 | Create Memo Record |

Use this transaction to post a credit memo for cash and liquidity planning purposes. You differentiate between the payment advice relevant for the cash position and the planned items relevant for the liquidity forecast. Alternatively you can create memo records from the screen DISPLAY CASH MANAGEMENT AND FORECAST of the cash position to the liquidity forecast.

| FF67 | Process Manual Bank Statement |

Use this transaction to manually enter bank account statements you receive. Statement entry usually occurs in two steps. First, enter the account line items in the system. Various facilities support you during this step so that the line layout for entering account line items can be varied. In addition, the system supports individual account determination and checks data consistency. Second, you post the line items you have entered. When you enter your data, payment advices that are created in Cash Management using memo record entry can be automatically transferred to the bank statement.

| FF68 | Edit Check Deposit List |

This transaction is used to enter checks you receive. After the input is complete, you can access additional functions to further process the entered checks. On the entry screen, the system will display different fields for each account assignment variant you choose. Depending on the number of account assignment fields in a variant, up to three lines are available for entering a memo record.

| FF6B | Memo Records: List |

Use this transaction for listing planning memo records of the cash position and the liquidity forecast created using transaction FF63.

| FF73 | Automatic Cash Concentration |

Use this transaction to concentrate all of your cash account balances into one target account. The system generates a proposal for concentrating cash that is based on a predefined grouping. This proposal contains the day-end balance and the cash planning results, in other words, the expected account transfers. You can correct the proposal at any stage. The system prints the outcome of the cash concentration process in the form of payment orders to banks. It also creates the payment advices needed to determine the new bank account balances.

| FF74 | Access Automatic Cash Concentration Using a Program |

This transaction calls up transaction FF73, cash concentration and therefore allows you to use variants in cash concentration. However, this process has the minor disadvantage that you see the start screen twice and so you must execute the program twice.

FF7A   Cash Position

Use this transaction to gain an understanding of a company's liquidity status. The system offers you two evaluation reports, with which you can edit various views. Use transaction FF7A to view the cash position, which provides a short-term view for monitoring the liquidity in bank accounts. Use transaction FF7B, the liquidity forecast to evaluate information for certain customers, vendors or sub ledgers in the mid/long term. The cash position and liquidity forecast together amount to the total liquidity of the company

FF7B   Liquidity Forecast

Use this transaction to gain an understanding of a company's liquidity status. The system offers you two evaluation reports, with which you can edit various views. Use transaction FF7A to view the cash position, which provides a short-term view for monitoring the liquidity in bank accounts. Use transaction FF7B, the liquidity forecast to evaluate information for certain customers, vendors or sub ledgers in the mid/long term. The cash position and liquidity forecast together amount to the total liquidity of the company.

FGI0   Execute Drill-Down Report

This transaction is used to execute a drill-down report using the new general ledger functionality. This type of interactive report allows drill-down capability from a basic list. You can also switch the order in which you drill down on the characteristics within the report. Use transaction FGI1 to create the report.

FGI1   Create Drill-Down Report

Use this transaction to create a drill-down report in the new general ledger. This type of interactive report allows drill down capability from a basic list. You can define default values when creating the report and navigation options for how the drill-down list is displayed.

FGI2   Change Report: Settings

Use this transaction to change a new general ledger drill-down report. This type of interactive report allows drill-down capability from a basic list. You can define default values when creating a report and navigation options for how the drill-down list is displayed.

FGI3   Display Report: Settings

Use this transaction to display the settings of a new general ledger drill down report. This type of interactive report allows drill-down capability from a basic list. You can define default values when creating a report and navigation options for how the drill-down list is displayed.

FGI4   Report Painter: Create Form

This transaction is used to create a form for a new general ledger drill-down reporting. In a form you define the content and formal structure, which is displayed in the report in the detail list. Here you determine the characteristics and key figures that you want to display in the report.

FGI5   Report Painter: Change Form

Use this transaction to change the settings of a form used in a new general ledger drill down report. In a form you define the content and formal structure, which is displayed in the report in the detail list. Here you determine the characteristics and key figures that you want to display in the report.

FGI6   Report Painter: Display Form

Use this transaction to display the settings of a form used in a new general ledger drill-down report. In a form you define the content and formal structure, which is displayed in the report in the detail list. Here you determine the characteristics and key figures that you want to display in the report.

FI01   Create Bank

This transaction is used to create the master data for banks that you require for payment transactions with your business partners. This includes both your banks and the banks of your business partners. Enter the country key where the bank is located. The country key defines the rules for validating the bank data such as the bank key and bank account number. Normally, you manage banks using their bank number. The bank number in the control data for the bank is then displayed twice, that is, as the bank key too. In certain countries, the bank account number takes on this function; then there are no bank numbers and the bank data is managed using the account number. To manage bank data using another key, for example, the SWIFT code, external number assignment can also be used. Click ENTER and maintain bank data, such as name and address, etc.

FI02   Change Bank

Use this transaction to change master data for banks. Your house bank and/or the banks of your business partners can be changed using this transaction. Your business partners' bank details are entered in the customer or vendor master record and linked to the bank master data via the bank country key and the bank key. The bank master will also contain the address of the bank.

FI03   Display Bank

Use this transaction to display master data for banks. Your house bank and/or the banks of your business partners can be displayed using this transaction. Your business partners' bank

details are entered in the customer or vendor master record and linked to the bank master data via the bank country key and the bank key. The bank master will also contain the address of the bank.

FI04   Bank Data Changes

Use this transaction code to report all changes to the bank master. The report is by company code. There is an option to select from a specific date, time and user ID of the individual making the change. The report output will display the fields changed with the option to drill down and display the old/new field value and date changed.

FI06   Set Bank Deletion Flag

Use this transaction to flag a bank master for deletion. The deletion flag can be set by company code. The deletion flag will ensure that the bank master cannot be used in financial transactional processing and can be included in the archiving process.

FK01   Vendor Create

This transaction is used to create the general and company code views of the vendor master record. Vendor master fields that are either optional or required fields, as determined by the account group, can be maintained. Use transaction XK01 to create the purchasing area data of the vendor master.

FK02   Vendor Change

This transaction is used to change the vendor master record general and company code level data. Vendor master data fields that are either optional or required, as determined by the account group will be available to change. Use transaction XK02 to change the purchasing area data.

FK03   Vendor Display

This transaction is used to display the vendor master general and company code level data only. To view the purchasing area data for business partners, use transaction code XK03.

FK04   Vendor Account Changes

Use this transaction code to report changes to the vendor master general and company code level data. The report is by vendor and company code. There is an option to select from a specific date, time and user ID of the individual making the change. The report output will display the fields changed with the option to drill down and display the old/new field value and date changed. Use transaction XK04 to view changes at the purchasing area data level.

FK05   Vendor Block/Unblock

This transaction is used to block the vendor master from various transactions such as processing financial transactions. Use transaction XK05 to block/unblock at the purchasing area level.

FK06   Vendor Flag for Deletion

Use this transaction to flag a vendor master for deletion. The deletion flag can be set by company code or all company codes. Furthermore, the deletion flag can be set at the general area data and general area data including selected company code area data. The deletion flag will ensure that the vendor cannot be used in transactional processing and can be included in the archiving process. Use transaction XK06 to flag the vendor at the purchasing area level.

FK08   Vendor Confirm Change

This transaction is used when the dual master data control functionality has been activated and you want to confirm the change to a sensitive field for a single vendor. Certain fields can be flagged as sensitive fields, which will require a second user, using this transaction, to confirm the change. Creating or changing sensitive fields can block a vendor from payment until the changes have been confirmed.

FK09   Display/Confirm Critical Vendor Changes

This transaction is used when the dual master data control functionality has been activated and you want to confirm the change to a sensitive field for a list of vendors. Certain fields can be flagged as sensitive fields, which will require a second user, using this transaction, to confirm the change. Creating or changing sensitive fields can block a vendor from payment until the changes have been confirmed.

FK10N   Vendor Balance Display

Use this transaction to display a vendor account balance. The account balance will show the opening balance (which is the carry forward balance from last year), total transactions per posting period broken down by debits and credits, balance per posting period and accumulated account balance. In addition to the above balances, the system displays the gross sales/purchases per period for each account. The balances from special G/L account transactions are also included in an account balance. The drill-down function enables the display of the line items that make up the account balance.

FK10NA Vendor Balance Display
with Worklist

Use this transaction to display a vendor
account balance with a worklist. A worklist
allows you to display a range of vendors.
The account balance will show the opening
balance (carry forward balance for last year),
total transactions per posting period broken
down by debits and credits, balance per posting period and accumulated account balance.
In addition to the above balances, the system
displays the gross sales/purchases per period
for each account. The balances from special
G/L account transactions are also included
in an account balance. The drill-down function enables the display of the line items that
make up the account balance.

FK15 Transfer Vendor Master Data
from Source Company Code

This transaction is used to transfer vendor
master data maintained in a source company
code to other target company codes. Due to
run time considerations there is a selection
option to select only those vendors where
company code dependent data has changed
since a specific date. Only data fields that are
ready for input may be transferred, so it is
recommended that the field control be the
same. Execute the program in direct transfer
mode and a batch input session is created and
ready for processing. Vendor master data can
be written to a sequential file and processed
via transaction FK16.

FK16 Transfer Vendor
Changes: Receive

Use this transaction to transfer vendor master
data to an external system. Once transaction
FK15 has been executed to create a sequential
file this transaction can be used to import the
data and create a batch input session.

FKI0 Execute Drill-Down Report

This transaction is used to execute a drill-
down report for vendor account financial
reporting. This type of interactive report
allows drill-down capability from a basic
list. You can also switch the order in which
you drill down on the characteristics within
the report. Use transaction FKI1 to create
the report.

FKI1 Create Drill-Down Report

Use this transaction to create a drill-down
report in vendor account financial reporting. This type of interactive report allows
drill-down capability from a basic list. You
can define default values when creating a
report and navigation options for which a
drill-down list can be displayed.

FKI2 Change Report: Settings

Use this transaction to change a vendor
account financial report. This type of interactive report allows drill down capability from a
basic list. You can define default values when
creating a report and navigation options for
which a drill-down list can be displayed.

FKI3 Display Report: Settings

Use this transaction to display the settings of
a vendor account financial drill down report.
This type of interactive report allows drill
down capability from a basic list. You can
define default values when creating a report
and navigation options for which a drill-
down list can be displayed.

FKI4 Report Painter: Create Form

This transaction is used to create a form for
a vendor account financial drill-down reporting. In a form you define the content and
formal structure, which is displayed in the
report in the detail list. Here you determine

the characteristics and key figures that you want to display in the report.

FKI5   Report Painter: Change Form

Use this transaction to change the settings of a form used in a vendor account financial drill-down report. In a form you define the content and formal structure, which is displayed in the report in the detail list. Here you determine the characteristics and key figures that you want to display in the report.

FKI6   Report Painter: Display Form

Use this transaction to display the settings of a form used in a vendor account financial drill-down report. In a form you define the content and formal structure, which is displayed in the report in the detail list. Here you determine the characteristics and key figures that you want to display in the report.

FKMT   Account Assignment Model

Use this transaction to create a reference/template with default values for financial postings. An account assignment model can contain any number of G/L account receivables/account payables account items, and can be changed or supplemented at any time. During document entry, the end user can change, add to, or delete the proposed data. The account assignment model can be called up at financial document entry time.

FLB1   Post Processing Lockbox Data

Use this transaction to process any checks that could not be fully applied by the Lockbox Import Program via transaction FLB2. Lockbox processing creates payment advices for any payment that cannot be applied fully and uses a "lockbox clearing" account to post all payments directly to the bank G/L account. This allows the bank account to have a correct balance while the clearing account has non-

zero balance until all payments are applied to customers or written off. Payment advices are stored and post processing uses these advices to correctly apply payments to the customer. You can make changes to advices if needed, or just use the advice to show the customer invoices and apply as partial or residual items.

FLB2   Main Lockbox Program

This transaction is used to process the lockbox file received from the bank (typically in BAI or BAI2 format). The SAP lockbox program translates the file and posts to a G/L cash account, creates payment advices that are matched against accounts receivable open items and clears those items. Use transaction FLB1 to access the lockbox post process transaction to process any checks that could not be fully applied by the Lockbox Import Program.

FLBP   Main Lockbox Program

Use this transaction to process the lockbox when using an IDoc interface. Data is read automatically and stored in the bank data. This transaction is then scheduled, which processes the lockbox data (by producing payment memos and postings, creating the check and posting logs, generating batch input for creating new bank details). Use transaction FLB1 to access the lockbox post process transaction to process any checks that could not be fully applied by the Lockbox Import Program.

FM5I   Create Fund

This transaction is used to create a fund that represents financial resources that are provided for a specific purpose by a sponsor and managed separately. This enables the exact source of the funds to be determined. Input the fund management area (to be entered once only, after which the system will remember) and the fund number. The validity of the fund can be determined by definition in the master record or determined by the fund application. Other input data can include fund type and budget profile, which determines the basis for budgeting and availability control.

FM5S	Display Fund

Use this transaction to display a fund master. You can display the validity of the fund and the budget profile.

FM9B	Copy Budget Version

This transaction supports budget planning. You can use this function to, for example, copy budget data from the old year, as the first version of the budget, for the new year. You can adjust the data to take account of inflation and other factors in the new year.

FM9C	Plan Data Transfer from CO

Use this transaction to copy data from the plan version from the controlling module to the budget version in funds management. This utility allows for an easy way of creating similar budget versions in funds management from the data transferred from the controlling module.

FM9D	Lock Budget Version

This transaction is used to lock the budget version in funds management.

FM9E	Unlock Budget Version

This transaction is used to unlock the budget version in funds management.

FMN0	Transfer Documents from Financial Accounting

This transaction is used to post or repost financial documents to funds management. This transaction can be used if there is a need to correct funds management data by recreating the financial documents after corrections have been made or to construct funds management when implementing funds management in a productive system. After the construction or reconstruction you must also reconstruct assigned values to determine excessive funds centers and commitment item hierarchies in funds management and execute a payment conversion to update the actual data in funds management in accordance with the time sequence.

FMR3	Plan/Actual/ Commitment Report

Use this transaction to report on plan, actual and commitment comparisons. This report will show all commitment/actual postings per funds management area, version, period and fiscal year. One or more commitment items can also be selected.

FMSA	Create Funds Center in FM Area

This transaction is used to create a funds center, which represents the structure of an organization (areas of responsibility, departments and projects) in the form of a hierarchy. You can assign a budget to funds centers in funds management. The budget is used up as postings are made to funds centers with commitments and actual values. Input the fund center number, funds management area and valid to/from dates, click ENTER and complete the master data set-up.

FMSU	Change Fund

Use this transaction to change the fund master. You can use this transaction, for instance, to assign a fund sponsor to the fund.

FMX1	Funds Reservation:
	Create InitScrn

This transaction is used to create a reservation for future budget consumption, within which all purchasing and financial activities take place. When posting a purchasing document (purchase order) or financial accounting document (i.e., vendor invoice) by referencing a funds reservation document number and the earmarked funds field of the account assignment coding block, the system automatically transfers the funds management account assignment from the funds reservation. Once a purchase order or finance document is registered, the funds reservation is consumed. Input the header data on the document, click ENTER, and then enter the overall amount, amount to be reserved, commitment item, funds center, other finance data such as G/L account, cost center, etc. and save.

FMX2	Funds Reservation:
	Change InitScrn

Use this transaction to change a reservation for future budget consumption.

FMX3	Funds Reservation:
	Display InitScrn

Use this transaction to display a reservation for future budget consumption.

FMY1	Funds Pre Commitment:
	Create InitScrn

This transaction is used to create a reservation for future budget consumption. By referencing a funds reservation (created using transaction FMX1) you can portray the funds reservation/budgeting process. Therefore, a funds pre commitment can reference a funds reservation and therefore reduce it.

FMY2	Funds Pre Commitment:
	Change InitScrn

Use this transaction to change the pre commitment reservation.

FMY3	Funds Pre Commitment:
	Display InitScrn

Use this transaction to display the pre commitment reservation.

FMZ1	Funds Commitment:
	Create InitScrn

This transaction is used to earmark funds for future budget consumption. Used in reference to a pre commitment the funds reservation can reduce the pre commitment and reservation for future budget consumption.

FMZ2	Funds Commitment:
	Change InitScrn

Use this transaction to change the commitment reservation.

FMZ3	Funds Commitment:
	Display InitScrn

Use this transaction to display the commitment reservation.

FPS3	Same Day Statement:
	Create Memo Records

This transaction used as a tool for updating the cash position in cash management. The uploading of an intraday statement will display a list of transactions that may or may not be selected to be included in the cash position for that day.

FSP4   G/L Account Changes in Chart of Accts

Use this transaction to report changes to the G/L account master at the chart of accounts level. Select the G/L account and chart of accounts. Further selection options include: from a specific date, time and the user ID of the individual making the change. The report output will display the fields changed with the option to drill down and display the old/new field value and date changed.

FS00   Edit G/L Account Centrally

Use this transaction to edit the G/L master record centrally at the chart of accounts level and the company code level. The chart of accounts data includes the description of the G/L account, a profit and loss or balance sheet indicator, and the account group field (which determines the fields that will be input at the company code level). The company code level data includes settings such as the currency the G/L account is managed in, an open item management indicator and the field status group, which determines the input fields when making financial postings to the G/L account. You can also use this transaction to block a G/L account from posting financial transactions and flag it for deletion.

FS10N   G/L Account Balance Display

This transaction is used to display the G/L account balance by month for a particular year. One or multiple G/L accounts can be selected. The user can drill down on any period to view the transactional detail.

FSE2   Change Financial Statement Version

Use this transaction to make a change to the financial statement version, i.e., the structure of financial statements. This transaction is by default a customization transaction, but some companies choose to make this a business user transaction in the productive client.

FSI0   Execute Drill-Down Report

This transaction is used to execute a drill-down report using the classic general ledger functionality. This type of interactive report allows drill-down capability from a basic list. You also have the option to switch the order in which the drill-down occurs. Use transaction FSI1 to create the report.

FSI1   Create Drill-Down Report

Use this transaction to create a drill down report in the classic general ledger. This type of interactive report allows drill down capability from a basic list. You can define default values when creating a report and navigation options for which a drill-down list can be displayed.

FSI2   Change Report: Settings

Use this transaction to change a classic general ledger drill down report. This type of interactive report allows drill down capability from a basic list. You can define default values when creating a report and navigation options for which a drill-down list can be displayed.

FSI3   Display Report: Settings

Use this transaction to display the settings of a classic general ledger drill down report. This type of interactive report allows drill down capability from a basic list. You can define default values when creating a report and navigation options for which a drill-down list can be displayed.

FSI4   Report Painter: Create Form

This transaction is used to create a form for a classic general ledger drill-down report. In a form you define the content and formal structure, which is displayed in the report in the detail list. Here you determine the characteristics and key figures that you want to display in the report.

FSI5	Report Painter: Change Form

Use this transaction to change the settings of a form used in a classic general ledger drill-down report. In a form you define the content and formal structure, which is displayed in the report in the detail list. Here you determine the characteristics and key figures that you want to display in the report.

FSI6	Report Painter: Display Form

Use this transaction to display the settings of a form used in a classic general ledger drill-down report. In a form you define the content and formal structure, which is displayed in the report in the detail list. Here you determine the characteristics and key figures that you want to display in the report.

FSP0	Edit G/L Account Chart of Accts Data

Use this transaction to create a G/L account in the chart of accounts only. Input the G/L account number, chart of accounts and click ENTER. Select the account group (this will determine the fields required at the company code level), the profit and loss account indicator and the text of the G/L account. Additionally, if the consolidation module is used, the trading partner account and group account may be selected.

FSS0	Edit G/L Account In Company Code

This transaction is used to create a new G/L at the company code level. Enter the G/L account and the company code the new G/L account is to be created in and then click

the CREATE icon. The company code level data includes settings such as the currency the G/L account is managed in, open item management indicator and the field status group, which determines the input fields when making financial postings to the G/L account. You can also use this transaction to block a G/L account from posting financial transactions and flag it for deletion.

FSS4	Central G/L Account Changes In Company Code

Use this transaction to report changes to the G/L account master at the company code level. Select the G/L account and company code and click EXECUTE. Further selection options include a specific date, time and the user ID of the individual making the change. The report output will display the fields changed with the option to drill down to display the old/new field value and date changed. You can also use this transaction to block a G/L account from posting financial transactions and flag it for deletion.

FV50	Park G/L Account Document

Use this transaction to enter and store (park) incomplete general ledger postings without carrying out extensive entry checks, such as the document balance check. Parked documents can be completed, checked and then posted at a later date, if necessary by a different individual, using transaction FBV0. Parked documents can be evaluated online for reporting purposes from the moment they are parked. Transaction FV67 can also be used.

FV60	Park Vendor Invoice

Use this transaction to enter and store (park) incomplete vendor invoices without carrying out extensive entry checks, such as the document balance check. Parked documents can be completed, checked and then posted at a later date, if necessary by a different individual, using transaction FBV0. Parked documents can be evaluated online for reporting purposes from the moment they are parked. Transaction F-65 can also be used.

FV65   Park Vendor Credit Memo

Use this transaction to enter and store (park) incomplete vendor credit memos without carrying out extensive entry checks, such as the document balance check. Parked documents can be completed, checked and then posted at a later date, if necessary by a different individual, using transaction FBV0. Parked documents can be evaluated online for reporting purposes from the moment they are parked. Transaction F-66 can also be used.

FV70   Park Customer Invoice

Use this transaction to enter and store (park) incomplete customer invoices without carrying out extensive entry checks, such as the document balance check. Parked documents can be completed, checked and then posted at a later date, if necessary by a different individual, using transaction FBV0. Parked documents can be evaluated online for reporting purposes from the moment they are parked. Transaction F-64 can also be used.

FV75   Park Customer Credit Memo

Use this transaction to enter and store (park) incomplete customer credit memos without carrying out extensive entry checks, such as the document balance check. Parked documents can be completed, checked and then posted at a later date, if necessary by a different individual, using transaction FBV0. Parked documents can be evaluated online for reporting purposes from the moment they are parked. Transaction F-67 can also be used.

IM01   Create Inv. Program Definition

This transaction is used to create an investment program for planned or budgeted costs for capital investments (or other projects) in the form of a hierarchical structure. The hierarchical structure is definable and is not dependent of any organizational units. You can assign investment measures and appropriation requests to the investment program positions. Input the program definition (program type, key, description and approval year), the program structure and program positions (organizational assignments, person(s) responsible). Note: use IM01 only once and then use IM27 for every approval year thereafter so that you can report on programs over multiple years.

IM02   Change Inv. Program Definition

Use this transaction to change an investment program for capital investments (or other projects). Enter the investment program number and the approval year and click ENTER. Input fields available for changing include program description, person responsible, etc.

IM03   Display Inv. Program Definition

Use this transaction to display an investment program for capital investments (or other projects). Enter the investment program number and the approval year and click ENTER.

IM05   Reassignment of Measures/App. Requests

This transaction is used to reassign investment measures and appropriation requests from one investment program position to another. Enter the sending program position and the receiving program position. There is also the ability to specify whether the system should automatically modify the plan and budget values on the sending and receiving program positions, as well as the next position above them in the hierarchy. You can start the reassignment in test mode or execute the function immediately.

| IM22 | Change Inv. Program Structure |

This transaction is used to sub divide the investment hierarchy below the enterprise structure. Enter the program, leave the position ID blank, approval year, leave hierarchy level blank and click ENTER. Position the cursor on the investment program and click CREATE. Enter the position ID and description and click ENTER. You can then continue to create subordinate levels in the structure. Note that only the end node of the program position can be assigned with investment measures.

| IM23 | Display Inv. Program Structure |

Use this transaction to display the investment program structure. Within the transaction enter the program, leave the position ID blank, enter approval year, leave hierarchy level blank and click ENTER. You can then drill down on the investment program structure.

| IM27 | Open New Approval Year |

Use this transaction to carry forward the original budget (after a fiscal year change) of the new investment program (rather than the current budget). SAP manages the budget carried forward separately from the current budget of the new investment program, so you must use this transaction to combine the two.

| IM30 | Change Program Budget Supplement |

This transaction is used to change the program budget from the original budget for both the investment program budget and for the measure budget. Changes are managed as line items in the system and are therefore managed separately from the original budget. Enter the program, position ID or the program node instead, approval year and click ENTER. The supplement budget can then be entered.

| IM31 | Display Program Budget Supplement |

Use this transaction to display a program budget supplement. You can also display budget supplements as an explanation of the current budget.

| IM32 | Change Original Program Budget |

This transaction is used to enter a program budget, typically for a new program year. You can enter budget values for all program positions in this transaction. Note that it is possible to adopt the planned values of the investment program as the budget values and change these values as needed. Once planning is completed, it is common to perform the budgeting process, which is usually distributed top down.

| IM33 | Display Original Program Budget |

Use this transaction to display the budget for a program and program positions. You are able to review the budget totals, the program position and level, the planned total version, previous year total and amount distributed.

IM34   Rollup of Plan Values

Use this transaction to roll up plan values to the current year. Old programs are treated as if they are in the new approval year, so if you want to report carried forward programs from a current year program, it is not recommended that you use this transaction.

IM35   Change Program Planning

Use this transaction to plan values for investment measures and appropriation requests independently of the investment programs. Before you can budget and approve your investment program, you perform the planning function and then use the plan values as the basis for the binding budget. You can use the functions of the project systems module and the overhead costing module to structure the planning process and roll up the plan values into program positions. Another utility is to use the carry forward plan from the previous year plan or actual as a basis for planning the current year.

IM36   Display Program Planning

This transaction is used to display the program plan values. You are able to review the plan totals, the program position and level, the planned total version, the carried forward total and amount distributed.

IM38   Change Program Budget Return

This transaction is used to change the program budget from the original budget for both the investment program budget and for the measure budget. Changes are managed as line items in the system and are therefore managed separately from the original budget. Enter the program, position ID or the program node instead, approval year and click ENTER. The return budget can then be entered.

IM39   Display Program Budget Return

Use this transaction to display a program budget return. You can also display budget returns as an explanation of the current budget.

IM52   Budget Distribution

This transaction is used to distribute a budget from program positions to measures. There are a few different ways to distribute the budget, but the system ensures that no more budget can be distributed to the lower positions than is available on the next higher level position. Enter the investment program, position ID, approval year, measure type, distribution of original budget indicator, display transaction and execute. Then assign the supplements/returns for the overall budget or the annual budget of the assigned measures.

IM53   Display Budget Distribution

Use this transaction to display the budget distributed. Enter the investment program, position ID, approval year, measure type, distribution of original budget indicator, display transaction and execute. Then review the distributed values for the assigned supplements/returns for the overall budget or the annual budget of the assigned measures.

IMA11   Display Appropriation Request

This transaction is used to manage appropriation requests, which is a measure such as an investment that is individually assessed and approved primarily because of the high cost. An appropriation request consists of a master record with basic information and control data, such as the program assignment, organizational unit assignments and measure assignment. An appropriation request can be planned using different measures such as a WBS element or internal order.

IMCAOV	Investment Program Budget Carry Forward

Use this transaction for the budget carry forward in the investment program function, i.e., transfer unused budget to the next fiscal year (annual values) within an investment program. Unused budget is the remaining distributable budget on a program position and all subordinate program positions. The program can be run in test mode or update mode.

IMCCV1	Copy Plan Version (Investment Program)

This transaction is can be used for copying plan values from one plan version to another. Planning for investments in an approval year is often not a one-step process. Instead, it involves a series of steps or versions. These versions represent various stages in the development of planning, or various stages in the approval process of the selected objects to the budget values. Thus, this transaction can be used to transfer planned values to budgeted values for selected objects.

IMR4	Master Data List – App. Requests w/o %Distrib., w/o Variants

Use this transaction to report master data of appropriation requests along with their plan values, without sub-totals. This listing is intended for reporting without summarization.

IMR5	Master Data List – App. Requests with %Distrib., w/o Variants

Use this transaction to report master data of appropriation requests along with their plan values, without sub-totals. This listing is intended for reporting without summarization.

IMR6	Master Data List – App. Requests w/o %Distrib., w/Variants

Use this transaction to report master data of appropriation requests along with their plan values, without sub-totals. This listing is intended for reporting without summarization.

IMR7	Master Data List – App. Requests with %Distrib., w/Variants

Use this transaction to report master data of appropriation requests along with their plan values, without sub-totals. This listing is intended for reporting without summarization.

MIR4	Display Invoice Document

This transaction is used to display a logistics vendor invoice. Enter the invoice number, fiscal year and click ENTER. You have the ability to drill down into the financial document to review the accounting entries.

MIR6	Invoice Overview – Selection Criteria

Use this transaction to report on a worklist of logistics vendor invoices. Selection includes document number or range, fiscal year, invoicing party, document date and posting date. In addition, you can further restrict the invoice list by selecting various types of invoice, such as an EDI invoice, invoices that have been held/parked or the status of an invoice. Invoices that are in error status, parked status or require further processing can be amended and posted using this transaction.

MIR7   Park Incoming Invoice

This transaction is used to park a logistics vendor invoice. A parked document can be used as part of an authorization/review process where one individual inputs the invoice and parked the document while a supervisor can review/authorize and post the document using transaction MIR6. Input the vendor invoice or credit memo as usual and then click SAVE. Workflow functionality can also be used with this process in order to automatically route the invoice to the appropriate individual for approval.

MIRO   Enter Incoming Invoice

This transaction is used for logistics invoice verification. Typically, the vendor invoice is matched against a purchase order and a goods receipt, which is more commonly known as three-way matching. Enter the invoice header information and then enter the purchase order(s) that the invoice relates to. SAP will then propose the invoice amount and quantity. Tolerance limits will determine whether the invoice can be processed or blocked, or if there are any discrepancies between the invoice amount/quantity and the purchase order amount/goods receipt quantity. Once posted, the logistics vendor invoice creates an additional financial document for the financial posting.

MR8M   Cancel Invoice Document

Use this transaction to reverse a logistics vendor invoice. Enter the invoice number, fiscal year, reversal reason and posting date (which must be open financial period for posting). If a posting date is not entered, then the current date is used as a default. Click SAVE and the logistics invoice is reversed, together with a reversed financial posting.

MRBR   Release Blocked Invoices

Use this transaction to review and release logistics invoices that have been blocked for payment (due to perhaps the invoice amount being greater than the purchase order amount and outside the tolerance limit). Enter the invoice header data to determine the worklist, select whether block removal is to be a manual step after program execution or an automatic block removal is required, select the type of blocked invoices and then execute the program.

MRKO   Consignment and Pipeline Settlement

This transaction is used to process an invoice/settlement document for a special type of procurement involving consignment and pipeline materials. In this process the vendor logistics invoice is created based on the consumption of the pipeline material or consignment material. The vendor then sends an invoice based on this settlement document to the vendor for reference.

MRRL   Evaluated Receipt Settlement (ERS) with Logistics Invoice Verification

Use this transaction to process logistics vendor invoices based on the goods received from a vendor. In this process the vendor relationship is such that the purchasing company will pay for any and all goods received from the vendor at predetermined prices. This transaction will create vendor invoices based on those goods receipts.

OB52   Open/Close Financial Posting Period

Use this transaction to open and close the financial posting period. The general ledger and sub ledgers such as accounts payable/receivable, asset management, inventory management, can be opened and closed separately as part of the period end closing process.

XD01   Customer Create

This transaction is used to create centrally all the customer master record views at the same time, i.e., general, company code and sales area level data. Customer master fields that are either optional or required fields, as determined by the account group, can be maintained. All business partners, such as sold-to, ship-to, payer and bill-to, can be created using this transaction code.

XD02   Customer Change

This transaction is used to change any of the customer master record views, i.e., general, company code or sales area level data. Customer master data fields that are either optional or required, as determined by the account group are available to change. All business partners, such as sold-to, ship-to, payer and bill-to, can be changed using this transaction code.

XD03   Customer Display

This transaction is used to display any of the customer master record views, i.e., general, company code or sales area level data. All business partners, such as sold-to, ship-to, payer and bill-to, can be displayed using this transaction code.

XD04   Customer Account Changes

Use this transaction code to report all changes to the customer master. The report is by customer and sales area. There is an option to select from a specific date, time and the user ID of the individual making the change. The report output will display the fields changed with the option to drill down and display the old/new field value and date changed.

XD05   Customer Block/Unblock

This transaction is used to block the customer master from various transactions, such as sales order processing, financial postings, etc.

XD06   Customer Flag for Deletion

Use this transaction to flag a customer master for deletion. The deletion flag can be set by company code, sales area or all company code and/or sales areas. Furthermore, the deletion flag can be set at the general area level data and general area level data, including selected company codes. The deletion flag will ensure the customer cannot be used in transactional processing and can be included in the archiving process.

XD07   Change Account Group

This transaction can be used to change the customer account group under certain circumstances. However, in order to be able to make the change from old to new account group, you must have field level compatibility.

XD99   Mass Maintenance: Customers

This transaction is used to make mass changes to the customer master. The process involves selecting the tables and fields used in order to input the selection criteria. Once the selection criteria have been input and the customer(s) to be changed and fields to be changed are listed, then the mass changes can be executed and saved.

XK01   Vendor Create

This transaction is used to centrally create all the vendor master record views at the same time, i.e., general, company code and purchasing level data. Vendor master fields that are either optional or required fields, as determined by the account group, can be maintained. All business partners can be created using this transaction code.

XK02   Vendor Change

This transaction is used to change any of the vendor master record views, i.e., general, company code or purchasing area level data. Vendor master data fields that are either optional or required, as determined by the account group will be available to change. All business partners can be changed using this transaction code.

XK03   Vendor Display

This transaction is used to display any of the vendor master record views, i.e., general, company code or purchasing area level data. All business partners can be displayed using this transaction code.

XK04   Vendor Account Changes

Use this transaction code to report all changes to the vendor master. The report is by vendor and purchasing area. There is an option to select from a specific date, time and the user ID of the individual making the change. The report output will display the fields changed with the option to drill down and display the old/new field and date changed.

XK05   Vendor Block/Unblock

This transaction is used to block the vendor master from various transactions, such as purchase order processing, financial postings, etc.

XK06   Vendor Flag for Deletion

Use this transaction to flag a vendor master for deletion. The deletion flag can be set by company code, purchasing area or all company code(s) and/or purchasing area. Furthermore, the deletion flag can be set at the general data level and/or at the company code(s) data level. The deletion flag will ensure that the vendor cannot be used in transactional processing and can be included in the archiving process.

XK07   Change Account Group

This transaction can be used to change the vendor account group under certain circumstances. However, in order to be able the make the change, the old and the new account group must have field level compatibility.

XK99   Mass Maintenance: Vendor

This transaction is used to make mass changes to the vendor master. The process involves selecting the tables and fields used in order to input the selection criteria. Once the selection criteria have been input and the vendor(s) to be changed and fields to be changed are listed, then the mass changes can be executed and saved.

2 Controlling (CO)

1KE4	Profit Center Accounting: Assignment Monitor

This transaction is used to monitor the assignment of master data to profit centers. Internal orders, business processes, cost centers, cost objects, materials and work breakdown structure lists can be displayed for master data that has been assigned a profit center and for non assignments to a profit center. Profit centers are posted via these assignments, so it is important to ensure that all master data has been assigned.

1KEK	Profit Center Accounting: Transfer Payables/Receivables

This transaction is used to pull accounts payable and receivable line items into profit center accounting. The line items are created from the profit center accounting assignment on the offset posting to the accounts payable and accounts receivable posting. Select the period and fiscal year to be posted and the relevant company codes and then execute.

2KEU	Copy Cost Center Groups

Use this transaction to copy cost center groups to profit center groups within the same controlling area. This is a useful utility if your cost center groups are similar to your profit center groups. Enter the cost center group and execute. Once created, the profit centers within the profit center group can be changed. The utility also gives you the ability to select the standard hierarchy only and then assign the profit centers into groups in a second step.

2KEV	Copy Cost Centers

Use this transaction to create profit centers from cost centers within the same controlling area. Select the cost center group and execute. This transaction will create profit centers for all the cost centers within the cost center group selected.

6KEA	Display Profit Center Change Documents

This transaction will report on changes made to the profit center master. A date range can be selected. The changes are date and time stamped and you can drill down to review the old/new field value input.

7KE1	Change Plan Costs/ Revenues: Characteristics

This transaction is used to plan costs and revenue elements at the profit center level. Enter the version of the plan, the period range, the fiscal year, the company code, the profit center and the account for a default planning layout. The layout can be changed via the menu path GO TO • NEXT LAYOUT. Select ENTER IN FREE FORM INPUT MODE and you can enter the plan by period.

7KE2	Display Plan Costs/ Revenues: Characteristics

Use this transaction to display the plan costs and revenues by profit center(s) entered via transaction 7KE1. Enter the version of the plan, the period range, the fiscal year, the company code, the profit center and the account for the default planning layout. The layout can be changed via the menu path GO

TO • NEXT LAYOUT. Select ENTER to display the plan by period.

9KE9   Display Document

Use this transaction to display a profit center accounting document. Select one of the standard delivered layouts, the document number range, fiscal year, leave the document type as the default and click EXECUTE to display the document data.

CK11N   Create Cost Estimate with Quantity Structure

This transaction is used to create a standard cost estimate for a material with a quantity structure. Enter the material and plant for the cost estimate. Then enter the costing variant, which controls the type/cost components to be included in the estimate and the quantity structure (i.e., BOM's and Routings). Enter the costing version and the costing lot size (if left blank, the material master will determine the costing lot size) and click ENTER. The standard cost estimate will be calculated which can be analyzed by cost component or by cost element.

CK13N   Display Cost Estimate with Quantity Structure

Use this transaction to display the cost estimate for a material with a quantity structure. Enter the material and plant for the cost estimate, the costing variant, version and click ENTER. The standard cost estimate will be displayed which can be analyzed by cost component or by cost element.

CK24   Price Update

This transaction is used to mark and release a standard cost estimate for a material that has been created using transaction CK11N. Before marking can take place, the period for marking must be activated. Enter the posting period, fiscal year and activate marking. Then choose the company code and plant for the update; you can further restrict the selection by entering a material number range. Then execute marking, which typically is for a future period and then follow up with releasing the standard cost, which typically results in a revaluation of the materials inventory.

CK40N   Edit Costing Run

This transaction is used to create a standard cost estimate, report, mark and release for a range of materials with a quantity structure. This transaction is the same as transaction CK11N and CK24 but for multiple materials at the same time. Enter a costing run number and date, click CREATE and enter a description. Then proceed to enter the control settings (e.g., costing variant) in the GENERAL sub area, then run the cost estimate, mark and release in the PROCESSING sub area and review the results in the COSTING RESULTS area.

CK74N   Create Additive Cost

This transaction is used to create a manual cost estimate for a material, save it and have it be included in a standard cost estimate using transaction CK11N. Enter the material and plant, the costing variant and click ENTER. Then various costing methods can be chosen and then saved. Note that to have the additive cost estimates included in the standard cost estimate using transaction CK11N, the cost variant must be customized to allow it to accept additive cost estimates.

CK75N   Change Additive Cost

Use this transaction to change a manual cost estimate for a material. Enter the material and plant, the costing variant and click ENTER. Then various costing methods can be chosen and then saved. Note that to have the additive cost estimate included in the standard cost estimate using transaction CK11N, the cost variant must be customized to allow it to accept additive cost estimates.

CK76N Display Additive Cost

Use this transaction to display a manual cost estimate for a material. Enter the material and plant for the cost estimate, the costing variant and click ENTER.

CO43 Actual Overhead Calculation: Collective Processing

This transaction is used to apply overhead costs to multiple production orders based upon an overhead costing sheet as part of the product costing period end closing process. The overhead costing sheet will calculate the overhead cost based on a base cost element and an overhead rate. The production order will typically be debited and a cost center (defined on the costing sheet) will be credited. Enter the plant, the type of production object, period, fiscal year and execute to apply the overhead. To execute the function for one production order use transaction KGI2.

KA01 Create Cost Element

This transaction is used to create a primary cost element. There are two types of cost element. First, a primary cost element, which is typically a one to one match to a general ledger profit and loss account and relates to costs and revenues that are incurred externally to the organization. Additionally, there are secondary cost elements, which are costs incurred internal to the organization and are represented by transactions that exist only in the controlling module. You can create the primary cost elements directly from the profit and loss general ledger master record or you can use this transaction but you first must create a general ledger account. Enter the name and description and then ensure that the correct cost element category is selected (i.e., different cost element categories relate

to primary costs, assessments, overhead cost etc.) and then click SAVE.

KA02 Change Cost Element

This transaction is used to change a cost element. There are two types of cost element. First, a primary cost element, which is typically a one to one match to a general ledger profit and loss account and relates to costs and revenues that are incurred externally to the organization. In addition, there are secondary cost elements, which are costs incurred internally to the organization and are represented by transactions that exist only in the controlling module.

KA03 Display Cost Element

This transaction is used to display a cost element. There are two types of cost element. First, a primary cost element, which is typically a one to one match to a general ledger profit and loss account and relates to costs and revenues that are incurred externally to the organization. In addition, there are secondary cost elements, which are costs incurred internally to the organization and are represented by transactions that exist only in the controlling module.

KA04 Delete Cost Element

This transaction is used to delete a cost element however you can only delete a cost element if no postings have been made to it in the productive client. If postings have been made to the cost element then you must set the deletion flag on the cost element and then execute the archiving process.

KA05 Display Cost Element Changes

Use this transaction to display changes to the cost element master data. A change date from can be selected and/or the user ID, both of which can be left blank to display all changes. Once in the report you can drill down on any changes to display the old/new field value, date of change and the user ID of the individual making the change.

KA06	Create Secondary Cost Element

This transaction is used to create a secondary cost element. There are two types of cost element. First, a primary cost element, which is typically a one to one match to a general ledger profit and loss account and relates to costs and revenues that are incurred externally to the organization. In addition, there are secondary cost elements, which are costs incurred internally to the organization and are represented by transactions that exist only in the controlling module. Enter the name and description and then ensure that the correct cost element category is selected (i.e., different cost element categories relate to primary costs, assessments, overhead cost etc.) and then click SAVE.

KA23	Display Cost Element Collective

Use this transaction to display/report on multiple cost elements. You have the option to select cost elements individually, by cost element group, by a selection variant or all cost elements within a controlling area within a certain validity period. The list displays the master data information and you have the option to drill down into the actual master record.

KA24	Delete Cost Elements Collective

Use this transaction to delete multiple cost element master record. However, you can only delete a cost element if no postings have been made to it in the productive client. If postings have been made to the cost element then you must set the deletion flag on the cost element and then execute the archiving

process. You have the option to select cost elements individually, by cost element group, by a selection variant or all cost elements within a controlling area within a certain validity period.

KABL	Planning Report

Use this transaction to report on overall planning for an internal order. Select an individual internal order, fiscal year, period from/to and plan version. The report can also be displayed in ALV format. The default layout will display plan data by cost element with drill down capability.

KAH1	Create Cost Element Group

This transaction can be used to create a cost element group. The cost element group can be created in a hierarchy with nodes and sub nodes with the cost element assigned to the lowest level. Cost element groups can be used for reporting purpose in order to summarize data.

KAH2	Change Cost Element Group

This transaction can be used to change a cost element group. The cost element group can be created in a hierarchy with nodes and sub nodes with the cost element assigned to the lowest level. Cost element groups can be used for reporting purpose in order to summarize data.

KAH3	Display Cost Element Group

Use this transaction to display a cost element group. The cost element group can be created and displayed in a hierarchy with nodes and sub nodes with the cost elements assigned to the lowest level. Cost element groups can be used for reporting purpose in order to summarize data.

KAK2	Change View "Statistical Key Figures": Overview

This transaction is used to change multiple statistical key figure master records at one time. A statistical key figure is part of cost center accounting master data and is used in key figure analysis and as a basis for internal allocation such as distributions and assessments. You can also create new statistical key figures using this transaction. Furthermore, you can change existing statistical key figures text, unit of measure and category.

KAK3	Display View "Statistical Key Figures": Overview

This transaction is used to display multiple statistical key figure master records. A statistical key figure is part of cost center accounting master data and is used in key figure analysis and as a basis for internal allocations such as distributions and assessments. You can display existing statistical key figures text, unit of measure and category.

KB11N	Enter Manual Reposting of Costs

This transaction is used to repost costs manually whereby the original cost element is always retained. This function is designed mainly to adjust posting errors. You should normally adjust posting errors in the application component where they originally occurred. This transaction ensures that external and internal accounting postings are reconciled. You can only adjust posting errors involving one cost accounting object (a cost center or internal order for example) using a transaction-based reposting. Enter the document date, posting date, select the screen variant, the cost object, the receiving cost object and the amount to be posted and save.

KB13N	Display Manual Reposting of Costs

Use this transaction to display a reposting of costs. Correction postings are normally adjusted in the application component where they originally occurred. This transaction ensures that external and internal accounting postings are always reconciled. The adjusted posting errors involve one cost accounting object (a cost center or internal order for example) using a transaction-based reposting. Enter the document number and click ENTER.

KB14N	Reverse Manual Reposting of Costs

Use this transaction to reverse a reposting of cost. Correction postings are normally adjusted in the application component where they originally occurred. This transaction ensures that external and internal accounting postings are always reconciled. The adjusted posting errors involve one cost accounting object (a cost center or internal order for example) using a transaction-based reposting. Input the document number and click ENTER. The reposting sending and receiving cost objects are reversed and then save the document.

KB21N	Enter Direct Activity Allocation

Use this transaction for direct activity allocation, which involves the measuring, recording, and allocating of business services performed. To do this, you must create the appropriate cost activities and tracing factors (allocation bases, which can be used as cost drivers). These are known as activity types in cost center accounting. Activity allocation occurs, for example, when business transactions are confirmed or activities are recorded. The system multiplies the activity produced by the activity price of the activity type.

KB23N	Display Direct Activity Allocation

Use this transaction to display an activity allocation. Activity allocation involves the measuring, recording, and allocating of business services performed. To do this, you must create appropriate cost activities and tracing factors (allocation bases, which can be used as cost drivers). These are known as activity types in cost center accounting. Input the document number and click ENTER.

KB24N	Reverse Direct Activity Allocation

This transaction is used to reverse a direct activity allocation made using transaction KB21N. Enter the document date, posting date and document number of the transaction you want to reverse. Execute the transaction and the reverse activity allocation will be displayed. Save the posting and a new document number will be issued for the reversal.

KB31N	Enter Statistical Key Figures

This transaction is used to enter actual statistical key figures, which can be used as a basis for internal allocations, such as distributions and assessments and key figure analysis. Statistical key figures can be planned and actuals posted on a cost center, internal order, or other cost object. Enter actual statistical key figures to cost centers or internal orders using this transaction. Enter the document date, posting date, select the screen variant, the statistical key figure, the receiving cost center or internal order and the quantity to be posted and save.

KB33N	Display Statistical Key Figures

This transaction is used to display the actual statistical key figures entered, which can be used as a basis for internal allocations, such as distributions and assessments and key

figure analysis. Statistical key figures can be planned and actuals posted on a cost center, internal order, or other cost object. Input the document number and click ENTER to display the posting.

KB34N	Reverse Statistical Key Figures

Use this transaction to reverse a statistical key figure posting made using transaction KB31N. Enter the document date, posting date and document number of the transaction you want to reverse. Click ENTER to display the reverse statistical key figure posting. Click SAVE to post the new document number for the reversal.

KB41N	Enter Manual Reposting of Revenues

This transaction is used to repost revenues whereby the original cost element is always retained. This function is designed mainly to adjust posting errors. You should normally adjust posting errors in the application component where they originally occurred. This transaction ensures that external and internal accounting postings are always reconciled. You can only adjust posting errors involving one cost accounting object (a cost center or internal order for example) using a transaction-based reposting. Enter the document date, posting date, select the screen variant, the cost object, the receiving cost object and the amount to be posted and save.

KB43N	Display Manual Reposting of Revenues

Use this transaction to display a reposting of revenues. Correction postings are normally adjusted in the application component where they originally occurred. This transaction ensures that external and internal accounting postings are always reconciled. The adjusted posting errors involve one cost accounting object (a cost center or internal order for example) using a transaction-based reposting. Input the document number and click ENTER.

KB44N   Reverse Manual Reposting of Revenues

Use this transaction to reverse a reposting of revenues. Correction postings are normally adjusted in the application component where they originally occurred. This transaction ensures that external and internal accounting postings are always reconciled. The adjusted posting errors involve one cost accounting object (a cost center or internal order for example) using a transaction-based reposting. Input the document number and click ENTER. The reposting sending and receiving cost object reversal is then displayed, click SAVE to post the document.

KB65   Enter IAA Reposting: Document Row Selection

Use this transaction to repost cost from one cost object to another that has previously been posted using activity allocation. This function is designed mainly to adjust posting errors. You should normally adjust posting errors in the application component where they originally occurred. When reposting a line item, the full amount and quantity is reposted. Note: once a document has been "reposted" it cannot be corrected by another reposting transaction. Input the original document number that needs to be corrected, click ENTER to display and correct and then save the document.

KB66   Display IAA Reposting: Document Row Selection

Use this transaction to display a reposting of an internal activity allocation. Correction postings are normally adjusted in the application component where they originally occurred. This transaction ensures that

external and internal accounting postings are always reconciled. The adjusted posting errors involve one cost accounting object (a cost center or internal order for example) using a transaction-based reposting. Enter the document number and click ENTER.

KB67   Reverse IAA Reposting: Document Row Selection

Use this transaction to reverse a reposting of an internal activity allocation. Input the document number and click ENTER. The reposting sending and receiving cost objects are reversed and then save the document to post the reversal.

KBH1   Create Statistical Key Figure Group

This transaction is used to create a statistical key figure group. When several statistical key figures have been created, a statistical key figure group may be necessary for reporting and monitoring the contents of the group. For example, a statistical key figure (SKF) type group could be created for all SKFs managed by manufacturing or all SKFs managed by finance, etc. This will help assign responsibility for large numbers of SKFs. Enter the SKF group name, click ENTER, assign the SKF's to nodes in the group and save.

KBH2   Change Statistical Key Figure Group

Use this transaction to change a statistical key figure group. Enter the SKF group name, click ENTER, change the SKF assignment and save your changes.

KBH3   Display Statistical Key Figure Group

Use this transaction to display a statistical key figure group. Enter the SKF group name, click ENTER, and review the SKF assignment.

KCH1   Create Profit Center Group

This transaction is used to create a profit center group, which is a hierarchy structure of profit centers. Profit center groups are used for profit reporting, allocations or in various planning functions, where it is desirable to display profit data at a high level of detail. Enter the profit center group key, which will be the top level of the hierarchy, click ENTER, create lower level nodes, assign profit centers to the lowest node and click SAVE.

KCH2   Change Profit Center Group

Use this transaction to change a profit center group, which is a hierarchy structure of profit centers. Profit center groups are used for profit reporting, allocations or in various planning functions, where it is desirable to display profit data at a high level of detail. Enter the profit center group key, which will be the top level of the hierarchy, click ENTER, create or change lower level nodes, assign/reassign profit centers to nodes and click SAVE.

KCH3   Display Profit Center Group

Use this transaction to display a profit center group, which is a hierarchy structure of profit centers. Profit center groups are used for profit reporting, allocations or in various planning functions, where it is desirable to display profit data at a high level of detail. Enter the profit center group key and click ENTER to display the hierarchical structure.

KCH5N   Standard Hierarchy for Profit Centers Change

This transaction is used to change the standard hierarchy for profit centers, which is a special type of profit center group that contains all the profit centers in a controlling area. Profit center master data is required to be assigned to at least one level in the profit center standard hierarchy. The standard hierarchy is set up in customizing and you have two options to change it, first, when maintaining the profit center master data and second, using this transaction you can also maintain the profit centers master data.

KCH6N   Standard Hierarchy for Profit Centers Display

Use this transaction to change the standard hierarchy for profit centers, which is a special type of profit center group that contains all the profit centers in a controlling area. Profit center master data is required to be assigned to at least one level in the profit center standard hierarchy. Input the profit center group key and click ENTER to display the hierarchical structure.

KE21N   CO-PA Line Item Entry

This transaction is typically only used in exception circumstances since data is usually transferred to Profitability Analysis (CO-PA) automatically. However, if a correction posting is required then use this transaction. Enter the appropriate document type, the posting date, select the valuation type, currency setting, click ENTER, input the characteristics, value fields and origin data, if necessary and then click SAVE.

KE24   Line Item Display – Actual Data

This transaction is used to report on actual line item postings in Profitability Analysis (CO-PA). Selection criteria include record type, which will narrow the list to the origin of the posting. The layout display can be changed to suit user requirements.

KE25   Line Item Display – Plan Data

This transaction is used to report on plan line item postings in Profitability Analysis (CO-

PA). Selection criteria include record type, which will narrow the list to the origin of the posting. The layout display can be changed to suit user requirements.

KE27	Periodic Valuation

Use this transaction is used to periodically valuate actual data, which has previously been posted to Profitability Analysis (CO-PA). The system posts the difference between the original values of the line item and the new values in a new, separate line item. For valuation using material cost estimates, you can choose the alternative option of displaying the periodically calculated values separately from the original values. This function is available for the record types A (incoming sales orders) and F (billing data) as well as user-defined record types, which you select on the initial screen. Also, at execution time select the period for valuation. The program can be executed in update or test mode. Once you have performed periodic valuation in update mode, you can display the new values in the information systems reports.

KE2B	Subsequent Posting Incoming Sales Orders

Use this transaction to retransfer incoming sales order from SD to Profitability Analysis (CO-PA). Errors may occur for example, if the standard cost valuation of a material has not been released at the time of the transfer. The system saves the "original" records that contain errors in a separate table, which can be viewed using this transaction. Once the error has been corrected you can use this transaction to retransfer the sales order to CO-PA.

KE2C	Delete Incoming Sales Orders Containing Errors

Use this transaction to delete any errors from the transfer of incoming sales orders from SD

to Profitability Analysis (CO-PA). The system saves the "original" records that contain errors in a separate table, which can be viewed using transaction KE2D. Once the error has been corrected and retransferred using transaction KE2B you can use this transaction to delete the sales order from the error table.

KE2D	Display Incoming Sales Orders Containing Errors

This transaction is used to analyze errors from the transfer of incoming sales orders from SD to Profitability Analysis (CO-PA). You can value incoming sales orders (as expected revenues) and transfer them from SD to CO-PA in order to obtain an early estimate of anticipated profits. Errors may occur for example, if the standard cost valuation of a material has not been released at the time of the transfer. The system saves the "original" records that contain errors in a separate table, which can be viewed using this transaction. Once the error has been corrected you can use transaction KE2B to retransfer the sales order.

KE30	Execute Profitability Report

This transaction is used to access and execute Profitability Analysis (CO-PA) reports. When you call up a drill-down report, you can have the system either select new data or read saved report data that was selected and saved at an earlier point in time. In order to make it as easy as possible for users to execute a report, SAP lets you make most of the settings when you define the report. When you execute the report, you can also determine how the report is displayed and make the appropriate settings. Select the report, click EXECUTE, input section criteria and then execute the report.

KE31	Create Profitability Report

Use this transaction to create a Profitability Analysis (CO-PA) report. CO-PA allows the user to "slice and dice" information derived from other SAP modules (customer billing, internal orders, direct FI postings) to provide a view of customer and product profitability. When creating a report, the user will select which variables, characteristics and value fields are contained in the report. A CO-PA report can be created without or with a form. A form will allow the user, to create separately, a form/report layout that can be standardized and used across multiple reports.

KE32   Change Profitability Report

Use this transaction to change a Profitability Analysis (CO-PA) report. CO-PA allows the user to "slice and dice" information derived from other SAP modules (customer billing, internal orders, direct FI postings) to provide a view of customer and product profitability. The user can change which variables, characteristics and value fields are contained in the report.

KE41   Create Condition Records

This transaction is used to create condition records for use in Profitability Analysis (CO-PA) for valuation purposes. For example, when transferring SD Billing documents for SD to CO-PA a valuation for sales commission or freight expense can be calculated and added to the valuation of the CO-PA posted line item. Enter the condition type, click ENTER, select the key combination for the condition record, enter your selection criteria, click ENTER and then maintain the condition record.

KE42   Change Condition Records

Use this transaction to change a condition record which is used for valuation purposes in Profitability Analysis (CO-PA). For example, when transferring SD Billing documents from SD to CO-PA a valuation for

sales commission or freight expense can be calculated and added to the valuation of the CO-PA posted line item. Enter the condition type, click ENTER, select the key combination for the condition record, enter your selection criteria, click ENTER and then maintain the condition record.

KE4L   Create Pricing Report

Use this transaction to create a report on the condition records you created using transaction KE41. Enter the two-character code and name of the report and click SELECT FIELDS. Select the fields for the report and then select the tables that contain the condition records. Lastly, select the format and save the report. You can execute the report using transaction KE4Q.

KE4N   Change Pricing Report

This transaction is used to change a report on the condition records that were created using transaction KE4L. Enter the two-character code and name of the report and click ENTER. Select the fields to be deleted or add new fields for the report and the tables that contain the condition records. Lastly, select the format and save the report. You can execute the report using transaction KE4Q.

KE4Q   Execute Pricing Report

Use this transaction to execute a report created using transaction KE4L. Input the 2-character report code and execute.

KE51   Create Profit Center

This transaction is used to create a profit center, which classifies income and expense transactions according to the internal responsibility of the organization, for example, by product lines, geography, division etc. To accomplish this, all internal orders and cost centers are attached to a single profit center, while all revenue-related items (including cost of goods sold at standard) are posted directly to a single profit center. Apart from the profit center number itself, the following fields are also maintained as part of the profit center master data: analysis period from/to, name, user responsible, lock indicator and assignment to company codes.

KE52 Change Profit Center

Use this transaction to change a profit center. The following fields are maintained as part of the profit center master data: analysis period from/to, name, user responsible, lock indicator and assignment to company codes.

KE53 Display Profit Center

Use this transaction to display a profit center. The following fields are displayed as part of the profit center master data: analysis period from/to, name, user responsible, lock indicator and assignment to a company codes.

KE54 Delete Profit Centers

This transaction is used to delete a profit center but before the system can do this it carries out the following checks; the profit center cannot be deleted if transaction data has already been posted to it and/or the profit center is assigned to the following objects: cost center, material and/or business processes.

KE56 Assignment of Profit Centers to Company Codes – Change

This transaction allows you to change the company code assignments for a large quantity of profit centers without having to access master data maintenance for each single profit center. If you do not change the company code assignments the profit center is assigned to all the company codes. A column is inserted for each company code selected

indicating for each profit center whether or not it is assigned to the company code in question. Note that you can select no more than 20 company codes at a time. To process any further company codes, repeat the transaction. Note that a company code assignment cannot be undone if the profit center has cost centers assigned to it, which are contained in the company code in question or the profit center has materials assigned to it, which are contained in the company code in question.

KE5Y Profit Center: Plan Line Items

Use this transaction to provide a list of all profit center plan posting documents and line items matching the user's selection criteria. This report can be used as an aid in researching problems driven by postings in particular accounts and profit centers. The list layout can be changed to suit business requirements.

KE5Z Profit Center: Actual Line Items

Use this transaction to provide a list of all profit center actual posting documents and line items matching the user's selection criteria. This report can be used as an aid in researching problems driven by postings in particular accounts and profit centers. The list layout can be change to suit business requirements.

KEDE Maintain Derivation Rules

This transaction is used to maintain the rules for deriving a Profitability Analysis (CO-PA) characteristic to be used in CO-PA postings. The characteristics value is maintained using transaction KES1.

KEPM CO-PA Planning

This transaction contains a user friendly way of executing the process for revenue planning including the ability to copy the plan values from last year's sales data, display the data, increase or decrease the plan amounts using a %, integrate plan quantities with manufacturing (i.e., LIS /spreadsheets), perform top down planning, manual manipulation for customer/product plan sales quantities and save a copied version of the plan.

KES1	Change Characteristic Values

Use this transaction to maintain characteristic values for new characteristics defined in Profitability Analysis (CO-PA). Once maintained you can define derivation rules using transaction KEDE to assign these characteristics to postings in CO-PA. Double-click the characteristic and input the characteristics and maintain the values.

KEU1	Create CO-PA Actual Assessment Cycle

This transaction is used to create an assessment cycle that can be used transfer actual overhead costs to Profitability Analysis (CO-PA) for customer product profitability analysis below the contribution margin line. Enter the cycle name and the start date and click ENTER. Then enter the controlling area and the type of CO-PA analysis used, i.e., costing or account based. Then create a segment for the assessment, which involves selecting the sender objects and receiving CO-PA segments and the method of assessment. Execute the assessment cycle using transaction KEU5.

KEU2	Change CO-PA Actual Assessment Cycle

Use this transaction to change the assessment cycle created using transaction KEU1.

KEU4	Delete CO-PA Actual Assessment Cycle

Use this transaction the delete the assessment cycle created using transaction KEU1.

KEU5	Execute CO-PA Actual Assessment Cycle

This transaction is used to transfer overhead costs to Profitability Analysis (CO-PA) for customer product profitability analysis below the contribution margin line. Enter the period start from/to, fiscal year and enter the cycle name and start date. The program can be run in test mode and/or in background. Leave the DETAIL LIST SELECTION checked to see the details of the sender and receiver posted amounts in the program output.

KEU7	Create CO-PA Plan Assessment Cycle

This transaction is used to create an assessment cycle that can be used to transfer plan overhead costs to Profitability Analysis (CO-PA) for customer product profitability analysis below the contribution margin line. Enter the cycle name, start date and click ENTER. Then enter the controlling area and the type of CO-PA analysis used, i.e., costing or account based. Then create a segment for the assessment, which involves selecting the sender objects and receiving CO-PA segments and the method of assessment. Execute the assessment cycle using transaction KEUB.

KEU8	Change CO-PA Plan Assessment Cycle

Use this transaction to change the assessment cycle created using transaction KEU7.

KEUA   Delete CO-PA Plan
Assessment Cycle

Use this transaction the delete the assessment cycle created using transaction KEU7.

KEUB   Execute CO-PA Plan
Assessment Cycle

This transaction is used to transfer plan overhead costs to Profitability Analysis (CO-PA) for customer product profitability analysis below the contribution margin line. Enter the period start from/to, fiscal year, cycle name and the start date. The program can be run in test mode and/or in background. Leave the detail list selection checked to see the detail of the sender and receiver posted amounts in the program output.

KGI2   Actual Overhead
Calculation: Order

This transaction is used to apply overhead costs to an individual production order based upon an overhead costing sheet as part of the product costing period end closing process. The overhead costing sheet will calculate the overhead cost based on a base cost element and an overhead rate. The production order will typically be debited and a cost center (defined on the costing sheet) will be credited. Enter the production order, period, fiscal year and execute to apply the overhead. To execute the function for multiple production orders, use transaction CO43.

KK01   Create Statistical Key Figure

This transaction is used to create a statistical key figure (SKF) master data, which can be used as the basis for internal allocations. For example, you assess the costs for the cafeteria to the individual cost centers, based on the number of employees in each cost center. To do this, you need to enter the number of employees in each cost center as a statistical key figure. Input the SKF name and click ENTER. Then enter the name of the SKF, the unit of measure, and the SKF category, i.e., if the SKF is fixed and will be stored in each period until changed or if the SKF is specific to individual periods.

KK02   Change Statistical Key Figure

Use this transaction to change the statistical key figure (SKF) master data, which is used as the basis for internal allocations. Input the SKF name and click ENTER to make an update.

KK03   Display Statistical Key Figure

Use this transaction to display the statistical key figure (SKF) master data, which is used as the basis for internal allocations. Input the SKF name and click ENTER to display the master data details.

KK04   Master Data Report:
Statistical Key Figures

This transaction is used to display a report of statistical key figures (SKF). Selection criteria include the SKF name, SKF group, unit of measure and SKF category.

KK87   Actual Settlement:
Product Cost Collector

This transaction is used for actual settlement of a single product cost collector, which is part of the period end closing process. A product cost collector is used in product costing by period and so the cost object in this case is the material. This transaction is used after other period end processes have been executed, such as applying overhead, WIP calculation, and variance calculation. The settlement will clear the cost object at period end. Use transaction CO88 for the settlement of multiple cost collectors.

KK88   Actual Settlement: Cost Object

This transaction is used for actual settlement of a single cost object, which is part of the period end closing process. A cost object is used in product costing but does not control the costs at the production order level or material level; rather it uses as a CO cost object such as an internal order. This transaction is used after other period end processes have taken place such as applying overhead, WIP calculation and variance calculation. The settlement will clear the cost object at period end. Use transaction KK89 for the settlement of multiple cost objects.

KK89   Actual Settlement: Cost Object Collective

This transaction is used for actual settlement of multiple cost objects, which is part of the period end closing process. A cost object is used in product costing but does not control the costs at the production order or material level; rather, it uses a CO cost object such as an internal order. This transaction is used after other period end processes have been executed such as applying overhead, WIP calculation, and variance calculation. The settlement will clear the cost object at period end.

KKA0   Change Cutoff Period

Use this transaction to establish the cut off period for the work in progress (WIP) calculation. Work in process is the difference between the debits and credits of a cost object that has not been fully delivered. When it calculates the work in process, the system does not overwrite the results analysis data that proceeds the cutoff period. Enter the results analysis version, click ENTER, change the cut off period and click SAVE.

KKA3   Results Analysis for Sales Order

This transaction calculates results analysis for a single sales order line item (i.e., the sales order line item is the cost object). The valuation for each sales order item can be used to capitalize costs, create reserves or reconcile postings made in FI and Profitability Analysis (CO-PA). Enter the sales order, the item number on the sales order, period, fiscal year, results analysis version and execute to run the calculation.

KKA6   Results Analysis for Sales Order: Enter Data

Use this transaction to manually enter results analysis data when transferring legacy data. Enter the sales order, the item number on the sales order, period, fiscal year, results analysis version and click enter.

KKAK   Actual Results Analysis: Sales Orders

This transaction calculates results analysis for multiple sales order line items (i.e., the sales order line item is a cost object). The valuation for each sales order item can be used to capitalize costs, create reserves or reconcile postings made in FI and Profitability Analysis (CO-PA). Enter the sales order, the item number on the sales order, period, fiscal year, results analysis version and execute to run the calculation.

KKAO   Calculate Work in Progress: Collective Processing

This transaction is used to calculate work in progress (WIP) on multiple open production orders/process orders/product cost collectors. The WIP calculation is based on actual costs and is the difference between the debits and credits posted to the order/cost collector. Enter the plant, the cost object type, WIP calculation period, fiscal year, results analysis version and execute the calculation.

KKAS — Calculate Work in Progress: Individual Processing; Material

This transaction is used to calculate work in progress on an individual material. In this case cost object controlling is conducted by period at the product cost collector/material level. The WIP calculation is based on actual costs and is the difference between the debits and credits posted to that period by product cost collector. Enter the material, plant, WIP calculation period, fiscal year, results analysis version and execute the calculation. Use transaction KKAO for multiple materials.

KKAX — Calculate Work in Progress: Individual Processing; Order

Use this transaction to calculate work in progress (WIP) on an individual open production order/process order. The WIP calculation is based on actual costs and is the difference between the debits and credits posted to the order. Enter the order, WIP calculation period, the fiscal year, the results analysis version and execute the calculation. Use transaction KKAO for multiple production/process orders.

KKC1 — Create Cost Object

This transaction is used to create a general cost object that is not represented by a cost object generated by other SAP applications like production orders or sales order line items. A cost object may be created, for example, to track resources used to create an intangible asset. Creating a general cost object will enable you to calculate planned costs and actual costs, transfer costs to other SAP cost objects and analyze plan vs. actual costs. The master data contains the following information: text/naming of the cost object, object currency, name of person responsible,

control parameters for the calculation of overhead and a deletion indicator flag.

KKC2 — Change Cost Object

Use this transaction to change a cost object previously created using transaction KKC1. The master data contains the following information, text/naming of the cost object, object currency, name of person responsible, control parameters for the calculation of overhead and a deletion indicator flag.

KKC3 — Display Cost Object

Use this transaction to display a cost object previously create using transaction KKC1. The master data contains the following information, text/naming of the cost object, object currency, name of person responsible, control parameters for the calculation of overhead and a deletion indictor flag.

KKC7 — Create Product Group

This transaction is used to create a product group for drill down and summarization reporting analysis. You may choose to use the product group/hierarchy created in the logistics modules for CO reporting but, in addition, you may create a separate product group just for product cost controlling use only using this transaction. Create the product group number and then proceed to assign materials to hierarchy nodes. Note: each material can only be assigned to one CO product group.

KKC8 — Change Product Group

Use this transaction to change the product group that is used solely in the CO product cost controlling application. Enter the product group number and then proceed to change/add materials to hierarchy nodes. Note: each material can only be assigned to one CO product group.

KKC9	Display Product Group

Use this transaction to display the product group that is used solely in the CO product cost controlling application. Enter the product group number and then proceed to display materials to hierarchy nodes. Note: each material can only be assigned to one CO product group.

KKCS	Display Actual Cost Line Items for Cost Objects

Use this transaction to report on cost object line items, which provides a detailed analysis of the posted documents. Furthermore, drill-down capability enables a review of the actual document posted.

KKF1	Create CO Production Order

This transaction is used to create a CO production order for use with other master data in the CO module. You can create a CO production order without a quantity structure and enter the costs using unit costing. Unit costing is a type of spreadsheet that, due to its integration, can be used with existing master data and prices, such as activity prices from cost center accounting. Enter the order type, material number and plant and click ENTER. Then enter data such as text, assignments to organizational units and control data such as currency, a statistical indicator and plan integration indicator.

KKF2	Change CO Production Order/QM Order

Use this transaction to change a CO production order for use with other master data in the CO module. Input the order number and click ENTER. Review the material number and plant and enter/change data such as text, assignments to organizational units and control data such as currency, a statistical indicator and plan integration indicator.

KKF3	Display CO Production Order/QM Order

Use this transaction to display a CO production order. Input the order number and click ENTER. Then display data such as material, plant, text, assignments to organizational units and control data such as currency, a statistical indicator and plan integration indicator.

KKF4	Change Order Planning

This transaction is used to plan the CO production order without a quantity structure using unit costing. Unit costing is a type of spreadsheet that, due to its integration, can be used with existing master data and prices, such as activity prices from cost center accounting. Enter the CO production order, click ENTER, and then proceed to manually plan the order.

KKF6M	Create Multiple Product Cost Collectors for Production Versions

This transaction is used to create multiple product cost collectors typically used in a repetitive manufacturing environment/period costing scenario. A product cost collector is like a production order costing object but is not limited in lifespan. Enter the plant, material(s) and product cost collector order type and execute.

KKF6N	Display Product Cost Collector

Use this transaction to display multiple product cost collectors that are typically used in a repetitive manufacturing environment/period costing scenario. A product cost collector is like a production order costing object but is not limited in lifespan. Input the plant and material(s), click ENTER and use the left hand window pane to navigate the product cost collector list.

KKFB   Display Variance Line Items for Orders

This transaction is a report online items that are based on the variance calculation. The variances calculated represent the difference between target costs and control costs (the control costs can be the net actual costs, for example). The report will show the lines related to the variances categories, which are the causes for the variances.

KKG1   Order: Enter Cost of Sales

This transaction is useful in a scenario where you want to input the cost of sales amount calculated from a non SAP system. Results analysis can then calculate work in progress and reserves for unrealized costs using the actual costs and the cost of sales you entered.

KKG2   Project: Enter Cost of Sales

This transaction is useful in a scenario where you want to input the cost of sales amount calculated from a non SAP system. Results analysis can then calculate work in progress and reserves for unrealized costs using the actual costs and the cost of sales you entered.

KKG3   Sales Order: Enter Cost of Sales

This transaction is useful in a scenario where you want to input the cost of sales amount calculated from a non SAP system. Results analysis can then calculate work in progress and reserves for unrealized costs using the actual costs and the cost of sales you entered.

KKH1   Create Cost Object Group

Use this transaction to create a cost object group using general cost objects created via transaction KKC1, for example, on the basis

of responsibility. This is useful for grouping cost objects for reporting purposes. Enter the cost object group number and then change/add cost objects to hierarchy nodes.

KKH2   Change Cost Object Group

This transaction is used to change a cost object group. Enter the cost object group number and then change/add cost objects to hierarchy nodes.

KKH3   Display Cost Object Group

This transaction is used to display a cost object group. Enter the cost object group number and then change/add cost objects to hierarchy nodes.

KKPH   Fast Entry for Cost Object Hierarchy

Use this transaction to create a cost object hierarchy that can be used to analyze target costs, actual costs, and variances in situations where costs are not collected at the level of orders or materials. With the fast entry function, you create the cost object nodes of a cost object hierarchy in a list screen. You can specify the level of the cost object nodes and define the top of the hierarchy.

KKPHIE   Edit: Cost Object Hierarchy

Use this transaction to create a cost object hierarchy that can be used to analyze target costs, actual costs, and variances in situations where costs are not collected at the level of orders or materials. With the structured entry method, the cost object hierarchy is shown as a graphic. You can specify the levels of the cost object nodes, define the top of the hierarchy, and assign single objects.

KKR0   Create Summarization
Hierarchy

This transaction is used to create a summarization hierarchy, which is an analysis tool you can use to summarize values upwards in a hierarchical structure that you define. This makes it possible to analyze values and quantities at higher levels, such as at a plant level. Values in object currency are only summarized if the summarization hierarchy contains a plant or company code node. Summarized data can include planned, actual, target costs, variances and work in progress. Click the CREATE icon, enter the name and description of the summarization and then proceed to define the object types, the totals records and hierarchy to be summarized. Fill the summarization with data using transaction KKRC.

KKRC   Summarization: CO Object

Use this transaction to fill the summarization tables created using transaction KKR0. The data collection run is usually carried out for each summarization hierarchy after period-end closing in cost object controlling. The system reads the quantities and values of the selected objects as defined by the summarization hierarchy for the period being closed. This data is summarized upwards according to the structure of the hierarchy, and it is updated by period and cost element in the summarization objects. A summarization object is built for each field characteristic for all fields in a summarization hierarchy.

KKS1   Variance Calculation
Cost Object Controlling
by Order; Collective

This transaction is used to calculate production variances for a whole plant at one time. Production orders are the mechanism used to monitor the consumption of raw materials and plant expenses in the production

of other inventories such as finished goods. Once overhead has been applied to a production order, production order variances can be calculated and then settled. Variances are calculated and reported in eight categories divided by input and output variances, such as price and quantity variance on the input side and lot size and output price variance on the output side.

KKS2   Variance Calculation
Cost Object Controlling
by Order; Individual

Use this transaction to calculate production variances for an individual production order. Production orders are the mechanism used to monitor the consumption of raw materials and plant expenses in the production of other inventories such as finished goods. Once overhead has been applied to a production order, production order variances can be calculated and then settled. Variances are calculated and reported in eight categories divided by input and output variances, such as price and quantity variance on the input side and lot size and output price variance on the output side.

KKS5   Variance Calculation
Cost Object Controlling
by Period; Collective

This transaction is used to calculate production variances for a whole plant at one time. This transaction is used to calculate variances for product cost collectors in a period based cost object controlling scenario typically at the material level in a repetitive manufacturing environment. Once overhead has been applied to a product cost collector for the period, production variances can be calculated and then settled. Variances are calculated and reported in eight categories divided by input and output variances, such as price and quantity variance on the input side and lot size and output price variance on the output side.

KKS6	Variance Calculation Cost Object Controlling by Period; Individual

Use this transaction to calculate production variances for an individual product cost collector/material. This transaction is used to calculate variances for a product cost collector in a period based cost object controlling scenario typically at the material level in a repetitive manufacturing environment. Once overhead has been applied to a product cost collector for the period, production variances can be calculated and then settled. Variances are calculated and reported in eight categories divided by input and output variances, such as price and quantity variance on the input side and lot size and output price variance on the output side.

KL01	Create Activity Type

This transaction is used to create an activity type master record, which can be used, for example, in routings and production orders for machine time. These quantities of time (both planned quantities and actual quantities confirmed), when combined with activity prices drive the application of direct machine costs for product costing and production orders. Activity types are assigned to one controlling area and have a valid from/to date. Activity types typically contain a name, person responsible and category, which determines the method of activity quantity planning and activity allocation

KL02	Change Activity Type

Use this transaction to change the activity type master record. When combined with activity prices, activity types drive the appli-

cation of activity costs for product costing and production orders.

KL03	Display Activity Type

Use this transaction to display the activity type master record. When combined with activity prices, activity types drive the application of activity costs for product costing and production orders.

KL04	Delete Activity Type

Use this transaction to delete an activity type master record individually. Note that there must be no plant transactional data existing in the controlling area.

KL05	Display Change Documents: Activity Type

Use this transaction to report all changes to an activity type. There is an option to select from a specific date, time and user ID of the individual making the change. The report output will display the fields changed with the option to drill down and display the old/new field value and date changed.

KL13	Display Activity Types

This transaction is used to display a list of activity types with the list being all activity types, an activity type group or an individual activity type.

KL14	Delete Activity Types

Use this transaction to delete an activity type master record individually, collectively or in a group. Note that there must be no plant transactional data exiting in the controlling area.

KLH1   Create Activity Type Group

This transaction is used to create an activity type group, which is a hierarchy structure of activity types. Activity type groups are used for reporting, allocations and/or in various planning functions, where it is desirable to display data at a high level of detail. Input the profit center group key and then click ENTER to create the hierarchical structure with activity types assigned to the lowest level node.

KLH2   Change Activity Type Group

This transaction is used to change an activity type group, which is a hierarchy structure of activity types. Activity type groups are used for reporting, allocations and/or in various planning functions, where it is desirable to display data at a high level of detail. Input the profit center group key and click ENTER to change the hierarchical structure.

KLH3   Display Activity Type Group

This transaction is used to display an activity type group, which is a hierarchy structure of activity types. Activity type groups are used for reporting, allocations and/or in various planning functions, where it is desirable to display data at a high level of detail. Input the profit center group key and click ENTER to display the hierarchical structure.

KO01   Create Internal Order

Use this transaction to create an internal order/cost object that collects actual and plan revenues and costs, statistical and activity data. Internal orders typically collect and analyze actual and planned costs related to a specific project, event or asset under construction. The project/event will span several accounting periods and all costs can be settled in the period they were incurred. Internal orders typically contain a name, person

responsible, assignment to an organizational unit and an order type, which determines the method of settlement.

KO02   Change Internal Order

This transaction is used to change an internal order/cost object that collects actual and plan revenues and costs, statistical and activity data. Internal orders typically collect and analyze actual and planned costs related to a specific project, event or asset under construction. Input the internal order number, click ENTER and update the internal master record data fields.

KO03   Display Internal Order

This transaction is used to display an internal order/cost object that collects actual and plan revenues and costs, statistical and activity data. Internal orders typically collect and analyze actual and planned costs related to a specific project, event or asset under construction. Enter the internal order number, click ENTER and display the internal master record data fields.

KO04   Order Manager

This transaction is used to create/change an internal order using a graphical user interface. An internal order worklist can be created and used to facilitate changes to multiple orders at the same time. You can also create new orders or copy an existing order in the worklist. You can also select single orders and process them using collective processing for orders, which enables multiple changes at one time.

KO12   Change Overall Planning

Use this transaction to input an overall plan for the internal order. This type of planning is performed independently from cost elements. You can enter the plan for the lifetime of the order or an annual plan in each fiscal year. Note: An overall plan can be changed using this transaction; however, the original values are not maintained separately.

KO13 Display Overall Planning

This transaction is used to display an overall plan for an internal order. This type of planning is performed independently from cost elements. The plan may be for the lifetime of the order or an annual plan entered in each fiscal year.

KO14 Copy Planning

Use this transaction to create a new plan for internal orders by copying an existing plan version. You can copy primary costs, revenues, secondary costs, activity data, fiscal year dependent and independent overall planning values, unit cost values, detailed planning and statistical key figure values together or in any combination. Additionally, data can be copied period by period, several periods at a time or for an entire year. Before a version can be referenced, the "copying allowed" parameter must be activated in the planning version parameters.

KO15 Copy Actual to Plan

This transaction is similar to transaction KO14 but allows you to create an internal order plan from actual costs. All data types can be copied individually, all together or in many combinations. Additionally, data can be copied period by period, several periods at a time or for an entire year.

KO22 Change Original Budget

Use this transaction to change the original budget, which is an approved cost structure for an internal order or an order group. A budget is more controlled and binding than a plan and can be subject to availability control. The original budget should be changed,

using this transaction, with the best estimation of costs. Unforeseen events, such as price increases, and so on, may require corrections to the original budget, which can be maintained using supplements (transaction code KO24) and returns (KO26). Use a supplement to increase the current budget or a return to decrease the current budget.

KO23 Display Original Budget

This transaction is used to display the original budget. A budget is more controlled and binding than a plan and can be subject to availability control. Input the internal order or internal order group and internal order type and click the ORIGINAL BUDGET icon.

KO24 Change Supplement

Use this transaction to make changes to the original budget. If the funds provided in the original budget are not sufficient, the system enables you to use budget supplements. Changes are managed as line items in the system and are therefore managed separately from the original budget. The time to lock down a budget as an original budget, and to update it with supplements, returns and transfers depends on when you want to log data origins, in other words the sender-receiver relationships for the updates. You therefore use budget updates to prove where supplements and returns originated, and where they are to be used. You do this using status management.

KO25 Display Supplement

This transaction is used to display changes to the original budget. If the funds provided in the original budget are not sufficient, the system enables you to use budget supplements. Changes are managed as line items in the system and are therefore managed separately from the original budget. Input the internal order or internal order group and type and click the SUPPLEMENT icon.

KO26   Change Return

Use this transaction to make changes to the original budget. Using this transaction you can return funds, i.e., reduce the original budget for unused funds. Changes are managed as line items in the system and are therefore managed separately from the original budget. You therefore use budget updates to prove where supplements and returns originated, and where they are to be used.

KO27   Display Return

This transaction is used to display changes to the original budget. Using this transaction you can display reductions to the original budget for unused funds. Changes are managed as line items in the system and are therefore managed separately from the original budget. You therefore use budget updates to prove where supplements and returns originated, and where they are to be used.

KO30   Activate Availability Control

Use this transaction to activate availability control for one or more internal orders. Within the framework of budget monitoring, availability control informs you promptly when a budget is exceeded (either by actual costs or commitments). When purchase requisitions or purchase orders, for example, are posted to an investment order that has been budgeted, the system checks whether the posting causes the predefined tolerance limits to be exceeded. If it does, then the system automatically issues either a warning or error message (depending on customizing settings).

KO32   Deactivate Availability Control

Use this transaction to deactivate availability control previously activated using transaction KO30.

KO88   Actual Settlement: Order

Use this transaction to settle actual primary and secondary costs and revenues (if applicable) to the receivers established in a production/internal order's settlement rules. In costing, production/internal orders are interim cost collectors that are used to plan, record actual costs and monitor costs until certain activities have been completed and the costs move to their final destination. This movement of the costs to their final destination is called settlement. The order's settlement rules are dependent on the parameters established in the settlement structure, settlement profile, and order type (all defined in customizing and in the master data itself).

KO8B   Display Settlement Document

Use this transaction if you know the settlement document number posted via transaction KO88. However, an alternative way to review the settlement posting is going to transaction KO88, inputting your selection criteria and via the menu path selecting GO TO • PREVIOUS SETTLEMENT. Either way, the information about the settlement is displayed such as the settlement senders/receivers, the amount calculated and distributed.

KO8G   Actual Settlement: Orders

This transaction is used to settle actual costs of multiple internal orders at the same time. A selection variant has to be created beforehand in order to select the internal order range. The selection method can be changed to internal orders used in CRM or cProjects order if these components are being used.

Select the settlement period and fiscal year variant and click EXECUTE.

KO9E	Planned Settlement: Internal Orders; Individual

Use this transaction to settle plan primary and secondary costs and revenues to the receivers established in an internal order's settlement rules. In costing, production/internal orders are interim cost collectors that are used to plan, record actual costs and monitor costs until certain activities have been completed and the costs move to their final destination. This movement of the costs to their final destination is called settlement. This transaction is the plan cost (as opposed to actual cost) equivalent of transaction KO88.

KO9G	Planned Settlement: Internal Orders; Collective

This transaction is used to settle plan costs of multiple internal orders at the same time. A selection variant has to be created beforehand in order to select the internal order range. The selection method can be changed to internal orders used in CRM or cProjects order if these components are being used. Select the settlement period and fiscal year variant and click EXECUTE. This transaction is the plan cost (as opposed to actual cost) equivalent of transaction KO8G.

KOB1	Display Actual Cost Line Items for Orders

Use this transaction to display detailed line items for internal order actual posting documents. Actual line items are created with every posting of actual costs. They contain information about the posted amount, the posting date, and the user who posted the line item. When you start an actual line item report, you need to limit the line items to be read by entering an order (or order group), a cost element (or cost element group), and

a posting period. Additionally, you can configure different layouts to control the appearance of the report.

KOB2	Display Commitment Line Items for Orders

Use this transaction to display the details for commitment line items that are created as a commitment in the set up, for example, for a purchase order. The line item contains information about the posted amount, the posting date, and the user who posted the item. When you start a line item report, you need to limit the line items to be read by entering an order (or order group), a cost element (or cost element group) and a posting period. Additionally, you can configure different layouts to control the appearance of the report.

KOB3	Display Variance Line Items for Orders

Use this transaction to display details for variance line items created via the variance calculation function (transaction KKS1 and KKS2). The line items can display, by target cost version the variance categories calculated. The line item contains information about the posted amount, the posting date, and the user who posted the item. When you start a line item report, you need to limit the line items to be read by entering an order (or order group), a cost element (or cost element group) and a posting period. Additionally, you can configure different layouts to control the appearance of the report.

KOB4	Display Budget Line Items for Orders

This transaction displays budgeting documents in ascending order. This way you can see how a particular budget came about. This report is therefore particularly suitable for monitoring the budgeting process. However, it cannot be used to display how much budget a particular funds management account assignment actually has.

KOB8	Display Results Analysis Line Items for Orders

Use this transaction to display the line items generated from the results analysis/work in progress calculation via transaction KKAX or KKAO. Results analysis valuates the relationship between the costs and a measure of the order's progress toward completion and thus the amount that can be capitalized as work in progress. This transaction displays the results of the results analysis execution. Note: In customizing the GENERATE LINE ITEM indicator must be turned on for the results analysis version report to display the line items.

KOC4	Order Selection

This transaction is used to generate a list of orders with the associated master data fields and key figures. The results list has a number of navigation and formatting options and can be modified by the user. From the results list in the detailed report, you can branch off to single orders or to a comparison of two orders, in order to examine these orders more closely. You can also go to the master data display for characteristics from the results list. Furthermore, you can drill down into the material master record for an order to be analyzed. Order selection is not a summarized analysis and is not based on classification. It mainly serves to answer specific questions/queries that arise in cost object controlling.

KOCF	Fiscal Year Close: Carry Forward Commitment

Use this transaction to carry forward commitments (for example, purchase requisitions, purchase orders, earmarked funds) posted in the current fiscal year but not reduced until the following fiscal year. The commitment carried forward then debits the budget in the new fiscal year.

KOCO	Budget Carry Forward for Orders

This transaction enables you to carry forward budget remainders from projects, internal orders, and plant maintenance orders to the following fiscal year. A budget that has not been used up is mainly defined here as the difference between the planned budget and incurred actual costs. Budgets carried forward to the following year can also be posted to the previous year in certain circumstances.

KOH1	Create Order Group

Use this transaction to create internal order groups. Internal order groups are very flexible structures and can be used in collective processing (master data and transactional data), reporting, allocations, and authorization objects. Each sub group represents a level of summarization. Internal order groups are unique within a controlling area.

KOH2	Change Order Group

Use this transaction to change an internal order group. Internal order groups as well as orders can be added, deleted or reassigned using this transaction. Order groups are very flexible structures and can be used in other order groups, collective processing (master data and transactional data), reporting, allocations, and authorization objects. Each sub group represents a level of summarization. Internal order groups are unique within a controlling area, but client dependent.

KOH3	Display Order Group

This transaction is used to display an internal order group. Internal order groups are very flexible structures and can be used in collective processing (master data and transactional data), reporting, allocations, and authorization objects. Each sub group represents a level of summarization. Internal order groups are unique within a controlling area.

KOK2	Collective Processing for Internal Orders

Use this transaction to make changes to multiple internal order master records using manual collective processing. Change any available field (as defined in customizing) or create/change settlement distribution rules. This transaction works especially well when every order in an order group requires the same change.

KOK3	Collective Display for Internal Orders

Use this transaction to display multiple internal order master records using manual collective processing. The user can toggle between available line display variants or drill down to the specific internal order master data and settlement rule.

KOK4	Automatic Collective Processing for Internal Orders

Use this transaction to make changes to multiple internal order master records using automatic collective processing. This transaction differs from the manual collective processing using transaction KOK2 in that both the order selection and the change function are performed within one transaction.

KP04	Set Planner Profile

This transaction is used to set the default planner profile to be used with transactions such as KP06 and KP26. Perform this procedure when the planner profile default needs to be changed to accommodate subsequent

planning activities. When planning in cost center accounting and profit center accounting, a planning profile is used to direct the kind of information the user enters. The planning template aids the user's planning process since not all fields need to be available for every planning activity.

KP06	Change CElem/Activity Input Planning

Use this transaction for primary cost planning, i.e., costs due to external procurement or material withdrawals. Activity-independent (only to cost center) and activity-specific (to cost center/activity type) primary costs can be planned. In order to calculate activity prices automatically you have to plan activity-specific primary costs with corresponding activity outputs that have been planned for the sender cost center. In other words, within an agreed activity plan, the sender cost centers provide activity quantities because other cost centers have planned to consume them. You use transaction KSC6 to calculate activity prices automatically.

KP07	Display Planning CElem/Act. Input

Use this transaction to display primary cost planning, i.e., costs due to external procurement or material withdrawals. Activity-independent (only to cost center) and activity-specific (to cost center/activity type) primary costs can be planned.

KP26	Change Activity Type/ Price Planning

Use this transaction to plan activity prices manually for cost centers. You plan the activity price of an activity type of a sender cost center, which can be used as the basis for cost allocations to receiver cost objects via a secondary cost element posting. If you have not manually planned the prices during activity type planning, SAP can calculate the debit for the receiver cost centers using an iteratively calculated price via transaction KSC6.

KP27	Display Activity Type/ Price Planning

Use this transaction to display plan activity prices for cost centers. You plan the activity price of an activity type of a sender cost center, which can be used as the basis for cost allocations to receiver cost objects via a secondary cost element.

KP46	Change Statistical Key Figure Planning

This transaction is used to plan for statistical key figures. For example, as a key figure, you can plan costs per the number of employees using this transaction. Furthermore, you can use the number of employees as an allocation base, i.e., to allocate cafeteria costs among cost centers based on number of employees in that cost center.

KP47	Display Statistical Key Figure Planning

This transaction is used to display a plan for statistical key figures.

KP90	Delete Planned Costs (All Integrated Planning Objects)

Use this transaction to delete particular planning data (including very large amounts) from the CO tables. This deletes the planning data on objects that are integrated with planning. This includes the following objects, cost centers, business processes, internal orders and projects, for which planning integration is active in both the version and the master data.

KP98	Copy Actual to Plan

This transaction is used during the planning process and offers a method of reusing large parts of your actual data to generate plan data. It allows actual data to be transferred to plan values within a fiscal year, across different periods or within different versions. You can copy within fiscal years, periods, versions, and cost centers. Try to avoid using the RESET AND OVERWRITE option because the system needs to read all the data in the target version in order to clear it.

KP9R	Copy CO Resource Prices

Use this transaction to copy resource prices, which are the equivalent of activity prices but for external activities. Resource prices are used to plan/valuate the cost of consuming business activities by cost object such as cost centers. The transaction enables you to copy resource prices from one target plan version/ fiscal year to another.

KPD6	Change Statistical Key Figure Planning

This transaction is used to enter plan statistical key figure data for internal orders, which can be used as a basis for internal allocations, such as distributions and assessments and key figure analysis. Statistical key figures can be planned on a cost center, internal order, or other cost objects. Enter the document date, posting date, select the screen variant, the statistical key figure, the receiving cost center or internal order and quantity to be posted and save.

KPD7	Display Statistical Key Figure Planning

This transaction is used to display plan data for statistical key figures for internal orders, which can be used as a basis for internal allocations, such as distributions and assessments and key figure analysis. Statistical key figures can be planned on a cost center, internal order, or other cost objects. Input the document number, click ENTER and the posting is displayed.

| **KPF6** | Planning CElem/Activity Input |

Use this transaction to plan primary costs for internal orders. You can plan an overall value for the internal order or plan annual values. Enter a plan version, from/to period, fiscal year, internal order from/to or internal order group and cost element from/to or cost element group, click OVERVIEW and proceed to the planning screen.

| **KPF7** | Display CElem./Acty Input Planning |

This transaction is used to display plan primary costs of for internal orders. You can display the plan at an overall plan for the internal order or for an annual plan. Enter a plan version, from/to period, fiscal year, internal order from/to or an internal order group and cost element from/to or cost element group, click OVERVIEW and proceed to the planning screen.

| **KPG5** | Report Painter: Create Orders: Planning Layout for Cost Elements/Active |

Use this transaction to create a planning layout for internal order planning. The planning layout can be customized to suit your planning requirements. This involves selecting a lead column, typically the cost element characteristic, and then the planning key figures, such as the total plan in the controlling area currency or total plan in the transaction currency. Furthermore, a number of formatting options are also available. Once saved, the planning layout can then be used via transaction KPF6 (Change CElem/Activity Input Planning).

| **KPG6** | Report Painter: Change Orders: Planning Layout for Cost Elements/Active |

This transaction can be used to change the planning layout, previously created using transaction KPG5.

| **KPSI** | Execute Plan Reconciliation |

Use this transaction to reconcile plan activity input and output. Because activity output and input can be planned separately there can be differences if, for example, only the activity output is changed. In this case the planning networked has to be reconciled again. This transaction will show how the planning change affects the planning network.

| **KRMI** | Display Actual Cost Line Items for Orders |

Use this transaction to display detailed line items for product cost collector actual postings. Actual line items are created with every posting of actual costs. They contain information about the posted amount, posting date, and the user who posted the item. Enter the material, plant, production process and date from/to an order and execute. Additionally, you can configure different layouts to control the appearance of the report.

| **KS01** | Create Cost Center |

This transaction is used to create a cost center, which is part of the controlling module master data. Cost centers are distinct cost objects/cost collectors that can sub divide the organization by function, process and responsibility. Cost centers can be planned, actual postings recorded and used for cost allocations. Cost centers can be grouped for summarization and hierarchically structured for drill down reporting. Enter the cost center number, valid from/to dates, click ENTER and maintain master data fields such as description/name, cost center category and person responsible. Note that one easy way to create a new cost center is to use an existing cost center as a reference and then change the few fields required for the new cost center and save it.

KS02   Change Cost Center

Use this transaction to change a cost center previously created using transaction KS01.

KS03   Display Cost Center

Use this transaction to display a cost center previously created using transaction KS01.

KS04   Delete Cost Center; Individual

This transaction is used to delete a cost center but deletion is only effective if there are no postings to the cost center. In other words, it is simply not enough to reverse any postings to the cost center in order to delete it. One option, as an alternative to deleting the cost center, would be to render the cost center inactive by shortening its effective to date, so that the cost center cannot be posted to from that date onwards.

KS05   Display Change Documents: Cost Center

Use this transaction to report all changes to a cost center. There is an option to select from a specific date and the user ID of the individual making the change. The report output will display the fields changed with the option to drill down and display the old/new field value and date changed.

KS12   Change Cost Centers

This transaction can be used to change multiple cost centers at one time. Select cost centers in a specific valid from/to period and then change the cost centers to overwrite the entries in the available for input fields and save your entries.

KS13   Display Cost Centers

Use this report to display a list of cost centers that may have been changed using transaction KS12.

KS14   Delete Cost Centers; Collective

This transaction is used to delete multiple cost centers at the same time but is effective only if there are no postings to the cost center. In other words, it is simply not enough to reverse any postings to the cost center in order to delete it. One option, as an alternative to deleting the cost center, would be to render the cost center inactive by shortening its effective to date, so that the cost center cannot be posted to from that date onwards.

KSB1   Display Actual Cost Line Items for Cost Centers

Use this transaction to display detailed line items for cost center actual postings. Actual line items are created with every posting of actual costs. They contain information about the posted amount, the posting date, and the user who posted the item. When you start an actual line item report, you need to limit the line items to be read by entering a cost center (or cost center group), a cost element (or cost element group) and a posting period. Additionally, you can configure different layouts to control the appearance of the report.

KSB2   Display Commitment Line Items for Cost Centers

Use this transaction to display detailed line items for commitment line item postings on a cost center that has been created for commitments, for example, for a purchase order.

The line item contains information about the posted amount, the posting date, and the user who posted the item. When you start a line item report, you need to limit the line items to be read by entering a cost center (or cost center group), a cost element (or cost element group) and a posting period. Additionally, you can configure different layouts to control the appearance of the report.

KSBP	Display Plan Cost Line Items for Cost Centers

Use this transaction to display detailed line items for cost center plan postings. The line item displays information about the planned amount, the posting date, and the user who posted the item. When you start a plan line item report, you need to limit the line items to be read by entering a cost center (or cost center group), a cost element (or cost element group) and a posting period. Additionally, you can configure different layouts to control the appearance of the report.

KSBT	Activity Type Price Report

Use this transaction to report on cost center activity prices created automatically by activity price calculation or manually created by activity price input planning using transaction KP26. Input the cost center, activity type, planning version, fiscal year, from period and click EXECUTE to display the results.

KSC1	Create Cycle for Actual Indirect Activity Allocation

Use this transaction to create a cost allocation cycle for actual indirect activity allocation, which is a method of allocating total activity quantity from senders cost centers to the receiver cost centers based on the receiver activity posted in the receiver cost center. For example, in manufacturing, you can allocate overhead costs from a cost center from which

the expenses are posted, to a production cost center that uses the overhead.

KSC2	Change Cycle for Actual Indirect Activity Allocation

This transaction is used to change an actual indirect activity allocation cycle previously created using transaction KSC1.

KSC3	Display Cycle for Actual Indirect Activity Allocation

This transaction is used to display an actual indirect activity allocation cycle previously created using transaction KSC1.

KSC4	Delete Cycle for Actual Indirect Activity Allocation

This transaction is used to delete an actual indirect activity allocation cycle previously created using transaction KSC1.

KSC5	Execute Cycle for Actual Indirect Activity Allocation

Use this transaction to execute an actual indirect activity allocation, which is a method of allocating total activity quantity from senders cost centers to the receiver cost centers based on the receiver activity posted in the receiver cost center. For example, in manufacturing, you can allocate overhead costs from a cost center from which the expenses are posted, to a production cost center that uses the overhead. Enter the period you want to run the allocation for, the cycle created using transaction KSC1 and execute. The program can also run in test mode with or without a detail list showing the allocation in the output.

KSC6	Act. Indirect Acty Alloc.: Overview

This transaction can be used to list an overview of the indirect activity allocation postings executed using transaction KSC5.

KSC7	Create Cycle for Planned Indirect Activity Allocation

Use this transaction to create an allocation cycle for plan cost indirect activity allocation, which is a method of allocating total activity quantity from senders cost centers to the receiver cost centers based on the receiver activity planned in the receiver cost center. For example, in manufacturing, you can allocate plan overhead costs from a cost center from which the expenses are posted, to a production cost center that uses the overhead.

KSC8	Change Cycle for Planned Indirect Activity Allocation

This transaction is used to change a plan cost indirect activity allocation cycle previously created using transaction KSC7.

KSC9	Display Cycle for Planned Indirect Activity Allocation

This transaction is used to display a plan cost indirect activity allocation cycle previously created using transaction KSC7.

KSCB	Execute Plan Indirect Acty Alloc.

Use this transaction to execute an allocation cycle for plan cost indirect activity allocation, which is a method of allocating total activity quantity from senders cost centers to the receiver cost centers based on the receiver activity planned in the receiver cost center. For example, in manufacturing, you can allocate plan overhead costs from a cost center

from which the expenses are posted, to a production cost center that uses the overhead. Enter the period you want to run the allocation for and the cycle created using transaction KSC7 and execute. The program can also run in test mode with or without a detail list showing the allocation in the output.

KSCC	Document List for Selected Cycle

This transaction can be used to list an overview of the indirect activity allocation postings executed using transaction KSCB.

KSH1	Create Cost Center Group

This transaction is used to create a cost center group, which is used for reporting and allocation purposes. Simply put, a cost center group is just a named range (or it may contain several ranges) of cost centers. These groups can be used as selection criteria when executing reports or may be imbedded in the reports themselves.

KSH2	Change Cost Center Group

Use this transaction to change a cost center group previously created using transaction KSH1.

KSH3	Display Cost Center Group

Use this transaction to display a cost center group previously created using transaction KSH1.

KSII	Actual Price Calculation

This transaction calculates an activity price by taking into account the exchange of activity between cost centers. Actual price calculation, which you can carry out during planning, is based on planned costs and activity. The resulting prices are used to valuate actual activity. After running actual price calculation, you can choose to recalculate actual activity based on actual prices.

KSS2 — Actual Cost Splitting

This transaction is used to split activity independent costs into activity type dependent costs if more than one activity type exists on the cost center. Costs can be split according to costs from the cost center to different activities based on equivalence numbers or actual activity. You must split plan costs before executing activity price calculation and plan/target/actual comparison reporting.

KSS4 — Plan Cost Splitting

Use this transaction to split the activity-independent plan costs of a cost center among the activity types of this cost center. You must split plan costs before executing plan activity price calculation and plan/target/actual comparison reporting. To split plan costs, you must first plan the corresponding values in activity type planning.

KSU1N — Create Actual Assessment Cycle

This transaction is used to set up the senders, receivers and distribution rules for an actual assessment posting using transaction KSU5. Assessments apportion costs collected within a cost center during the accounting period to receiver cost centers according to user-defined distribution rules. The difference between a distribution and an assessment is that assessments use a secondary cost element to post to the receiver cost center, which leaves the original posting visible in the sender cost center.

KSU2N — Change Actual Assessment Cycle

Use this transaction to change an assessment cycle previously created using transaction KSU1N.

KSU3N — Display Actual Assessment Cycle

Use this transaction to display an assessment cycle previously created using transaction KSU1N.

KSU4N — Delete Actual Assessment Cycle

Use this transaction to delete an assessment cycle previously created using transaction KSU1N.

KSU5 — Execute Actual Assessment

This transaction is used to allocate/apportion actual costs collected within a cost center during the accounting period to receiver cost centers according to user-defined distribution rules. The difference between a distribution and an assessment is that assessments use a secondary cost element to post actual costs to the receiver cost centers, which leaves the original posting visible in the sender cost center.

KSU6 — Document List for Selected Cycle

Use this transaction to review the controlling documents posted as a result of executing KSU5 in update mode.

KSU7N — Create Plan Assessment Cycle

This transaction is used to set up the senders, receivers and distribution rules for a plan assessment posting using transaction KSUB. Assessments apportion plan costs within a cost center in a period to receiver cost centers according to user-defined distribution rules. The difference between a distribution and an assessment is that assessments use a secondary cost element to post plan costs to the receiver cost centers, which leaves the original plan posting visible in the sender cost center.

KSU8N   Change Plan Assessment Cycle

Use this transaction to change a plan assessment cycle previously created using transaction KSU7N.

KSU9N   Display Plan Assessment Cycle

Use this transaction to display a plan assessment cycle previously created using transaction KSU7N.

KSUAN   Delete Plan Assessment Cycle

Use this transaction to delete a plan assessment cycle previously created using transaction KSU7N.

KSUB   Execute Plan Assessment

This transaction is used to allocate/apportion plan costs within a cost center during an accounting period to receiver cost centers according to user-defined distribution rules. The difference between a distribution and an assessment is that assessments use a secondary cost element to post plan costs to the receiver cost centers, which leaves the original plan posting visible in the sender cost center.

KSUCN   Plan Assessment: Overview

Use this transaction to review the controlling documents posted as a result of executing KSUB in update mode.

KSPI   Plan Price Calculation

This transaction is used to determine prices for the plan activity types of each cost center. The system calculates the prices iteratively by dividing the plan costs by the plan activity quantity. It is also possible to determine the fixed portion of the price as the quotient (ratio) of plan costs and capacity.

KSV1N   Create Actual
            Distribution Cycle

This transaction is used to set up the senders, receivers and distribution rules for a distribution actual posting using transaction KSV5. Distributions allocate primary costs collected within a cost center during the accounting period to receiver cost centers according to user-defined distribution rules. The difference between a distribution and an assessment is that a distribution posts using the primary cost element, which means the original cost gets posted into the receiving cost centers.

KSV2N   Change Actual
            Distribution Cycle

Use this transaction to change an actual distribution cycle previously created using transaction KSV1N.

KSV3N   Display Actual
            Distribution Cycle

Use this transaction to display an actual distribution cycle previously created using transaction KSV1N.

KSV4N   Delete Actual
            Distribution Cycle

Use this transaction to delete an actual distribution cycle previously created using transaction KSV1N.

KSV5   Execute Actual Distribution

This transaction is used to allocate/apportion actual costs collected within a cost center during the accounting period to receiver cost centers according to user-defined distribution rules. Distributions allocate primary costs collected within a cost center during the accounting period to receiver cost centers according to user-defined distribution rules. The difference between a distribution and an assessment is that a distribution posts costs using the primary cost element, which means the original cost gets posted into the receiving cost centers.

KSV6N   Actual Distribution: Overview

Use this transaction to review the controlling documents posted as a result of executing KSV5 in update mode.

KSV7N   Create Plan Distribution Cycle

This transaction is used to set up the senders, receivers and distribution rules for a plan distribution posting using transaction KSVB. Distributions allocate plan costs posted within a cost center during the accounting period to receiver cost centers according to user-defined distribution rules. The difference between a distribution and an assessment is that a distribution posts plan costs using the primary cost element, which means the original plan gets posted into the receiving cost centers.

KSV8N   Change Plan Distribution Cycle

Use this transaction to change a plan distribution cycle previously created using transaction KSV7N.

KSV9N   Display Plan Distribution Cycle

Use this transaction to display a plan distribution cycle previously created using transaction KSV7N.

KSVAN   Delete Plan Distribution Cycle

Use this transaction to delete a plan distribution cycle previously created using transaction KSV7N.

KSVB   Execute Plan Cost Distribution

This transaction is used to allocate/apportion plan costs within a cost center to receiver cost centers according to user-defined distribution rules. The difference between a distribution and an assessment is that a distribution posts plan costs using the primary cost element, which means the original cost gets posted into the receiving cost centers.

KSVC   Plan Distribution: Overview

Use this transaction to review the controlling documents posted as a result of executing KSVB in update mode.

KSW1   Create Actual Periodic Reposting Cycle

This transaction is used to create a cycle for reposting actual costs. Reporting costs is an easy way to repost costs from, for example, an administration cost center to cost centers that consume the costs, such as manufacturing departments. The sender cost center is not updated with this method. To define a periodic reposting, create a cycle, create segments for the cycle to specify the sender/receiver cost center relationship and specify the tracing factors for the apportionment.

KSW2	Change Actual Periodic Reposting Cycle

Use this transaction to change the reposting cycle created using transaction KSW1.

KSW3	Display Actual Periodic Reposting Cycle

Use this transaction to display the reposting cycle created using transaction KSW1.

KSW4	Delete Actual Periodic Reposting Cycle

Use this transaction to delete the reposting cycle created using transaction KSW1.

KSW5	Execute Actual Periodic Reposting Cycle

This transaction is typically used as an easy way to repost actual costs from, for example, an administration cost center to cost centers that consume the costs, such as manufacturing departments. Periodic reposting uses the original cost element, meaning the primary cost element remains intact. When you allocate telephone costs, for example, the allocating cost center is unimportant for the receiving cost centers. The system therefore stores data records for periodic reposting in a way that uses less memory than a distribution. The sender cost center is not updated with this method. To define a periodic reposting, use the cycle created via transaction KSW1 with segments for the cycle and also tracing factors for the apportionment.

KSW7	Create Plan Periodic Reposting Cycle

This transaction is used to create a cycle for reposting plan costs. Reposting costs is an easy way to repost costs from, for example, an administration cost center to cost centers that consume the costs, such as manufacturing departments. The sender cost center is not updated with this method. To define a periodic reposting, you create segments and tracing factors for the apportionment. Use transaction KSWB to execute the reposting.

KSW8	Change Plan Periodic Reposting Cycle

Use this transaction to change the reposting cycle created using transaction KSW7.

KSW9	Display Plan Periodic Reposting Cycle

Use this transaction to display the reposting cycle created using transaction KSW7.

KSWA	Delete Plan Periodic Reposting Cycle

Use this transaction to delete the reposting cycle created using transaction KSW7.

KSWB	Execute Plan Periodic Reposting

This transaction is used as an easy way to repost plan costs from, for example, an administration cost center to cost centers that consume the costs, such as manufacturing departments. Periodic reposting uses the original cost element, meaning the primary cost element remains intact. When you allocate plan telephone costs, for example, the allocating cost center is unimportant for the receiving cost centers. The system therefore stores data records for periodic reposting in a way that uses less memory than a distribution. The sender cost center is not updated with this method. To define a periodic reposting, use the cycle created via transaction KSW7 with segments for the cycle and also tracing factors for the apportionment.

| **KVA5** | Transfer Actual Data from LIS Activity-Independent Statistical Key Figures, LIS |

This transaction is used to transfer statistical key figure data collected in the logistics information system to cost center accounting. This data can then be used, for example, in allocations. This transaction transfers data that is not linked to any particular activity type.

| **KVD5** | Transfer Actual Data from LIS Activity-Dependent Statistical Key Figures, LIS |

This transaction is used to transfer statistical key figure data collected in the logistics information system to cost center accounting.

This data can then be used, for example, in allocations. This transaction transfers activity dependent statistical key figures.

| **OKP1** | Maintain Period Lock |

This transaction is used to open and close the controlling area posting periods. This is a separate table from the finance posting period table maintained via transaction OB52. The period lock in the controlling module can be maintained for both actual and plan postings.

| **OKP2** | Display Period Lock |

Use this transaction to display the controlling period lock table maintained via transaction OKP1.

3   Inventory Management (IM)

MB00   Inventory Management Menu

This transaction is used to access the inventory management menu. The areas accessible from this menu include Goods Movements, Material Documents, Reservations, Periodic Processing and the environment area, which includes stock overview reports, list displays and the inventory controlling transactions.

MB01   Goods Receipt For
            Purchase Order

This transaction is used to perform a goods receipt for a Purchase Order. The movement type that is entered in this transaction determines the process involved in the goods receipt, which can include goods receipt into blocked stock, return delivery to a vendor, receipt without a purchase order and goods receipt reversals.

MB02   Change Material Document

This transaction is used to change a material document that has been generated. The transaction allows some fields to be changed in the material document, such as recipient of a service, unloading point and general text fields, depending on the movement type that generated the document.

MB03   Display Material Document

This transaction is similar to MB02 except that it allows users only to display the material document that is specified. If the material movement generated accounting documents, those documents can be accessed via this transaction.

MB04   Subcontracting Subsequent
            Adjustment

This transaction is used for a subsequent adjustment with reference to a subcontracting purchase order. If material is sent to a subcontractor to perform an external operation and the vendor requires additional material due to damaged items, this transaction is used to adjust the quality. This transaction has been superseded by MIGO_GS.

MB0A   Goods Receipt – PO Unknown

This transaction is used to perform a goods receipt when the purchase order is unknown. If you do not know the purchase order number, you can enter the vendor that provided the items, as well as the material and quantity that has been received. This transaction has been superseded by transaction MIGO.

MB1A   Enter Goods Issue

This transaction is used to perform a goods issue. The material in a goods issue is consumed, and a reduction in stock level is performed. For example, the material consumption can be against a cost center, sales order, sample or scrap. This transaction has been superseded by transaction MIGO_GI.

MB1B   Enter Transfer Posting

This transaction is used to transfer material from one physical or logical location to another. For example, a material can be transferred between two storage locations, or between two logical states such as quality inspection to unrestricted. This transaction has been superseded by transaction MIGO_TR.

MB1C   Enter Other Goods Receipts

This transaction is used for goods receipts that are not associated with purchase orders or production orders, such as a goods receipt of a by-product. This transaction can be used when initially loading inventory into the system. This transaction has been superseded by transaction MIGO_GI.

MB21   Create Reservation

This transaction is used to create a reservation of material. A reservation document is a formal request to retain materials in the warehouse so that they are ready for withdrawal at a later date and for a specific purpose.

MB22   Change Reservation

This transaction is used to change an existing material reservation. The quantity of the material to be reserved and the location where it is to be reserved from. A reservation can be changed only if it is created manually and not automatically generated.

MB23   Display Reservation

This transaction is used when it is necessary to display the details of a material reservation.

MB24   Reservation List Inventory Management

This transaction is used to produce a list of material reservations. A large number of selection criteria can be entered. The reservation list shows reservation number, item number, requirement date, movement type, material number, reserved quantity, reservation category and account assignment.

MB26   Pick List

This transaction is used to produce a pick list based on reservation information. The pick list shows quantity of material to be picked, reservation number, order number, required date and quantity already withdrawn. The transaction is very similar to CO27, but that transaction is based on order information. The other difference between MB26 and CO27 is that MB26 can be scheduled as a background job and CO27 cannot.

MB51   Material Document List

This transaction is used to create a list of material documents based on selection parameters. The list shows material documents per material, which includes movement type, plant, storage location, posting date and quantity posted.

MB52   Display Warehouse Stocks of Material

This transaction is used to create a report that shows the inventory levels of materials within a plant. The report shows the totals for each material in a plant, including unrestricted stock, stock in transit, stock in quality, restricted stock, blocked stock, returns and unrestricted stock. The report also shows the value of the material for each of the individual totals.

MB53   Plant Availability

This transaction is used to show the availability of a specific material at one or more plants. The transaction displays the unrestricted total for the material at each plant as well as the unrestricted consignment total, unrestricted sales order total, and the unrestricted project total.

MB54   Display Consignment Stocks

This transaction is used to display the unrestricted consignment stock at one or many plants. The display shows the material at each plant that is supplied by one or more vendors. The unrestricted consignment stock is shown by quantity, price per unit and overall value of the stock for each storage location and batch.

MB56   Display Batch Where-Used List

This transaction is used to find where a batch of material is used. The display requires a material, plant number and batch number. The display shows where the batch has been used including inspection lots, transfer posting, orders, and purchase orders. The user has the choice whether the analysis is top-down or bottom-up.

MB58   Display Consignment and Returnable Packaging Stocks at Customer

This transaction is used when consignment or returnable packaging is required to be located at a customer. The selection criteria are not mandatory but this will give a report of all materials at customer locations. The report shows the material located at each customer with totals for unrestricted, restricted and quality inspection stock.

MB59   Material Document List

This transaction is used to display a selection of material documents. The selection criteria require at least one entry, for example, plant, material or posting date. The display will show the material documents for the selection criteria entered in material order indicating movement type, posting date and quantity posted.

MB5B   Stocks on Posting Date

This transaction is used to ascertain the stock levels on a specific posting date. The transaction requires one entry in the selection criteria, such as company code, material or plant. If no selection dates are entered, the report will show current stock levels and all material movements up to the current date for the selection criteria supplied.

MB5C   Pick-Up List for Batch Where-Used List

This transaction is used to produce a pick-up list for where a batch of material is used. This transaction is similar to MB56; however, with this transaction, a list of all relevant batches are produced, rather than a single display, which is obtained using MB56. The same result can be achieved using MB5C by selecting a batch from the pick-up list.

MB5K   Stock Consistency Check

This transaction is used to check the consistency of stocks at company code level, valuation area level, and material level. The report shows if there are errors, such as that the actual quantity of material does not equal the total of stock records or that a table entry, such as in table MARC, does not exist.

MB5L   List of Stock Values: Balances

This transaction is used to display a list of account balances for inventory stock. The transaction requires that a selection is made for the current period, a previous period or a previous year. No other selection is required, but the report can be restricted by material, company code or accounts. This report can show differences between the stock accounts and material value if manual changes have been made to the General Ledger stock accounts.

MB5M   Shelf Life List

This transaction is used to display the batch shelf life of unrestricted stock in the plant. The report requires that a selection is made to determine whether remaining shelf life in the warehouse or total remaining shelf life is to be shown. The report shows a red stop light for batches that have expired, the date on which the batch expires, the quantity of the batch to expire and the number of days that have passed since expiry or the number of days until the batch expires.

MB5S   List of GR/IR Balances

This transaction is used to show the details of goods receipt and invoice balances. There is no mandatory selection for this report, but the result can be restricted by vendor, purchasing organization, purchasing group, purchasing document or material. The list produced by this transaction shows the details for each purchase order: quantity received, quantity invoiced and invoice amount. Invoices that are in excess of the quantity received are highlighted.

MB5T   Display Stock in Transit

This transaction is used to display material that is identified as stock in transit processed, using a two-step stock transport order. There is no mandatory selection for this report, but the report can be restricted by material, supplying plant, receiving plant, and special stock.

MB5U   Analysis of Conversion Differences

This transaction is used to analyze differences that are due to conversions between a material's unit of entry and base unit of measure. Typically, differences are produced when rounding differences occur between metric and imperial units of measure.

MB90   Output from Goods Movements

This transaction is used to produce output for a goods movement. The selection criteria for this transaction include output type, transmission medium and processing mode. It is possible to restrict the output by entering a single or range of material documents.

MBBM   Batch Input: Post Material Document

This transaction is used to create a batch input session, in order to post material documents for goods movements. The data for the batch input session is imported from the file that is entered in the selection criteria. A flag exists in the transaction, so the batch can be run in test only mode.

MBBR   Batch Input: Create Reservation

This transaction is used to create a batch input session, in order to create material reservations. The data for the batch input session is imported from the file that is entered in the selection criteria. A flag exists in the transaction, so the batch can be run in test only mode.

MBBS   Valuated Sales Order and Project Stock

This transaction is used to display the stock for material associated with a project. There are no mandatory selection criteria for this transaction. The result of the transaction shows the material quantity and value for each individual WBS element.

MBC1   Create Batch Search Strategy

This transaction is used to create a batch search strategy. The search strategy can be created using a strategy type, for example

ME02, which is used for a plant search strategy, or ME01, which is used for movement type, plant and material combinations. If there are user-defined strategy types, these can be used.

| **MBC2** | Change Batch Search Strategy |

This transaction is used to change an existing batch search strategy. If an existing batch search strategy requires a modification, such as to allow overdelivery or batch splits, then this can be performed using this transaction.

| **MBC3** | Display Batch Search Strategy |

This transaction is used to display batch search strategies.

| **MBGR** | Material Documents with Reason for Movement |

This transaction is used to display material documents that have an assigned reason for movement. There are no mandatory selection criteria for this transaction, but it is possible to enter a reason for movement for a given movement type. Other selection criteria include material, plant, and posting date.

| **MBLB** | Stocks at Subcontractor |

This transaction is used to display stocks that are currently located at a subcontractor. There are no mandatory selection criteria for this transaction, but it is possible to restrict the result by material, vendor, plant or company code. The resulting display shows the unrestricted, quality inspection and restricted stock at each subcontractor.

| **MBPM** | Manage Held Data |

This transaction is used to display any inventory management data that has been held. There are no mandatory selection criteria for

this transaction, but it is possible to restrict the result by username, creation date or the number of days the data has been held. It is possible to delete held data from this transaction.

| **MBRL** | Enter Return Delivery |

This transaction is used to enter a return delivery for a material document. The material document is required to create the return, but the quantity to be returned can be changed from the amount on the original material document. When complete, a new material document will be posted, which shows the return movement.

| **MBSF** | Release Blocked Stock |

This transaction is used to release blocked stock for a material document. The blocked stock is released, and a material document is created for the movement.

| **MBSL** | Copy Material Document |

This transaction is used to copy an existing material document. When an existing material document is copied, it is possible to change the material quantity to be posted. For example, if a material document for a movement type 101 of a quantity of 100 is copied, the new material document can be for the same or a different quantity.

| **MBSM** | Cancelled Material Documents |

This transaction is used to display cancelled material documents. Each line of the display shows the two material documents that correspond to the cancelled material document. For example, a line on the display may show a material document with a 262 movement type and a corresponding material document that shows a 261 movement type.

MBST   Cancel Material Document

This transaction is used to cancel a material document. If a material document has been created or copied incorrectly, for example using transaction MBSL, this transaction allows the user to cancel that material document.

MBSU   Place in Storage for Material Document

This transaction is used to place material into storage that is described on a material document. For example, a material document for a movement type 303, plant to plant transfer posting, can be received into storage using the material document.

MC.1   Plant Analysis: Stock: Selection

This transaction is used to display the stock quantity and value. The report can be restricted to a single plant or a selection of plants. The report shows the valuated stock, consignment stock and total value. This report is similar to the MB5B transaction, but this transaction brings data from Inventory Controlling information structures S032 and S034, while MB5B uses material documents to create the stock analysis.

MC.2   Plant Analysis: Receipts/ Issues: Selection

This transaction is used to show the value of receipts and issues for a single or multiple plants. The report shows the value of the receipts, value of issues and number of movements for a plant over a given period. It is possible to drill down on each plant to show the value of receipts and issues for each storage location. This transaction uses data from information structures S031 and S034.

MC.3   Plant Analysis: Inventory Turnover: Selection

This transaction is used to show the inventory turnover of valuated stock and the average valuated stock value at a plant over a given period. It is possible to restrict the selection to a single or a range of plants. This transaction uses data from information structure S032.

MC.4   Plant Analysis: Range of Coverage: Selection

This transaction is used to display the range of coverage for valuated stock. The range of coverage is calculated as the value of the valuated stock divided by the value of the average total daily usage. The report also shows the value of the valuated stock for the plant selected. This transaction uses data from information structure S032.

MC.5   Storage Location Analysis: Stock: Selection

This transaction is used to show the valuated stock for storage locations at a plant. The report shows the quantity of valuated stock, the quantity of consignment stock and the value of the valuated stock for each storage location selected. This transaction uses data from information structure S032.

MC.6   Storage Location Analysis: Receipts/Issues: Selection

This transaction is used to show the value of receipts and issues for storage locations at a plant. The report shows the value of the receipts, value of issues and number of movements for each storage location over a given period. It is possible to drill down on each storage location to show the value of receipts and issues for each material. This transaction uses data from information structures S031 and S034.

MC.7   Storage Location Analysis: Inventory Turnover: Selection

This transaction is used to show the inventory turnover of valuated stock and the average valuated stock value for storage locations over a given period. It is possible to drill down on each storage location to show the inventory turnover of valuated stock and the average valuated stock for each material. This transaction uses data from information structure S032.

MC.8   Storage Location Analysis: Coverage: Selection

This transaction is used to display the range of coverage for valuated stock for storage locations. The range of coverage is calculated as the value of the valuated stock divided by the value of the average total daily usage. The report also shows the value of the valuated stock for the storage location selected. This transaction uses data from information structure S032.

MC.9   Material Analysis: Stock: Selection

This transaction is used to show the valuated stock for materials. The report shows the quantity of valuated stock, the quantity of consignment stock and the value of the valuated stock for each material. The report can be restricted by entering a plant, storage location, MRP Controller, material type or date range. This transaction uses data from information structure S032.

MC.A   Material Analysis: Receipts/ Issues: Selection

This transaction is used to display the value of receipts and issues for materials. The report shows the value of the receipts, value of issues and number of movements for each material over a given period. The report can be restricted by using selection criteria including plant, storage location, MRP controller and material type. This transaction uses data from information structures S031 and S034.

MC.B   Material Analysis: Inventory Turnover: Selection

This transaction is used to show the inventory turnover of valuated stock and the average valuated stock value for materials over a given period. The report can be restricted by using selection criteria including plant, storage location, MRP controller and material type. This transaction uses data from information structure S032.

MC.C   Material Analysis: Range of Coverage: Selection

This transaction is used to display the range of coverage for valuated stock for materials. The range of coverage is calculated as the value of the valuated stock divided by the value of the average total daily usage. The report also shows the value of the valuated stock for the material selected. This transaction uses data from information structure S032.

MC01   Key Figure Retrieval Using Info Sets

This transaction is used to find data by searching through info sets. The transaction allows users to click on info sets until they reach the key figure they require, such as net order value or mean delivery time from vendor. Once users have found the correct key figure they can select that line and the appropriate transaction will be displayed that can then be executed.

MC02   Key Figure Retrieval Using Text Strings

This transaction is used to find data by entering text strings. The transaction allows the user to enter a number of text strings with AND, OR operands. After the user enters the appropriate text, strings, the transaction will return a key figure list from which the user can choose.

MC03	Key Figure Retrieval Using Classification

This transaction is used to find data by selecting classification characteristics. After the user enters the required classification characteristics, the transaction will return a key figure list from which the user can choose.

MC04	Create Info Set

This transaction is used to create a user-defined info set. The user is able to create an info set by selecting one or many key figures, which are values used to evaluate performance. A key figure can be a percentage or value, such as purchase order quantity, lead time, range of coverage, etc.

MC05	Change Info Set

This transaction is used to change an info set that has been created. Key figures can be deselected from the info set or new key figures can be added.

MC06	Display Info Set

This transaction is used to display current info sets. The transaction shows the last time the info set was updated and what user last updated the info set.

MC07	Create Key Figure

This transaction is used to create a new key figure. The new figure requires a description and needs to be assigned to a unique application area, such as Purchasing, Inventory Controlling, Invoice Verification, etc.

MC08	Change Key Figure

This transaction is used to change an existing key figure. The user can change the description of the key figure and details within the key figure.

MC09	Display Key Figure

This transaction is used to display the details of an existing key figure.

MC40	Usage-Based ABC Analysis

This transaction is used to perform usage-based ABC analysis on materials at a single or range of plants. The transaction allows the ABC analysis to be performed at a number of different levels: user-defined percentages, usage as a number, percentage of materials or number of materials per level. The resulting display will show the old and new ABC indicator for each material.

MC41	Requirement-Based ABC Analysis

This transaction is used to perform requirement-based ABC analysis on materials at a single or range of plants. Similar to transaction MC40, the ABC analysis can be performed at a number of different levels: user-defined percentages, usage as a number, percentage of materials or number of materials per level. The resulting display will show the old and new ABC indicator for each material.

MC42	Key Figure: Range of Coverage Based on Usage Values

This transaction is used to analyze the range of coverage based on usage. The transaction allows the user to choose to display the range of coverage for sales organizations, purchase organizations or plants. The report can be restricted by a number of criteria, including material, ABC indicator, purchasing group, and MRP type. The report shows the number of days of coverage for each material based on the selection criteria.

MC43	Key Figure: Range of Coverage Based on Requirement Values

This transaction is used to analyze the range of coverage based on future requirements. The user can specify the period to be used for the analysis. Similar to transaction MC42, the user can choose to display the range of coverage for sales organizations, purchase organizations or plants. The report shows the number of days of coverage for each material based on the selection criteria.

MC44	Key Figure: Inventory Turnover

This transaction is used to analyze inventory turnover for sales organizations, purchase organizations or plants. The user can specify the period to be used for the inventory turnover analysis. It is possible to restrict the report to show only materials that have greater than a certain number of turnovers or to show the materials with the highest and lowest turnovers.

MC45	Key Figure: Usage Value

This transaction is used to analyze the usage value for sales organizations, purchase organizations or plants. The user can specify the period to be used for the usage value analysis. It is possible to restrict the report to show only materials that have a usage value over a specified amount or to show the materials with the highest and lowest usage value.

MC46	Key Figure: Slow-Moving Items

This transaction is used to analyze slow-moving materials for sales organizations, purchase organizations or plants. The transaction allows the user to enter a number of

days to analyze. The resulting display shows the number of days since any consumption was posted for each material.

MC47	Key Figure: Requirements Value

This transaction is used to analyze the requirement value for sales organizations, purchase organizations or plants. The requirements value is derived from the requirements quantity and the current price of the material. The transaction allows the user to enter the future period to analyze. The resulting display shows the requirements value for each material by currency and percentage.

MC48	Key Figure: Stock Value

This transaction is used to analyze the current material stock value for sales organizations, purchase organizations or plants. It is possible to restrict the output by material, material type, ABC indicator and MRP Type. The resulting display shows the current stock value and percentage of stock figure for each material.

MC49	Key Figure: Average Stock Value

This transaction is used to analyze the material average stock value for sales organizations, purchase organizations or plants. The transaction allows the user to enter a date period for the average stock analysis. It is possible to restrict the output by material, material type, ABC indicator, purchasing group and MRP Type. The resulting display shows the average stock value for the period entered and percentage of stock figure for each material.

MC50	Key Figure: Dead Stock

This transaction is used to show the dead stock analyzed over a given period. Dead stock is where the stock level is greater than zero, but no goods issues have been posted in the specified period. This report is useful, as dead stock impacts the company's cash flow and profitability in a negative way. The report shows the value of the dead stock for each material.

MCBA   Plant Analysis

This transaction is used to generate a plant analysis report. This report is part of the Inventory Controlling standard analyses. The report can be restricted by plant, storage location, material or MRP controller. The analysis shows, for each plant, the quantity of goods issues from valuated stock, quantity of goods receipts from valuated stock, the total of planned and unplanned consumption, and the total quantity of valuated stock.

MCBC   Storage Location Analysis

This transaction is used to generate a storage location analysis report. This report is part of the Inventory Controlling standard analyses. The report can be restricted by plant, storage location, material or MRP controller. The analysis shows, for each storage location, the quantity of goods issues from valuated stock, quantity of goods receipts from valuated stock, and the total of planned and unplanned consumption.

MCBE   Material Analysis

This transaction is used to generate a material analysis report. This report is part of the Inventory Controlling standard analyses. The report can be restricted by plant, storage location, material or MRP controller. The analysis shows, for each material, the quantity of goods issues from valuated stock, quantity of goods receipts from valuated stock, and the total of planned and unplanned consumption.

MCBG   MRP Controller Analysis

This transaction is used to generate an MRP controller analysis report. The report can be restricted by plant or MRP controller. The analysis shows, for each MRP controller, the quantity of goods issues from valuated stock, quantity of goods receipts from valuated stock, and the total of planned and unplanned consumption.

MCBI   Business Area Analysis

This transaction is used to generate a business analysis report. The report can be restricted by plant or business area. The analysis shows, for each business area, the quantity of goods issues from valuated stock, quantity of goods receipts from valuated stock, and the total of planned and unplanned consumption.

MCBK   Material Group Analysis

This transaction is used to generate a material group analysis report. The report can be restricted by plant or material group. The analysis shows, for each material group, the quantity of goods issues from valuated stock, quantity of goods receipts from valuated stock, and the total of planned and unplanned consumption.

MCBM   Division Analysis

This transaction is used to generate a division analysis report. The report can be restricted by plant or division. The analysis shows, for each division, the quantity of goods issues from valuated stock, quantity of goods receipts from valuated stock, and the total of planned and unplanned consumption.

MCBO   Material Type Analysis

This transaction is used to generate a material type analysis report. The report can be restricted by plant or material type. The analysis shows, for each material type, the quantity of goods issues from valuated stock, quantity of goods receipts from valuated stock, and the total of planned and unplanned consumption.

MCBR	Batch Analysis

This transaction is used to generate a batch analysis report. The report can be restricted by plant, storage location, batch or material. The analysis shows, for each batch, the quantity of goods issues from valuated stock, quantity of goods receipts from valuated stock, and the quantity of valuated stock.

MCBZ	Current Requirements/ Stock Analysis

This transaction is used to generate a current requirements analysis. The report can be restricted by plant, material, MRP controller and MRP type. The analysis for each plant shows the total stock, which is calculated from valuated stock and consignment stock, total quantity of future goods issues and total future goods receipts.

MCL1	Stock Placements and Removals

This transaction is used to show stock placements and removals for a given period. The result can be restricted by warehouse, material, plant or period. If the report returns no data, then you should ensure that the Logistics Information System configuration is set so that the updates are activated, using transaction OMO9.

MCL5	Quantity Flows

This transaction is used to show the quantity of material that is moved through a warehouse over a given period. The result can be restricted by warehouse, material, plant or period. The resulting display shows for

each warehouse, the moved quantity, moved weight, number of movements, the time to convert a transfer requirement to a transfer order and time to confirm a transfer order.

MCL9	Material Stock Placements and Removals

This transaction is used to show the placements and removals in a warehouse for a given period. The resulting data can be restricted by warehouse, material, plant or period. The report shows the quantity and weight of material placed in the warehouse and the quantity and weight of material removed from the warehouse over a given period.

MCLD	Material Quantity Flows

This transaction is used to show the quantity of material that flows through a warehouse. The resulting display can be restricted by warehouse, material, movement type and period. The resulting data shows for each warehouse the quantity and weight of material moved, the time to convert a transfer requirement to a transfer order, the time to confirm a transfer order, and the time to convert a delivery note to a transfer order.

MCLH	Movement Types

This transaction is used to show the movements per movement type for each warehouse. The result of the transaction can be restricted by warehouse, movement type, material and period. The resulting display shows for each movement type in a warehouse; the number of movements, quantity and weight of material moved, and the number of transfer order items with reference to a transfer requirement.

MCYG   Exception Analysis

This transaction is used to produce reports based on exception analyses. The transaction requires that an exception is entered on which to perform an analysis. The exception is defined using a number of characteristics, such as price or quantity. The exception occurs when one or more of the characteristics exceeds a specified threshold, for example, if a goods issue quantity exceeds 500 or a purchase order value exceeds $1000.

MD04   Stock/Requirements List

This transaction is used to produce a requirements list for an individual material or collectively for a plant or MRP area. The individual requirements report for a material requires a plant or MRP area to be entered. The result shows stock and requirements that have been allocated against the material. The collective requirements report shows the materials in a plant or MRP area with their respective stock level, days supply without receipts, first receipt days supply and second receipt days supply.

MI00   Physical Inventory Menu

This transaction is used to access the physical inventory menu. The areas accessible from this menu include the physical inventory documents, inventory counts, inventory differences, and the environment area which includes the physical inventory overview, physical inventory list, stock overview and serial numbers.

MI01   Create Physical
Inventory Document

This transaction is used to create a physical inventory document. To create the document, it is necessary to enter a planned count date, a plant number and storage location. The user can indicate that a posting block is to

be in place for the duration of the count or a freeze is to be placed on inventory balance of material not counted. The physical inventory document allows the user to enter a list of material numbers and batch numbers to be counted.

MI02   Change Physical
Inventory Document

This transaction code is used to change an existing physical inventory document. It is possible to change the physical inventory document by changing the planned count date or adding further materials to be counted. It is possible to delete a physical inventory document using this transaction.

MI03   Display Physical
Inventory Document

This transaction code is used to display an existing physical inventory document. It is possible to review the materials that are to be counted and the date on which the count is to occur. Using this transaction, it is also possible to display the history of the physical inventory document, including the current status of the document.

MI04   Enter Inventory Count

This transaction is used to enter a count for a physical inventory document. The transaction requires a valid physical inventory document number and count date to be entered. The user can then enter a quantity value for each of the materials in the physical count document.

MI05   Change Inventory Count

This transaction is used to change the values for a count that has been entered in a physical inventory document. A valid physical inventory document is required and a variance percentage can be entered on the initial screen. The variance is entered if the user will allow a percentage variation between the count and the book inventory. The user can change the count total for the materials entered in the physical inventory document.

| MI06 | Display Inventory Count |

This transaction code is used to display an existing physical inventory count. It is possible to review the materials that have been counted. Using this transaction, it is also possible to display the history of the items in the physical inventory document, including the count date, count quantity, book quantity, book value, difference and who entered the count.

| MI07 | Post Inventory Difference |

This transaction is used to post an inventory count where there is a difference between the count and the book quantity. The transaction shows the user the quantity that is the difference between the count and the book quantity. If the user decides to post the count despite the variance, the user can enter a reason code if any have been configured.

| MI08 | Post Count and Difference |

This transaction is used to enter a count for a physical inventory document and post the difference in one step. The count quantity and reason code for any difference, if required, can be entered for each line item of the physical inventory document. A reason code can be entered only if it has previously been configured. If a difference is posted a material document is created showing the addition or subtraction from stock.

| MI09 | Enter Count Without Reference to Document |

This transaction is used to enter a physical inventory count without using a physical inventory document. The count date, plant and storage location are mandatory selections, but the user can also enter a special stock indicator and the acceptable variance percentage. The material number, batch number (if appropriate), count quantity and unit of measure are required for each line item entered into this transaction. Subsequent to posting, the transaction will display the generated physical inventory document number.

| MI10 | Post Document, Count and Difference |

This transaction is used to enter a physical inventory count without using a physical inventory document and then post the count value. The count date, plant and storage location are mandatory selections, but the user can also enter a special stock indicator and the acceptable variance percentage. The material number, batch number (if appropriate), count quantity and unit of measure are required for each line item entered. Subsequent to posting, the transaction will display the generated physical inventory document number and a material document number if a change in stock levels occurred.

| MI11 | Create Recount Document |

This transaction is used to create a recount document for a physical inventory count that has already been entered. To create the recount document, the user has to enter the original physical inventory document and the planned date for the recount. The transaction allows the user to review the details of the original document and by executing the transaction a recount document is generated.

MI12   Display Changes to Physical
             Inventory Documents

This transaction is used to display the changes
that have occurred with a single or range of
physical inventory documents. The transaction will display the changes made to physical
inventory documents such as change document number, date and time of the change
and the transaction in which the change was
made.

MI20   List of Inventory Differences

This transaction is used to display a list of
physical inventory documents that were
posted with differences. The transaction
allows the user to restrict the result by material, plant, physical inventory document
range, fiscal year, count date, and reason
code. The resulting display shows, for each
physical inventory document, the material,
the book quantity, count quantity, difference,
and the value of the difference.

MI21   Print Physical Inventory
             Document

This transaction is used to print physical
inventory documents that have been created.
The transaction allows the user to restrict
the number of documents to be printed by
entering a single or range of physical inventory documents, plant, storage location, and
planned count date.

MI22   Display Physical Inventory
             Documents for Material

This transaction is used for finding and displaying physical inventory documents that
have been created for a single or range of
materials. The user can restrict the resulting
display by selecting a plant, storage location,
batch, count date and posting period. The
resulting display shows the relevant physical inventory documents per material, the

posting period, count date, and whether the
document is still active.

MI23   Display Physical Inventory
             Data for Material

This transaction is used for finding and displaying physical inventory data associated
with a single or range of materials. The user
can restrict the resulting display by selecting
a plant, storage location, batch, and date of
last physical inventory. The resulting display
shows the data associated with each material
including the storage location, current stock
and whether a physical inventory has been
carried out in the current period.

MI24   Physical Inventory List

This transaction is used for displaying the
physical inventory documents for the selection criteria entered. The user can restrict
the physical inventory documents displayed
by entering a single or range of materials,
plant, storage location, batch, count date, and
reason code. The resulting display shows a
list of relevant physical inventory documents,
item number and the status of the physical
inventory item, e.g., counted or adjusted.

MI31   Create Physical Inventory
             Documents in Batch

This transaction allows users to create physical inventory documents with a batch input.
The user can enter a single or range of materials, plant, material type or material group. It
is possible to create a batch input or create the
physical inventory documents directly.

MI32   Batch Input – Block Material
             for Physical Inventory

This transaction allows the user to block
material for physical inventory by batch
input. The selection criteria allows the user to
enter a single or range of physical inventory

documents, plant, storage location, planned count date and fiscal year. After executing the transaction, it will return with the physical inventory documents that can be blocked.

MI33	Batch Input – Freeze Book Inventory Balance for Physical Inventory

This transaction is used to freeze the book inventory balance for physical inventory documents. The user can restrict this by a single or range of physical inventory documents, plant, and planned count date. The transaction will not allow the freezing of book inventory at a storage location level unless the system is configured to allow it. The configuration to allow this to occur at the storage location is found in transaction OMBP.

MI34	Batch Input – Enter Count with Reference to Document

This transaction is used for entering physical inventory counts in batch mode. This method requires a file to be created for the batch input and is useful if the inventory count is performed outside of SAP, for example by using RF technology.

MI35	Batch Input – Post Zero Count for Uncounted Materials

This transaction is used to post a zero count for uncounted materials using a batch input. There is no mandatory selection, but a number of fields can be used to restrict the selection such as plant, planned count date, physical inventory document number and fiscal year. After executing the transaction a display will appear that shows the inventory documents that are relevant for posting.

MI37	Batch Input – Post Differences

This transaction is used to post inventory differences in batch. There is no mandatory selection, but a number of fields can be used to restrict the selection such as plant, planned count date, physical inventory document number and fiscal year.

MI38	Batch Input – Enter Count With Reference to Document

This transaction is used to enter inventory counts with reference to physical inventory documents in batch. This transaction generates a batch input session that enters the count results when the user processes the batch session.

MI39	Batch Input – Enter Count Without Reference to Document

This transaction is used to enter inventory counts without reference to physical inventory documents in batch. This transaction generates a batch input session that enters the count results when the user processes the batch session.

MI40	Batch Input – Enter Count Without Reference to Document Post Differences

This transaction is used to enter inventory counts and post any differences without reference to physical inventory documents in batch. This transaction generates a batch input session that enters the count results and posts inventory differences when the user processes the batch session.

MIBC	ABC Analysis for Cycle Counting

This transaction is used to perform an ABC analysis for materials at a given plant. The user is required to enter a plant for the analysis and can select from a number of criteria, such as material type and date range for consumption. The resulting analysis displays the old and new ABC indicator, total value and total stock for each material.

MICN	Batch Input: Create Physical Inventory Documents For Cycle Counting

This transaction is used to post physical inventory documents for cycle counting using a batch input. There is no mandatory selection, but a number of fields can be used to restrict the selection such as material, plant, planned count date, batch and material type. After executing the transaction, a display will appear that shows the materials that are relevant for posting.

MIDO	Display Physical Inventory Overview

This transaction is used to display for each company code the status of the physical inventory for available materials. The transaction requires a company code to be entered, but the report can be further restricted by entering a plant, storage location, material type or material group.

MIGO	Goods Receipt for a Purchase Order

This transaction is used to perform a goods receipt for a purchase order and other goods receipts. This transaction can be used instead of other goods receipt transactions such as MB01 and MB0A. The goods receipt can be performed for a number of documents, including inbound deliveries, material documents and orders.

MIGO_ GI	Goods Movement

This transaction is used to perform a goods issue. It is possible to use this transaction for a goods issue to an order, purchase order and a reservation. The material in a goods issue is consumed and a reduction in stock level is performed. For example, the material consumption can be against a cost center, sales order, sample or scrap. This transaction can be used instead of MB1A.

MIGO_ GS	Subsequent Adjustment

This transaction is used for a subsequent adjustment with reference to a subcontracting purchase order. If material is sent to a subcontractor to perform an external operation and the vendor requires additional material due to damaged items, this transaction is used to adjust the quality. This transaction can be used instead of MB04.

MIK1	Selected Data for Physical Inventory Documents – Vendor Consignment

This transaction is used to create physical inventory documents in batch for vendor consignment stock. The user can restrict the selection by vendor, material, plant, material type and planned count date. The transaction will check each relevant material to make sure it has not been counted in the current period. If not, the material will be added to the batch file for processing.

MIQ1	Selected Data for Physical Inventory Documents for Project

This transaction is used to create physical inventory documents in batch for project stock. The user can restrict the selection by WBS element, material, plant, material type and planned count date. The transaction will check each relevant material to make sure it has not been counted in the current period. If not, the material will be added to the batch file for processing.

MMBE	Stock Overview

This transaction is used to view stock at different organizational levels: company code, plant, storage location and batch level. The material number is mandatory for this transaction. The user can choose to restrict the resulting display by entering a plant, storage location or batch number. On the selection screen, the user has the ability to hide levels from the final display.

MR51	Accounting Documents for Material

This transaction allows the user to display all the accounting documents for a specific material. The results can be restricted by entering a company code, valuation area, posting date or document type. The resulting display shows the document type, accounting document number, posting date, quantity of material posted and the value of the posted material.

4   Materials Management (MM)

ME00   Purchasing Menu

This transaction gives users access to the purchasing menu. The areas accessible from this menu include the purchase order, purchase requisition, outline agreement, request for quotation, master data and purchasing reports.

ME01   Maintain Source List

This transaction is used to create a source list for a material at a specified plant. The selection screen requires a material and a plant to be entered. On the detail screen, the user can add a list of available sources of supply for a material, entering the periods during which procurement from each vendor is possible. The user can flag a vendor as the preferred source of supply for the material and also flag vendors as blocked for procurement.

ME03   Display Source List

This transaction is used to display the source list for a material at a specific plant. The selection screen requires a material and a plant to be entered. The display will show a list of vendors if a list has been maintained. The source list shows the valid from and to dates for each vendor, the vendor number, purchasing organization and outline agreement, if relevant.

ME04   Changes to Source List

This transaction shows the changes that have been made to a source list for a specific material. The selection requires a material and plant to be entered. The user can restrict the resulting display by entering the person's name whose changes to the source list are to be shown and a date from which all changes are to be viewed. The resulting display shows the details of the change to the source list including user ID, date and time of the change, document change number and the values that were changed.

ME05   Generate Source List

This transaction is used to generate a source list using the system rather than manually entering values. The initial screen allows a single or range of materials to be selected and the dates from which the system will review the transactions to develop the source list. If the test run indicator on the selection screen is highlighted, the system will display a simulation of the source list changes, rather than make the changes.

ME06   Analyze Source List

This transaction is used to analyze the source list for a material or range of materials. The selection screen allows the user to enter a range of dates between which the analysis should be performed. The resulting display will show, for each material/plant combination, whether there is a source list missing.

ME07   Reorganize Source List

This transaction is used to reorganize the source list. The user is required to enter a material and the date before which all records are to be deleted. The transaction will delete all source list entries before the date entered and is used to remove out of date source list records.

ME08   Send Source List

This transaction is used to send source lists to another system via ALE. It is possible to restrict the source lists to be sent by entering a material, material class or plant. The user can enter the logical system where the source list is to be sent.

ME0M   Source List for Material

This transaction is used to display the source lists for a given material. The selection screen allows the user to enter a material or range of materials, and a plant or range of plants. If no values are entered, the resulting display will show all the source lists for all materials.

ME11   Create Purchasing Info Record

This transaction is used to create a purchasing information record for a material. The info record can be for a material/vendor combination or for a material group/vendor combination. The user can select the type of info record to be created: standard, subcontracting, pipeline or consignment. The info record can contain the net price for the material or material group charged by the specified vendor, as well as other information on delivery time, minimum quantity, purchasing group and shelf life.

ME12   Change Purchasing Info Record

This transaction allows the user to change an existing purchasing info record. The info record number can be entered or the user can enter a combination of vendor number, plant, material and purchasing organization to access the record. The user can change values in the info record, such as net price for the material or material group charged by the specified vendor, as well as other information on delivery time, minimum quantity, and purchasing group.

ME13   Display Purchasing Info Record

This transaction is used to display the details of an existing purchasing info record. The info record number can be entered or the user can enter a combination of vendor number, plant, material and purchasing organization to display the info record.

ME14   Changes to Purchasing
             Info Record

This transaction is used to display changes that have been made to a purchasing info record. The selection screen requires that a purchasing info record number is to be entered, but the results can be restricted by entering the user ID of the person who made the change and the change date. The resulting display shows the entry and the change details of the info record, including the date of change, document change number and the table and field that was changed.

ME15   Flag Info Record for Deletion

This transaction is used to flag a purchasing info record for deletion. The info record number can be entered or the user can enter a combination of vendor number, plant, material and purchasing organization to flag the info record for deletion. The user can select either the complete info record for deletion or just the data for the purchasing organization.

ME16   Deletion Proposals
             for Info Records

This transaction is used to delete purchasing info records based on the selection entered. The transaction allows the user to enter the vendor, material, material group, purchasing organization, plant and purchasing group. The key date for the document or the entry date must be entered for this transaction. This process is useful to delete info records for vendors who are no longer used by your company.

ME17	Archive Purchasing Info Records

This transaction is used to archive purchasing info records. Before a record is ready to be archived, it must have the deletion flag set, which can be achieved using transaction ME15.

ME18	Send Purchasing Info Records

This transaction is used to send purchasing info records to another system via ALE. It is possible to restrict the purchasing info records to be sent by entering a vendor, material, material class or info record number. The user can enter the logical system where the source list is to be sent.

ME1A	Archived Purchasing Info Records

This transaction is used to access archived purchasing info records. The archived info records can only be accessed if read from a flat file, which has to be on an application server. If the archived records are held externally, then they will need to be loaded onto the server in order to be accessed.

ME1E	Quotation Price History

This transaction is used to display price history from the purchasing info record. The resulting display can be restricted by entering a vendor, material, material group, purchasing organization, plant or purchasing group. The report will show the current price for each relevant purchasing info record. The price details can be accessed from the results screen.

ME1L	Info Records per Vendor

This transaction is used to display all the purchasing info records for a single or range of vendors. The output can be restricted by entering a material, material group, purchasing organization, plant or purchasing group. The output shows the purchasing info record details for each vendor within the selection criteria.

ME1M	Purchasing Info Records per Material

This transaction is used to display all the purchasing info records for a single or range of materials. The output can be restricted by entering a vendor, material group, purchasing organization, plant or purchasing group. The output shows the purchasing info record details for each material within the selection criteria.

ME1P	Purchase Order Price History

This transaction is used to display the purchase order price for each purchase info record. The selection can be restricted by vendor, material, material group, purchasing organization and plant. The output is in purchase info record sequence and shows the purchase order detail for each purchase info record. The date, net price, quantity, purchase order number and variance are shown for each purchase order.

ME1W	Purchasing Info Records per Material Group

This transaction is used to display the purchasing info records for a material group. The selection can be restricted by material group, vendor, purchasing organization, plant and purchasing group. The output is in material group order and shows all the relevant purchasing info records for each material group. The details of the purchasing info record include the net price from the info record and the net price from purchase orders.

ME1X	Print Buyer's Negotiation Sheet for Vendor

This transaction is used to display the purchasing information record data for each material that has been purchased from the vendor selected. The selection criteria can be restricted by entering the vendor, purchasing organization, and material.

ME1Y	Print Buyer's Negotiation Sheet for Material

This transaction is used to display the purchasing information record data for vendors based on the material that has been entered. The output shows the information on the vendors who have been used to purchase the material, including the terms of payment, terms of delivery, and vendor evaluation scores.

ME21	Create Purchase Order

This transaction is used to create a purchase order. The initial screen requires a vendor, purchasing organization, purchasing group, and delivery date to be entered. The transaction requires that a material, quantity, plant and price are entered. The transaction has been superseded by transaction ME21N.

ME21N	Create Purchase Order

This transaction is used to create a purchase order. This transaction superseded transaction ME21. The difference between this transaction and ME21 is that this transaction shows the data on a single screen rather than a number of separate screens.

ME22	Change Purchase Order

This transaction is used to change a purchase order. The initial screen requires a purchase order number to be entered. The transaction allows the user to change the purchase order quantity for each line item as well as the price. The transaction has been superseded by transaction ME22N

ME22N	Change Purchase Order

This transaction is used to change a purchase order and has superseded transaction ME22. The transaction allows the user to change the purchase order quantity for each line item as well as the price. The details of the purchase order are on one screen, unlike ME22 where information is on separate screens.

ME23	Display Purchase Order

This transaction is used to display a purchase order. The initial screen requires a purchase order number to be entered. The transaction allows the user to display the details of the purchase order. The transaction has been superseded by transaction ME23N.

ME23N	Display Purchase Order

This transaction is used to display a purchase order and has superseded transaction ME23. The transaction allows the user to display the details of the purchase order on a single screen, rather than separate screen as with transaction ME23.

ME24	Maintain Purchase Order Supplement

This transaction is used to add or change header texts for an existing purchase order. The initial screen requires a single purchase order number to be entered. The transaction allows the user to add text in a number of fields: header text, header note, pricing types, deadlines and terms of delivery.

ME25	Create Purchase Order with Source Determination

This transaction allows the user to create a purchase order where the vendor can be determined by the transaction. The initial screen requires the user to enter an order type, purchase order date, and purchasing group. The user can highlight the source determination flag, which allows the system to suggest a vendor if one source of supply exists, or, if a number of sources exist, the user can select a vendor.

ME26	Display Purchase Order Supplement

This transaction is used to display header texts for a purchase order. The user is required to enter a single purchase order number. The transaction will display the header texts for the purchase order number that was entered.

ME27	Create Purchase Order with Transfer Order

This transaction is used to create a stock transport order between two plants. The initial screen requires the supplying plant, purchasing organization, purchasing group and purchase order date to be entered. The detail screen requires the receiving plant, material and quantity to be entered.

ME28	Release Purchasing Documents

This transaction allows the user to release purchase orders that are subject to a release strategy. If purchase orders need to be approved before being sent to the vendor, then a release strategy can be configured. This transaction is used by approvers to release purchase orders that they approve.

The purchase order is then released to the vendor or to the next level of approval in the release strategy.

ME29N	Release Purchasing Documents

This transaction is used to release a purchase document, such as a purchase order or a stock transport order. This transaction is similar to ME28, but shows all the information for the purchasing document on a single screen.

ME2A	Monitor Vendor Confirmations

This transaction is used to display vendor confirmations. The initial screen requires a confirmation category to be entered, such as order acknowledgement or shipping notification. The output can be restricted by purchasing document, purchasing organization, purchasing group or vendor.

ME2B	Purchasing Documents per Requirement Tracking Number

This transaction is used to display the purchasing documents with a specific requirement tracking number. The initial screen has a number of criteria that can be entered to restrict the output, including purchasing organization, purchasing group, plant, delivery date, vendor, material and material group.

ME2C	Purchasing Documents for Material Group

This transaction is used to display the purchasing documents with a specific material group. The initial screen has a number of criteria that can be entered to restrict the output, including purchasing organization, purchasing group, plant, delivery date, vendor, material, and item category.

ME2J	Purchasing Documents per Project

This transaction is used to display the purchasing documents with a specific project. The initial screen has a number of criteria that can be entered to restrict the output, including WBS element, network, activity, purchasing organization, purchasing group, and plant.

ME2K	Purchasing Documents per Account Assignment

This transaction is used to display the purchasing documents with a specific account assignment. The initial screen has a number of criteria that can be entered to restrict the output, including WBS element, order, asset, network, activity, purchasing organization, purchasing group, plant, and vendor.

ME2L	Purchasing Documents for Vendor

This transaction is used to display the purchasing documents with a specific vendor. The initial screen has a number of criteria that can be entered to restrict the output, including purchasing organization, purchasing group, plant, material, material group, and delivery date.

ME2M	Purchasing Documents for Material

This transaction is used to display the purchasing documents with a specific material. The initial screen has a number of criteria that can be entered to restrict the output, including plant, purchasing organization, purchasing group, delivery date, vendor, and material group.

ME2N	Purchasing Documents per Document Number

This transaction is used to display the purchasing documents with a specific document number. The initial screen has a number of criteria that can be entered to restrict the output, including purchasing organization, plant, purchasing group, vendor, and delivery date.

ME2O	Subcontractor Stock Monitoring for Vendor

This transaction is used to display the materials that have been sent to a subcontracting vendor. The output shows the material details, batch number and quantity of material at each subcontracting vendor. The selection criteria can be restricted by vendor, material, plant and requirement date.

ME2S	Purchase Order Reporting with Services

This transaction shows purchase orders that contain services. The initial screen shows a number of selection criteria that can restrict the output including vendor, purchasing organization, purchasing group, plant, purchase order number, service number, and service type. The output shows each purchase order and the entered quantity and value, accepted quantity, settled value, and invoiced quantity, and value for each line item.

ME2V	Expected Goods Receipts

This transaction shows the expected goods receipts for a specific or range of plants. The initial screen shows a number of selection criteria that can restrict the output including plant, delivery date, vendor and material. The output shows the plant and the expected date for the receipt.

ME2W	Purchasing Documents per Supplying Plant

This transaction is used to display the purchasing documents for a supplying plant. The initial screen shows a number of selection criteria that can restrict the output including purchasing organization, purchasing group and plant. The output is shown in vendor/supplying plant order, with each purchasing document displayed. Each line item shows the purchasing document type, purchasing organization, purchasing group, material group, quantity and net price.

ME31	Create Outline Agreement

This transaction is used to create an outline agreement, which can be referenced to a purchase requisition or a request for quotation. The outline agreement can be either a contract or a scheduling agreement. A contract can be for predetermined quantity or predefined value. A scheduling agreement is a long term purchase agreement with a vendor to supply a quantity of material or material up to a certain value.

ME31K	Create Contract

This transaction is used to create a contract, which can be for a specific value of material or quantity of material. The initial screen requires a vendor, agreement type, purchasing organization and purchasing group to be entered. Depending on the agreement type, the user is required to enter either a target value or a target quantity for the contract.

ME31L	Create Scheduling Agreement

This transaction is used to create a scheduling agreement with a vendor. The initial screen requires a vendor, agreement type, purchasing organization and purchasing group to be entered. The user will need to enter a validity end date, the material and material target quantity.

ME32	Change Outline Agreement

This transaction allows the user to change the details of an outline agreement. The initial screen requires a single outline agreement number to be entered. The target quantity for a line item can be changed as well as underdelivery and overdelivery percentages, tax code, shipping instructions and tracking number.

ME32K	Change Contract

This transaction allows the user to change the details of a value or quantity contract. The initial screen requires a single contract number to be entered. The target quantity for a line item can be changed as well as underdelivery and overdelivery percentages, tax code, shipping instructions and tracking number.

ME32L	Change Scheduling Agreement

This transaction allows the user to change the details of a scheduling agreement. The initial screen requires a single scheduling agreement number to be entered. The target quantity for a line item can be changed as well as underdelivery and overdelivery percentages, tax code, shipping instructions and tracking number.

ME33	Display Outline Agreement

This transaction allows the user to display the details of an outline agreement. The initial screen requires a single outline agreement number to be entered. The details of the outline agreement can then be displayed.

ME33K Display Contract

This transaction allows the user to display the details of a value or quantity contract. The initial screen requires a single contract number to be entered. The details of the contract can then be displayed.

ME33L Display Scheduling Agreement

This transaction allows the user to display the details of a scheduling agreement. The initial screen requires a single scheduling agreement number to be entered. The details of the scheduling agreement can then be displayed.

ME34 Maintain Outline Agreement Supplement

This transaction is used to change header texts for an outline agreement. The user is required to enter a single outline agreement number. The transaction will display the text supplements for the outline agreement number that was entered, including the header text, header note, pricing types, deadlines, and terms of delivery.

ME34K Maintain Contract Supplement

This transaction is used to maintain header texts for a contract. The user is required to enter a single contract number. The transaction will display the text supplements for the contract number that was entered, including the release order text, header text, header note, pricing types, and deadlines.

ME34L Maintain Scheduling Agreement Supplement

This transaction is used to change header texts for a scheduling agreement. The user is required to enter a single scheduling agreement number. The transaction will display the text supplements for the scheduling agreement number that was entered, including the header text, header note, pricing types, deadlines, and terms of delivery.

ME35 Release Purchasing Documents

This transaction allows the user to release outline agreements that are subject to a release strategy. If outline agreements need to be approved before being sent to the vendor, then a release strategy can be configured. This transaction is used by approvers to release outline agreements that they approve. The outline agreement is then released to the vendor or to the next level of approval in the release strategy.

ME35K Release Contracts

This transaction allows the user to release contracts that are subject to a release strategy. If contracts need to be approved before being sent to the vendor, then a release strategy can be configured. This transaction is used by approvers to release contracts that they approve. The contract is then released to the vendor or to the next level of approval in the release strategy.

ME35L Release Scheduling Agreements

This transaction allows the user to release scheduling agreements that are subject to a release strategy. If scheduling agreements need to be approved before being sent to the vendor, then a release strategy can be configured. This transaction is used by approvers to release scheduling agreements that they approve. The scheduling agreement is then released to the vendor or to the next level of approval in the release strategy.

ME36   Display Outline Agreement Supplement

This transaction is used to display header texts for an outline agreement. The user is required to enter a single outline agreement number. The transaction will display the text supplements for the outline agreement number that was entered, including the header text, header note, pricing types, deadlines, and terms of delivery.

ME37   Create Transport Scheduling Agreement

This transaction is used to create a transport scheduling agreement between plants. The initial screen requires a supplying plant, agreement type (LU), purchasing organization and purchasing group to be entered. The user will need to enter a validity end date, receiving plant, the material and material target quantity.

ME38   Maintain Scheduling Agreement Schedule

This transaction allows the user to change the details of a transport scheduling agreement. The initial screen requires a single transport scheduling agreement number to be entered. The target quantity for a line item can be changed as well as underdelivery and overdelivery percentages, tax code, shipping instructions and tracking number.

ME39   Display Scheduling Agreement Schedule

This transaction allows the user to display the details of a transport scheduling agreement. The initial screen requires a single transport scheduling agreement number to be entered. The details of the transport scheduling agreement can then be displayed.

ME3B   Purchasing Documents per Requirement Tracking Number

This transaction is used to display outline agreements with a specific requirement tracking number. The initial screen has a number of criteria that can be entered to restrict the output, including purchasing organization, purchasing group, plant, delivery date, vendor, material, and material group.

ME3C   Purchasing Documents for Material Group

This transaction is used to display outline agreements for a specific material group. The initial screen has a number of criteria that can be entered to restrict the output, including purchasing organization, purchasing group, plant, delivery date, vendor, material and item category.

ME3J   Outline Agreements per Project

This transaction is used to display outline agreements for a specific project. The initial screen has a number of criteria that can be entered to restrict the output, including WBS element, network, activity, purchasing organization, purchasing group and plant.

ME3K   Purchasing Documents per Account Assignment

This transaction is used to display outline agreements with a specific account assignment. The initial screen has a number of criteria that can be entered to restrict the output, including WBS element, order, asset, network, activity, purchasing organization, purchasing group, plant, and vendor.

ME3L   Purchasing Documents per Vendor

This transaction is used to display outline agreements for a specific vendor. The initial screen has a number of criteria that can be entered to restrict the output, including purchasing organization, purchasing group, plant, material, material group, and delivery date.

ME3M	Purchasing Documents for Material

This transaction is used to display outline agreements for a specific material. The initial screen has a number of criteria that can be entered to restrict the output, including plant, purchasing organization, purchasing group, delivery date, vendor, and material group.

ME3N	Purchasing Documents per Document Number

This transaction is used to display outline agreements with a specific document number. The initial screen has a number of criteria that can be entered to restrict the output, including purchasing organization, plant, purchasing group, vendor, and delivery date.

ME3S	Contract Reporting with Services

This transaction is used to display contracts for services. The initial screen requires that a contact number is entered. The output can be restricted by service number, service type or service catalog number.

ME41	Create Request for Quotation

This transaction is used to create a request for quotation. The initial screen requires that the user enter a date by which vendors must return a quotation, a purchasing organization and purchasing group. A collective number can be entered in the RFQ header so RFQs and other purchasing documents can be grouped together. The RFQ should include the material and quantity required, as well as the date the items should be delivered.

ME42	Change Request for Quotation

This transaction is used to change a request for quotation. The initial screen requires that a single RFQ number is entered. The detail of the RFQ can be changed, such as the RFQ quantity and delivery date. Other details that can be maintained include the tracking number and the reminder values.

ME43	Display Request for Quotation

This transaction is used to display a request for quotation. The initial screen requires that a single RFQ number is entered. The details of the RFQ can be displayed, such as the material, short text, RFQ quantity and delivery date.

ME44	Maintain Request for Quotation Supplement

This transaction is used to display header texts for a request for quotation. The user is required to enter a single request for quotation number. The transaction will display the text supplements for the request for quotation number that was entered, including the header text, header note, pricing types, deadlines, and terms of delivery.

ME45	Release Request for Quotation

This transaction allows the user to release request for quotations that are subject to a release strategy. If RFCs need to be approved before being sent to the vendor then a release strategy can be configured. This transaction is used by approvers to release RFCs that they approve. The RFC is then released to the vendor or to the next level of approval in the release strategy.

ME47	Maintain Quotation

This transaction is used to enter the quotation sent from a vendor who had received a request for quotation. The initial screen requires a single request for quotation number to be entered. The detail screen allows the user to enter the net price of each line item on the quotation.

ME48	Display Quotation

This transaction is used to display the details from a vendor's quotation. The initial screen requires a single request for quotation number to be entered. The transaction shows the information from the RFQ and the vendor's quotation such as the material, RFQ quantity, delivery date and net price.

ME49	Price Comparison List

This transaction is used to compare quotations to give the purchasing department a price comparison. The initial screen requires a purchasing organization to be entered as well as quotations or collective request for quotation numbers. The output shows the details from the quotations and gives a ranking for the quotations displayed.

ME4B	Purchasing Documents per Requirement Tracking Number

This transaction shows the request for quotations for a single or range of requirement tracking numbers. The initial screen displays a number of criteria that can restrict the output. These criteria include purchasing organization, purchasing group, plant, delivery date, plant and material.

ME4C	Purchasing Documents for Material Group

This transaction shows the request for quotations for a single or range of material groups.

The initial screen displays a number of criteria that can restrict the output. These criteria include purchasing organization, purchasing group, plant, delivery date, plant, vendor, and material.

ME4L	Purchasing Documents per Vendor

This transaction shows the request for quotations for a single or range of vendors. The initial screen displays a number of criteria that can restrict the output. These criteria include purchasing organization, purchasing group, plant, delivery date, plant, material group, and material.

ME4M	Purchasing Documents for Material

This transaction shows the request for quotations for a single or range of materials. The initial screen displays a number of criteria that can restrict the output. These criteria include purchasing organization, purchasing group, plant, delivery date, plant, vendor, and material.

ME4N	Purchasing Documents per Document Number

This transaction shows the request for quotations for a single or range of RFQ numbers. The initial screen displays a number of criteria that can restrict the output. These criteria include purchasing organization, purchasing group, plant, delivery date, plant, vendor, and material.

ME4S	RFQ's per Collective Number

This transaction shows the request for quotations for a single or range of collective numbers. The initial screen displays a number of criteria that can restrict the output. These criteria include purchasing organization, purchasing group, plant, delivery date, plant, vendor, and material.

ME51   Create Purchase Requisition

This transaction is used to create a purchase requisition. The initial screen requires a document type of NB to be entered. The detail screen requires the entry of a material or account assignment category, if the material is not known. The user is required to add the price for each line item. This transaction has been superseded by transaction ME51N.

ME51N   Create Purchase Requisition

This transaction is used to create a purchase requisition and has superseded transaction ME51. This transaction requires that the information is entered in a single screen, while the old ME51 transaction is split across several screens. This transaction requires the entry of a material or account assignment category.

ME52   Maintain Purchase Requisition

This transaction is used to change a purchase requirement but has been superseded by transaction ME52N. The initial screen requires the entry of a single purchase requisition. The detail screen shows the line item details, and it is possible to change the quantity to be delivered and the delivery date.

ME52N   Maintain Purchase Requisition

This transaction is used to change a purchase requisition and has superseded transaction ME52. This transaction allows the information to be changed in a single screen, while the old ME52 transaction is split across several screens. With this transaction, it is possible to change line item details, such as the quantity to be delivered and the delivery date.

ME53   Display Purchase Requisition

This transaction is used to display a purchase requirement but has been superseded by transaction ME53N. The initial screen requires the entry of a single purchase requisition. The detail screen shows the line item details.

ME53N   Display Purchase Requisition

This transaction is used to change a purchase requisition and has superseded transaction ME53. This transaction allows the information to be displayed in a single screen, while the old ME53 transaction is split across several screens.

ME54   Release Purchase Requisition

This transaction allows the user to release a single purchase requisition that is subject to a release strategy. If the purchase requisition needs to be approved before being sent to the vendor then a release strategy can be configured. This transaction is used by approvers to release purchase requisitions that they approve. The purchase requisition is then released to the vendor or to the next level of approval in the release strategy. This transaction has been superseded by ME54N.

ME54N   Release Purchase Requisition

This transaction allows the user to release a single purchase requisition that is subject to a release strategy. If the purchase requisition needs to be approved before being sent to the vendor then a release strategy can be configured. This transaction is used by approvers to release purchase requisitions that they approve. The purchase requisition is then released to the vendor or to the next level of approval in the release strategy. This transaction has superseded transaction ME54.

ME55	Collective Release of Purchase Requisitions

This transaction is used to release a number of purchase requisitions at one time that are subject to a release strategy. For this transaction the user is required to enter a release code and can also enter other criteria to restrict the number of purchase requisitions to release. The output will show all purchase requisitions that can be released based on the criteria entered.

ME56	Assign Source to Supply to Requisitions

This transaction is used to assign a source of supply to existing purchase requisitions. The number of purchase requisitions can be restricted by the selection criteria, such as purchasing group, material, material group and plant. The output shows a list of purchase requisitions that can then be selected and a source of supply can be assigned automatically by the system.

ME57	Assign and Process Purchase Requisitions

This transaction is used to assign a source of supply to existing purchase requisitions and process them. The number of purchase requisitions can be restricted by the selection criteria, such as purchasing group, material, material group and plant. The output shows a list of purchase requisitions that can then be selected; a source of supply can be assigned, and then processed by the system.

ME58	Ordering: Assigned Purchase Requisitions

This transaction allows the user to select assigned purchase requisitions and manually convert them into purchase orders. The initial screen has selection criteria to restrict the output such as purchasing group and purchasing organization. The output is grouped by vendor and the user can select the line item to convert into a purchase order.

ME59	Automatic Creation of Purchase Orders from Requisitions

This transaction is used to automatically convert purchase requisitions to purchase orders. The initial screen shows a list of selection criteria to restrict the number of requisitions to be converted, such as purchasing group, purchasing organization, vendor, plant and material group. The system will automatically create the purchase orders based on the selection criteria.

ME5A	List Display of Purchase Requisitions

This transaction is used to display a list of purchase requisitions based on the selection criteria entered. The initial screen shows a list of criteria to restrict the output, such as purchasing group, material, material group, plant, and delivery date. The output is shown in purchase requisition order.

ME5F	Release Reminder: Purchase Requisitions

This transaction is used to display purchase requisitions that are subject to a release strategy and have yet to be released. The initial screen offers the user a list of selection criteria to restrict the output. The selection criteria include material, purchasing group, plant, delivery date, or cost center. The output shows the purchase requisitions to be released and the user can choose requisitions to release.

ME5J	List Display of Purchase Requisitions for Project

This transaction shows a list of purchase requisitions that are attached to a project. The initial selection screen shows a list of criteria that can restrict the requisitions shown. The criteria include project, WBS element, network, activity, purchasing group, material, and material group.

ME5K	List Display of Purchase Requisitions by Account Assignment

This transaction is used to display purchase requisitions associated with a single or range of cost centers. The initial screen offers the user a number of selection criteria to restrict the output. The selection criteria include cost center, WBS element, order, asset, network, operation, material, material group and purchasing group. The output is shown in cost center order.

ME5W	Resubmission of Purchase Requisitions

This transaction is used to generate a list of purchase requisitions that are to be resubmitted for processing. The initial screen shows a list of criteria that can restrict the output, including requisition number, purchasing group, material, material group, plant, and delivery date. The output shows requisitions that have a release date, plus resubmission interval, that has been passed.

ME61	Maintain Vendor Evaluation

This transaction is used to manually maintain the evaluation scores for a vendor. The initial screen requires the user to enter a vendor and a purchasing organization. The transaction allows the user to manually enter scores for the different criteria, such as price, quality, delivery and service.

ME62	Display Vendor Evaluation

This transaction is used to display the evaluation scores for a vendor. The initial screen requires the user to enter a vendor and a purchasing organization. The transaction allows the user to see the overall vendor evaluation score and to display the scores for the different criteria, such as price, quality, delivery and service.

ME63	Calculate Scores for Semi-Automatic and Automatic Sub-Criteria

This transaction is used to calculate the vendor evaluation scores for a vendor. The initial screen requires the user to enter a vendor and a purchasing organization. The transaction will then automatically calculate the vendor evaluation scores for the automatic and semi-automatic sub-criteria and display the new and old scores for each sub-criteria.

ME64	Evaluation Comparison

This transaction allows you to compare a vendor's evaluation general score against that vendor's score for a specific material. The initial screen requires a vendor, purchase organization and material to be entered. The output shows the overall score for the vendor and the vendor's score for the specific material. The individual criteria also show the vendor's general score and the score for the material.

ME65	Ranking List of Vendors

This transaction is used to rank a specific list of vendors. The initial screen requires the user to enter a purchasing organization and a list or range of vendors to be ranked. The output shows the vendors ranked by their overall evaluation score, but also shows the scores for the main criteria.

ME6A   Display Change Documents

This transaction is used to display changes that have been made to a vendor's evaluation score. The initial screen allows the user to enter a vendor and purchasing organization. The output shows the changes to the vendor evaluation scores and which criteria were changed.

ME6B   Ranking List of Vendor Evaluations Based on Material/Material Group

This transaction shows the ranking of vendors for a material or material group based on their vendor evaluation scores. The initial screen requires the user to enter a purchasing organization and a material or material group. The output shows a list of vendors

ME6C   Vendors without Evaluation

This transaction is used to show vendors that have not been evaluated. The initial screen allows the user to enter a single or range of purchasing organizations and a single or range of vendors. If a vendor has already been evaluated, the system will display a message indicating that fact. The output will show a list of vendors, which can then be evaluated.

ME6D   Vendors not Evaluated Since

This transaction will show a list of vendors who have not been evaluated since a specific date, which the user can enter. The initial screen allows a vendor or range of vendors to be entered, as well as a purchasing organization and the cut-off date for the evaluation. The output shows the vendor, the purchasing organization, and the date the last evaluation was created.

ME6E   Evaluation Records without Weighting Key

This transaction is used to display evaluation records that have no weighting key. The initial screen allows the user to enter a single or range of vendors and a single or range of purchasing organizations.

ME6F   Print Vendor Evaluation Sheet

This transaction allows the user to print a vendor evaluation sheet. The initial screen requires the user to enter a vendor and a purchasing organization. The output shows the overall vendor evaluation score, the scores for the main criteria and the scores for the sub-criteria.

ME6H   Vendor Evaluation Analysis

This transaction is used to perform analysis on vendor evaluation for a given set of vendors. The initial screen allows the user to enter a range of purchasing organizations and vendors for a given period of time. The output shows the list of vendors and their scores over that period. There is a drill-down facility to allow details for each vendor to be examined.

ME80   General Analysis of Purchasing Documents

This transaction is used to perform an analysis of purchasing data. The initial screen allows the user to enter a vendor, material, material group and purchasing group. The user can also enter the scope of selection, such as purchase orders, contracts, scheduling agreements and requests for quotation, as well as a date range for the analysis. The output shows the purchasing documents and the details from those documents, such as material, quantity, unit of measure, and net value.

ME80A	General Analysis of RFQs

This transaction is used to perform an analysis of purchasing data, specifically requests for quotation. The initial screen allows the user to enter a vendor, material, material group and purchasing group. The transaction is similar to ME80, except that ME80A defaults the analysis to be performed on RFQ documents.

ME80AN	General Evaluations of RFQs

This transaction is used to evaluate the requests for quotation for a given set of criteria. The initial screen allows the user to enter a material, vendor, material group, plant, purchasing organization and purchasing group. The output shows the details for each of the requests for quotation, including vendor, material, purchasing group, purchasing organization, document date, quantity, and order value.

ME80F	General Analysis of Purchase Orders

This transaction is used to perform an analysis of purchasing data, specifically purchase orders. The initial screen allows the user to enter a vendor, material, material group and purchasing group. The transaction is similar to ME80, except that in ME80F the analysis to be performed is set on purchase order documents by default.

ME80FN	General Evaluations of Purchase Orders

This transaction is used to evaluate the purchase orders for a given set of criteria. The initial screen allows the user to enter a material, vendor, material group, plant, purchasing organization and purchasing group. The output shows the details for each of the purchase orders, including vendor, material, purchasing group, purchasing organization, document date, quantity, and order value.

ME80R	General Analysis of Outline Agreements

This transaction is used to perform an analysis of purchasing data, specifically outline agreements. The initial screen allows the user to enter a vendor, material, material group and purchasing group. The transaction is similar to ME80, except that ME80R defaults the analysis to be performed on outline agreement documents.

ME80RN	General Evaluations of Outline Agreements

This transaction is used to evaluate the outline agreements for a given set of criteria. The initial screen allows the user to enter a material, vendor, material group, plant, purchasing organization and purchasing group. The output shows the details for each of the outline agreements, including vendor, material, purchasing group, purchasing organization, document date, quantity, and order value.

ME81N	Analysis of Purchase Order Values

This transaction is used to perform a financial analysis of purchase orders. The initial screen requires the user to enter a currency and to narrow the search selection by entering a comparison period, material, purchasing organization, purchasing group, vendor or material group. The output shows the purchase orders for the selected criteria. The details on the output include the purchase order number, document date and net value of the purchase order.

ME84   Create Releases

This transaction is used to create scheduling agreement releases after delivery schedules have been created. The initial screen gives the user the option to create a release type, plant, MRP area, MRP controller, material, vendor, and scheduling agreement. The output can be flagged to be in test mode only or releases can be directly created.

ME84A   Individual Display of
             Scheduling Agreement Release

This transaction is used to display the releases for a scheduling agreement. The initial screen offers the user the opportunity to enter a scheduling agreement number, a line item number, a release type, and a release number. The output shows the schedule lines, including the delivery date and time, and scheduled quantity.

ME85   Re-number Scheduling
             Agreement Delivery
             Schedule Lines

This transaction is used to re-number the scheduling agreement delivery schedule lines. The initial screen allows the user to enter a plant, purchasing organization, and purchasing group. The re-numbering can be further restricted by entering a vendor or material.

ME86   Aggregation/Disaggregation
             of Scheduling Agreement
             Schedule Lines

This transaction is used to aggregate or disaggregate the scheduling agreement delivery schedule lines. The initial screen gives the user an option to aggregate or disaggregate. The next screen shows the user a number of selection criteria that can restrict the schedule lines to be aggregated or disaggregated, including plant, purchasing organization, and purchasing group.

ME87   Summarization and Removal
             of PO History Records

This transaction is used to summarize and remove purchase order history records. The initial screen gives the user the option to restrict the purchase orders, using selection criteria including plant, purchasing organization, and purchasing group. The output shows the purchase order history records for each of the purchase orders selected. The user can then save the aggregation if required.

ME88   Set/Reset Agreed
             Cumulative Quantity and
             Reconciliation Date

This transaction is used set or reset the agreed cumulative quantity and reconciliation date. The initial screen offers the user selection criteria to restrict the output. The user can also select a transaction category, set agreed cumulative quantity, reset agreed cumulative quantity and reconciliation date, or mass maintenance of control parameters.

ME91   Purchasing Documents:
             Reminders/Expediters

This transaction is used to generate reminders and urging letters. The initial screen allows the user to enter a number of selection criteria, including purchasing document, purchasing organization, purchasing group, vendor, delivery date, and a reference date for the reminders. The output shows the purchasing documents that can be selected and messages can be generated.

ME91A   Quotations: Reminders/
              Expediters

This transaction is used to generate reminders and urging letters for quotations. The initial screen allows the user to enter a number of selection criteria including purchasing document, purchasing organization, purchasing group, vendor, delivery date, and a reference date for the reminders. The output shows the quotations that can be selected and messages can be generated.

ME91E	Scheduling Agreement: Reminders/Expediters

This transaction is used to generate reminders and urging letters for scheduling agreements. The initial screen allows the user to enter a number of selection criteria, including purchasing document, purchasing organization, purchasing group, vendor, delivery date, and a reference date for the reminders. The output shows the scheduling agreements that can be selected and messages that can be generated.

ME91F	Purchasing Orders: Reminders/Expediters

This transaction is used to generate reminders and urging letters for purchase orders. The initial screen allows the user to enter a number of selection criteria including purchasing document, purchasing organization, purchasing group, vendor, delivery date, and a reference date for the reminders. The output shows the purchasing orders that can be selected and messages that can be generated.

ME92	Monitor Receipt of Order Acknowledgments

This transaction is used to display purchase documents that have not received an order acknowledgment. The initial screen allows the user to enter selection criteria, including purchasing document number, purchasing organization, purchasing group, vendor, and document date. The output shows the purchase documents without

order acknowledgement, which can then be selected and reminder messages can be generated.

ME92F	Monitor Receipt of Order Acknowledgments (Purchase Order)

This transaction is used to display purchase orders that have not received an order acknowledgment. The initial screen allows the user to enter selection criteria, including purchasing document number, purchasing organization, purchasing group, vendor, and document date. The output shows the purchase orders without order acknowledgement, which can then be selected and reminder messages can be generated.

ME92K	Monitor Receipt of Order Acknowledgments (Contract)

This transaction is used to display contracts that have not received an order acknowledgment. The initial screen allows the user to enter selection criteria, including purchasing document number, purchasing organization, purchasing group, vendor, and document date. The output shows the contracts without order acknowledgement, which can then be selected and reminder messages can be generated.

ME92L	Monitor Receipt of Order Acknowledgments (Scheduling Agreement)

This transaction is used to display scheduling agreements that have not received an order acknowledgment. The initial screen allows the user to enter selection criteria, including purchasing document number, purchasing organization, purchasing group, vendor, and document date. The output shows the scheduling agreements without order acknowledgement, which can then be selected and reminder messages can be generated.

ME99	Output from Purchase Orders

This transaction is used to create output for purchase orders. The initial screen allows the user to enter an output type, transmission medium, processing mode, as well as a single or range of purchasing documents. The result of the selection criteria shows a list of purchasing documents, which can be selected and output can be processed.

ME9A	Request for Quotation Output

This transaction is used to create message output for requests for quotation. The initial screen allows the user to enter selection criteria to restrict the list of RFCs to select from. The selection criteria include document number, vendor, purchasing organization, purchasing group, document type, and document date. The output shows the RFCs that can be selected and output can be generated.

ME9E	Scheduling Agreement Output

This transaction is used to create message output for scheduling agreements. The initial screen allows the user to enter selection criteria to restrict the list of scheduling agreements to select from. The selection criteria include document number, vendor, purchasing organization, purchasing group, document type, and document date. The output shows the scheduling agreements that can be selected and output can be generated.

ME9F	Purchase Order Output

This transaction is used to create message output for purchase orders. The initial screen allows the user to enter selection criteria to restrict the list of purchase orders to select from. The selection criteria include document

number, vendor, purchasing organization, purchasing group, document type, and document date. The output shows the purchase orders that can be selected and output can be generated.

ME9K	Contract Output

This transaction is used to create message output for contracts. The initial screen allows the user to enter selection criteria to restrict the list of contracts to select from. The selection criteria include document number, vendor, purchasing organization, purchasing group, document type, and document date. The output shows the contracts that can be selected and output can be generated.

ME9L	Outline Agreement Output

This transaction is used to create message output for outline agreements. The initial screen allows the user to enter selection criteria to restrict the list of outline agreements to select from. The selection criteria include document number, vendor, purchasing organization, purchasing group, document type, and document date. The output shows the outline agreements that can be selected and output can be generated.

MEB0	Cancel Settlement Runs

This transaction is used to cancel settlement runs. The initial screen offers the user the opportunity to enter a settlement run or a rebate agreement number. If you enter a rebate agreement number, then the settlement runs for that agreement will be shown.

MEB1	Create Rebate Agreement

This transaction is used to create a rebate agreement. The initial screen requires that an agreement type is entered, e.g., rebates. The detail screen requires a condition granter is entered, which is the company who the rebate was negotiated with, commonly a vendor. The rebate agreement will also require a validity period during which the agreement is valid.

MEB2	Change Rebate Agreement

This transaction is used to change the details of a rebate agreement. The initial screen will require a single rebate agreement number to be entered. The user can change some fields on the rebate agreement, such as the validity periods, payment method, agreement status, and terms of payment.

MEB3	Display Rebate Agreement

This transaction is used to display the details of a rebate agreement. The initial screen will require a single rebate agreement number to be entered. The user can display the details of the rebate agreement, such as the condition granter, currency, validity periods, payment method, agreement status, and terms of payment.

MEB4	Settlement: Vendor Rebate Arrangements Purchasing

This transaction is used to settle a rebate arrangement with a vendor for a specific period. The selection screen gives the user the ability to enter the rebate arrangement number, the settlement date, and the billing date. The output shows the agreement details and the total income from the rebate arrangements.

MEB5	List of Vendor Rebate Arrangements: Purchasing

This transaction shows a list of vendor rebate arrangements based on the selection criteria entered. The final output can be restricted by entering a single or range of rebate agreement numbers, the arrangement type, validity period, purchasing organization, and purchasing group. The output is displayed in condition granter order.

MEB8	Detailed Statement: Vendor Business Volumes: Rebate Arrangements Purchasing

This transaction shows the detailed settlements of the vendor rebate arrangements based on the selection criteria entered. The final output can be restricted by entering a single or range of rebate agreement numbers, the arrangement type, validity period, purchasing organization, and purchasing group. The detailed settlements are shown in condition granter order.

MEI1	Changes to Purchasing Documents Due to Changes in Conditions

This transaction is used to display changes to purchasing documents due to changes in conditions. The selection screen allows the user to restrict the output. The selection criteria include document type, vendor, material, purchasing organization, purchasing group, and plant.

MEI2	Mass Adjustment of Documents Due to Changes in Conditions

This transaction allows a mass adjustment of purchasing documents due to changes in conditions. The selection screen allows the user to restrict any adjustment to those purchasing documents that are selected. The selection criteria include purchasing document number and price determination date.

MEI3	Recompilation of Document Index for Purchasing Documents

This transaction is used to recompile purchasing documents. The transaction updates the change pointers such as when master data and conditions are updated. The documents to be updated can be restricted by the selection criteria, which include document type, purchasing document number, vendor, and document date.

MEI4	Automatic Document Adjustment: Create Worklist

This transaction creates a worklist for the automatic adjustment of purchasing documents. The selection screen can restrict the documents in the worklist by selecting one or more document categories, such as purchasing documents or pricing documents.

MEI5	Automatic Document Adjustment: Delete Worklist

This transaction is used to delete a worklist that has been created for the automatic adjustment of purchasing documents. The worklist can be selected by entering a document category and a price determination date.

MEI6	Delete Document Index

This transaction is used to delete document indexes that may have been created. The selection screen offers the user a number of options, such as purchasing documents, payment documents, vendor billing documents, and customer settlements.

MEI7	Make Price Change in Open Purchase Orders

This transaction allows price changes in open purchase orders. The number of purchase orders to be changed can be restricted by the selection fields, such as vendor, purchasing organization, purchasing group, material, material group, and plant. After the transaction is executed, the system will display a list of the purchasing documents that have been changed.

MEI8	Recompilation of Document Index for Payment Documents

This transaction is used to recompile payment documents. The transaction updates the change pointers such as when master data and conditions are updated. The settlement requests to be updated can be restricted by the selection criteria, which include payment type, billing type, posting date, invoicing party, and payer.

MEI9	Recompilation of Document Index for Vendor Billing Documents

This transaction is used to recompile vendor billing documents. The transaction updates the change pointers such as when master data and conditions are updated. The vendor billing documents to be updated can be restricted by the selection criteria, which include vendor billing document number, posting date, invoicing party, and document date.

MEK1	Create Condition Records

This transaction is used to create a condition record. The initial screen requires the user to enter a condition type. The following screen allows the user to add the condition details based on the condition type that was entered.

MEK2	Change Condition Records

This transaction allows the user to change an existing condition record. The initial screen requires the user to enter the condition type. The following screen offers the user the option to change a single condition record or a number of condition records. The user can then amend the elements in the condition record that are required to be changed.

MEK3	Display Condition Records

This transaction is used to display existing condition records. The initial screen requires the user to enter the condition type. The following screen offers the user the option to display a single condition record or a number of condition records.

MEK4	Create Condition Records with Reference

This transaction is used to create condition records with reference to an existing condition record. The initial screen requires the user to enter the condition type. The following screen allows the user to enter the information of the existing condition. When the information is displayed, the user can enter new condition records based on the reference condition.

MEKA	Purchasing Conditions

This transaction is used to display purchasing conditions based on the selection criteria entered. The initial screen shows a number of selection criteria, including purchasing organization, vendor, material, material group, plant, and material type. The purchasing organization is a mandatory field. The system will display any relevant conditions and allows conditions to be created from the output screen.

MEKB	Conditions by Contract

This transaction is used to display contract conditions based on the selection criteria entered. The initial screen shows the selection criteria, including purchasing

organization, agreement, and agreement item. The purchasing organization is a mandatory field. The system will display any relevant conditions.

MEKC	Conditions by Info Record

This transaction is used to display purchasing info record conditions based on the selection criteria entered. The initial screen shows the selection criteria, including purchasing organization, vendor, material, material group, plant, and purchasing info record. The purchasing organization is a mandatory field. The system will display any relevant conditions.

MEKD	Conditions for Material Group

This transaction is used to display material group conditions based on the selection criteria entered. The initial screen shows the selection criteria, including purchasing organization, vendor, material group, and plant. The purchasing organization is a mandatory field. The system will display any relevant conditions.

MEKE	Conditions by Vendor

This transaction is used to display vendor conditions based on the selection criteria entered. The initial screen shows the selection criteria of the purchasing organization and vendor. The purchasing organization is a mandatory field. The system will display any relevant conditions.

MEKF	Conditions for Material Type

This transaction is used to display material type conditions based on the selection criteria entered. The initial screen shows the selection criteria of the purchasing organization and material type. The purchasing organization is a mandatory field. The system will display any relevant conditions.

MEKG	Conditions by Condition Group of Vendor

This transaction is used to display condition group of the vendor conditions based on the selection criteria entered. The condition group of the vendor is entered into the purchasing info record. The initial screen shows the selection criteria of the purchasing organization, vendor, and condition group. The purchasing organization is a mandatory field. The system will display any relevant conditions.

MEKH	Conditions by Market Price

This transaction is used to display market price conditions based on the selection criteria entered. The initial screen shows the selection criteria of the purchasing organization, material, and material group. The purchasing organization is a mandatory field. The system will display any relevant conditions.

MEKI	Conditions by Incoterms

This transaction is used to display incoterms conditions based on the selection criteria entered. The initial screen shows the selection criteria of the purchasing organization, incoterms, and plant. The purchasing organization is a mandatory field. The system will display any relevant conditions.

MEKJ	Conditions for Invoicing Party

This transaction is used to display invoicing party conditions based on the selection criteria entered. The initial screen shows the selection criteria of the purchasing organization, invoicing party, and vendor. The purchasing organization is a mandatory field. The system will display any relevant conditions.

MEKK	Conditions by Vendor Sub-Range

This transaction is used to display vendor sub-range conditions based on the selection criteria entered. The initial screen shows the selection criteria of the purchasing organization, vendor, and vendor sub-range. The purchasing organization is a mandatory field. The system will display any relevant conditions.

MEKL	Price Change Involving Vendor's Scheduling Agreements

This transaction should be used when changes are required to be made to a vendor's scheduling agreements. The initial screen shows a number of selection criteria, including purchasing organization, vendor, material, material group, and scheduling agreement. In addition, the user needs to enter an absolute amount or a percentage change. The system will display the affected scheduling agreements and the changes in price shown on the document.

MEKLE	Currency Change for Scheduling Agreement Conditions of Vendor

This transaction should be used if the currency on a vendor's scheduling agreement is to be changed. The initial screen shows a number of selection criteria, including purchasing organization, vendor, and scheduling agreement. In addition, the user needs to enter the old and the new currency. The system will display the affected scheduling agreements and the changes in currency.

MEKP	Price Change Involving Vendor's Info Records

This transaction should be used when changes are required to be made to a vendor's purchasing info records. The initial screen shows a number of selection criteria, including purchasing organization, vendor, material, and material group. In addition, the user needs to enter an absolute amount or a percentage change. The system will display the affected purchase info records and the changes in price shown on the document.

MEKPE	Currency Change for Info Record Conditions of Vendor

This transaction should be used if the currency on a vendor's purchasing info record is to be changed. The initial screen shows a number of selection criteria, including purchasing organization and vendor. In addition, the user needs to enter the old and the new currency. The system will display the affected purchasing info record and the changes in currency.

MEKR	Price Change Involving Vendor's Contracts

This transaction should be used when changes are required to be made to vendor's contracts. The initial screen shows a number of selection criteria, including purchasing organization, vendor, contract, material, and material group. In addition, the user needs to enter an absolute amount or a percentage change. The system will display the affected contracts and the changes in price shown on the document.

MEKRE	Currency Change for Contract Conditions of Vendor

This transaction should be used if the currency on vendor's contracts is to be changed. The initial screen shows a number of selection criteria, including purchasing organization, contract, and vendor. In addition, the user needs to enter the old and the new currency. The system will display the affected contracts and the changes in currency.

MELB	Purchasing Transactions per Requirement Tracking Number

This transaction is used to find and display all the purchasing transactions that contain a specific requirement tracking number. The initial screen allows the user to enter a number of selection criteria, including requirement tracking number, purchasing organization, purchasing group, plant, material, and material group. The output shows all the purchasing documents for each requirement tracking number.

MEPA	Order Price Simulation/ Price Information

This transaction is used to display price information for a specific set of selection criteria. The selection screen has a number of fields that need to be entered, including vendor, order type, purchasing organization, purchasing group, material, plant, and company code. The system will display the price information overview for the selection fields, including purchase order item data, net price, order quantity, and price date.

MEPB	Price Information/Vendor Negotiation Sheet

This transaction is used to display the price information for a vendor that can be used for vendor negotiation. The initial selection screen has a number of fields that the user can enter, including vendor, material, material group, purchasing organization, and plant. The system will display the price information for the selection fields entered.

MEPO	Display Purchase Order

This transaction is used to display and change a purchase order. This transaction is the same as transaction ME22N.

| **MEQ1** | Maintain Quota Arrangement |

This transaction is used to maintain quota arrangements. A material can be used in a quota arrangement only if the quota arrangement usage key on the purchasing screen of the material master has been entered. The initial screen allows the user to enter a material and a plant. The detail screen shows the validity period of the quota and permits the user to enter the minimum quantity split for the quota arrangement.

| **MEQ3** | Display Quota Arrangement |

This transaction is used to display quota arrangements. The initial screen allows the user to enter a material and a plant. The detail screen displays the validity period of the quota, the minimum quantity split for the quota arrangement and the quota arrangement number.

| **MEQ4** | Changes to Quota Arrangement |

This transaction is used to display changes that have been made to a quota arrangement. The initial screen allows the user to enter a material, plant, user who made the change, and the change date. The detail screen displays all changes that have been made to the quota arrangement based on the selection criteria. The output shows date and time of the change, transaction used, document change number, and the action that was taken.

| **MEQ6** | Analyze Quota Arrangement |

This transaction is used to analyze existing quota arrangements. The initial screen allows the user to enter the material, plant, and validity dates. The output shows the quota arrangement information.

| **MEQ8** | Quota Arrangement for Material |

This transaction is used to check whether the quota arrangements are being adhered to by vendors. The initial screen has a number of selection fields that can be entered, such as material, plant, quota arrangement, and minimum percentage variance. The transaction checks the target values of the quota arrangement against actual values, and any variances are shown when processing this transaction.

| **MEQM** | Quota Arrangement for Material |

This transaction is used to display quota arrangements for a material. The selection screen allows the user to enter a material, plant, and quota arrangement. The output shows the quota arrangement details in material order.

| **MK01** | Create Vendor (Purchasing) |

This transaction is used to create the purchasing elements of a vendor. The initial screen requires a purchasing organization and account group. The vendor can be left blank if the vendor number is internally generated. The address can be added with account control information, tax information, conditions, control data, sales data and partner functions. If the vendor number is internally generated, it will be shown after the transaction is saved.

| **MK02** | Change Vendor (Purchasing) |

This transaction is used to change the purchasing details of a vendor. The initial screen requires the vendor number to be entered along with selecting one of the four options: address data, control data, purchasing data, or partner functions. The purchasing organization field on the initial screen is optional.

MK03 Display Vendor (Purchasing)

This transaction is used to display the purchasing details of a vendor. The initial screen requires the vendor number to be entered along with selecting one of the four options: address data, control data, purchasing data, or partner functions. The purchasing organization field on the initial screen is optional.

MK04 Vendor Account Changes (Purchasing)

This transaction is used to display changes made to the purchasing data of a vendor. The initial screen requires a vendor number is entered. The selection can be restricted by entering a purchasing organization, vendor sub-range or plant. The system will display the areas where the data has been changed. These can be selected and the details of any changes are displayed.

MK05 Block/Unblock Vendor (Purchasing)

This transaction is used to block or unblock purchasing functions for a vendor. The initial screen requires a vendor number to be entered, while the purchasing organization is optional. The vendor can be totally blocked for all purchasing organizations or blocked for purchase orders, goods receipt, RFQ or source determination.

MK06 Flag Vendor for Deletion (Purchasing)

This transaction is used to flag a vendor for deletion. The initial screen requires a vendor number to be entered, while the purchasing organization is optional. The user can set the deletion flag for all areas or set a deletion block to stop the general data of the vendor from being deleted.

MK12 Plan Vendor Change

This transaction is used to plan the vendor changes for a future date. The initial screen allows the user to enter a vendor, purchasing organization and change planned for the date. The user can also select one of the four options: address data, control data, purchasing data, or partner functions. The data can be changed and, after saving, the data the system will display the planned date for the change.

MK14 Planned Vendor Account Changes

This transaction is used to display changes that have been planned for the vendor master. The initial screen requires the vendor number to be entered; the purchasing organization, vendor sub-range, plant and planned change date fields are optional. The transaction shows the areas that are scheduled for change, and the details can then be shown.

MK19 Display in Future Vendor

This transaction is used to display vendor details at a future date. The initial screen requires a vendor number and a key date to be entered. The system will show the vendor data that will be in the master record on that date. If no planned changes are scheduled, then the data shown will be the same as the current data.

MKVG Vendor's Settlement and Condition Groups

This transaction is used to display a vendor's settlement and condition groups. The initial screen does not require an entry, but the resulting output can be restricted by entering a vendor, material, material group, vendor material number, vendor sub-range, or vendor material group. The output shows the settlement groups and condition groups for each vendor.

MKVZ	List of Vendors: Purchasing

This transaction is used to produce a list of vendors. The output can be restricted by entering a vendor number, purchasing organization, search term, or account group. The output is shown in vendor order and the details listed include the vendor's name and address, account group, search term, purchasing organization, terms of payment, incoterms, minimum order value, and currency.

MM00	Material Master Menu

This transaction is used to display the material master menu. The transactions you can access from this menu include material transactions, profile transactions, batch transactions, special stock transactions, and report transactions.

MM01	Create Material

This transaction is used to create a material master record. The initial screen requires a material number to be entered if the number is externally assigned or can be left blank if the numbering is internally assigned. The screen also requires the user to enter an industry sector and a material type. A change number can be entered if change master record is to be referenced. The user can also enter the number of a material that is to be used to copy from.

MM02	Change Material

This transaction is used to change the details of an existing material number. The initial screen will allow the user to enter a single material number and a change number, if required. The user can select the material master screens to be changed and can enter

the appropriate organizational level, for example, plant, storage location, warehouse, valuation type, sales organization, and distribution channel.

MM03	Display Material

This transaction is used to display the details of an existing material number. The initial screen will allow the user to enter a single material number. The user can then select the material master screens to be changed and can enter the appropriate organizational level, for example, plant, storage location, warehouse, valuation type, sales organization, and distribution channel.

MM04	Display Changes

This transaction allows the user to display changes to a material master record. The initial screen requires that the user enter a material number, but other fields can be entered, such as a change number, plant, valuation type, sales organization, distribution channel, warehouse number or storage type. The output shows a list of the changes for a material, which can be selected and the details displayed.

MM06	Flag Material for Deletion

This transaction is used to flag a material for deletion. The deletion flag can be set at a certain level, for example, the deletion flag can be set for a single storage location and not for the plant. The initial screen allows the user to determine the level at which the deletion flag is set by entering a plant, storage location, valuation type, sales organization, distribution channel, warehouse number or storage type.

MM11	Schedule Creation of Material

This transaction allows the creation of material to be scheduled for a future date. The initial screen requires the user to enter a material number, if externally assigned, or left blank for internal number assignment. The user will need to enter an industry sector and a material type. A change number can be entered if change master record is to be referenced. The user will need to enter a future date for which the material creation is scheduled.

MM12   Schedule Changing of Material

This transaction is used to schedule a change to the material master record on a future date. The initial screen will allow the user to enter a single material number, the future date for which the material change is scheduled, and a change number, if required.

MM16   Schedule Material for Deletion

This transaction is used to schedule a deletion to a material master record. The initial screen allows the user to determine the level at which the deletion flag is set by entering a plant, storage location, valuation type, sales organization, distribution channel, warehouse number or storage type. In addition, the future date for which the material change is scheduled is required, and a change number, if relevant.

MM19   Display Material at Key Date

This transaction is used to display a material master record for a specific date. The user is required to enter a material number and a key date, which can be either in the past or the future. The user can then select the material master screens to be display and can enter the appropriate organizational level, for example, plant, storage location, warehouse, valuation type, sales organization, and distribution channel.

MM50   Extend Material View(s)

This transaction allows the user to extend the views of existing materials. The initial screen gives the user the opportunity to enter the view, such as costing, storage, MRP, etc. The user can then restrict the number of materials to be extended by entering a plant, sales organization, distribution channel, material, material type, warehouse number or industry sector. The output will show a list of materials where the views are extended.

MM60   Materials List

This transaction is used to display a list of materials based on the values entered. The initial screen allows the user to enter a single or range of materials, plant, material type, material group and the user who created the material master record. The user has the option of retrieving valuated materials only. The output shows the material details, including date of last change, material type, material group, unit of measure, purchasing group, MRP Type, valuation class and price.

MMAM   Change Material Type

This transaction allows the user to change the material type of an existing material. The initial screen requires the material number and the new material type. If the material type cannot be changed, the system will display details about the reason why, such as whether a purchase order exists or whether plant stock exists.

MMH1   Create Trading Goods

This transaction is used to create a material that is a trading good. The transaction automatically creates the material with a material type HAWA. The initial screen requires the user to enter a material number, if externally assigned, or left blank if the material number is assigned internally. The user will need to enter an industry sector and an optional change number.

MMI1   Create Operating Supplies

This transaction is used to create a material that is an operating supply. The transaction automatically creates the material with a material type HIBE. The initial screen requires the user to enter a material number, if externally assigned, or left blank if the material number is assigned internally. The user will need to enter an industry sector and an optional change number.

MMN1   Create Non-Stock Material

This transaction is used to create a material that is a non-stock material. The transaction automatically creates the material with a material type NLAG. The initial screen requires the user to enter a material number, if externally assigned, or left blank if the material number is assigned internally. The user will need to enter an industry sector and an optional change number.

MMPI   Initialize Period for Material Master Records

This transaction is used to initialize the period for material master records. This is part of the month end closing that is performed by the finance department. This program sets the current period and should be used in combination with the period closing program, RMMMPERI. This transaction should not be run if the material ledger is active.

MMPV   Close Period for Material Master Records

This transaction is used to close a period for material master records. This transaction is run at month end closing and will be part of the financial monthly close. This transaction will normally be run as a background job.

MMR1   Create Raw Material

This transaction is used to create a material that is a raw material. The transaction automatically creates the material with a material type ROH. The initial screen requires the user to enter a material number, if externally assigned, or left blank if the material number is assigned internally. The user will need to enter an industry sector and an optional change number.

MMRV   Allow Posting to Previous Period

This transaction can be used to allow posting to a previous period. The initial screen requires the user to enter a company code. The following screen shows the current period, the previous period, and the last period in the previous year. The user can then select the option to allow posting to the previous period or to disallow backposting.

MMS1   Create Service

This transaction is used to create a material that is a service. The transaction automatically creates the material with a material type DIEN. The initial screen requires the user to enter a material number, if externally assigned, or left blank if the material number is assigned internally. The user will need to enter an industry sector and an optional change number.

MMSC   Enter Storage Locations Collectively

This transaction allows the user to extend materials to additional storage locations at a plant. The initial screen requires a material number and a plant to be entered. The user can then choose to list all existing storage locations or to list extendable storage locations only. The resulting screen allows the user to enter the storage location or storage locations where the material needs to be extended to.

MMU1   Create Non-Valuated Material

This transaction is used to create a material that is a non-valuated material. The transaction automatically creates the material with a material type UNBW. The initial screen requires the user to enter a material number, if externally assigned, or left blank if the material number is assigned internally. The user will need to enter an industry sector and an optional change number.

MMV1   Create Packaging

This transaction is used to create a material that is a packaging material. The transaction automatically creates the material with a material type VERP. The initial screen requires the user to enter a material number, if externally assigned, or left blank if the material number is assigned internally. The user will need to enter an industry sector and an optional change number.

MMVD   Change Material

This transaction allows a user to change data in the sales views of a material master record. The initial screen requires the user to enter a material number, and the system will display the views to be changed, if they have been previously created. The views displayed include sales 1, sales 2, sales/plant data, sales text and foreign trade.

MMVH   Create Material

This transaction allows a user to change data in the engineering and sales views of a material master record. The initial screen requires the user to enter a material number, and the system will display the views to be changed, if they have been previously created. The views displayed include the engineering/

sales screen, storage, sales 1, sales 2, sales/plant data, sales text and foreign trade.

MN01   Create Output – Condition Records: Purchasing RFQ

This transaction is used to create a condition record for an output message relating to a request for quotation. The initial screen requires the user to enter an output type, such as ABSA for a rejection or MAHN for a reminder. The next screen will show the user a key combination to select from. After the selection screen the user can enter the details to create the condition record, such as document type, vendor, purchasing group, partner function and the medium of the output, for example, fax or EDI.

MN02   Change Output – Condition Records: Purchasing RFQ

This transaction is used to change details on a condition record for an output message relating to a request for quotation. The initial screen requires the user to enter an output type, such as ABSA for a rejection or MAHN for a reminder. The next screen will offer the user a key combination to select from. The following screen offers the user selection fields based on the key combination; the resulting output will show the condition record details that can be changed.

MN03   Display Output – Condition Records: Purchasing RFQ

This transaction is used to display details on a condition record for an output message relating to a request for quotation. The initial screen requires the user to enter an output type, such as ABSA for a rejection or MAHN for a reminder. The next screen will show the user a number of key combinations to select from. The following screen offers the user selection fields based on the key combination; the resulting output will display the details of the condition records selected.

MN04	Create Output – Condition Records: Purchase Order

This transaction is used to create a condition record for an output message relating to a purchase order. The initial screen requires the user to enter an output type, such as NEU for purchase order print. The next screen will offer the user a key combination to select from. After the selection screen, the user can enter the details to create the condition record, such as purchase organization, partner function, and the medium of the output, for example, fax or EDI.

MN05	Change Output – Condition Records: Purchase Order

This transaction is used to change details on a condition record for an output message relating to a purchase order. The initial screen requires the user to enter an output type, such as NEU for purchase order print. The next screen will show the user a key combination to select from. The following screen offers the user selection fields based on the key combination; the resulting output will show the condition record details that can be changed.

MN06	Display Output – Condition Records: Purchase Order

This transaction is used to display details on a condition record for an output message relating to a purchase order. The initial screen requires the user to enter an output type, such as NEU for purchase order print. The next screen will offer the user a key combination to select from. The following screen offers the user selection fields based on the key combination; the resulting output will display the details of the condition records selected.

MN07	Create Output – Condition Records: Outline Agreement

This transaction is used to create a condition record for output message relating to an outline agreement. The initial screen requires the user to enter an output type, such as NEU for an outline agreement print. The next screen will offer the user a key combination to select from. After the selection screen, the user can enter the details to create the condition record, such as document type, partner function, and the medium of the output, for example, fax or EDI.

MN08	Change Output – Condition Records: Outline Agreement

This transaction is used to change details on a condition record for an output message relating to an outline agreement. The initial screen requires the user to enter an output type, such as NEU for an outline agreement print. The next screen will show the user a key combination to select from. The following screen offers the user selection fields based on the key combination; the resulting output will show the condition record details that can be changed.

MN09	Display Output – Condition Records: Outline Agreement

This transaction is used to display details on a condition record for an output message relating to an outline agreement. The initial screen requires the user to enter an output type, such as NEU for an outline agreement print. The next screen will offer the user a key combination to select from. The following screen offers the user selection fields based on the key combination; the resulting output will display the details of the condition records selected.

MN10	Create Output – Condition Records: Scheduling Agreement Release

This transaction is used to create a condition record for output message relating to a scheduling agreement release. The initial screen requires the user to enter an output type, such as LPH1 for a scheduling agreement release print. The next screen will offer the user a key combination to select from. After the selection screen, the user can enter the details to create the condition record, such as partner function, and the medium of the output, for example, fax or EDI.

MN11	Change Output – Condition Records: Scheduling Agreement Release

This transaction is used to change details on a condition record for an output message relating to a scheduling agreement release. The initial screen requires the user to enter an output type, such as LPH1 for a scheduling agreement release print. The next screen will show the user a key combination to select from. The following screen offers the user selection fields based on the key combination; the resulting output will show the condition record details that can be changed.

MN12	Display Output – Condition Records: Scheduling Agreement Release

This transaction is used to display details on a condition record for an output message relating to a scheduling agreement release. The initial screen requires the user to enter an output type, such as LPH1 for a scheduling agreement release print. The next screen will offer the user a key combination to select from. The following screen offers the user selection fields based on the key combination; the resulting output will display the details of the condition records selected.

MN13	Create Output – Condition Records: Service Entry Sheet

This transaction is used to create a condition record for output message relating to a service entry sheet. The initial screen requires the user to enter an output type, such as NEU for a service entry sheet release print. The next screen will offer the user a key combination to select from. After the selection screen, the user can enter the details to create the condition record, such as partner function, and the medium of the output, for example, fax or EDI.

MN14	Change Output – Condition Records: Service Entry Sheet

This transaction is used to change details on a condition record for an output message relating to a service entry sheet. The initial screen requires the user to enter an output type, such as NEU for a service entry sheet print. The next screen will show the user a key combination to select from. The following screen offers the user selection fields based on the key combination; the resulting output will show the condition record details that can be changed.

MN15	Display Output – Condition Records: Service Entry Sheet

This transaction is used to display details on a condition record for an output message relating to a service entry sheet. The initial screen requires the user to enter an output type, such as NEU for a service entry sheet print. The next screen will offer the user a key combination to select from. The following screen offers the user selection fields based on the key combination; the resulting output will display the details of the condition records selected.

MN21	Create Output – Condition Records: Inventory Management

This transaction is used to create a condition record for output message relating to an inventory management movement, such as a goods issue or goods receipt. The initial screen requires the user to enter an output type, such as WE01 for a goods receipt note. The next screen will offer the user a key combination to select from. After the selection screen, the user can enter the details to create the condition record, such as partner function, and the medium of the output, for example, fax or EDI.

MN22	Change Output – Condition Records: Inventory Management

This transaction is used to change details on a condition record for an output message relating to an inventory management movement, such as a goods issue or goods receipt. The initial screen requires the user to enter an output type, such as WE01 for a goods receipt note. The next screen will show the user a key combination to select from. The following screen offers the user selection fields based on the key combination; the resulting output will show the condition record details that can be changed.

MN23	Display Output – Condition Records: Inventory Management

This transaction is used to display details on a condition record for an output message relating to an inventory management movement, such as a goods issue or goods receipt. The initial screen requires the user to enter an output type, such as WE01 for a goods receipt note. The next screen will offer the user a key combination to select from. The following screen offers the user selection fields based on the key combination; the resulting output will display the details of the condition records selected.

MN24	Create Output – Condition Records: Inbound Delivery

This transaction is used to create a condition record for output message relating to an inbound delivery. The initial screen requires the user to enter an output type, such as OPOD for a vendor proof of delivery. The next screen will offer the user a key combination to select from. After the selection screen, the user can enter the details to create the condition record, such as partner function, and the medium of the output, for example, fax or EDI.

MN25	Change Output – Condition Records: Inbound Delivery

This transaction is used to change details on a condition record for an output message relating to an inbound delivery. The initial screen requires the user to enter an output type, such as OPOD for a vendor proof of delivery. The next screen will show the user a key combination to select from. The following screen offers the user selection fields based on the key combination; the resulting output will show the condition record details that can be changed.

MN26	Display Output – Condition Records: Inbound Delivery

This transaction is used to display details on a condition record for an output message relating to an inbound delivery. The initial screen requires the user to enter an output type, such as OPOD for a vendor proof of delivery. The next screen will offer the user a key combination to select from. The following screen offers the user selection fields based on the key combination; the resulting output will display the details of the condition records selected.

MP01	Maintain Approved Manufacturer Parts List

This transaction is used to maintain the manufacturer parts list for a specific material. The initial screen requires that a material number is entered. The detail screen allows the user to enter a manufacturer part number, a manufacturer, plant number, valid to and from dates, and revision number.

MP02	Display Approved Manufacturer Parts List

This transaction is used to display the manufacturer parts list for a specific material. The initial screen requires that a material number is entered. The detail screen allows the user to display the details for the manufacturer part numbers associated with a material, including manufacturer, plant number, valid to and from dates, and revision number.

MR00	Invoice Menu

This transaction is used to display the invoice menu. The transactions you can access from this menu include document entry, processing transactions, document parking transactions and reports.

MR02	Invoice Items Release

This transaction is used to release blocked invoices that were posted. The initial screen shows a number of selection fields that can be entered to restrict the number of invoices to be released. The selection fields include company code, fiscal year, vendor, purchasing group and payment block. The user can allow the transaction to consider all blocking reasons or the user can select one or many blocking reasons.

MR03	Display Original Document

This transaction is used to display an invoice verification document. The initial screen requires an invoice verification document, a company code and the fiscal year to be entered. The output shows each line item with the posting key, quantity and amount.

MR08	Cancel Invoice Document

This transaction is used to cancel an invoice document. This transaction has been superseded by transaction MR8M. The selection screen requires the user to enter the invoice document number, fiscal year and reversal reason.

MR11	Maintain GR/IR Clearing Account

This transaction is used to maintain the goods receipt/invoice receipts account. The transaction is used to monitor purchase orders, as it shows the goods receipts and invoice receipts entered. The report shows when a goods receipt has been made and an invoice has not been received. The initial screen requires the user to enter a company code and posting data, while the report output can be restricted by entering a vendor, purchasing organization, plant, PO date, or order type.

MR21	Price Change – Overview Screen

This transaction is used to change the price of a single or number of materials. The new price that is entered for the material will directly change the moving average price or standard price. The initial screen allows the user to enter a posting date, company code, and plant. The detail screen gives the user the opportunity to enter a material, valuation type and new price.

MR42   Change Parked Document

This transaction allows the user to make changes to a parked document. If the user knows the document number, then that number should be entered with the company code and fiscal year. The overview screen shows the details of the parked document and changes can be made by switching to the fast data entry mode. An existing line can be changed or a new line can be added by entering a posting key, account number, amount, cost center, and business area.

MR43   Display Parked Document

This transaction allows the user to display a parked document. If the user knows the document number then that number should be entered with the company code and fiscal year. The overview screen shows the line items of the parked document including the posting key, account number, amount, cost center, and business area.

MR44   Post Parked Document

This transaction is used to post a parked document. If the user knows the document number then that number should be entered with the company code and fiscal year. The overview screen shows the line items of the parked document including the posting key, account number, amount, cost center, and business area. The parked document can be posted from the overview screen.

MR8M   Cancel Invoice Document

This transaction is used to cancel an invoice document. This transaction has superseded transaction MR08. The selection screen requires the user to enter the invoice document number, fiscal year and reversal reason.

MR90   Output Messages in Logistics
              Invoice Verification

This transaction can be used to produce output for a single or multiple logistics invoice verification documents. The initial screen allows the user to enter a single or range of output types, the transmission medium, and processing mode. The output can be restricted by entering a single or range of invoices, fiscal year, company code, and invoicing party. This transaction is very similar to MR91, but with MR90 it is not possible to restrict the output by document date.

MR91   Messages for Invoice
              Verification

This transaction can be used to produce output for a single or multiple logistics invoice verification documents. The initial screen allows the user to enter a single or range of output types, the transmission medium, and processing mode. The output can be restricted by entering a single or range of invoices, fiscal year, company code, and invoicing party. This transaction is very similar to MR90, but with MR91 it is possible to restrict the output by document date.

MRM0   Logistics Invoice
              Verification Menu

This transaction is used to access the Logistics Verification Menu. From this menu it is possible to access transactions on document entry, automatic settlement, GR/IR account maintenance, and archiving.

MRM1   Create Message:
              Invoice Verification

This transaction is used to create a condition record for output message relating to invoice verification. The initial screen requires the user to enter an output type, such as INS for an evaluated receipts settlement procedure.

The next screen will offer the user a key combination to select from. Following the selection screen, the user can enter the details to create the condition record, such as partner function, and the medium of the output, for example, fax or EDI.

MRM2	Change Output – Condition Records: Invoice Verification

This transaction is used to change details on a condition record for an output message relating to invoice verification. The initial screen requires the user to enter an output type, such as INS for an evaluated receipts settlement procedure. The next screen will show the user a key combination to select from. The following screen offers the user selection fields based on the key combination; the resulting output will show the condition record details that can be changed.

MRM3	Display Output – Condition Records: Invoice Verification

This transaction is used to display details on a condition record for an output message relating to invoice verification. The initial screen requires the user to enter an output type, such as INS for an evaluated receipts settlement procedure. The next screen will offer the user a key combination to select from. The following screen offers the user selection fields based on the key combination; the resulting output will display the details of the condition records selected.

MRNB	Revaluation with Logistics Invoice Verification

This transaction is used to perform revaluation on purchasing documents where there has been a price change. The initial screen requires a purchasing document to be entered.

MSRV2	Reporting on Services (Purchase Requisition)

This transaction is used to display services from purchase requisition documents. The initial selection screen allows the user to enter a service number, and the output can be restricted by entering a purchasing organization, purchasing group, document number or plant. The resulting display shows the activity number, quantity, origin, document number and line item.

MSRV4	Reporting on Services (RFQ)

This transaction is used to display services from request for quotation documents. The initial selection screen allows the user to enter a service number, and the output can be restricted by entering a purchasing organization, purchasing group, document number or plant. The resulting display shows the activity number, quantity, origin, document number and line item.

5   Warehouse Management (WM)

LB01   Create Transfer Requirement

This transaction is used to create a warehouse transfer requirement. The initial screen requires the user to enter a warehouse number and a WM movement type that allows a manual transfer requirement to be created. The detail screen allows the user to enter the plant and storage location details as well as line item details such as material, quantity and batch number.

LB02   Change Transfer Requirement

This transaction allows the user to change an existing transfer requirement. The initial screen requires a warehouse number and a transfer requirement number. The transaction will then display the details of the transfer requirement, from which the user can view the line details and change the transfer requirement quantity.

LB03   Display Transfer Requirement

This transaction is used to display the details of a transfer requirement. The initial screen requires a warehouse number and a transfer requirement number. The transaction will then display the details of the transfer requirement, such as the material, quantity, plant, and storage location.

LB10   Display Transfer Requirement: List for Storage Type

This transaction is used to provide the user with a list of transfer requirements for a specific source or destination storage type. The initial screen allows the user to enter a warehouse number, source storage type or a destination storage type. The output can be restricted by entering a value for shipment type. The user can determine whether to see transfer requirements with a status of open, partially delivered, or completed.

LB11   Display Transfer Requirement: List for Material

This transaction is used to provide the user with a list of transfer requirements for a specific material. The output can be restricted by entering a value for plant, storage location, batch, shipment type, stock category, and special stock. The user can determine whether to see transfer requirements that have been completely processed.

LB12   Process Material Document

This transaction is used to process an inventory management material document and the subsequent warehouse transfer order. The transaction requires the material document number and the material document year. The transaction processes the inventory management movement first and then completes the warehouse movement.

LI01N   Create System Inventory Record

This transaction is used to create a warehouse count document. The initial screen requires a warehouse number and storage type to be entered. The user can opt to enter a planned count date, an inventory reference, and an inventory method. The subsequent screen allows the entry of a number of storage bins to be counted and the name of the counter, if known.

LI02N	Change System Inventory Record

This transaction is used to change a warehouse count document. The initial screen requires a warehouse and the count document number to be entered. The detail screen shows the existing storage bins to be counted; these bins can be either or new storage bins can be added to the count document.

LI03N	Display System Inventory Record

This transaction is used to display a warehouse count document. The initial screen requires a warehouse and the count document number to be entered. The detail screen shows all the storage bins to be counted as well as a count date and name of the counter, if entered.

LI04	Print Inventory List

This transaction allows activated count documents to be printed. The user can enter the warehouse number, the count document number, and the printer to be used. The user does have options for how the document is to be printed, such as print in landscape, print immediately, delete after output, etc.

LI05	Inventory History for Storage Bin

This transaction is used to show the inventory count documents that have been relevant for a specific storage bin. The initial screen requires the warehouse number, storage type and storage bin. The output shows the count documents for that specific storage bin, including the material number, count date and inventory document status, for example counted, cleared, and not counted.

LI06	Change View "Block/Unblock Storage Type for Annual Inv"

This transaction is used to block storage types when an annual inventory is being performed. For each warehouse and storage type combination, the user can manually enter a block on the entire storage type for stock placement and stock removal.

LI11N	Enter Inventory Count

This transaction is used to enter the count for a warehouse count document. The user can enter a warehouse number and a warehouse count document number. The transaction will allow the user to enter a quantity for the material in the bin. If the count document indicates that the bin is empty, but the user finds material in the bin, the found material quantity can be added into the warehouse count document.

LI12N	Change Inventory Count

This transaction allows a user to change the count details of a warehouse count document. The user is required to enter the warehouse number and count document. The transaction shows the line items in the count document and the user can change the counted quantity or flag the line as zero.

LI13N	Display Inventory Count

This transaction allows a user to display the count details of a warehouse count document. The user is required to enter the warehouse number and count document. The transaction shows the line items in the count document, such as the storage bin, material, batch, plant, counted quantity, and quant number.

LI14	Start Recount

This transaction is used to start a recount for a specific count document. The user is required to enter the warehouse number and count document. In addition, the user can enter a percentage that would be allowed between the book quantity and the counted quantity. For example if 2% is entered then the recount would not require any more processing if the deviation were less than 2%. Instead of a percentage, the user can also enter a specific value for an allowed deviance, for example, $50.

LI20	Clear Inventory Differences WM

This transaction is performed to clear any inventory differences in a warehouse count document. The user is required to enter the warehouse number and count document. The user can enter a variance in percentage, under which the difference is cleared or enter a specific value, for example, $50. The transaction will show the line items, including the value difference between the book value and the counted value. Each line can be selected and the differences be written off.

LI21	Clearing of Differences in Inventory Management

This transaction is similar to LI20, but instead of clearing WM differences, it deals with inventory management differences. The user is required to enter the warehouse number and the interim storage type where the WM differences have been posted. The transaction will post the WM difference—logically existing in the interim storage type—in the IM system, so the warehouse totals and IM totals are the same.

LICC	Execute Inventory with Cycle-Counting Method and by Quants

This transaction is used to execute cycle counting for a warehouse and a material or range of materials. The initial screen requires

a warehouse number and a material or range of materials to be entered. The output screen shows the storage bins to be counted with a comment, such as overdue, and a new physical inventory date. The user can activate the documents from the output screen.

LL01	Warehouse Activity Monitor

This transaction is used to execute the warehouse activity monitor. The warehouse entered must be configured to have active warehouse activity monitor objects. The activity monitor gives the user the option to see unconfirmed transfer orders, open transfer requirements, open posting change documents, open deliveries, negative stocks, stock in interim storage types, and critical stock in production.

LLVS	SAP Easy Access Warehouse Management

This transaction is used to display the warehouse management menu. The menu offers the user a number of options such as master data transactions, transfer requirement transactions, transfer order transactions, physical inventory transactions, posting change transactions, and report transactions.

LM00	Logon to RF

This is the standard SAP transaction for the logon for mobile data entry. The transaction can be performed on the SAP system or a mobile data entry device. The standard logon requires a warehouse number to be entered.

LM01	Dynamic Menu

This is the transaction for RF devices that shows the standard menu layout. The standard menu options offered are inbound process, outbound process, stock transfer, internal warehouse processes and inquiries.

This can be modified for a user's specific mobile data entry needs.

LM02   Putaway by Storage Unit

This is the transaction for RF devices that allows a storage unit to be putaway. The transaction requires that a storage unit be entered on the mobile device. The transaction will show the details and allow the user to process the putaway.

LM03   Putaway by Transfer Order

This is the transaction for RF devices that allows a putaway for a transfer order. The transaction requires a transfer order number be entered. The transaction shows the source bin for the transfer order, which has to be confirmed on the mobile device and then the destination bin is selected and confirmed by the user.

LM04   Putaway – System Guided

This is the transaction for RF devices where the system processes the putaway for a transfer order according to specific sorting criteria.

LM05   Picking by Transfer Order

This is the transaction for RF devices that is used for the picking of a transfer order. The transaction requires a transfer order number be entered. The transaction shows the source bin for the transfer order which has to be confirmed on the mobile device and then the destination bin is selected and confirmed by the user.

LM06   Picking by Delivery

This is the transaction for RF devices that is used for the picking of a delivery. The user is required to enter an outbound delivery number for this transaction.

LM07   Picking – System Guided

This is the transaction for RF devices where the system processes the picking of a transfer order according to specific sorting criteria.

LM09   Putaway by Delivery

This is the transaction for RF devices that is used for the putaway of a delivery. The user is required to enter a delivery number for this transaction.

LM11   Posting Changes

This is the transaction for RF devices where the system processes a posting change transfer order according to specific sorting criteria.

LM12   Material Inquiry

This is the transaction for RF devices where a user can make a material inquiry. The transaction requires a material number, plant and storage type to be entered. The user can select a number of options, such as sort by storage bin location, sort by goods receipt date, and sort by expiration date.

LM13   Clustered Putaway

This is the transaction for RF devices where a user can process a clustered putaway. The transaction requires a storage unit number to be entered for processing. The transaction selects a group of transfer order items by the storage unit number for simultaneous putaway.

LM18   Handling Unit Inquiry

This is the transaction for RF devices where a user can make a handling unit inquiry. The transaction requires a handling unit to be entered. The transaction allows the user to print the shipping unit label, print the handling unit label or display the material in the handling unit.

LM19 Handling Unit – Pack

This is the transaction for RF devices where a user can pack a handling unit. The transaction requires a handling unit to be entered, along with the plant, storage location and storage bin. The transaction packs materials into an existing HU or creates a new HU.

LM22 Handling Unit – Unpack

This is the transaction for RF devices where a user can unpack a handling unit. The transaction requires a handling unit to be entered.

LM24 Packing Handling Unit by Delivery

This is the transaction for RF devices where a user can pack a handling unit by delivery. The transaction requires a handling unit to be entered, along with the plant, storage location and storage bin. The transaction packs the selected items of a delivery.

LM25 Unpack Handling Unit by Delivery

This is the transaction for RF devices where a user can unpack a handling unit by delivery. The transaction requires a handling unit to be entered and will unpack the selected items of a delivery.

LM26 Picking by Delivery – Without Selection Screen

This is the transaction for RF devices where picking can be instigated without the user entering any details on a selection screen. If there are no relevant deliveries for the warehouse, the transaction will inform the user that no deliveries are available.

LM27 Putaway by Delivery – Without Selection Screen

This is the transaction for RF devices where putaway can be instigated without the users entering any details on a selection screen. If there are no relevant deliveries for the warehouse, the transaction will inform the user that no deliveries are available.

LM30 Load Control – Load by Shipment

This is the transaction for RF devices where a load is created for a shipment. The user is required to enter a shipment number and a relevant handling unit number. The transaction selects the goods to be loaded by the shipment number.

LM31 Load Control – Load by Delivery

This is the transaction for RF devices where a load is created for a delivery. The user is required to enter a delivery number and a relevant handling unit number. The transaction selects the goods to be loaded by the delivery number.

LM32 Load Control – System Guide Load

This is the transaction for RF devices where the system creates a load for a shipment. The system proposes the next shipment to be loaded.

LM33 Load Control – Unload by Shipment

This is the transaction for RF devices where a shipment is unloaded. The user is required to enter a shipment number and a relevant handling unit number. The process selects the materials to be unloaded by the shipment

LM34	Load Control – Unload by Delivery

This is the transaction for RF devices where a delivery is unloaded. The user is required to enter a delivery number and a relevant handling unit number. The process selects the materials to be unloaded by the delivery.

LM35	Load Inquiry by Handling Unit

This is the transaction for RF devices where the user can inquire about the load status of a specific handling unit. The transaction requires the user to enter a handling unit number.

LM36	Load Control – Detail by Delivery

This is the transaction for RF devices where a user can inquire about the load status of a specific delivery and the transaction will display the relevant handling units. The transaction requires the user to enter a handling unit number.

LM37	Load Control – Detail by Shipment

This is the transaction for RF devices where a user can inquire about the load status of a specific shipment and the status of the respective deliveries. The transaction requires the user to enter a shipment number.

LM45	Pick and Pack

This is the transaction for RF devices where a user can pick and pack materials in one step. The transaction requires the user to enter a handling unit number and the materials to pack.

LM46	Pick and Pack by Delivery

This is the transaction for RF devices where a user can pick and pack materials in one step for a delivery. The transaction requires the user to enter a delivery number, a handling unit number and the materials to pack.

LM50	Count Inventory by Storage Unit – System Guided

This is the transaction for RF devices where the system will propose a storage unit to be counted. The system will display a message if there are no relevant inventory documents to be counted by the user.

LM51	Count Inventory by Storage Unit – User Selection

This is the transaction for RF devices where the user can count storage units based on user input. The transaction requires the user to enter a storage bin for the storage unit count.

LM56	Interleaving – Select by Storage Unit

This transaction for RF devices is used to perform interleaving using a storage unit. The transaction requires the user to enter a storage unit number, which is used to identify transfer order for putaway. After the transfer order for putaway has been confirmed, the system proposes a transfer order for picking from the same queue. Interleaving reduces warehouse movement, making warehouse operations more efficient.

LM57	Interleaving – System Guided Putaway

This transaction for RF devices allows interleaving to be performed by the system proposing a transfer order for putaway; after its confirmation, the system then proposes a transfer order for picking. Interleaving reduces warehouse movement, making warehouse operations more efficient.

LM61   Goods Issue by Delivery

This is the transaction for RF devices where a goods issue is performed for a selected delivery. The transaction requires the user to enter an outbound delivery number.

LM62   Goods Issue by Staging Area

This is the transaction for RF devices where a goods issue is performed for an outbound delivery based on staging area. The transaction requires the user to enter a staging area number.

LM63   Goods Issue by Shipment

This is the transaction for RF devices where a goods issue is performed for an outbound delivery based on shipment number. The transaction requires the user to enter a shipment number.

LM64   Goods Issue by All

This is the transaction for RF devices where a goods issue is performed for an outbound delivery. The user can enter one of a number of selection fields, such as material number, ship-to party, delivery date, external delivery number, or service agent.

LM65   Goods Issue by Group

This is the transaction for RF devices where a goods issue is performed for an outbound delivery based on a group. The transaction requires the user to enter a group number.

LM66   Goods Issue by Handling Unit

This is the transaction for RF devices where a goods issue is performed for an outbound

delivery based on a handling unit number. The transaction requires the user to enter a handling unit number.

LM71   Goods Receipt by Delivery

This is the transaction for RF devices where a goods receipt is performed for an inbound delivery based on a delivery number. The transaction requires the user to enter a delivery number.

LM72   Goods Receipt by Staging Area

This is the transaction for RF devices where a goods receipt is performed for an inbound delivery based on staging area. The transaction requires the user to enter a staging area number.

LM73   Goods Receipt by Shipment

This is the transaction for RF devices where a goods receipt is performed for an inbound delivery based on shipment number. The transaction requires the user to enter a shipment number.

LM74   Goods Receipt by All

This is the transaction for RF devices where a goods receipt is performed for an inbound delivery. The user can enter one of a number of selection fields, such as material number, vendor, delivery date, external delivery number, or service agent.

LM76   Goods Receipt by Handling Unit

This is the transaction for RF devices where a goods receipt is performed for an inbound delivery based on a handling unit number. The transaction requires the user to enter a handling unit number.

LM77	Queue Assignment

This is the transaction for RF devices where the user can modify the warehouse or queue that they are working with. The transaction allows the user to enter a modified warehouse number or a modified queue number.

LM80	Serial Number Capture

This is the transaction for RF devices where the user can enter a delivery number to capture the serial numbers from that delivery.

LP11	WM Staging of Crate Parts

This transaction is used to create production staging for crate parts. This transaction requires that a control cycle has been created for the crate parts. The transaction allows the user to enter the material, plant and supply area.

LP12	WM Material Staging of Release Order Parts

This transaction is used to create production staging for release order parts. The transaction allows the user to enter the plant and supply area. There are a number of selection screens that can be entered, including material, order and requirement date.

LP21	Replenishment for Fixed Bins in Warehouse Management

This transaction is used to replenish the fixed bins in the warehouse based on the current stock position and the settings in the material master records. The transaction requires a plant, storage location, warehouse number and storage type to be entered. The storage type must be configured to allow replenishment of fixed bins.

LP22	Replenishment Planning for Fixed Bins

This transaction is used to plan replenishment of the fixed bins in the warehouse. The transaction requires that the user enter a plant, warehouse number and storage type. A replenishment movement type must be configured for the entered warehouse and storage type combination. When the transaction is executed, the system will display the number of transfer requirements that were created.

LP24	Replenishment for Storage Types with Random Space Management

This transaction is used to control replenishment in the warehouse. The transaction calculates the replenishment quantity based on current stock in the storage type and the replenishment quantity defined in the material master record. The transaction requires that the user enter a plant, warehouse number and storage type. When the transaction is executed, the system will display the number of transfer requirements that were created.

LPIN	Information on Material Status in Production

This transaction is used to display reservations for material in production. The user must enter a plant number and select one of four options: order number, supply area, work center, or raw material number.

LPK1	Create Control Cycle

This transaction is used to create a control cycle, which is used in the plant to define the production storage bin where material is to be staged for production. The initial screen requires the material number, plant number and supply area. The detail screen allows the user to enter the number of kanbans and quantity.

LPK2 — Change Control Cycle

This transaction is used to change a control cycle. The initial screen requires the material number, plant number and supply area. The transaction allows the user to change the details in the control cycle, such as the number of kanbans, quantity and the storing position.

LPK3 — Display Control Cycle

This transaction is used to change a control cycle. The initial screen requires the material number, plant number and supply area. The transaction displays the control cycle data and the destination storage bin data.

LPK4 — Automatic Creation of Control Cycles for Release Order Parts

This transaction automatically creates control cycles for release order parts. The initial screen requires the user to enter the material type, material number, plant, supply area, warehouse, storage type, and storage bin. There are three options that the user can enter: list the control cycles to be created, delete control cycles or a database update.

LQ01 — Posting Change Storage Location to Storage Location in Inventory Management

This transaction is used to post a change in inventory management that has been made in warehouse management. The initial screen requires the user to enter the warehouse number, storage type and plant. The output can be restricted by entering a quant, storage bin, or material number. A list of quants applicable for posting is displayed, and the user can then execute the posting changes.

LQ02 — Posting Change in WM and IM

This transaction allows the user to transfer quants in warehouse management and make a simultaneous inventory management change. The initial screen requires a warehouse number and movement type. The output shows a list of posting change quants that can be selected and processed.

LRF1 — RF Monitor, Active

This transaction is used by the warehouse supervisor to monitor the RF queues of warehouse operators. The transaction shows the queues and, by drilling down, the user can see the transfer orders in each queue along with the date and time the transfer order was created. The user can drag and drop transfer orders from one queue to another, allowing them to balance the work in the warehouse.

LRF2 — RF Monitor, Passive

This transaction is used by the warehouse supervisor to monitor the RF queues of warehouse operators. The transaction shows the queues and, by drilling down, the user can see the transfer orders in each queue, along with the date and time the transfer order was created. Unlike transaction LRF1, the user cannot move transfer orders from one queue to another.

LS01N — Create Storage Bin

This transaction is used to create a storage bin in the warehouse. The user is initially required to enter the warehouse number, storage type and the storage bin to be created. After entering those details, the storage bin will require a storage section to be entered and optional information, such as picking area, maximum weight, total capacity, storage bin type and a block for putaway or removal, if required.

LS02N   Change Storage Bin

This transaction is used to change a storage bin in the warehouse. The user is initially required to enter the warehouse number, storage type and the storage bin to be created. After entering the storage bin details, the transaction allows a storage section to be changed, as well as the picking area, maximum weight, total capacity, storage bin type and a block for putaway or removal, if required.

LS03N   Display Storage Bin

This transaction is used to display a storage bin in the warehouse. The user is initially required to enter the warehouse number, storage type and the storage bin to be created. The transaction will display the storage section, the picking area, maximum weight, total capacity, storage bin type and any blocks entered.

LS04   Display Empty Storage Bins

This transaction is used to display empty storage bins for a specific location. The initial screen requires a warehouse number and storage type to be entered. The output can be restricted by entering some option information, such as storage section, storage bin or storage bin type. The output shows the empty bins by storage section. The output information includes the storage bin type, putaway block, removal block, maximum weight, and maximum capacity.

LS05   Automatic Creation
of Storage Bins

This transaction is used to automatically generate storage bins with similar characteristics. The system displays a screen with the storage bin characteristics and the coordinates of all the bins that will be generated based on your entries.

LS06   Block/Unblock Several
Storage Bins Simultaneously

This transaction is used to block or unblock storage bins within the same storage type. The initial screen requires a warehouse and storage type to be entered. The bins to be blocked or unblocked can be restricted by entering values in other selection criteria, such as storage section or picking area. From the output screen, the user can select one or more storage bins to process.

LS07   Block and Unblock
Quants for Material

This transaction allows the user to block or unblock quants for a specific material. The user is required to enter the warehouse number and material number. The selection can be further restricted by entering the plant, batch number, stock category, special stock indicator or special stock number. From the output screen, the user can select one or more quants which they can block or unblock.

LS08   Block and Unblock a
Range of Storage Bins

This transaction is used to block or unblock a range of storage bins in a warehouse. The initial screen requires the user to enter the warehouse number and storage type. The output can be restricted by entering a single or range of storage bins. The system will display a message informing the user if any bins are blocked. If users wants to block any bins, they can select the block icon and enter a putaway or removal block and, if required, a block reason.

LS09   WM Material Data
per Storage Type

This transaction is used to display what storage types are associated with a particular material in a warehouse. The initial screen allows the user to enter a material, warehouse and storage type, but no fields are mandatory. If a material only is entered, then the output will show what warehouses and storage types are associated with that material.

LS10	Change View "Storage Bin Structure for Automatic Creation"

This transaction allows the entry of the data required to automatically create storage bins. For each warehouse/storage type combination, the user can configure the template used for new storage bins. If there is more than one template, then these are given different sequence numbers. Each template has a structure, a start and end value, as well as the increment between storage bin numbers.

LS11	Change Several Storage Bins Simultaneously

This transaction is used to change the same values for a number of storage bins simultaneously. The warehouse number and storage type is required, and the output can be restricted by entering storage bins, storage section or picking area. The output shows a list of storage bins that can be selected. The fields that can be changed for the storage bins include the storage section, picking area, storage bin type, maximum weight, and total capacity.

LS12	Change View "Block/Unblock Storage Type": Overview

This transaction is used to block or unblock a specific storage type. The transaction allows the user to enter a placement or removal block, as well as a blocking reason for a single or many storage types.

LS22	Change Quant

This transaction is used to change the details of a quant of material. The initial screen requires the user to enter a warehouse number and a quant number. The transaction shows the quant details, such as material number, plant, storage location, batch, storage type, storage bin and total stock. The user can change a number of fields, such as goods receipt date, certificate number, and the blocking indicators.

LS23	Display Quant

This transaction is used to display the details of a quant of material. The initial screen requires the user to enter a warehouse number and a quant number. The transaction shows the quant details, such as material number, plant, storage location, batch, storage type, storage bin, total stock, goods receipt date, goods receipt number, last movement date, certificate number, and blocking indicators.

LS24	Stock per Material

This transaction is used to show the stock for a specific material in a warehouse. The initial screen requires a material, warehouse and plant to be entered. The output can be restricted by entering other fields, such as storage type, storage bin, goods receipt date and goods receipt number. The output is shown in storage type, storage bin order, and shows the stock in each bin as well as the goods receipt date.

LS25	Stock per Storage Bin

This transaction is used to show the stock for a specific storage bin. The initial screen requires a warehouse number, storage type, and storage bin to be entered. The transaction shows the quant details, such as material number, plant, storage location, batch, storage type, storage bin, total stock, goods receipt date, goods receipt number, last movement date, certificate number, and blocking indicators.

LS26   Stock Overview

This transaction is used to show the stock overview for a specific material in a warehouse. The output can be restricted by entering other selection criteria, such as plant, storage location, and storage type. The stock overview output shows the material in the warehouse in stock type order.

LS27   Stock per Storage Unit

This transaction is used to show the stock that is associated with a specific storage unit. The initial screen requires that the user enter a specific storage unit.

LS28   Storage Units per Storage Bin

This transaction is used to display the storage units for a specific storage bin. The initial screen requires that the user enter a warehouse number, storage type, and storage bin. The output shows the storage units associated with the specific storage bin.

LS32   Change Storage Unit

This transaction is used to change a storage unit. The initial screen requires the user to enter a specific storage unit. A storage unit is a group of one or more amounts that are managed in the warehouse as one unit.

LS33   Display Storage Unit

This transaction is used to display a storage unit. The initial screen requires the user to enter a specific storage unit. A storage unit is a group of one or more amounts that are managed in the warehouse as one unit.

LS41   List of Control Cycles

This transaction is used to display a list of control cycles that are associated with a material, plant or production supply area (PSA). The initial screen has no mandatory fields, so, by leaving the fields blank, a list of all control cycles will be displayed. The output can be restricted by entering a material, plant, PSA, warehouse number or storage type. The output shows the supply area, material, plant, warehouse, storage type, storage bin, and the material staging indicator.

LS51   Create Batch Search Strategy

This transaction is used to create a batch search strategy. The initial screen requires the user to enter a search strategy type, which controls the batch determination, including selection criteria and quantity proposal. Depending on which search strategy type is entered, the user will be required to enter a number of fields, which could include warehouse number, movement type or customer number.

LS52   Change Batch Search Strategy

This transaction is used to change a batch search strategy. The initial screen requires the user to enter a search strategy type, which controls the batch determination, including selection criteria and quantity proposal. Depending on which search strategy type is entered, the user will be required to change the fields in the strategy, which could include warehouse number, movement type or customer number.

LS53   Display Batch Search Strategy

This transaction is used to display a batch search strategy. The initial screen requires the user to enter a search strategy type. Depending on which search strategy type is entered, the user will have to enter a number of selection fields, such as warehouse number, movement type or customer number. The transaction will then display the batch search strategies for the criteria entered.

| LT01 | Create Transfer Order |

This transaction is used to create a transfer order. The initial screen requires the user to enter the movement type, material number, quantity, and plant. The following screen allows the user to enter a source storage type and storage bin, and a destination storage type and storage bin. The transfer can be created from the detail screen.

| LT02 | Create Transfer Order for Inventory Difference |

This transaction allows you to clear inventory differences by creating a transfer order. The initial screen allows the user to enter a warehouse number, movement type, material, plant, and quantity required to be cleared. The following screen allows the user to enter a source storage type and storage bin, and a destination storage type and storage bin. The transfer can be created from the detail screen.

| LT03 | Create Transfer Order for a Posting Change Delivery |

This transaction is used to create a transfer order for a posting change delivery. The initial screen requires the user to enter a warehouse number and a delivery number. The following screen will propose the source storage type and storage bin, and a destination storage type and storage bin. The transfer can be created from the detail screen.

| LT04 | Create Transfer Order from Transfer Requirement |

This transaction is used to create a transfer order from a transfer requirement. The initial

screen requires the user to enter a warehouse number and the transfer requirement number. The following screen shows the material from the transfer requirement and the amount to be moved. The user can change the destination bin or allow the system to determine that. The transfer order can be created from this screen.

| LT05 | Process Posting Change Notice |

This transaction is used to process a posting change notice. The initial screen requires the user to enter a warehouse number and a posting change notice. The following screen shows the details of the posting change notice, and the document can be saved from this screen.

| LT06 | Create Transfer Order for Material Document |

This transaction allows a user to create a transfer order for an inventory management material document. For example, if material was consumed and the consumption was recorded in the inventory management system, then this transaction would allow a transfer order to be created to replicate the inventory management movement. The initial screen requires a material document, material document year and a warehouse number to be entered.

| LT07 | Create Transfer Order for Storage Unit |

This transaction is used to place a storage unit into stock by creating a transfer order. The initial screen requires the user to enter the warehouse number and movement type. The storage unit does not exist until this transfer order is created, as the actual movement of the material with its container requires that the transfer order create the storage unit as part of the process. If the storage unit is numbered externally, the relevant number can be added on the initial screen.

| LT08 | Manual Addition to Storage Unit |

This transaction allows the user to add stock to an existing storage unit. The initial screen requires that the storage unit be entered along with the movement type and plant number. This transaction is used when material arrives in the receiving area after it should have, and the storage unit it was to be in was already created with some of the material scheduled to be in the storage unit. This transaction creates a transfer order to add stock to the existing storage unit.

| LT09 | Move Storage Unit |

This transaction is used to move a storage unit from one location to another. The initial screen requires the user to enter the storage unit number and the movement type. By default, the movement type in this transaction is set to 999. The user should replace the 999 movement type with a new ID point movement type.

| LT0A | Create Transfer Order to Pre-Plan Storage Unit |

This transaction allows the user to manually create a transfer order associated with a storage unit. The initial screen requires the entry of a warehouse number, warehouse movement type, material, quantity, plant, and storage location. The following screen allows the user to enter the target quantity as well as the destination storage bin and destination storage unit.

| LT0B | Putaway of Pre-Picked Handling Units |

This transaction is used to control the putaway of a pre-picked handling unit. The initial

screen requires that the user enter the goods issue date, the warehouse number, plant, and movement type. To restrict the number of handling units to be put away, the user can enter values for customer, delivery, handling unit, or storage unit type. The transaction will display a list of handling units that can be put away by creating transfer orders.

| LT0C | Removal of Pre-Picked Handling Units |

This transaction is used to remove a pre-picked handling unit. The initial screen requires that the user enter the specific warehouse number, although other selection criteria can be entered, such as storage type, goods issue date, customer, delivery, handling unit, and movement type.

| LT0D | Transferring Pre-Picked Handling Units |

This transaction is used to transfer a pre-picked handling unit. The initial screen requires that the user enter the specific warehouse number, although other selection criteria can be entered such as storage type, goods issue date, customer, delivery, handling unit, and movement type.

| LT0E | Create Removal Transfer Order for Two-Step Picking |

This transaction is used for creating two-step transfer orders for a group that is used to reference several unique documents. The initial screen requires a warehouse number and a group number to be entered. The transaction will use the movement type 850, which references two-step picking.

| LT0F | Create Transfer Order for Inbound Delivery |

This transaction is used to put away a handling unit using an inbound delivery. A transfer order is created to put away the handling unit. The user should enter a warehouse and an inbound delivery number. The handling unit overview screen will be displayed from which a transfer order can be created.

LT0G	Return to Stock from Delivery

This transaction is used to return to the warehouse material that has already been picked and confirmed for a delivery. The transaction requires that the user enter a warehouse number, a single or range of delivery numbers, and a relevant movement type. The display screen allows the user to select the delivery or transfer order to be returned to the warehouse.

LT0H	Putaway/Transfer Handling Units

This transaction is used to put away or transfer handling units in the warehouse. The initial screen requires a warehouse number to be entered as well as the movement type. The output shows a list of suitable handling units from which users can select those they require to be put away. The system will then create transfer orders based on the user's selection.

LT0I	Removal of Handling Units from Stock

This transaction is used for the picking of handling units in the warehouse. The initial screen requires the warehouse number and the movement type to be entered. The output shows a list of suitable handling units from which users can select those they require to be picked. The system will then create transfer orders based on the user's selection.

LT0J	Create Transfer Order for Storage Unit

This transaction is used to create a transfer order for a storage unit. The initial screen requires that the user enter a specific storage unit.

LT0R	Request Replenishment Manually

This transaction is used to replenish warehouse material manually. The initial screen requires a warehouse number, storage type and the material number to be entered. The user can add other information, such as storage bin, plant and storage location. The transaction checks to ensure that there is a fixed bin assigned to the material.

LT0S	Create Transfer Order for Multiple Orders

This transaction is used to create transfer order for multiple orders using a group. The initial screen requires a user to enter a warehouse number and a group number. The transaction will create a single transfer order for the multiple deliveries.

LT10	Create Transfer Order from List

This transaction allows the user to move materials from one storage bin to another by generating one or more transfer orders. The initial screen requires that the user enter a warehouse and storage type. The output shows all the storage bins for the respective storage type and indicates whether the bin is blocked from movement. Users can select the material from the unblocked bin they require and can create transfer orders in the foreground or background.

LT11   Confirm Transfer Order
Item – In One Step

This transaction allows a user to confirm a line item on a transfer order using one step. The initial screen requires a transfer order, transfer order item, and warehouse number to be entered. The default setting in this transaction is the PICK AND TRANSFER option, but the user can select one of three options: PICK AND TRANSFER, PICK only, or TRANSFER only. After entering the necessary data, the following screen allows the user to enter the actual quantity that was moved.

LT12   Confirm Transfer Order –
In One Step

This transaction is used to confirm a complete transfer order in one step. The initial screen allows a user to enter a transfer order number and warehouse number. The default setting in this transaction is the PICK AND TRANSFER option, but the user can select one of three options: PICK AND TRANSFER, PICK only, or TRANSFER only. After entering the necessary data, the following screen allows the user to confirm the actual quantity that was moved.

LT13   Confirm Transfer Order for
Storage Unit – In One Step

This transaction is used to confirm a transfer order for storage unit items in one step. The initial screen allows a user to enter a storage unit number. The default setting in this transaction is the PICK AND TRANSFER option, but the user can select one of three options: PICK AND TRANSFER, PICK only, or TRANSFER only. After entering the necessary data, the following screen allows the user to confirm the actual quantity that was moved.

LT14   Confirm Preplanned
Transfer Order Item

This transaction allows a user to confirm a line item on a transfer order. The initial screen requires a transfer order, transfer order item, and warehouse number to be entered. The default setting in this transaction is the PICK AND TRANSFER option, but the user can select one of three options: PICK AND TRANSFER, PICK only, or TRANSFER only. After entering the necessary data, the following screen allows the user to enter the actual quantity that was moved.

LT15   Cancelling Transfer Order

This transaction is used to cancel a transfer order. The initial screen requires a transfer order number and a warehouse number to be entered. If users choose to perform this transaction in the foreground, then they can select the line items they wish to cancel on the transfer order.

LT16   Cancelling Transfer Order
for Storage Unit

This transaction is used to cancel a transfer order for a storage unit. The initial screen requires a storage unit number to be entered. If users choose to perform this transaction in the foreground, then they can select the items they wish to cancel on the transfer order.

LT1A   Change Transfer Order Header

This transaction is used to change the header for a transfer order. The initial screen requires the user to enter a transfer order and a warehouse number. The following screen allows the user to change the data in the confirmation, planned and actual data section, such as personnel number, HR status of the transfer order, planned processing time for the transfer order, and the actual time of the transfer order.

LT1B	Confirm Transfer Order Item – Pick Step

This transaction is used to confirm the pick step for an item on a transfer order. The initial screen requires a user to enter a transfer order number, item number and warehouse number. The transaction defaults to a pick option, but the user can select one of three options: pick and transfer, pick only, or transfer only. After entering the necessary data, the following screen allows the user to enter the actual quantity that was moved.

LT1C	Confirm Transfer Order Item – Transfer Step

This transaction is used to confirm the transfer step for an item on a transfer order. The initial screen requires a user to enter a transfer order number, item number and warehouse number. The transaction defaults to the transfer option, but the user can select one of three options: pick and transfer, pick only, or transfer only. After entering the necessary data, the following screen allows the user to enter the actual quantity that was moved.

LT1D	Confirm Transfer Order – Pick Step

This transaction is used to confirm the pick step for a complete transfer order. The initial screen allows a user to enter a transfer order number and warehouse number. The default setting in this transaction is the PICK option, but the user can select one of three options: PICK AND TRANSFER, PICK only, or TRANSFER only. After entering the necessary data, the following screen allows the user to confirm the actual quantity that was moved.

LT1E	Confirm Transfer Order – Transfer Step

This transaction is used to confirm the transfer step for a complete transfer order. The initial screen allows a user to enter a transfer order number and warehouse number. The default setting in this transaction is the TRANSFER option, but the user can select one of three options: PICK AND TRANSFER, PICK only, or TRANSFER only. After entering the necessary data, the following screen allows the user to confirm the actual quantity that was moved.

LT1F	Confirm Transfer Order Items for Storage Unit – Pick Step

This transaction is used to confirm the pick step for storage unit items in transfer order. The initial screen allows a user to enter a storage unit number. The default setting in this transaction is the PICK option, but the user can select one of three options: PICK AND TRANSFER, PICK only, or TRANSFER only. After entering the necessary data, the following screen allows the user to confirm the actual quantity that was moved.

LT1G	Confirm Transfer Order Items for Storage Unit – Transfer Step

This transaction is used to confirm the transfer step for storage unit items in transfer order. The initial screen allows a user to enter a storage unit number. The default setting in this transaction is the TRANSFER option, but the user can select one of three options: PICK AND TRANSFER, PICK only, or TRANSFER only. After entering the necessary data, the following screen allows the user to confirm the actual quantity that was moved.

LT21	Display Transfer Order

This transaction is used to display the details of a transfer order. The initial screen requires a transfer order and warehouse number to be entered. The following screen shows the transfer order details such as the header data: material, plant, storage location, weight and storage unit type. The screen also shows the item data, which includes the source and destination data.

LT22	Display Transfer Orders for a Storage Type

This transaction is used to display transfer orders for a single or range of storage types. The initial screen requires the user to enter a warehouse number and the results will be for all storage types. The user can allow all transfer orders to be shown or can allow only open or confirmed transfer orders. The output shows the details for each transfer order, such as plant, material, source bin, destination bin, quantity, and whether the transfer order is confirmed or open.

LT23	Display Transfer Orders by Transfer Order Number

This transaction is used to display transfer orders for a single or range of transfer orders. The initial screen requires the user to enter a warehouse number, and the results will be for all relevant transfer orders. The user can allow all transfer orders to be shown or can allow only open or confirmed transfer orders. The output shows the details for each transfer order, such as plant, material, source bin, destination bin, quantity, and whether the transfer order is confirmed or open.

LT24	Display Transfer Orders for Material Number

This transaction is used to display transfer orders for a single or range of material numbers. The initial screen requires the user to enter a warehouse number and the results will be for all relevant material numbers. The user can allow all transfer orders to be shown

or can allow only open or confirmed transfer orders. The output shows the details for each transfer order, such as plant, material, source bin, destination bin, quantity, and whether the transfer order is confirmed or open.

LT25	Display Transfer Orders By Groups

This transaction is used to display transfer orders for a single or range of groups. The initial screen requires the user to enter a warehouse number and the results will be for all relevant groups. The user can allow all transfer orders to be shown or can allow only open or confirmed transfer orders. The output shows the details for each transfer order, such as plant, material, source bin, destination bin, quantity, and whether the transfer order is confirmed or open.

LT25A	Display Transfer Order for a Group

This transaction is used to display transfer orders for a specific group. The initial screen requires the user to enter a warehouse number and a group. The user can allow all transfer orders to be shown or can allow only open or confirmed transfer orders. The output shows the details for each transfer order, such as plant, material, source bin, destination bin, quantity, and whether the transfer order is confirmed or open.

LT25N	Confirm Transfer Orders By Group

This transaction is used to display transfer orders for a single or range of groups. The initial screen requires the user to enter a warehouse and this will show the transfer orders for all groups. The user can select all transfer order items or only open items. The initial screen also gives the user the option to enter a storage type and a picking area to restrict the output.

LT26	Display Transfer Orders for Storage Bin

This transaction is used to display transfer orders for a specific storage bin. The initial screen requires the user to enter a warehouse number, a storage type, and a storage bin. The user can allow all transfer orders to be shown or can allow only open or confirmed transfer orders. The output shows the details for each transfer order, such as plant, material, source bin, destination bin, quantity, and whether the transfer order is confirmed or open.

LT27	Display Transfer Orders for Storage Unit

This transaction is used to display transfer orders for a specific storage unit. The initial screen requires the user to enter a warehouse number and a storage unit number. The user can allow all transfer orders to be shown or can allow only open or confirmed transfer orders. The output shows the details for each transfer order, such as plant, material, source bin, destination bin, quantity, and whether the transfer order is confirmed or open.

LT28	Display Transfer Orders for a Group

This transaction is used to display transfer orders for a single or range of groups. The initial screen requires the user to enter a warehouse and this will show the transfer orders for all groups. The user can select all transfer order items or only open items. The initial screen also gives the user the option to enter a storage type and a picking area to restrict the output.

LT31	Print Transfer Order Manually

This transaction is used to manually print a transfer order. The transaction requires a warehouse number and a transfer order number to be entered. The user can enter print parameters such as the printer number and print code.

LT32	Print Transfer Order for Storage Unit

This transaction is used to manually print a transfer order for a specific storage unit. The transaction requires a storage unit to be entered. The user can enter print parameters such as the printer number and print code.

LT41	Prepare Transfer Requirements for Multiple Processing

This transaction is used to prepare a number of transfer requirements for processing. The initial screen requires a warehouse number to be entered and a shipment type such as A, for stock removal and E, for stock placement. The transaction will group together the transfer requisitions for further processing.

LT42	Create Transfer Orders by Multiple Processing

This transaction will create transfer orders for groups. The initial screen requires users to enter a warehouse number and they have the option to enter a specific group. If users want to select a group from a list, they can leave the group number blank or can search for a group via text search. After users have selected a group, they can then execute the multiple processing.

LT43	Creating Groups for Deliveries

This transaction will assign a group to all the transfer orders of a delivery. The initial screen requires a warehouse number to be entered. The selection can be restricted by entering a shipping point, route, shipment number or picking date.

LT44   Release for Multiple Processing

This transaction allows a user to release groups for processing. The initial screen requires a warehouse number to be entered and the user has the option to enter a group or a reference document category: L for grouped deliveries and B for grouped transfer requirements. The following screen shows the groups for the selection criteria entered.

LT45   Analysis of Groups

This transaction is used to evaluate the groups for a specific warehouse. The initial screen requires a warehouse number to be entered and the user has the option to enter a group or range of groups. In addition the user can enter a date range for the creation of the group. The transaction output shows the analysis for the different type of groups with totals for the number of new groups, active groups, completed groups, and released groups.

LT63   Control: Single Entry of Actual Data

This transaction is used to enter actual data. The initial screen allows the user to enter a warehouse number and a transfer order number or range of transfer orders. In addition, on the initial screen the user can enter values for processing control, entry of actual time, selection of transfer orders and automatically printing of transfer orders. After the selections are made, the next screen shows allows the user to enter a personnel number prior to the actual data being entered.

LT72   Determine Two-Step Relevance

This transaction is used to determine the two-step relevance for a group. The initial screen requires a warehouse number and a group number to be entered. The output screen shows the materials that are relevant for two-step picking. Users have the option of selecting a material, and then they can redetermine two-step picking, activate two-step picking or deactivate two-step picking.

LT73   Display Two-Step Picking Relevance for a Group

This transaction is used to display the two-step relevance for a group. The initial screen requires a warehouse number and a group number to be entered. The output screen displays the materials that are relevant for two-step picking.

LU01   Create Posting Change Notice

This transaction is used to create a posting change notice. The initial screen requires a warehouse number and movement type to be entered. The movement type must be relevant for a posting change, such as 309 or 321. The following screen requires the details of the posting change to be entered, such as material, plant, storage location, batch, and the post change quantity.

LU02   Change Posting Change Notice

This transaction is used to change a posting change notice. The initial screen requires a warehouse number and a posting change number. The next screen allows the user to change the details of the posting change notice, such as text, goods receipt number, inspection lot number, and storage location.

LU03   Display Posting Change Notice

This transaction is used to display a posting change notice. The initial screen requires a warehouse number and a posting change number. The next screen displays the details of the posting change notice, such as material, plant, storage location, batch, post change quantity, goods receipt number, inspection lot number, and storage location.

LU04	Display Posting Change Notice: Overview

This transaction is used to display the posting change notices for a specific warehouse or movement type. The initial screen allows the entry of just a warehouse number, or the user can restrict the display by entering a movement type, material, plant, storage location, stock category or batch. The output shows the posting change notices from which transfer orders can be generated for those change notices that have not been processed.

LX01	List of Empty Storage Bins

This transaction shows a list of empty storage bins for the selection criteria entered. The initial screen requires the entry of a warehouse number, and the entry of a storage type or a storage bin are optional. The transaction allows the user to highlight the fields to allow only unlocked bins or only bins without an inventory count. The output shows a list of empty bins, including the warehouse number, storage type and storage section.

LX02	Warehouse Management Stock

This transaction displays the warehouse stock at the storage bin level. The initial screen requires the entry of a warehouse number, while the entry of a storage type or a storage bin is optional. The initial screen allows the user to restrict the output by entering a plant, goods receipt date, stock category, special stock indicator, or special stock number. The output is displayed in material order, and shows the material stock for each storage bin.

LX03	Bin Status Report

This transaction is used to display an overview of the contents of selected storage bins. The initial screen requires a warehouse number to be entered, while the entry of

a storage type or a storage bin is optional. The user can restrict the output by entering values for other selection criteria, such as inventory method, days since putaway, stock category, special stock indicator, or special stock number. The output is shown in storage type order and shows the material in each of the occupied storage bins.

LX04	Capacity Load Utilization

This transaction is used to calculate the warehouse capacity that has been used. The initial screen requires a warehouse number to be entered while the entry of a storage type or a storage bin is optional. The output of this transaction shows the capacity used by storage type. The display shows the number of storage bins occupied, the number of empty storage bins, and the usage as a percentage.

LX05	Block Bins in Bulk Storage

This transaction allows the user to block bins in bulk storage immediately or at a later date. The initial screen requires a warehouse number and bulk storage type to be entered. A selection of storage bins to be blocked can be entered, as well as the flag to block the bins immediately.

LX06	Fire Department Inventory List

This transaction is used to supply the fire department with a list of hazardous materials in the warehouse. The initial screen requires a specific warehouse number to be entered. The report can be restricted by entering a storage type or range of storage types as well as fire containment areas.

LX07	Check Storage of Hazardous Materials

This transaction is used to check that hazardous materials are stored correctly in the warehouse. The initial screen requires a warehouse number to be entered, while the storage type and storage bin fields are optional. The transaction will display an error log and shows the number of storage bins that were checked and the number that are incorrect for each storage type.

| LX08 | Hazardous Substance List |

This transaction produces a report of all the hazardous material stored in a particular warehouse or storage type or fire containment area. The initial screen requires a warehouse number to be entered, while the storage type and storage bin fields are optional. The report shows the fire containment area the material is located in as well as the hazardous storage class and water pollution class.

| LX09 | Transfer Requirements with Processed Quantities as Percentages |

This transaction is used to display the processed quantities of transfer requirements as a percentage. The initial screen requires a warehouse number to be entered. The user can enter a transfer requirement or range of transfer requirements. The user can also restrict the output by entering a shipment type, movement type, and transfer requirement date. The output shows the relevant transfer requirements with the processed quantities shown as percentages.

| LX10 | Activities per Storage Type |

This transaction is used to display the types of movements that were processed for a storage type. The selection screen requires a warehouse number to be entered. The report output can be restricted by entering a range of transfer orders, storage type, plant or transfer order date. The report can be processed for all transfer orders, open transfer orders or confirmed transfer orders. The output shows the number of stock removals, putaways

and returns for each storage type in the warehouse.

| LX11 | Transfer Orders: Resident Documents |

This transaction is used to display a list of transfer orders for a specific warehouse. The selection screen requires a warehouse number to be entered. The output can be restricted by entering a transfer order date, requirement type and requirement number. The output shows a list of transfer orders, including the creation date, confirmation date, requirement type, requirement number, material document and the user who created the transfer order.

| LX12 | Transfer Orders: Resident Documents (Detailed View) |

This transaction is used to display a detailed list of transfer orders for a specific warehouse. The selection screen requires a warehouse number to be entered. The output can be restricted by entering a transfer order date, warehouse management movement type, source storage type, destination storage type, and material number. The output shows the line item detail for each transfer order.

| LX13 | Transfer Order with Differences |

This transaction is used to display transfer order differences summarized by storage type and transfer type. The selection screen requires a warehouse number to be entered. The final output can be restricted by entering a specific or range of transfer orders. The output is produced in storage type order and displays the number of line items for each specific movement. If there are any items with differences, the total is shown per movement as an actual figure and a percentage of the total line items.

LX14	Material Movement Frequency

This transaction is used to display the movement rate of materials within a specific warehouse for a given period. The selection screen requires a warehouse number to be entered. The final output can be restricted by entering a transfer order date or storage type. The report shows the number of movements for each material in a given storage type.

LX15	Selection of Storage Bins for Annual Inventory Count

This transaction allows you to select a number of storage bins for an annual inventory count. The transaction requires that the warehouse and storage type is entered. The number of storage bins selected can be restricted by selecting only bins not yet counted, only bins that have been counted, or dynamic storage bins. The transaction will display the number of bins that have been selected for the annual inventory count.

LX16	Carry out Continuous Inventory

This transaction is used to produce the count documents for continuous inventory. The warehouse number and storage type are entered, and a range of storage bins can be selected. Other selection parameters can be entered, such as only empty bins, only bins not yet counted, only bins that have been counted, or dynamic storage bins. The output shows a list of storage bins that can be counted in the selected warehouse and storage type. These bins can be selected and activated for the count.

LX17	Differences List per Storage Type

This transaction is used to display any existing inventory differences. The initial screen requires that the warehouse number and storage type are entered. The output can be restricted by entering a single or range of storage bins. The user has the opportunity to enter a variance, either an absolute value or a percentage, below which the difference does not trigger a recount and is cleared.

LX18	Statistics for Inventory Differences

This transaction is used to generate inventory statistics for each storage type in a warehouse. The initial screen requires a warehouse number, while the storage type and storage bins are optional fields. The output shows five statistics for each storage type: number of storage bins with completed inventory, number of storage bins with difference, number of storage bins not counted, number of storage bins counted, and the number of storage bins without inventory.

LX20	Create Bins for Interim Storage Types

This transaction allows you to create bins for the interim storage bins in the warehouse. The initial screen has only one field to enter: the warehouse number. The output shows the storage bins for each interim storage bin. If the bin exists, then the report will display the value "exists"; if it does not exist, then the report will display "missing."

LX21	Combined Pick List

This transaction is used to create a pick list for a group or range of groups. The initial screen allows the user to choose only open transfer orders, only confirmed transfer orders, or all transfer order items. You can print the transfer orders from the transaction based on the selection fields entered.

LX22	Inventory Overview

This transaction gives an overview of the physical inventory count situation. The user can view the display and complete any open processes including clearing differences. The initial screen requires the user to enter a warehouse number. The user can enter various selection criteria to reduce output, such as physical inventory document number, storage type and inventory status. The output shows the inventory documents, their status, storage type, and count date.

LX23	Stock Comparison Inventory Management/ Warehouse Management

This transaction is used to produce an inventory comparison between the Inventory Management and Warehouse Management systems. The user can restrict the area for comparison by entering the plant and storage location, plant and warehouse number or only the warehouse number. The comparison shows the stock for the plant, storage location and warehouse, at the IM level and the WM level, and calculates the difference quantity.

LX24	Display of Hazardous Material Numbers

This transaction produces a report of the hazardous material numbers for a specific or range of region codes. The user can leave all the selection fields blank and all hazardous materials will be displayed. The output can be restricted by entering a range of hazardous materials numbers, and a single or range of region codes. The output shows the region code, storage class, and water pollution class for each hazardous material selected.

LX25	Inventory Status

This transaction shows a user the number of inventory counts that have been taken in a specified storage type in a given period. The selection screen allows the user to enter a specific warehouse number, a single or range of storage types and a single or range of storage bins. The output shows the information for each storage type, which includes the absolute and percentage totals for the following areas: total number of bins, active inventory, planned inventory, and no inventory executed.

LX26	Carry Out Inventory Using the Cycle Counting Method

This transaction is used to display a list of storage bins that need to be inventoried. The initial screen allows the user to enter a warehouse number, relevant for cycle counting, a storage type and storage bins. The output shows the storage bins, in storage type order, that need to be counted. For example, if a bin needs to be counted because it is overdue, the transaction will propose a new physical inventory date.

LX27	SLED Control List

This transaction is used to show material with critical shelf life expiration date for a specific warehouse number. The initial screen requires the user to enter a specific warehouse number. The output can be restricted by entering an upper limit for the remaining shelf life of the materials, plant number, storage location or a storage type. The list displays the remaining shelf life for the materials relevant for the shelf life expiration date, the status of which is displayed using a traffic light.

LX29	Fixed Bin Supervision

This transaction is used to monitor the use of fixed bins in the warehouse. The initial screen requires the user to enter a warehouse number and to highlight at least one selection criteria for fixed storage bin evaluation, such as to display storage bins without assignment, or storage bins with assignment but without stock. The output displays a list of fixed storage bins with specific characteristics, according to the indicators set in the selection screen.

LX30	Overview of WM Messages Transmitted to External Systems

This transaction provides an overview of warehouse management messages that have been sent to an external system via the warehouse control unit (WCU) interface. The display shows the transfer orders, cancellations and group data that were sent.

LX31	Analysis of Customized Print Control Tables

This transaction displays the printer determination information for a warehouse. The initial screen requires a warehouse number to be entered as well as optional information, such as transfer order number. The output shows the name of the table that was read with key fields and lists the results for the transfer order printout, such as form, printer and spool data.

LX32	Read Transfer Orders from Archive

This transaction is used to display transfer orders that have been archived. The initial screen allows the user to enter a warehouse number and a transfer order, or range of transfer orders. Additional criteria can be entered, such as plant, storage bin and transfer order date.

LX33	Read Transfer Requirements from Archive

This transaction is used to display transfer requirements that have been archived. The initial screen allows the user to enter a warehouse number and a transfer requirement, or range of transfer requirements. Additional criteria can be entered, such as shipment type, WM movement type, and transfer requirement date.

LX34	Archived Posting Change Notices

This transaction is used to display posting change notices that have been archived. The initial screen allows the user to enter a warehouse number and a posting change notice, or range of posting change notices.

LX35	Archived Physical Inventory Records

This transaction is used to display physical inventory documents that have been archived. The initial screen allows the user to enter a warehouse number and a physical inventory document, or range of physical inventory documents.

LX36	Archived Inventory Histories

This transaction is used to display physical inventory counts that have been archived. The initial screen allows the user to enter a warehouse number and a physical inventory document, or range of physical inventory documents.

LX40	Material Situation Prod. Storage Bins

This transaction is used to provide an overview of the quantity situation in production storage bins. The initial screen allows the user to enter the warehouse number, storage type, storage bin, plant, material, and batch. The report calculates figures for the stock in the storage bin, the open quantities in transfer requirements for the storage bin, and the requirements situation based on the components that are needed at the production storage bin.

LX41	WM-PP Evaluation Report

This transaction is used to evaluate the stock situation for storage bins in production. The initial screen allows the user to enter a warehouse number, a range of storage types and storage bins. The report shows bin status using a traffic light to indicate whether or not there is available stock.

LX42	Evaluation PP Order from WM View

This transaction is used to evaluate a production order based on transfer requirements. The initial screen allows a user to enter a single or range of production orders. The

transaction determines whether the transfer requirement or transfer order has been created or whether the requirement does not equal the transfer order. The output shows the production order with either a red, yellow, or green traffic light to show whether the production order is OK or has an error.

LX43	Consistency Check for Control Cycles

This transaction is used to check the consistency in the definitions of control cycles, production supply areas and the associated reservations. The initial screen requires that the user enters a specific plant. The user can restrict the output by entering other selection criteria such as production supply area or material. The transaction checks whether the plant/storage location combination from the production supply area is allowed. The output shows the control cycles along with their status.

6 Production Planning (PP)

C201 — Create Master Recipe

This transaction is used to create a master recipe for a finished or semi-finished material. The material, plant, version, and profile should be added on the initial screen. On the RECIPE screen, the resource and the control should be added. On the OPERATIONS screen, the operation, description and the duration should be entered and these should be repeated for each phase of the operation.

C202 — Change Master Recipe

This transaction is used to change a master recipe for a finished or semi-finished material. On the initial screen, the user should enter the recipe group. The transaction will display the OPERATIONS screen where the user can change the existing operation or add additional operations.

C203 — Display Master Recipe

This transaction is used to display a master recipe for a finished or semi-finished material. On the initial screen, the user should enter the recipe group. The transaction will display the operations screen, where the user can review the operations. The user can review the materials in the recipe by clicking on the MATERIALS tab. Recipe header information and administrative data can also be reviewed.

C223 — Production Version: Mass Processing

This transaction is used to modify production versions based on certain selection criteria. The initial selection screen requires the user to enter a plant, but other selection criteria can be entered, such as material, MRP controller, key date, or production line. The transaction then will display the production versions, and the user can modify data for each, such as text, validity dates, lot size, planning group, production line, receiving storage location, and issuing location

C251 — Master Recipe Print List

This transaction is used to print master recipes. The selection screen allows the user to enter a material, plant, recipe group, key date, planner group, recipe status, and usage. From the selection screen, the output shows all the relevant recipes based on the selection criteria. Each recipe shows the operation details, including the resource and activity types.

C252 — Print List for Production Versions with Consistency Check

This transaction is used to print the details of a production version for a material. The selection screen allows the user to enter a material, plant, production version, task list type and type list group. The transaction output shows the production versions for each material, including the detailed planning and bill of materials information. The output will also display warning or error messages if there is an discrepancy with a production version.

C260 — Task List Changes

This transaction displays any changes that have been made to a task list. The initial screen allows the user to enter a material, plant, recipe group, and a date range. The output shows the changes per object, which can include the item, the date change, and the user who made the change.

C261	Display Change Documents for a Recipe Group

This transaction displays the changes made to a recipe group. The initial screen allows the user to enter the recipe group, a date range for changes to be displayed, and the user who made the change. The output shows the date and time a change was made, the user who made the change, and the transaction used to make the change.

C298	Deletion of Task Lists without Archiving

This transaction is used to delete task lists but without archiving. The initial selection screen allows the user to enter a material, plant, group, status, task list usage or planner group. The transaction will propose a number of relevant task lists from which the user can deselect those that do not need to be deleted.

CA01	Create Routing

This transaction is used to create a routing, which is a description of which operations have to be carried out, and in what order, to produce a material. On the initial screen, the user needs to add a material and plant. On the next screen, the user needs to enter a value for the usage and a status. Operations can be added to the routing, including the work center, control key and description.

CA02	Change Routing

This transaction is used to change an existing routing. The initial screen requires a material and plant to be entered or a group number. The OPERATION OVERVIEW screen

is displayed, where the user can add new operations or change existing ones.

CA03	Display Routing

This transaction is used to display an existing routing. The initial screen requires a material and plant to be entered or a group number. The transaction displays all the operations for the routing. The user can review other aspects of the routing, such as production resource/tool and inspection characteristics.

CA10	Standard Text

This transaction is used to create, change or display standard texts. The initial screen allows the user to enter a new standard text by entering a standard text key and a description. The next screen gives the user the option of entering a full screen of free-format text. If a standard text exists, then the screen will show the existing text, which can be changed.

CA11	Create Reference Operation Set

This transaction is used to create a reference operation set. The initial screen does not require a group number to be entered. The HEADER DETAILS screen requires the user to enter the task list usage and the status key. Operations can be added with on the OPERATION OVERVIEW screen. Inspection characteristics can be entered for each operation.

CA12	Change Reference Operation Set

This transaction allows the user to change an existing reference operation set. The initial screen requires the user to enter a group number. The OPERATION OVERVIEW screen allows the user to enter a new operation or change an existing one. For each operation, the inspection characteristics can be changed or added.

CA13	Display Reference Operation Set

This transaction is used to display an existing reference operation set. The initial screen requires the user enter a group number. The transaction shows the operations associated with the group number. The user can review other aspects of the routing, such as production resource/tool and inspection characteristics.

CA21	Create Rate Routing

This transaction is used to create a rate routing, which is used when you plan on a quantity basis, for example in repetitive manufacturing. The initial screen does not require a group number to be entered. The HEADER DETAILS screen requires the user to enter the task list usage and the status key. Operations can be added on the OPERATION OVERVIEW screen. Inspection characteristics can be entered for each operation.

CA22	Change Rate Routing

This transaction allows the user to change an existing rate routing. The initial screen requires the user to enter a group number. The OPERATION OVERVIEW screen allows the user to enter a new operation or change an existing one. For each operation, the inspection characteristics can be changed or added.

CA23	Display Rate Routing

This transaction is used to display an existing rate routing. The initial screen requires the user to enter a group number. The transaction shows the operations associated with the group number. The user can review other aspects of the routing, such

as production resource/tool and inspection characteristics.

CA31	Create Reference Rate Routing

This transaction is used to create a reference rate routing, which is used when you plan on a quantity basis, for example in repetitive manufacturing. The initial screen does not require a group number to be entered. The HEADER DETAILS screen requires the user to enter the task list usage and the status key. Operations can be added with on the OPERATION OVERVIEW screen. Inspection characteristics can be entered for each operation.

CA32	Change Reference Rate Routing

This transaction allows the user to change an existing reference rate routing. The initial screen requires a group number to be entered. The OPERATION OVERVIEW screen allows the user to enter a new operation or change an existing one. For each operation, the inspection characteristics can be changed or added.

CA33	Display Reference Rate Routing

This transaction is used to display an existing reference rate routing. The initial screen requires the user to enter a group number. The transaction shows the operations associated with the group number. The user can review other aspects of the routing, such as production resource/tool and inspection characteristics.

CA60	Task List Changes

This transaction is used to display the changes made to a task list. The initial screen requires the recipe group to be entered. The output screen shows each change by object, item, validity date, and the user who made the change.

| CA62 | Display Change Documents for Reference Operation Set Group |

This transaction is used to display the changes for a reference operation set group. The initial screen requires a reference operation set group to be entered as well as an optional date range. The output screen shows each change to the reference operation set group. The details of each change are shown, including the change date and time, the user who made the change, and the date the change is valid from.

| CA63 | Display Change Documents for a Rate Routing |

This transaction is used to display the changes for a rate routing. The initial screen requires a rate routing to be entered as well as an optional date range. The output screen shows each change to the rate routing. The details of each change are shown, including the change date and time, the user who made the change, and the date the change is valid from.

| CA64 | Display Change Documents for a Reference Rate Routing Group |

This transaction is used to display the changes for a reference rate routing. The initial screen requires a reference rate routing to be entered as well as an optional date range. The output screen shows each change to the reference rate routing. The details of each change are shown, including the change date and time, the user who made the change, and the date the change is valid from.

| CA70 | Use of PRT in Task Lists |

This transaction is used to find which task lists a production/resource tool is used in. On the initial screen, the user will need to enter the PRT material number, the plant number, and which task list types should be searched. The user can enter other optional search criteria to restrict the output, such as status, usage, and planner group.

| CA75 | Replace PRT in Task Lists |

This transaction is used to make a mass change of a production resource/tool in selected task lists. On the initial screen, the user will need to enter the PRT material number, the plant number, and which task list types should be searched. The user can enter other optional search criteria to restrict the output, such as status, change number, usage, and planner group.

| CA75N | Mass Change of PRT |

This transaction is used to make a mass change of a production resource/tool in selected task lists. The user can enter the information on four screens. The initial screen allows the user to enter the material and plant. The second tab is for the task list screen, where the user can enter the task list or the task list types to be searched. The third tab is where the user can enter the new values, such as the material number. The final tab gives the user the option to delete multiple entries.

| CA80 | Work Center Where-Used |

This transaction is used to display the task lists in which a specific work center is used. The initial screen requires the user to enter a work center, plant, and the task list types to be searched. The user can optionally enter other search criteria, such as status, usage, and planner group. The resulting display shows the task lists in which the work center is used in material order. The details displayed include the task list usage, validity dates, and control key.

CA81   Resource Where-Used

This transaction is used to display the task lists in which a specific resource is used. The initial screen requires the user to enter a resource, plant, and the task list types to be searched. The user can optionally enter other search criteria, such as status, usage, and planner group. The resulting display shows the task lists in which the resource is used in material order.

CA85   Replace Work Center

This transaction is used when a work center needs to be replaced in a selection of task lists. The initial screen requires the old and the new work center to be entered as well as the task list type. The user can optionally enter other search criteria, such as status, usage, and planner group. The resulting display shows the task lists in which the old work center is used, and the user can select the task lists in which the old work center needs to be replaced.

CA85N   Mass Change Work Center

This transaction allows the user to perform a mass change of work centers. The initial screen allows the user to enter a number of fields, such as material, plant, task list type, and planner group. The next screen gives the user the option to enter the new values for the work center and other data, such as control key, standard text key, and wage group.

CA87   Replace Work Center

This transaction is used when a work center needs to be replaced in a selection of task lists. The initial screen requires the old and the new work center to be entered as well as the task list type. The user can optionally enter other search criteria, such as status, usage, and planner group. The resulting

display shows the task lists in which the old work center is used; the user can select the task lists in which the old work center needs to be replaced.

CA90   Use of Reference Operation Set in Task Lists

This transaction is used to find which task lists use a particular reference operation. On the initial screen the user will need to enter the group number, group counter, and which task list types should be searched. The user can enter other optional search criteria to restrict the output, such as status, usage, and planner group.

CA95   Replace Reference Operation Set

This transaction allows a user to replace a reference operation with a new reference operation. The initial screen requires the user to enter the old reference operation, the new reference operation, and the operation increment. The user can optionally enter other search criteria, such as status, usage, and planner group. The resulting display shows the task lists in which the old reference operation is used; the user can select the task lists in which the old reference option needs to be replaced.

CA95N   Mass Change Ref. Operation Set Reference

This transaction allows a user to replace a reference operation with a new reference operation. The initial screen requires the user to enter the old reference operation, the new reference operation. The next screen provides the user the opportunity to enter the task list type, status, usage, plant, and planner group. The final screen gives the user the option to delete multiple entries.

CA96	Update Material Master with Scheduling Results

This transaction is used to transfer scheduling results to a material master record. The initial screen requires the user to enter a plant and the production scheduler. The next screen displays the scheduling results for materials that can be updated. The set-up time, processing time, interoperation time, and assembly scrap can be updated in the material master record.

CA97	Update Material Master with Scheduling Results

This transaction is used to transfer scheduling results to a material master record. The initial screen requires the user to enter a single or range of material numbers, a plant, and a production scheduler. The user can select to have the material master records updated directly, updated with assembly scrap, or have the transaction carry out a CAPP calculation.

CA98	Deletion of Task Lists without Archiving

This transaction allows the user to delete task lists for a material. The initial screen requires the user to enter a material number, plant, and task list type. When executed, the transaction will delete the relevant task lists for the material, but there is no archiving of task lists, unlike transaction CA99.

CC01	Create a Change Master

This transaction is used to create a change master record. The initial screen allows the user to enter whether the change is a change master or an engineering change record. The following screen requires the user to enter a description for the change master record, a date from when the change is valid, and a status for the change master. The next screen gives the user the ability to determine which objects are valid for the change master, such as material, task list, or bill of materials.

CC02	Change a Change Master

This transaction is used to change a change master record. The initial screen requires the user to enter a change number. The following screen allows the user to change the validity date, authorization group and the reason for the change.

CC03	Display a Change Master

This transaction is used to display a change master record. The initial screen requires the user to enter a change number. The next screen will display the details of the change record, such as description, validity date, authorization group, status, and the reason for the change.

CC04	Product Structure Browser

This transaction is used to display the details for the product. The initial screen has a number of tabs from which the user can choose. These tabs are for the material, document, change number, characteristic, class, equipment, and functional location. The user can enter information into one of the screens and the output will show the structure. For example, if a material is entered, the output will show a where-used list including the bill of materials it can be found within.

CC05	Change Overview

This transaction is used to display details relating to the change number. The initial screen has no mandatory selection fields, but the user can enter a change number, validity date, status, or a change type. The output shows the objects that have been affected by the individual change number. The output is shown in change number order.

CC07 Change Number Selection

This transaction is used to display the details of a change number. The initial screen allows the user to enter a single or range of change numbers, as well as other selection criteria, such as validity date, and the user who created the change. The output screen shows the change number from which you can drill down to materials, bills of materials, or routings, where it was used.

CK11N Create Material Cost Estimate with Quantity Structure

This transaction is used to create a material cost estimate. The initial screen requires the user to enter the material, plant number, and the costing variant. The next screen allows the user to enter the to and from dates for the validity of the cost estimate as well as the quantity structure date and the validation date. The transaction then shows the costing structure and the costs for each element in the structure.

CK13N Display Material Cost Estimate with Quantity Structure

This transaction is used to display the material cost estimates for a material at a specific plant. The initial screen requires the user to enter a material, plant and a costing variant. The subsequent screen shows the costing structure and the costs for each element in the structure.

CK24 Price Update: Mark Standard Price

This transaction is used to update the standard price of materials. The initial screen requires the user to enter a posting period and fiscal year for the price update. The user can enter a specific company code, plant or material. There is also the option to flag the transaction so that the transaction will be run

in test run mode only. The output screen of this transaction shows the future planned price for each material selected.

CK31 Print Error Log for Costing Run

This transaction is used to print any error log for a specific costing run. The initial screen requires the user to enter a costing run along with the relevant costing run date. The user can indicate which log he or she wants to print, such as the log for selection, costing, marking, release, or structure explosion. The transaction requires a printer to be entered, and the result is sent to the spool queue. The output will show the information, warning, and error logs for the costing run.

CK33 Comparison of Itemizations

This transaction is used to compare two costing estimates. The initial screen allows the user to enter the details of the two cost estimates, such as material, plant, costing variant, costing version and date. After the two cost estimates are entered, the transaction shows the details of the two cost estimates with differences shown as an absolute value or a percentage.

CK40N Edit Costing Run

This transaction is used to edit an existing costing run. The initial screen requires the user to enter a costing run. The transaction allows the user to create a cost estimate for the selection, as well as a structure explosion, costing, analysis of material cost estimates, marking and release.

CK41 Create Costing Run (Material)

This transaction is used to create a costing run. The initial screen requires the user to enter a title for the costing run and a costing run date. The next screen requires a description to be added as well as a costing variant and a company code. The update parameters and print parameters need to be completed before the transaction is executed.

CK42 — Change Costing Run (Material)

This transaction is used to change a costing run. The initial screen requires the user to enter the costing run and a costing run date. On the subsequent screen, the user can change the costing variant, controlling area, and the company code. The print parameters can also be changed so that the user can select which costing report to print.

CK43 — Display Costing Run (Material)

This transaction is used to display a costing run. The initial screen requires the user to enter a costing run and the costing run date. The next screen shows the general data for the costing run, such as the costing variant, costing version, transfer control, and company code. The user can select to display the update parameters and the print parameters.

CK44 — Delete Costing Run

This transaction is used to delete a costing run. The initial screen requires the user to enter a costing run and the costing run date. The other option the user has on the initial screen is to execute the transaction as a background job. When the transaction is executed, the details of the costing run are displayed. The user then has the option to confirm the deletion of the costing run.

CK80 — Cost Component Report for Product Cost Estimate

This transaction shows the cost component report for a cost estimate. The initial screen requires the user to enter a material, plant and costing variant. The transaction displays the line item report for the material showing the overall, fixed and variable cost for each component.

CK82 — List of Existing Material Cost Estimates

This transaction displays the cost estimates for a material. The initial screen requires the user to enter a plant, material, and costing variant. When the transaction is executed, the resulting screen shows details for the cost estimate, such as costing status, costing version, overall cost, and fixed cost.

CK84 — Line Items in Cost Estimate for Product

This transaction shows the line items in the cost estimate for a material. The initial screen the user to enter a material, plant and costing variant. The output screen displays the line item report for the material showing the total and fixed value for each item.

CK85 — Line Item Report Costing Items

This transaction is used to display the costing report for each item on a sales order. The initial screen requires the user to enter a sales order number. When the transaction is executed, the output screen displayed shows the line items relevant to the sales order. Each item shows the item category, resource, cost element, total value, fixed value and quantity.

CK86 — Costed Multilevel BOM, Material Cost Estimate

This transaction shows the bill of materials hierarchy for the cost estimate for a material. The initial screen requires the user to enter a material, plant and costing variant. The next screen shows the hierarchy of the bill of materials explosion. The user can choose other options from the hierarchy screen, such as the cost component view or line items for the material view.

CK87	Costed Multilevel BOM, Sales Order Cost Estimate

This transaction shows the bill of materials hierarchy for the cost estimate for a sales order. The initial screen requires the user to enter a sales order number and the item number. The next screen shows the hierarchy of the bill of materials explosion. The user can choose other options from the hierarchy screen, such as the cost component view or line items for the material view.

CK88	Partner Cost Component Split

This transaction is used to produce a report that shows the partner component split. The initial screen requires the user to enter a plant, material and costing estimate. The user can enter a cost component view, such as for the cost of goods manufactured, cost of goods sold, inventory, etc.

CK89	Cost Component Report for Sales Document Cost Estimate

This transaction is used to display the cost component report for the sales document cost estimate. The initial screen allows the user to enter a sales order and a sales order item number. The line item report displays the cost components for the sales order. Each cost component shows the overall, fixed, and variable costs.

CK91	Create Procurement Alternative

This transaction is used to create a procurement alternative for a material. The initial screen requires a material and a plant to be entered. In addition, the initial screen allows the user to select a process category, such as production, purchase order, subcontracting, etc. The subsequent screen reflects the process

category that was entered; the user needs to enter the specific information required.

CK91N	Display Procurement Alternatives

This transaction is used to display the procurement alternatives for a specific material at a plant. The initial screen requires a material and a plant to be entered. The resulting screen shows the procurement alternatives for the material and plant combination. The information can be seen by drilling down on the list of procurement alternatives.

CK92	Change Procurement Alternatives

This transaction is used to change procurement alternatives for a specific material at a plant. The initial screen requires a material and a plant to be entered. The subsequent screen shows the process categories for the material and plant combination. The user can select the appropriate process category and display the details to be changed.

CK93	Display Procurement Alternatives

This transaction is used to display the procurement alternatives for a specific material at a plant. The initial screen requires a material and a plant to be entered. The subsequent screen shows the process categories for the material and plant combination. The user can select the appropriate process category and display the details.

CK94	Change Mixing Ratios

This transaction is used to change the mixing ratios for procurement alternatives. The initial screen requires a material, plant, quantity structure type and fiscal year to be entered. The next screen shows the procurement alternatives and a mixing ratio can be entered for each. The mixing ratio is a weighting that is applied when the cost estimate of a procurement alternative is factored into the mixed cost estimate.

CK95	Display Mixing Ratios

This transaction is used to display the mixing ratios for procurement alternatives. The initial screen requires a material, plant, quantity structure type and fiscal year to be entered. The next screen shows the procurement alternatives and the mixing ratio for each.

CKC1	Check Costing Variant

This transaction is used to display the parameters that are linked to the costing variant and the assigned cost component layout. The initial screen requires the user to enter a costing variant, company code, and plant. The output shows a list of parameters for the costing variant, which allows you to check your settings for product costing.

CKR1	Reorganization of Cost Estimates

This transaction is used to reorganize the cost estimates for a company code, plant or material number. The initial screen allows the user to enter a company code, plant or material number. The user can also enter a control parameter and an option for processing. When executed, the transaction will display the cost estimates that have been reorganized.

CKW1	Create Cost Estimate for Production Lot

This transaction is used to create a cost estimate for a production lot. The initial screen requires the user to enter a costing variant, WBS element, material and plant. The next screen requires the user to enter the quantity structure date and a validation date. The

transaction displays the costing data for the WBS element, and the cost estimate can then be saved.

CKW3	Display Cost Estimate for Production Lot

This transaction is used to display a cost estimate for a production lot. The initial screen requires the user to enter a costing variant, WBS element, material and plant. The next screen shows the costing estimate for the WBS element.

CKW4	Activate Cost Estimate for Production Lot

This transaction is used to activate a cost estimate for a production lot. The initial screen requires the user to enter a costing variant, WBS element, material and plant. The transaction will show a pop-up screen that asks whether the user wishes to activate the costing estimate. If the user selects YES then cost estimate will be activated.

CM01	Capacity Planning: Selection (Work Center – Load)

This transaction is used for analysis purpose and capacity leveling. The initial screen allows the user to enter a work center and a plant number. The output display gives an overview of the available capacity, the capacity requirements for planned and production orders, and the capacity load in percentage for the next 60 working days summarized in a weekly format. If there is an overload, this is displayed with a red figure.

CM02	Capacity Planning: Selection (Orders)

This transaction is used for analysis purpose and capacity leveling. The initial screen requires a work center and plant to be entered. The output display shows the capacity details, which gives an overview of the planned and production orders that form the capacity requirement for the next 60 working days.

CM03	Capacity Planning: Selection (Work Center – Pool)

This transaction is used for analysis purposes and capacity leveling. The initial screen requires a work center and plant to be entered. The output will display an overview of the available capacity, the capacity requirements for released production orders, and the capacity load in percentage for the next 14 working days in a daily format. If there is an overload, this is displayed with a red figure.

CM04	Capacity Planning: Selection (Work Center – Backlog)

This transaction is used for analysis purposes and capacity leveling. The initial screen requires a work center and plant to be entered. The transaction output shows the capacity details, which gives an overview of the planned and production orders that should have been finished at least one day ago.

CM05	Capacity Planning: Selection (Work Center – Overload)

This transaction is used for analysis purpose and capacity leveling. The initial screen requires a work center and plant to be entered. The transaction shows an overview of the available capacity, the capacity requirements for planned and production orders, and the capacity load in percentage for the next 60 working days summarized in a weekly format. Only weeks with overload are displayed.

CM22	Capacity Leveling: SFC Planning Table

This transaction is used for capacity leveling, which overloads and underloads at work centers, achieving optimum commitment of machines and production lines, and selection of appropriate resources. The initial screen allows the user to enter a work center, plant, capacity category, and a capacity planning group. On the output screen, which shows the period requirements per resource, the user can dispatch, dispatch manually, or deallocate.

CM23	Capacity Leveling: SFC Orders Tab

This transaction is used for capacity leveling, which overloads and underloads at work centers, achieving optimum commitment of machines and production lines, and selection of appropriate resources. The initial screen allows the user to enter an order or a planned order. On the output screen, the user can dispatch, dispatch manually, or deallocate.

CM24	Capacity Leveling (Individual Capacity – Tabular)

This transaction is used for capacity leveling, which overloads and underloads at work centers, achieving optimum commitment of machines and production lines, and selection of appropriate resources. The initial screen allows the user to enter a work center, plant, and capacity category. On the output screen, which shows the period requirements per resource, the user can dispatch, dispatch manually, or deallocate.

CM26	Capacity Leveling: Project View Tabular

This transaction is used for capacity leveling, which overloads and underloads at work centers, achieving optimum commitment of machines and production lines, and selection of appropriate resources. The initial screen allows the user to enter a single or range of WBS elements. On the output screen, which shows the period requirements per resource, the user can dispatch, dispatch manually, or deallocate.

CM28	Capacity Leveling: SFC Individual Capacity Tab

This transaction is used for capacity leveling, which overloads and underloads at work centers, achieving optimum commitment of machines and production lines, and selection of appropriate resources. The initial screen allows the user to enter a work center, plant, and capacity category. On the output screen, which shows the period requirements per resource, the user can dispatch, dispatch manually, or deallocate.

CM34	Capacity Leveling (Work Center – Tabular)

This transaction is used for capacity leveling, which overloads and underloads at work centers, achieving optimum commitment of machines and production lines, and selection of appropriate resources. The initial screen allows the user to enter a work center and a plant. On the output screen, which shows the period requirements per resource, the user can dispatch, dispatch manually, or deallocate.

CM35	Capacity Leveling (Resource View – Table)

This transaction is used for capacity leveling, which overloads and underloads at work centers, achieving optimum commitment of machines and production lines, and selection of appropriate resources. The initial screen allows the user to enter a work center, plant and capacity category. On the output screen, which shows the period requirements per

resource, the user can dispatch, dispatch manually, or deallocate.

CM36	Capacity Leveling (Process Order View)

This transaction is used for capacity leveling, which overloads and underloads at work centers, achieving optimum commitment of machines and production lines, and selection of appropriate resources. The initial screen allows the user to enter a single or range of orders and a single or range of planned orders. On the output screen, which shows the period requirements per resource, the user can dispatch, dispatch manually, or deallocate.

CM50	Capacity Leveling: SFC Work Center List

This transaction is used for capacity leveling, which overloads and underloads at work centers, achieving optimum commitment of machines and production lines, and selection of appropriate resources. The initial screen allows the user to enter a work center, plant and capacity category. The output screen shows the remaining capacity requirements per period, the available capacity per period, and the remaining available capacity for each work center.

CO01	Create a Production Order

This transaction is used to create a production order. The user is required to enter a material number and a plant. The user can enter an order type, such as a standard order, costing order or kanban order. The next screen requires a total quantity to be entered for the order as well as a start and end date for the order. The transaction will copy the BOM and routing into the order and then carry out the scheduling. The order can then be saved, causing the costs to be determined, and the transaction will finally display an order number.

CO01S — Create a Simulation Order

This transaction allows a user to create a simulation order. A simulation order enables a user to see how changes to initial data, e.g. a sales order, affect a production order. A user can use the simulation order to find errors in the material configuration. The simulation order is structured like a production order but has no effect on operations.

CO02 — Change a Production Order

This transaction is used to change an existing production order. The initial screen requires the user to enter a production order. The next screen shows the header information with a number of tabs that can be selected to view other screens, such as ASSIGNMENT, CONTROL DATA, MASTER DATA and ADMINISTRATION. On the GENERAL screen, the user can change the order quantity, scrap portion, and the start and finish dates for the production order.

CO02S — Change a Simulation Order

This transaction allows a user to change an existing simulation order. A simulation order enables a user to see how changes to initial data, e.g. a sales order, affect a production order. A user can use the simulation order to find errors in the material configuration. The simulation order is structured like a production order but has no effect on operations. The user can change the same data that he or she would find in a production order, such as order quantity, and start and finish dates.

CO03 — Display a Production Order

This transaction is used to display an existing production order. The initial screen requires the user to enter a production order. The user can then display details from any of the accessible screens, such as assignment, control data, master data and administration.

CO03S — Display a Simulation Order

This transaction allows a user to display an existing simulation order. A simulation order enables a user to see how changes to initial data, e.g. a sales order, affect a production order. A user can use the simulation order to find errors in the material configuration. The simulation order is structured like a production order but has no effect on operations. The user can display details from any of the accessible screens such as assignment, control data, master data and administration.

CO04 — Print Shop Papers

This transaction gives the user the ability to print or reprint shop papers for orders at a specific plant. The initial screen requires the user to enter a plant number and choose whether the original print-out or a reprint is required. The user can enter other selection criteria such as MRP controller, production scheduler, order type, material or order number. The next screen shows a number of relevant production orders where the shop papers can be printed.

CO04N — Print Production Orders

This transaction gives the user the opportunity to print details for a single or range of production orders. The initial screen requires the user to enter at least one selection criterion, such as material, order type, MRP controller, sales order, WBS element or work center. The next screen shows a list of production orders that can be printed. The user can select the required orders and print the required document.

CO05N Release Production Orders

This transaction is used to release production orders. The initial screen requires the user to enter at least one selection criterion, such as material, order type, MRP controller, sales order, WBS element or work center. The next screen shows a list of production orders that can be released. The user can select the relevant orders and the background processing will release the orders if there are no errors.

CO06 Backorder Processing

This transaction is used to perform backorder processing for a material. The initial screen requires a user to enter a material and a plant. The overview screen shows the available to promise (ATP) situation for the material at the plant. If necessary, the user can change the confirmation and reschedule.

CO07 Create a Production Order
(Without Material)

This transaction is used to create a production order where no material number is entered. The initial screen requires the plant and order type to be entered. The user has the option to enter a sales order number, WBS element or a production order number. The next screen requires the user to enter a description for the material to be produced, the total quantity to be produced, the start and finish dates, and any scrap percentage. The transaction will return a production order number when processed.

CO08 Create a Production Order
(For Sales Order)

This transaction is used to create a production order for a sales order. The initial screen requires the user to enter the sales order and sales order item number. The user can add other selection criteria, such as material, plant and order type. The next screen requires a total quantity to be entered for the order as well as a start and end date for the order. The transaction will copy the BOM and routing into the order and then carry out the scheduling. The order can then be saved, causing the costs to be determined, and the transaction will finally display an order number.

CO09 Availability Overview

This transaction is used to display an overview of the availability of a material. The initial screen requires the user to enter a material and a plant. The overview screen shows the available to promise (ATP) situation for the material at the plant. The transaction shows the MRP elements, such as production orders, purchase requirements, sales orders, etc.

CO10 Create a Production Order
(For WBS Element)

This transaction creates a production order for a WBS element. The initial screen requires the user to enter a WBS element, a material number and a plant. The next screen requires a total quantity to be entered for the order as well as a start and end date for the order. The order can then be saved, causing the costs to be determined, and the transaction will finally display an order number.

CO11 Enter Production Order
Confirmation

This transaction is used to enter the confirmation details for a production order. The initial screen requires the user to enter a confirmation number or an order number and operation. The next screen allows the user to enter the confirmation type and the confirmation details, such as yield, scrap and rework. The confirmation can then be saved, during which the costs are calculated.

CO11N	Enter Time Ticket for Production Order

This transaction allows the user to enter a time ticket for a production order. The initial screen requires the user to enter either a confirmation number or an order number and operation. In addition, the user can enter the confirmation details, such as yield, scrap and rework, in addition to the time spent on the activities performed during the operation.

CO12	Collective Entry: Time Ticket

This transaction is used to enter the time ticket information for a number of confirmations. The initial screen allows the user to enter the confirmation number, yield, scrap quantity, rework quantity, posting date, personnel number, work center, and the details for the activities.

CO13	Cancel Production Order Confirmation

This transaction is used to cancel a confirmation for a production order. The initial screen allows the user to enter a confirmation number or a production order and operation number. The user can enter the reason that the confirmation needs to be cancelled. After processing, the transaction will display a message indicating that the confirmation has been cancelled.

CO14	Display Production Order Confirmation

This transaction is used to display a production order confirmation. The initial screen allows the user to enter a confirmation number or a production order and operation number. The transaction will display the information entered for the confirmation such as yield, scrap and rework, in addition to the time spent on the activities performed during the operation.

CO15	Enter Production Order Confirmation

This transaction is used to enter the confirmation details for a production order. The initial screen requires a user to enter the relevant production order number. The next screen allows the user to enter the type of confirmation, the yield, confirmed scrap, rework, and the execution start and end date.

CO16N	Reprocessing Incorrect Confirmations

This transaction allows the user to reprocess incorrect confirmations for a production order. The initial screen allows the user to enter a production order number, a plant, confirmation number, WBS element, sales order, production scheduler or work center. The transaction will then reprocess the incorrect confirmations based on the selection criteria.

CO27	Picking List for Production Orders

This transaction can generate picking lists for a single or range of production orders. The initial screen allows the user to enter a number of selection criteria, including production order, material, plant, order type, MRP controller, sales order, WBS element, and work center. After the user has entered the selection criteria, the transaction will display a list of relevant production orders. The user can then select which orders should be picked.

CO40	Create a Production Order (Planned Order)

This transaction is used to create a production order from an existing planned order. The initial screen requires the user to enter a planned order number and an order type. The next screen allows the user to change the total quantity and the scrap percentage. After the user has entered any further information, the transaction can be saved and a production order number will be generated.

CO41	Collective Conversion of Planned Orders

This transaction is used to create production orders from a number of planned orders. The initial screen requires the user to enter a planning plant or production plant. The transaction will return a list of planned orders for the selection criteria that were entered. The user can select the relevant planned orders and then convert them to production orders.

CO43	Actual Overhead Calculation: Production/Process Orders

This transaction is used to calculate the actual overhead for production and process orders. The initial screen requires the user to enter a plant number, period, and fiscal year, and to select which types of orders are to be included, such as production orders, process orders and QM orders. The user can also select whether to run the transaction as a test run. The subsequent screen shows the processing details, such as number of orders for which the overhead was calculated, the number of orders that are not relevant, and the number of errors.

CO44	Mass Processing for Orders

This transaction is used to perform a processing on a number of orders. The transaction executes a number of functions for a range of process orders and production orders. The processing functions include scheduling, costing, capacity requirements, WM material staging, complete technically, and close the order. The user can enter a wide range of selection criteria, such as order type, plant, MRP controller, material number, order

number, and sales order. The user can select which functions to process and can run the transaction in test mode if desired.

CO46	Order Progress Report: Selection Screen

This transaction is used to display the progress of a sales order, project, WBS element, production order, planned order or network. The initial screen has the option to enter a value for one of the choices, for example, a production order, and the transaction will display the progress of the order and show any exceptions that may have occurred, such as a delay because of a missing material.

CO48	Create a Production Order (Partial Conversion of Planned Order)

This transaction is used to create a production order by partially converting a planned order. The initial screen requires the user to enter a planned order number and an order type. The next screen allows the user to change the order quantity, along with the start and finish dates. Production order can then be generated and a production order number will be displayed.

CO78	Archiving of Production Orders

This transaction allows the user to archive production orders. The initial screen gives the user a selection so that he or she can set the deletion flag on orders, archive the orders, delete the orders and retrieve orders from archive. The user can set the deletion flag on a range of production orders by using a variant with the first option of this transaction.

CO88	Actual Settlement: Production/Process Orders

This transaction is used to perform the actual settlement for a range of production and process orders. The initial screen requires the user to enter a plant number, period, and fiscal year, and to select which types of orders are to be included, such as production orders, process orders and QM orders. The user can also select whether the transaction should be processed automatically or by period; in addition, the user can run the transaction as a test run. The subsequent screen shows the processing details, such as number of orders where the overhead was calculated, the number of orders that are not relevant, and the number of errors.

COB1	Create Batch Search Strategy

This transaction is used to create a batch search strategy. The initial screen requires the user to enter a strategy type, which controls the selection criteria, sort rule and the quantity proposal. The subsequent screen allows the user to enter validity dates for the strategy and then a number of materials can be added that will be relevant for the batch search strategy.

COB2	Change Batch Search Strategy

This transaction is used to change an existing batch search strategy. The initial screen requires the user to enter a strategy type, which controls the selection criteria, sort rule and the quantity proposal. The next screen allows the user to enter a single or range of materials can be changed. The subsequent screen shows the information for each material and the user can change the details, such as the number of batch splits, the quantity proposal, and the selection type.

COB3	Display Batch Search Strategy

This transaction is used to display an existing batch search strategy. The initial screen requires the user to enter a strategy type, which controls the selection criteria, sort rule and the quantity proposal. The next screen allows the user to enter a single or range of materials can be changed. The subsequent screen shows the information for each material and the user can review the details, such as the number of batch splits, the quantity proposal, and the selection type.

COFC	Reprocessing of Confirmations with Errors

This transaction is used to reprocess confirmations that have errors in the calculation of actual costs. The initial screen allows the user to enter a number of selection criteria to restrict the reprocessing; these include the order category, order number, confirmation number, and the date created. The subsequent screen shows the orders that have been found using the selection criteria. These orders can then be reviewed and reprocessed if appropriate.

COHV	Mass Processing Production Orders

This transaction allows the user to perform mass processing on a number of production orders. On the initial screen, the user can select the MASS PROCESSING tab and choose which process to complete, such as confirmation, costing, release, scheduling, etc. The user can then access the selection screen and enter data into the selection criteria fields to choose the appropriate orders. The transaction will display the relevant orders. The user can select those orders that require the necessary processing.

COMAC	Collective Availability Check

This transaction allows the user to perform mass processing on a number of production orders for the material availability check. On the initial screen, the user can select the MASS PROCESSING tab and choose which scope of processing is required, such as ATP check for all materials or individual checks. The user can then access the selection screen and enter data into the selection criteria fields to choose the appropriate orders. The transaction will display the relevant orders and the user can select the orders for which the availability check should be performed.

COOIS	Production Order Information System

This transaction allows the user to review information on a number of selected production orders. The initial screen requires the user to enter selection criteria to restrict the number of production orders to be reviewed. The subsequent screen shows the production orders relevant to the search. The user can then select the orders to be reviewed and then select to see the operation overview, component overview, status, configuration, stock/requirements list, and the stock overview.

COPD	Print Process Order

This transaction is used to print process orders. The initial screen gives the user a number of selection criteria to enter to restrict the number of process orders to select from. These criteria include the process order number, plant, production scheduler, MRP controller and order type. The transaction will display the orders based on the criteria and the user can select the relevant orders for printing.

COPI	Print Process Order Shop Floor Papers

This transaction gives the user the ability to print or reprint shop papers for orders at a specific plant. The initial screen requires the user to enter a plant number and to choose the original print-out or a reprint. The user can enter other selection criteria, such as MRP controller, production scheduler, order type, material or order number. The next

screen shows a number of relevant production orders where the shop papers can be printed.

COR1	Create Process Order

This transaction is used to create a process order. The initial screen requires the user to enter a material number, a plant and an order type. The next screen requires the user to enter the total quantity of the process order, the start and finish dates, and the type of scheduling required, such as backwards or forwards scheduling. After processing, the transaction will display the process order number that has been generated.

COR2	Change Process Order

This transaction is used to change an existing process order. The initial screen requires the user to enter a process order number. The next screen is the GENERAL DATA screen, on which the user can change the total quantity of the process order, the start and finish dates, and the type of scheduling required, such as backwards or forwards scheduling. The other screens that can be accessed are the ASSIGNMENT, GOODS RECEIPT, CONTROL DATA, and MASTER DATA screens.

COR3	Display Process Order

This transaction is used to display a process order. The initial screen requires the user to enter a process order number. The next screen is the GENERAL DATA screen, on which the user can display the total quantity of the process order, the start and finish dates, and the type of scheduling required, such as backwards or forwards scheduling. The other screens that can be displayed are the ASSIGNMENT, GOODS RECEIPT, CONTROL DATA, and MASTER DATA screens.

COR5	Release Process Order

This transaction is used to release process orders that have been created. The initial screen requires the user to enter a plant; the user can also enter optional selection criteria, such as order type, MRP controller, production scheduler, process order number and release date. The transaction will show relevant process orders based on the selection criteria and the user can select the required process orders and release them. If there are any errors, the transaction will indicate that the release has been refused.

COR6	Create Process Order Confirmation

This transaction is used to confirm operations in a process order. The initial screen requires the user to enter a confirmation number or a process order number. The confirmation can be made for an operation in the process order.

COR6N	Enter Time Ticket for Process Order

This transaction allows the user to enter the time ticket information for a process order. The initial screen requires the user to enter a process order number or an order/sequence/operation combination. The user can choose between final and partial confirmation. The total yield and scrap can be entered for the process order.

COR7	Create Process Order from a Planned Order

This transaction allows the user to create a process order from an existing planned order. The initial screen requires the user to enter a planned order number and a process order type. The user has the ability to create a process order based on a partial conversion of the planned order. The next screen allows the user to change the total quantity, start and finish dates of the order, and the type of scheduling.

COR8	Collective Conversion of Planned Orders

This transaction is used to create process orders for a number of planned orders. The initial screen requires the entry of a plant, MRP area or planning plant. The next screen shows all of the planned orders for the selection criteria entered. The user can then select the required planned orders and convert them to process orders. The transaction will process the request, and any errors will be displayed.

CORA	Process Order: Scheduling External Relationships

This transaction is used to schedule external relationships for a process order. The initial screen requires the user to enter a process order. The next screen allows the user to change the start and finish dates of the process order.

CORK	Enter Process Order Confirmation

This transaction is used to enter a confirmation for a process order. The initial screen requires the user to enter the process order number. The next screen allows the yield to be entered as well as the personnel number, execution start and finish times, and any confirmation text.

CORO	Create Process Order without Material

This transaction is used to create a process order without a material number. The initial screen requires the user to enter a recipe group, recipe, plant number, and order type. The next screen shows the general data, where the user can enter the total quantity to be produced, as well as the start and finish dates for the order. Additional data can be entered before the process order is generated.

CORR	Collective Entry of Confirmations

This transaction is used to enter the information for a number of confirmations. The initial screen allows the user to enter the confirmation number, yield, scrap quantity, posting date, personnel number, and the details for the activities.

CORS	Cancel Process Order Confirmation

This transaction is used to cancel a confirmation for a process order. The initial screen allows the user to enter a confirmation number or a process order and operation number. The user can enter the reason that the confirmation is to be cancelled. After processing, the transaction will display a message indicating that the confirmation has been cancelled.

CORT	Display Process Order Confirmation

This transaction is used to display a process order confirmation. The initial screen allows the user to enter a confirmation number or a process order and operation number. The transaction will display the information entered for the confirmation, such as yield, scrap and rework, in addition to the time spent on the activities performed during the operation.

CORZ	Enter Confirmation of Process Order: Create Time Event

This transaction is used to enter a confirmation for a process order. The initial screen allows the user to enter a specific time event,

such as start processing, processing partial finish, interrupt processing, or finish processing. The other information required on the initial screen is either a confirmation number or a process order number.

CR01	Create Work Center

This transaction is used to create a work center at a plant. The initial screen requires the user to enter a plant number, a work center category, and an eight-character work center number. The next screen requires a forty-character work center description, the responsible personnel, the location, task list usage, and rules for standard value maintenance, as it pertains to the set-up, machine and labor standard values. Other information, such as capacities, scheduling, and costing data, can be added before the work center is created.

CR02	Change Work Center

This transaction is used to change a work center at a plant. The initial screen requires a plant and work center to be entered. The next screen allows the user to change the work center description, the responsible personnel, the location, task list usage, and rules for standard value maintenance, as it pertains to the set-up, machine and labor standard values. Other information, such as capacities, scheduling, and costing data, can be changed.

CR03	Display Work Center

This transaction is used to display a work center at a plant. The initial screen requires a plant and work center to be entered. The user can then display information, including general data, default values, capacities, scheduling, costing, and technical data, on a number of screens.

CR05	Work Center List

This transaction is used to display a list of work centers based on the selection criteria entered. The initial screen does not require any mandatory entries, but the list of work centers can be reduced by entering selection criteria such as plant, work center, work center category, and person responsible. The resulting list will show the work centers based on the selection criteria. A work center can be selected and further details on that work center can be displayed.

CR06	Assignment of Work Centers to Cost Centers

This transaction is used to display which cost centers are assigned to a work center. The initial screen has no mandatory fields, but the output can be reduced by entering data into the selection criteria fields, which include the plant, work center, work center category, controlling area, and cost center. The resulting display shows the cost centers assigned to the work centers that are relevant to the search criteria.

CR07	Work Center Capacities

This transaction is used to display the capacity of a work center. The initial screen has no mandatory fields, but the output can be reduced by entering data into the selection criteria fields, which include the plant, work center, work center category, controlling area, and cost center. The resulting display shows work centers and the capacity categories for the work center. The user can select data on the output, such as work center, work center category, or the capacity category, to obtain further information.

CR08	Work Center Hierarchy

This transaction is used to view a work center hierarchy. The initial screen requires the user to enter a plant and hierarchy name. The resulting display shows the whole hierarchy, with the hierarchy level, work center, plant, work center category, and description. More information on each work center can be obtained by selecting a work center from the hierarchy list.

CR09	Standard Text

This transaction is used to create, change, delete, and display a standard text key. The initial screen requires the user enter a new standard text key if one is to be created, or an existing standard text key, if changes are to be made. If a new standard text key is entered, the transaction will display an empty screen where text can be entered. If the standard text key exists, the screen will display the existing text to be changed. The user also has the option to delete existing standard text keys.

CR10	Work Center Change Documents

This transaction is used to display work center change documents. The transaction will display change documents only if the configuration has been set to allow their creation for the work center category. In the initial screen, there are no mandatory fields, but the user can enter selection criteria data to restrict the number of change documents displayed, such as work center and work center category.

CR11	Create Capacity

This transaction is used to create capacity without assigning it to a work center. The initial screen requires the user to enter the plant where the capacity is to be assigned, the capacity category, such as labor or machine, and the name of the new capacity. The next screen provides the user the ability to enter a capacity planner group, factory calendar, start and finish time for the capacity and break times.

CR12 Change Capacity

This transaction is used to change existing capacity. The initial screen requires the user to enter a plant, capacity category and a capacity. The user can then change the capacity description, factory calendar, start and finish time for the capacity and break times.

CR13 Display Capacity

This transaction is used to display existing capacity. The initial screen requires the user to enter a plant, capacity category and a capacity. The user can then display the details of the capacity, such as the capacity description, factory calendar, start and finish time for the capacity and break times.

CR15 Capacity: Where Used

This transaction shows where a capacity has been used. The initial screen requires the user to enter a capacity name, although the user can enter other selection criteria, such as plant, category group, and planner group. The where-used list shows whether the capacity has been used as pooled capacity, basis for scheduling, or as reference available capacity.

CR21 Create Hierarchy

This transaction is used when a work center hierarchy is to be created. The initial screen requires the user to enter a ten-character hierarchy name and a plant number. The next screen requires a description for the hierarchy to be entered; the user can then assign work centers to the hierarchy. The user can assign the work centers to the hierarchy until the structure is complete.

CR22 Change Hierarchy

This transaction is used to change a work center hierarchy. The initial screen requires the user to enter a hierarchy name and a plant number. On the next screen, the user can change the hierarchy description. The user can then review the structure and add or change work center assignment as needed.

CR23 Display Hierarchy

This transaction allows a user to display a work center hierarchy. The initial screen requires a hierarchy name and a plant number to be entered. On the next screen, the user can display the hierarchy description. The user can then review the work center structure as a list or graphically.

CR60 Work Center Information System

This transaction displays the work center information system, which shows information on work centers. The initial screen has no mandatory fields, but there are number of selection criteria that will narrow the resulting display, such as capacity, hierarchies and cost centers. The output shows the work centers that are relevant for the selection criteria entered.

CS01 Create Material Bill of Material

This transaction is used to create a material bill of materials (BOM). The initial screen requires the user to enter a material number, plant number and a BOM usage key, which determines whether a BOM is used universally or just for production, plant maintenance, costing, etc. The next screen allows the user to enter the component materials and the quantities for the new BOM.

CS02	Change Material Bill of Material

This transaction is used to change a material bill of materials (BOM). The initial screen requires the user to enter a material number, plant number and a BOM usage key, which determines whether a BOM is used universally or just for production, plant maintenance, costing, etc. The next screen shows the component materials that have been assigned to the BOM. The user can add a new component material, change the values for an existing component, or delete a component material from the BOM.

CS03	Display Material Bill of Material

This transaction is used to display a material bill of materials (BOM). The initial screen requires the user to enter a material number, plant number and a BOM usage key. The next screen shows the component materials assigned to the material bill of materials.

CS05	Change Bill of Material Group

This transaction allows the user to change a bill of materials group, which is a material bill of materials that is not assigned to a plant. The initial screen requires a bill of materials group or a material/plant/BOM usage key to be entered. The next screen shows the assigned work centers, which can be changed as appropriate.

CS06	Display Bill of Material Group

This transaction allows the user to display a bill of materials group, which is a material bill of materials that is not assigned to a plant. The initial screen requires a bill of materials group or a material/plant/BOM usage key to be entered. The next screen shows the work centers assigned to the bill of materials.

CS07	Create Plant Assignment

This transaction is used to assign a bill of materials group to a plant. The initial screen allows the user to enter a bill of materials group, BOM usage key, and a plant number to assign the BOM group to. On the next screen, the user can select the BOM and execute the transaction to assign it to the relevant plant.

CS08	Change Plant Assignment

This transaction is used to change the assignment of a bill of materials group to a plant. The initial screen allows the user to enter a bill of materials group, BOM usage key, and the plant number that the BOM group is assigned to. The user can delete an assignment to a plant if the bill of materials is no longer required at that facility.

CS09	Display Plant Assignment

This transaction is used to display the assignments for a bill of materials group. The initial screen allows the user to enter a bill of materials group, BOM usage key, and the plant number that the BOM group is assigned to. The next screen shows the allocations for the bill of materials.

CS11	Explode BOM: Level by Level

This transaction allows the user to explode a bill of materials to view the component materials level by level. The initial screen requires the user to enter the material, the plant number and the BOM application, such as plant maintenance, costing, rework, and production. The next screen displays the exploded bill of materials level by level.

CS12	Explode BOM: Multi-Level BOM

This transaction allows the user to explode a bill of materials to view the component materials on a multi-level basis. The initial screen requires the user to enter the material, the plant number and the BOM application, such as plant maintenance, costing, rework, and production. The next screen displays the exploded multi-level bill of materials.

CS13	Explode BOM: Summarized BOM

This transaction allows the user to explode a bill of materials to view a summarized display of the component materials. The initial screen requires the user to enter the material, the plant number and the BOM application, such as plant maintenance, costing, rework, and production. The next screen displays a summarized bill of materials.

CS14	Bill of Material Comparison

This transaction is used to compare two bills of materials and show the display as a summarized comparison, multi-level comparison, or a differentiated comparison. The initial screen requires the user to enter the details for the two bills of material, such as material, plant, BOM usage key. The output shows the differences between the two BOMs.

CS15	Material Where-Used List: Bill of Material

This transaction allows the user to investigate where a material is used, as it pertains to the bill of materials. The user can enter a material into the initial screen, in addition to the type of where-used list required and the type of BOMs to be reviewed. The resulting screen shows the entire bill of materials that the material is used in.

CS20	Mass Changes: Material BOM

This transaction is used to perform a mass change on work centers related to a specific material. The initial screen allows the user to enter a component material number and the user has to select whether the change is for existing item data, add a material, add a document, add a class, or delete an item.

CS21	Mass Changes: Material Selection

This transaction is used to perform a mass change on work centers related to a specific material. The initial screen allows the user to enter a component material number and the user has to select whether the change is for existing item data, add a material, add a document, add a class, or delete an item. This transaction is similar in processing to CS20.

CS22	Mass Changes: Document Selection

This transaction is used to perform a mass change on documents related to a specific document structure. The initial screen allows the user to enter a document number and the user has to select whether the change is for existing item data, add a material, add a document, add a class, or delete an item.

CS23	Mass Changes: Class Selection

This transaction is used to perform a mass change on a class related to a specific material BOM. The initial screen allows the user to enter a class number and the user has to select whether the change is for existing item data, add a material, add a document, add a class, or delete an item.

CS40	Creating Bill of Materials Configurable Link

This transaction is used to create a bill of materials configurable material link. On the initial screen, the user should enter the material, plant and the BOM usage key. On the next screen, the CURRENT ASSIGNMENTS screen, the user selects the material and processed the transaction so that the bill of materials is assigned to the configurable material.

CS41	Change Bill of Materials Configurable Link

This transaction allows the user to delete the bill of materials configurable material link. On the initial screen, the user should enter the material, plant and the BOM usage key. On the next screen, the CURRENT ASSIGNMENTS screen, the user chooses the option to delete and process the transaction so that the bill of materials is no longer assigned to the configurable material.

CS42	Display Bill of Materials Configurable Link

This transaction allows the user to display the bill of materials configurable material link. On the initial screen, the user should enter the material, plant and the BOM usage key.

CS51	Create Standard Bill of Material

This transaction is used to create a standard bill of materials. The initial screen requires a standard object, which does not have a material master record, and a BOM usage key. On the next screen, the user can enter a number of material components with the relevant quantities. After processing, the transaction will display a message indicating that the standard BOM has been created.

CS52	Change Standard BOM

This transaction is used to change a standard bill of materials. The initial screen requires a standard object, which does not have a material master record, and a BOM usage key. On the next screen, the user can enter additional material components with the relevant quantities, change existing components or delete existing components. After processing, the transaction will display a message indicating that the standard BOM has been changed.

CS53	Display Standard BOM

This transaction is used to display a standard bill of materials. The initial screen requires a standard object, which does not have a material master record, and a BOM usage key. On the next screen, the user can review the contents of the standard bill of materials.

CS61	Create Order BOM

This transaction is used to create a bill of materials for a sales order. The initial screen requires the user to enter the sales order number, the sales order item number, the material number and the BOM usage key. The next screen allows the user to enter the component materials and quantities for the bill of materials. After processing, a message will be displayed indicating that a BOM has been created for a customer order.

CS62	Change Order BOM

This transaction is used to change a bill of materials for a sales order. The initial screen requires the user to enter the sales order number, the sales order item number, the material number and the BOM usage key. The next screen allows the user to enter additional component materials and quantities, edit existing components or delete existing components. After processing, a message will be displayed indicating that a BOM has been changed for the customer order.

CS63 Display Order BOM

This transaction is used to display a bill of materials for a sales order. The initial screen requires the user to enter the sales order number, the sales order item number, the material number and the BOM usage key. The next screen allows the user to review the components on the bill of materials for the customer order.

CS71 Create WBS BOM

This transaction is used to create a bill of materials for a WBS element. The initial screen requires the user to enter the WBS element number, material number, plant number, and the BOM usage key. The next screen allows the user to enter the component materials and quantities for the bill of materials. After processing, a message will be displayed indicating that a BOM has been created for the WBS element.

CS72 Change WBS BOM

This transaction is used to change a bill of materials for a WBS element. The initial screen requires the user to enter the WBS element number, the material number, plant number, and the BOM usage key. The next screen allows the user to enter additional component materials and quantities, edit existing components or delete existing components. After processing, a message will be displayed indicating that a BOM has been changed for the WBS element.

CS73 Display WBS BOM

This transaction is used to display a bill of materials for a WBS element. The initial screen requires the user to enter the WBS element, material number, plant number, and the BOM usage key. The next screen allows the user to review the components on the bill of materials for the WBS element.

CS80 Display Change Documents: Material BOM

This transaction is used to display change documents for a material bill of materials. The initial screen requires the user to enter a material number, plant number, and BOM usage key. The next screen gives the user the option to display a document overview or display the full document. The document overview shows the user the document number, date and object ID. The full document display shows all details from the change document.

CS81 Display Change Documents: Standard BOM

This transaction is used to display change documents for a standard bill of materials. The initial screen requires the user to enter a standard object and BOM usage key. The next screen gives the user the option to display a document overview or display the full document. The document overview shows the user the document number, date and object ID. The full document display shows all details from the change document.

CS82 Display Change Documents: Order BOM

This transaction is used to display change documents for a sales order bill of materials. The initial screen requires the user to enter the sales order, the sales order item number, the material number, and BOM usage key. The next screen gives the user the option to display a document overview or display the full document. The document overview shows the user the document number, date and object ID. The full document display shows all details from the change document.

| **CS83** | Display Change Documents: WBS BOM |

This transaction is used to display change documents for a WBS element bill of materials. The initial screen requires the user to enter the WBS element, the material number, the plant number, and BOM usage key. The next screen gives the user the option to display a document overview or display the full document. The document overview shows the user the document number, date and object ID. The full document display shows all details from the change document.

| **CSK1** | Explode BOM: Level by Level |

This transaction explodes the sales order bill of materials, level by level. The initial screen requires the user to enter the sales order number, sales order item number, material number, and application. The next screen displays the sales order bill of materials, level by level.

| **CSK2** | Explode BOM: Multi-Level BOM |

This transaction explodes the multi-level sales order bill of materials. The initial screen requires the user to enter the sales order number, sales order item number, material number, and application. The next screen displays the multi-level sales order bill of materials.

| **CSK3** | Explode BOM: Summarized BOM |

This transaction explodes the sales order bill of materials and displays it in a summarized mode. The initial screen requires the user to enter the sales order number, sales order item number, material number, and application.

The next screen displays the summarized sales order bill of materials.

| **MB11** | Enter Goods Movement |

This transaction is used to enter a goods movement, specifically consumption for a cost center, receipt without a purchase order, or a transfer posting plant to plant. On the initial screen, the user needs to enter the movement type and plant number. The next screen requires the user to enter the material information and to process the goods movement.

| **MB31** | Goods Receipt for Production Order |

This transaction is used to enter a goods movement, specifically for the receipt of a production order. On the initial screen, the user needs to enter the movement type, which is 101, the production order number, and plant number. The next screen requires the user to enter the material quantity and to process the goods movement.

| **MBVR** | Manage Reservations |

This transaction is used to manage existing reservations and to delete those that are obsolete. The initial screen does not have any mandatory fields, but the user can enter data into the selection criteria, such as cost center, production order, project, sales order, etc., to reduce the list of reservations. The next screen shows the reservations that have been selected to be deleted. The user can select which reservations he or she wishes to delete and execute the transaction.

| **MC35** | Create Rough-Cut Planning Profile |

This transaction is used to create a rough-cut planning profile, which can be used to plan work center capacities, raw materials, costs, and production resources and tools. The initial screen requires the user to enter a product group with a plant, a material with a plant, or an information structure. If a material and plant are entered, a pop-up screen will show the general data, which will require some data to be entered such as status and usage. The next screen allows the user to enter resources and the quantity for the periods in the planning profile.

MC36	Change Rough-Cut Planning Profile

This transaction is used to change a rough-cut planning profile. The initial screen requires a user to enter a product group with a plant, a material with a plant, or an information structure. If a material and plant are entered, the planning profile will be displayed so that the user can change the values for the resources for the periods entered. Resources can be added or deleted in the planning profile.

MC37	Display Rough-Cut Planning Profile

This transaction is used to display a rough-cut planning profile. The initial screen requires the user to enter a product group with a plant, a material with a plant, or an information structure. If a material and plant are entered, the planning profile will be displayed so that the user can review the values for the resources for the periods entered.

MC61	Create Planning Hierarchy

This transaction is used to create a planning hierarchy, which represents the organizational levels and units in the company to be planned. A planning hierarchy is a combination of characteristic values based on the characteristics of one information structure, which the user enters on the initial screen. Depending on the information structure entered, a dialog box is displayed

that requires the user to enter values for the characteristics from the information structure. After the characteristics are entered, the hierarchy can be saved.

MC62	Change Planning Hierarchy

This transaction is used to change a planning hierarchy, which represents the organizational levels and units in the company to be planned. A planning hierarchy is a combination of characteristic values based on the characteristics of one information structure. On the initial screen, the user is required to enter the information structure number. The subsequent screens reflect the information that was entered into the characteristics and this information can be changed using this transaction.

MC63	Display Planning Hierarchy

This transaction is used to display a planning hierarchy, which represents the organizational levels and units in the company to be planned. A planning hierarchy is a combination of characteristic values based on the characteristics of one information structure. On the initial screen, the user is required to enter the information structure number. The subsequent screens will display the information that was entered into the characteristics.

MC64	Create Event

This transaction is used to create an event, for example, a planned sales promotion that is entered to show the impact on the forecast. The initial screen can be left blank so the transaction displays an event number. The user can add an event description, status, event type, and event length. The user can then enter an absolute change that would be caused by the event. This change can then be assigned to a key figure in an information structure.

MC65	Change Event

This transaction is used to change an event, for example, a planned sales promotion that is entered to show the impact on the forecast. The initial screen requires the user to enter an event number. The next screen allows the user to change the values caused by the event, which can be assigned to a key figure in an information structure.

MC66	Display Event

This transaction is used to display an event, for example, a planned sales promotion that is entered to show the impact on the forecast. The initial screen requires the user to enter an event number. The next screen allows the user to display the values caused by the event, which have been assigned to a key figure in an information structure.

MC67	Planning Hierarchy Graphic

This transaction is used to display the planning hierarchy in a graphical form. The initial screen requires the user to enter the information structure. The transaction then displays a pop-up screen that offers the user a number of selection criteria. Based on the selection criteria, the transaction graphically displays the hierarchy.

MC71	Product Group Hierarchy

This transaction is used to display a product group hierarchy. The initial screen requires the user to enter a product group number, the relevant plant, and the display level, which can be a structural display or single-level display. The resulting output shows the product group in the format required, including the material number, plant and description. The user can then request additional information, such as unit conversion, version, material type, and proportion.

MC72	Product Group Usage

This transaction is used to display a product group usage. The initial screen requires the user to enter a product group number, the relevant plant, and the display level, which can be a structural display or single-level display. The resulting output shows the product group in the format required, including the material number, plant and description. The user can then request additional information, such as unit conversion, version, material type, and proportion.

MC73	Product Group Usage (Material)

This transaction is used to display a product group usage for a material. The initial screen requires the user to enter a material, the relevant plant and the display level, which can be a structural display or single-level display. The resulting output shows the material and the product group it is associated with in the format required, including the material number or product group, plant and description. The user can then request additional information, such as unit conversion, version, material type, and proportion.

MC74	Transfer Planning Data to Demand Management (Material)

This transaction is used to transfer planning data for a material to demand management. The initial screen requires the user to enter a material and plant. The user is also required to choose which transfer strategy to use, such as the sales plan or production plan. In addition, the user must enter the date period for the data that the user wishes to transfer to demand management.

MC75	Transfer Planning Data to Demand Management (Product Group)

This transaction is used to transfer planning data for a product group to demand management. The initial screen requires the user to enter a product group and plant. The user is also required to choose which transfer strategy to use, such as the sales plan or production plan. In addition the user must enter the date period for the data that the user wishes to transfer to demand management.

MC76	Change Plan

This transaction is used to change an existing active or inactive plan. The initial screen requires the user to enter the product group number and the plant number, and to choose an inactive or active plan. The transaction displays a screen where the user can choose to create a sales plan, disaggregate the production plan, disaggregate target stock, or disaggregate a sales plan.

MC77	Display Plan

This transaction is used to display an existing active or inactive plan. The initial screen requires the user to enter the product group number and the plant number, and to choose an inactive or active plant. The transaction displays a screen where the product group members are shown.

MC78	Copy Planning Version

This transaction is used to copy a planning version. The initial screen shows by default information structure S076, and requires the user to enter a source planning version and a target planning version with a description.

MC79	Change SOP: User Settings

This transaction is used to change SOP settings for a user. The initial screen shows the users, which can be changed. A user can be selected and then the settings, such as the planning start date and information structure, can be amended.

MC80	Delete Planning Version

This transaction is used to delete a planning version for information structure S076. The initial screen shows all the planning versions and the user can select a version or versions that the user wishes to delete.

MC81	Create Rough-Cut Plan

This transaction is used to create a rough-cut plan based on a product group and plant. The initial screen requires the user to enter the specific product group and associated plant number. The transaction displays a pop-up screen where the user can enter a version number and description. The next screen allows the user to enter values for each period of the plan, for sales, production, target stock level and target day's supply.

MC82	Change Rough-Cut Plan

This transaction is used to change a rough-cut plan. The initial screen requires the user to enter the specific product group and associated plant number. The user can choose between the active version and inactive versions of the plan. Once a plan is selected, the user can change the values for each period of the plan, for sales, production, target stock level and target day's supply.

MC83	Display Rough-Cut Plan

This transaction is used to display a rough-cut plan. The initial screen requires the user to enter the specific product group and associated plant number. The user can choose between the active version and inactive versions of the plan. Once a plan is selected, the user will be able to review the values in the rough-cut plan.

MC84	Create Product Group

This transaction is used to create a product group. The initial screen requires the user to enter a product group number, the plant where the product group will exist, and a unit of measure that will be used for the items in the product group. On the next screen, the materials, or product groups, that will be part of the product group can be entered. An aggregation factor and the factor for disaggregation can be entered for each entry.

MC85	Display Product Group

This transaction is used to display a product group. The initial screen requires the user to enter a product group number and a plant. The next screen shows the details of the product group. Each product group member is displayed along with its associated aggregation factor and the factor for disaggregation.

MC86	Change Product Group

This transaction is used to change a product group. The initial screen requires the user to enter a product group number and a plant. The next screen shows the details of the product group. Each product group member is displayed and the user can change the values for the aggregation factor and the factor for disaggregation. Additional product group members can be added to the product group or the existing members can be deleted.

MC87	Create Rough-Cut Plan (Material)

This transaction is used to create a rough-cut plan based on a material and plant. The initial screen requires the user to enter the specific material and associated plant number. The transaction displays a pop-up screen where the user can enter a version number and description. The next screen allows the user to enter values for each period of the plan, for sales, production, target stock level and target day's supply.

MC88	Change Rough-Cut Plan (Material)

This transaction is used to change a rough-cut plan. The initial screen requires the user to enter the specific material and associated plant number. The user can choose between the active version and inactive versions of the plan. Once a plan is selected, the user can change the values for each period of the plan, for sales, production, target stock level and target day's supply.

MC89	Display Rough-Cut Plan (Material)

This transaction is used to display a rough-cut plan. The initial screen requires the user to enter the specific material and associated plant number. The user can choose between the active version and inactive versions of the plan. Once a plan is selected, the user will be able to review the values in the rough-cut plan.

MC8A	Planning Type: Create

This transaction is used to create a new planning type. The initial screen requires the user to enter a planning type number. The transaction requires the user to enter an information structure and will then display a screen to allow the entry of a description, single or dual level planning, planning horizon values and standard calculations.

MC8B   Planning Type: Change

This transaction is used to change a new planning type. The initial screen requires the user to enter an existing planning type number. The user can then add a new structure into the planning type, as well as an event and actual data.

MC8C   Planning Type: Display

This transaction is used to display a new planning type. The initial screen requires the user to enter an existing planning type number. The user can then review the aggregate information for the planning type.

MC8D   Create Planning Job

This transaction is used to create a planning job. The initial screen requires the user to enter a ten-character job number and a job name. The next screen requires the user to enter an information structure and a version number. A pop-up screen will be displayed showing the planning types; the user is required to select one. The next screen will display the relevant variants and the user one can select one.

MC8E   Change Planning Job

This transaction is used to change a planning job. The initial screen requires the user to enter a ten-character job number and a job name. The next screen will allow the user to enter characteristics for the variant. Once the fields in the variant have been entered, the variant can be saved.

MC8G   Schedule Background Run for Selected Planning Objects

This transaction is used to schedule background jobs for planning objects. The initial screen requires a job number to be entered. Once executed, the transaction will allow the user to enter information about when the job is to be run, such as immediately, or to schedule it for a later time.

MC8J   List of Planning Objects

This transaction is used to display a list of materials and product groups associated with a planning job. The initial screen requires the user to enter a job name. The output display shows a list of the materials and product groups associated with the planning job. The user can then select a material or product group and delete that object from the job, if required.

MC8V   Copy Planning Version

This transaction is used to copy a planning version. The initial screen shows by default information structure S076, and requires the user to enter a source planning version and a target planning version with a description.

MC8W   Delete Planning Version

This transaction is used to delete a planning version for information structure S076. The initial screen will show all the planning versions and the user can select a version or versions for deletion.

MC90   Transfer Planning Data to Demand Management

This transaction is used to transfer planning data for a material to demand management. The initial screen requires the user to enter a material, plant, information structure and version. The user is also required to enter the key figure from the information structure, along with a relevant date range.

| MC91 | Product Hierarchy Graphic |

This transaction is used to display a product hierarchy in a graphical form. The initial screen requires the user to enter a product group and plant. The user can indicate that he or she requires the display to show descriptions and the materials to be displayed.

| MC93 | Create Rough-Cut Plan in Flexible Planning |

This transaction is used to create a rough-cut plan in flexible planning. The initial screen requires the user to enter a planning type. The next screen requires a material and plant to be entered. A pop-up screen will appear so that the user can enter a version number. The detail screen shows the objects from the planning table and the user can enter values into the periods of the rough-cut plan for each object.

| MC94 | Change Rough-Cut Plan in Flexible Planning |

This transaction is used to change a rough-cut plan in flexible planning. The initial screen requires a planning type to be entered. The next screen requires a material and plant to be entered as well as a choice of the active or inactive versions. The detail screen shows the objects from the planning table and the user can amend values into the periods of the rough-cut plan for each object.

| MC95 | Display Rough-Cut Plan in Flexible Planning |

This transaction is used to display a rough-cut plan in flexible planning. The initial screen requires a planning type to be entered. The next screen requires a material and plant to be entered as well as a choice of the active or inactive versions. The detail screen shows the objects from the planning table and the user can review the values into the periods of the rough-cut plan for each object.

| MC9K | Maintain Available Capacity for Material |

This transaction is used to amend the available capacity for a material. The initial screen requires the user to enter a material number, plant number and version number. The next screen allows the user to enter a number of period dates and the availability capacity value for each of the periods.

| MCP1 | Operation Analysis |

This transaction is used to perform an analysis on operation data. The initial screen allows the user to enter a number of selection criteria, such as plant, material, work center, date range, and order. The resulting display is based on the selection criteria that the user entered. It shows the target lead time, which is the time period between the scheduled input date at the work center and the latest scheduled finish of the operation, and the actual lead time, which is the time between the input date at the work center and the completion confirmation date.

| MCP3 | Production Order Analysis |

This transaction is used to perform an analysis on production order data. The initial screen allows the user to enter a plant, material and production order. The resulting display is based on the selection criteria that the user entered and shows the target lead time and actual lead time. The user can drill down on the results to find data on materials and order numbers.

MCP5   Material Analysis

This transaction is used to perform an analysis on material data. The initial screen allows the user to enter a plant, MRP controller and material. The resulting display is based on the selection criteria that the user entered and shows the target lead time and actual lead time. The user can drill down on the results to find data on MRP controller and materials.

MCP7   Work Center Analysis

This transaction is used to perform an analysis on work center data. The initial screen allows the user to enter a plant, planner group, and work center. The resulting display is based on the selection criteria that the user entered and shows the target lead time and actual lead time. The user can drill down on the results to find data on the planner groups.

MCRE   Material Usage Analysis

This transaction is used to perform an analysis on material usage data. The initial screen allows the user to enter a plant, material, bill of materials component, and production order. The resulting display is based on the selection criteria that the user entered and shows the target lead time and actual lead time. The user can drill down on the results to find data on the material, BOM component, and production order.

MCRI   Product Costs Analysis

This transaction is used to perform an analysis on product costing data. The initial screen allows the user to enter a plant, material, bill of materials component, costing activity type, and production order. The resulting display is based on the selection criteria that the user entered and shows the total value in the controlling area, fixed value in the controlling area, and the variable value in the controlling area. The user can drill down on the results to find data on the material, BOM component, and costing activity type.

MCRX   Material Usage Analysis

This transaction is used to perform an analysis on material usage data. The initial screen allows the user to enter a plant, material, bill of materials component, and production order. The resulting display is based on the selection criteria that the user entered and shows the requirement quantity and the withdrawal quantity. The user can drill down on the results to find data on the material, BOM component, and production order.

MCRY   Product Costs Analysis

This transaction is used to perform an analysis on product costing data. The initial screen allows the user to enter a plant, material, bill of materials component, costing activity type, and production order. The resulting display is based on the selection criteria that the user entered and shows the total value in the controlling area, fixed value in the controlling area, and the variable value in the controlling area. The user can drill down on the results to find data on the material, BOM component, and costing activity type.

MD01   MRP Run

This transaction is used to generate an MRP run. On the initial screen, the user can enter a scope of planning value, a plant number, processing key, creation indicator for purchase requisitions, automatic scheduling line indicator, planning mode value, and planning date. The resulting display shows details on the planning run, such as the number of materials planned and the number of any errors generated.

MD02 Single-Item, Multi-Level (MRP)

This transaction is used to perform a single item, multi-level MRP run. On the initial screen, the user can enter a material, MRP area, a plant number, processing key, creation indicator for purchase requisitions, automatic scheduling line indicator, planning mode value, and planning date. The resulting display shows details on the planning run, such as the number of materials planned and the number of any errors generated.

MD03 Single-Item, Single-Level (MRP)

This transaction is used to perform a single item, single-level MRP run. On the initial screen, the user can enter a material, MRP area, a plant number, processing key, creation indicator for purchase requisitions, automatic scheduling line indicator, planning mode value, and planning date. The user can also flag the indicator that displays the results before they are saved. If required, the resulting display shows the planning result for the individual lines.

MD05 MRP List (individual Display)

This transaction is used to display the MRP list for an individual material. The initial screen allows the user to enter a material, MRP area, and a plant. The transaction will then show the MRP list for the material, showing each of the MRP elements such as purchase requisitions, safety stock, production orders, consignment material, etc.

MD06 MRP List (Collective Display)

This transaction is used to display the MRP list for an MRP area or plant. The initial screen allows the user to enter an MRP area or a plant. In addition, the user can enter an MRP controller, a product group or a vendor. The next screen shows a list of materials with MRP lists that can be selected, and the MRP list can be reviewed.

MD07 Stock/Requirements List (Collective Display)

This transaction is used to display a stock/requirements list for a number of materials. The initial screen allows the user to enter MRP area or a plant. In addition, the user can enter an MRP controller, a product group or a vendor. The next screen shows a list of materials with stock/requirements lists that can be selected, and an individual stock/requirements list can be reviewed.

MD08 Delete MRP Lists

This transaction is used to delete MRP lists. The initial screen allows the user to enter a plant, MRP area, MRP controller, or MRP date. The user can flag that the executed transaction be run in test mode. The next screen shows the MRP lists that can be deleted.

MD09 Determine Pegged Requirements

This transaction is used to determine the pegged requirements. The initial screen allows the user to enter one of the following: a planned order, production order, purchase requisition, purchase order or scheduling agreement.

MD11 Create Planned Order

This transaction is used to create a planned order. The initial screen requires the user to enter a planned order profile or reference another planned order. The next screen requires the user to enter the material, MRP area, and order quantity; the start and finish dates for the order can also be entered. The data can be saved and the transaction will display the planned order.

MD12   Change Planned Order

This transaction can be used to change a planned order. The initial screen requires the user to enter a planned order number. The user can then change the planned order quantity, start and finish dates, and the source of supply.

MD13   Display Planned Order

This transaction can be used to display a planned order. The initial screen requires the user to enter a planned order number. The user can then display the planned order quantity, start and finish dates, and the source of supply.

MD14   Convert Planned Order to Purchase Requisition

This transaction is used to convert an existing planned order to a purchase requisition. The initial screen requires the user to enter a planned order. The next screen allows the quantity to be changed; the plant, storage location, delivery date, release date, MRP controller, and purchasing group can also be changed. When the transaction is posted, a message will appear with the purchase requisition number.

MD15   Collective Conversion of Planned Order to Purchase Requisition

This transaction is used to convert a number of planned orders to purchase requisitions. The initial screen requires the user to enter a plant along with an MRP controller, a material or a WBS element. The next screen shows the relevant planned orders and the user can select the planned orders he or she wishes to convert to purchase requisitions.

MD16   Display Planned Orders

This transaction is used to display planned orders. The initial screen gives the user the choice to display planned orders, by MRP controller, material, production version, line from production version, or WBS element. The user can select one of the options and the transaction displays the relevant planned orders.

MD17   Collective Requirements Display

This transaction shows the collective requirements for a material. The initial screen requires the user to enter a material, plant and a production version. The transaction will show the collective requirements for the entered criteria. This transaction is mainly used in repetitive manufacturing.

MD20   Create Planning File Entry

This transaction is used to create a planning file entry for a single material. The transaction can be used when a new material that has not been in the MRP run can be added. The initial screen requires the user to enter a material, and the MRP area or plant. Users can then select which planning file entry they require and then press ENTER. The transaction will display that the material has been marked for the MRP run.

MD21   Display Planning File Entries

This transaction is used to display planning file entries. The initial screen requires the user to enter a material and either a plant or an MRP area. Other selection data can be entered, such as a low-level code, re-explode BOM indicator, or the MPS item indicator. The output shows the planning file entries for the material.

MD25   Create Planning Calendar

This transaction is used to create a planning calendar. The initial screen requires the user to enter a plant and a planning calendar number. The next screen requires a description to be added for the planning calendar. The user can select the option for the transaction to calculate the periods and can select weeks, months, workdays, or years.

MD26   Change Planning Calendar

This transaction is used to change a planning calendar. The initial screen requires the user to enter a plant and a planning calendar number. The next screen allows the user to change the planning calendar description and the user can then change the existing periods of the planning calendar.

MD27   Display Planning Calendar

This transaction is used to display a planning calendar. The initial screen requires the user to enter a plant and a planning calendar number. The next screen shows the planning calendar header, and the user can then review the defined periods.

MD43   Single Item Planning – Interactive

This transaction is used to plan a single material. The initial screen requires the user to enter the material and plant. A number of selection values can be entered, such as the processing key, creation indicator for purchase requisitions, automatic schedule line indicator, and the planning mode indicator. The next screen shows the planning result for the material, and the user has the ability to execute the planning run or to reschedule, set firming dates, create a procurement proposal, or create a production order.

MD44   Evaluation of the Planning Situation

This transaction is used to evaluate a planning situation for a material. The initial screen requires the user to enter a material, plant and a layout for the MPS evaluation. The planning situation for the material is shown in the output screen: the warehouse stock, planned receipts, issues, available quantity and ATP quantity for the periods of the evaluation.

MD45   Evaluation of the Planning Result

This transaction is used to evaluate a planning result for a material. The initial screen requires the user to enter a material, plant and a layout for the MPS evaluation. The planning result for the material is shown in the output screen: the warehouse stock, planned receipts, issues, available quantity and ATP quantity for the periods of the evaluation.

MD46   Evaluation of the Planning Result for MRP Controller

This transaction is used to evaluate the planned result for a specific MRP controller. The initial screen requires the user to enter the MRP controller with either a MRP area or plant. It is possible to restrict the values by entering selection criteria, such as MRP date, processing date or stock coverage. The output shows the MRP list for materials associated with the MRP controller.

MD47   Evaluation of Product Group Planning

This transaction is used to evaluate a planning result for a product group. The initial screen requires the user to enter a product group, plant and a layout for the MPS evaluation. The planning result for the product group is shown in the output screen: the warehouse stock, planned receipts, issues, available quantity and ATP quantity for the periods of the evaluation.

MD48 Cross-Plant Evaluation

This transaction is used to evaluate a planning situation for a material across plants. The initial screen requires the user to enter a material and a layout for the MPS evaluation. The planning situation for the material is shown in the output screen: the warehouse stock, planned receipts, issues, available quantity and ATP quantity for the periods of the evaluation.

MD4C Multi-level Order Report

This transaction is used to display the stock requirements for materials from a sales order, project, WBS element, planned order, production or process order. The initial screen shows a number of tabs where the user can enter a sales order, a WBS element, etc. After the user has entered in an order, the next screen shows the materials that are required by the order and the stock/requirements for the material.

MD50 Make-To-Order Planning – Multi-Level

This transaction is used to plan the details for a make-to-order sales order. The initial screen requires the user to enter the sales order and the sales order item number. This transaction generates the sales order specific requirement or planning only.

MD51 Project Planning – Multi-Level

This transaction is used to plan material requirement for a project or WBS element. The initial screen requires the user to enter a project or a WBS element; in addition, the

user can enter a number of MRP control parameters.

MD61 Create Planned Independent Requirements

This transaction allows the user to create planned independent requirements for a material or product group. The initial screen requires a product group or a material to be entered, along with the MRP area, plant number and the planning horizon. The next screen lets the user enter independent requirement values into the planning table for the periods specified. After the values have been entered, the requirements can be saved.

MD62 Change Planned Independent Requirements

This transaction allows the user to change the planned independent requirements for a material or product group. The initial screen requires a product group or a material to be entered, along with the MRP area, plant number and the planning horizon. The next screen lets the user revise the independent requirement values into the planning table for the periods specified. After the necessary changes have been made, the requirements can be saved.

MD63 Display Planned Independent Requirements

This transaction allows the user to display the planned independent requirements for a material or product group. The initial screen requires a product group or a material to be entered, along with the MRP area, plant number and the planning horizon. The next screen lets the user review the independent requirement values into the planning table for the periods specified.

MD64	Standard Independent Requirements (Create)

This transaction allows the user to create standard independent requirements for a material or product group. The initial screen requires a product group or a material to be entered, along with the MRP area, plant number and the planning horizon. The next screen lets the user enter independent requirement values into the planning table for the periods specified. After the values have been entered, the requirements can be saved.

MD65	Change Standard Independent Requirements

This transaction allows the user to change the standard independent requirements for a material or product group. The initial screen requires a product group or a material to be entered, along with the MRP area, plant number and the planning horizon. The next screen lets the user revise the independent requirement values into the planning table for the periods specified. After the necessary changes have been made, the requirements can be saved.

MD66	Display Standard Independent Requirements

This transaction allows the user to display the standard independent requirements for a material or product group. The initial screen requires a product group or a material to be entered, along with the MRP area, plant number and the planning horizon. The next screen lets the user review the independent requirement values into the planning table for the periods specified.

MD73	Display Total Requirements

This transaction shows the total requirements for a material, requirements plan or an MRP controller. The initial screen requires the user to enter either a material, requirements plan or an MRP controller, along with a plant and a display option. The next screen shows the planned independent requirements with any assigned customer requirements for the upcoming periods.

MD74	Reorganizing Independent Requirements – Adjusting Requirements

This transaction is used when there is a need to reorganize existing independent requirements for a plant. The initial screen requires the user to enter a plant, material, requirement types, version, MRP area or key date. In addition, the user can set the TEST MODE flag to stop unnecessary updates. The next screen shows the number of independent requirements that were selected and the number of requirements that are to be adjusted.

MD75	Independent Requirements Reorganization – Delete Old Requirements

This transaction is used when there is a need to reorganize existing independent requirements for a plant. The initial screen requires the user to enter a plant, material, requirement types, version, MRP area or key date. In addition, the user can set the TEST MODE flag to stop unnecessary updates. The next screen shows the number of independent requirements that were selected and the number of requirements that are to be deleted.

MD76	Reorganizing Independent Requirements – Delete History

This transaction is used when there is a need to reorganize existing independent requirements for a plant and delete history records. The initial screen requires the user to enter a plant, material, requirement types, version, MRP area or key date. In addition, the user can set the TEST MODE flag to stop unnecessary updates. The next screen shows the number of independent requirements that were selected and the number of history records that are to be deleted.

MD79	PP Demand Management – Microsoft Excel List Viewer

This transaction is used to display the demand requirements for the selection criteria and download to Microsoft Excel. The initial screen allows the user to enter a material number or a requirements plan in addition to the requirements type, plant, or requirements date. The transaction displays a pop-up screen, which offers the user a choice of processing mode: table or pivot table. The transaction will then download the information to an Excel spreadsheet.

MD81	Create Customer- Independent Requirements

This transaction is used to enter the customer requirement directly instead of using a sales order. The initial screen requires the user to enter the delivering plant; the user can optionally enter the delivery date and the requirements type. The next screen requires the user to enter the materials associated with the independent requirements as well as the total quantity. The transaction displays the customer-independent requirements number when the values are posted.

MD82	Change Customer- Independent Requirements

This transaction is used to change existing customer-independent requirements. The initial screen requires the user to enter a requirements plan number. The next screen shows the existing customer-independent requirements, and the user can change the value of the requirement, delete existing line items or create new customer-independent requirements.

MD83	Display Customer Independent Requirements

This transaction is used to display existing customer-independent requirement. The initial screen requires the user to enter a requirements plan number. The next screen shows the existing customer-independent requirements, and the user can review the line items in the customer-independent requirement.

MDL1	Create Production Lot

This transaction is used to create a production lot, which is a quantity of an assembly that is planned and produced together. The initial screen requires the user to enter a production lot number and a production lot profile. The next screen allows the user to enter a material number, and the production lot can be saved. The production lot number is a system-generated WBS element.

MDL2	Change Production Lot

This transaction is used to change a production lot, which is a quantity of an assembly that is planned and produced together. The initial screen requires the user to enter a production lot number. The next screen allows the user to change the description of the production lot or material number.

MDL3	Display Production Lot

This transaction is used to display a production lot, which is a quantity of an assembly that is planned and produced together. The initial screen requires the user to enter a production lot number. The next screen allows the user to display the production lot details.

MDLD	Print MRP List

This transaction is used to print an existing MRP list. The initial screen allows the user to enter a single or range of plants, an MRP area, MRP controller, as well as selection criteria to reduce the output selection. The transaction will display a pop-up screen and will require the user to enter a printer number.

MDVP	Collective Availability Check

This transaction is used to perform a collective availability check on planned orders. The initial screen allows the user to enter selection criteria, such as planned order, production plant, MRP controller, production scheduler, and production version.

MF12	Display Document Log Information

This transaction is used to display document log information. The initial screen allows the user to enter selection criteria to reduce the number of document logs displayed. The selection criteria include plant, material, posting date, sales order, and production lot. The output shows the document logs for the selection criteria and the user can choose to select the log and review the log details.

MF26	Display Reporting Point Information

This transaction is used to display the confirmations for reporting point backflushing. The initial screen requires a plant to be entered, and selection criteria can also be entered such as material, MRP controller and production version. The output shows the reporting points per material. The user can select a reporting point and view the detailed information.

MF30	Creation of Preliminary Cost Estimates for Product Cost Collectors

This transaction is used to create preliminary cost estimates for product cost collectors. The initial screen requires the user to enter a costing date, plant and material. The transaction processes the information in the background and displays a message log, indicating if there is any warning or error messages. In addition the transaction will display the number of product cost collectors costed.

MF41	Document Specific Backflush Reversal

This transaction is used to reverse a backflush for a specific document. The initial screen requires the user to enter a reversal date, a reversal selection, such as make to stock, make to order, kanban or production lot, and other selection criteria. The transaction will display all the relevant documents based on the selection criteria. The user can then select the documents he or she requires and reverse the backflush.

MF42N	Collective Entry of Backflushes

This transaction is used to perform the backflushing of products. The transaction requires the user to enter the material and quantity of the items to be backflushed. The user can also enter a plant, planned order number, production version and a quantity of scrap if appropriate. When all the materials to be backflushed have been entered, they can be posted.

MF45	Post Process Backflush Items

This transaction is used to perform individual backflushing in repetitive manufacturing. The initial screen allows the user to enter a material, plant, production version, or a production line.

MF46   Collective Post Processing

This transaction is used to perform collective backflushing in repetitive manufacturing. The initial screen allows the user to enter the posting date and plant number. The next screen lets the user enter a number of materials, along with the relevant sales order information.

MF50   Change Planning Table

This transaction is used to change a planning table. The initial screen requires the user to enter a plant or MRP area along with a material, product group, production line, or MRP controller. The next screen allows the user to enter values for the capacity and the materials in the planning table.

MF51   Production List for Repetitive Manufacturing

This transaction is used to display production lists for repetitive manufacturing. The initial screen requires the user to enter a plant, examination period, and production line. The next screen shows the production list, which shows the production line, the total quantity, order number and end date.

MF52   Display Planning Table

This transaction is used to display a planning table. The initial screen requires the user to enter a plant or MRP area along with a material, product group, production line, or MRP controller. The next screen allows the user to review values for the capacity and the materials in the planning table.

MF57   Planning Table by MRP Lists

This transaction is used to display the planning table by MRP lists. The initial screen requires the user to enter the plant and MRP controller. A number of other selection criteria fields can be entered, such as MRP date, processing date or day's supply. The next screen shows the materials associated with the planning table.

MF60   Material Staging – Pull List

This transaction is used to create the pull list for material staging; it can create stock transfer requirements to stage the materials to the production storage locations. The initial screen requires the user to enter a specific plant, the date for the requirements, as well as a number of selection criteria that can be entered to restrict the processing. The next screen shows the total requirements, and for each line item the user can enter the quantity staged or create replenishment proposals.

MF63   Material Staging Situation

This transaction is used to display the staging situation and post material to the production storage location. The initial screen requires the user to enter a specific plant, the date for the requirements, as well as a number of selection criteria that can be entered to restrict the processing. The output screen shows the requirements details and the missing quantities for the planned orders.

MF65   Stock Transfer for Reservation

This transaction is used to display and post the existing stock transfers for reservations. The initial screen has no mandatory fields, but the user can enter a range of selection criteria, such as material, plant, MRP controller, WBS element, or sales order. The next screen shows the material for the reservations that can be posted. The user can use batch determination if the material is batch managed, or the goods movements can be posted immediately.

MF68	Message Logs for Material Staging

This transaction is used to display the material staging message logs for a specific period. The initial screen allows the user to enter a date range and user names for the message logs. The next screen shows the message logs for the users entered within the date range.

MF70	Aggregate Collective Backflush

This transaction is used when a large volume of backflushing needs to be processed. The initial screen requires the user to enter the plant or plants for the backflushing, as well as the backflush processes to be carried out and the production type. By separating the backflush processes, the user can instruct the system to post the goods receipts, and reduce the production quantities and capacity requirements immediately. The partial or less critical functions can then be carried out at a later time.

MP30	Execute Material Forecast

This transaction is used to execute a forecast for a material. The FORECAST screen in the material master must be completed in order to execute a forecast. The initial screen requires the user to enter a material number and plant number. The next screen shows the forecast data from the material master and the user can then display the historical values or execute the forecast. A pop-up screen will offer periods that the user can select from. The transaction will then display the forecast for next twelve periods, which can then be saved.

MP31	Change Material Forecast

This transaction is used to change an existing material forecast. The initial screen requires the user to enter a material and a plant. The next screen shows the forecast details for the material, and the user can select to view the historical values or the forecast values. By selecting the forecast values, the user can then make changes to the forecast values for the material.

MP32	Display Material Forecast

This transaction is used to display an existing material forecast. The initial screen requires the user to enter a material and a plant. The next screen shows the forecast details for the material, and the user can select to view the historical values or the forecast values.

MP33	Forecast Reprocessing

This transaction is used to reprocess a forecast for a plant and an MRP controller. The user must enter a plant and an MRP controller on the initial screen. In addition, the user can select an error class to process, such as reorder level, model selection, initializations, etc. The next screen shows the materials that are available to be reprocessed. The user can select a material and the forecast can be reprocessed.

MP38	Execute Mass Forecast

This transaction allows the mass execution of forecasts for a plant or range of plants. The initial screen allows the user to enter the plant or plants, MRP areas, materials and ABC indicator. The transaction will show on the initial screen the number of plants and materials selected. The user can then choose to restrict the entries further or to execute the mass forecast. The output screen shows the information for the forecasts processed.

MP39	Material Forecast Printing

This transaction is used to print the materials forecasts for a specific plant. The initial screen requires the user to enter a plant number and period indicator. The transaction will generate a pop-up screen that will require that the user to enter a printer number. Subsequently, the transaction will indicate that the printing has been completed.

MP80   Forecast Profile Create

This transaction allows the creation of a forecast profile, which can be used in the material master record. The initial screen requires the user to enter a four-character profile number. The next screen requires a forty-character description; the user can select the fields the profile should contain, specifying whether each field is to be copied to the material master record as a fixed value or as a default value. The data screen allows the user to enter the fixed values for the fields selected.

MP81   Forecast Profile Change

This transaction allows the user to change a forecast profile, which can be used in the material master record. The initial screen requires a forecast profile to be entered. The user can then change the profile description and then add or change the values in the profile. If additional fields were selected to have a fixed value or as a default value, then the user must enter the fixed values for the fields selected.

MP82   Forecast Profile Delete

This transaction allows the user to delete a forecast profile, which was used in the material master record. The initial screen requires a forecast profile to be entered. The transaction will display a message to confirm that the forecast profile is to be deleted.

MP83   Forecast Profile Display

This transaction allows the user to display a forecast profile, which can be used in the material master record. The initial screen requires a forecast profile to be entered. The

user can then display the profile description and review the values in the profile.

MS31   Create Planning Scenario

This transaction is used to create a planning scenario. The initial screen requires a three-character planning scenario number and a forty-character description. The user can also define the default settings for the control parameters, such as long-term planning, gross long-term planning or short term simulation. The next screen allows the user to enter planning period, control parameters, gross requirements planning, receipts, or BOM explosion. The planning scenario can then be assigned to a planned independent requirement, and then the user can release and save the planning scenario.

MS32   Change Planning Scenario

This transaction is used to create a planning scenario. The initial screen requires the user to enter a planning scenario number. The following screen shows all the parameters that can be amended. The user can also change the assignment to a planned independent requirement.

MS33   Display Planning Scenario

This transaction is used to display a planning scenario. The initial screen requires the user to enter a planning scenario number. The following screen shows all the parameters that can be displayed. The user can also review the assignment of planned independent requirements.

MS44   Long-Term Planning
         Evaluation for Material

This transaction is used to create a long-term planning evaluation for a material based on a planning scenario. The initial screen requires the user to enter a planning scenario, material, plant and a layout. The user can also select an option to compare the evaluation with the planning situation or planning result. The output screen shows planning evaluation with the receipts, planned issues, available quantity and ATP quantity shown for the forecasted periods.

MSC1N   Create Batch

This transaction is used to create a batch for a material. The initial screen requires the user to enter the material number, batch number, plant, and storage location. The transaction takes the user to the first data screen, where the user can enter details on shelf life, expiration date, and trading data information. The user can also assign the batch to a class so that additional data can be added to characteristics describing the batch.

MSC2N   Change Batch

This transaction is used to change a batch for a material. The initial screen requires the user to enter the material number, batch number, plant, and storage location. The transaction takes the user to the first data screen, where the user can enter or change details on shelf life, expiration date, and trading data information. The user can also assign the batch to a class so that additional data can be added to characteristics describing the batch.

MSC3N   Display Batch

This transaction is used to display a batch for a material. The initial screen requires the user to enter the material number, batch number, plant, and storage location. The transaction takes the user to the first data screen, where the user can review details on shelf life, expiration date, and trading data information. The user can also review the classification information assigned to the batch.

MSC4N   Display Change Documents for Batch

This transaction is used to display changes that have been made to a specific material batch. The initial screen requires the user to enter the material number, batch number, plant, and storage location. The next screen shows the changes made to the batch, such as the data and time the changes were made, and what objects were changed. The screen also shows the old data and the new data of each of the fields that have been changed.

PK01   Create Control Cycle

This transaction is used to create a kanban control cycle. The initial screen requires the user to enter a material, plant, and a supply area. The next screen allows the user to enter the number of kanbans and the kanban quantity as well as the control cycle replenishment strategy. Once all the values are entered, the control cycle can be saved, and the transaction will display the control cycle number that has been created.

PK02   Change Control Cycle

This transaction is used to change a kanban control cycle. The initial screen requires the user to enter a material, plant, and a supply area. On the next screen, the user can then change the number of kanbans, the quantity, and add a new control cycle replenishment strategy.

PK03   Display Control Cycle

This transaction is used to display a kanban control cycle. The initial screen requires the user to enter a material, plant, and a supply area. On the next screen, the user can then display the number of kanbans, the quantity, and review the control cycle replenishment strategy.

PK03NR Display Control Cycle

This transaction is similar to transaction PK03, but instead of accessing the control cycle using the material, plant, and a supply area, the user can directly enter the control cycle number on the initial screen. On the next screen, the user can then display the number of kanbans, the quantity, and review the control cycle replenishment strategy.

PK05 Maintain Supply Area

This transaction is used to maintain the supply areas for a plant. The initial screen requires the user to enter a plant. The next screen shows the user the production supply areas for the plant. The user can change the description of the production supply areas already configured; the user can also add a new production supply area or delete an existing production supply area.

PK05S Quick Entry Supply to Production Area

This transaction allows the user to enter supply area information into the system. The initial screen requires the user to enter a plant number. The next screen shows the existing supply areas for the plant and the storage location they are assigned to. The user can enter the responsible party, the unloading point and supply area description for existing supply areas. The transaction allows the user to enter new supply areas for the plant and assign them to a storage location.

PK06 Display Supply Area

This transaction is used to display the supply areas for a plant. The initial screen requires the user to enter a plant. The next screen shows the user the production supply areas that have been created for the plant. The user can select a supply area and review detailed information about the supply area.

PK10 Kanban Board Status

This transaction allows the maintenance of the user authorization for the kanban table. The initial screen requires entry of either the demand view of the kanban board or the supply view. The next screen shows the users and the statuses that can be set by them. Additional changes can be made for each user, or new users can be added to this transaction.

PK11 Kanban Plant Overview

This transaction is used to display where the kanbans are in the plant. The initial screen requires the user to enter a plant number and an optional supply area. The output can be sorted by material or supply area. The next screen shows the overview of the control cycles at the plant, with the output showing the material, supply area, kanban quantities, and kanban containers.

PK12N Kanban Board: Supply Source Overview

This transaction is used for monitoring and changing kanban status for the supply source. The initial screen requires the user to enter the plant and either the person responsible, vendor, issuing plant, or storage location. The transaction will graphically show the kanbans that are "in process" and those "in transit." The user can trigger replenishment for a kanban if required.

PK13N Kanban Board: Demand Source Overview

This transaction is used for monitoring and changing kanban status for the demand source. The initial screen requires the user to enter the plant and either the person responsible, vendor, issuing plant, or storage location. The transaction will graphically show the supply area, material and kanban quantity. The user can select kanbans and save them to full or to empty.

PK17   Collective Kanban Print

This transaction allows kanbans for a plant to be printed. The initial screen requires the user to enter a printer and a plant. The user can restrict the kanban to be printed by entering selection criteria, such as storage location, supply area, vendor, material, or kanban status. The output screen shows the supply areas and kanban that are relevant to the selection criteria entered. The user can select the kanban for the supply area he or she wishes to print or individual kanbans.

PK18   Control Cycle Evaluation

This transaction is used to evaluate the control cycles for a plant. The initial screen requires the user to enter a plant number. The user can restrict the kanban to be printed by entering selection criteria, such as storage location, supply area, vendor, material, or kanban status. The output shows the supply areas relevant to the selection criteria. By selecting a supply area, the relevant kanban are shown and the user can see their status, i.e. whether they are in wait, empty, or full status.

PK21   Manual Entry of a Kanban Signal

This transaction allows the user to manually trigger a kanban signal. The initial screen allows the user to enter a kanban identification number, a control cycle number and kanban number, or a plant, supply area and kanban number. Once the information is entered, the user can either allow the transaction to automatically assign the next status, or manually enter a status, for example: wait, empty, in transit, full, or in use.

PK22   Enter Quantity Signal

This transaction allows the entry of a quantity signal for a control cycle. The initial screen requires the user to enter either a control cycle, or a plant, material and supply area. The transaction also requires a withdrawal quantity to be entered that will be removed from the kanbans. In this transaction, only kanbans with a full or in use status can be used.

PK23   Create an Event-Driven Kanban

This transaction is used to create an event-driven kanban, which is where material is not continually provided and replenished at a supply area, but replenished only when specifically triggered. The initial screen requires the user to enter either a control cycle number, or a material, plant and supply area. The user can enter the quantity to be released as well as the delivery date and time.

PK23L   Delete Event-Driven Kanbans

This transaction is used to delete an event-driven kanban. The initial screen requires the user to enter a plant, as well as selection criteria such as supply area, vendor, person responsible, storage location, etc. The user also has the option to run the transaction as a simulation so that no database updates are made.

PK31   Kanban Correction

This transaction is used to correct a kanban. The initial screen requires the user to enter a plant, material and supply area. The next screen shows the relevant kanbans, and the user can select the appropriate kanban and correct the kanban status, actual quantity or batch number.

PK41   Kanban Backflush

This transaction is used to backflush kanbans. The initial screen requires the user to enter a control cycle number or a plant and material. The next screen shows the relevant kanbans, and the user can post the backflush. This will confirm either a goods receipt or goods issue posting.

PK50   Kanban Processing: Error Display

This transaction allows the user to display the error messages for a kanban at a specific plant. The initial screen requires the user to enter a plant and any relevant selection criteria. The output screen shows the errors for each of the control cycles. The user can select a specific error message and review a detailed message on the kanban or the error. The user has the option to select the error and transfer to transaction PK31.

PK52   Kanban Calculation: Display Error Log

This transaction is used to display error logs for any kanban calculations for a specific plant. The initial screen requires the user to enter a plant and selection criteria, such as supply area or storage location, if required. The next screen will display the kanban calculation error logs for the plant entered.

PKMC   Control Cycle Maintenance: Display

This transaction gives an overview of the control cycles at a plant. The selection part of the screen requires the user to enter a plant; the user also can enter the supply area, the person responsible, or the control cycle number. The screen shows the control cycles for the selection entered. The details for each line include the supply area, material, number of kanbans, kanban quantity, storage location, control cycle status, and control cycle category.

7   Sales and Distribution (SD)

COGI	Automatic Goods Movements: Error Handling

This transaction is used to correct errors that have resulted from automatic goods movements. Automatic goods movement errors occur, for example, when a production order is being confirmed and components are backflushed from a storage location that does not have the required quantity in inventory. Selection criteria include plant, storage location, material, error date from/to range, and other relevant inventory document data. The output is an aggregated list of goods movement errors. Once the error has been reviewed and resolved, the inventory movement will be processed.

DGP1	Create Dangerous Goods Master

This transaction is used to create a dangerous good master, which is an extension of the material master. The master record contains information required to carry out automatic checks in the sales and distribution and materials management processes and generate documents required by local regulators. Input an existing material master and the dangerous goods regulation code (in customizing the dangerous goods regulation code contains the mode of transport and validity area, for example, Germany). Enter the master data and save.

DGP2	Change Dangerous Goods Master

Use this transaction to change a dangerous good master previously created using transaction DGP1.

DGP3	Display Dangerous Goods Master

Use this transaction to display a dangerous good master previously created using transaction DGP1.

DGR1	Dangerous Goods Master: Display with Descriptions

Use this transaction to display a list of dangerous goods master data from the dangerous goods master data table DGTMD. Input selection includes material, regulation key, and valid from/to date range. The output can be listed by material, mode of transport category, and validity area; all change statuses, which are identified by validity area or change number, can be read at the item level. Display layout can be changed and saved as a default, according to user requirements.

DP91	Resource-Related Billing Request

This transaction is used to create a resource-related billing request, which is a special type of billing based on resources consumed by the organization. For example, a consulting company agrees to sell services based on time spent on a sales order. Time is recorded to the sales order and then the customer is billed based on the hours charged to the sales order. This transaction generates the resource-related billing request, which is followed up by an actual billing document. Input the sales order and line items, pricing date, posting date and posting period, and execute.

| DP93 | Resource-Related Billing Request Between Company Codes Sales and Distribution |

Use this transaction to create an intercompany billing document for the purposes of billing one company for using the resources of another company code in order to bill an end customer. In this scenario an intercompany sales order is generated for using the resources. Once time and/or expenses are charged to a project, the selling company code can bill the end customer. The next step is to use this transaction to create the intercompany billing request, which is then followed by an intercompany billing document. This in turn facilitates the payment from the selling company code to the company code providing the resources. Input the intercompany sale document, period, fiscal year, and posting to date, choose a sales price and click ENTER. On the SALES screen, expand the items and chose the cross-company line item and then chose BILLING REQUEST and click YES to confirm the billing request creation.

| DP96 | Collective Processing Resource-Related Billing Request |

This transaction is used to create a resource-related billing request for multiple resource usage postings across multiple sales orders. Resource-related billing is a special type of billing based on resources consumed by an organization. For example, a consulting company agrees to sell services based on time spent on a sales order. Time is recorded to the sales order and then the customer is billed based on the hours charge to the sales order. This transaction generates a resource-related billing request, which is followed by the actual billing document. Input the sales order and line items, pricing date, posting date and posting period and execute.

| MCTA | Customer Analysis: Selection |

This transaction uses the sales information system application to report sales activities. This transaction specifically uses information structure S001 (Customer). An information structure contains characteristics (fields that are reported on) and key figures (results of the report). This transaction has the following standard delivered characteristics: sold-to, sales organization, division, distribution channel and material. The standard delivered key figures include, for example, sales order values and quantity, open sales order values, sales order cost, returns order values, billing values and sales order subtotal values. Input customer, sales area and posting period from/to range, and execute. Multiple display functions are available, including the ability to switch the drill order, the characteristic key and value display, and key figures related to top % values.

| MCTC | Material Analysis (SIS): Selection |

This transaction is similar to transaction MCTA but focuses on the material characteristic and uses information structure S004 (Material). An information structure contains characteristics (fields that are reported on) and key figures (results of the report). This transaction has the following standard delivered characteristics: material, sales organization, division and distribution channel. The key figures include, for example, sales order values and quantity, open sales order values, sales order cost, returns order values, billing values and sales order subtotal values. Input customer, sales area, posting period from/to range, and execute. Multiple display functions are available including the ability to switch drill-down order, the characteristic key and value display, and key figures related to top % values.

MCTE	Sales Organization Analysis: Selection

This transaction is similar to transaction MCTA but focuses on the sales organization characteristic and uses information structure S003 (Sales Organization). An information structure contains characteristics (fields that are reported on) and key figures (results of the report). This transaction has the following standard delivered characteristics: sales organization, division, distribution channel and sales district. The key figures include, for example, sales order values and quantity, open sales order values, sales order cost, returns order values, billing values and sales order subtotal values. Input customer, sales area and posting period from/to range, and execute. Multiple display functions are available, including the ability to switch drill-down order, the characteristic key and value display, and key figures related to top % values.

TK11	Create Condition Records Shipment Costs

This transaction is used to maintain pricing condition records for shipment costs that access pricing information automatically when creating a shipment cost document via transaction VI01. Input a condition type, for example FB00, and click ENTER. Next select the condition table to be maintained (each condition type will be customized with an access sequence and condition tables with the condition fields) and click ENTER. In order to calculate freight costs based on scales, you also need to assign the scale to the freight condition type in customizing (transaction T_06). Maintain the condition record fields, rate, unit of measure and valid from/to fields, and save.

TK12	Change Condition Records Shipment Costs

Use this transaction to change pricing condition records for shipment costs, which may be required if you need to change the rate, extend the valid to date, or place a deletion indicator on the condition record. Input the condition type, click ENTER, select the condition table that contains the condition fields (note that in customizing you do have some flexibility as to changing some of the required fields for the purposes of maintenance, which can be useful if you want the change multiple condition records at the same time) and click EXECUTE. Then maintain the condition record and click SAVE.

TK13	Display Condition Records Shipment Costs

Use this transaction to display a condition record previously created using transaction TK11.

V.01	Incomplete SD Documents

Use this transaction to list all sales documents that are incomplete according to the incomplete procedure assigned to the sales document header or line item. Check the box for the document type(s) selected, the status code, sales area information, and execute. The output will list the incomplete documents with the follow-on documents affected and provide the ability to select the document, complete the missing data, and save the document.

V.02	Incomplete SD Documents (Incomplete Orders)

This transaction is used in the same way as transaction V.01 except the default field selection for the SD transaction group is "0," which means that all incomplete sales orders will be selected.

V.03	Incomplete SD Documents (Sales Inquiry)

This transaction is used in the same way as transaction V.01 except the default field selection for the SD transaction group is "1," which means that all incomplete sales inquiries will be selected.

V.04	Incomplete SD Documents (Sales Quotation)

This transaction is used in the same way as transaction V.01 except the default field selection for the SD transaction group is "2," which means that all incomplete sales quotations will be selected.

V.14	Sales Orders/Contracts Blocked for Delivery

Use this transaction to report all sales order/ contracts blocked for delivery according to the delivery block indicator. Note: The values are determined from the confirmed quantities of the order items. Also note, by selecting the new data selection indicator, the program reads the whole database and so if there is a large data set being processed it is recommended not to select this indicator. Therefore, it is recommended that you save the output. Selection criteria include delivery block indicator and sales area. The display variant can be changed, saved, and used as a default at run time.

V.15	Backorders

This transaction is used for backorder processing, where you can list the materials that are on backorder and confirm them manually using available to promise inventory quantities. Input your selection criteria (for example, the plant, sold-to party, purchase order number) and click EXECUTE. The output displays your list of sales order line items and materials. Then you can branch to the sales order change function. To process the backorder from the list, select your line item and select EDIT • BACKORDER, select the MRP element, and click EDIT • CHANGE CONFIRMATION. Then in the SALES REQUIREMENTS section, you can distribute available to promise quantities or redistribute confirmed quantities.

V.21	Log of Collective Run

Use this transaction to review a log of the billing collective run, which is generated by collective run transactions such as billing run via transaction VF04 or delivery run via transaction VL10. Selection criteria include the number of the collective run, the type of collective run (e.g., billing, delivery, etc.) and the user ID that started the run. The output shows the documents created and/ or any errors that occurred during the collective run.

V.23	Release Sales Orders for Billing

This transaction is used to release any blocked orders for billing document processing. Note that if you select the confirmation prompt parameter, a dialog box appears for each order, so when you confirm again, the document should be released. Selection criteria include customer, sales order number range, sales area information, user ID that created the document, and creation date range.

V_17	Create Condition Record Using Index

This transaction is used to create condition records using an index which is an aid to condition record updates. An index is set up by selecting fields that are relevant to the index and then flagging a condition type (in customizing) as relevant to condition index update. Once this has been set up, you can use this transaction to create new condition records via the index. For example, you create prices and discounts for all materials within a group. Select the condition table that contains the index fields, input selection criteria and then click EXECUTE. On the next screen, input the condition record values, and save.

V_NL	Create Net Price List

Use this transaction to create a net price list based on the pricing conditions already maintained in the system. Selection criteria include sales area information, sold-to party, plant, material from/to range, order type, billing type, item category, and pricing date (note that the only optional field is the material number). Input required fields and click EXECUTE to display the list of materials net price calculation. The display format can be changed and saved to include subtotal amounts, unit quantity, customer groups, and many more fields commonly used in net pricing calculation.

V_R2	Rescheduling of Sales and Stock Transfer Documents: Evaluation

This transaction is used to evaluate the list of rescheduled sales and stock transfer documents generated via transaction V_V2. A list of changed documents and documents in which an error occurred during processing are displayed. If, in the subsequent evaluation, a restricted selection is carried out, a note appears at the end of the list saying that not all document line items are displayed. You can set the scope of the list under the menu option LIST in the list display. You can view improvements, deteriorations, and the entire list. Before the documents can be included in one or either of the restricted lists, the date or quantity has to have changed so that the item can be contained in both the list of improved or deteriorated documents. Selection criteria include material from/to range, plant, sales orders and/or stock transport orders range from/to, delivering plant, sales organization, distribution channel and customer.

V_UC	Selection of Incomplete SD Documents

Use this transaction to list all sales documents that are incomplete according to the incomplete procedure assigned to the sales document header or line item. Check the box for the document type(s) selected and other selection criteria, for example, status code, sales area information, overall document status code, sales document from/to, and execute. The output will list incomplete documents with the follow-on document affected and provide the ability to select the document, complete the missing data, and save the document.

V_V2	Rescheduling of Sales and Stock Transfer Documents: by Material

This transaction is used to reschedule open sales and stock transfer documents. A checking rule is used as a basis for the check, for example, check delivery schedules. Line items are sorted into priorities, delivery priority, schedule line date, etc. The rescheduling can be run in simulation mode or in update mode, which means the program changes the confirmation/delivery date. Line items are read and quantities are transferred to availability to promise checking, and delivery dates can be rescheduled and saved in a log. Input material from/to range, plant, sales order and/or stock transport order and list sorting requirements and execute. Results showing old new delivery scheduled date are displayed and can be saved. Note: due to system performance concerns, you should narrow selection criteria as much as possible.

V/I5	Change Condition Record Using Index

This transaction is used to change condition records using an index. An index is set up by selecting fields that are relevant to the index and then flagging a condition type (in customizing) as relevant to condition index update. Once this has been set up, you can use this transaction to change condition records via the index. For example, you can change price and discount conditions for all materials within a material group. Select the table that contains the index fields, input selection criteria, click EXECUTE CHANGE, input condition record values, and save.

V/I6	Display Condition Record Using Index

Use this transaction to display condition records via an index. An index is set up by selecting fields that are relevant to the index and then flagging a condition type (in customizing) as relevant to condition index update. For example, you can display all price and discount conditions for materials within a material group. Select the table that contains the index fields, input selection criteria, and click EXECUTE to display the list of condition records.

V/LD	Execute Pricing Report

This transaction is used to display a list of pricing records based on a pricing report table set up in customizing. In customizing, select the key fields and condition tables that contain the selected fields and save the report table under a two-character ID. In this transaction, input the two-character ID of the reporting table and click EXECUTE. On the next screen, input the selection criteria from the selected fields and execute to display the pricing report.

VA01	Create Sales Order

This transaction is used to set up a contractual agreement between your sales organization (typically aligned with a company code) and a sold-to party (the customer/business partner you have the agreement with). A sales order can be sub divided into a distribution channel and/or division, which, together with the sales organization, combine to make up the sales area. The sales area will determine some of the master data that will be used on the sales order. Various sales order types come standard with the system, including a regular order, cash sale, return order, debit/credit memo requests, etc. The sales order has functionality to determine pricing for materials being sold, as well as availability and shipping date. Furthermore, the sales order is integrated with manufacturing and purchasing in order to plan fulfillment of the sales order requirements. Furthermore, the sales order is integrated with the finance module and credit management, checking, for example, whether the customer's sales order value is within their credit limit. The sales order is split into header information and line item information. Input the sales order type, sales area, click ENTER and then select customer/business partners, materials/services to be sold, requested delivery date and pricing information, and save.

VA02	Change Sales Order

Use this transaction to change a sales order, such as adding or deleting items. Input the sales order number and click ENTER. If you need to make changes to multiple items, the FAST CHANGE function can be used via the menu path EDIT • FAST CHANGE OF. The FAST CHANGE function can change data such as the plant, delivery block indicator and the reason for rejection status change. Other functions, such as executing the available to promise check and updating pricing details, can also be performed.

VA03	Display Sales Order

This transaction is used to display a sales created using transaction VA01.

VA05	List of Sales Orders

Use this transaction to list sales orders using a material or business partner as one of the selection criteria. You can select just the sales orders that you created, all open sales orders, or all orders within a date created range. Various output display options are available, which can be saved and used as a default. Note that a special authorization parameter ID is required in your user profile in order to make and save changes to the display layout.

VA07	Selection: Comparison of Orders with Purchase Requisitions and Purchase Orders

This transaction is used to report on inconsistencies between the sales order quantity and the purchase order quantity in a third party order sales process. Selection includes sales order and deviation category. For example, if a sales order is created for 20 ea and the purchase requisition/purchase order that was subsequently created from the sales order was changed to 30 ea, this report would highlight the difference. It also offers the ability to drill down on the documents to facilitate changing the quantity. Other deviation categories are also available.

VA08	Adjustment Sales-Purchasing (Selection Using Organizational Data)

This transaction is used to report on inconsistencies between the sales order quantity and the purchase order quantity in a third party order sales process. Selection includes sales organization, sales office, sales group and deviation category. For example, if a sales order is created for 20 ea and the purchase requisition/purchase order that was subsequently created from the sales order was changed to 30 ea, this report would highlight the difference. It also offers the ability to drill down on the documents to facilitate changing the quantity. Other deviation categories are also available. It is recommended to use transaction VA08 in background mode for large amounts of data.

VA11	Create Inquiry

This transaction is used to record an inquiry as part of the pre sales process. Functionality similar to the SALES ORDER CREATE function is also available to the INQUIRY CREATE function, such as pricing information and delivery date scheduling. A sales inquiry is entered by sales area, which includes the sales organization, distribution channel and division. Also input an inquiry type, such as an available stock inquiry or price list inquiry, and click ENTER. Within the inquiry function, the customer can be informed of available stock on hand, the shipping date timeline, and the price of materials. By saving the inquiry, reports can be created such as an analysis of the number of inquires that have been converted to sales orders or materials that customers are most interested in. Input the inquiry type, sales area, click ENTER, and then select customer/business partners, materials/services to be sold, requested delivery date and pricing information, and save.

VA12	Change Inquiry

Use this transaction to change an inquiry previously created using transaction VA11.

VA13	Display Inquiry

Use this transaction to display an inquiry previously created using transaction VA11.

VA14L — Sales Documents
Blocked for Delivery

This transaction is used to review any sales documents that have been blocked for delivery. Sales documents may be blocked for delivery if they are on credit hold where a customer has exceeded their credit limit. Selection options include the customer, sales area (sales organization, distribution channel and division), all sales documents, or only sales documents that are open. The report output displays sales document number and category, sold-to and ship-to customer number, and the various blocks that can exist. There is an option to change the layout and drill-down capability into the sales document in order to facilitate delivery dates change, remove manual blocks, etc.

VA15 — List of Inquiries

Use this transaction to list sales inquiries using a material or business partner as one of the selection criteria. You can select just the sales inquiries that you created, all open inquiries, or all inquiries within a date created range. Various output display options are available, which can be saved and used as a default. Note: a special authorization parameter ID is required in your user profile in order to make and save changes to the display layout.

VA21 — Create Quotation

This transaction is used to create a document that is a legally binding offer for a material or provision of service according to some fixed terms. Functionality similar to the SALES ORDER CREATE function is also available to the QUOTATION CREATE function, such as pricing information and delivery date scheduling. A sales area (sales organization, distribution channel and division) is required and the quotation can be created in reference to a customer inquiry. Typically, the quotation has

a specified valid from/to date. Input the quotation type (e.g., in reference to an inquiry or marketing activity), sales area information, click ENTER, then select the customer/business partners, materials/services to be sold, requested delivery date(s) and pricing information, and save.

VA22 — Change Quotation

Use this transaction to change a quotation previously created using transaction VA21.

VA23 — Display Quotation

Use this transaction to display a quotation previously created using transaction VA21.

VA25 — List of Quotations

Use this transaction to list quotations using a material or business partner as one of the selection criteria. You can select just the quotations that you created, all open quotations, or all quotations within a date created range. Various output display options are available, which can be saved and used as a default. Note: a special authorization parameter ID is required in your user profile in order to make and save changes to the display layout.

VA26 — List of Quotations
(Follow-up Actions)

This transaction is used to display a list of open quotations for a particular sold-to party up to a valid to date. Furthermore, a document date from/to can also be selected in order to narrow the output list. After the list is displayed, quotations can then be processed and converted into sales orders.

VA31 — Create Scheduling Agreement

This transaction is used to create an agreement with a customer to deliver materials with specific delivery quantities and dates which are created in a delivery schedule. Scheduling agreements are integrated with production planning so that material components/production can be appropriately scheduled in order to fulfill agreed upon delivery dates. Input the agreement type, for example, a just-in-time scheduling agreement, sales area information, and click ENTER. Input the business partner data, the materials to be delivered, and the forecast or fixed delivery dates, and save.

VA32	Change Scheduling Agreement

Use this transaction to change the scheduling agreement, perhaps as a result of the customer informing you that the delivery dates require changing. Scheduling agreements can be integrated with EDI functionality whereby the customer can send forecast delivery dates for production planning purposes and then send follow-up notices of firm delivery dates.

VA33	Display Scheduling Agreement

Use this transaction to display a scheduling agreement previously created using transaction VA31.

VA35	List of Scheduling Agreements

Use this transaction to display a list of scheduling agreements using a material or business partner as one of the selection criteria. You can select just the scheduling agreements that you created, all open scheduling agreements, or all scheduling agreements within a date created range. Various output display options are available, which can be saved and used as a default. Note: a special authorization parameter ID is required in your user profile in order to make and save changes to the display layout.

VA41	Create Contract

This transaction is used to create a contract with your business partner. There are various types of contract, namely a master contract or a value, quantity, and service contract. A master contract will contain general terms such as a master agreement number, perhaps special payment terms, and it offers a way to group follow-on contracts for reporting purposes. A value, quantity and service contract will contain information about the material/service quantities and pricing, and it will facilitate copying information into released sales orders where delivery dates and prices can be finalized. Contracts are valid for a specified time period. Input the contract type, sales area information and click ENTER. Then input business partner information, valid from/to dates, material/service materials, quantities/values, and save.

VA42	Change Contract

Use this transaction to change a contract previously created using transaction VA41. Note that any changes to contracts, as with most other master data and transactional documents, are logged in a change document that can be viewed within the contract document via the menu path ENVIRONMENT/CHANGES.

VA42W	Change Contract

This transaction is the same as transaction VA42 but is used in conjunction with workflow functionality for the completion and approval of a master contract setup.

VA43	Change Contract

Use this transaction to display a contract previously created using transaction VA41.

VA44   Actual Overhead: Calculation: Sales Order

This transaction is used to calculate overhead on sales order costs as part of cost object controlling functionality for sales orders. An overhead costing sheet can be assigned directly in the sales order, in the ACCOUNT ASSIGNMENT tab, or derived via customizing to facilitate the overhead calculation. Note: As with valuated sales order stock, overhead is allocated to the cost element for the cost of sales calculation. But with a non-valuated sales order stock, overhead is allocated when the consumption cost elements are posted or to the cost elements upon the inventory movement posting when the materials are consumed.

VA45   List of Contracts

Use this transaction to display a list of contracts using a material or business partner as one of the selection criteria. You can select just the contracts that you created, all open contracts, or all contracts within a date created range. Various output display options are available, which can be saved and used as a default. Note: A special authorization parameter ID is required in your user profile in order to make and save changes to the display layout.

VA46   List of Contracts (Follow-up Actions)

This transaction is used to display a list of open contracts for a particular sold-to party up to a valid to date. Furthermore, a subsequent process valid to date can also be selected in order to narrow the output list. After the list is displayed, contracts can be processed and converted into released sales orders.

VA51   Create Item Proposal

This transaction is used to create a proposed list of materials that can be stored and easily retrieved at sales order processing time. For example, if a customer typically orders the same list of materials, this list of materials can be stored in an item proposal document and then, at sales order processing time, the list of materials can be retrieved via the menu path EDIT • ADDITIONAL FUNCTIONS • PROPOSE ITEMS. Input the proposal list type, sales area information, description of the list, valid from/to date, materials to be proposed, and save the document.

VA52   Change Item Proposal

Use this transaction to change an item proposal previously created using transaction VA51.

VA53   Display Item Proposal

Use this transaction to display an item proposal previously created using transaction VA51.

VA55   List of Item Proposals

Use this transaction to list item proposals using the material number as the selection criteria. You can select just the item proposals that you created or all item proposals within a date created range or valid from/to range. Various output display options are available, which can be changed, saved, and used as a default. Note: A special authorization parameter ID is required in your user profile in order to make and save changes to the display layout.

VA88   Actual Settlement: Sales Orders

Use this transaction to settle actual primary and secondary costs and revenues (if applicable) to the receivers established in the sales order line item (which is a cost object) settlement rules. In cost object controlling for sales orders, the sales order is an interim cost collector that can be used to plan, record actual costs, and monitor costs until certain activities have been completed and costs moved to their final destination. This movement of the costs to their final destination is called settlement. The sales order settlement rules are dependent on the parameters established in the settlement structure, settlement profile, and order type (all defined in customizing and in the master data itself).

VACF	Fiscal Year Close: Carry Forward Commitment

This transaction is used to carry forward commitments values, in this case open sales orders posted in the current year but not reduced until the following year. The commitment carried forward updates the budget in the new fiscal year. Input the sale order number range, the carry forward from fiscal year, and execute in test or update mode.

VB01	Create Listing/Exclusion

This transaction is used to control the materials you sell to your customers. In other words, you create a material listing for a particular customer and only sell materials to that customer that are on the list. Furthermore, you can create a material exclusion that prevents a customer from buying particular materials. The listing/exclusion functionality utilizes the condition technique to accommodate this process. Input the listing/exclusion type, make the table entries, such as the selected materials, and save.

VB02	Change Listing/Exclusion

Use this transaction to change a material listing/exclusion previously created using transaction VB01.

VB03	Display Listing/Exclusion

Use this transaction to display a material listing/exclusion previously created using transaction VB01.

VB11	Create Material Determination

This transaction is used to determine materials based on some predefined conditions. For example, a material that has been replaced by a new material can be automatically substituted, using material determination during sales order input. Another typical use for this functionality involves using the customer's material number to automatically determine SAP's system-generated material number. The material determination functionality utilizes the condition technique to accommodate this process. Input the material determination type, valid from/to date range and the relevant condition entries, and save.

VB12	Change Material Determination

Use this transaction to change a material determination condition previously created using transaction VB11. This transaction is typically used when the valid from/to date range has expired and needs extending.

VB13	Display Material Determination

Use this transaction to display a material determination condition previously created using transaction VB11.

VB21	Create Sales Deal

This transaction is used to create master data for a sales deal, which includes general data and associated pricing information, such as a flat rate discount or volume-related discount. A sales deal can be created in reference to a promotion (created using transaction VB31), in which case the payment terms can also be defaulted into the sales deal. Input the agreement type, click ENTER, and enter general data such as the valid from/to date range and description of the deal. Complete the master data by clicking the CONDITION RECORD icon to input the pricing/discount information, for example, a discount on a product line or individual materials. This condition will now be shown in the sales order if that product line or material is being sold.

VB22   Change Sales Deal

Use this transaction to change a sales deal previously created using transaction VB21. This transaction may be used, for example, if the sales deal needs to be discontinued prematurely, which can be accomplished by changing the valid to date.

VB23   Display Sales Deal

Use this transaction to display a sales deal previously created using transaction VB21.

VB25   List of Sales Deals

This transaction is used to display a list of sales deals using the following selection criteria: sales deal number, sales deal description, valid from/to date range, assigned promotion, and sales area information. The output display can be changed and used as a default to suit user requirements.

VB31   Create Promotion

This transaction is used to create a promotion, which can represent a broad marketing plan used to connect multiple sales deals (created using transaction VB21). Sales deals can be created in reference to a promotion, which facilitates the link to the promotion. Furthermore, the promotion contains payment terms and valid from/to dates which, by default, contain the information from the sales deal. Input the agreement type, click ENTER, and

input the description. Then enter the payment terms, valid from/to date range and internal comment, if required, and save.

VB32   Change Promotion

Use this transaction to change a promotion previously created using transaction VB31. This transaction may be used, for example, if the promotion needs to be discontinued prematurely, which can be accomplished by changing the valid to date.

VB33   Display Promotion

Use this transaction to display a promotion previously created using transaction VB31.

VB35   Promotions List

This transaction is used to display a list of promotions using the following selection criteria: promotion number, promotion description, validity from/to date range, and sales area information. The output display can be changed and used as a default to suit user requirements.

VB41   Create Cross-Selling

This transaction is used to create a master data link for materials that are frequently sold together. This information is commonly used in mail order sales scenarios wherein a customer calls to order a material and once the material is entered into the sales order, a dialog box appears enabling the order entry clerk to suggest an additional material the customer might consider buying. Input the material determination type, click ENTER, select a condition type, click ENTER, enter a valid from/to date range, and then enter the materials sold/to be suggested. Note: to get a sales analysis of materials that are frequently sold together, you can use report program SDCRSL01.

VB42	Change Cross-Selling

Use this transaction to change the material determination master data previously created using transaction VB41.

VB43	Display Cross-Selling

Use this transaction to display the material determination master data previously created using transaction VB41.

VBN1	Create Free Goods Determination

This transaction is used to create master data to determine free goods during sales document processing. Free goods are those that the customer does not pay for and may be one of two types: inclusive (the free goods are within the same line on the sales order) or exclusive (a separate line on the sales document is created where the free material does not have to take the same material number as the original material ordered). The condition technique is used to facilitate this functionality. Input the condition type (which may be by material, customer/material etc.), click ENTER, select the key combination, materials etc., the valid from/to date range of the condition, and save. The free goods will now be selected during sales document processing if the condition is fulfilled.

VBN2	Change Free Goods Determination

Use this transaction to change a free goods condition record previously created using transaction VBN1. This transaction may be used, for example, if the free good deal needs to be discontinued prematurely, which can be accomplished by changing the valid to date.

VBN3	Display Free Goods Determination

Use this transaction to display the free goods condition record previously created using transaction VBN1.

VBO1	Create Rebate Agreement

This transaction is used to create a special type of agreement/discount with the customer involving the settlement of a discount/rebate retroactively. An agreement for a rebate is entered into with the customer or another rebate recipient, and rebate volume/accrual amounts are recorded as sales document/ deliveries are processed. Then, on a one-time or periodic basis, the rebate amount is settled by creating a rebate request and rebate settlement document. The rebate agreement has header data and uses the condition technique to accrue for the rebate amount and capture the rebate volume. Input the agreement type, click ENTER, enter the valid from/to date range, rebate recipient, description, type of settlement, click the CONDITION icon and then enter the condition records that will be called during sales document processing and save.

VBO2	Change Rebate Agreement

Use this transaction to change a rebate agreement previously created using transaction VBO1. This transaction is also used to perform the following functions: change the rebate amount or validity date range, perform settlement and report on previous settlement amounts and rebate volume.

VBO3	Display Rebate Agreement

Use this transaction to display a rebate agreement previously created using transaction VBO1. This transaction can be used to report on previous settlement amounts and rebate volume.

VBOF   Update Billing Documents

This transaction is used to update billing documents for rebate conditions that have been created with a valid date in the past or pricing condition changes that will affect billing documents already created. The program updates the billing document pricing procedure for changes to rebate conditions and then posts an accrual if required. Selection criteria include rebate agreement number, rebate recipient, validity end date before, sales area information and posting date. The program can be run in test or update mode.

VC/2   Sales Summary

Use this report to prepare for sales activities. The report is split into a header and main section. The header contains a VIEW FIELD icon, which allows you to group the information you require and an INFORMATION BLOCK field, which enables you to go directly to the information block you require. The main body of the report contains blocks of information, such as the customer address, partner contacts, sales volume/key figures, credit information, promotional agreements, and any payment card information.

VC01N   Create Sales Activity

Use this transaction to record sales activities you engage in with a customer. Record the sales activity type such as a phone call, sales letter, etc., date and time from/to the activity took place, company information, contact person and description of the activity. The screen can be customized by sales activity type to suit business requirements. Sales information can be displayed and you can branch to the address data of the customer. Follow-on activities can also be created, such as a sales letter to follow up on a phone call or sales order processing.

VCC1   Payment Cards: Worklist

This transaction lists all sales orders and deliveries with payment cards. The report selection criteria include sales area information, sales document and various status indicators, such as the sales document's overall status and credit hold status. The output display enables you to process a sales document, release documents and carry out authorizations.

VD01   Customer Create (Sales)

This transaction is used to create the customer master record sales and distribution views, which are stored at the sales area level. The customer master sales and distribution view contains data relevant to sales, shipping, billing and business partner determination functionality. Customer master data fields that are either optional or required fields, as determined by the account group, can be maintained. All business partners, such as sold-to, ship-to, payer and bill-to, can be created using this transaction code. Input the customer master sales area information and the customer master number if the GENERAL DATA views have already been maintained; if not, leave blank and the GENERAL DATA will need input also. Then click ENTER. Input relevant customer master data and save. Note that there is a comparison report via transaction F.2D that displays customer master records that have not been created in finance or sales and distribution to ensure that all data have been set up in the relevant modules.

VD02   Customer Change (Sales)

This transaction is used to change any of the customer master record views in the GENERAL or SALES AREA DATA views. Customer master data fields that are either optional or required, as determined by the account group, are available to change. All business partners, such as sold-to, ship-to, payer and bill-to, can be changed using this transaction. Note that there is a change log on the customer master that can be accessed within the customer master via menu path ENVIRONMENT • ACCOUNT CHANGES in order to review changes by user ID, date and old/new values.

| VD03 | Customer Display (Sales) |

This transaction is used to display the customer master record views at the general and/or sales area level. All business partners, such as sold-to, ship-to, payer and bill-to, can be displayed using this transaction.

| VD04 | Customer Account Changes |

Use this transaction to report all changes to the customer master. The report is organized by customer and sales area. There is an option to select a specific date, time, and user ID of the individual making the change. The report output will display the fields changed, with the option to drill down and display the old/new field value and date changed.

| VD05 | Customer Block/Unblock |

This transaction is used to block the customer master from various transactions, such as sales order processing, financial postings, etc.

| VD06 | Customer Flag for Deletion |

Use this transaction to flag a customer master for deletion. The deletion flag can be set by sales area or all sales areas. Furthermore, the deletion flag can be set at the general area level and general area level including selected sales areas. The deletion flag will ensure that the customer cannot be used in transactional processing and can be included in the archiving process.

| VD51 | Create Customer-Material Info Record |

This transaction is used to stored customer-specific material master data, such as the customer's material number and description. Furthermore, customer-specific data on deliveries and delivery tolerances can also be stored. This data can be used during sales order entry whereby if you input the customer's material number, your company's material number will be pulled into the sales order. Also, during EDI incoming sales order processing, your company's material number can be derived from this master data.

| VD52 | Selection of Customer-Material Info Records (Change) |

Use this transaction to change a customer's material info record previously created using transaction VD51. This may be required if, for example, more materials need to be added.

| VD53 | Selection of Customer-Material Info Records (Display) |

Use this transaction to display a customer's material info record previously created using transaction VD51.

| VD59 | List Customer-Material Info |

Use this transaction to display a list of customer-material info records. Input selection criteria include sales organization, your company's material number, the customer's material number, and the customer number. Display variants can be created, saved, and used as a default.

| VDH1N | Edit Customer Hierarchy |

This transaction is used to create and change levels on a customer hierarchy, which is used to reflect the structure of a customer organization. For example, a customer may have several buying companies that all receive the same pricing/discounts: you can maintain this hierarchical structure and maintain pricing records at that higher level. The same hierarchy can be used for rebate processing and profitability analysis. Input the hierarchy type (which controls how the hierarchy is used, for example, pricing, account groups and organizational data restrictions), the customer or customer number range, sales area information and execute. On the next screen, highlight the customer and click the CREATE button or the CHANGE button to maintain the hierarchy assignment in the right-hand window pane and save.

VDH2	Display Customer Hierarchy

Use this transaction to display a customer hierarchy previously created using transaction VDH1N.

VF01	Create Billing Document

This transaction is used to process the billing document, which represents the final step in the sales and distribution ordering cycle. This transaction is used to process an individual billing document; however, transaction VF04 is used to process multiple billing documents. Billing document types, including invoices, credit memos, cancellations, rebate settlements and pro forma invoices, are typically defaulted from the previous document type/copy control settings in customizing. The billing document is fully integrated with the financial module and, upon posting, creates financial postings to the general ledger and management reporting modules (if required). Input the billing type (if needed) and billing date (current date is defaulted) and then input the reference document, which could be a delivery document, sales order (if non-delivery relevant) or rebate settlement request, and click ENTER. The billing information can be reviewed before saving.

VF02	Change Billing Document

Use this transaction to change a billing document, which may be required, for example, if the billing document had not been processed in the financial modules because perhaps the posting period had been incorrectly closed. In this case, you need to reopen the accounting period and, using this transaction, input the billing document number, click ENTER, and save the document, which will ensure that the accounting documents have been created.

VF03	Display Billing Document

Use this transaction to display the billing document previously created using transaction VF01 or VF04. From the display function, you can click the ACCOUNTING DOCUMENT icon in order to drill down into the general ledger or management financial postings.

VF04	Maintain Billing Due List

This transaction is used to process multiple billing documents at one time. Selection is by billing date, reference document or sales area. You can change the default data, proposed by copy control, by clicking the DEFAULT SETTINGS tab and selecting a different billing type or billing date. Document selection enables the choice of sales process you want to bill, such as order-related or delivery-related billing. After executing the program and before you create the billing documents, you have the option to bill individually for each reference document or perform collective billing, where the system tries to combine billing documents as much as possible, by sold-to, payment terms, etc.

VF05	List of Billing Documents

Use this transaction to list billing documents using a material or business partner, typically payer, as one of the selection criteria. You can select all open billing documents or all billing documents within a date created range. Various output display options are available, which can be saved and used as default. Note: A special authorization parameter ID is required in your user profile in order to make and save changes to the display layouts.

| **VF11** | Cancel Billing Document |

This transaction is used to cancel a billing document, which may be required if, for example, there was an error in posting to the incorrect customer account in finance. An additional cancellation billing document is created reversing the accounting entries, allowing the corrections to be made to the reference document and allowing for the recreation of the billing document. Input the billing document number and save. The cancellation will also be displayed in the document flow.

| **VF21** | Create Invoice List |

This transaction is used to create invoice lists, at specified time intervals or on specific dates, in order to send to a particular payer business partner. This may be required where a central payer collects and pays invoices for a group of companies. Typically, the group payer pays the invoices and in return for this service earns a factoring discount. Note that there are a number of prerequisites to enabling this functionality that must be set up in customizing, such as a special condition type for the factoring discount, use of special billing document type, customer calendar setting (in the customer master), etc. Input the billing documents individually or via a worklist and save your selection.

| **VF22** | Change Invoice List |

Use this transaction to change an invoice list, for example, if one of the billing documents had been incorrectly input into the list. Input

the invoice list number, remove the billing document, and save the list.

| **VF23** | Display Invoice List |

Use this transaction to display an invoice list previously created using transaction VF21.

| **VF25** | List of Invoice Lists |

Use this transaction to list invoice lists using the business partner payer. You can select all open invoice lists or all invoice lists within a date created range. Various output display options are available, which can be saved and used as a default.

| **VF26** | Cancel Invoice List |

Use this transaction to cancel invoice lists, which reverses financial postings and renders the billing documents available for posting again.

| **VF31** | Output from Billing |

This transaction is used to process the billing output as a separate step from the billing document creation function. Input the output type (which is the billing document layout form), the transmission medium (e.g., printout or fax), the sort order in which the output is created and printed, and the processing mode (e.g., whether this is the first billing output or repeat output). In addition, the billing document range, billing date, reference type document and sales area information can be selected before you click EXECUTE.

| **VF43** | Posting Documents for Revenues |

Use this transaction to report on revenue recognition postings for an individual sales order or accounting document, which is useful if document summarization is active since it is not possible to retrace the postings by sales order line item from the accounting document. The revenue posting document can also be found by looking at the document flow and also by drilling back to the original document from the accounting document. Selection criteria include sales documents or the ACCOUNTING DOCUMENT radio buttons and the document number. The display offers the ability to navigate to postings at the line item level and then to the revenue accounts with the revenue update status. Click the ALL REVENUE POSTING icon to display all postings for a collective run. Drill-down capability is available to view the sales order and follow-on documents.

VF44	Edit Revenue List

This transaction is used to recognize revenue separately from the standard billing document, once the process is initialized (depending on the revenue recognition method). Revenue recognition functionality is activated by item category in customizing. Sales order line items with an item category activated for revenue recognition will control when revenue is recognized as opposed to recognizing revenue when invoicing the customer (which is the standard SAP process). Input the company code, sales document number range (if required), the posting period/fiscal year, posting date, and execute. The output displays the revenue recognition relevant line items from which you can select the lines and process the financial posting documents individually or collectively.

VF45	Revenue Report

Use this transaction to report on revenue recognition postings for multiple sales orders. The revenue posting document can also be found by looking at the document flow and by drilling back to the original document from the accounting document. Selection criteria include sales and distribution documents or the ACCOUNTING DOCUMENT radio button and

the document number. The display list offers the ability to navigate to postings at the line item level and then to the revenue accounts with the revenue update status. Click the ALL REVENUE POSTINGS icon to display all postings for a collective run. Drill-down capability is available to view the sales order and the follow-on documents.

VF46	Maintain Cancellation List

Use this transaction to cancel any revenue recognition postings incorrectly generated from transaction VF44. This transaction reverses the original financial postings, marks both the original line and the reversed line with a cancellation indicator in the revenue recognition tables, and creates new lines ready for use again with transaction VF44.

VF47	Revenue Recognition; Inconsistency Check in Revenue Table

Use this transaction as the main tool in the analysis of the revenue recognition data from a technical view of the revenue recognition tables. Sales orders may contain errors, which can cause inconsistencies in the revenue recognition tables (VBREVK, VBREVE and VBREVR). Selection criteria include company code, sales document range, number of lines to read (to improve performance) and types of checks (for example, checking control lines in the revenue recognition tables and whether the control lines have errors). The report can be executed in test mode (which is recommended until errors are analyzed) and update mode.

VF48	Compare Report

This transaction is used to compare finance and sales and distribution balances on the accrual accounts (i.e., deferred revenue and unbilled revenue). The program looks at the account balance in finance and compares this to the balance in the revenue recognition tables (VBREVE and VBREVR) for selected periods. This report simply compares balances; to determine the reasons for any issues, VF47 can be used. Selection criteria include the company code, an individual accrual account, posting period, and fiscal year from/to. The executed report provides a header part that shows the balances determined for the selected accrual account and a detail part that provides a worklist with sales document line items used when the accrual account was posted via billing or revenue recognition.

VFRB	Retro-billing

Use this transaction in a scenario where new pricing has been agreed upon with the customer and is valid for billing documents that have already been processed. You can run this transaction to list the billing documents affected by the new pricing conditions and to create new billing documents for the differences. Input the payer, sales organization, billing date range, execute transaction, and then process the additional invoices.

VFX3	Release Billing Documents for Accounting

This transaction enables the release of billing documents that, for whatever reason, have not been passed to finance for posting. For example, if the financial posting period had been incorrectly closed. Once the posting period has been reopened, you can use this transaction to release the billing document to accounting. Input the payer or payer range, sales organization, select various incomplete posting indicators, and then execute the program.

VG01	Create Group

This transaction is used to group delivery documents for collective processing. Input the group type, which determines the type of document that can be processed in this collective manner, i.e., group deliveries that refer to sales order or returns only, and click ENTER. On the next screen, enter the documents numbers that are to be grouped and save.

VG02	Change Group

Use this transaction to change a delivery group previously created using transaction VG01.

VG03	Display Group

Use this transaction to display a delivery group previously created using transaction VG01.

VI01	Create Shipment Costs

This transaction is used to create an individual shipment cost document for a shipment or shipment stage. Input the shipment document number, which must have a transportation status of "planned" (defined in customizing) and click ENTER. The shipment cost document has header information, such as pricing/settlement date, which will be set to the default value (defined in customizing). The shipment cost document also has line item information, which includes a pricing procedure that calculates costs using the pricing condition technique and settlement data. The shipment cost document also has sub items that represent the calculation basis for the cost. Upon saving the shipment cost document, costs are automatically calculated and settlement data is assigned and transferred to accounting.

VI02   Change Shipment Costs

Use this transaction to change an individual shipment cost document, which may be required, for example, if further calculation of shipment costs is needed or settlement data need to be assigned. Input the shipment document number, click ENTER, make the necessary changes and save.

VI03   Display Shipment Costs

Use this transaction to display a shipment cost document previously created using transaction VI01.

VI04   Shipment List: Create Shipment Costs

Use this transaction to create multiple shipment cost documents at one time. Input selection criteria include service agent, route, shipment document range, status of the shipment document and many attributes of the shipment document. The shipment cost document header information includes pricing date and settlement date, which will default (defined in customizing). The shipment cost document line item information includes a pricing procedure calculating costs using the pricing condition technique and settlement data. The shipment cost document also has sub items that represent the calculation basis for the cost. Upon program execution and list generation, the saved shipment cost document can have the costs automatically calculated, settlement data assigned, and be transferred to accounting.

VI05   List Shipment Costs: Change Worklist

This transaction is used to change shipment cost documents via a worklist. Individual shipment cost documents may require changing, for example, if further calculation of shipment costs is needed or settlement

data need to be assigned. Input the shipment document number, click ENTER, make the necessary changes and save.

VI07   List Shipment Costs: Change Worklist in Background

This transaction is used to change shipment cost documents via a worklist with background processing. Shipment cost documents may require changing, for example, if further calculation of shipment costs needs updating, and the updates can be performed in background.

VI12   List Shipment Costs: Settlement

Use this transaction to settle shipment cost documents that have not been fully calculated, for example, shipment cost documents created with line items with automatically calculated shipment costs. On a periodic basis, this program is executed, and line items are reviewed and batched together for settlement to accounting.

VI16   Logs in the Application Log

Use this transaction to review the log for shipment cost document changes via a worklist in background executed using transaction VI07. The log can be displayed with or without warnings and errors.

VK11   Create Condition Records

This transaction is used to maintain pricing condition records that access pricing information automatically in sales documents. Input a condition type, for example PR00 for price, and click ENTER. Next, select the condition table to be maintained (each condition type will be customized with an access sequence and condition tables with the condition fields) and click ENTER. Maintain the condition record fields, price, unit of measure and valid from/to fields and save.

| VK12 | Change Condition Records |

Use this transaction to change pricing condition records, which may be required if you need to change the price, extend the valid to date, or place a deletion indicator on the condition record. Input the condition type, click ENTER, select the condition table that contains the condition fields. (Note: In customizing, you do have some flexibility as to changing some of the required fields for the purposes of maintenance, which can be useful if you want to change multiple condition records at the same time.) Click EXECUTE. Then maintain the condition record and click SAVE.

| VK13 | Display Condition Records |

Use this transaction to display a condition record previously created using transaction VK11.

| VK14 | Create Condition Records with Reference |

This transaction is used to create pricing condition records with reference to existing pricing condition records. Input the pricing condition type, select the table used for the reference, input the reference pricing condition record, select the option to keep the reference valid from/to date, if required, and execute. On the next screen, enter the new entries at the line item level and save.

| VKM1 | Blocked SD Documents |

This transaction is used to review sales documents, including sales orders and deliveries, that have been blocked via credit control. Customers can be set up with a credit master and with DYNAMIC CREDIT CHECKING turned on at the sale document level, sales documents can be checked for credit control

purposes. For example, a sales order placed by customer who has exceeded his or her credit limit can be blocked. After the sales order has been blocked, the customer may settle his or her account receivable and/or the credit department may grant the customer more credit, which means that you can use this transaction to release the blocked sales order(s). Input the credit control area and credit representative group, credit account (customer) and click EXECUTE. On the next screen, select the blocked sales order, click the RELEASE flag, and save the document.

| VKM2 | Released SD Documents |

Use this transaction to display a list of sales documents that have been released via transaction VKM1.

| VKM3 | Sales Document |

This transaction is used to review only sales orders that have been blocked via credit control, as opposed to transaction VKM1, which reviews both sales orders and deliveries. There is also a selection option for the sales order document number. Customers can be set up with a credit master and with DYNAMIC CREDIT CHECKING turned on at the sale document level, sales documents can be checked for credit control purposes. For example, a sales order placed by a customer who has exceeded his or her credit limit can be blocked. After the sales order has been blocked, the customer may settle his or her account receivable and/or the credit department may grant the customer more credit, which means you can use this transaction to release the blocked sales order(s). Input the sales order document number, if known, and click EXECUTE. On the next screen, select the blocked sales order, click the RELEASE flag, and save the document.

VKM4   SD Documents

Use this transaction to review both blocked and released sales documents: this transaction is a combination of transactions VKM1 and VKM2.

VKM5   Deliveries

This transaction is used to review only deliveries that have been blocked via credit control, as opposed to transaction VKM1, which reviews both sales orders and deliveries. There is also a selection option for the delivery document number. Customers can be set up with a credit master with DYNAMIC CREDIT CHECKING functionality at the sale document level. For example, at delivery time a customer who has overdue accounts receivable and has exceeded his or her credit limit will have any future deliveries blocked for credit control purpose. Subsequently, the customer may settle his or her account receivable and/or the credit department may grant the customer more credit, which means that you can use this transaction to release the blocked deliveries. Input the delivery document, if known, and click EXECUTE. On the next screen, select the blocked delivery document, click the RELEASE flag, and save the document.

VL01N   Create Outbound Delivery with Order Reference

This transaction is used to create a delivery document in reference to a single sales document. Delivery documents can serve as the basis for planning material requirements, picking, creating shipping units and billing. A delivery will be issued out of one shipping point. When you create the delivery document, some of the activities that will take place include checking for delivery blocks, calculating weight and volume, checking for any partial delivery requirements on the sales order, redetermining the shipping route,

assigning pick locations, and updating the sales order status. Input the shipping point, selection date (this will select all material available on those dates and transportation scheduling up to this date) and click ENTER. Review the delivery quantity and default information and click SAVE.

VL01NO   Create Outbound Delivery without Order Reference

Use this transaction to create a delivery document without reference to a sales order, which may be required if sales orders are processed outside of SAP and you want to create a delivery document manually just for printing delivery output. In this scenario, there will be no default information flow from the sales order, so all information will need to be entered manually and there will be no system checks (for example, checking to see whether the data are complete with plant and material storage information). Input the shipping point, delivery document type, sales area information, click ENTER, and manually enter materials, quantities, etc.

VL02N   Change Outbound Delivery

Use this transaction to change an outbound delivery document, which can include inputting the pick quantity, changing the shipping route for the delivery, transportation scheduling dates, deleting or adding line items to the delivery, etc. Input the delivery document and click ENTER. Make changes to the header or line item information and click SAVE. If the delivery document is complete and the goods have been shipped, you can also post the goods issue inventory movement from this transaction, which will relieve and update inventory balances and process the associated financial transactions. For the ability to process multiple documents via a worklist, you can use transaction VL06.

VL03N	Display Outbound Delivery

Use this transaction to display the delivery document, which also includes drill-down capability to view any follow-on documents, such as inventory and financial postings. Input the delivery document number and click ENTER.

VL06	Delivery Monitor

Use this transaction to access the delivery monitor, which is a central transaction for monitoring and subsequent collective processing of inbound and outbound delivery documents. This transaction lists completed and open deliveries. Delivery documents can be listed depending on their status, such as all deliveries ready for picking or goods issue. Deliveries can be selected for collective processing using multiple selection options, but some of the selection options are preset, such as those dependent on the status of the delivery document. Select the type of collective processing required, for example, click the TRANSPORTATION PLANNING icon and on the next screen input selection options, such as shipping point or shipping planning date range, and execute.

VL06C	Outbound Deliveries for Confirmation

Use this transaction for the collective processing of delivery documents that require confirmation, such as those requiring confirmation of transfer orders for picking or put away entries. As with creation of a transfer order, the color of the confirmation indicates its status. Input selection criteria, such as shipping point and planned goods movement date range, and execute. If you have set the processing of subsequent functions to background mode, you can specify whether the picking or put away quantity should be copied into the delivery quantity or whether

you want to post goods issue/goods receipt immediately following confirmation.

VL06D	Outbound Deliveries for Distribution

This transaction is used when integrating SAP with a decentralized warehouse management system (WMS) where you can choose at which point the delivery document is ready for distribution to the WMS. In customizing, you set decentralized WHS to ACTIVE for the warehouse number; for the delivery type, you set at what point the distribution occurs. Furthermore, if you set the distribution option to DELAYED for the delivery type, then you can use this transaction to execute the distribution of the delivery document to the decentralized WMS. Selection criteria include sales area, shipping point, delivery date range, delivery status (e.g. "D" for delayed), warehouse number, delivery number, material number range, and most of the common data referenced on a delivery document.

VL06F	General Delivery List – Outbound Deliveries

Use this report for a general list of outbound delivery documents. Selection criteria include sales area, shipping point, delivery date range, delivery status (e.g. transportation planning, goods issue, etc.), warehouse number, delivery number, material number range, and most of the common data referenced on a delivery document.

VL06G	Outbound Deliveries for Goods Issue

Use this transaction to process the outbound delivery post goods issue function. Selection options include shipping point and the actual goods movement date. Execute the program. If the goods issue posting was successful, the processed deliveries appear in green; if errors occurred, they appear in red. The delivery also appears in green if the goods issue was already posted for the delivery document in question (this may occur because the same delivery was accidentally selected twice, for example).

VL06I   Inbound Delivery Monitor

Use this transaction to access the delivery monitor, which is a central transaction for monitoring and subsequent collective processing of inbound delivery documents. This transaction can list completed and open deliveries. Delivery documents can be listed depending on their status, such as all deliveries ready for put away or goods receipt. Deliveries can be selected for collective processing using multiple selection options, but some of the selection options are preset, such as those dependent on the status of the delivery document. Select the type of collective processing required, for example, click the TRANSPORTATION PLANNING icon and, on the next screen, input selection options such as purchase order, delivery date range, and execute.

VL06IC   Inbound Deliveries for Confirmation

Use this transaction for the collective processing of delivery documents that require confirmation, such as transfer orders for picking or put away entries. As with the creation of a transfer orders, the color of the confirmation indicates its status. Input selections include purchase order document number, inbound delivery document number, planned goods movement date range. Then you can execute. If you have set the processing of subsequent functions to background mode, you can specify whether the picking or put away quantity should be copied into the delivery quantity or whether you want to post goods issue/goods receipt immediately following confirmation.

VL06ID   Inbound Deliveries for Distribution

This transaction is used when integrating SAP with a decentralized warehouse management system (WMS) where you can choose at which point the delivery document is ready for distribution to the WMS. In customizing, you set decentralized WHS to ACTIVE for the warehouse number; in the delivery type, you set at what point the distribution occurs. Furthermore, if you set the distribution option to DELAYED for the delivery type, then you can use this transaction to execute the distribution of the delivery document to the decentralized WMS. Selection criteria include sales area, shipping point, delivery date range, delivery status (e.g. "D" for delayed), warehouse number, delivery number, material number range, and most of the common data referenced on a delivery document.

VL06IF   List of Inbound Deliveries

Use this report for a general list of inbound delivery documents. Selection criteria include shipping point/receiving point, purchase order, document creation date range, vendor status, status of the inbound delivery document, delivery number, material, and most of the common data referenced on a delivery document.

VL06IG   Inbound Deliveries for Goods Receipt

Use this transaction to process the inbound delivery goods receipt function. This transaction may be used, for instance, in the sales return process where a delivery document is processed with the relevant information for receiving the returned materials back into the plant. Selection options include the receiving shipping point and the actual goods return date. Execute the program. If the goods return posting was successful, the processed deliveries appear in green; if errors occurred, they appear in red. The delivery also appears in green if goods return was already posted for the delivery document in question (this may occur because the same delivery was accidentally selected twice, for example).

VL06IP	Inbound Deliveries for Putaway

This transaction is used to process an inbound goods receipt and put the stock into the warehouse supported by the Warehouse Management system (WM). For example, a company issues a purchase order that is confirmed by the vendor using a shipping notification. When the shipping notification is received, the data are transferred to an inbound delivery document so that you can put the inventory away into the warehouse when it arrives. Input selection criteria include purchase order document number, inbound delivery document number, planned goods movement date range; then you can execute. If you have set the processing of subsequent functions to background mode, you can specify whether the picking or put away quantity should be copied into the delivery quantity or whether you want to post the goods receipt immediately following confirmation.

VL06L	Outbound Deliveries for Loading

Use this transaction to generate a list of deliveries ready for loading into a truck or shipment container prior to goods issue. The vehicle or transport equipment sealing activity is also supported. Selection options include shipping point and the actual loading date. Execute the program and update the loading date as necessary and save. The processed deliveries appear in green; if errors occurred, they appear in red.

VL06O	Outbound Delivery Monitor

Use this transaction to access the delivery monitor, which is a central transaction for monitoring and the collective processing of outbound delivery documents. This transaction lists completed and open deliveries. Delivery documents can be listed depending on their status, such as all deliveries ready for picking or goods issue. Deliveries can be selected for collective processing using multiple selection options, but some of the selection options are preset, such as those dependent on the status of the delivery document. Select the type of collective processing required, for example, click the TRANSPORTATION PLANNING icon and, on the next screen, input selection options, such as shipping point and shipping planning date range, and execute.

VL06P	Outbound Deliveries for Picking

Use this transaction to execute the picking process, which involves taking goods from a storage location and staging the materials in a picking area where the goods can be prepared for shipping. Picking can be set up to post automatically at delivery document creation time or processed manually using this transaction, according to the daily workload. There is a picking status in the delivery document that indicates what stage of picking the delivery is at, such as started or completed. Selection options include shipping point, picking delivery date range, and warehouse number. Execute to display a list of deliveries ready for picking. Then select the delivery documents, enter picking quantity, and save.

VL06T	Outbound Deliveries for Transportation Planning

This transaction is used to display a worklist of deliveries ready for transportation planning, i.e., those deliveries that are ready to be assigned a route for the delivery and a forwarding agent for transportation. A prerequisite for this functionality is that the delivery type is flagged in customizing as TRANSPORTATION-PLANNING RELEVANT and routes are set up. Input the shipping point and transportation planning date or organize the worklist by selecting the route and/or forwarding agent and then click EXECUTE. Once the worklist is displayed, you can then assign delivery documents to shipments manually or have them automatically assigned to shipment documents.

VL06U	Unchecked Outbound Deliveries

Use this transaction to display a worklist of unchecked deliveries, which are deliveries with a reduced scope of check in relation to the main availability checking functionality. An unchecked delivery is only created in reference to a preceding document that has shipping requirement dates on it. Use this transaction to convert unchecked deliveries into checked deliveries by performing all necessary checks that were explicitly switched off when you created the unchecked delivery, especially the availability checking. Input the sales area, shipping point, planned goods movement date, and click EXECUTE. The delivery now confirms the delivery quantities to the sales order and updates the status. You can now perform all the follow-on functions, such as picking, packing, and goods issue.

VL08	Report Results of Pick Order

This transaction is used to report picked quantities. Input the delivery number and the picking request number and click ENTER. On the next screen, you can confirm amounts for individual items in the picking request. Items that are subject to confirmation are automatically confirmed.

VL09	Reverse Goods Movement

Use this transaction to reverse a goods movement such as a goods issue posted in reference to an outbound delivery document. This may be required if the goods movement was posted in error. Enter the shipping point, goods movement date, inbound/outbound delivery document number, and click EXECUTE. Then select the delivery document/goods movements you want to reverse and click SAVE. Select ENTER through the confirmation message to confirm the reversal and post the reversing goods movements.

VL10	Sales and Purchase Orders, Fast Display

This transaction is used to create multiple delivery documents in reference to a sale and/or purchase order. Sales and purchase orders are analyzed and delivery documents are created according to the planned delivery date. Collective processing of deliveries may be required if you want to combine deliveries for a ship-to party. Input the shipping point, the delivery creation date (which is the earliest of the material availability date or transportation planning date), the rule for determining the delivery date, and click EXECUTE. You can then manually process the delivery document by selecting the line and clicking the DIALOG or you can select the lines and click the CREATING THE DELIVERIES IN BACKGROUND icon.

VL10A	Sales Orders, Fast Display

This transaction is used to create multiple delivery documents in reference to a sales order only. Sales orders are analyzed and delivery documents are created according to the planned delivery date. Collective processing of deliveries may be required if you want to combine deliveries for a ship-to party. Input the shipping point, the delivery creation date (which is the earliest of the material availability date or transportation planning date), the rule for determining the delivery date, and click Execute. You can then manually process the delivery document by selecting the line and clicking the Dialog icon or you can select the lines and click the Creating the Deliveries in Background icon.

VL10B	Purchase Orders, Fast Display

This transaction is used to create multiple delivery documents in reference to purchasing documents only. This may be required, for instance, when delivering interplant transfers using stock transport orders. Stock transport orders are analyzed and delivery documents are created according to the planned delivery date. Collective processing of deliveries may be required if you want to combine deliveries for a ship-to plant location. Input the shipping point, the delivery creation date (which is the earliest of the material availability date or transportation planning date), the rule for determining the delivery date, and click Execute. There are also further selection options for narrowing the list of stock transport orders on the Purchase Orders tab. On the next screen, you can manually process the delivery document by selecting the line and clicking the Dialog icon or you can select the lines and click the Creating the Deliveries in Background icon.

VL10H	Sales Order and Purchase Order Items

This transaction is used to create multiple delivery documents in reference to a sales/purchase order at the line item level. The delivery list output gives you the option to select specific quantities, at the line item level, when combining and creating deliveries. Sales and purchase orders are analyzed and delivery documents are created according to the planned delivery date. Collective processing of deliveries may be required if

you want to combine deliveries for a ship-to party. Input the shipping point, the delivery creation date (which is the earliest of the material availability date or transportation planning date), the rule for determining the delivery date, and click Execute. You can then manually process the delivery document by selecting the line and clicking the Dialog icon or you can select the lines and click the Creating the Deliveries in Background icon.

VL10I	Sales and Purch. Order Item Sched. Lines

Use this transaction to create multiple delivery documents in reference to a sales or purchasing schedule line agreement. Schedule line agreements contain details of a delivery schedule. Some scheduling agreements contain two sets of delivery date: one is a forecast delivery date and the other is a firm delivery date that can be sent by the customer via EDI. Once the firm delivery dates are received, you can use this transaction for the automatic creation of the delivery documents for subsequent shipment processing. Collective processing of deliveries can also facilitate combining deliveries for a ship-to party. Input the shipping point, the delivery creation date (which is the earliest of the material availability date or transportation planning date), the rule for determining the delivery date, and click Execute. You can then manually process the delivery document by selecting the line and clicking the Dialog icon or you can select the lines and click the Creating the Deliveries in Background icon.

VL21	Create Background Jobs for Goods Issue Posting

This transaction can be used for collectively posting the goods issue for delivery documents and can be set up to run in background mode. Selection criteria include shipping point, route, goods issue date, delivery document number, grouped delivery document number and shipment number.

VL22	Display Change Documents of Delivery

Use this transaction to display a list of delivery document change documents that are posted when details of a delivery are changed. The system records changes to the header or line item data, partner roles, status, and to management data. You can also call up this report when processing the delivery document in change or display mode. Selection criteria include one delivery document number at a time. Selection criteria can also include item number, date and user ID of the individual making the change. The report output will display the fields changed with the option to drill down and display the old/new field value and date changed.

VL31N	Create Inbound Delivery

This transaction is used to create an inbound delivery document, which may be required to document delivery confirmation from the vendor. Input the vendor number, purchase order number, expected delivery date, expected delivery time, any external ID numbers, means of transport and click ENTER. The purchase order lines will be displayed; then select the line item, input the quantity confirmed, and save.

VL32N	Change Inbound Delivery

Use this transaction to change an inbound delivery document, which may be required to input a change in the planned delivery date, change the confirmed vendor delivery quantity or process the goods receipt. Input the inbound delivery document number, click ENTER, make changes to the delivery date or quantity received, for example, and save.

VL33N	Display Inbound Delivery

Use this transaction to display an inbound delivery document previously created via transaction VL31N.

VL35	Create Picking Waves According to Delivery Compare Times

This transaction is used to assign deliveries to picking waves. The warehouse is divided into picking timeslots, and the assignment of a delivery to a timeslot is dependent on the time when the order is recorded. Input the warehouse number, reference date (used to compare with the delivery date), timeslot group, timeslot, and other selection related to delivery data and execute. The program can be executed with the wave groups saved automatically or wave groups displayed before saving.

VL35_ST	Create Pick. Waves Acc. To Shipments

Use this transaction the create wave picks automatically according to time criteria, with reference to shipments. Input the warehouse number, reference date (used to compare with the delivery date), timeslot group, timeslot, shipment number from/to range and execute. The program can be executed with the wave groups saved automatically or wave groups displayed before saving.

VL36	Change Wave Picks

This transaction is used to make changes to wave picks. Input the warehouse number, reference date (used to compare with the delivery date), timeslot group, timeslot and the numbers of the wave picks in the group field. On the next screen, the wave picks appear. Waves and deliveries that were saved with capacity problems are marked in yellow. You can move deliveries from one wave to another and deselect waves and deliveries and then save the changes.

VL37	Wave Pick Monitor

Use this transaction to monitor the status of wave picks. Input the warehouse number, reference date (used to compare with the delivery date), timeslot group, timeslot and the numbers of the wave picks in the group field and click EXECUTE. The display list gives you an overview of the processing status of wave picks.

VL41	Create Rough Goods Receipt

This transaction is used to split the goods receiving process into two steps: one a rough goods receipt and the other an exact goods receipt. This allows for the matching of a shipping notification or purchase order with a delivery note while triggering the printing of documents to enable the physical receiving of the goods (counting). You can enter a rough goods receipt only if the purchasing information record has the confirmation category (confirmation control) turned on. Input the delivery number, vendor, purchase order number, and delivery date and then click the INBOUND DELIVERY DOCUMENT icon

VL64	Generation of Inbound Deliveries

This transaction is used to search for a delivery schedule of a purchase order line item or schedule line of a scheduling agreement where the flag is set for AUTOMATIC INBOUND DELIVERY CREATION. If the delivery date for the schedule line is older than or equal to the delivery date entered by the user, the system generates a new inbound delivery for each purchase order and/or scheduling agreement. Selection criteria include vendor, plant, purchasing document number and delivery to date. The program can be run in test or update mode.

VL65	Inbound Delivery Purge Report

This transaction is used to purge old inbound deliveries for which no more goods receipts are expected. For this program to work, the purge offset in days needs to be entered in customizing for the warehouse in question. The goods movement status of the inbound delivery at the header level and for each item is set to C (completely processed) if the offset days are reached for the purge scenario. Selection criteria include purge scenario (e.g., third part process or stock transport order), warehouse number and delivery number. The program can be executed in test or update mode.

VL66	Delete Inbound Delivery

Use this transaction to delete an inbound delivery document. Note that the inbound delivery document must not have any goods receipts posted to it or any handling units assigned to it. Selection criteria include delivery document and the created on date. The program can be executed in test or update mode.

VLSP	Subsequent Outbound-Delivery Split

This transaction is used to subsequently split a delivery into multiple deliveries, which is required if you discover that one delivery has too many items or the quantity is too large for the means of transport. This functionality has to be activated in customizing. During the subsequent outbound-delivery split, the status of the delivery document is checked to ensure that subsequent functions, such as goods movements or billing documents, have not been created. Also, the system confirms characteristics (delivery groups and correlation), copies data (texts), calculates attributes (volume and weight), and carries out determinations (outputs). Selection criteria include shipping point, outbound delivery document, handling unit, ship-to party, shipment data and split profile, which contains the control settings for how the split deliveries will be grouped.

VM01	Create Hazardous Material

This transaction is used to create hazardous material master records that contain special handling instructions in the warehouse management system. Information in the master record can include storage class (how the material should be stored), hazardous material storage warning (warnings that can be issued when handling the material in the warehouse) and, if the material is liquid, what concentration of a hazardous substance (as a percentage) is in the material. Regulations governing hazardous material vary by national laws, so the master record data can be customized to include any extra data required. Input the hazardous material number and the region code that governs the hazardous material regulations and click ENTER. Maintain the relevant data and save.

VM02	Change Hazardous Material

Use this transaction to change hazardous material master records that contain special handling instructions in the warehouse management system. This may be required if, for example, regulations governing the hazardous material were to change. Input the hazardous material number and the region code that governs the hazardous material regulations and click ENTER. Maintain the relevant data and save.

VM03	Display Hazardous Material

Use this transaction to display a hazardous material previously created using transaction VM01.

VRRE	Create Returns Delivery for Repair Order

This transaction is used to create a returns delivery document in reference to a single returns request. This transaction is similar to transaction VL01N (Create Delivery Document) except that you can cannot process the post goods movement (instead, you have to use transaction VL02N the post the goods receipt). The delivery document can serve as the basis for planning the material return and for processing the credit memo. Input the shipping point, return request, delivery type, click ENTER, review the delivery quantity and default information, and click SAVE.

VS01	Create Scale

This transaction is used to create a scale for calculating shipment costs, for example, a scale to calculate a freight rate depending on the combination of a distance scale (scale base type distance) and weight scale (scale base type weight). In order to calculate freight costs based on scales, you also need to assign the scale to the freight condition type using transaction T_06. Input the scale basis, click ENTER, and on the next screen enter a description for the scale, scale type (controls scale level, e.g., "scale basis" or "to scale"), enter scale levels, and save.

VS02	Change Scale

Use this transaction to change the scale rate for calculating shipment costs, for example, a scale to calculate a freight rate depending on the combination of a distance scale (scale base type distance) and weight scale (scale base type weight). Input scale ID, click ENTER, change rates and save.

VS03	Display Scale

Use this transaction to display scales for calculating shipment costs, for example, a scale to calculate a freight rate depending on a combination or a distance scale (scale base type distance) and weight scale (scale base type weight). Input scale ID and click ENTER to review the rates.

| **VS04** | Create Scale with Reference |

Use this transaction to create a scale with reference to an existing scale. Input the scale ID and click ENTER. Then, on the next screen, make changes for the new scale and save.

| **VS06** | List Scales |

Use this transaction to report on a list of scales and rates. Selection options include scale basis, scale description, scale type, created by and date of creation. Input selection criteria and click EXECUTE. The display output can be changed to suit user requirements and saved for future reporting.

| **VT01N** | Create Shipment |

This transaction is used to create an individual shipment document, which controls the transportation planning process, including acquiring the services of a forwarding agent, organizing the means of transportation, specifying the route of the shipment, and defining the stages covering the route in the most efficient way. In customizing, the delivery type must be relevant for transportation planning and, for outbound deliveries, the routes have to be defined. Input the transportation point, shipment type (what type of transportation is to be processed, for example, shipment by road), selection variant (can default values for transportation planning) and click ENTER. On the next screen, assign deliveries to the shipment, select a forwarding agent, plan the transportation times/dates, and save the document.

| **VT02N** | Change Shipment |

Use this transaction to change an individual shipment document, which controls the transportation planning process, including acquiring the services of a forwarding agent, organizing the means of transportation, specifying the route for the shipment, and defining the stages covering the route in the most efficient way. Input the shipment document, click ENTER, make the necessary changes, such as assign additional deliveries documents, adjust transportation times/date, etc. and save.

| **VT03N** | Display Shipment |

Use this transaction to display a shipment document previously created using transaction VT01N.

| **VT04** | Create Shipments in Collective Proc. |

This transaction is used to create multiple shipment documents automatically at one time depending on grouping rules that you define. The shipment document controls the transportation planning process, including acquiring services of a forwarding agent, organizing the means of transportation, specifying the route for the shipment, and defining stages covering the route in the most efficient way. In customizing, the delivery type must be relevant for transportation planning and, for outbound deliveries, routes have to be defined. Select whether inbound or outbound shipment documents are to be created and then define which deliveries will be considered by maintaining a selection variant. Then you can define the grouping criteria for the shipment documents, such as grouping by shipping point, ship-to party and route with minimum and maximum values for weight, volume and number of deliveries. You can also define some default values for shipment dates and times. There is also an option to process transportation chains when shipments consist of multiple shipment documents. Execute the program with an option to log the results, which can be viewed via transaction VT05.

VT05   Logs in the Application Log

Use this transaction to display the log resulting from the collective shipment create program executed via transaction VT04. The amount of detail in the log depends on your selection when executing transaction VT04; for example, you can save the log with a normal amount of detail or with very detailed information, including messages of a technical nature.

VT06   Shipment List: Collective Change Shipment

This transaction is used for mass changes to shipment documents, for example, if you need to change the forwarding agent on multiple shipments. Instead of changing each document individually, you can make a mass change in multiple shipment documents in one step. This change function allows you to enter changes in a sample line and then carry those changes over multiple shipment documents. Selection criteria include forwarding agent, route, shipping conditions, container ID, overall transport status and various transportation planning dates. Execute the program and, on the next screen, enter your changes in the default line and choose reference document. New value(s) will update the selected shipment documents and then you can save your changes.

VT11   Shipment List: Planning

Use this transaction for reporting on shipments to be planned or scheduled. For example, a shipment planner can select, as selection criteria, the overall transport status

0 (Planned), transportation planning point, planned check-in date, and the shipment type. Input selection criteria and execute to display the list. On the next screen, the planner can select a shipment and branch to the shipment document for processing and save the document. This report is displayed in advanced list viewer (ALV) format, which means there are advanced view options that can be customized by the user and saved for future reporting.

VT12   Shipment List: Shipment Completion

This transaction is similar to transaction VT11 but has an extra option related to status reporting of the shipment document, in particular, transportation status and dates for planned and actual shipment completion.

VT16   Shipment List: Check-in

Use this transaction to report on shipments that you want to check in. You can report on all shipments that are expected to arrive on that day, for instance, so that you can check in the shipments as the trucks arrive. Selection criteria important for check-in include planned deadlines and service agents. Input selection criteria and execute the report. From the displayed list, you can set the check-in status for all selected documents. Provided that the relevant setting was made in the activity profile, a dialog box will appear in which the truck's license plate number and driver's name can be entered. Once you have made changes to a shipment document in the list and then returned to the list, you can use the REFRESH function to update the list.

VT20   Overall Shipment Status Monitor

This transaction gives a good overview of the transportation execution process, displaying shipments grouped by status, time, and date and how much workload exists. For example, the transportation planner can review a particular shift in terms of workload and react to a busy schedule. In this way, the work can be distributed more evenly. Selection criteria include transportation planning point, shipment type, shipping point, forwarding agent, transportation planning date and time range, status groups, and an option to select the critical number of shipments per hour.

VT22	Selection Screen: Change Document Shipment

Use this transaction to report a list of shipment document changes. Selection criteria include user ID of the individual making the change, date and time of change, shipment number, shipment document table/field, and an option to display the changes per shipment or by field grouping. The report output will list the fields changed grouped by shipment document or table field and the old/new field values and date changed.

VT32	Selection Criteria for Forwarding Agent

This transaction is used to report on the tendering status of shipment order where one or more potential transportation service providers submit a quote for the transportation service. Selection criteria include tender status, such as accepted or rejected by forwarding agent, date of tender status, forwarding agent, shipment type, and overall status of the shipment document. Once the quote is accepted, the shipment order is updated with the terms and conditions of the transportation service and the service is carried out.

VT70	Messages for Shipments

Use this transaction to print output from shipment documents. The types of documents that can be output include general shipping

documents, labels to attach to the side of containers, shipment notifications and pro forma billing documents to accompany export shipments across country borders. Input the shipment document number, planned shipment completion date, transportation planning point, business partners (including ship-to party and forwarding agent), output type (documents), the transmission medium (such as printout and email), output device (such as a printer), and execute. The next screen will show the status of the output.

VV21	Create Output – Condition Records: Shipping

This transaction is used to create conditions for the automatic generation of output (such as printed documents/sending emails) for shipping documents. Input the output type and click ENTER to select the condition table. Then choose the condition table that will store the condition records and click ENTER. The condition record will be those conditions that, if fulfilled, will automatically generate the output. On the next screen, input the conditions, the valid from/to date range and save.

VV22	Change Output – Condition Records: Shipping

Use this transaction to change conditions for the automatic generation of output (such as printed documents/sending emails) for shipping documents, which may be required to extend the validity period for the condition record. Input the output type and click ENTER to select the condition table. Then choose the condition table that will store the condition records and click ENTER. Make changes to the condition record and save.

VV31	Create Output – Condition Records: Billing

This transaction is used to create conditions for the automatic generation of output (such as printed documents/sending emails) for billing documents. Input the output type and click ENTER to select the condition table. Then choose the condition table that will store the condition records and click ENTER. The condition record will be those conditions that, if fulfilled, will automatically generate the output. On the next screen, input the conditions and the valid from/to date range and save.

VV32	Change Output – Condition Records: Billing

Use this transaction to change conditions for the automatic generation of output (such as printed documents/sending emails) for billing documents, which may be required to extend the validity period for the condition record. Input the output type and click ENTER to select the condition table. Then choose the condition table that will store the condition records and click ENTER. Make changes to the condition record and save.

8 Plant Maintenance (PM)

CA85	Replace Work Center in Task Lists

You can use this transaction to replace the Work Center. In the selection screen, enter the plant, the key for the work center and the key for the new work center. If a key date is not entered, all operations where the work center is used are displayed. You can restrict the selection by entering additional search filters such as key date, status, usage, planner group and material number.

Transaction CA85 has disadvantages such as poor performance and lack of background processing capability; hence, a new transaction, CA85N — Mass Replacement: Work Center, is available. While using transaction CA85N, if the target work center is same as the source work center but contains different validities for cost centers and activity types, the system issues an error message. Refer to SAP Note 1454538 – CA85N: Incorrect error message CR 061 for information on how to correct this error message. You can refer to SAP Note 543400 – New: Mass Replacement Work Center for more details about transaction CA85N.

CL02	Classes

You can use this transaction to create, change (edit and maintain) and display the master data of classes. You can create a new class either directly or with a template. Classification of equipment, functional locations, and BOMs are often used to identify additional technical specifications for maintenance objects. The Product Structure Browser displays which objects are assigned to the class. In the initial screen, follow the menu path

ENVIRONMENT • PRODUCT STRUCTURE to display the product structure browser.

COIB	As-Built for Serialized Material

You can use this transaction to create as-built configurations from production data. An as-built configuration describes the structure of a serialized assembly that has been produced or the history of the individual components used in the product. An as-built configuration can be created after each individual order or at the end of the production of a finished product.

CS01	Create Material BOM

You can use this transaction to create the data that identify the maintenance bill of material. The maintenance BOM is different than production or engineering BOMs because it contains only items relevant to maintenance. The maintenance BOM has two main functions: structuring a technical object (equipment or functional location assemblies) and spare parts planning in the order. While creating the BOM, you can specify the effective date as well. You can enter the plant if you want the BOM to be effective in this specific plant. If the material for which you are creating the BOM has a material type that cannot be combined with the BOM usage, an error message is displayed.

CS02	Change Material BOM

You can use this transaction to edit and maintain the BOM data. If the BOM you are maintaining is allocated to multiple plants, the changes are relevant to all plants. If you process a BOM that is part of a BOM group with a change number, you must use a change number to process all BOMs in the group.

CS03 Display Material BOM

You can use this transaction to display the bill of material. In the selection screen, you can enter the plant data as a search filter. Based on the entered search filter, the contents of the BOM are displayed.

CS14 BOM Comparison

You can use this transaction to compare two different BOMs. This functionality is particularly useful, if there are multiple BOMs for a specific material. The comparison is done per item. In the BOM comparison initial screen, enter the primary BOM, secondary BOM, the validity dates, and select the explosion level (single-level or multi-level). If there are differences between BOMs, a BOM COMPARISON – RESULT screen will be displayed. You can compare different categories of BOMs with each other.

CS15 Single-Level Where-Used List – Material

You can use this transaction to get a listing of all the BOMs in which the material is used. The output listing will include the material BOMs and the equipment BOMs that use the material. The material where-used list can be displayed either as single-level or multi-level. In a single-level listing, only BOMs where the material is directly used as components are displayed. The BOMs will be displayed with explosion level 1. In a multi-level listing, you get an overview of all levels where the BOMs (which contain the specified material) are used.

CS20 Mass Changes – Material Selection

You can use this transaction to make changes to multiple BOMs at once. Using the mass change functionality, you can perform one of the following: Change—You can change an item in multiple BOMs at once or change an item's data; Delete—You can delete an item from multiple BOMs at once; Create—You can create a new material item in several BOMs that contain a specific reference object.

CS80 Change Documents for Material BOM

If you edit or maintain a BOM without a change number, the system logs these changes in a change document. SAP stores the data related to BOMs in different tables. SAP writes the changes made to the BOM data to the relevant tables and change documents are generated based on these tables. You can use this transaction to display the change document for the specified material BOM. Change documents give an overview of the old and new field values.

You can use transaction IB81—Functional Location BOM Change Documents to display change documents related to Functional Location BOM. You can use transaction IB80—Change Documents for Equipment BOM to display changes documents related to Equipment BOM.

CR05 Work Center List

You can use this report to display a listing of work centers. If you want a listing of work centers in a hierarchy, then in the selection screen, enter data in the fields grouped under the SELECTION BY HIERARCHY group.

CR06	Work Center Assignment to Cost Center

You can use this report to get a listing of work centers and the cost centers they are assigned to.

CV01N	Create Document

Information about technical objects to be maintained can also exist in the form of electronic documents (for example, maintenance manuals, instructions, pictures). Documents are managed using the SAP logistics common component "document management system." These documents are associated with and linked to various plant maintenance objects. You can use this transaction to create a document info record. A document info record stores all the data required to process and manage a document. For the specified document number and document type, you can use transaction CV03N—Display Document to display the document info record and original application files that belong to the document.

CV02N	Change Document

You can use this transaction to edit and make changes to a document. Prior to making changes to a document, the following needs to be considered:

1. If the document is in status "Locked" or "Original in Process," many of the fields in the document cannot be changed. Hence, the document status need to be changed prior to making edits to the document info record.

2. All changes to the document will generate a workflow event.

3. Changes to the document are not historical. If you prefer to maintain historical status, it is a suggested practice to create a newer version of the document.

4. If preferred, during customizing of the Cross-Application Components, you can specify whether change documents need to be created for all changes to the document info record.

CV03N	Display Document

For the specified document number and document type, you can use this transaction to display the document info record and original application files that belong to the document.

CV04N	Find Document

You can use this transaction to search and find documents. You can use any of the following as a search filter: data from the document info record, text elements, signature data, etc. You can create a task list to describe a sequence of individual maintenance activities that must be performed at regular intervals. The next few transactions describe how to create, maintain, and display equipment task list, general task list and functional location task list.

IA01	Create Equipment Task List

You can use this transaction to create an equipment task list. In the initial screen, enter the equipment and, if required, an existing profile number. If an equipment task list exists, the TASK LIST OVERVIEW screen is displayed. If no task list exists, the GENERAL OVERVIEW screen is displayed. Using the equipment task list, you can define and manage maintenance tasks for your equipment in one central place. The equipment task list can be used to prepare maintenance plans and orders as well. You can combine several task lists into one group. Within the group, a unique sequential number called the group counter is assigned to each individual equipment task list.

Spare parts and material components can also be included in maintenance task lists. The basis for component parts list is the relevant maintenance BOM defined in the ASSEMBLY field on the task list header. If no assembly is referenced on the task list, then only items with a material category of L (stock items) can be included as components.

IA02	Change Equipment Task List

You can use this transaction to edit and maintain an equipment task list.

IA03	Display Equipment Task List

You can use this transaction to display an equipment task list. This is a display-only screen, and no maintenance can be performed.

IA05	Create General Task List

You can use this transaction to create a general maintenance task list. You can create a new general task list by entering an existing group number or an existing profile number. You can also create a new general task list by not entering any data. For the entered data, if a general task list exists, an OPERATIONS OVERVIEW screen is displayed. If no general task list exists, then a GENERAL OVERVIEW screen is displayed.

General maintenance task lists do not refer to any specific technical object and are task lists that are used for general maintenance tasks. In the general maintenance task list, you can define and manage the sequence of maintenance tasks centrally and use them for work scheduling as well. Within each group, you can create several individual general task lists. Within the group, a unique sequential number called the group counter is assigned to each individual general maintenance task list.

IA06	Change General Maintenance Task List

You can use this transaction to edit and maintain a general maintenance task list.

IA07	Display General Task List

You can use this transaction to display a general task list. This is a display-only view and no maintenance can be performed on the task list.

IA08	Change PM Task Lists

You can use this transaction to generate a listing of maintenance task lists or service plans. The report output will display the task list type, the maintenance strategy (if assigned), task list group, group counter and the description of the task list. From the report output, you can navigate to the TASK LIST DETAILS screen, where you can edit and maintain the task lists.

IA09	Display Task Lists

You can use this transaction to display a listing of maintenance task lists or service plans. The different task list types are functional location task list, equipment task list, and general task list. The report displays the task list type, task list group, group counter and task list description, and, where available, the maintenance strategy. From the report output, you can navigate to the TASK LIST DETAILS screen, to get an overview of the task list. This is a display-only view and no maintenance can be performed.

IA10	Display Task Lists (Multi-Level)

You can use this transaction to generate a multi-level listing of maintenance task lists or service task lists. In the selection screen, you can select which objects need to be displayed in the listing. Where required, you can generate this listing independently of operations and display operations/sub-operations separately.

IA11   Create Functional Location Task List

You can use this transaction to create a functional location task list. In the initial screen, enter the identification of the functional location and, if required, an existing profile number. For the entered data, if a task list exists, the TASK LIST OVERVIEW screen is displayed. If no functional location task list exists, the GENERAL OVERVIEW screen is displayed. Using this task list, you can centrally define and manage maintenance tasks for the specific functional location. The task list also helps to prepare maintenance plans and maintenance orders for functional locations. Similar to the other task lists, you can combine several functional location task lists into one group. Within the group, a unique sequential number, called the group counter, is assigned to each individual functional location task list.

IA12   Change Functional Location Task List

You can use this transaction to edit and maintain a functional location task list.

IA13   Display Functional Location Task List

You can use this transaction to display a functional location task list. This is a display-only process and no maintenance can be performed on the task list.

IA16   Cost Maintenance Task Lists

You can use this report to conduct cost analysis for maintenance task lists, service task lists or operations in a task list.

IA17   Print Maintenance Task Lists

For the specified task list type, you can use this report, to print the maintenance task lists and service task lists.

IB01   Create Equipment BOM

You can use this transaction to create an equipment BOM. Using this transaction, you can also create a new equipment BOM by using another material BOM as a reference. In the initial screen, the EQUIPMENT field and the BOM USAGE field are required fields.

IB11   Create Functional Location BOM

In Plant Maintenance, a functional location BOM is a type of BOM. You can use this transaction to create a functional location BOM. You can also create a functional location BOM using another BOM as a reference. To create a functional location BOM by reference, you can use a material BOM or an equipment BOM or another functional location BOM. You can create the BOM with or without a change number. You can create a BOM with a change number only if you want the BOM to have a history requirement upon creation. After a BOM is released for production, you can maintain and process a BOM only with a valid change number.

IB12   Change Functional Location BOM

You can use this transaction to edit and maintain the functional location BOM. You can make changes to a functional location BOM in one of two ways: without a history or with a history. In the latter, enter the change number in the CHANGE NUMBER field belonging to the validity group. The VALID FROM field is populated with the validity date from the change master record.

You can use this transaction to perform any of the following functions: extend the BOM to include items from other BOMs, add/delete BOM items, or add/delete BOM sub-items.

IB13	Display Functional Location BOM

For the specified validity period, you can use this transaction to display a functional location BOM. A number of options are available in the GO TO and EXTRAS menus. You will be able to navigate to the different screens using these menu options.

IB51	Create Installed Base

You can use this transaction to create the master record of an installed base (IBase) of a certain category. It is a prerequisite that the master record of each component used in the IBase, such as a piece of equipment, functional location, or material document, is already created and exists in the system.

IB52	Change IBase

You can use this transaction to edit and maintain the master record of a specific IBase.

IB53	Display IBase

You can use this transaction to display the general data of the specified IBase. This is a display-only transaction and no maintenance is possible.

IB55	Display Two Installations

You can use this transaction to display and compare any two specific IBases. For a specific time point and other selection filter, the system will output the IBase data in multi-level.

IB61	Create Installation from Sales/Production Data

You can use this transaction to create an IBase from a sales order. Through this process, you can record the status of the object in the sales phase as "as_sold." In the initial screen, choose SALES in the SELECTION OPTIONS group. Enter the number of the sales document and, where required, enter the item number. Click the CREATE AND PROCESS INSTALLATION icon. Based on the entries, the system generates an IBase and navigates to the CHANGE INSTALLED BASE: DETAILS screen where you can fill the remaining general data. The system automatically copies sales relevant data from the BOM. You can also create an IBase based on the production data. In the initial screen, select the option PRODUCTION, and follow the above procedure.

IB80	Change Documents for Equipment BOM

You can use this transaction to display changes documents related to an equipment BOM.

IB81	Functional Location BOM Change Documents

You use this transaction to display change documents related to a functional location BOM.

IE01	Create Equipment

You can use this transaction to create a master record for a piece of equipment. If you are using another piece of equipment or material as a reference for the new piece of equipment, you can enter the reference equipment number in the EQUIPMENT field or the reference material number in the MATERIAL field belonging to REFERENCE group. During processing, you can choose which data pertaining to the reference equipment need to be copied to the new equipment.

IE02	Change Equipment

You can use this transaction to edit and maintain the master record of a piece of equipment.

IE03	Display Equipment

You can use this transaction to display the master record of a piece of equipment. This is a display-only process and no maintenance can be performed.

IE05	Change Equipment – Equipment Selection

You can use this transaction to get a listing of equipment. The listing can include general data about the equipment, serial number data, location data, maintenance data, and sales & distribution data. The data that will be displayed depend on the search filter in the selection screen. You can use the equipment listing to search for equipment numbers where required or to display an equipment listing based on certain selection filters and use the selected list for collective processing, such as mass changes to the fields or data on multiple pieces of equipment at the same time.

To perform mass changes for equipment or functional locations (using transactions IE05 or IL05), it is a prerequisite that you have the proper authorizations to perform mass changes. The authorizations object I_MASS should be assigned to your profile to enable you to perform mass changes.

IE07	Equipment List (Multi-Level)

You can use this transaction to output a multi-level listing of equipment. In multi-level listing, you can display fields from other master records that are involved in the functional process for a piece of equipment. In multi-level listing, you can compile a list of equipment with specific characteristics and perform collective processing such as maintenance of the master records.

IE10	Multiple Equipment Entry (List Editing)

You can use this transaction to enter multiple pieces of equipment in the SAP system, with their required data. Where required, you can use an existing equipment of material master record as a reference. When the entries are saved, the system will display a message informing the number of pieces of equipment that were created.

IE20	Replacement Equipment Search (List Editing)

You can use this transaction to generate a listing of equipment. The system uses the classification data as a basis for the search. Based on the search filter, you can generate a listing of equipment with same characteristics. Details of equipment, such as equipment general data, serial number data, location data, maintenance data, sales & distribution data, are displayed.

IE25	Create Production Resource/Tools

You can use this transaction to create an equipment master record for production resources/tools (PRT). In the initial screen, it is important that you enter a valid equipment category. By creating a counter for the PRT equipment master record, you can track the wear and tear of the production resources/tools.

IE31	Create Fleet Object

You can use this transaction to create a vehicle as a piece of equipment based on a specific equipment category and vehicle type. In the master record, you can maintain vehicle-related data such as maintenance intervals, average fuel consumption, weight, speed, etc.

IE37 — Change Vehicles – Vehicle Selection

You can use this transaction to display a listing of vehicles. To get a detailed view of an equipment, you can select a piece of equipment from the displayed list, and the system will navigate to display the general data of the equipment. In the general data screen, you can edit and maintain the master record of that particular piece of equipment. For this report, you can specify the selection filter to be either general equipment data or vehicle-specific data. The report output will display vehicle-specific data, as well consumption data. The display of consumption data in the report output is very performance intensive since the values are calculated during report generation.

IE4N — Equipment Dismantling with Goods Movement

You can use this transaction to dismantle, install, or exchange equipment with simultaneous goods movements. This transaction has the following constraints:

1. Does not support goods receipt for the purchase order or stock transfers.

2. Multiple pieces of equipment cannot be simultaneously installed and removed.

3. Does not support batch input or the CALL TRANSACTION command.

4. Does not support forced installation for non-serialized materials.

IFCU — Consumption Transaction

In the selection screen, you can enter the search filter with or without a gas station. You can use this transaction:

1. To record consumption for vehicles such as counter readings, enter the amount of oil or fuel consumed, or update material documents for vehicle consumption.

2. Display consumption data of a vehicle.

3. Reverse documents such as measurement and material documents.

It is a prerequisite that you have created at least one fuel counter. A primary counter to measure the distance traveled or the operating time should exist as well.

IH01 — Functional Location Structure List

For the specified functional location, the report displays the hierarchy of the functional location. You can expand the hierarchy to view higher and lower functional locations. By setting the proper parameters, the following data are also displayed: the equipment installed at the functional locations, the hierarchies below the equipment, and the BOMs that belong to the equipment. Common maintenance operations (create notification, create order, etc.) can be launched directly from the Functional Location Structure List.

IH03 — Equipment Structure

Based on the specified piece of equipment and validity date, this transaction outputs a structure display in list format. In the output list you can determine the position of the equipment within a functional location hierarchy, the position of the equipment within an equipment hierarchy, the equipment with its BOM, and the position of the equipment within an installed base. In the selection screen, if you select the option AS GRAPHIC, the output is displayed in graphic format.

IH06 — Display Functional Location

You use this transaction to display a listing of functional locations.

IH08   Display Equipment

For the specified selection filter, you can use this report to generate a listing of a piece of equipment. The report will display the following: general data pertaining to the equipment, functional location data, serial number data, maintenance data, and sales & distribution data.

IH09   Display Material

You can use this report to generate listing of material data. The report displays the material general data and the material type.

IH12   Functional Location Structure

For the specified functional location, you can use this transaction to display the hierarchy of the functional location. You can explode the hierarchy display to display the equipment installed at the functional locations, BOMs that belong to the equipment, etc.

IH18   Reference Location List (Multi-Level)

You can use this transaction to display a multi-level listing for reference functional locations. In multi-level listing, you can display data from other master records in functional sequence for a reference location.

IH20   Where-Used List Time

You can use this transaction to display a listing of which components are available in which IBase, at the exact time that you specify in the selection screen. You specify the exact time in the VALID-ON DATE, VALID-ON TIME fields. Both fields are mandatory for data selection. The components displayed in the "Where-Used List Time" report could include equipment, materials, serial numbers, and documents.

IH22   Where-Used List Time Interval

You can use this transaction to display a listing of which components are available in which IBase during the time interval you specify in the selection screen. You specify the time interval in the VALID-FROM DATE, VALID-FROM TIME and VALID-TO DATE, VALID-TO TIME. These fields are mandatory for data selection.

IK01   Create Measuring Point

You can use this transaction to create measuring points directly. In the initial screen, specify whether the measuring point objects is equipment or a functional location. Enter details such as the number of the technical object for which you are creating the measuring point and the required measuring point category. In the GENERAL DATA screen, enter the details to create the master record.

Prior to creating the measuring point, the following prerequisites must be completed:

1. You have created the measuring point categories.

2. You have configured the characteristics that you might assign to the measuring points and counters.

The code groups must be created. Using these codes, you can qualitatively evaluate measurement and counter readings.

IK02   Change Measuring Point

You can use this transaction to edit and maintain the measuring point general data.

IK03   Display Measuring Point

You can use this transaction to display only the general data of the specified measuring point.

IK08	Change Measuring Points (List Editing)

You can use this transaction to display a listing of measuring points and counters. Based on the search filter, you can generate a listing of measuring points and perform collective processing, such as mass changes to the general data of the measuring points at the same time.

IK11	Create Measurement Document

You can use this transaction to create Measurement Document general data for a measuring point. The measurement documents are used for regular readings and measurement. In the CREATE MEASUREMENT DOCUMENT: GENERAL DATA screen, you can enter a valuation code, only if the indicator VAL CODE SUFFICIENT has been set in the master record of the measuring point.

IK12	Change Measurement Document

You can use this transaction to edit and maintain the measurement document. Some of the editing functions that can be performed include changing the text for the measurement document and changing the processing status.

IK13	Display Measurement Document

You can use this transaction to display a measurement document. In this transaction, you cannot edit the measurement document.

IK16	Collective Entry of Meas. Documents (List Editing)

You can use this transaction to enter multiple measurement documents with the required data at the same time. You can use transaction IK21 to enter measurement documents for the specified functional location.

IK17	Display Measurement Documents (List Editing)

For displaying the specified measuring point, or functional location or a piece of equipment, you can use this transaction to display a listing of measurement documents for measuring points/counters.

IK18	Change Measurement Documents (List Editing)

You can use this transaction to get a listing of measurement documents for measuring points/counters. Based on the search filter, you can generate a listing of measurement documents with the same characteristics, and perform collective processing, such as mass changes to the general data of the measurement documents, at the same time. For displaying the specified measuring point, or functional location or piece of equipment, you can use transaction IK17—Display Measurement Documents (List Editing).

IK21	Collective Entry of Meas. Documents

You can use this transaction to enter measurement documents for the specified functional location.

IK41	Display MeasDocs From Archive

You can use this transaction to produce a listing of archived measurement documents. For example, in the selection screen, you can enter the search filter for any of the following criteria: listing of measurement documents for a specific measuring point/counter, listing of measurement documents for a specific technical object, or listing of measurement documents for a specific time period.

IL01	Create Functional Location

You can use this transaction to create a new functional location. Functional location is an organizational unit within logistics and represents the place where a maintenance task might be performed. In the initial screen, you enter the details required for a functional location master record. You can create a functional location by any of the following processes: create a functional location, create a functional location based on a reference functional location, create a functional location by the copy method, create a subordinate functional location within a hierarchy of another functional location.

It is a prerequisite that you have completed customizing in the IMG for defining the structure indicator.

IL02	Change Functional Location

You can use this transaction to edit and maintain a functional location master record.

IL03	Display Functional Location

You can use this transaction to display the master record of a functional location. This is display-only and maintenance cannot be performed.

IL04	Create Functional Location (List Entry)

You can use this transaction to enter multiple functional location labels, along with the corresponding descriptions in the listing screen, at the same time. When you save the entries, if mandatory data are missing, the system will navigate to the corresponding master record and force you to make the entries. Details such as the structure indicator or function location category must be entered prior to making the list entries. After you have created the functional locations in List Entry, you can execute transaction IL02 — Change Functional Location and enter the additional details for the master record. You can use transaction IL05 to display a listing of functional locations. You can also use transaction IH06 to display a listing of functional locations.

IL05	Change Functional Location

You can use this transaction to carry out mass changes to the fields or data of multiple functional locations at the same time. To perform mass changes for equipment or functional locations (using transactions IE05 or IL05), it is a prerequisite that you have the proper authorizations to perform mass changes. The authorizations object I_MASS should be assigned to your profile to enable you to perform mass changes.

IL06	Data Transfer from Functional Location

You can use this transaction to perform a hierarchical data transfer. Data changes at a higher hierarchical level are automatically transferred to the objects maintained at the lower level of the hierarchy. You can use the data transfer to maintain data at a higher level for objects lower in the hierarchy, maintain data centrally for objects assigned to a reference functional location, or, when creating a new technical object, you have the option to copy or omit portions of general data.

IL07	Functional Location Listing (Multi-Level)

You can use this transaction to generate a multi-level listing of functional locations. In a multi-level listing, fields from other master records included in the processing for a functional location are also displayed.

IL09 — User Profile for Labeling

You can use this transaction to perform alternate labeling of functional locations. This process can also be used to create secondary functional location structural views.

IL10 — Reusability of Historical Labels

SAP system saves all previously used functional location labels as historical labels. If there is a need to reuse historical labels, then the historical label needs to be released. You can use this transaction to explicitly release a historical label for reusage.

IL11 — Create Reference Location

You can use this transaction to create a master record for the reference functional location. Reference functional locations have their own master records in the system. However, reference functional locations do not actually exist as locations. They are assigned to real functional locations as references. A reference functional location contain data that are valid for the functional locations that are assigned to it.

IL12 — Change Reference Location

You can use this transaction to make changes to the master record of a reference location. Any changes that are made to the master data of a reference functional location affect the data of all functional locations assigned to this particular reference functional location.

IL13 — Display Reference Location

You can use this transaction to display the master data of the specified reference location.

IL14 — Create RefLocation – List Entry

You can use this transaction to quickly create multiple reference functional locations at the same time. You can enter the structure and the essential data in one step and, where required, enter the detailed data at a later time. You can create a new reference functional location using another reference functional location as a copy reference for new functional locations. The system allows copying sub-objects, such as the classification or measuring points/counters, into the new reference functional location.

IN07 — Create Object Link for Equipment

You can use this transaction to create and maintain an object link master record. The newly created object links are assigned a unique number (external or internal). In Plant Maintenance, the object links are used to represent the dependencies between the specified technical objects. The master record of an object link contains data about the object link, data about the link and linked objects, and link description data. Object links can be created from one functional location to another functional location or between one piece of equipment and another piece of equipment. You cannot form object links between different technical objects.

IN08 — Change Object Link for Equipment

You can use this transaction to maintain object links for equipment.

IN09 — Display Object Link for Equipment

You can use this transaction to display the master record of an object link.

IN15 | Change Functional Location Object Network

You can use this transaction to display a listing of object links between functional locations. From the displayed list, you can select one or more object links for maintenance or for further processing.

IN18 | Change Object Network for Equipment

Based on the search filter entered in the initial screen, you can use this transaction to display a listing of links between pieces of equipment. This listing helps you analyze the object networks in your company. The analysis that can be performed includes determining which object links are defined and exist in the system for a particular piece of equipment and which are incoming or outgoing links. From the listing, you can select a particular object link for further processing or for editing and maintenance. From the object link listing, select a particular column, and then click LIST • GRAPHIC in the menu bar, for a graphic representation.

IN19 | Display Object Network for Equipment

You can use this transaction to display a listing of object links in the system. The report output displays the link ID, network ID, link from equipment number, and the link to equipment number.

IP01 | Create Maintenance Plan

A maintenance plan contains the description of the maintenance and inspection tasks to be performed at the maintenance objects. The scope of the tasks and the dates on which these tasks need to be performed are listed as well. You can use this transaction to create a complete maintenance plan. You can schedule this maintenance plan to generate maintenance call objects such as maintenance orders. At least one maintenance item must be assigned to a maintenance plan.

IP04 | Create Maintenance Item

A maintenance item describes what maintenance tasks should be performed regularly at a technical object or a group of technical objects. You can use this transaction to create a maintenance item. Where required, you enter the maintenance strategy in the maintenance item general data. If you wish to assign the maintenance item to a time-based or a performance-based maintenance plan, then a maintenance strategy needs to be entered during the maintenance item creation. If the maintenance strategy is not specified, then the maintenance item can be assigned only to a single-cycle plan or multiple counter plans.

IP05 | Change Maintenance Item

For the specified maintenance item, you can use this transaction to display the details of the maintenance item. In the detail screen, you can edit and maintain the maintenance item. If you do not specify a maintenance item, click the F4 button and the system displays a selection screen for Change Maintenance Item. (This screen is very similar to transaction IP17—Change Maintenance Item.) For the entered search filter, you can use this transaction to generate a listing of maintenance items. The report displays the maintenance item, maintenance item description, maintenance plan and, where available maintenance strategy. From the listing, you can navigate to the detail screen (displaying the general data) and edit/maintain the maintenance item.

IP06   Display Maintenance Item

You can use this transaction to display the general data of the specified maintenance item.

IP10   Schedule Maintenance Plan

For the specified maintenance plan, you can use this transaction to manually start, restart, or schedule maintenance call objects. You can also use this transaction to monitor and manage maintenance plan call objects.

IP11   Maintain Maintenance Strategies

A maintenance strategy contains scheduling information for the planned maintenance work. You can use this transaction to create and maintain maintenance strategies. A maintenance strategy can be assigned to multiple maintain plans simultaneously

IP12   Display Maintenance Strategies

You can use this transaction to display maintenance strategies and maintenance packages assigned to these maintenance strategies.

IP13   Package Order

You can use this transaction for a graphical display of the package sequence of a maintenance strategy. From the graphical output, you can get an overview of the individual maintenance packages in the maintenance strategy. The hierarchy of the packages is displayed as well.

IP14   Where-Used List by Strategy

For the specified maintenance strategy, you can use this transaction to generate a listing of all maintenance plans to which this maintenance strategy is assigned. The report output will display the number of the maintenance

plan, the description of the maintenance plan, the assigned strategy, and the number of maintenance items. From the list output, you can navigate to the detail screen of the maintenance plan.

IP15   Change Maintenance Plan (List Editing)

You can use this transaction to generate a listing maintenance plans. The report output will display the maintenance plan number, the description of the maintenance plan, and the maintenance strategy assigned to the maintenance plan. From the listing, you can navigate to the detail screen of the maintenance plan or the maintenance call objects for the maintenance plan. The list generated for this report is derived from a user-defined display variant. All fields associated with the maintenance plan are available for display in the list.

IP16   Display Maintenance Plan

You can use this report to generate a listing of maintenance plans. The report displays the maintenance plan number, maintenance plan description and, where available, the maintenance strategy. From the listing, it is possible for you to select a specific maintenance plan and navigate to the detail screen.

IP17   Change Maintenance Item

You can use this transaction to generate a listing of maintenance items in the system. The report is generated based on the search filter entered in the initial screen. The report output will display the maintenance item, maintenance plan, short text, and, where available, the maintenance strategy. From the report output, you can navigate to the maintenance plan, detail screen of the maintenance item, maintenance call object, or the assigned technical objects, where you can edit and make changes.

IP18 Display Maintenance Item

You can use this report to generate a listing of maintenance items. The report will display the maintenance item, maintenance plan, and, where required, the maintenance strategy and the maintenance item description. From the listing, you can select a particular value and navigate to the detail screen of the particular object.

IP19 Maintenance Scheduling Overview and Simulation

You can use this report to get a graphical overview of the maintenance plans scheduling. Using this report, you can simulate the current and future maintenance plans that are becoming due and get a graphic overview of the changes.

IP24 Scheduling Overview List Form

You can use this report to generate a listing of scheduling overview for maintenance plans. The report will display the number of the maintenance item, the maintenance plan, and, where available, the maintenance strategy, description of the maintenance item, the plant and the start date. By clicking an item, you can call up the detail screen of that particular item. Start date is the date on which the maintenance call object was created.

IP30 Maintenance Schedule – Date Monitoring

You can use this report to generate the maintenance call objects that are due for maintenance plans. A report is created to list the plans that were reviewed, the call objects that were created, and any errors detected. It is a suggested best practice to start deadline monitoring on a regular basis.

IP41 Add Single Plan

You can use this transaction to create a single cycle maintenance plan. In the initial screen, select a maintenance plan category and click ENTER. In the detail screen, enter the required general data and save your entries.

IP42 Add Strategy-Controlled Plan

You can use this transaction to create a maintenance plan and assign a maintenance strategy while creating the plan. The maintenance strategy can either be time-based or performance-based. Assigning a maintenance strategy is considered a best practice because you can reduce maintenance plan creation time: The same scheduling information need not be created for each maintenance plan. You can update scheduling information easily. Any changes you make to the maintenance strategy are valid for all maintenance plans, which contains this maintenance strategy.

Strategy-based maintenance plans must reference a maintenance task list that includes the same maintenance strategy. Additionally, maintenance packages must also be assigned for the selected task list.

IQ01 Create Material Serial Number

You can use this transaction to create a single serial number against a material. In the initial screen, enter the material for which you are creating the serial number and press ENTER. In the detail screen, enter the required data and save the master record. Using this transaction, you can create a material serial number by reference. In the initial screen, enter the material and serial number (that you wish to copy from) in the reference group and follow the process described above.

IQ02	Change Material Serial Number

You can use this transaction to edit and maintain the material serial number general data. In the initial screen, enter the combination of material and serial number that you wish to edit.

IQ03	Display Material Serial Number

For the specified material and serial number, you can use this transaction to display the general data of the material serial number.

IQ04	Create Material Serial Number (List Editing)

For the specified material, you can use this transaction to create multiple serial numbers at the same time. In the list entry screen, you can enter data in the FROM SERIAL NUMBER and TO SERIAL NUMBER fields, to specify the serial number range you wish to create. Alternatively, you can manually enter an alpha-numeric number range in the SERIAL No. field.

IQ08	Change Material Serial Number (List Editing)

You can use this transaction to generate a listing of serial numbers. The report output will display the material number, serial number, plant, storage location, etc. From the listing, you can select a record and navigate to the detail screen to edit and maintain the data.

IQ09	Display Material Serial Number

You can use this report to generate a listing of serial numbers. The report will display the material number, serial number, plant, storage location, etc. Where required, from the listing, you can select a record to navigate to the detail screen and perform maintenance of the data.

IR01	Create Work Center

Maintenance work centers represent the resources involved in the planning of work activities. You can use this transaction to create a maintenance work center. A maintenance work center can also be created by copying an existing work center; to create a new work center navigate to the COPY FROM group on the CREATE WORK CENTER initial screen, and enter an existing PLANT and the REF. WORK CENTER that you can copy.

IW12	Document Flow List

You can use this transaction to generate a listing of all objects involved in a document flow. The report output displays the document type, document number, date and status of the document. From the output listing, you can use the DISPLAY DOCUMENT function to navigate to the original document. A maintenance notification forms the basis for creating maintenance orders. Maintenance notifications are used to describe a technical condition execption of an object, request maintenance department to perform a maintenance task or document the completed task. These notifications can be used to identify and plan tasks in detail, track progress of the identified tasks, and identify costs for the maintenance tasks.

IW13	Material Where-Used List

For the specified order status, you can use this report to generate a listing of materials used in specific orders. The report listing compares the following material quantities: reserved quantity, issued quantity, quantity with/without reservation reference. Transaction S_ALR_87013434 provides the exact same functionality.

IW21	Create PM Notification – General

You can use this transaction to create a new plant maintenance notification. In the initial screen, the notification type is a required field. You can also create a notification with reference. Through this process, you use an existing notification as a copy model. The reference notification can be of any notification type, irrespective of which notification type the new notification should have. In the initial screen, enter the notification that you wish to use as a reference in the notification field belonging to reference group.

If you select MALFUNCTION REPORT as the notification type in the initial screen, it will navigate you to CREATE PM NOTIFICATION: MALFUNCTION REPORT details screen (transaction IW24). If you select ACTIVITY REPORT as the notification type, it will navigate you to the CREATE PM NOTIFICATION: ACTIVITY REPORT detail screen (transaction IW25). If you select MAINTENANCE REQUEST as the notification type, it will navigate you to the CREATE PM NOTIFICATION: MAINTENANCE REQUEST details screen (transaction IW26).

IW22	Change PM Notification

In the CHANGE PM NOTIFICATION initial screen, you can enter a specific notification that you want to edit and maintain. The system will then navigate to the CHANGE PM NOTIFICATION: MAINTENANCE REQUEST screen, where PM notification data can be edited and maintained.

IW23	Display PM Notification

You can use this transaction to generate a listing of maintenance or service notifications. From the listing, you can select a specific notification and navigate to the detail screen to get an overview of the notification. This is display-only and no maintenance can be performed.

IW24	Create PM Malfunction Report

Use this transaction to enter the required data and create the malfunction report.

IW25	Create PM Activity Report

Use this transaction to enter the required data and create the activity report.

IW26	Create Maintenance Request

Use this transaction to enter the required data and create the maintenance request.

IW28	Change Notifications (List Editing)

For the specified notification status, you can use this transaction to generate a listing of maintenance or service notifications existing in the system. The report will display the notification number, the short text of the notification, and the date on which the notification was created. Among other things, you can use this list to edit and maintain the notifications or perform status changes for multiple notifications simultaneously. Additionally, you can create or assign a maintenance order based on a notification from the list.

IW29	Display Notifications (List Editing)

You can use this transaction to display a listing of notifications (service/maintenance) existing in the system. From the displayed list, you can navigate to the detail screen to get an overview of the notification. This is display-only and no maintenance can be performed. The report output will display the notification number, the date of creation and the description of the notification. You can also use this report to change the status of several notifications at the same time. The list generated for this report is derived from a user-defined display variant. All fields associated with the notification header are available for display in the list.

IW30	Notification List (Multi-Level)

For the specified notification status and filter, you can use this transaction to generate a multi-level listing of service notifications or maintenance notifications. Depending on the search criteria and filter(s) you have set in the displayed report, the first level displays the notification number and the short text of the notification. The second level will contain details about the functional location, equipment, orders, tasks, activities, classification information, and partners for all selected notifications. Other information available for display includes partner information for the notification, assigned work orders, classification information, and notification cause codes, activities, and tasks. It is a suggested best practice to limit the data selected for the report. Performance issues might arise if a large number of data need to be selected for the report output.

IW31	Create Order [Order type description appears here. Name changes depending on order type.]

You can use this transaction to create an order directly. These repair orders are usually created when a malfunction is detected in a technical object and the employee creates an order to plan the required repair tasks. You can also create a new order by the reference method. In this method, you enter the order number in the REFERENCE group. Important data are copied to the newly created order from this reference order. To be able to create orders for notifications, the application component Maintenance Notifications or Service Notifications must be configured and be used in your enterprise.

IW32	Change Order

You can use this transaction to edit and maintain a maintenance work order.

IW33	Display PM Order

For the specified order, you can use this transaction to display an overview of the header data, operations, components and costs. In the initial screen, enter the order for which you wish to get an overview and click the specific buttons displayed in the menu bar.

IW34	PM Order for PM Notification

You can use this transaction to create an order for the notification. In the initial screen, enter the plant, order type and the notification number for which you want to create an order. The system will navigate to the HEADER DATA screen for the new order. In the data screen, the system will automatically enter the reference object for the notification as the reference object for the order. Other data, such as basic dates, short text, and planner group, are copied as well.

IW36	Create PM Sub-Order

You can use this transaction to create sub-orders for a superior order. In the initial screen, enter the superior order for which you want to create the sub-order. The system will navigate to the HEADER DATA screen for the sub-order; you will notice that the system has automatically filled the order type, superior order and the reference object. (Where required, you can change or remove the reference object data in the SUB-ORDER HEADER DATA screen.) Fill in the required data to create the sub-order.

IW37   Change Operations

You can use this transaction to generate a listing of operations for service or maintenance orders. The report will display data for the order number to which an operation is assigned, the operation number, work center and the operation short text. From the listing, you can select a specific order and you can make changes to the detail data of the order or the work center.

IW37N   Change Orders and Operations

For the specified order status (at least one order status must be selected), you can use this transaction to generate a listing of orders and operation items, currently existing in the system. The report output will display details containing the order number, description of the order, the operation number, the description of the operation, and the work center where this operation will be performed. You can use this report to get an overview of the orders and operations, confirm tasks, monitor planning deadlines, where required make status changes, or display the work list for your work center. The list generated for this report is derived from a user-defined display variant. All fields associated with maintenance orders and operations are available for display in the list.

IW38   Change PM Orders

You can use this transaction to edit and maintain PM orders. For the specified order status and order number, the system will navigate to the CENTRAL HEADER DATA screen, where you can edit and maintain the required changes. If you do not specify an order number, based on the search filter, the system will display a listing of service and maintenance orders that satisfy the search filter. In the displayed list, you can select a specific order and navigate to the CENTRAL HEADER DATA

screen to maintain the order. The report output will displays the following details: order number, order type, basic start data and the short text of the order. The list generated for this report is derived from a user-defined display variant. All fields associated with the maintenance order header are available for display in the list.

IW39   Display PM Orders

You can use this transaction to generate a listing of service and maintenance orders available in the system. From the displayed list, you can select a specific order and navigate to the CENTRAL HEADER DATA screen to get an overview of the order. The initial report output is display-only and no maintenance can be performed. If you wish to edit and make changes, in the report output, select the particular PM order and click the pencil icon displayed in the menu bar. This will transition the system to edit mode. When you navigate to the detail screen, you will be able to edit and make changes.

The report output will display the order number, order type, basic start date and the short text of the order. When you select a particular order, it will navigate to the ORDER DATA DETAILS screen. This provides details such as the time at which the services should be provided, utilities required, order costs, etc. It is a prerequisite that at least one order status is selected to execute this report.

IW40   Display Orders (Multi-Level)

You can use this transaction to generate a multi-level listing of service and maintenance orders. In the report output, the first level will display the order number, short text of the order and the system status. The second level will display details for functional location, equipment, notification, operations, and the costs/revenues.

IW41	Enter PM Order Confirmation

You can use this transaction to create an order confirmation. An order confirmation is created every time the team has completed the services that were assigned to them in the work order. Prior to creating the order confirmation, it is a prerequisite that the order to be confirmed is released for processing.

IW42	Overall Completion Confirmation

You can use this transaction to create an overall completion confirmation. You can use the overall completion confirmation to confirm the following: tasks/services activities, measured values/counter readings, items, causes, goods movements and work times. The overall completion confirmation combines details of the time confirmation, technical confirmation, and confirmation of goods movements and services. It is a prerequisite that the order to be confirmed is released for processing. Another prerequisite is that the confirmation profile is configured and is assigned to the user who will be creating the overall completion confirmation.

IW44	PM Order Collective Confirmation

You can use this transaction for collective time confirmation without selections. If you are using specific orders or operations several times, it is a suggested best practice to use pool function. It is a prerequisite that the orders to be confirmed are released for processing. You use collective time confirmation if you are entering large number of time completions confirmations into the SAP system. Collective time confirmations are used to confirm times for operations and sub-operations.

IW45	Cancel PM Order Confirmation

You can use this transaction to cancel an order confirmation. In the initial screen, enter the search filter. Depending on what your search filter is, one of these screens might be displayed: COMPLETION CONFIRMATION DATA screen, a listing of operations and sub-operations for a maintenance order and the completion confirmation entered for these, the selected operation and its sub-operations and the completion confirmations entered for these, or the selected sub-operation and the completion confirmation entered for these.

Choose the specific confirmation that you wish to cancel. You will be required to enter a cancellation reason for cancelling the confirmation. Where required, you can select multiple order confirmations for cancellation. In that scenario, the system will display the individual confirmation one after another.

IW46	Post processing of PDC Error Records

You can use this transaction to display the pool of incorrect completion confirmations and to post process these confirmations. The system generates such incorrect records if the order data are incorrect and cannot be posted in the completion confirmation processing.

IW47	Confirmation List

You can use this transaction to display a list of completion confirmations. You can use the confirmations generated in the report output to perform the following activities: cancel confirmations, get a detailed overview of the completion confirmation, display the order for the completion confirmation, display the long text of the completion confirmation or display equipment, functional locations for completion confirmation.

IW48	Confirmation Using Operation List

You can use this transaction to generate a listing of operations waiting to be confirmed. From the output list, you can call the order to which the operations belong, and get a detailed overview, generate a confirmation pool, and execute transactions to perform individual and collective confirmation of operations. In the selection screen, if you select the option ONLY PM ORDERS the report output will display maintenance and service orders; if you select COLLECTIVE ENTRY it navigates directly to the collective confirmation screen.

IW49	Display Operations

You can use this report to generate a listing of operations for service and maintenance orders. Where required, you can use this listing to edit and maintain the operations. The report will display the order number to which an operation is assigned, the operation number, the work center and the operations description.

IW51	Create Service Notification – General

You can use this transaction to create the general data of a service notification. In the initial screen, enter the notification type for which you want to create the service notification. The notification number will be automatically assigned by the system. You can also create a new notification with reference. Through this process, you use an existing notification as a copy model. In the CREATE SERVICE NOTIFICATION initial screen, enter a pre-existing notification number in the notification field—displayed under REFERENCE GROUP.

IW52	Change Service Notification

For the specified notification, you can use this transaction to edit and maintain the service notification. If the notification is completed, then the notification is display-only and no maintenance can be performed.

IW53	Display Service Notification

For the specified notification, you can use this transaction to provide an overview of the notification. If you choose ACTIVITY REPORT as the notification type in the initial screen, the system will navigate to the CREATE SERVICE NOTIFICATION: ACTIVITY REPORT details screen (transaction IW55) If you choose SERVICE REQUEST as the notification type, the system will navigate to the CREATE SERVICE NOTIFICATION: SERVICE REQUEST details screen (transaction IW56).

IW54	Create Service Notifications – Malfunction

You can use this transaction to create a service notification. The notification number is automatically assigned by the system. You can also use this transaction to create the spare parts order for the piece of equipment directly from the service notification: follow the menu path SERVICE NOTIFICATION • CREATE SALES ORDER • STANDARD.

IW55	Create Activity Report

Use this transaction to create the activity report for a notification created with transaction IW53.

IW56	Create Service Request

Use this transaction to create the service request for a notification created with transaction IW53.

IW57	Set Deletion Flag for Notification

In the SAP system, you cannot delete a notification directly. You can use this transaction to set the delete flag in the notification. The archiving program checks for notifications with deletion flags, converts these flags into deletion indicators, and deletes these notifications from the database. The archiving program copies these deleted notifications into an archive as well. Prior to setting the delete flag for a notification, you need to confirm that the notification is no longer required. While in change mode, you can set the delete flag directly from a notification details screen by following the menu path NOTIFICATION • FUNCTIONS • DELETION FLAG • SET.

IW58   Change Service Notification

You can use this transaction to generate a listing of service notifications or maintenance notifications. The report output will display the notification number, short text of the notification, as well as the date on which the notification was created. From the output list, you can select a specific notification and navigate to the detail screen, where the service notification can be edited and maintained. The list generated for this report is derived from a user-defined display variant. All fields associated with the notification header are available for display in the list. To be able to execute this report, it is a prerequisite that at least one notification status is selected.

IW59   Display Service Notifications

You can use this transaction to generate a listing of service notifications or maintenance notifications. From the output list, you can select a specific notification and navigate to the detail screen for an overview.

IW64   Change Activities

You can use this report to display a listing of service notifications or maintenance notifications and the related activities. Using this report, you can access the notification details screen and edit/maintain the activities. The report output will display the notification number, activity code group, activity code, and the short text of the activity. If the notification is completed, then the notification overview will be display-only, and no maintenance can be performed.

IW65   Display Activities

You can use this transaction to generate a listing of notifications (service or maintenance) and the related activities. From the output list, you can navigate to the notification details screen and get an overview. This is display-only and no maintenance can be performed.

IW66   Change Tasks

You can use this transaction to generate a listing of service notifications/maintenance notifications and the tasks assigned to these notifications. From the report output, you can select a specific notification, navigate to the detail screen and edit/maintain those tasks. The report output will display the notification number, task, task code and the description of the task. The list generated for this report is derived from a user-defined display variant. All fields associated with the maintenance tasks are available for display in the list.

IW67   Display Tasks

You can use this transaction to display a listing of notifications (maintenance or service) and the tasks assigned to these notifications. From the report output, you can select a specific notification, navigate to the detail screen and get an overview of the notifications and the tasks as well. This is a display-only functionality and no maintenance can be performed.

IW68	Change Notification Items

You can use this transaction to generate a listing of service notifications/maintenance notifications, items assigned to these notifications, and the damages for which these items require maintenance. The report output displays the notification number, item, short text of the item, damage code group and the damage key. From the report output, you can select a specific notification and navigate to the notification details screen. In the detail screen, you can edit and maintain the notification items.

IW69	Display Notification Items

You can use this transaction for a display-only overview of the notification details screen.

IWBK	Material Availability Information

You can use this report to get an overview of the availability of materials required for an earliest/latest start of operations.

MCI1	PMIS: Object Class Analysis

You can use this report to perform analysis based on equipment classification and material number.

MCI2	PMIS: Manufacturer Analysis

You can use this report to perform analysis based on equipment manufacturer and material number.

MCI3	PMIS: Location Analysis

You can use this report to perform analysis based on equipment/function location, maintenance plant, location, company area and assembly group.

MCI4	PMIS: Planner Group Analysis

You can use this report to perform an analysis based on equipment/functional location, maintenance plan, planner group, location, company area and assembly group.

MCI5	PMIS: Object Damage Analysis

You can use this report to perform an analysis based on PM order, PM notification, damage or cause codes and activities.

MCI6	PMIS: Object Statistic Analysis

You can use this report to perform an analysis based on equipment classification, material number and manufacturer. Key figures include acquisition value, number of pieces of equipment/functional locations, number of installed equipment/functional locations.

MCI7	PMIS: Breakdown Analysis

You can use this report to perform an analysis of equipment/functional locations. Key figures include number of breakdowns, Mean Time to Repair (MTTR), Mean Time Between Repairs (MTBR).

MCI8	PMIS: Cost Evaluation

You can use this report to perform an analysis based on order category, maintenance activity type, equipment and functional location.

MCIZ	PMIS: Vehicle Consumption Analysis

You can use this report to perform an analysis of fleet equipment based on vehicle consumption statistics.

MCJB	MTTR/MTBR for Equipment

You can use this report to perform an evaluation for equipment, with regard to the key figures Mean Time to Repair (MTTR) and Mean Time Between Repair (MTBR).

MCJC	Functional Location: Mean Time Between Repair

You can use this report to perform an evaluation for functional locations with regard to the key figures Mean Time to Repair (MTTR) and Mean Time between Repair (MTBR).

MM01	Create Material

You can use this transaction to create a material master record. You can create a new material master record for any of the following situations: if no master record exists for the specified material; if the material master record exists but the master data for the user department are incomplete (in this scenario, you can extend the material master record); if the material master record exists but the master data for the user department are entered at the wrong organizational level (in this scenario, you can extend the material master record). You can also create a material master record by reference model.

MM02	Change Material

You can use this transaction to make changes to a material master record. You can make changes in one of the two ways: immediately or by scheduling the change. All changes to the master record are recorded in the change documents. It is a prerequisite that the material master record you are planning to maintain already exists in the material master. If you are not able to access the data screen for your department, it might be because no data have been entered for your department. In such a scenario, you must extend the material master record to include data for your department.

MM03	Display Material

You can use this transaction to display the material master record. You can display the data as they exist or as they will appear on a key date. If you want to display the data for a key date, then the system will read all the change documents for the material master record, from the current date through to the key date. The system will use these data (recorded change documents) to simulate the situation as they will appear on the key date.

MMBE	Stock Overview

You can use this transaction to get a listing of the stocks of the materials across all organizational levels. From the listing, you can select a specific stock type and double-click it to get a detailed overview. You can also use this overview to perform the following:

1. Display stocks of the materials for a specific organizational level.

2. Display the alternative units of measures (if it is defined) for the material.

3. Display the stocks of the materials in the alternative units of measure.

4. Display the stock overview for a different material.

OINI	Network ID

Object networks are used to represent a link between technical objects. You can use this transaction to create new network IDs.

OIOB	Revisions

For the specified plant, you can use this transaction to create revisions. The newly created revisions have a unique ID. Revisions are used to group maintenance tasks, so they can be scheduled and executed as a group. Revisions have a definite time periods assigned to them. If you get a short dump while executing transaction OIBO, implement SAP Note 929161 – Dump in Transaction OIOB. This note is applicable only if you create revisions by using transaction OIOB.

S_ALR_87013426	Maintenance Plan Costing

For the specified time period, you can use this report to determine the expected costs for maintenance plans. Prior to executing this report, the following prerequisites should be satisfied:

1. Maintenance plans are scheduled.

2. The maintenance plans do not have status inactive or set for deletion.

3. For the maintenance plan category, the maintenance order or service order is set as the maintenance call object.

4. In the maintenance task list, the times for operations should be maintained.

Materials with prices should be assigned to the operations as well.

This report can be executed only in the background.

S_ALR_87013432	Display Confirmations

You can use this report to generate a listing of completion confirmations. You can use this listing to perform the following activities: cancel completion confirmations, display actual data of completion confirmations, display the maintenance order for a completion confirmation, display the long text of a completion confirmation, and display functional locations and a piece of equipment for completion confirmations.

S_ALR_87013434	Material Where-Used List

See transaction IW13 for more details.

9 Quality Management (QM)

CA70   PRT Where-Used Lists

You can use this transaction to generate a usage listing of the task lists where PRT (Production Resources/Tool) is used. In the report output, you can select a specific task list: To display the PRT general views use the menu path GO TO • DETAIL. To display the PRT overviews use the menu path GO TO • CHOOSE.

Users can access this transaction only if the parameter ACC_MODE is set to x in the user profile. If this parameter is not set for the user, the user can select an overview variant that determines what task list objects and fields of the objects are displayed to the user.

CC04   Display Product Structure

You can use this transaction to start the Product Structure Browser. For the specified object, this report displays an overview of the product defined data. You can navigate within the product structure, access data, and perform the required functions. For example, the following tasks can be performed in the Product Structure Browser: You can change and maintain the statuses or maintain the master data of the product from a central point.

CF01   Create Production Resource/Tool

Production Resource/Tool (PRT) is an object that denotes a moveable operating resource used in plant maintenance. You can use this transaction to manually create a new PRT master record. You can also create a new PRT master record by copying an existing PRT. Enter an existing PRT in the field COPY FROM PROD. RESOURCE/TOOL and click on the button BASIC DATA. In the displayed dialog box, you can select what components you want to copy and click on the COPY FROM icon. The CREATE PRODUCTION RESOURCE/TOOL: BASIC DATA screen is displayed, where you can make the required changes and save the new PRT record. You can create language-dependent short text by following the menu path EXTRAS • SHORT TEXT.

CF25   PRT: Usage of PRT Master in PM Order

You can use this transaction to generate a listing of service and maintenance orders. From the report output, you can select a specific order and navigate to the order general data screen to get an overview or to make changes to the general data. The report output displays the order number, order type, basic start date and the short text of the order.

CJ00   Digital Signature – Find

See transaction DSAL for details.

CT01   Create Characteristics

See transaction CT04 for details.

CT04   Characteristics

You can use this transaction to create characteristics, which describe the properties of objects. Characteristics are created centrally and then assigned to classes. When a characteristic is assigned to a class, you can overwrite the characteristic. In the initial screen, you can enter the change number, if you plan to create a characteristic using engineering change management. You are required to maintain the basic data of the characteristics; all other data, such as values, are optional. You can also create a new characteristic by copying an existing characteristic. Click on the icon CREATE BY COPYING and enter the name of the characteristic that you wish to copy. SAP recommends using transaction CT04 to create Characteristics rather than using transaction CT01

CWB QM — QM – Engineering Workbench

You can use this transaction to create a new inspection plan; to create a new task list and assign maintenance packages to it; or to transfer QM data to an SAP system. You can do a data transfer of master inspection characteristics, data transfer of inspection methods, and data transfer of inspection plans.

DSAL — Digital Signature – Logs

You can use this transaction to display the digital signatures log. Using the log, you can get an overview and analyze all activities that were performed during the signature process. The following data are displayed in the log: For each signature, the header data includes the date/time/signatory, number of log-messages and the reason for the signature. For the selected signature record, the signature steps and other signature data are displayed at the bottom of the screen. Messages displayed in the log are marked according to the type (information or warning or error or abandon).

As per SAP Note 586914 – Workaround for printing signature via CJ00 or DSAL, SAP recommends using transaction DSAL (Digital Signature Logs) instead of transaction CJ00: Digital Signature – Find.

IP10 — Schedule Maintenance Plan

You can use this transaction to schedule a maintenance plan, which the system will use to generate maintenance call objects, such as maintenance orders or service orders, for the defined cycles.

IP14 — Where-Used List by Strategy

For the specified strategy, you can use this report to generate a listing of maintenance plans in which the strategy is used. The report output displays the maintenance plan, the short text, the strategy and the number of maintenance items. From the report output, you can navigate to the detail screen of the maintenance plan.

IP16 — Display Maintenance Plan

You can use this report to generate a listing of maintenance plans in the system. The report output displays the maintenance plan number, the short text and, where available, the maintenance strategy. From the report output, you can navigate to the detail screen of the maintenance plan or the maintenance call objects for a maintenance plan.

IP19 — Maintenance Scheduling Overview

You can use this report to generate a scheduling overview of the maintenance plans in a graphical format. The graph displays the maintenance call date, equipment, and maintenance call objects for the maintenance plans. You will be able to simulate changes to the maintenance plans in the graph as well.

IP24 — Scheduling Overview List Form

You can use this transaction to generate a listing of a scheduling overview for maintenance plans. The report output contains the maintenance item number, maintenance plan, maintenance strategy, short text of maintenance item, call number and the date on which the maintenance call object was generated (listed in the report as start date). From the report, you can navigate to get a detailed overview of maintenance plan or maintenance item. From the report output, you can also display a graphical scheduling overview.

IQS12 Process Task

You can use this transaction to process specific tasks in a notification. You can process immediate tasks and corrective tasks as well. In the PROCESS TASK screen, you can do the following actions (select menu TASK or the displayed push buttons): release task, complete task, set the task as successful, set user status. In the PROCESS TASK screen, you can also display the associated notification (the notification that contains the task), the associated objects (reference objects specified in the notification), or the action log. In the initial screen, the notification number and task number are required fields.

IQS21 Create Notification – Simplified View

You can use this transaction to create a simplified notification. Based on the customizing settings, the notification type is displayed in the CREATE NOTIFICATION initial screen. In the CREATE NOTIFICATION screen, you can perform the following functions: make changes to the current notification, display a notification, or switch to extended notification processing mode, change the processing status of the notification, approve or refuse approval to a notification, set user default values, change notification address or display the current catalog profile assigned to the notification type.

IQS8 Worklist: Notifications (General)

For the specified search filter, you can use this transaction to select and process notifications that exist in the system. To maximize performance, it is a suggested best practice that you specify a layout in the selection screen.

IQS9 Worklist: Tasks (General)

For the specified search filter, you can this transaction to select and process tasks for notifications that exist in the system. To maximize performance, it is a suggested best practice that you specify a layout in the selection screen.

KKF2 Change CO Production Order

For the specified CO production order or QM order, you can use this transaction to maintain the general data of the order and verify the default settlement rule as well. Hence, when you create a CO production order, a settlement rule is generated automatically by the system.

MB1A Goods Withdrawal

You can use this transaction to generate a material withdrawal posting, post a material issue or post the shipment of goods to a customer. When you post a goods issuance, the warehouse stock will be reduced simultaneously.

MB5M Shelf Life List

You can use this report to get an overview of the remaining shelf-life of batches. In the selection screen if you do not enter a remaining shelf life, the report will display batches with past expiration dates. For batches to be included in this report, the shelf life expiration date/production date must be maintained in the batch master record.

MCXA	QMIS – Material Analysis (Lot Overview)

For the specified analysis period, you can use this report to get an overview of mean value of quality score, percentage rejection rate, percentage skip rate, and lead time of the number of inspection lot that is generated. Similar data are displayed against the respective inspection types as well. You can drill down the report based on material, plant, quality score or month as well. You can generate a similar report based on quantities (rather than percentages) by executing transaction MCXI: QMIS – Material Analysis (Quantities).

MCXV	QMIS – Material Analysis Overview Quality Notification

For the specified analysis period, you can use this report to display the notification status at the plant and material level. The report displays the total number of notifications, notifications outstanding, notifications being processed, notifications completed and notifications reset. Analyses about tasks are also displayed. Similar data are displayed against the respective notification types as well.

PLM_ AUDITMONITOR	Start Audit Monitor

You can use this transaction to get an overview of the number of outstanding corrective/preventive actions, display all audits, and display all question lists. Using this report you can also get a listing of all audit plans and their valid time periods. In the selection screen, you can select which audit component you would like to search for and get an overview. In the report listing, you can select a specific record and display its general data.

PLMD_ AUDIT	Audit Management

You can use this transaction to perform the following actions: process an audit component – create new audit component, search an existing audit component, delete the selected audit component or maintain an existing audit component; process an audit plan; process a question list; execute an audit; process corrective/preventive actions; assign documents to an audit component.

Q000	Quality Management

You can use this transaction to display the SAP Easy Access: Quality Management menu. The SAP Easy Access menu tree structure displays the transactions related to Quality Management.

QA00	Quality Inspection

You can use this transaction to display the SAP Easy Access: Quality Inspection menu. The SAP Easy Access menu tree structure displays the transactions related to Quality Inspection.

QA01	Create Inspection Lot

You can use this transaction to manually create a new inspection lot. For the specified inspection lot, you can use this transaction to display the inspection lot or to edit and maintain the inspection lot. The other processing that can be performed using this transaction are: block/unblock an inspection lot; cancel an inspection lot; create a new batch in an inspection lot; perform stock transfers in an inspection lot; where required, make corrections to inspection lot quantities; create a new QM order; and where required, approve the task list to be assigned to an inspection lot.

QA05	Job Planning: Periodic Inspection

You can use this transaction to create a variant for deadline monitoring of batches (materials maintained in batches and stored in a warehouse). The system can automatically perform deadline monitoring of batches for batch expiration dates and recurring inspections.

For the system to perform deadline monitoring, the following prerequisites should be satisfied in the material master record: You should have defined an inspection interval and activated "recurring inspection" in the inspection set-up. The initial screen displays the variants that are already created and existing in the system. Where required, you can select a specific variant and get a detailed overview or schedule the variant or start it immediately.

QA06	Job Overview: Periodic Inspection

You can use this transaction to get an overview of jobs scheduled for recurring inspection. You can also use this transaction to delete a specific job variant.

QA07	Trigger for Recurring Inspection

You can use this transaction for deadline monitoring of batches, specifically for monitoring the batch expiration date or monitoring recurring expirations. In the report output, you can view the batches that were processed. Actions performed and special notifications are displayed as well. Only data that satisfies the search filter is displayed in the output. The batches should also meet the following prerequisites: The batch status should be in "released" status; the stock should not be a special stock and should not be in an HU storage location.

QA08	Collective Processing of Inspection Set-up

You can use this report to perform mass activation or de-activation of an inspection type for materials, or to process the inspection set-up for an individual or several materials.

QA32	Change Data for Inspection Lot

You can use this transaction to display or maintain the following inspection lot data: inspection lot general data; inspection lot specifications; defect records; quality certificates; characteristics results; usage decision (UD) data. The report will output all inspection lots that satisfy the search filter.

QA33	Display Data for Inspection Lot

You can use this report to maintain and process inspection lots. You can edit and change the following data: inspection lot data, inspection lot characteristics, usage decision data, characteristics results, defect records and quality certificates.

QA51	Scheduling Source Inspections

You can use this transaction to generate a listing of materials (that have outstanding purchase orders and scheduling agreements) that are scheduled for source inspections. For a material to be included in the source inspection listing, the following prerequisites should be satisfied: quality information records should exist and the inspection type should be defined in the material master record.

QAC1	Change Insp. Lot Actual Quantity

You can use this transaction to make changes to the actual quantity of materials in an inspection lot. When you make a correction, you can also specify a correction reason. After you have made the correction, the system will make a posting to the Materials Management application, and a material document with the corrected quantity will be created.

QAC2	Transfer Stock to Insp. Lot

You can use this transaction to transfer material stocks in an inspection lot from one location to another, while the goods are still managed in inspection stock. While performing the stock transfer, you can mention the new physical location where you want to transfer the material stocks, specify a transfer reason, and the posting date for the stock transfer.

You can perform a stock transfer only if the inspection lot is in "Created" or "Released" status, the inspection lot does not have origin 17, a usage decision is not made for the inspection lot, and the specified inspection lot quantity is not in goods-receipt blocked stock. After you have performed the transfer, the system will make a posting to the Materials Management application and a new material document will be created to record the stock transfer. The inspection lot record will contain all information related to the new and original material documents for historical purposes.

QAC3	Reset Sample

You can use this transaction to reset or cancel the sample determination for an inspection lot. When you perform this process, the system will automatically set the inspection lot status to the status that had existed prior to the sample size determination. To be able to execute this process, the following prerequisites must be satisfied: the inspection lot should not have origin 17, the inspection lot should not be marked for cancellation, a usage decision is not made for the inspection lot, and inspection results or defects are not recorded for the inspection lot.

QC32	Archive Display – Inspection Lot

You can use this report to retrieve and display certificates that were archived using ArchiveLink. You might have created these certificates for a delivery item or an inspection lot. In the Business Document Navigator screen, use object type LIPS as class name for all delivery item certificates, and use object type BUS2045 as class name for inspection lot certificates.

QC55	QM Worklist – Quality Certificates in Procurement

Based on the search filter, this report generates a listing of procurement certificates available in the system. From the report output, you can navigate to the initial screen of the certificate where you can edit and make changes to the general data. The certificate status is indicated by a traffic light in the report output. It is a prerequisite that the procurement certificates and certificate type are defined as "Enhanced certificate processing" during customizing.

QCC0	QM – Direct Access to IMG

You can use this transaction to access the QM related customizing steps in IMG. The IMG structure displays all the customizing steps for Basic Settings, QM in Logistics, Quality Planning, Quality Inspection, Quality Certificates, Quality Notifications, Quality Control, Test Equipment Management, and Stability Study; settings to maintain the environment are displayed as well.

QCC1	Direct Access to IMG – Notification

You can use this transaction to access the Notifications related customizing steps in IMG. The IMG structure displays the customizing steps related to notification creation and notification processing. You can also access the customizing step OVERVIEW OF NOTIFICATION TYPE to get an overview of the notifications in the system.

QCC2	IMG Direct Access: QM Q – Notification

You can use this transaction to access the Quality Notifications related customizing steps in IMG. The IMG structure displays the customizing steps related to notification creation, notification processing, defects processing, and information systems (reports) related to Quality Notification. You can also access the customizing step OVERVIEW OF NOTIFICATION TYPE to get an overview of the quality notifications in the system.

QCC3	IMG Direct Access: QM Q – Inspection

You can use this transaction to access the Quality Inspection related customizing steps in IMG. The IMG structure displays the customizing steps related to inspection lot creation, inspection lot completion, status management, sample management, and results recording, as well as reports related to Quality Inspection.

QCC4	IMG Direct Access: QM Q – Planning

You can use this transaction to access the Quality Planning related customizing steps in IMG. The IMG structure displays the customizing steps related to setting up the Basic Data for Quality Planning. The customizing steps related to Inspection Planning, Engineering Workbench, Failure Mode and Effects Analysis (FMEA), and Control Plan are displayed as well.

QCC5	IMG Direct Selection – QM Business Add-In

You can use this transaction to view all the delivered BAdIs (Business Add-Ins) in SAP Quality Management. The tree structure displays the BAdIs in Quality Planning, Quality Inspection, Quality Certificate, Quality Notification, QM in Logistics, Stability Study, and Quality Control.

QDP1	Create Sampling Scheme

A sampling scheme is a collection of sampling plans. You can use this transaction to create a new sampling scheme manually. Using this transaction, you can also create a new sampling scheme, by copying an existing sampling scheme and making changes where required. In the header data, you can set the usage indicator SCHEME BLOCKED if you do not want the sampling scheme to be assigned to a sampling procedure.

QDV1	Create Sampling Procedure

You can use this transaction to create a sampling procedure. Using this transaction, you can also create a new sampling procedure, by copying an existing sampling procedure and making changes where required.

QDV6	Uses – Sampling Procedures

For the specified sampling procedure and key date, you can use this transaction to display an usage overview of the sampling procedure. The report output will display the task lists, material specifications and inspection set-ups where the specified sampling procedure is used.

The report output will display the total number of times the sampling procedure is used, and the number of uses in the task lists, material specifications and inspection set-ups. From the report output, if required, you can replace the sampling procedure by following the menu path SAMPLING PROCE-DURE • REPLACEMENT initial screen. From the report output, you can also display the data of the sampling procedure, task list, material specification and inspection type.

QE00	Quality Planning

You can use this transaction to display the SAP Easy Access: Quality Planning menu. The SAP Easy Access menu tree structure displays the transactions related to Quality Planning.

QF01	Record Defect Data

Defects can be recorded using

▶ defects recording – You can record defects for an inspection lot or an inspection operation or inspection characteristic.

▶ results recording – You can record defects for an inspection lot or an inspection operation or inspection characteristic.

▶ usage decision – You can record defects only for an inspection lot.

You can use this transaction to manually record defects that get identified. The defect records thus created are saved and processed in the system as a quality notification. Defects can be recorded with or without reference to serial numbers.

A defect record contains the following data: defect type, defect location, cause of the defect, what corrective action needs to be/ is taken, and valuation of the defect. It is a prerequisite that you have defined the defect codes prior to recording defects.

QF11	Record Defects for Inspection Lot

You can use this transaction to manually create defects at the inspection lot level. You can record defects only for the inspection lot if

no inspection plan or material specification is available.

QF21	Record Defects for Operation

You can use this transaction to manually create defects at the inspection operation level.

QF31	Record Defects for Characteristic

If an inspection plan is not available, you can record defects using the material specifications. If you have created an inspection lot for materials that have material specification, then you can use this transaction to record defects. If an inspection is carried using an inspection plan, then defects can be recorded either for inspection lot (transaction QF11), inspection operation (transaction QF21) or inspection characteristic (transaction QF31). Regardless of the level at which you record the defects, you can use the confirmation profile to define a summarization recording form.

QGA1	Display Quality Score Time Line

For the specified time period, you can use this report to provide a graphical overview of the changes to the quality scores of inspection lots. In the graphical output, you can double-click the quality score to get an overview of the inspection lot. Only inspection lots with usage decisions are considered for the report.

QGA3	Print Inspection Results

This report reads inspection lot information from the logical database PGQ and generates a printout of the inspection results for the lots. The report executes the program RQGAAM31.

QGA4   General QM Evaluations

You can use this transaction to create evaluations of quality inspections with informative graphics. You can use the QM Cockpit for Evaluations to process the following functionalities: Select inspection lots, inspection characteristics, and inspection results; create table views and graphic views; use quality control charts for evaluations; using QM-STI interface to export data and view external evaluations; evaluate defects; evaluate quality notifications; evaluate quality related data for components or preliminary products for a material; determine table or graphic layouts; and determine key figures.

QGC1   Quality Control Charts for Inspection Lots

You can use this report to generate a configurable list of quality control charts for inspection lots. Using this transaction, you can call the individual control charts, activate the control charts, or edit/make changes to the control charts. You can access the different processing options by following the menu path EDIT • CONTROL CHART.

QGD1   Test Equipment Usage List

You can use this transaction to generate a listing of equipment in the system. The report output displays the equipment general data, system status, functional location data, maintenance data, etc. In the report output, you can select a specific equipment and navigate (use menu path GO TO • DETAILS) to view the general data of the equipment.

QGD2   Test Equipment Tracking

You can use this transaction to generate a listing of inspection lots and the respective inspection characteristics. For the specified test equipment, you can use this listing to determine which inspection characteristics

were inspected. The field TEST EQUIPMENT is a required field in the selection screen.

QGP1   Results History for Task List Characteristics

You can use this report to display inspection results for the task list characteristics. In the selection screen, you are required to enter the search filter for the inspection lots, task list, and task list characteristic. (You can also do task list selection for a material or in the PM component.) In the selection screen, PLANT is a required field.

QGP2   Results History for Task List Charac

You can use this transaction to generate a listing of inspection results for a task list characteristic. When you select a task list for the material, it is a prerequisite that you enter the plant and the material number.

QI06   QM Releases – Mass Maintenance

You can use this transaction to do mass maintenance to quality information records. The report generates a listing of quality information records that are available in the system and satisfy the search criteria entered in the selection screen.

QI07   Worklist for Source Inspections

You can use this transaction to generate source inspection lots for open purchase orders and scheduling agreements. From the report listing, you can select a specific purchase order and display the Q-Info record or the purchase order data. As a prerequisite to being considered for this report, the materials must have incoming inspection assigned as an inspection type, and also reference to quality info records.

| QK01 | Assign QM Order to Material |

You can use this transaction to mass maintain the QM orders in the material master inspection set-up. You can use this transaction to perform the following functions: assign a QM order, delete an assignment, replace an existing QM order with another QM order, set or cancel the indicator for the individual QM order. In the report output, you can follow the menu path ENVIRONMENT to create a new QM order, edit or maintain a QM order, or display a QM order.

| QK02 | Display Assigned QM Orders |

You can use this report to generate a listing of QM orders in the material master. From the report listing, you can navigate to the QM master data to get a detailed overview. You can also display the material master data. For the report to be generated, it is a prerequisite that a QM order be assigned in the material master of a material/inspection type combination.

| QK04 | Create QM Order |

You can use this transaction to create a new QM order, edit an existing QM order, or display an existing QM order. In the inspection set-up of the material master, you can use this transaction to assign a QM order, replace an assigned QM order by assigning a new QM order, or delete an existing assignment. In the initial screen, PLANT is a required field.

| QM_FMEA | Cockpit |

The FMEA (Failure Mode Effect Analysis) Cockpit enables you to perform all of the processing functions for all FMEA components, such as Question List, FMEA, and Preventive or Detective action from one screen. Depending on the FMEA component, one of the following screens is displayed as tab pages: basic data, administration, texts, participant or contact person, status, valuation specs, result, control plan, and use.

| QM01 | Create Quality Notification |

You can use this transaction to create a new quality notification. The NOTIFICATION TYPE field in the initial screen is a required field. Depending on your customization, an additional dialog box might get displayed, where you will be required to enter the material number and other details. After this entry, the system navigates to the notification general data screen, where you can enter the data required to create the notification.

You can also create a new notification by by copying an existing notification as a reference. When you save the newly created notification, the existing notification that you used as a reference is saved in the notification. This enables you to search for notifications, using the reference notifications as a search filter. You can use any notification type as a reference notification, irrespective of the notification type of the new notification that you are creating.

| QM10 | Change List of Quality Notifications |

For the specified notification status (at least one status indicator should be selected), you can use this transaction to generate a listing of quality notifications that exist in the system. The report will output only quality notifications that satisfy the search filter you entered in the selection screen. You can use this report output to display or maintain quality notifications in the system.

| QM11 | Display List of Qualification Notifications |

You can use this report to display a listing of qualification notifications available in the system. In the selection screen, at least one notification status indicator must be selected. Where required, from the report output you can navigate to the QUALIFICATION NOTIFICATION initial screen where you can display the general data or make changes to the general data. If a QM order is maintained for the notification, you can navigate to the master data screen of the QM order, and you can get a detailed overview or maintain the master data of the QM order.

QM12	Change List of Tasks

You can use this transaction to generate a listing of quality notification tasks available in the system. The report will output only quality notification tasks that satisfy the search filter you entered in the selection screen. You can use this report output to display or maintain quality notification tasks in the system. From the report output, you can navigate and get an overview of the notification, item, task, activity or the associated order.

QM13	Display List of Tasks

You can use this report to display a listing of qualification notification tasks available in the system. From the report output, you can navigate to the initial screen of the associated notification, order, item or task. If you are in edit mode, you can make changes to the general data of these objects. If you are in display mode, then no maintenance can be performed.

QM14	Change List of Items

You can use this transaction to generate a listing of quality notification items available in the system. The report will output only quality notification items that satisfy the search filter you entered in the selection screen. You can use this report output, to display or maintain quality notification items in the system. From the report output, you can navigate and

get an overview of the notification, item, task, activity or the associated order.

QM16	Change Activity List

You can use this transaction to generate a listing of quality notification activities available in the system. The report will output only quality notification activities that satisfy the search filter you entered in the selection screen. You can use this report output to display or maintain quality notification activities in the system. From the report output, you can navigate and get an overview of the notification, item, task, activity or the associated order.

QM19	List of Q Notifications, Multi-Level

You can use this transaction to generate a multi-level listing of quality notifications in the system. In the report output, if you wish to display the notification header, select the notification number and click DISPLAY OBJECT (menu path: ENVIRONMENT • DISPLAY OBJECT). To display any of the reference objects, select the object and click DISPLAY OBJECT (menu path: ENVIRONMENT • DISPLAY OBJECT).

QM50	Time Line Display Q Notifications

For the specified notification status, you can use this transaction to graphically display the number of qualifications notifications created over the specified time period.

QP01	Create Inspection Plan

You can use this transaction to create a new inspection plan manually, or by copying an existing inspection plan, or copy a reference operation set to an inspection plan, or create a reference to an inspection plan. It is a prerequisite that, prior to creating an inspection plan, you have defined the work centers where the inspection will take place, the test equipment to be used for inspection must exist in the system and be in released status, and the materials to be inspected must exist in the system and be in released status. How this inspection plan will be used and the validity of this inspection plan must be pre-defined as well.

QP05	Print Inspection Plan

You can use this transaction to print an existing inspection plan. In the selection screen, if you do not mention a group counter, then all inspection plans for the group and the dependent characteristic specifications for the plan will be printed. In the selection screen, TASK LIST TYPE and KEY DATE are mandatory fields.

QP06	Missing or Unusable Task Lists (General)

You can use this report to generate a listing of missing inspection plans for materials. The report displays the material, material short text, plant and the error message related to inspection plan search. From the report, you can navigate to the material master record or the inspection plan.

QP48	Number Range for Physical Samples

You can use this transaction to create and maintain the internal number range for physical samples. The system will use this number range to automatically number the physical samples when they are created.

QP49	Number Range for Physical Sample Drawing

You can use this transaction to create and maintain the internal number range for physical sample drawing.

QP60	Display Task List Changes

You can use this report to edit and maintain currently existing inspection plans or reference operation sets. You can make changes by key date or by changing the master record.

QPCP	Control Plan

For the specified plan type, you can use this transaction to create a new control plan. In the initial screen, after you have specified the plan type, the system will navigate to the basic data screen, where you can enter the data required to create a control plan.

In the CONTROL PLAN initial screen, PLAN TYPE is a required field. If you have a control plan template, you can specify the template in the initial screen and the new control plan will be created based on the template. You can use this transaction to edit and make changes to an existing control plan or to display the basic data of an existing control plan. You can use this transaction to simulate a control plan as well.

QPNQ	Number Ranges for Inspection Plans

You can use this transaction to maintain the internal number range for inspection plans. The system will use this number range to automatically number the inspection plans when they are created.

QPR1	Create Physical Sample

You can use this transaction to manually create new, unplanned physical samples for an inspection lot. You can also create a new physical sample, by copying an existing physical sample record and making changes where required. In the initial screen, you can mention how you want to create the new physical sample; if you want to create it by copying, select the radio button NEW WITH

COPY MODEL and enter the physical sample that you wish to copy. The newly created physical sample will be assigned the status "CRTD" (created).

You can create a new physical sample with or without reference to an existing physical sample drawing number. If a physical sample drawing number is not referenced, then the system will automatically assign a new physical sample drawing number to the newly created physical sample.

QPR4	Confirm Physical Sample Drawing

For the specified physical sample drawing, you can use this transaction to perform additional processing. In the report output, you can select one or more physical samples and perform the following: release a physical sample, block or unblock a physical sample, set the delete flag or cancel the deletion of a physical sample, and double-click a physical sample and view its details.

QPR5	Manual Inspection Lots for Physical Samples

You can use this transaction to create inspection lots for physical samples of origin 15. Based on the search filter, the report output displays a listing of physical samples. In the report output, you can select a specific physical sample and create inspection lots or display the general data of the physical sample.

The following prerequisites must be fully met prior to creating the inspection lots: the specified physical sample must be released; the material and plant for the physical sample must be known; inspection type 15 must be active.

QPR6	Create New Physical Sample Drawing w. Ref

For the specified inspection lot, or order or production version, you can use this transaction to create a new physical sample drawing. You can also process the newly created physical sample drawing and release the physical samples.

QPR7	Storage Data Maintenance

You can use this transaction to maintain storage data for physical samples. The PLANT field is a required field in the selection screen. If a physical sample is referenced in another object, then that physical sample is blocked and is not displayed in the listing. From the report listing, you can select a physical sample and display its general data.

QPV2	Maintain Sample Drawing Procedure

You can use this transaction to create and maintain sample drawing procedures. You can also create a new sample drawing procedure by copying an existing sample drawing procedure and making the required changes. In the initial screen, you can select a specific sample drawing procedure and maintain the existing sample drawing items. You can also create a new sample drawing item for the sample drawing procedure.

QS21	Create Master Inspection Characteristic

You can use this transaction to create a new master inspection characteristic. Using this transaction you can perform the following: create a new validity period for an existing master inspection characteristic; display or maintain an existing master characteristic. In the initial screen, PLANT and VALID FROM are required fields.

QS22	Create Master Inspection Characteristic Version

You can use this transaction to create a new version of an existing master inspection characteristic. In the initial screen, select an existing master inspection characteristic and enter a new key date to create a new version.

QS26	Display Characteristic Use

You can use this report to generate a listing of task lists, material specifications and certificate profiles where the specified master inspection characteristic (MIC) is used. If you do not specify an MIC version in the selection screen, the report generates the usage overview for all versions of the MIC.

QS28	Display Inspection Characteristic List

You can use this report to generate a listing of all master inspection characteristics available in the system. In the selection screen, if you checkmark the field MONITOR CONTROL, the status of the inspection characteristic is displayed in the report in the form of a monitor. If the monitor displays RED, the inspection characteristic is not valid; YELLOW, the inspection characteristic is created but not Released yet; GREEN, the inspection characteristic is Released.

QS29	Maintain Characteristic Number Range

For the specified plant, you can use this transaction to maintain the internal number ranges for inspection characteristics.

QS31	Create Inspection Method

You can use this transaction to create a new inspection method. In the initial screen, PLANT and VALID FROM are required fields.

You can use this transaction to edit/maintain an existing inspection method or display an existing inspection method.

QS32	Create Inspection Method Version

You can use this transaction to create a new version of an existing inspection method. In the initial screen, enter the plant, inspection method and valid from date. The general data screen will be displayed, where you can fill in the required details and create a new version. In the general data screen, if you click the pushbutton TIMELINE, the system will display a listing of all valid versions of the specified inspection method.

QS37	Central Replacement of Methods

You can use this transaction to replace an inspection method used in task list characteristics. If you use help ($\boxed{\text{F4}}$) to display a list of inspection methods, only the current version will be displayed. If you use a change number, then the date of this change number is the key date on which the replacement becomes effective.

QS38	Display Inspection Method List

You can use this report to generate a listing of all inspection methods available in the system. In the selection screen, if you checkmark the field MONITOR CONTROL, the status of the inspection method is displayed in the report in the form of a monitor.

QS39	Maintain Method Number Range

For the specified plant, you can use this transaction to maintain internal number ranges for inspection methods.

QS41 — Maintain Catalog

For the specified catalog, you can use this transaction to create a code group. In the OVERVIEW screen, you can enter the short text of the code group, the long text of the code group and set the status of the code group. For the specified catalog and code group, this transaction can also be used to create new codes. This transaction can also be used to edit/maintain the code group and codes. Using this transaction, a code group can be deleted if it does not contain any codes and is not used anywhere else.

QS47 — Central Replacement of Code Groups

For the specified catalog type, you can use this transaction to replace the specified code group with a new code group that you specify in the initial screen. In the initial screen, you can also specify the key date on which this replacement becomes effective. Using the menu path CODE GROUP • DISPLAY USAGE, you can get a listing of where the code group is currently used.

QS48 — Usage Indicator – Code Groups

You can use this transaction to check the usage indicator of code groups and make adjustments where required. The system sets the usage indicator if a code group is used in another task. If you delete the reference to the code group, the usage indicator is not reset immediately. A code group cannot be deleted from the system if its usage indicator is set. This report will check if the code group is being used anywhere; if it is not being used anywhere, this report will reset the usage indicator

QS51 — Edit Selected Sets

For the specified plant and catalog, you can use this transaction to create selected sets and selected set codes for the specific selected sets. Using this transaction, you can also enter a classification for the specific selected set. You can use this transaction to delete a selected set if it is not being used elsewhere. Deleting a selected set will also delete the associated set codes.

QS53 — Maintain Individual Selected Set

For the specified catalog and plant, you can use this transaction to make changes and to maintain the already existing selected sets and the associated set codes.

QS58 — Usage Indicator – Selected Sets

You can use this transaction to check the usage indicator of selected sets and make adjustments where required. The system sets the usage indicator if a selected set is used in another task. If you delete the reference to the selected set, the usage indicator is not reset immediately. A selected set cannot be deleted from the system if its usage indicator is set. This report will check whether the selected set is being used anywhere; if it is not being used anywhere, this report will reset the usage indicator.

QS61 — Maintain Material Specification

An inspection can be performed based on an inspection plan or based on a valid material specification. Using this transaction, you can perform the following functions: create new master inspection characteristics, assign a new master inspection characteristic to a class characteristic, reference a master inspection characteristic or cancel a reference to a master inspection characteristic, delete an assignment, display the material.

QST01	Create Stability Study

You can use this transaction to create a stability study. A stability study is a quality notification of the notification type QS or QR and it is the central object for the stability testing of physical materials. You use notification type "QS" if you conduct a stability study with reference to a material. You use notification type "QR" if you conduct a stability study without reference to a material.

QST03	Stability History

You can use this transaction to generate a listing of stability studies. From the report listing, you can display the stability history for each study by clicking the button STABILITY HISTORY.

QST04	Packages in Inspection Plans

You can use this transaction to display a listing of packages used in inspection plans. The listing includes all inspection plans that have "released" status and are assigned the same maintenance strategy as the maintenance plans from which the selection was called. The report listing also shows scheduling intervals assigned to each operation in inspection plan.

QST06	Scheduling Overview List

You can use this transaction to generate a listing of dates for selected testing schedule items for stability studies. The report displays only active testing schedules. In the selection screen, you can enter the search filter and the report selection is based on the entered search filter.

QST07	List of Testing Schedule Items – Change Data

You can use this transaction to generate a listing of testing schedule items for stability studies. The report will display the testing schedule item number, the testing schedule, the strategy, short text of the testing schedule item, and the inspection plan. From the report output, you can click the pushbutton TESTING SCHEDULE ITEM to maintain (make changes and edit) the testing schedule item. If you click the pushbutton STORAGE CONDITION, you can get an overview of the storage condition for the respective testing schedule item.

QST09	Maintain Planning Building Block

You can use this transaction to maintain planning building blocks for stability studies. The primary usage is for setting up templates for stability studies created through trials.

QV01	Create Quality Assurance Agreement

You can use this transaction to create a new quality assurance agreement. In the initial screen, enter the document of which you wish to create a new version. The system will then navigate to the basic data screen, where you can enter the basic data for the new quality assurance agreement. If a template is available, you can specify the template in the initial screen, and the quality assurance agreement will be created based on the specified template.

QV04	Find Quality Assurance Agreement

You can use this transaction to display the quality assurance agreements currently available in the system. You can specify the search filter in the selection screen and the report will display all quality assurance agreements that meet the search criteria.

QV11	Create Technical Delivery Terms

You can use this transaction to create technical delivery terms in the document management system. The process is similar to creating a new quality assurance agreement. (Refer to transaction QV01 for more details.)

QV51	Create Control for QM in SD

You can use this transaction to create a new customer info record. In the initial screen, enter the customer and sales organization and click the CONTROL DATA push button; the system will navigate to the overview screen. Here, click the NEW INFO RECORD push button and the system will display the CREATE QM CONTROL DATA IN SD dialog box. Enter the required details and save the custom info record.

QZ00	Quality Certificates

You can use this transaction to display the SAP Easy Access: Quality Certificate menu. The SAP Easy Access menu tree structure displays the transactions related to Quality Certificates.

SAP1	SAP Easy Access Report Selection

You can use this transaction to display the SAP Easy Access Report menu. Under QUALITY MANAGEMENT node, you will see all reports related to Quality Management. The reports are categorized under Quality Planning, Quality Inspection, Quality Certificates, Quality Notification, Quality Control, and Test Equipment Management.

SBWP	SAP Business Workplace

SAP Business Workplace is a working environment where SAP users receive their assigned work items and process all documents they receive from other users and from the SAP system. The workplace provides folders where work items and documents can be managed. Any messages that were published within their work group, or enterprise wide can be accessed and read from the workplace.

10 Project System (PS)

CJ01 Create Project (Work Breakdown Structure)

Use this transaction to create a project definition with a work breakdown structure(s). A project structure consists of a project definition (which can also be maintained via transaction CJ06) and work breakdown structure (WBS) elements (which can be created individually via transaction CJ11) arranged in a hierarchical manner. The project definition, as well as WBS elements, will have master data associated with it. Input the project definition number and text of the project profile and click ENTER. Other section options include the ability to create a project definition in reference to an existing project or a standard project and also an indicator for copying the WBS elements and project data with a project definition. Maintain project definition and/or WBS elements and save your project. Projects can also be maintained centrally in transaction CJ20N.

CJ02 Change Project (Work Breakdown Structure)

Use this transaction to expand the project definition to include work breakdown structure elements. A project structure consists of a project definition (which can also be maintained via transaction CJ06) and work breakdown structure (WBS) elements (which can be created individually via transaction CJ11) arranged in a hierarchical manner. Input the project definition number and click ENTER. On the BASIC DATA tab, start to enter the levels of the WBS elements, the number, description and other settings, such as relevancy to account assignment (actual costs are charged to the WBS elements), billing element indicator, organizational assignments (ASSIGNMENT tab), start/finish dates (DATES tab), overhead costing sheet and results analysis (for calculation of work in progress, CONTROL tab), and person responsible (RESPONSIBILITIES tab) and save your project.

CJ03 Display Project (Work Breakdown Structure)

Use this transaction to display the project previously created/changed via transaction CJ01 and CJ02.

CJ06 Create Project Definition

This transaction is used to create the project definition, which is a framework for all organizational elements within a project. When you create a work breakdown structure, the corresponding project definition is created automatically. In this transaction, you can maintain default values for a project, such as the settlement rule and default values, which are copied for new WBS elements created for the project. Input the project definition number and click ENTER. Other section options include the ability to create a project definition in reference to an existing project or a standard project and also an indicator for copying WBS elements and project data with a project definition. Maintain project definition elements and save your project. Projects can also be maintained centrally in transaction CJ20N.

CJ07	Change Project Definition

Use this transaction to change the project definition, which may be useful because you can maintain default values for a project, such as a settlement rule and default values, which are copied into new WBS elements that you create for a project definition.

CJ08	Display Project Definition

Use this transaction to display the project definition previously created/changed via transaction CJ01, CJ06 or CJ20N.

CJ11	Create WBS Element

This transaction is used to create a work breakdown structure assigned to a project definition that already exists. This may be useful for conversion purposes where you define the overall project definition but require an LSMW to convert the WBS element details. To use this transaction, manually input the project definition, WBS element number, project profile and click ENTER. On the BASIC DATA screen enter the description and other settings, such as the project priority, person responsible, relevancy to account assignment (actual costs are charged to the WBS elements), billing element indicator, organizational assignments (ASSIGNMENT tab), start/finish dates (DATES tab), overhead costing sheet and results analysis key (for calculation of work in progress, CONTROL tab), and save your project.

CJ12	Change WBS Element

Use this transaction to change the work breakdown structure previously created/changed via transaction CJ02, CJ11 or CJ20N.

CJ13	Display WBS Element

Use this transaction to display the work breakdown structure previously created/changed via transaction CJ02, CJ11 or CJ20N.

CJ20	Structure Planning: Change

This transaction is the old transaction used to centrally maintain a project structure but CJ20N is more commonly used.

CJ20N	Project Builder

This transaction is the updated version of transaction CJ20 with an improved user method of editing projects. The project builder integrates all functions necessary to process your project. Within project builder you can create, change or display all project structure data, such as the project definition, WBS element and network in one transaction. Furthermore, you can schedule projects with a direct link to the project planning board. Also, you can define user-specific work lists and user-specific templates, which you can then use to process your projects. Project builder has three displays: a structure display (project you are working on), a display to access a work list/template, and a work area where the details of your project can be changed. Various display options can be changed via the menu path SETTINGS • OPTIONS with some user-friendly processing options, such as the drag and drop feature of moving an object from one display window to another.

CJ21	Change Time Scheduling: Basic Dates

Use this transaction to change the basic dates in your work breakdown structure (WBS) element, which are binding dates for functions such as time scheduling and capacity planning. You can also input these dates during the initial project setup. Input the project definition and leave the WBS ELEMENT field blank if you want to change the whole project (click the WITH ACTIVITIES indicator if you want all network activities to be taken into account when time scheduling) and then click ENTER. On the next screen, input the basic dates, and then there are various time scheduling tasks that can be executed, including checking dates (for example, checking WBS element dates that are within a superior WBS element date range). Time scheduling will calculate scheduled dates based on the planning method (top-down, bottom-up or free scheduling). The planning method can be defaulted onto the project from a project profile defined in customizing. Once the schedules dates have been calculated, you can save the dates.

CJ22	Display Time Scheduling: Basic Dates

Use this transaction to display the basic dates and calculated scheduled dates changed via transaction CJ21.

CJ23	Change Time Scheduling: Forecast Dates

Use this transaction to change forecast dates in your work breakdown structure (WBS) element, which are dates you expect tasks to be completed. Note that these dates have no influence on reservations, purchase requisitions or capacity planning. You have the option of using the forecast for scheduling and can schedule a network using the forecast dates. Furthermore, you can copy the forecast dates into the basic dates in the WBS element or activity and then use them as the basis for further planning. Input the project definition and leave the WBS element field blank if you want to change the whole project (click the WITH ACTIVITIES indicator if you want all network activities taken into account when

time scheduling) and then click ENTER. On the next screen, input the forecast dates, and then there are various time scheduling tasks that can be executed, including checking dates (for example, checking WBS element dates that are within a superior WBS date range) and scheduling. Time scheduling calculates scheduled dates based on the planning method (top-down, bottom-up or free scheduling). The planning method can be defaulted onto the project from a project profile defined in customizing. Once the schedules dates have been calculated, you can save the dates.

CJ24	Display Time Scheduling: Forecast Dates

Use this transaction to display the forecast dates and any calculated scheduled dates changed via transaction CJ23.

CJ25	Change Time Scheduling: Actual Dates

Use this transaction to input manually actual dates, which provide you with information on the state of the project. You enter them in the WBS element manually using this transaction, or you can let the system calculate them using confirmation data. Input the project definition and leave the WBS element field blank if you want to change the whole project and click the WITH ACTIVITIES indicator if you want all network activities taken into account when time scheduling and then click ENTER. On the next screen, input the actual dates, and then there are various time scheduling tasks that can be executed, including checking dates (for example, checking WBS element dates that are within a superior WBS date range) and scheduling. Time scheduling calculates scheduled dates based on the planning method (top-down, bottom-up or free scheduling). The planning method can be defaulted onto the project from a project profile defined in customizing. Once the schedules dates have been calculated, you can save the dates.

CJ26	Display Time Scheduling: Actual Dates

Use this transaction to display the actual dates and any calculated scheduled dates changed via transaction CJ25.

CJ27	Create Project (Project Planning Board)

This transaction is used to create the settings for the project planning board, which is a tool for planning and controlling the project. The appearance of the project planning board can be changed to suit user requirements. You review progress and access all the important data on your project, including calculated costs, plan costs, check dates, schedule resources, distribute work and level capacities. You can also branch to functionality that simulates changes and provides further graphics, such as a hierarchical view of the project structure. The layout of the project planning board consists of a table area and a graphic area. The graphic area displays a Gantt chart within which you can edit your project. Input you project definition and click OPEN PROJECT.

CJ29	Project Scheduling

This transaction can be used to schedule projects with maintenance and service orders. Maintenance orders and service orders can be included as sub networks in a network and can be taken into account during WBS scheduling and overall network scheduling. Input a project definition or a WBS element and then click BASIC DATES or FORECAST DATES, depending on the set of dates you want to schedule. An option screen appears with the option to choose the schedule selection box either by networks only, maintenance and service orders only, or networks and maintenance/service orders. Make your selection and execute.

CJ2A	Structure Planning: Display

Use this transaction to display a structure planning project previously created via transaction CJ2D.

CJ2B	Change Project Planning Board

Use this transaction to change the project planning board previously created via transaction CJ27.

CJ2C	Display Project Planning Board

Use this transaction to display a structure planning project previously created via transaction CJ27.

CJ2D	Create Project (Structure Planning)

This transaction is used to structure a project by creating the WBS elements and network data together, as opposed to maintaining the structure separately. You may use structure planning particularly when you have a more precise idea of the structure of the project, for example, where WBS elements are detailed by activities. You can maintain default parameters in the project profile, such as scheduling methods for WBS elements and scheduling parameters for activities. When you create an activity for a WBS element, the system will automatically create the network in the background. Input the project (or use a template), click CONTINUE, maintain WBS element via the WBS tab and activities/activity elements via the ACTIVITY tab, and click SAVE.

CJ30	Change Original Budget

Use this transaction to change the original budget, which is an approved cost structure for an internal WBS element. A budget is more controlled and binding than a plan and can be subject to availability control. The original budget can be changed, using this transaction, with the best estimation of costs. Unforeseen events, such as price increases, and so on, may require corrections to the original budget, which can be maintained using supplements (transaction code CJ36) and returns (transaction code CJ35). Use a supplement to increase the current budget or a return to decrease the current budget. Input the project number and WBS element and click the ORIGINAL BUDGET icon, enter your budget and click SAVE.

CJ31   Display Original Budget

This transaction is used to display the original budget. A budget is more controlled and binding than a plan and can be subject to availability control. Input the project number and WBS element and click the ORIGINAL BUDGET icon.

CJ32   Change Release

This transaction is used to release a budget on a total or an annual level. The release is based on the current budget, which includes the original budget +/- any supplements, returns or transfers. Input the project number, click the RELEASE icon, and now you can release the budget for all WBS elements or individual WBS elements. On the next screen, input the released budget amount and click SAVE.

CJ33   Display Release

Use this transaction to display the released budget previously released via transaction CJ32.

CJ34   Transfer Budget

Use this transaction to transfer a budget from one WBS element to another. The WBS element must have the appropriate status to

enable this. The transfer posting works the same way as a supplement to a project (transaction code CJ36) or a return from a project (transaction CJ35), except that you specify a sender and receiver WBS element.

CJ35   Post Return

Use this transaction to make returns from the original project budget. Using this transaction you can return funds, i.e., reduce the original budget of the overall project for unused funds. Changes are managed as line items in the system and are therefore managed separately from the original budget. You therefore use budget updates to prove where supplements and returns originated and where they are to be used.

CJ36   Post Supplement

Use this transaction to make supplements to the original project budget, which means you make supplements to particular WBS elements independent of the higher level WBS elements. The system updates the supplemented budget on the WBS at the higher level. Changes are managed as line items in the system and are therefore managed separately from the original budget. The time to lock down a budget as an original budget, and to update it with supplements, returns and transfers depends on when you want to log data origins, in other words, the sender-receiver relationships for the updates. You therefore use budget updates to prove where supplements and returns originated, and where they are to be used. You can accomplish this by changing the status on the project via transaction CJ20N.

CJ37   Change Supplement

Use this transaction to make supplements to the original budget within a project, which means the supplement is top-down, i.e., from a higher level WBS element to the one below. You can supplement only as much budget on a WBS element as is contained in the higher level. Changes are managed as line items in the system and are therefore managed separately from the original budget. The time to lock down a budget as an original budget, and to update it with supplements, returns and transfers depends on when you want to log data origins, in other words, the sender-receiver relationships for the updates. You therefore use budget updates to prove where supplements and returns originated and where they are to be used. You can accomplish this by changing the status on the project via transaction CJ20N.

CJ38   Change Return

Use this transaction to make returns from the original project budget, which means you return from the bottom-up from a lower-level WBS element to the next one up. You can return only a budget that is distributable or available. Changes are managed as line items in the system and are therefore managed separately from the original budget. You therefore use budget updates to prove where supplements and returns originated and where they are to be used.

CJ3A   Change Document

This transaction is used to change the standard text during budgeting. When entering the budget via transaction CJ30, you can enter text then or via this transaction. Input the budget document number, click ENTER, enter the standard text and save.

CJ3B   Display Document

Use this transaction to display the standard text on a budget document, which can also be viewed via transaction CJ30 and selecting the appropriate layout. Input the budget document number and click ENTER to display.

CJ40   Change Cost Planning

Use this transaction to input an overall cost plan for the WBS element. This type of planning is performed independently from cost elements. You can enter the plan for the lifetime of the project/WBS element or an annual plan in each fiscal year. Note that an overall plan can be changed using this transaction; however, the original values are not maintained separately.

CJ41   Display Project Plan

This transaction is used to display an overall plan for a WBS element. This type of planning is performed independently from cost elements. The plan may be for the lifetime of the project or an annual plan entered in each fiscal year.

CJ42   Change Revenue Planning

This transaction is used to plan revenues on a project/WBS element manually, but the WBS element must be flagged as a billing element to do so. Input the project number, currency, planning version and click ENTER. On the next screen, you can enter the plan for the lifetime of the project or an annual plan in each fiscal year. Also, you can switch between the WBS elements, which are planned hierarchically, meaning a lower level WBS element cannot have a greater plan than the higher level WBS element. Note that an overall plan can be changed using this transaction; however, the original values are not maintained separately. It is possible to plan revenue automatically by indicating, in the project profile, that billing data from sales orders assigned to WBS elements should update the planned revenue lines for the WBS elements.

CJ43	Display Revenue Planning

This transaction is used to display the revenue plan for a WBS element. The plan may be for the lifetime of the order or an annual plan entered in each fiscal year. Input the project, currency, planning version and click ENTER. On the next screen, you can review the plan for the lifetime of the project or the annual plan in each fiscal year. Also, you can switch between the WBS elements, which have been planned hierarchically.

CJ44	Actual Overhead Calculation: Project/WBS Element/Network

This transaction is used to apply actual overhead costs to WBS elements/networks based on an overhead costing sheet assignment as part of the costing period end closing process. The overhead costing sheet will calculate the overhead cost based on a base cost element and an overhead rate. The WBS element/network will typically be debited, and a cost center (defined in the costing sheet) will be credited. Enter the WBS element, period, fiscal year, include the WBS element hierarchy/with order indicators and you can execute in test or update mode. To execute the function for multiple WBS elements, use transaction CJ45.

CJ45	Actual Overhead Calculation: Projects/WBS Elements/Networks

This transaction is used to apply actual overhead costs to multiple WBS elements/networks based on an overhead costing sheet assignment as part of the costing period end closing process. In order to use this function, you must first create a selection variant that specifies the WBS element/network range required (i.e., click the CREATE button to the left of the selection variant, name your variant, select CREATE/CHANGE, click ENTER, select your range, and save your variant).

The overhead costing sheet will calculate the overhead cost based on a base cost element and an overhead rate. The WBS element/network will typically be debited, and a cost center (defined in the costing sheet) will be credited. Enter the selection variant, period, fiscal year and then you can execute in test or update mode. To execute the function for an individual WBS element, use transaction CJ44.

CJ46	Plan Overhead Calculation: Project/WBS Element

This transaction is used to calculate plan overhead costs to WBS elements/networks based on an overhead costing sheet assignment as part of the costing period end closing process. The overhead costing sheet will calculate the overhead cost based on a base cost element and an overhead rate. Enter the WBS element, period, fiscal year, include the WBS hierarchy/network indicators and you can execute in test or update mode. To execute the function for multiple WBS elements, use transaction CJ45.

CJ47	Plan Overhead Calculation: Projects/WBS Elements

This transaction is used to calculate plan overhead costs to multiple WBS elements/networks based on an overhead costing sheet assignment as part of the costing period end closing process. In order to use this function, you must first create a selection variant that specifies the WBS element/network range required (i.e., click the CREATE button to the left of the selection variant, name your variant, select CREATE/CHANGE, click ENTER, select your range and save your variant). The overhead costing sheet will calculate the overhead cost based on a base cost element and an overhead rate. Enter the selection variant, period, fiscal year, and then you can execute in test or update mode. To execute the function for individual WBS elements, use transaction CJ46.

CJ48	Payment Planning Change

This transaction is used to manually plan project payments, enabling cash flow reporting for both plan and actual data. You can then report on how much you are expecting to receive and pay. If you enter the plan payments for the whole year, then a distribution rule will allocate the amounts to periods. This transaction is useful in the beginning of a project for planning revenues and expenditure since during the project other SAP components, such as payment data from sales documents and commitment values from materials management, are fully integrated. Input the controlling area on the initial screen and click CONTINUE. Enter the project data you want to plan and select either free or form-based entry and click OVERVIEW. Input a negative amount for plan payments and a positive amount for plan revenues, and save your plan.

CJ49	Payment Planning Display

Use this transaction to display payments/revenues planned via transaction CJ48.

CJ7E	Transfer of Planning Data: Projects/WBS Elements

This transaction is used for plan settlement from individual projects to CO-Profitability Analysis (CO-PA). In customizing go to CREATE CO VERSIONS and then within the controlling area settings by fiscal year the INTEGRATED PLANNING flag must be selected. For projects, the individual WBS elements must also be flagged as PLAN-INTEGRATED in the project. When you settle planning data, the sender objects are credited. Input the sender project or WBS element, plan version, period, fiscal year and click EXECUTE in test or updated mode.

CJ7G	Transfer of Planning Data: Projects/WBS Elements Collective

This transaction is used for plan settlement from multiple orders or projects to CO-Profitability Analysis (CO-PA). In customizing go to CREATE CO VERSIONS and then within the controlling area settings by fiscal year the INTEGRATED PLANNING flag must be selected. For projects, the individual WBS element also must be plan-integrated. When you settle planning data, the sender objects are credited. Create and input a selection version for projects or WBS elements, plan version, period, fiscal year and click EXECUTE in test or updated mode.

CJ88	Actual Settlement: Project/WBS Element/Network

Use this transaction to settle actual primary and secondary costs and revenues (if applicable) to the receivers established in a WBS element/network settlement rule. In costing, WBS element/networks are interim cost collectors that are used to plan, record actual costs and monitor costs until certain activities have been completed and the costs can move to their final destination. This movement of the costs to their final destination is called settlement. The WBS element/network settlement rules are dependent on the parameters established in the settlement structure, settlement profile, and project profile (all defined in customizing and in the project itself).

CJ8G	Actual Settlement: Projects/WBS Elements/Networks

This transaction is used to settle actual costs of multiple WBS elements/networks at the same time. In costing, WBS element/networks are interim cost collectors that are used to plan, record actual costs and monitor costs until certain activities have been completed and the costs can move to their final destination.

This movement of the costs to their final destination is called settlement. The WBS element/network settlement rules are dependent on the parameters established in the settlement structure, settlement profile, and project profile (all defined in customizing and in the project itself). A selection variant has to be created beforehand in order to select the project/WBS element/network range. The selection method can be changed to projects used in CRM or cProjects if these components are being used. Select the settlement period and fiscal year and click Execute.

CJ91	Create Standard WBS

This transaction is used to create a standard WBS element to be used as a template for creating operative WBS elements. A standard WBS element can be created for projects that have a similar structure. This saves time setting up projects. Input the standard WBS number and project profile and click Enter. On the Project Definition Basic Data screen, input the organizational data and then click the WBS Element Overview screen to enter the detail data for the WBS element and click Save. Note that when you use a standard network that is assigned to a standard network to create an operative network, an operative WBS element is also created. However, if you create an operative WBS element from a standard WBS element to which a standard network is assigned, an operative network is not created.

CJ92	Change Standard WBS

Use this transaction to change a standard WBS element previously created via transaction CJ91.

CJ93	Display Standard WBS

Use this transaction to display a standard WBS element previously created via transaction CJ91.

CJ9B	Copy WBS Plan to Plan (Collective)

This transaction is used during the planning process and offers a method of generating a plan data version from plan data that already exists for an individual WBS element. This may be needed in order to track actual performance against an original plan and a modified plan version. It allows plan data posted to your WBS elements to be copied to plan values within a fiscal year, across different periods or within different versions. You can copy within fiscal years, periods and versions. Try to avoid using the Reset and Overwrite option because the system needs to read all the data in the target version in order to clear it.

Create and input the selection variant, which includes project, sales document, WBS element, network, activity or materials in the network. Select the plan version, period/fiscal year transferring from and the target plan version, period/fiscal year transferring to and click Execute.

CJ9BS	Copy WBS Plan to Plan (Individual)

This transaction is used during the planning process and offers a method of reusing large parts of your planning data in WBS elements to generate additional plan data versions. This may be needed in order to track actual performance against an original plan and a modified plan version. It allows plan data posted to your WBS elements to be copied to plan values within a fiscal year, across different periods or within different versions. Try to avoid using the Reset and Overwrite option because the system needs to read all the data in the target version in order to clear it. Input the project definition or WBS element and select the plan version, period/fiscal year transferring from and the target plan version, period/fiscal year transferring to and click EXECUTE.

CJ9C	Copy WBS Actual to Plan (Collective)

This transaction is used during the planning process and offers a method of reusing large parts of your actual data in WBS elements to generate plan data. It allows actual data posted to your WBS elements to be transferred to plan values within a fiscal year, across different periods or within different versions. Try to avoid using the RESET AND OVERWRITE option because the system needs to read all the data in the target version in order to clear it. Create and input the selection variant, which includes project, sales document, WBS element, network, activity or materials in the network. Select the actual period/fiscal year transferring from and the target plan version, period/fiscal year transferring to and click EXECUTE.

CJ9CS	Copy WBS Actual to Plan (Individual)

This transaction is used during the planning process and offers a method of generating plan data from actual postings to individual WBS elements in a project. It allows actual data posted to your WBS elements to be transferred to plan values within a fiscal year, across different periods or within different versions. Try to avoid using the RESET AND OVERWRITE option because the system needs to read all the data in the target version in order to clear it. Input the project definition, WBS element and select the actual period/fiscal year transferring from and the target plan version, period/fiscal year transferring to and click EXECUTE.

CJ9D	Orders/Networks for Project: Copy Plan Version

This transaction is used during the planning process and is a utility for copying one plan version to another for individual orders/networks. Selection criteria include a project, sales document, WBS element and network. Try to avoid using the reset and overwrite option because the system needs to read all the data in the target version in order to clear it. Select the reference plan version and the target version and click EXECUTE IN TEST OR UPDATE MODE.

CJ9E	Planned Settlement: Projects/WBS Elements

This transaction is used to allocate planned cost to cost centers, business processes and profitability segments for an individual project or WBS element so that you can get a holistic view of the organizations plan for the business, for example, the profit plan for a service product line of business. Planned settlement is used when integrated cost object planning has been set up in customizing. Input the project or WBS element, plan version, period/fiscal year and click EXECUTE IN TEST OR UPDATE MODE.

CJ9F	Copy Project Costing (Collective)

This transaction is used during the planning process and offers a method of reusing large parts of your planning data in a project to generate additional plan data versions. This may be needed in order to track actual performance against an original plan and a modified plan version. It allows plan data posted to your WBS elements/networks/activities within a project to be copied to plan values within a fiscal year, across different periods or within different versions.

Try to avoid using the Reset and Overwrite option because the system needs to read all the data in the target version in order to clear it. Create and input the selection variant, which includes project, sales document, WBS element, network, activity and materials in the network. Select the plan version, period/fiscal year transferring from and the target plan version, period/fiscal year transferring to and click Execute.

CJ9FS	Copy Project Costing (Individual)

This transaction is used during the planning process and is a utility for copying one plan version to another for individual projects with WBS elements/networks/orders/activities. Selection criteria include a project, reference plan version and target version. Execute in test or update mode.

CJ9G	Planned Settlement: Projects/WBS Elements Collective

This transaction is used to allocate planned costs to cost centers, business processes and profitability segments for a range of projects and/or WBS elements so that you can get a holistic view of the plan for the business, for example, the profit plan for a service product line of business. Planned settlement is used when integrated cost object planning has been set up in customizing. Create and input a selection variant for the range of projects or the WBS elements, plan version, period/fiscal year and execute in test or update mode.

CJ9K	Asynchronous Network Costing: Planned Costs and Payments

Use this transaction for asynchronous network costing, which calculates or updates the plan values for several activities that are assigned to networks, simultaneously.

Updates are determined for all planned costs, planned outgoing payments (if project cash management is active) and costing for configurable materials in valuated project stock, per the configuration settings entered. Selection criteria include a project, sales document, WBS element and network. Select the indicator read purchasing info records if you want the system to read the purchase info record and update data for planned costs and planned payments. Execute in test or update mode.

CJ9L	Cost Forecast (Individual Processing)

This transaction is used to generate a cost forecast for an individual project, which is calculated by adding actual and commitment costs to the cost to complete the project (the cost to complete the project is determined by valuating the activities remaining on the project on the basis of the plan, forecast, and actual values in the network). Input the project definition and the version for the forecast, which in the standard system is version 110 for the exclusive use of forecast costs. Execute in test or update mode.

CJ9M	Cost Forecast (Collective Processing)

Use this transaction to generate a cost forecast for multiple projects calculated by adding actual and commitment costs to the cost to complete the project (the cost to complete the project is determined by valuating the activities remaining on the project on the basis of the plan, forecast, and actual values in the network). Create and input a selection variant, which includes a project, sales document, WBS element, network, activity and materials in the network. The version for the forecast in the standard system is version 110 for the exclusive use of forecast costs. Execute in test or update mode.

CJA1	Project-Related Incoming Orders (Collective Processing)

Use this transaction to transfer key figures (revenues, costs and quantities) from multiple incoming sales orders and open sales order values assigned to projects. Open sales order values are determined by the incoming sales order value less the value of any billing documents. Create and input the selection variant for a range of projects, sales orders, WBS elements, network/orders, activity or materials in a network. Input a period/fiscal year and execute in test or update mode.

CJA2	Project-Related Incoming Orders (Individual Processing)

This transaction is used to transfer key figures (revenues, costs and quantities) from individual incoming sales orders and open sales order values assigned to projects. Open sales order values are determined by the incoming sales order value less the value of any billing documents. Input the sales order number, project, WBS element, period, fiscal year and execute in test or update mode.

CJB1	Generate Settlement Rules: WBS Elements (Collective Processing)

This transaction is used to generate settlement rules automatically for multiple projects, sales orders or WBS elements, which is recommended because the settlement of projects can become very complex. Settlement posts actual costs incurred in the project to one or more receivers. For example, if you have already carried out results analysis, you can capitalize costs capable of being capitalized by settling them to financial accounting. The settlement rules are dependent on the parameters established in the settlement structure, settlement profile, and project profile (all defined in customizing and in the project itself). Create and input the selection variant

for a range of projects, sales orders, WBS elements, network/orders, activity or materials in a network. Input a period/fiscal year and execute in test or update mode.

CJB2	Generate Settlement Rules: WBS Elements (Individual Processing)

This transaction is used to generate settlement rules automatically for individual projects, sales orders or WBS elements, which is recommended because the settlement of projects can become very complex. Settlement posts actual costs incurred in the project to one or more receivers. For example, if you have already carried out results analysis, you can capitalize costs capable of being capitalized by settling them to financial accounting. The settlement rules are dependent on the parameters established in the settlement structure, settlement profile, and project profile (all defined in customizing and in the project itself). Selection criteria include a project, sales order or WBS element. Input a period/fiscal year and execute in test or update mode.

CJBV	Project Availability Control Background Job Activation

Use this transaction to activate availability control, which prevents the assignment of too many funds by checking the budget release to lower level WBS elements and assigned values (actual costs, commitments). Settings for availability control are contained within the budget profile assigned to the project. Input the project number range, click DETAIL LOG (logs the activated objects) and click EXECUTE. Upon activation, the system determines WBS elements that carry a budget and has assigned funds and carries out availability checking. Availability checking checks to see, for example, if there is enough budget available in the higher level WBS element to be assigned to a lower level WBS element. Furthermore, after the activation, each posting to the project is checked by availability control.

| CJBW | Deactivate Availability Control for Projects |

This transaction is used to deactivate availability control for one or more projects, which may be required if availability control was activated by mistake or if the current year control is not required until the budget has been approved. Input the project number range and click EXECUTE.

| CJCF | Fiscal Year Close: Carry Forward Commitment |

Use this transaction to carry forward commitments (for example, purchase requisitions, purchase orders, earmarked funds) posted in the current fiscal year but not reduced until the following fiscal year. The commitment carried forward then debits the budget in the new fiscal year. Input the project number/range, the network number/range, fiscal year carry from and execute in test or update mode.

| CJCO | Carrying Forward Project Budget |

This transaction enables you to carry forward budget remainders from projects to the following fiscal year. A budget that has not been used up is mainly defined here as the difference between the planned budget and incurred actual costs. Budgets carried forward to the following year can also be posted to the previous year in certain circumstances. Input the project number/range, sender fiscal year, document date and execute in test or update mode.

| CJCS | Display Change Documents: Reference WBS |

Use this transaction to report all changes to reference WBS elements. Selection criteria include a standard project definition number, user ID of the individual making the change and the change date from/to. The report output will display the project data object ID such as WBS element, field changed, old/new field value, date changed and user ID of the individual making the change.

| CJE0 | Execute Hierarchy Report |

Use this transaction to run a hierarchy report previously created via transaction CJE1. The analysis is based on data within the project information database (RPSCO). The project information database contains all costs, revenues and payment data summarized by value category (groupings of cost elements and commitment items). Double-click the report name in the left hand window pane, select the database profile, click ENTER, select the report criteria, and execute the report.

| CJE1 | Create Hierarchy Report |

This transaction is used to create a report of costs, revenues and payments from a hierarchical point of view for projects, partial projects and across projects. The analysis is based on data within the project information database (RPSCO). The project information database contains all costs, revenues and payment data summarized by value category (groupings of cost elements and commitment items). Various standard hierarchy reports have been predefined, but using this transaction you can define your own. Input the report type (i.e., a report from RPSCO or a summarized report from RPSCO) and the report ID . When defining a report you choose the drill-down order for the detail listing and attributes of the report, such as format. In addition, you create a report form in which you select the contents and structure of the report and the report value types, for example, plan, actual, budget values, etc. Click the CREATE icon to make your selections and save the report.

CJE2	Change Hierarchy Report

Use this transaction to change a hierarchy report previously created via transaction CJE1.

CJE3	Display Hierarchy Report

Use this transaction to display a hierarchy report previously created via transaction CJE1.

CJEA	Selection: Plan/Actual/ Commitment/Rem. Plan/Assigned

This transaction is used to report on project financials, but the selection is dependent on your database profile. The database profile will determine the objects that are selected; for example, you can exclude components/ materials in networks. The database profile will also determine the view in which the data is displayed (PROJECT STRUCTURE view, PROFIT CENTER STRUCTURE view, etc.) and the fields in the OVERVIEW screen. On the initial screen, select your range of objects (projects, WBS elements, etc.) and the plan/actual version and click EXECUTE. The report output has drill-down capability to line item reports and you can create and save your layouts.

CJF1	Create Transfer Price Agreement

This transaction is used where one business unit/profit center is providing a service for another business unit/profit center. In project systems, this scenario would be a WBS element structured directly beneath another WBS element. The service provided by the subordinate WBS element would be valued with a special profit center transfer price. Input the WBS element, click LIST OVERVIEW, and the system displays a list of document items for the transfer price agreement. The system determines the transfer price agreement receiver in line with the project hierarchy and displays it in the document header. Enter items for the transfer price agreement and the necessary data and save the agreement.

CJF2	Change Transfer Price Agreement

Use this transaction to change a transfer price agreement, which may be required if additional services are required or if the project schedule changes. Input the document number created via transaction CJF1, make the changes and save.

CJF3	Display Transfer Price Agreement

Use this transaction to display a transfer price agreement previously created via transaction CJF3.

CJI3	Display Project Actual Cost Line Items

Use this transaction to display detailed line items for project systems actual posting documents. Actual line items are created with every posting of actual costs. They contain information about the posted amount, the posting date, and the user who posted the line item. When you start an actual line item report, you need to limit the line items to be read by entering a project/range, sales document/range, WBS element/range, network/ order/range, activity/range, material number/range, a cost element (or cost element group) and a posting period. Additionally, you can configure different layouts to control the appearance of the report.

| CJI4 | Display Project Planned Cost Line Items |

Use this transaction to display detailed line items for project systems plan posting documents. Plan line items are created with every posting of plan costs. They contain information about the posted amount, the posting date, and the user who posted the line item. When you start a plan line item report, you need to limit the line items to be read by entering a project/range, sales document/range, WBS element/range, network/order/range, activity/range, material number/range, a cost element (or cost element group) and a posting period. Additionally, you can configure different layouts to control the appearance of the report.

| CJI5 | Display Project Commitment Line Items |

Use this transaction to display the details for commitment line items that are created as a commitment in the set-up, for example, for a purchase order. The line item contains information about the posted amount, the posting date, and the user who posted the line item. When you start a commitment line item report, you need to limit the line items to be read by entering a project/range, sales document/range, WBS element/range, network/order/range, activity/range, material number/range, a cost element (or cost element group) and a posting period. Additionally, you can configure different layouts to control the appearance of the report.

| CJI8 | Display Project Budget Line Items |

This transaction is used to display budgeting documents in ascending order for projects. This way, you can see how a particular budget came about. This report is therefore particularly suitable for monitoring the budgeting process. However, it cannot be used to display how much budget a particular funds management account assignment actually has.

| CJI9 | Display Project Hierarchy Cost Planning Line Items |

Use this transaction to display detailed line items for project systems plan posting documents in a hierarchical view format. Plan line items are created with every posting of plan costs. They contain information about the posted amount, the posting date, and the user who posted the line item. When you start the planning line item report, you need to limit the line items to be read by entering a project/range, sales document/range, WBS element/range, network/order/range, activity/range, material number/range, plan version and posting period. Additionally, you can configure different layouts to control the appearance of the report.

| CJIA | Display Project Actual Payment Line Items |

Use this transaction to display detailed line items for project systems actual payment posting documents. Line items are created with every posting of actual payment costs. They contain information about the posted amount, the posting date and the user who posted the line item. When you start the report, you need to limit the line items to be read by entering a project/range, sales document/range, WBS element/range, network/order/range, activity/range, material number/range and payment date range. Additionally, you can configure different layouts to control the appearance of the report.

| CJIB | Display Project Planned Payment Line Items |

Use this transaction to display detailed line items for project systems plan payment posting documents. Plan line items are created with every posting of plan costs. They may be created manually via transaction CJ48 or via integrated components, such as payment data from commitment values from materials management. They contain information about the posted amount, the posting date, and the user who posted the line item. When you start the report, you need to limit the line items to be read by entering a project/range, sales document/range, WBS element/range, network/order/range, activity/range, material number/range and expected payment date range. Additionally, you can configure different layouts to control the appearance of the report.

CJID	Display Project Settlement Line Items

Use this transaction to display detailed line items for project systems settlements documents. Settlement is posted via transaction CJ88 and this report contains information about the posted amount, the posting date, the user ID of the individual who posted the line item and makes the distinction between primary (external to the organization) and secondary (within the organization) cost element postings. When you start an actual line item report, you need to limit the line items to be read by entering a WBS element/range, activity/range, material number/range and depreciation area. Additionally, you can configure different layouts to control the appearance of the report.

CJK2	Change Statistical Key Figure Planning

This transaction is used to plan for statistical key figures for a WBS element. For example, with a statistical key figure, you can plan costs per the number of employees assigned to a WBS element using this transaction. Furthermore, you can use the number of employees as an allocation base, i.e., allocating the cost of recruiting fees among the WBS elements

based on number of employees in the WBS element.

CJK3	Display Statistical Key Figure Planning

Use this transaction to display the plan statistical key figure for a WBS element entered using transaction CJK2.

CJR2	Change Cost and Activity Inputs

Use this transaction for primary cost planning on WBS elements, i.e., costs due to external procurement or material withdrawals. Activity-independent (only to a WBS) and activity-specific (to a WBS element/activity type) primary costs can be planned. Input the plan version, period from/to, fiscal year, WBS element/range, cost element/range and click ENTER. On the next screen, enter the sender cost center, sender activity type and total planned consumption and save. The system uses the planned prices of the activity types to calculate costs.

CJR3	Display Cost and Activity Inputs

Use this transaction to display the plan cost and activity inputs previously created via transaction CJR2.

CJS2	Change Planning Statistical Key Figures

This transaction is used to plan for statistical key figures for a network. For example, as a key figure, you can plan costs per the number of employees assigned to a WBS element. Furthermore, you can use the number of employees as an allocation base, i.e., allocating the cost of recruiting fees among the network activities based on number of employees in the network activity.

CJS3	Display Planning Statistical Key Figures

Use this transaction to display the plan statistical key figure for a network activity.

CJV1	Project Planning Board: Create Simulation

This transaction is used to simulate a version of your project based on changes in factors such as schedule and cost. Actual values from an operative project can be copied into a simulated version. Input the version key, project definition key, project profile and click CONTINUE. The project planning board appears enabling you to change dates, create activities, etc. Then you can save the simulated version.

CJV2	Project Planning Board: Change Simulation

Use this transaction to change a simulated project version previously created via transaction CJV1, which may be required if you need to make some further changes to the schedule, activities, etc.

CJV3	Project Planning Board: Display Simulation

Use this transaction to display a simulated project version previously created using CJV1.

CJV4	Transfer Project

This transaction is used to transfer actual values from an operative or simulated project version to another simulated project version. In the standard system, project elements, material components, invoicing, billing plans, costs, revenues and payments can be transferred. Input the project definition for the operative project or the simulation version, select the transfer option and click TRANSFER.

CJV5	Delete Simulation Version

Use this transaction to delete a simulated version. Input the version key, project definition and click DELETE.

CM53	Evaluating Capacity Load Project

This transaction is used to evaluate the capacity load for all the work centers for network activities assigned to the selected WBS elements. Input the WBS elements, click FIND, enter simulation key, and click EXECUTE.

CM54	Evaluating Capacity Load Simulation

This transaction is used to evaluate the capacity load for all the work centers assigned to the selected simulation versions/keys. Click FIND, enter simulation key, and click EXECUTE.

CM55	Evaluating Capacity Load Work Center

This transaction used to evaluate the capacity load for all work centers for criteria selected. Input the work center, plant, capacity category, capacity planner group, click FIND, enter simulation key, and click EXECUTE.

CN01	Standard Network Create

This transaction is used to create a standard network to be used as a template for creating operative networks. A standard network can be created for processes within a project that have similar activities. A standard network saves time and promotes consistency when setting up projects. Input the standard network number or leave blank and let the system generate the number, input the project profile and click ENTER. The standard network header, which contains data that is valid for the entire standard network, appears. Enter the detail data for the network and click SAVE. Note that when you use a standard network assigned to a standard WBS element and you create an operative network, an operative WBS element is also created. However, if you create an operative WBS from a standard WBS to which a standard network is assigned, an operative network is not created.

CN02	Standard Network Change

Use this transaction to change a standard network previously created via transaction CN01.

CN03	Standard Network Display

Use this transaction to display a standard network previously created via transaction CN01.

CN04	PS Text Catalog: Change

This transaction is used to maintain project systems texts. Input the language key, the text type (e.g., project team structure or project status report), text description and text format. Other text data selection options available include an option to find existing texts such as by user ID. Click the CREATE icon and if a text exists, you can change it or copy it and save it. Also, you have the ability to assign and delete assignment of texts to project system objects, such as WBS elements or an activity.

CN05	PS Text Catalog: Display

Use this transaction to display project system texts previously created via transaction CN04.

CN08	Allocate Material to Standard Network Change: Overview

This transaction is used to update network parameters for the sales order assembly process using project systems networks. Use this transaction to make the link between the standard network used for the assembly order and the material components used. If you do not make this link, then a dialog box appears when creating the sales document asking for the standard network. Input the material, order type, standard network and other relevant parameters such as MRP controller and save.

CN09	Allocate Material to Standard Network Display: Overview

Use this transaction to display a list of material allocated to standard network/order types previously created via transaction CN08. Click the CHANGE icon to maintain the parameters.

CN11	Create Standard Milestone

Use this transaction to create a standard milestone, which can be used as a template when copying standard milestones in WBS elements and networks. Input the name of the standard milestone and click ENTER (you can also create a standard milestone in reference to an existing standard milestone). Click FUNCTIONS (if used) and input a function from a predefined list (i.e., INCLUDES STANDARD NETWORKS, CREATE NETWORKS, INCLUDES SUB NETWORK or START WORKFLOW). Maintain user status if a status profile has been assigned and save.

CN12	Change Standard Milestone

Use this transaction to change a standard milestone previously created via transaction CN11.

CN13	Display Standard Milestone

Use this transaction to display a standard milestone previously created via transaction CN11.

CN21	Create: Network

Use this transaction to create a network, which represents the process structure of a project. The network can be used to plan the time required to complete tasks and scheduled dates, allocate resources to the individual operations and define the sequence of operations. Select a network profile (which will default values such as plant, control keys for activities and activities), network type, plant and MRP controller and click ENTER. You also have the option of creating with reference to an existing network. In the following screen, input the network description, start date, finish date, scheduling type and click CONTINUE. On the ASSIGNMENTS tab, enter the project definition of your project and save the network. Note that warnings may appear in the message area if any prices, activity types or plan versions are not maintained for the complete duration of the project, so click ENTER and ensure that the integrated data is maintained accordingly.

CN22	Change: Network

Use this transaction to change a network, which includes adding and changing activities on a network. To do this, input the network number and choose ACTIVITY OVERVIEW and then, on the BASIC DATA OVERVIEW screen, activities for the network can be created and assigned to a single WBS elements. Enter the activity data and save the network.

CN23	Display: Network

Use this transaction to display a network previously created via transaction CN21.

CN24N	Overall Network Scheduling

This transaction is used for scheduling multiple networks that have linked relationships. Network scheduling will determine the earliest and latest start and finish dates for completing activities and calculate the required capacity requirements as well as the slack/float time. Slack/float time is time that may be required to transfer from one activity to another. Input the network/range, select either basic or forecast dates and then enter the necessary start or finish dates and execute.

CN25	Enter Network Confirmation

This transaction is used to confirm activity and activity element completion on an individual network. Confirmations control business functions such as backflushing material components consumed for an assembly to order process, posting actual costs based on activities completed, and updating network data such as duration, date and status. Some important customizing settings for this process include decoupling the confirmation transaction from automating goods movements (if there is a negative impact on performance) and linking causes for variances with a user status. Also, in customizing there are settings for confirmation parameters, such as generating an error log for cost calculation errors and indicating dates of confirmations that may lie in the future. Input the network and click CONTINUE. If multiple network activities are listed, choose one to confirm and enter the actual date and then enter the activity data such as dates, duration, status, and goods movements, and save. This transaction can also be carried out in project builder transaction CJ20N.

CN27 Network Confirmation: Collective Confirmation

Use this transaction to confirm activity and activity element completion on multiple networks. Confirmations control business functions such as backflushing material components consumed for an assembly to order process, posting actual costs based on activities completed and update network data such as duration, date and status. Some important customizing settings for this process include decoupling the confirmation transaction from automating goods movements (if there is a negative impact on performance) and linking causes for variances with a user status. Also, in customizing there are settings for confirmation parameters, such as generating an error log for cost calculation errors and indicating dates of confirmations that may lie in the future. The input screens of transaction CN27 has two parts, an upper part and lower part. The upper part includes an input area for default values which can be copied into networks in the lower part of the table via the menu path EDIT • DEFAULT VALUES • SET ALL ENTRIES. You can enter activity/confirmation data into the lower part of the table such as dates, duration, status, and goods movements, and then you can save your confirmation entries. This transaction can also be carried out in project builder transaction CJ20N.

CN28 Display Network Confirmation

Use this transaction to display a network confirmation previously created via transaction CN25 or CN27. Input the network or confirmation number and click ENTER to display the confirmed data.

CN29 Cancel Network Confirmation

Use this transaction to cancel a confirmation. Input the confirmation number, click CONTINUE and save the cancellation. It is also possible to cancel all confirmations for a network by inputting the network number and clicking ENTER. On the next screen, you can choose which confirmations to cancel by selecting the line items and then select GO TO • ACTUAL DATA so that the CANCEL NETWORK CONFIRMATION: ACTUAL DATA screen appears. On this screen, check the data to be cancelled and save. Then enter text for your cancellation and save.

CN41 Structure Overview

Use this transaction to report on the structure of a project(s). After releasing a project, the structured overview of the project can be generated. This report covers most of the technical settings for project monitoring and control. Input the database overview profile, which is the key to identifying data from project information systems information structure, and click ENTER. On the next screen, selection options include all or specific objects in a project, such as WBS elements or components of the WBS elements, basic date information, project assignments, etc. and then execute the report. The output display shows the structure of a project with key fields at each level. At execution time, you can change the layout; for example, to change the fields selected, choose the FIELD icon and select/deselect key fields. However, for permanent report settings, you save the settings in a series of report profiles, such as the PS info profile (used to store the overall profile for working with project systems information data), the database profile (determines project system objects included in the report) and displayed fields profile (key figures/data displayed in the report). The report can also be used to call up further overviews, such as complete line item cost report.

CN41N   Overview: Project Structure

This transaction is used to report on the structure of a project(s) similar to transaction CN41. After releasing a project, the structured overview of the project can be generated. This report covers most of the technical settings for project monitoring and control. Input the database overview profile, which is the key to identifying data from project information systems information structures, and click ENTER. On the next screen, the selection options include all or specific objects in a project, such as WBS elements or components of the WBS elements, such as basic date information, project assignments, etc. Execute the report and the output display shows the structure of a project with key fields at each level. With this report you can create, change and manage the report layout by clicking the LAYOUT icon. Report layouts can also be saved as user specific and used as a default whenever the report is executed. This report can also call up individual project objects (such as WBS element, network, etc.) reports, which can also be accessed via transaction CN42N through CN55N.

CN60   Change Documents for Projects/Netw.

Use this transaction to report all changes to project objects. Selection criteria include a project number/range, WBS element/range, network/order/range or activity/range. You can also select the user ID of the individual making the change and the date from (i.e., ignore changes before this date). The report output will display the project data object ID, such as WBS element or network, field changed, old/new field value, date changed and user ID of the individual making the change.

CN61   Display Change Documents: Library Network

This transaction is used to display all changes on a standard network. Selection criteria include standard network, the user ID of the individual making the change and the date from (i.e., ignore changes before this date). The report output will display the standard network, field changed, old/new field value, date changed and user ID of the individual making the change.

CN65   Display Change Document: Network

This transaction is used to display all changes on an individual network. Selection criteria include network (required input), the user ID of the individual making the change and the date from (i.e., ignore changes before this date). The report output will display the network, field changed, old/new field value, date changed, user ID of the individual making the change and the transaction codes used to make the change.

CN71   Project Info System: Save Project Version Initial Screen

Use this transaction to save a project version, which involves deciding whether to save all the project data or a subset. Project versions are snapshots of a project at a certain point in time and are used for example to make comparisons to other projects at different time intervals or as part of a milestone trend analysis. Input the project data objects, such as sales document number/range, WBS element/range and network/range and click EXECUTE. Then click SAVE and select SAVE PROJECT VERSION.

CN72   Create Project Version

Use this transaction to save a project version, which involves deciding whether to save all the project data or a subset. Project versions are snapshots of a project at a certain point in time and are used for example to make comparisons to other projects or at different time intervals or as part of a milestone trend analysis. Input the project data objects, such as sales document/range, WBS element/range and network/range, version key (or click the icon FIND OPEN NUMBER for a system assigned number) and version group (facilitates combining multiple versions for reporting) and click ENTER to save the project version.

CN98	Delete Standard Networks Without Archiving

This transaction is used to delete a standard network, which may be required if the data will no longer be used for future network maintenance. Note that by deleting without archiving you, will lose data, so it is recommended to delete only those standard networks you created for testing purposes. Selection criteria include the last date the standard network was used, standard network number/range and a deletion flag indicator (all routings with a deletion flag are selected). Click the EXECUTE icon to delete.

CNB1	List Display of Purchase Requisitions for Project

Use this report to display a list of all projects that have generated and assigned purchase requisitions. Selection criteria include project number/range, WBS element/range, purchase requisition/range, material number/range, and plant/range. The list can be displayed by WBS element and the materials to be procured with assigned purchase requisition. From the list display, the purchase requisition can be processed and assigned a source of supply ready for conversion into a purchase order.

CNB2	Purchasing Documents per Project

Use this report to display a list of all projects that have assigned purchasing documents. Selection criteria include project number/range, WBS element/range, purchasing document/range, material number/range, and plant/range. The list displays a purchase order summary report with purchase order number/WBS element assignment and purchase order items still to be received and still to be invoiced in quantities and amounts.

CNC4	Master Data Reconciliation Report: Consistency Within Project Struct.

This transaction is used to carry out a consistency check within the project structure. The program can check the settlement rules depending on the settlement rule strategy (i.e., check whether the settlement receivers are at the same level as the WBS element level, at a higher level, or all WBS elements settling to the top level only) and checks any validations (set up in customizing). Selection options include the list of objects to be checked and whether consistency and existence are checked. Selection options also include fields for consistency. The program generates a log showing any errors and inconsistencies found where you can branch to the object concerned to check the error and correct as necessary.

CNC5	Master Reconciliation Report: Consistency Sales Order/Project

This transaction is used to carry out a consistency check between sales documents and projects. The program can check whether there is a one-to-one match only between a sales document line item and a WBS element. The program can check the settlement rule depending on the settlement rule strategy (i.e. only one settlement, settlement only to CO-Profitability Analysis (CO-PA) and characteristics in the settlement rule) and checks on any validations (set up in customizing). Selection options include the list of sales documents to be checked and whether consistency and existence are checked. Selection options also include fields for consistency. The program generates a log showing any errors and inconsistencies found where you can branch to the object concerned to check the error and correct as necessary.

CNE1	Project Progress (Individual Processing)

This transaction is used to transfer projects progress calculation to statistical key figures, for an individual project. Reporting on project progress can be accomplished via transaction CNE5. The project progress can be dependent on actual hours posted to the project as compared with the planned hours, or project progress can be estimated directly in the PROJECT/PROGRESS tab of the work breakdown structure (WBS). Select the project number, WBS element or network, progress version and to period/fiscal year and execute.

CNE2	Project Progress (Collective Processing)

This transaction is used to transfer a project progress calculation to statistical key figures, for multiple projects. Reporting on project progress can be accomplished via transaction CNE5. The project progress can be dependent on actual hours posted to the project as compared with the planned hours, or project progress can be estimated directly in the PROJECT/PROGRESS tab of the work breakdown structure (WBS). Create and select a selection variant, which will contain the project, WBS element or networks to be calculated, progress version and to period/fiscal year and execute.

CNE5	Project Info System: Progress Analysis Initial Screen

Use this transaction to report on the progress calculated using transaction CNE1 or CNE2. The report displays a structured overview of the percentage of completion (POC) and earned value figures. It shows values in total and by period, and you can call up a period breakdown directly from the graphical value display. Input the project objects, such as project number and WBS element, and execute.

CNL1	Create Delivery Info

This transaction is used to create an individual delivery in project systems to deliver material components that are allocated to a project. This may be required if you need to deliver material components allocated to different network activities at different dates. These requirement dates can be linked with a phase of the project, for instance in a pre-assembly and assembly process. Input the name of the delivery and click ENTER. Input the project number assigned to the delivery, delivery information such as delivery date and ship to address, assign the delivery to a WBS element or activity (via menu path GO TO • ASSIGNMENTS), and save the delivery. The delivery document can now be processed via follow-on processes in shipping.

CNL2	Change Delivery Info

Use this transaction to change delivery information previously created via transaction CNL1. This may be required if the planned goods issue date changes. Input delivery information and click ENTER to change relevant data and save.

CNL3   Display Delivery Info

Use this transaction to display delivery information previously created via transaction CNL1.

CNMASS   Mass Changes in the Project System

This transaction is used to mass change project object data. The process involves selecting the project objects that require a mass change, such as the project number/range and the WBS element/range and then click ENTER. Then select the tables and fields used in order to input the selection criteria to select the fields to change. After selection options have been input and the data to be changed is listed, then the mass changes can be executed and saved.

CNR1   Create Work Center

This transaction is used to create a work center, which is the physical unit within a company where an activity is performed. For example, a work center may be an individual, group of people, a work station or a production line. Data stored in the work center, together with activity types, is required for costing, scheduling and capacity planning. Input the plant, work center number and click ENTER. Input work center data, such as description, person responsible and usage code, which determines the task list. Also input costing data, such as a formula, activity

type and cost center assignment and capacity data.

CNR2   Change Work Center

Use this transaction to change a work center previously created via transaction CNR1. This could be required if additional tasks have to be added to the work center or activity types need to change. Input the plant, work center number, input changes and save the work center.

CNR3   Display Work Center

Use this transaction to display a work center previously created via transaction CNR1.

CNS0   Delivery from Project: Selection Initial Screen

This transaction is used to create multiple deliveries in project systems to deliver material components allocated to a project, which may be required if you need to deliver material components allocated to different network activities on different dates. These requirement dates can be linked with a phase of the project, for instance in a pre-assembly and assembly process. Input the project number/WBS element to deliver, delivery information, such as delivery date and ship to party, and click DELIVERY OVERVIEW to display the work list and process the delivery. The delivery document created can now be processed via follow-on processes in shipping.

11 Human Capital Management (HCM)

Since Human Capital Management is a module that consists of a multitude of specialized applications, this chapter is structured according to these sub-modules. If you are looking for a specific code or transaction title within HCM but are not sure to which sub-module it belongs, refer to the indices at the end of this book to find the exact page containing its explanation.

11.1 Organizational Management

DELETE_ OM_ SETTINGS	Delete Object Manager Settings

For the specified user, you can use this transaction to delete and reset the user settings in the Object Manager. In the initial screen, you can select which user settings you want to be deleted. Using this transaction, you can also reset the search variants, the size of the search area, or the selection area and Object Manager attributes.

PA15	Actions for Company

You can use this transaction to create and maintain the Company object. After you have created the Company object, you are required to maintain the company address and, where required, create the external training provider.

PO01	Maintain Work Center

You can use transaction PO01 to maintain a Work Center. In the PO01 screen, you can select the plan version, the Work Center that you wish to maintain, and create/maintain the different infotypes related to the Work Center.

PO01D	Display Work Center

You can use transaction PO01D to display a Work Center. The data in the PO01D screen are in display mode only. You can select a particular infotype and click the DISPLAY icon to display more details about the particular infotype. In the PO01D screen, you can click the EDIT icon to change to MAINTAIN mode. Similar to PO01D, you can use transaction POXXD to display the infotypes related to the particular object.

PO02	Maintain Training Program

You can use transaction PO02 to create and maintain the object Training Program. In the PO02 screen, you can select the plan version, the development plan that you wish to maintain, and create/maintain the different infotypes related to the development plan.

PO03	Maintain Job

You can use transaction PO03 to create and maintain the object Job. In the PO03 screen, you can select the plan version, the job that you wish to maintain, and create/maintain the different infotypes related to the Job object.

PO04 Maintain Business Event Type

You can use transaction PO04 to create and maintain the object Business Event Type. In the PO04 screen, you can select the plan version, the Business Event Type that you wish to maintain, and create/maintain the different infotypes related to the Business Event Type.

PO05 Maintain Business Events

You can use transaction PO05 to create and maintain the object Business Events. In the PO05 screen, you can select the plan version, the Business Event that you wish to maintain, and create/maintain the different infotypes related to the Business Event.

PO06 Maintain Location

You can use transaction PO06 to create and maintain the object Location. In the PO06 screen, you can select the plan version, the Location that you wish to maintain, and create/maintain the different infotypes related to the Location.

PO07 Maintain Resource

You can use transaction PO07 to create and maintain the object Resource. In the PO07 screen, you can select the plan version, the Resource that you wish to maintain, and create/maintain the different infotypes related to the Resource.

PO08 Maintain External Person

You can use transaction PO08 to create and maintain the object External Person. In the PO08 screen, you can select the plan version, the External Person that you wish to maintain, and create/maintain the different infotypes related to the External Person object.

PO09 Maintain Business Event Group

You can use transaction PO09 to create and maintain a Business Event Group. In the PO09 screen, you can select the plan version, the business event group that you wish to maintain, and create/maintain the different infotypes related to the Business Event Group object.

PO10 Maintain Organizational Unit

You can use transaction PO10 to create and maintain an Organizational Unit. In the PO10 screen, you can select the plan version, the Organizational Unit that you wish to maintain, and create/maintain the different infotypes related to the Organizational Unit object.

PO11 Maintain Qualifications

You can use transaction PO11 to create and maintain Qualifications in the system. In the PO11 screen, you can select the plan version, the Qualification object that you wish to maintain, and create/maintain the different infotypes related to the Qualification object. You use the qualification(s) created using transaction PO11 to build a qualifications catalog.

PO12 Maintain Organizational Resource Type

You can use transaction PO12 to create and maintain the object Organizational Resource Type: In the PO12 screen, you can select the plan version, the Resource Type object that you wish to maintain, and create/maintain the different infotypes related to the Resource Type object.

PO13 Maintain Position

You can use transaction PO13 to create and maintain the Position in the system. In the

PO13 screen, you can select the plan version, the position that you wish to maintain, and create/maintain the different infotypes related to the Position object. For example, if the position is vacant, you can use this transaction to update the IT VACANCY.

PO14	Maintain Task

You can use transaction PO14 to create a Task in the system. In the PO14 screen, you can select the plan version, the task that you wish to maintain, and create/maintain the different infotypes related to the Task object.

PO15	Maintain Company

You can use transaction PO15 to create the Company object in the system. In the PO15 screen, you can select the plan version, the company that you wish to maintain, and create/maintain the different infotypes related to the Company object.

PO16	Maintain Services

You can use transaction PO16 to create a Service object in the system. In the PO16 screen, you can select the plan version, the Service object that you wish to maintain, and create/maintain the different infotypes related to the Service object.

PO17	Maintain Requirements Profile

You can use transaction PO17 to create Requirements Profile in the system. In the PO17 screen, you can select the plan version, the Requirements Profile object, that you wish to maintain, and create/maintain the different infotypes related to the Requirements Profile object.

PO18	Maintain Resource Room

You can use transaction PO18 to create a Resource Room object in the system In the

PO18 screen, you can select the plan version, the Resource Room object that you wish to maintain, and create/maintain the different infotypes related to the Resource Room object. For example, you can create the A003 relationship to the Location object and the A021 relationship to the Resource Type object.

PO19	Maintain External Instructor

You can use transaction PO19 to maintain External Instructor(s) in the system. In the PO19 screen, you can select the plan version, the External Instructor object that you wish to maintain, and create/maintain the different infotypes related to the External Instructor object. For the relationship infotype, you can create the A832 relationship to the User object.

PP01	Maintain Plan Data (Menu Guided)

You can use this transaction to create, edit, or delete OM-related objects. In the MAINTAIN OBJECT initial screen, enter the plan version and the object type that you wish to create or maintain. Transactions such as PO01 (Maintain Work Center) or POxx are object-specific, where you can create or maintain only the specific objects. Using transaction PP01, you will be able to create or maintain any object. The disadvantage of transaction PP01 is that you will not be able to delimit any objects.

PP03	Maintain Plan Data (Event Guided)

You can use this transaction to execute actions that are related to creating and maintaining plan data. For example, to create a new position in the SAP system, you have to populate data for the following tables: HRP1000 – Object, HRP1001 – Relationships, HRP1008 – Account Assignment, HRP1032

– Employee group/sub-groups, and HRP1028 – Address. By executing an action, the system will display the required screens one after another, which will enable you to populate the required tables and create a new position in the organizational unit.

PP05	Number Ranges for Personnel Planning

You can use this transaction to maintain number ranges for Personnel Planning. You can click the OVERVIEW button or use menu path NUMBER RANGE OBJECT • OVERVIEW to get a listing of the sub-objects the number ranges (external or internal number range) they are assigned to, the intervals, as well the last assigned number. You can click the INTERVALS button to display the number range being used and the current number available for usage.

PP70	Area Menu for Organizational Management

You can use this transaction to display the area menu for Organizational Management. The SAP Menu tree structure displays the transactions that are related to OM, such as creating a new Organizational Unit by expert mode (transaction PO10).

PP90	Set Up Org. Unit

This transaction displays an initial screen, from which you can navigate to the different screens to create/maintain objects. For example, if you follow the menu path ORG. PLANNING • ORGANIZATIONAL UNIT • CREATE, the system will navigate to ACTIONS FOR ORGANIZATIONAL UNIT. While creating the relationships for the different objects, you can click the ALLOWED RELATIONSHIPS button, displayed on the RELATIONSHIP screen, to view a list of allowed relationships for that particular object.

PPCI	Copy Infotype

This transaction is primarily used by ABAP technical developers. They use this transaction to create a new custom infotype and transparent tables by copying an existing custom infotype.

PPCO	Organizational Management: Maintain Organizational Plan

The organizational structure that you specified in the selection screen is displayed in graphical mode when you click the DISPLAY or CHANGE buttons. You can maintain the organizational structure (for example, delimiting an organizational unit) by clicking the CHANGE button.

PPME	Change Matrix Organization

You can use this transaction to access a matrix organization and edit/make changes to it. In the initial screen, you can enter the plan version of the matrix setup, the validity period, as well as how you want the setup to be displayed.

PPMM	Personnel Planning

You can use this transaction to display the Personnel Planning menu. The SAP Easy Access menu tree structure displays the transactions that are related to Personnel Planning. The tree structure still displays transactions that are obsolete and no longer available.

PPO1	Change Cost Center Assignment

You can use this transaction to maintain a Cost Center (object type: K) assignment to an organizational unit. In the selection screen, enter the organizational unit for which you would like to maintain the Cost Center. When the report is rendered, select the organizational unit and click the MASTER

COST CENTER button to assign and maintain the Cost Center.

PPO2	Display Cost Center Assignment

You can use this transaction to display the Cost Center assignment to an Organizational Unit.

PPO3	Change Reporting Structure

You can use transaction PPO3 to create and maintain the reporting structure in an organizational unit. In the displayed report, you can create a new chief, delete a chief, maintain relationships, etc.

PPO4	Display Reporting Structure

You can use this transaction to display the reporting structure (including the chief) of an organizational unit for the specific reporting period.

PPO5	Attributes of Organizational Units and Positions/Change

You can use this transaction to create and maintain attributes of an organizational unit. For example, for an organizational unit, you can plan the number of required positions for the specified reporting period.

PPO6	Attributes of Organizational Units and Positions/Display

You can use this transaction to display the attributes of an organizational unit.

PPOC	Create Organizational Plan

You can use this transaction to create a root (or superior) organizational unit. When you execute this transaction, you will see a dialog box where you can maintain the validity period of the organizational unit. You will

then be navigated to the ORGANIZATION AND STAFFING (WORKFLOW) CREATE screen, where you can fill in the basic data, account assignment and tasks for the organizational unit.

PPOCA	Create Attributes

You can use this transaction to create a new organizational unit and its related attributes, including time management, positions, and job levels. In the initial screen, you will be required to enter the time period for which the new organizational unit is valid.

PPOCE	Create Organization and Staffing

You can use this transaction to create a new organizational structure and assign staff to the organizational units. When you execute the transaction, you will see a dialog box where you can maintain the validity of the organizational object. Using this transaction, you will also be able to fill in details such as the person responsible for financing (where required), address of the organizational unit, cost distribution, work schedule, etc. In the PPOCE screen, you can click the DETAILS buttons to display details about the specific object that you have selected.

While accessing this transaction, if you get a system dump, review SAP Note 1114954—HRPBCM: Dump when Displaying Unassigned Full-Time Equivalents and see whether it will resolve the issue.

PPOCW	Create Org. and Staffing (WF)

Refer to transaction PPOC (Create Organizational Plan) for details.

PPOM	Maintain Org. Plan

This is the initial screen for maintaining an enterprise organizational plan. You can use this transaction to create an organizational structure and make staff assignments to the individual organizational units. To create a new organizational structure, begin by creating a root organizational unit, then create the organizational structure and staff assignments.

PPOM_ DEL	Delete User Settings for Organizational Management

This transaction executes the report RH_DELETE_USER_SETTINGS. You can use this transaction to delete the user settings of a specified user. If you have slow system performance for a particular user (compared to other users who perform the same processes), one of the steps for troubleshooting the issue is to delete the user settings.

Refer to the following SAP Notes if you have data inconsistencies or performance issues: 363721—Long Runtimes When Calling Transaction PA20/PA30; 403526—Object Manager: Last Search Should Not Be Restored; 496718—Object Manager: Deactivation via User Parameter.

PPOM_ MODE	Org. Management Interface Maintenance

You can use this transaction to set the maintenance interface for organizational management. In the dialog box you can select one of two options: ORGANIZATION AND STAFFING or SIMPLE MAINTENANCE.

PPOMA	Attributes in Organizational Management Change

You can use this transaction to change and maintain attributes for the objects in the organizational structure.

PPOME	Change Organization and Staffing

You can use this transaction to maintain the organizational structure and assign employees to the organizational units. A root organizational structure needs to exist (see transaction PPOCE for more details) before you are able to maintain the organizational structure. In the PPOME screen, you can click the DETAILS button to display details about the specific object that you have selected.

PPOMW	Organization and Staffing (Workflow) Change

You can use this transaction to edit and maintain the organizational structure. You should create a superior organizational unit as a basis for building the organizational structure. You can create jobs, positions, and assign persons to the positions (where required) by highlighting the desired organizational unit (or object) and selecting the CREATE icon.

PPOS	Display Organizational Plan

You can use this transaction to display the organizational plan.

PPOSA	Attributes in Organizational Management Display

You can use this transaction to view and display the attributes of the objects in the organizational structure.

PPOSE	Display Organization and Staffing

Use this transaction to display the organizational structure and staffing. In the PPOSE screen, you can click the DETAILS buttons to display details about the specific object that you have selected.

PPSC   Create Structure

You can use this transaction to create a structure for an object. While creating, you can specify the object type, (object ID and name), the validity period, and the evaluation path.

PPSM   Change Structure

You can use this transaction to maintain objects and structures.

PPSS   Display Structure

You can use this transaction to display objects and structures.

PPST   Structure Display/Maintenance

This transaction executes the report RHSTRU00. The report considers the object specified in the selection screen as the root, accesses the structure, and displays all the related objects that are in the evaluation path. It is a prerequisite that the evaluation must exist in table T778A.

PPUP   Settings for Personnel Development

You can use this transaction to make user settings for Personnel Development. In the selection screen, you can specify the plan version as well the reporting period. For transactions PO01 through PO19, if you wish to create a new object, in the POxx screen, click the Object infotype, select the Create icon, and fill in the required details. You can also maintain the different statuses of the object, such as "Planned," "Submitted," "Approved," and "Rejected."

PQ01   Actions for Work Center

You can use this transaction to create a Work Center and execute all actions that are required

in the Work Center setup and maintenance. In the Actions for Work Center screen, you enter the plan version for which you are creating the Work Center and enter the selection criteria details. Click the Execute button. In the Create Object screen, enter the details of the Work Center object.

After you have created the object, the system will take you to additional screens such as Create Planned Compensation, Create Restrictions, Create Health Examinations, Create Authorities/Resources, and Create Relationships (A003 – Belongs to/A083 – Is Key Position of). You can enter the relevant details in these screens and complete the actions required to create and set up a Work Center.

PQ02   Actions for Training Program

You can use this transaction to execute the actions required to create and set up a Training Program.

PQ03   Actions for Job

You can use this transaction to execute the actions required for Job setup. After you have created the Job object, the action takes you to the Create Relationship screen, where can you create the required relationships (for example relationship B007 – Is Described by). You can also use this action to create job evaluation results, create survey results, and update infotype 1610 – US Job Attributes.

PQ04   Actions for Business Event Type

You can use this transaction to execute the actions required for Business Event Type setup. In the initial screen, in the selection criteria, you can select what action you would like to execute; this will determine what Business Event Type object is created.

PQ06	Actions for Location

You can use this transaction to execute the actions required to create and set up the Locations object. During the actions execution, you will be required to fill in data for CREATE SITE-DEPENDENT INFO, CREATE ADDRESS, and CREATE WEB LINK for the address.

PQ07	Actions for Resource

You can use this transaction to create the Resource object. After you have created the Resource object, you need to create the required relationships for the Resource object. The related objects for which you will create the relationships are Resource type, Cost Center, and Location. During the actions, you will be prompted to CREATE CAPACITY and CREATE COSTS for the newly created Resource object.

PQ08	Actions for External Person

You can use this transaction to execute the actions required to create and maintain the External Person object. After you have created the External Person object, the system will require you to create the required relationships, create an address, create a name format for the External Person.

PQ09	Actions for Business Event Group

You can use this transaction to execute the actions to create and maintain the Business Event Group object. After you have created the Business Event object, the actions will take you to these screens: CREATE DESCRIPTION, CREATE RELATIONSHIPS (where you can create relationships to the following objects – Course Group, Course Type, Curriculum Type, and Course Program), CREATE COURSE GROUP INFO, and CREATE COLLABORATION ROOM.

PQ10	Actions for Organizational Unit

You can use this transaction to create and maintain the object Organizational Unit. After you have created the Organizational Unit object, the actions will require you to create the essential relationships, to maintain the description of the Organizational Unit, and to create the department and staff for the Organizational Unit.

PQ12	Actions for Resource Type

You can use this transaction to create the Resource Type object. After you have created the Resource Type object, you will be required to maintain the availability indicators and the required relationships.

PQ13	Actions for Position

You can use this transaction to create and maintain the Position object. After you have created the Position object, you will be required to maintain relationship A003 (Belongs to) with the organizational unit to which the Position object belongs, relationship A002 (Reports to) with the position to which it reports, maintain position description, create department/staff, create planned compensation for the newly created object, create authorities/resources, create relationship B007 (Is Described by) to the job family it belongs, create job evaluation results, create survey results, and, where required, create a vacancy for the Position.

PQ14	Actions for Task

You can use this transaction to create and maintain the Task object. The task actions will require you to create a character for the Task object and to create the required relationship (B007 – Is Described by).

PQ17	Action for Requirement Profiles

You can use this transaction to create and maintain the Requirement Profiles. After you have created the object, you will be required to maintain the description of the object and maintain the relationship (A031 – Requires) to the Qualification object.

PQ18	Actions for Resource Room

You can use this transaction to create and maintain the Resource Room object. You will be required to maintain these essential relationships: A003 (Belongs to) to the Location object, A020 (Is a Specialization of), A021 (Is Equipped with) to the Resource Type object, A011 (Cost Center Assignment) to the Cost Center object. You will also be prompted to create capacity, create costs, and create an address where the resource room is located.

PQ19	Actions for External Instructor

You can use this transaction to create and maintain the External Instructor object. During the actions execution, you are required to create the A003 (Belongs to) relationship to the Company object and the B026 (Is the Instructor for) relationship to the Course Type. You are also required to maintain the address where the external instructor can be reached, as well as an acceptable name format.

PQAH	Infoset Query

You can use this transaction to create and maintain ad hoc queries that are based on infosets. The query screen is menu based: you can select the required fields to be included in the selection and get a preview of the query output.

S_AHR_61016354	Telephone Directory

This report displays an employee's telephone numbers; this includes both the internal and external lists. It is a prerequisite that the following infotypes are created and maintained: 0006 (Address), 0032 (Internal Control), and 0105 (Communication).

S_AHR_61016356	Time Spent in Each Pay Scale Area/Types/Group/Level

This report displays an employee's pay scale classification and the length of assignment at a particular pay scale/level. It is a prerequisite the employee is assigned to a pay scale structure. Infotype 0008 (Basic Pay) should also be maintained for the employee.

S_AHR_61016357	Defaults for Pay Scale Reclassification

This report displays the next pay scale reclassification for an employee. The report helps you to determine which employee needs to be reclassified and when. It is a prerequisite that the employee is assigned to a pay scale structure. The pay scale grouping should be defined as being relevant for automatic reclassification. Infotype 0008 (Basic Pay) should be maintained for the employees

S_AHR_61016358	Reference Personnel Numbers

If an employee is in more than one work contract, the report displays the reference personnel number for each work contract. The reference personnel number should be maintained in infotype 0000 (Actions) and infotype 0031 (Reference Personnel Number).

S_AHR_61016360	HR Master Data Sheet

This report displays an employee's HR Master Data information. When you execute the report, if you see an error message similar to "<no entry in ...>", it means the data are incomplete or are not configured.

S_AHR_61016362	Flexible Employee Data

In this report, you can choose what employee data should be displayed, by selecting the required fields. The report is displayed in the ALV grid control format. The fields that you selected in the fields catalog are displayed in the chosen sequence.

S_AHR_61016369	Employee List

This report displays an employee's data, including personnel ID number (the SSN in the US), date of entry, and leaving date (where applicable).

S_PH0_48000450	Date Monitoring

Depending on the specified reporting period, the report displays the employees and the tasks assigned to them. It is a prerequisite that infotype 0019 (Monitoring of Tasks) is created and maintained for the employees.

S_PH9_46000216	Service Anniversaries

This report displays an employee's name, the date of entry into employment, and the length of employment period.

S_PH9_46000220	Vehicle Search List

The report displays an employee's details and the license plate number of the company issued car. If the employee does not have a company issued car, the license plate number of the employee's personal car can be stored.

S_PH9_46000221	Birthday List

The report displays the birthday list for employees, as specified in the selection criteria.

S_PH9_46000222	Family Members

The report displays an employee's name and family member details, including family relationships.

S_PH9_46000223	EEs Entered and Left

The report displays an employee's date of entry, leaving date, and the organizational unit the employee was working for.

S_PH9_46000224	Education and Training

This report provides an overview of the education and training data of employees in the specified organizational unit.

S_PH9_46000225	Powers of Attorney

The report displays an employee's name, the power of attorney, and the power of attorney type. The org. unit details are displayed as well.

11.2 Personnel Administration

PA00	Initial PA Master Data Menu

You can use this transaction to display the SAP HCM Personnel Administration (PA) application menu. The SAP Menu tree structure displays the transactions that are related to Personnel Administration.

PA03	Maintain Personnel Control Record

The Payroll Control Record contains details about the payroll area, payroll status, payroll period, earliest retroactive accounting period, and the last change made to the control record. The payroll control record locks the personnel numbers against master data changes during a payroll run. Prior to a payroll run, the control record of that particular payroll area should be released. You can use this transaction to view the payroll control record, to set the payroll period, and to set the statuses of the payroll run.

PA04	Maintain PA Number Ranges

You can use transaction PA04 to maintain Personnel Administration number ranges. In the PA04 screen, you can click the INTERVALS button to find what number is currently in use. During the hiring event, you input the PERNR, which is checked against the existing PERNRs; it should fall within the defined number range. The intervals you have configured in PA04 should match the default value of the NUMKR feature check.

PA10	Personnel File

You can use this transaction to display the personnel file of an employee. In the PA10 screen, you enter the personnel number of the employee for whom you would like to view the details. Click the ASSIGNMENT OVERVIEW icon to display the assignment overview. Click the ASSIGNMENT DETAILS icon to display details of the assignments.

PA20	Display Personnel Master Data

You can use this transaction to display HR Master Data for an employee. This is a commonly used transaction and can be used to display the values of the various infotypes. In the INFOTYPE field, you can enter the infotype and click the DISPLAY icon to display details about the infotype. Alternatively, you can double-click the infotype text to display the details.

PA30	Maintain Personnel Master Data

You can use this transaction to maintain HR Master Data for an employee. This is a commonly used transaction. Select the employee for whom you wish to maintain the master data. (Change an existing detail or create new infotypes.) In the INFOTYPE field, you can enter the infotype that you wish to maintain and click the CHANGE icon. If you have to create a new infotype, enter the infotype in the INFOTYPE field and click the CREATE icon.

PA40	Personnel Actions

You can use this transaction to execute personnel actions for an employee. Some of the actions that can be executed are creating a new employee in the organization, re-hiring an employee, retirement termination, etc. In the ACTION screen, you select ACTION TYPE from the table to execute the action.

PA41	Change Start Date

You can use this transaction to change entry/leaving date of an employee. Transaction PA41 can also be used to change the personnel area of a newly hired employee. In the PA41 screen, enter the personnel number of the employee for whom you wish to change the dated and click the EXECUTE button. You can enter the CHANGE ENTRY/LEAVING DATE screen from PA30 too. In the PA30 screen, click UTILITIES in the menu and select CHANGE ENTRY/LEAVING DATE.

PA42   Fast Entry for Actions

You can use this transaction as a fast entry screen for hiring event. In the FAST ENTRY screen, you can enter the data for the hiring event related infotypes, in one screen. If the data are incomplete or incorrect, the system will take you to the particular screen, where you can make corrections. When you execute the personnel action, if you encounter the error CALL_DIALOG_NOT_FOUND, refer to SAP Note 691631 – PA42/OG42: CALL_DIALOG_NOT_FOUND, PG301, DH801, and XI004 for more details and for corrective action.

PA48   Hiring from External System

Transaction PA48 is a PA action type that can be executed to transfer candidate data from SAP HCM E-Recruiting to an SAP HCM application. During the PA48 action, if you encounter any problems due to the RFC connection, review SAP Note 1490895 – PA48—Problem with RFC Connection with Logical EREC System.

PA51/   Display Time Data
PA53

You can use transaction PA51 or PA53 to display time data for an employee. In the PA51 screen, enter the personnel number of the employee; the infotypes related to time management are categorized and displayed in different tabs.

PA61   Maintain Time Data

You can use transaction PA61 or PA63 to maintain time data for an employee. In the PA61 screen, enter the personnel number of the employee for whom you wish to maintain time-related infotypes. The infotypes are categorized and displayed in different tabs such as WORKING TIMES, ADDITIONAL ACCOUNT ASSIGNMENTS, TIME QUOTAS, TIME MANAGEMENT DATA, and SPECIAL ABSENCES.

PA62   List Entry of Additional Data

PA62 is a maintenance transaction that is used to maintain time-related data for your employees. In the PA62 screen, you can maintain additional data for the following infotypes: 2002: Activity Allocation (Attendances), 2010: Cost Allocation (EE Rem. Info), 2002: Cost Assignment (Attendances), 2052: Weekly Entry w/Activity Allocation, 2052: Weekly Calendar w/Cost Assignment, 2052: List Entry for Attendance/Absences.

PA63   Maintain Time Data

See transaction PA61 for details.

PA70   Fast Data Entry

You can use this transaction for fast entry of the following infotypes: 0014: Recurring Payments/Deductions, 0015: Additional Payments, 0012: Fiscal Data D, 0232: Child Allowance D, and 0105: Communication. In the selection screen, there are multiple options by which you can select the employee personnel numbers. Choose the option that suits you best. In the FAST ENTRY screen, you can enter the data for multiple employees in the same screen at the same instance.

PA71   Fast Entry of Time Data

You can use this transaction for fast entry of the following time management related infotypes: 2001: Absences, 2002: Attendances, 2003: Substitutions, 2004: Availability, 2005: Overtime, 2006: Absence Quotas, 2007: Attendance Quotas, 2010: Employee Remuneration Info, 2012: Time Transfer Specifications. In the selection screen, there are multiple options by which you can select the employee personnel numbers. Choose the option that suits you best. In the FAST ENTRY screen, you can enter the data for multiple employees in the same screen at the same instance.

PAAH	Call Ad-Hoc Query

You can use this transaction to call the Ad-Hoc query. The default setting of the ad-hoc query will be the HR Personnel Administration infoset.

PRMM	Personnel Actions

You can use this transaction to maintain an employee mini-master for travel management. In the PRMM screen, enter the personnel number of the employee, select an action type, and click the EXECUTE button. In the DETAIL screen, click the EXECUTE INFO GROUP button to maintain the master data.

PRMS	Display HR Master Data

You can use this transaction to display HR Master Data of travel related infotypes for an employee.

PU00	Delete Personnel Data

You can use this transaction to delete personnel data for an employee. In the intial screen, enter the PERNR of the employee whose personnel data you wish to delete. You will be able to delete the personnel data only if no payroll results were created. Also, you require sufficient authorizations to be able to delete personnel data.

11.3 Benefits

HRBEN0000	Benefits Application Menu

You can use this transaction to display the SAP HCM Benefits application menu. The SAP Menu tree structure displays the transactions that are related to benefits.

HRBEN0001	Benefits Enrollment

You can use this transaction to enroll an employee into benefits. If an employee is unable to make changes or make benefits elections through ESS and submits a paper enrollment form, you can use this transaction to make benefits elections. An employee and his or her dependents should be eligible for the benefits they elect to enroll. It is recommended that you do not use transaction PA30 for benefits enrollment. You can refer to SAP Note 124934—Q&A: Benefits InfoTypes Do Not Process Eligibility Rules for further details.

HRBEN0003	Benefits Participation Monitor

You can use this transaction to verify the eligibility of an employee and his or her dependents for various benefits for which they are currently enrolled. The benefits administrator will execute this transaction regularly to check eligibility or detect inconsistencies in the enrollments. It is a suggested best practice to execute HRBEN003 at least once every week. If you detect an inconsistency in an employee's election, the changes should be completed using adjustment reasons.

HRBEN0004	Benefits EOI Monitor

You can use this transaction to track the Evidence of Insurability for employees. You can use the EOI monitor to track employees who have outstanding EOI, to stop or suspend participation for employees who have not provided EOI within the time specified, or to approve coverage elections. It is a suggested best practice to execute HRBEN004 at least once every week. This will help detect employees who have outstanding EOI or stop participation for an employee if the plan administrator had denied insurability.

| HRBEN0005 | Print Enrollment Form |

You can use this transaction to print the benefits enrollment form for an employee(s). In the selection screen, enter the desired parameters—personnel number, benefits area, and adjustment reasons—and click the EXECUTE button. If you run into errors due to adjustment reasons, make sure that infotype 0378 is maintained for the employee.

| HRBEN0006 | General Overview of Benefit Plan Data |

You can use this transaction to display the benefits enrollments for an employee. Using this transaction, you can get an overview of the Plan Data (elected benefits options, dependents/beneficiaries, costs, employee/employer contributions), Employee Master Data, and Participation Overview. Benefits administrators can use transaction HRBEN0006 to get a general overview of an employee's benefits plan data when they receive enquiries from employees regarding their current enrollments.

| HRBEN0009 | Overview of Benefit Plans |

You can use this transaction to get an overview of benefits plans in your benefit area. In the selection screen, enter the plan area, plan category, plan type, plan status and selection period, and click the EXECUTE button. In the displayed results page, you can drill down for more details. This transaction is similar to the report RPUBEN09.

| HRBEN0012 | Automatic Plan Enrollment |

You can use this transaction for group processing of automatic plan enrollment. In automatic plan enrollment, an employee can be enrolled into a plan as long the employee is eligible for that plan. The employee is not required to submit enrollment forms, and the benefits administrator will be able to enroll the employee into the plan.

| HRBEN0013 | Default Plan Enrollment |

You can use this transaction for group processing of default plan enrollment. In default plan enrollment, an employee can be enrolled in a plan, unless the employee submits an enrollment for another plan in the same category. Using default plan enrollment, the benefits administrator can default employees into the basic or standard plan.

| HRBEN0014 | Termination of Participation |

You can use this transaction to manually terminate an employee's benefits participation. In the HRBEN0014 selection screen, the date entered should be same as the employees last day worked or the last day on the payroll. Do not use the SELECT ALL button unless termination dates are the same for all elected plans.

| HRBEN0015 | Print Confirmation Form |

You can use this transaction to print the confirmation statement and distribute it to the employees. This is a transaction that is frequently used by the benefits administrator when employees request benefits confirmation statements.

| HRBEN0042 | Benefits Configuration Consistency Check |

You can use this transaction to execute a benefits configuration check. In the HRBEN0042 selection screen, enter the benefits area (or a range of benefits areas) and click the EXECUTE button. In the next selection screen, select all configuration steps and click the PERFORM CHECKS button. The errors and warnings, if any, are displayed. This is a useful feature that helps determine whether there are any configuration mistakes.

HRBEN0043   Copy Benefit Area

You can use this transaction to copy a benefit area into another benefit area. In the HRBEN0043 screen, you can also create a name for the new target benefit area. If you are a large organization and have multiple benefits areas, this transaction provides useful functionality.

HRBEN0044   Delete Benefit Area

You can use this transaction to delete a benefit area.

HRBEN0045   Benefit Area Currency Conversion

You can use this transaction to convert a benefit area from one operating currency to another currency. You would have defined a currency for your benefit area as part of benefits customizing and setup. At a later date, if you have a business requirement to convert from one currency to another, you can execute this report. The report automatically converts all defined money and currency fields in customizing. After you have completed the currency conversion, it is a suggested best practice to manually check that all rounding rules (that you defined for your benefit plans) are valid in the new currency.

HRBEN0046   Plan Cost Summary

You can use this transaction to generate a report that will provide an overview of costs for benefit plans and setup of benefits in your organization. This report provides a detailed cost structure for health plans (BY PLAN AND PLAN option), insurance plans (BY PLAN AND COVERAGE), and miscellaneous plans (BY PLAN AND PLAN option).

HRBEN0047   Dynamic Eligibility Check

An employee's eligibility for certain benefits enrollment can be based either on actual hours worked or length of employment in the organization. You can use this transaction to perform this dynamic eligibility check. This report is executed in the background and it automatically updates the date types and the infotypes that monitor eligibility checks in benefits administration.

HRBEN0053   Copy Benefit Plan

You can use this transaction to copy a benefit plan existing in a benefit area into another benefit plan in the same benefit area. In the HRBEN0053 selection screen, you can also enter the name of the target benefit plan.

HRBEN0054   Delete Benefit Plan

You can use this transaction to delete a particular benefit plan from a benefit area.

HRBEN0056   Standard Plans Overview

For the specified benefit area and plan category, you can use this report to get an overview of the benefit plan, plan type, program grouping, enrollment type and the dependent coverage that is available.

HRBEN0071   Eligible Employees

You can use this transaction to display eligibility participation in specific benefit plans for one or more employees. In the HRBEN0071 selection screen, BENEFIT AREA is a key field that needs to be entered. The results will display the benefit plan, the name of the employee, the employee entry date and the calculated eligibility date. The calculated eligibility date is the date on which the employee is eligible for the specific benefit plan.

HRBEN0072	Benefits Participation

You can use this transaction to display employees who are participating in a specific benefit plan on a given date or in a given time period. In the selection screen, BENEFIT AREA is a mandatory field that needs to be entered. The results page displays the benefit plan, the name of the employee, the hiring date, the employee's participation date, and the plan begin date/end date.

HRBEN0073	Health Plan Costs

You can use this transaction to generate a report that shows the dependent coverage text and employee/employer cost for each health plan on a given date. For each payment period, the report also displays total cost for each plan and the grand total. This is a useful report for budgeting purposes, since it shows the total cost of each plan for the organization. In the selection screen, BENEFIT AREA is a mandatory field that needs to be entered prior to executing the report.

HRBEN0074	Insurance Plan Costs

You can use transaction HRBEN0074 to generate a report that shows the employee/employer cost for each insurance plan on a given date.

HRBEN0075	Savings Plan Contributions

You can use transaction HRBEN0075 to generate a report that shows the employee (pre-tax/post-tax) and employer total contributions to the saving plans on a given date.

HRBEN0076	Vesting Percentage

You can use transaction HRBEN0076 to generate a report that shows the employee, the hiring date (displayed as entry date in the report), the participation date in the specified savings plan and the percentage vested in the benefits plan.

HRBEN0077	Changes in Benefits Elections

You can use this transaction to generate a report that shows the changes in benefit plan elections on a given date or in a given time period. The changes in benefits elections can be new enrollments or a re-enrollment, inclusion of new beneficiary, employment terminations, or an employee changes in benefit elections.

HRBEN0078	FSA Contributions

If your organization offers Flexible Spending Account (FSA), you can use transaction HRBEN0078 – FSA Contributions to generate a report that shows the FSA plan text and the employee/employer contributions for each FSA plan on a given date.

HRBEN0079	Change of Eligibility Status

You can use this transaction to generate a report that shows employees who are not eligible for a specific benefit plan and the date (or the time period) on which they became ineligible. The reason text for the ineligibility is also displayed in the report.

HRBEN0083	Changes in Default Values for General Benefits Information

You can use this transaction to generate a report that shows deviations from the system generated default values in infotype 0171 (General Benefits Information). In the selection screen you can select the reason for deviation from default values as either due to manual override or change in default values. The report can be executed for any time period. The reports displays the name of the employee, the first program grouping,, the second program grouping stored in infotype 0171, the first program grouping, the second program grouping as determined by the benefits feature, begin date and end date of infotype 0171.

HRBEN0085	Costs/Contributions for Miscellaneous Plans

If your organization offers Miscellaneous Plans, you can use transaction HRBEN0085 to generate a report that shows the miscellaneous plan text, the employee cost, and employer credit for each miscellaneous plan on a given date.

HRBEN0086	Stock Purchase Plan Contributions

If your organization has a Stock Purchase Plan as an employee benefit, you can use transaction HRBEN0086 to generate a report that shows the employee/employer contributions for the specified plan on a given date. *This report is valid for the private sector only*.

HRBEN00CEWB	Concurrent Employment Workbench

If Concurrent Employment (CE) for benefits is activated, you can use this transaction for benefits administration and to process benefits for employees with concurrent employment assignments. In the Concurrent Employment (CE) environment, employees have multiple personnel assignments.

HRBENUS02	Account Balance and Claims

You can use this transaction to enter an employee's FSA claim, set the status of the FSA claim, process pending FSA claims, and enter an employee's agreement to FSA claim rejection.

HRBENUSCOB01	Collection of Qualifying COBRA Events

If a qualifying event occurs for an employee, the system detects whether the employee is enrolled in any plan that is subject to COBRA. Only those employees and their dependents/beneficiaries who might lose health coverage due to a qualifying event are COBRA beneficiaries. You can use this transaction to collect qualifying COBRA events and employees who are qualified COBRA beneficiaries. The collection of qualifying COBRA events is the first step in COBRA administration. It is suggested that you execute this report on a regular basis for all employees in your organization.

HRBENUSCOB02	Processing of Qualifying COBRA Events and Letters

You can use this transaction to create COBRA letters for qualifying COBRA beneficiaries. The COBRA letter will contain notice of the right to continue the benefits coverage under COBRA administration, COBRA election forms and enrollment forms.

HRBENUSCOB03	COBRA Participation

You can use this transaction to process COBRA participation by employees and their beneficiaries. This transaction can also be used to terminate COBRA participation, display COBRA elections of an employee, and print enrollment/confirmation forms of COBRA participants.

HRBENUSCOB04	COBRA Payments

You can use this transaction to record COBRA payments as they are received, as well to identify pending COBRA payments. COBRA payments are not deductible at source, and this includes even employees who are currently on the payroll.

HRBENUSCOB05	COBRA Cost Overview

You can use this transaction to display an overview of costs for COBRA-elected health plans. In the report, you will see the employees or their dependents/beneficiaries who are enrolled in a COBRA health plan and the associated cost of the plan.

HRBENUSCOB06	COBRA Enrollment Form

You can use this transaction to print COBRA enrollments forms after they have been printed in the COBRA letter.

HRBENUSCOB07	COBRA Election Period

You can use this transaction to display qualified COBRA beneficiaries who did not elect COBRA coverage within the stipulated COBRA election period. In the report's output display screen, you can select the employees and click the REJECT button to confirm the forfeiture of COBRA benefits.

HRBENUSCOB08	COBRA Invoice

You can use this transaction to print COBRA invoices for employees and their beneficiaries who have elected COBRA coverage.

HRBENUSCOB09	COBRA Confirmation Form

You can use this transaction to print COBRA confirmation form, after an employee elects a COBRA plan or makes a change in COBRA election.

HRBENUSCOB10	IDoc Data Transfer to Provider

You can use this transaction to create an IDoc to communicate with external benefit providers. The IDoc will contain the employee's participation data as well as data required for benefits administration. While creating the IDoc you can choose to transfer all the data or only those data that were changed within the selected time period.

HRBENUSCOBOVERDUE	COBRA Overdue Payments Monitor

You can use this transaction to monitor COBRA-related payments that have not been made within the stipulated time period. In the results display screen, you can terminate COBRA participation for the delinquent employees and their beneficiaries by clicking the TERMINATION button.

HRBENUSCOBREGEND	End of Maximum Coverage Continuation Period for COBRA

You can use this transaction to notify COBRA beneficiaries in advance about the impending end of their COBRA benefits due to the end of the maximum coverage continuation period. In the selection screen, BENEFIT AREA is a mandatory field. In the NUMBER OF DAYS

BEFORE END selection field, you can enter the number days before the end of coverage within which the beneficiaries need to be notified.

HRBENUSFSACLM	FSA Claims Monitor

You can use this transaction to display all FSA claims and their statuses. In the FSA CLAIMS results display screen, you can select the claims and process them for approval. In the selection screen, you have the option to display FSA claims with the following status: "Not Yet Approved," "Approved," "Rejected," and "Agreement Given to Rejection." Flexible Spending Accounts (FSA) is a US-specific benefit plan. All FSA-related transaction codes can be used for US benefits only.

PTFMLA	FMLA Workbench

You can use the FMLA Workbench to manage all processes related to FMLA (Family Medical Leave). For example, while creating an FMLA request, the FMLA workbench will automatically check and validate the employee's eligibility for FMLA. After an employee has exhausted his or her FMLA leave entitlement, the FMLA workbench will manage the employee's eligibility for subsequent leave entitlements. An FMLA Event Maintainer can use this transaction to create an FMLA event. The FMLA Event Maintainer can also use this transaction to apply absences to an FMLA event

11.4 Time Management

BD82	Generate Partner Profile

You can use this transaction to generate profiles of the trading partners with whom you communicate using the IDoc interface. Refer to SAP Note 399271—CUA: Tips for

Optimizing Performance of ALE Distribution for more details about transaction BD82 and to generate a partner profile.

CAC1	Time Sheet: Maintain Profiles

You can use this transaction to set up data entry profiles for CATS for Service Providers. You are required to assign the right level of authorization to these profiles to prevent improper usage. SAP has provided a number of standard delivered profiles for common data entry scenarios.

CAC2	Time Sheet: Field Selection

You can use this transaction to customize the fields that should be maintained and displayed on a time sheet. You can also maintain the attributes of these fields. It is a suggested best practice to keep the number of fields on the time sheet to a minimum; hence, you should define only the required fields. This will reduce the scope of errors. It is a prerequisite that the customizing activity SET UP DATA ENTRY PROFILES is completed prior to this activity. As default, the indicator FIELD IS READY FOR INPUT is active for all fields.

CAC3	Time Sheet: Rejection Reasons

You can use this transaction to define reasons for rejecting a time record. During customizing, if you checkmark the field LT (Long Text) for a rejection reason, the user can enter a long text in the time sheet data detailing why the time record is being rejected. This long text is dynamic and is not stored anywhere else.

CAC4	CATS: Profile Authorization Groups

You can use this transaction to create profile authorization groups. Profile authorization groups are used to group data entry profiles with similar attributes. You can assign the profile authorization groups to the relevant data entry profiles through the customizing step MAINTAIN DATA ENTRY PROFILES.

CAC5   Define Customer Fields

You can use this transaction to create custom fields that are displayed in the time sheet. These custom fields are created to meet your business requirements. You can maintain/display these custom fields in the time sheet and the entered values can be validated by enhancements.

CADO   Display Time Sheet Data

You can use this transaction to display time data that were entered in the time sheet. The data can be displayed for an employee, for a group of employees, or for a particular work record. The selection screen is based on the Personnel Administration database. Transaction CADO is no longer listed in the SAP Easy Access menu but can be used.

CAOR   Display Time Sheet Data

This transaction is similar to transaction CADO. The selection screen is based on an organizational structure. Transaction CAOR is no longer listed in the SAP Easy Access menu but can be used.

CAPS   Time Sheet: Approve Times
(Selection by Master Data)

You can use this transaction to approve time sheets. The selection screen allows you to select the employee(s) based on the personnel number, organizational unit, payroll area, time recording administrator, etc. In the selection screen, you can also enter details on how to display the data and set tolerance for target hours.

CAT2   Time Sheet (Change)

You can use this transaction to call the time sheet and to maintain data. CAT2 is used to call the CATS initial screen and can be used to change the time data of the selected employee. In the selection screen, enter the data entry profile and the personnel number of the employee for whom you wish to maintain the CATS data. You can use the data entry profile selection to select the profiles that best suit your needs. The data entry profile is used to format the layout of the CATS time sheet.

CAT2_   CATS: Maintain Times
ISCR   (Init Screen)

This transaction is similar to CAT2. Hence, to maintain data for an employee, you can use either CAT2 or CAT2_ISCR.

CAT3   Time Sheet (Display)

You can use this transaction to call the time sheet and to display data. CAT3 is used to call the CATS initial screen to display the time data of the selected employee. In the selection screen, enter the data entry profile and the personnel number of the employee for whom you wish to display the CATS data.

CAT3_   CATS: Display Times
ISCR   (Init Screen)

This transaction is similar to CAT3. Hence, to display the CATS for an employee, you can use either CAT3 or CAT3_ISCR.

CAT4   Time Sheet: Approve Times
(Selection by Org. Assignment)

You can use this transaction to approve times. The selection screen allows you to select the employees whose time you want to approve, based on their organizational assignment.

In the selection screen, you can also enter details on how to display the data and set tolerance for target hours. This transaction is no longer listed in the SAP Easy Access menu but can be used

CAT5	Data Transfers CATS -> PS

You can use this transaction to transfer recorded times to the Project Systems. In the selection screen, enter the required parameters to initiate the transfer to Project Systems. The recorded times are confirmations for orders or networks.

CAT6	Transfer Time Data to HR Time Management

You can use this transaction to transfer recorded times to the HR system. In the selection screen, enter the required parameters to initiate the transfer to the HR system. The recorded times are the attendances, absences, substitutions, and the employee remuneration information.

CAT7	CATS: Transfer Data to Controlling (CO)

You can use this transaction to transfer recorded times to Controlling (CO). In the selection screen, enter the required parameters to initiate the transfer to CO system. The recorded times are the internal activity allocation and statistical key figures. Refer to SAP Note 369308 — CAT7: Problems w/Summarized Transfer and SAP Note 171762 — CATS CO Data Transfer: Do not Use Summarization! for details about CAT7 and data transfer from CATS to CO.

CAT8	Time Sheet: Document Display

You use this transaction to access information on a record saved in CATSDB. In the selection screen, enter the document number for which you wish to access information. You can also use transaction SA38 or SE38 and run the report RCATSBEL to access this selection screen.

CAT9	Data Transfer CATS -> PM/CS

You can use this transaction to transfer recorded times to the Project Maintenance (PM) or Customer Service (CS). In the selection screen, enter the required parameters to initiate the transfer to PM/CS systems. The recorded times are confirmations for orders or networks.

CATA	Time Sheet: Transfer to Target Components

You can use this transaction to transfer time sheet data records from the interface tables to the component systems like HR, CO, PS, and PM/CS. You can initiate the transfer of records to the different component systems in a single step. In the selection screen, enter the required parameters to select the time sheet data records. You can use transaction SE38 or SA38 and run the report RCATSTAL. In the selection screen (which is the same screen when you execute transaction CATA), you can select the time sheet data records based on the organizational assignment, for example.

CATC	Time Sheet: Time Leveling

You can use this transaction to find employees whose time entries are inconsistent. This is a leveling report RCATSCMP, which is used to find employees who have not reported any time and to find variance in time reporting trends. You can use transaction SE38 or SA38 and run the report RCATSCMP. The report can be run as a background job and emails can be sent automatically to employees whose time sheets are inconsistent.

CATI	SAP Easy Access: Time Recording

You can use this transaction to display the Time Recording menu. The SAP Easy Access menu tree structure displays the transactions that are related to CATS: Time Recording.

CATM	Selection From Time Recording

You can use this transaction to transfer data recorded in the time sheet to Materials Management (MM) system.

CATP	SAP Easy Access: Time Sheet

You can use this transaction to display the Time Sheet menu. The SAP Easy Access menu tree structure displays the transactions that are related to CATS.

CATR	Reorganize Time Sheet Interface Tables

This transaction executes the report RCATSRIF (Reorganize Time Sheet Interface Tables). The report deletes data records that have already been transferred to the target application from the respective time sheet interface tables. SAP recommends that you run this report periodically. Optimizing the interface tables greatly improves the performance of the transfer report.

CATS	SAP Easy Access Time Sheet

You can use this transaction to display the CATS menu. The SAP Easy Access menu tree structure displays the transactions that are related to CATS. The CATS menu tree displays more transactions than those displayed in the CATP menu tree.

CATS_APPR/ CATS_APPR_ LITE	Approve Working Times (Power User)

This transaction executes the report RCATS_APPROVE_ACTIVITIES (Approve Working Time). The report is used to approve and maintain statuses of time sheet data. For example, you can set the status of a data record as Rejected. While rejecting a data record, you can provide a rejection reason. (In customizing, you should have defined rejection reasons). You can change the status of the time sheet from "Rejected" to "Released for Approval."

In the selection screen of this transaction, the processing status is set to 20 ("Released for Approval"). Hence, the report will display data that need to be approved. However, you can change the status to display data with other statuses.

CATS_DA	Display Working Times

You can use this transaction to display working times. This report is primarily used by managers. In the report, the time data are displayed in the CATS Classic format.

CATSARCH	Archiving Time Sheet Data

This transaction executes the report RCATS_ARCH_ARCHIVING (Archiving Time Sheet Data). The reports read the data you want to archive from the CATSDB table (table for Time Sheets) and writes it into an archive file. In the selection screen, you can select the records you want to archive by entering the personnel numbers and the time period. Only records with the status "Approved" or "Canceled" are selected for archiving. To execute this transaction, it is a prerequisite that you maintain the required customizing settings in Archive Management.

CATSWF	Time Sheet: Approve Times

You can use this transaction to execute the report RCATSB01 (Time Sheet: Approve Times). The report displays the employee's name, date, and the number of hours recorded on that date. The status of the data record is "Released for Approval." The time administrator can select the employee he or she wants to approve and move the time sheet to status "Approved."

CATSXC	Customizing: CATS for Service Prov.

This transaction displays the customizing steps in the IMG for CATS for Service Providers.

CATSXC_ CHECK	Check Customizing

You can use this transaction to validate the customizing settings in CATS for Service Providers. In the CHECK CUSTOMIZING SETTINGS screen, you need to enter the data for CONTROLLING AREA and COUNTRY GROUPING prior to performing the validation.

CATSXT_DA	Display Work Time and Tasks

You can use this transaction to display working time data that were entered using CATSXT and CATSXT_ADMIN transactions. In the selection screen, you can enter the reporting period for which you wish to execute this report. The report will display data based on the entered search filter. For example, you can restrict data to a particular Cost Center or company code.

CATSXT_DTL	Work Times: Detail Display

You can use this transaction to display task components for working time data. You would have entered these data using CATSXT and CATSXT_ADMIN transactions. The different task components are normal working time, overtime, travel hours, etc.

OODY	Shift Planning: Time Types/Balances

See transaction S_AHR_61005002 for details.

OOT1	Shift Groups for Shift Planning

See transaction S_AHR_61004989 for details.

PE03	Maintain Features

You can use this transaction to display the FEATURES: INITIAL SCREEN. In the screen, you can maintain/display the features or create new custom features. New features can also be created using the copy function.

PE04	Create Functions and Operations

You can use this transaction to display the MAINTAIN FUNCTIONS AND OPERATIONS screen. In this screen, you can create new functions or operations for the object classes Payroll or Time Management. You can also display and maintain the object types Functions or Operations for the object classes.

PE50	Form Editor

You can use this transaction to create custom forms and to display and maintain the forms (delivered and custom) in the form editor. In the selection screen, enter the country grouping and the form name that you wish to create or maintain. If you are creating a new form, you are required to enter the form class too.

| PO10 | Maintain Shift Group Infotype for Organizational Unit |

See transaction S_AHR_61004980 for details.

| PP60 | Display Shift Plan |

You can use this transaction to display the personnel shift plans of an employee.

| PP61 | Change Shift Plan |

You can use this transaction to create and maintain a shift plan. As a prerequisite to starting shift planning, you must maintain the profile, shift groups, time intervals, and requirement types.

| PP62 | Display Requirements |

You can use this transaction to display a specific requirement record.

| PP63 | Change Requirements |

You can use this transaction to edit and maintain requirements. To change or edit a requirement, you overwrite the particular entry in that record.

| PP67 | Create Requirements |

You can use this transaction to create requirement records for selected requirement types. In the entry screen, enter the time period for which you are creating the requirement record. The current date is entered as the start date by default. It is a prerequisite that you have created and maintained the requirement types.

| PP6A | Display Personal Shift Plan |

You can use this transaction to display the personal shift plan of the selected employee. The displayed report provides details of day of the week, the date, the shift abbreviation, the shift name, and the shift time.

| PP6B | Display Attendance List |

You can use this transaction to display all employees assigned to shifts and requirements. The displayed report provides details of day of the week, the date, name of the employee, organizational unit, the shift abbreviation, and shift times.

| PP6C | Undo Completed Target Plan |

You can use this transaction to partially or completely delete a target plan for the specified time period. In the selection screen, you are required to enter the object type and object ID of the target plan.

| PP6I | Display Temporary Assignment List |

You can use this transaction to display a list of all employees in any organizational unit who are currently temporarily assigned. This transaction executes the temporary assignment report RHSP_TEMP_ASSIGNMENT. In the report, you can gather details such as the length of the temporary assignment and whether the temporary assignment is exclusive or the employee has shared responsibility (shared, for example, between the new organizational unit to which the employee is temporarily assigned and the parent organizational unit of the employee).

PT_ BAL00	Cumulated Time Evaluation Results: Time Balances/Wage Types

You can use this report to generate a listing of the day balances, period balances, and time wage types that were determined by time evaluation. You can also use this report to check the value limits for individual time types or wage types as configured during customizing. The report can also be used to get an overview of balances for each organizational unit.

PT_ BPC00	Generate Personal Calendar

This transaction executes the report RPTBPC00 (Generate Personal Calendar: International Version). The report generates a personal calendar. The generated calendar is stored in cluster PC on database PCL1.

PT_ CLSTB1	Temp. Time Eval. Results (Cluster B1)

You can use this transaction to display the current content of cluster B1 (time evaluation results) for an employee. In the selection screen, you have an option to select:

▶ LIST OF PERSONNEL NUMBERS: The initial screen will display a list of personnel numbers. Selecting a personnel number takes you to a screen that provides an overview of the tables in the cluster, including the number of entries created. Selecting a record that has an entry takes you to a screen that provides an overview of the entries in that table. You can select a record and get a detailed description of that entry or you can opt to see a detailed description of all entries by clicking the ALL TABLE ENTRIES button.

▶ DETAILED DESCRIPTION OF ALL TABLE ENTRIES: You can use this option to display the detailed description of entries of

the individual tables in the cluster for the selected personnel numbers.

PT_ CLSTB2	Display Time Evaluation Results (Cluster B2)

You can use this transaction to display the current content of cluster B2 for a selected employee.

PT_ CLSTG1	Display Group Incentive Wages (Cluster G1)

You can use transaction to display group incentive wages for individual groups.

PT_ CLSTPC	Display Personal Calendar (Cluster PC)

This transaction executes the report RPCL-STPC (Display Cluster PC: Personal Calendar and Cover Table). The report displays the personal calendar of an employee. In the selection screen, you can enter the personnel numbers for employees for whom you wish to generate a personal calendar. In SAP HCM Time Management, the personal calendar displays an employee's absence and attendance record.

PT_ CLSTL1	Display Individual Incentive Wages (Cluster L1)

This transaction executes the report RPCL-STL1 (Display Database PCL1, Cluster L1). The report displays incentive wages data for the selected personnel numbers. The data are stored in cluster L1 in the database PCL1. The list formatting selection is similar to that described for transaction PT_CLSTB1 – Temp. Time Eval. Results (Cluster B1).

PT_ DOW00	Time Accounts

You can use this report to generate a listing of current and selected time accounts for each employee. It is a prerequisite that time balances have been generated in time evaluation prior to executing this report. The time balances must also be available to be downloaded to the time recording systems.

PT_ DSH20	Daily Work Schedule

You can use this transaction to display the details of the daily working schedule of your organization. Using this transaction, you can get details of the working times, such as planned working time, normal working time, core time, tolerances, and compensation time.

PT_ EDT_TEDT	Time Statement

See transaction PT61 for details.

PT_ ERL00	Time Evaluation Messages

You can use this transaction to generate the Time Evaluation Messages report (RPT-ERL00). This report displays all the messages that were generated during time evaluation. You can use the selection criteria to restrict the messages to be displayed. As a prerequisite the time evaluation report should be executed for the specific day.

PT_ QTA10	Display Absence Quota Information

For the specified search filter, this report generates a listing of employee's absence quotas. The report displays the employee's personnel number, the employee's name, quota, unit (days or hours), total entitlement, used up to deduction key date, compensated up to deduction key date, and total reminder.

PT_ REOPC	Personal Calendar Reorganization (Cluster PC)

You can use this transaction to conduct logical checks for the personal calendar and, where required, set the deletion indicator in the database or delete the record(s) to be reorganized directly. This transaction executes the report RPUREOPC (Reorganization for Personal Calendar Cluster). It is a suggested best practice to execute this report periodically (every two years or so) to delete older database records related to employee work schedule in cluster PC.

PT_ UPD00	Revaluation of Attendance/ Absence Records

This transaction executes the report RPTUPD00 (Revaluation of Attendance/Absence Records using Batch Input). The report creates a batch input session for revaluating absence/attendance records. It is recommended that you execute the report RPTUPD00 periodically to revaluate your attendance/absence records. If your work schedule data change after the absences/attendances are inputted, then a revaluation is required. The attendances and absences should always be consistent with the entitlement quotas.

PT_ UWSH00	Revaluate Planned Working Time

This transaction executes the report RPU-WSH00 (Revaluation of the Planned Working Time Infotype 0007). The report determines which Planned Working Time records are inconsistent with the defined work schedule rule. You should execute this report whenever you make changes to the work schedule rule definition. The Planned Working Time and the Work Schedule definition should always be synched and consistent.

PT00	SAP Easy Access Time Management: Time Data Administration

You can use this transaction to display the area menu for Time Management. The SAP Easy Access menu tree structure displays the transactions that are related to Time Management/Time Data Administration. The nodes contain transactions to maintain time data, time evaluation, and work schedule, as well to generate reports and maintain the basic settings.

PT01	Create Work Schedule

You can use this transaction to create individual works schedules for the specified period. In the initial screen, you have the option of creating the work schedule by either of these options:

1. CREATE—if you wish to create the work schedule month by month in the specified time period.

2. CREATE ALL—if you wish to create the work schedule without calling up the individual months in the specified time period.

It is a prerequisite that you have completed customizing the work schedule rules before creating the individual work schedules.

PT02	Change Work Schedule

You can use this transaction to maintain or delete individual work schedules for the specified period.

PT03	Display Work Schedule

You can use this transaction to display work schedules for the specified period.

PT40	Time Management Pool

You can use this transaction to check, maintain and display time evaluated data for your employees. The time management pool provides a single interface that can be used by time administrators to process time evaluation messages.

PT50	Quota Overview

You can use this transaction to display an employee's attendance and absence quotas. It is a prerequisite that the employee's attendance and absence quotas are created and maintained in infotypes Attendance Quota (2007) and Absence Quota (2006).

PT60	HR Time: Time Evaluation

You can use this transaction to call the time evaluation report RPTIME00. The time evaluation driver RPTIME00 evaluates an employee's data. Time balances and wage types are formed while executing the time evaluation driver. In the PT60 screen, the evaluation schema's default setting is TM00. If you are using a custom evaluation schema, remember to replace it with the custom schema. This is a common cause of errors.

PT61	Time Statement

You can use this transaction to generate a Time Statement. A time statement can be used to validate time evaluation results and to provide time balances and time wage types results for each employee. Time statements can also be accessed from the ESS. The report RPTEDT00 displays the time statement.

PT62	Attendance Check

You can use this transaction to generate the Attendance Check report (RPTEAB00). The attendance check report lists employees who are at work, absent with reason, absent

357

without prior notification, and late beyond eligible time. This report is helpful in planning substitution for the absentees. Prior to running this report, the time events should be recorded and the Attendances (2002) and Absences (2001) infotypes should be maintained.

PT63	Personal Work Schedule

You can use this transaction to display detailed individual work schedules of an employee. The Personal Work Schedule displays the working times of the specific employee(s).

PT64	Attendance Data Overview

This report displays an employee's attendance and absences. In the selection screen you can make selections that determine the layout of the report. You can execute the report for a payroll period (instead of a specific time period)

PT65	Attendance Overview Graphic

The employee's recorded attendances and absences are displayed in a graphical interface. The attendances and absences are represented in color bars. You can use this report to plan leave scheduling.

PT80	Subsystem Connection

You can use this transaction to upload and download processes from external time recording applications. The communication logs provide an overview of all transactions conducted between the external systems and SAP HCM Time Management. The TIME EVENTS tab provides reports to download, upload, and post time events to SAP HCM Time Management. The EMPLOYEE EXPENDITURES tab provides reports to download, upload, and post employee expenditures to SAP HCM Time Management.

PT90/ PT90_ATT	Attendance/Absence Data: Calendar View

This report displays attendance and absence data for each employee in a calendar view. In the report, legend and statistics are also displayed for each employee; for example, public holidays are displayed in red.

PT91/ PT91_ATT	Attendance/Absence Data: Multiple Employee View

This report is similar to the RPTABS50 report, except that the report is displayed in multiple employee format. The attendances and absences are displayed in abbreviation. This report can also be accessed from within the RPTABS50 report.

PTMW	Time Manager's Workplace

In a decentralized environment, the Time Manager's Workplace (TMW) is used by time administrators to administer and manage time & labor and time evaluation messages for their employees. Prior to using the TMW you should have completed IMG configuration for the time manager's workplace, time recording and administration.

PU03	Change Payroll Status

You can use this transaction to manually edit an employee's payroll status. Normally, the Payroll Status infotype (0003) is updated by the system. This infotype contains data that control an employee's payroll runs and time evaluations. The infotype is updated during a payroll run and time evaluation. You need the required authorization to edit the HR Master Data.

PW01	Maintain Incentive Wages Data

Time tickets are used for incentive wages data. You use time tickets to record work performed and to be compensated. The time tickets can be automatically created or manually entered. In SAP, time tickets can be maintained in full-screen or list-screen mode and are used in individual or group incentive wages. You can use transaction PW01 to maintain incentive wages. In the MAINTAIN INCENTIVE WAGES screen, you can switch between full screen and list screen by clicking the FULL SCREEN OR LIST SCREEN icon.

PW02	Display Incentive Wages Data

You can use this transaction to display the incentive wage.

PW03	Record Incentive Wages Data

You can use this transaction to record time tickets for multiple users at the same time. Time tickets are recorded in full screen mode.

PW61	Time Leveling

The report generates a listing of employees to consider for time leveling. You can use this time leveling report to compare the actual working times with the time or incentive wage time data. Hence, where required, you can use the time leveling report to make corrections, so that time data correspond to the actual time worked (clocked).

PW62	Employment Percentage

You can use this transaction to generate a list of employees (these employees who are incentive or time wage earners), whose recorded time in incentive wages during the payroll period either falls short or exceeds certain percentage rates. In the selection screen, you can enter values for the field VALUE LIMITS FOR OUTPUT group. The displayed result will be restricted by this entered value. Incentive or time wage earners are identified by their employee sub-grouping and wage types.

PW63	Reassignment Proposals for Wage Groups

You can use this transaction to evaluate whether any of the employees working under incentive wage option should be assigned to a different master wage group for the next payroll period. In the selection screen, you can enter values for the ADDITIONAL DATA group. The report will evaluate only the time tickets meeting this selection criterion.

PW70	Recalculate Results and Cumulations for Individual Incentive Wages

If you make any changes to the customizing settings for premium formulas, you can use this transaction to recalculate the time ticket results, cumulations, and results in individual incentive wages. You need read authorization for infotypes Org. Assignment (0001) and Payroll Status (0003) for all personnel numbers in the group.

The output will display a value for each personnel number and period. In the Log group of the selection screen, you have different options: DISPLAY TIME TICKET RESULTS (the original and new time ticket results are displayed in the output), DISPLAY PERIOD RESULTS (the original and new cumulations and results are displayed in the output), and DISPLAY RESULT TYPES (the original and new result types and parameters are displayed in the output).

PW71	Recalculate Results and Cumulations for Group Incentive Wages

If you make any changes to the customizing settings for premium formulas, you can use this transaction to recalculate the cumulations, result types, and results in group incentive wages.

PW72	Withdrawal from Group

When an employee leaves the organization, you can use this transaction to update the group membership. Besides delimiting the group membership, you can use this transaction to delete all group time tickets in inactive times for this particular employee. The group time tickets are deleted from cluster L1.

S_AHR_61004980	Maintain Shift Group Infotype for Organizational Unit

You can use this transaction to create the Shift Group infotype (1039). You use this infotype to assign shift groups to an organizational unit. It is a prerequisite that the plan version, the org. unit, and the shift groups are created and maintained prior to maintaining infotype 1039. You can also access this transaction by the customizing activity in IMG • TIME MANAGEMENT • SHIFT PLANNING • MAINTAIN SHIFT GROUP INFOTYPE FOR ORGANIZATIONAL UNIT.

S_AHR_61004989	Specify Shift Groups

You can use this transaction to create shift groups. You create a shift groups to group together requirement types and shifts that are valid only for the shift group. The shift groups are then assigned to the entry object used in shift planning. You can also specify shift groups by the customizing activity in IMG • TIME MANAGEMENT • SHIFT PLANNING • SPECIFY SHIFT GROUPS.

S_AHR_61005002	Shift Planning: Time Types/Balances

If you use Excel to output the shift plan, use this transaction to specify the time type that you want to display in the first column of the shift plan. You can also define time types for connecting to MS Excel, by the customizing activity in IMG • TIME MANAGEMENT • SHIFT PLANNING • CONNECTING TO MICROSOFT EXCEL • DEFINE TIME TYPES FOR CONNECTING TO MICROSOFT EXCEL.

SCAL	Holiday Calendar

You can use this transaction to create a new public calendar. The public holiday calendar is used by the different components of SAP and is used in payroll and for work scheduling. In many organizations the holiday calendar is created and maintained by systems administrators.

11.5 Personnel Development

OOEC	Change Development Plan Catalog

You can use this transaction to create and maintain the Development Plan Catalog. Using this transaction, you can create both Development Plan Group (BL) and Development Plan (B) objects. While creating the development plan objects, you need to specify the validity period as well the qualifications and the proficiency required.

OOQA	Catalog: Change Qualification(s)

You can use this transaction to create and maintain Qualification Group (QK) and Qualification (Q). The qualification catalog (containing the Qualification Group and

Qualification objects) contains all the qualifications that are required for a company. A well defined qualifications catalog is essential to define the personnel development and talent management processes. The qualification object can be tied to a person (P) or to a position (S) object. If the qualification is tied to a position, it is called requirements. Requirements, qualifications, and competency all refer to the same objects Qualification Group (QK) and Qualification (Q).

The qualification catalog can be integrated into SAP HCM Performance Management, SAP HCM E-Recruiting, SAP HCM Enterprise Learning Environment, SAP HCM Organizational Management and SAP HCM Personnel Administration.

OOSB — Assign Authorization Profiles

You can use this transaction to assign users to the different authorization profiles. These assignments are time-dependent and you can specify the validity period during the assignment. If you check the EXCLUDE flag, you can exclude the sub-structures from the structural authorization check. (The exclusion of the small sub-structures can also potentially improve the performance of the structural authorizations.)

OOSP — Define Authorization Profiles

You can use this transaction to create and maintain authorization profiles required for authorizations related to Personnel Planning. You can create authorizations related to plan versions, object types and object IDs. During customization you are required to specify the validity period of the authorization profile.

PEPM — Profile Matchup

You can use this transaction to compare qualifications (or requirements) between two employees, two positions, or between an employee and a position. You can also have the system generate the qualifications deficits and training proposals. The profile matchup can be performed between two objects. In the DISPLAY PROFILE MATCHUP screen, you can click the dropdown list and see what different objects can be compared with each other.

PPCP — Career Planning

For the specified person (employee) and planning criteria, this report will generate a listing of positions that this person is qualified to occupy during the course of his or her career. This report can be used to determine the training requirements that need to be completed to occupy those positions.

PPCT — Task Catalog

You can use this transaction to create and maintain a task catalog. In the task catalog selection screen, enter the selection criteria and click the EXECUTE button. This will render the MAINTAIN TASKS screen. In the MAINTAIN TASKS screen, you can create new tasks or maintain/display existing tasks in the catalog.

PPDPCS — Display Development Plan Catalog

You can use this transaction to display the development catalog.

PPLB — Evaluate Careers

This report displays the careers available in your organization. Careers form the basis for succession planning.

PPPD — Display Profile

You can use this transaction to display the profile of the selected object.

PPPE	Area Menu: Personnel Development

You can use this transaction to display the SAP HCM Personnel Development (PD) application menu. The SAP Menu tree structure displays the transactions that are related to Personnel Development.

PPPM	Change Profile

You can use this transaction to create and maintain profiles for the different objects such as Person, Position, Job, Organizational Unit, etc. If you are maintaining the profile for an employee, you can include the qualifications the person currently possesses, the employee's potential, preferences, dislikes, individual development plan, and individual plan history. You can also view the appraisal documents of this employee.

PPQ1	Find Objects for Qualifications

For the selected qualifications, you can use this report to generate a listing of objects who have been assigned these qualifications. The basic data will display the name of the individual, the assigned qualification, and the proficiency level of the individual in that qualification. This report is particularly useful while maintaining the qualifications catalog. It helps to determine which qualifications can be retained and which are obsolete.

PPQD	Display Qualifications Catalog

You can use this transaction to display the qualifications catalog.

PPRP	Reporting – Personnel Development

When you execute this transaction, the system displays a dynamic menu with a listing of personnel development related reports that can be executed. The menu is categorized into ORGANIZATIONAL UNIT, PROFILE, and OTHERS.

The reports available under ORGANIZATIONAL UNIT are Profile Matchup: Positions/Holders, Profiles, Succession Overview, Expired Qualifications, and Qualifications Overview. The reports available under PROFILE are Objects Without Qualifications or Requirements and Objects with Non-Rated Qualifications or Requirements. The reports available under OTHERS are Listing of Vacant Positions, Prebookings per Attendee, and List of Alternate Qualifications.

PPUP	Settings for Personnel Development

You can use this transaction to make system settings specific to HCM Personnel Development application. In the settings dialog box, you can select the plan version and the time period for which these settings need to be applied.

S_AHR_61003929	Catalog: Change Qualification(s)

See transaction OOQA for details.

S_AHR_61003942	Assign Authorization Profiles

See transaction OOSB for details.

S_AHR_61007168	Change Development Plan Catalog

See transaction OOEC for details.

S_AHR_61007222	Define Authorization Profiles

See transaction OOSP for details.

S_AHR_ 61015532	Profile Matchup: Positions/Holders

You can use this report to compare the requirements of all the positions that exist in an organizational unit with the qualifications of the employees who are currently in that position.

S_AHR_ 61015533	Profiles

You can use this report to display the subprofiles of all the planning objects in an organizational unit. The report will also display the individual entries, the scales used, the proficiency and the validity period.

S_AHR_ 61015536	Expired Qualifications

You can use this report to display all planning objects in an organizational unit with qualifications that are going to expire in the specified reporting period.

S_PH9_ 46000016	Qualifications Overview

This report provides an overview of all the qualifications that the employees possess. The report also displays the qualifications group and the proficiency level of the qualifications. In the selection screen, you should specify the organizational unit(s) that you wish to report on.

S_PH9_ 46000018	Objects with Non-Rated Qualifications or Requirements

You can use this report to get a display of all objects of the specified object type whose qualifications (or requirements) status is "Unevaluated."

S_PH9_ 46000019	Objects Without Qualifications or Requirements

You can use this report to get a display of all objects of the specified object type that do not have any qualifications (or requirements) assigned to them.

S_PH9_ 46000022	List of Alternative Qualifications

This report provides a listing of all qualifications that has alternative qualifications assigned to them. The report also displays the validity of the alternative qualifications as well as the replacement percentage.

11.6 Enterprise Compensation Management (ECM)

HRCMP0000	SAP Easy Access – Compensation Management

You can use this transaction to display the SAP HCM Compensation Management application menu. The SAP Menu tree structure displays the transactions that are related to ECM.

HRCMP0001C	Change Compensation Adjustment

You can use this transaction to make compensation adjustments for an employee. After you have made the compensation adjustments for each adjustment type, the system creates Compensation Adjustment infotype (0380) record for the employee.

HRCMP0001D	Display a Compensation Adjustment

You can use this transaction to display details about the compensation adjustments made to an employee. In the selection screen, you can enter the employee for whom you wish to display the adjustment reason. In the menu, click SETTINGS • CHANGE PLANNING PERIOD and enter the time period for which you wish to display the adjustment reason. In the menu, click SETTINGS • CHANGE ADJUSTMENT REASON, and select an adjustment reason. You can click the INFORMATION button for compensation adjustment information.

HRCMP0011	Create Budget Structure: Initial Screen

You can use this transaction to create a budget structure. The basic data of the budget structure includes BUDGET TYPE, BUDGET ABBREVIATION AND NAME, and BUDGET PERIOD.

HRCMP0012	Display Budget Structure: Initial Screen

You can use this transaction to display the budget structure. In the selection screen, you can choose the display option to be BUDGET DISTRIBUTION (option displays the budget structures and the amounts) or FINANCING (displays the budget structures and the objects they finance).

HRCMP0013	Change Budget Structure: Initial Screen

You can use this transaction to make changes to a budget structure. Using this transaction you can also extend the validity period of the budget structure, thus enabling you to reuse a budget that has already been released. You can also copy a budget structure, edit budget values, or delete budget units and structures using this transaction. If the budget is consistent, then using transaction HRCMP0013 you can set the status of the budget structure as "Released." You cannot make changes to a budget structure if the budget has the status "Released."

PECM_ADJ_SAL_STRU	Update of Pay Grade Amounts from Market Data

You can use this transaction to execute a report (RHECM_ADJ_SALARY_STRUC) that will update the salary structure data in the customizing table T710 (Pay Grade Levels). The report will use the data proposed by the compensation analyst in the Job Pricing module. As a prerequisite that the compensation analyst has created at least one salary adjustment. The salary adjustments can be created and maintained in the portal in the delivered workset JOB PRICING • SALARY STRUCTURE ADJUSTMENT. The user must have the required authorizations to execute this report.

PECM_ADJUST_0759	Adjust Compensation Process Records

You can use this transaction to execute a report (RHECM_ADJUST_0759) to make changes to the compensation data in infotype 0759 (Compensation Process). The report can make changes only to the fields COMPENSATION AMOUNT (CPAMT), COMPENSATION PERCENT (CPPCT), and COMPENSATION NUMBER (CPNUM) in existing compensation records. It is a prerequisite that infotype 0759 (Compensation Process) is maintained prior to executing this report. This report is used for mass processing. Hence, it is recommended that you execute this report in the background.

PECM_CHANGE_ STATUS	Change Compensation Process Status

You can use this transaction to execute a report (RHECM_CHANGE_PROC_STATUS) to activate the compensation process for the selected set of employees. This report will consolidate the salary reviews maintained by the manager in MSS and update the status of the compensation process in infotype 0759 (Compensation Process). The report will also update secondary infotypes 0008 – Basic Pay, 0015 – Additional Payments, 0267 – Additional Off-Cycle Payments, and 0761 – LTI Granting.

Once the compensation process is activated, it cannot be reset or changed. It is a prerequisite that infotype 0759 (Compensation Process) is maintained prior to executing this report. This report is used for mass processing. Hence, it is recommended that you execute this report in the background.

PECM_CHK_ BUDGET	Check and Release Compensation Budgets

You can use this transaction to execute the report RHECM_BUDGET_CHK_RELEASE to check the accuracy of the compensation budget. For example, the report will check whether there are sub-budgets with negatives. Once the consistency check is completed, the budget can be released or you can reset the status to "Planning" if you wish to make changes to the budget. The status can be reset to "Planning" only if no budget amount has been spent.

PECM_CONV_ BDG_STKUN	Convert Budget Stock Unit

You can use this transaction to convert an existing budget structure from one stock unit to another stock unit. In the selection

screen, you can enter details for budget type, budget period, old and the new stock units. It is a prerequisite that you maintain data on infotype 1520 (Budget Definition) prior to executing this transaction. The transaction executes the report RHECM_CONV_BUDGET to perform the conversion.

PECM_CONV_ LTI_STKUN	Convert LTI Grant Stock Unit

You can use this transaction to perform a stock split. This transaction executes the report RHECM_CONVERT_STOCK_UNIT. The report will be sorted by employee personnel number, and will display the number of awards prior to the stock split and the number of awards after the stock split.

It is a prerequisite that you maintain infotype 0761 (LTI Grant) prior to executing this report. After completing the stock split, you should execute the report Convert Budget Stock Unit (to convert the corresponding budgets) and update the compensation guidelines in the customizing step DEFINE GUIDELINES. This report is used for mass processing. Hence, it is recommended that you execute this report in the background.

PECM_ CREATE_0758	Create Compensation Program Records

You can use this transaction to create infotype 0758 (Compensation Program) for the employees. This transaction executes the report RHECM_CREATE_0758. The report will read the values you enter in the selection screen for Compensation Area, 1st Program Grouping, and 2nd Program Grouping, and will populate the Compensation Program group in infotype 0758. This report is used for mass processing. Hence, it is recommended that you execute this report in the background. It is a recommended best practice that you execute this report on a regular basis for all new hires. For individual employees, it is suggested you use Personnel Actions.

PECM_CREATE_ COMP_PRO	Create Compensation Process Records

You can use this transaction to create infotype 0759 (Compensation Process). For creating infotype 0759, the transaction will read the guidelines you have defined in customizing. After infotype 0759 is created, you can execute the report Change Compensation Process Status for the manager's approval, as well to update the secondary infotypes 0008 – Basic Pay, 0015 – Additional Payments, 0267 – Additional Off-Cycle Payments and 0761 – LTI Granting.

It is a prerequisite that eligibility and guidelines are defined and maintained in customizing. If you have not implemented Manager Self-Services, execute transaction PECM_CREATE_COMP_PRO to create infotype 0759 (Compensation Process).

PECM_DEL_ HIST_DATA	Delete Comp. Planning History Data

After you have completed the compensation review, you can execute this transaction to delete all history data related to that specific compensation review, maintained in the following tables: Employee History (T71ADM_EE_HIST), Process History (T71ADM_PROCESS), Compensation Tracking of Employee Notes (T71ADM_EE_NOTE), Notes for Compensation Process Tracking (T71ADM_PROC_NOTE), and Compensation Planning: Spent Amounts (T71ADM_SPENT_AMT).

You can also execute this transaction from the customizing step Delete Comp. Planning History Data. Once you execute this transaction, the deleted data *cannot* be recovered;

hence, be very cautious about making the decision to delete history data.

PECM_DISP_ PROGRESS	Display Comp. Planning Progress

You can use this transaction to display the progress of compensation planning for an organizational unit during a specific compensation review. This report (RHECM_DISPLAY_PROGRESS) enables compensation administrators to monitor compensation reviews and to send reminders to managers who have not completed compensation planning. You can access and execute this report from the customizing activity Display Comp. Planning Progress.

PECM_DISPLAY_ BUDGETS	Display Budgets

For a specific organizational unit, budget period, budget types and budget unit, you can execute this report (RHECM_BUDGET_RPT) to get an overview of the budgeted amount, amount spent, amount rewarded, and the budget amount unspent.

PECM_DISPLAY_ CHANGES	Display Comp. Planning Changes

You can execute this transaction to display all changes made to infotype 0759 (Compensation Planning). The report will read the specific employee's compensation plan and review data from the Employee History table (T71ADM_EE_HIST) and display them in the report. You can also access and execute this report from the customizing step Display Comp. Planning Changes.

PECM_EVALUATE_ GRANT	Evaluate LTI Grants

You can execute this transaction to generate a report that lists all employees who have been granted LTI. The report also displays the number of awards granted and exercised by the employee. This transaction executes the report RHECM_EVALUATE_LTIDATA. It is a prerequisite that infotype 0761 (LTI Grant) is maintained.

PECM_ GENERATE_ BUDGET	Generate Budget from Org. Hierarchy

You can use this transaction to generate a budget structure for a specific organizational unit. This transaction executes the report RHECM_BUDGET_GENERATE. In the selection screen, enter the budget type, budget period, and the organizational unit for which you want to generate the budget structure.

PECM_INIT_ BUDGET	Upload Budget Values from PCP

You can use this transaction to import data from Personnel Cost Planning (PCP) into the ECM budget structure. You can use the imported data for budget planning. It is a prerequisite that the budget be in a "Planned" status. This transaction executes the report RHECM_BUDGET_INIT to perform the budget upload.

PECM_PREP_ ORGUNITS	Prepare Org. Units for Compensation Planning

You can use this report to identify organizational units to which no eligible employees are assigned for the selected compensation review. You can also use this report to suppress reviews for which the manager is not responsible. This information is particularly useful within the planning overview to suppress information that is irrelevant and not required for the planning overview. It is a suggested best practice to execute this report before the start of the planning overview.

PECM_PRINT_CRS	Print Comp. Review Statement

You can use this transaction to print the Compensation Review Statement (CRS) for your employees. You can use the standard delivered smartform HR_ECM_CRS to print the report. The transaction executes the report RHECM_PRINT_CRS to print the Comp Review Statement. You generate the report after the annual merit review to gain an overview of the compensation granted to your employees. The report will display the following: salary adjustment, regular bonus, off-cycle bonus, LTI grant, the new salary, and the effective date.

It is a prerequisite the following infotypes are maintained: Organizational Assignment (0001), Personal Data (0002), Address (0006), Planned Working Time (0007), Basic Pay (0008), and the Compensation Process (0759).

PECM_PROCESS_ EVENT	Process Event for LTI Grants

You can use this transaction to process LTI related events and update infotype 0761 (LTI Grants) to reflect the changes. The transaction executes the report RHECM_PRO-CESS_EVENT, to process LTI related events. In the selection screen, you can select different processing options: CANCEL ALL (cancel all LTI awards), CANCEL UNVESTED (cancel all unvested LTI awards), PROCESS LIFE EVENT (process the life event stored in infotype 0761 – LTI Grants), VEST PCT. OF GRANTED (vest a percentage of the LTI awards; you can enter the specific percentage in the field), VEST PCT OF UNVESTED (vest a percentage of the unvested award; you can enter the specific percentage in the field), and OVERRIDE VESTING RULE (enter the vest rule and this will override the vesting rule stored in infotype 0761 – LTI Grants).

This report is used for mass processing. Hence, it is recommended that you execute this report in the background.

| PECM_START_ BDG_BSP | Start Budgeting BSP |

You can use this transaction to display the Compensation Budgeting start page. The page (hrecm_bdg_start) will be displayed in the portal and will be BSP displayed.

| PECM_START_ JPR_BSP | Start Job Pricing BSP |

You can use this transaction to display the page containing the different options for Job Pricing. The page (hrecm_jpr_start) will be displayed in the portal and will be BSP based.

| PECM_ SUMMARIZE_ CHNGS | Summarize Compensation Planning Changes |

For the specified reporting period, compensation plan and compensation review, you can use this transaction to evaluate employee data. This transaction evaluates the data stored in the Employee History table and summarizes the compensation planning changes that have occurred as of the specified reporting period, compensation plan, and compensation review. In the initial screen, REPORTING, COMPENSATION PLAN and COMPENSATION REVIEW are required fields. You can also enter other selection criteria to narrow down the report output selection.

| PECM_ UPD_0008_1005 | Update IT0008 when IT0015 Changes |

You can execute this transaction to update infotype 0008 (Basic Pay) when infotype 1005 (Planned Compensation) is changed.

The transaction executes the report RHECM_ UPD_0008_FROM_1005 to perform the table updates. It is a prerequisite that infotypes 0008 (Basic Pay) and 1005 (Planned Compensation) are maintained prior to executing this transaction. This report is used for mass processing. Hence, it is recommended that you execute this report in the background.

11.7 SAP Learning Solution (LSO)

| LSO_ACTIVATE | Activate/Deactivate SAP Learning Solution |

SAP HCM Learning Solutions and SAP Training & Event Management use the same tables. You can use this transaction to adjust system settings and to resolve any system conflicts that might arise due to the common table usage between T&EM and LSO.

| LSO_EVAL_ADMIN | Administrator: Appraisal Document |

This transaction is used and executed by LSO administrators. You can use this transaction to maintain the LSO-related appraisals and course evaluation forms.

| LSO_EVAL_ CATALOG | Evaluation Catalog |

You can use this transaction to create the category group and the category. At least one category should be created under a category group. After creating the category, you create an appraisal template that is attached to a category. The category group and category help to structure the appraisal catalog.

LSO_EVAL_ CHANGE	Edit Appraisal Document

You can use this transaction to edit the course evaluation forms that are created and submitted by the course participants or by administrators. Changing the course evaluation ratings or notes are some of the common maintenance tasks that are performed.

LSO_EVAL_CREATE	Create Appraisal

You can use this transaction to manually enter the course evaluation results by participant and by course. This is particularly useful when you have to transfer course evaluation results submitted in pen and paper to SAP.

LSO_EVAL_ PREPARE	Prepare Appraisal

You can use this transaction to create a course appraisal form for each participant who has attended a training course. The appraisal creation is menu driven, and you can specify the name of the participant (appraiser) and the name of the course (appraisee) during the creation process. The appraisal template that you created using transaction LSO_EVAL_ CATALOG can be used during the appraisal preparation process.

LSO_EVAL_ SEARCH	Find Appraisal

You can use this transaction to evaluate course evaluation results. You can use the report to evaluate, perform ranking, and analyze the evaluation results. This transaction generates a report that displays the appraisal document (as a link), the participants, the course title, and the status of the course evaluation ("Completed," "In Process," etc.).

LSO_OORT	Create Resource Type

You can use this transaction to create resource types. If you wish to create a new resource type by copying an existing resource type, in the RESOURCE TYPE: INITIAL SCREEN enter the data in the resource type field displayed in the COPY FROM group and click the CREATE icon. The system will navigate to the data screen, where you can make the required changes and save the newly created resource type. The system will default the start date to the current date and end date to the SAP system end date (12/31/9999). Using this transaction, you can also maintain and display the resource type details and the associated infotypes.

LSO_PADBOOK	Database Conversion SAP LSO600

When you execute this transaction, the data maintained in the Training & Event Management application are converted to the data model for LSO 6.0. You need to execute this transaction if you are currently on Training & Event Management and planning to upgrade to LSO 600 or if you are on an earlier release of LSO and planning to upgrade to LSO 600. SAP recommends that you do not run T&EM and LSO600 in the same system because this might lead to data inconsistencies.

LSO_PSV1	Dynamic Participation Menu

The dynamic participation menu lists the course catalog. You can drill down to the individual courses and carry out day-to-day activities for bookings and participation. Select the course you wish to maintain, click the right mouse button and select the desired activity. The following participation activities can be maintained through the dynamic participation menu: Book Participation, Prebook Participation, Rebook Participation, Cancel Participation, and Replace Participation.

LSO_PSV2	Dynamic Course Menu

You can use this transaction to create and maintain courses. You can use the dynamic course menu to create courses, firmly book/cancel courses, lock/unlock courses, and follow up on courses.

LSO_PSV3	Dynamic Information Menu

You can use this transaction to generate reports for courses, resources and participation. From the DYNAMIC INFORMATION menu, you can also navigate to the DYNAMIC COURSE menu and DYNAMIC PARTICIPATION menu.

LSO_PSV5	Info: Participation

This transaction displays, in the form of a menu tree, the different reports that can be generated based on participation criteria. The reports that can be generated are Participant List, Attendance List, Employee List, Bookings per Participant, Participation Prerequisites, Attendee's Qualifications, Prerequisites Matchup, Attendee Appraisals, Prebookings per Course Type, Prebookings per Participant, Participants for Rebooking, Participation Statistics, Participation and Sales Statistics, Participation Cancellations per Course, Cancellations per Participant, Budget Comparison, and Participant Results Overview.

LSO_PSV6	Information: Courses

You can use this transaction to generate different types of reports that provide information regarding the courses. Some of the reports are for information only, some reports trigger other activities, and some reports create

objects. The reports that are available include Course Demand, Course Schedule, Course Appraisals, Course Hierarchy, Participation Statistics, Course Brochure, Course Information, Course dates, Resource List per Course, Resources not yet Assigned per Course, Material Requirements per Course, Course Prices, Course Results Overview, and Test Item Statistics.

LSO_PSV7	Reporting: Resources

You can use this transaction to generate different types of reports that provide information regarding the resources in your course types. The different reports that can be generated are Resource Equipment, Resource Reservation, Instructor Information, Graphical Resource Reservation, Available/Reserved Resources, Resource Reservation Statistics, Resources not yet Assigned per Resource Type. These reports provide information and data for the training administrator to plan for the required resources.

LSO_PSV8	Create Participant

You can use this transaction to create a participant. When you execute this transaction, a dialog box is displayed with the list of participant types that you can create. Select the participant type that you want to use for creating the participant. For example, you can select the participant type Person if the participant is an internal employee. Prior to executing this transaction, you must first maintain the customizing setting Specify Attendee Type Control Options in IMG.

LSO_PSV9	Change/Display Participant

You can use this transaction to display and maintain participants. From the dialog box, select the participant type you wish to display or maintain.

| LSO_PSVI | User-Defined Settings |

You can use this transaction to make user-defined settings specifying how you want the data to be displayed in dynamic menus and what infotypes you want displayed for the different objects.

| LSO_PSVP | Dynamic Planning Menu |

You can use this transaction to determine the demand for a course and also to plan for the course. This transaction is important because these functionalities (course demand and course planning) can be maintained only through this transaction.

| LSO_PSVO | Change/Display Training Provider |

You can use this transaction to display and maintain the internal/external training providers.

| LSO_PSVQ | Create Training Provider |

You can use this transaction to create internal or external training providers. For the external training provider, you create the object Company. In the CREATE COMPANY: DATA screen, you maintain the abbreviation, short text and the address of the company. You also assign the external training provider.

Prior to creating the training providers, you should have maintained the customizing settings SPECIFY EXTERNAL PROVIDER and SPECIFY EXTERNAL SERVICE. For the internal training provider, you create an organizational unit that is responsible for delivering the training requirements of your company.

| LSO_PSVR | Dynamic Resource Menu |

You can use this transaction to create and maintain resource objects in a structured hierarchy fashion. The resources are displayed at the top level and the resource types at the lower level of the hierarchy. If you have created a resource type and you do not see the object in the RESOURCE menu, check whether you have maintained the required relationships. For example, for the instructor, you need to maintain these relationships: A022 – Requires Resource Type and A026 – Is Held by.

| LSO_PSVT | Dynamic Tool Menu |

You can use this transaction to create and maintain infotypes for all objects displayed in the course hierarchy structure. These include the course groups, course types, courses and participants. In the DYNAMIC TOOL menu, you cannot create the Object infotype (1000).

| LSO_ PUBLISHER | Display Publisher Database |

This transaction is used by Basis administrators to display data from authoring environment, test author, the content player, and Training Management (contains information on learning objectives and qualification). This is a display-only data screen.

| LSO_PV00 | Book Participation |

You can use this transaction to book a participant in a course. You can make bookings only for planned courses and cannot make bookings for courses that are cancelled or locked. You can also make list bookings, where you book a single participant in multiple courses or multiple participants in a single course. If Learning Solution (LSO) is integrated with Time Management, then the attendance records of the participant are updated when the participant is booked in a course.

| LSO_PV01 | Rebook Participation |

You can use this transaction to rebook a participant booked in a course for a different date. When you rebook the participant for the same course type, the original booking is automatically deleted. If LSO is integrated with Time Management, the time records of the participant are automatically updated.

LSO_PV02	Prebook Participation

When no courses are currently being offered, you can prebook participants for a course type and for a specific time period. When the course is offered, the prebookings can be converted to bookings. Prebookings help in planning the number of days that the course type can be offered.

LSO_PV03	Replace Participation

You can use this transaction to replace a participant booked in a course with another participant. The replacement of a participant can be performed for both internal/external course and in any status. The replace participation can be performed for courses that are locked, cancelled or historically recorded.

LSO_PV04	Cancel Participation

If a participant who is booked cannot attend the course, you can use this transaction to cancel the participation.

LSO_PV06	Prebook: Multiple Participants for Course Type

You can use this transaction to prebook multiple participants for a particular course type in one step.

LSO_PV07	Book: Multiple Participants for Course

You can use this transaction to book multiple participants for a particular course in one step.

LSO_PV08	Book: Participant for Multiple Courses

You can use this transaction to book a participant in multiple courses in one step.

LSO_PV10	Create Course with Resources

You can use this transaction to create a course and assign the required resources that are required for the course. In the corresponding course type, the relationship Requires Resource Type must be maintained. If this relationship is not maintained, then the course can be created without resources only.

LSO_PV11	Create Course without Resources

You can use this transaction to create a course without resources. In the data screen, the fields are automatically pre-populated with data from the corresponding course type.

LSO_PV12	Firmly Book/ Cancel Course

Once you decide to deliver a course, you can use this transaction to firmly book or cancel a course. When the course is firmly booked, the SAP LSO system automatically sends confirmations to the participants. If the capacity of the course is not reached, the participants on the waiting list are automatically moved to the participation list until the optimum capacity is attained.

LSO_PV14	Lock/Unlock Course

You can use this transaction to lock/unlock a course. When the course is locked, no participant bookings are accepted. You need to unlock the course to accept participant bookings again. For a course to be locked or unlocked, the course should not be CAN-CELLED or HISTORICALLY LOCKED.

LSO_PV15	Follow Up Course

You can use this transaction to execute follow-up actions, once the course is firmly booked. Some of the follow-up activities are TRANSFER THE COURSE OBJECTIVES AS QUALIFICATIONS TO THE PARTICIPANTS PD RECORDS, CHANGE THE COURSE TO HISTORICALLY RECORDED, and SEND CONFIRMATION NOTIFICATIONS TO ALL PARTICIPANTS.

LSO_PV16	Prebook: Participant for Multiple Course Types

You can use this transaction to prebook a participant in multiple courses in one step.

LSO_PV18	Activity Allocation – Participation

You can use this transaction to allocate participation fees to the Cost Center that delivered the course. The transaction executes the report RHINLV0_LSO, which allocates the participation costs internally. During the activity, the Cost Center that delivered the course is credited with the course cost and the Cost Center of the course participant is debited. The Cost Center that delivered the course and the Cost Center of the participant should be in the same controlling area.

LSO_PV1A	Change Course

You can use this transaction to change data in a course. Only time-dependent courses can be changed.

LSO_PV1B	Display Course

You can use this transaction to display a course.

LSO_PV1C	Cost Transfer Posting

You can use this transaction to calculate the cost of delivering the course and to transfer the cost FI-CO. The Cost Center of the resource is credited and the Cost Center that is delivering the course is debited. Both the Cost Centers should be in the same controlling area. Prior to executing this transaction, you should have maintained the customizing activity COST TRANSFER POSTING in the IMG.

LSO_PV1D	Price Proposal

You can use this transaction to calculate the price proposal for a course. The price is calculated based on the cost items stored for the course, the reference units and reservation times. The following items are added to determine the cost: cost items of the course, cost items of the course type that the course is related to, cost items of the resource assigned to the course, cost items of the resource type assigned to the course type, cost items of the equipment available in the room and assigned to the course.

LSO_PV33	Create Appraisal

See transaction LSO_EVAL_CREATE for details.

LSO_PVCT	Master Data Catalog

A very important transaction, this transaction is used to create and maintain the different master data objects required in SAP HCM Learning Solutions. You can also maintain the relationships for the different objects in Master Data Catalog.

LSO_PVDC	Edit Curriculum Type

Curriculum types contain course types as elements. Curriculum types can be created with or without sequence rules. You use this transaction to create and maintain curriculum types. While creating the curriculum types, you have to maintain the following relationships: Belongs to course group, Has prerequisite course type, Has prerequisite qualification, Imparts qualification, and Is planned for job.

LSO_PVEC_CREATE	Access: Create/ Change Curriculum

You can use this transaction to create and maintain curricula. In the initial screen, specify the type of curriculum you are creating. The system will then navigate to the Curriculum Maintenance screen, where you can enter the required and basic data. In the initial screen, if you do not specify the validity period, the system will by default set the current date as the start date. You can also use this transaction to edit and maintain existing curricula.

LSO_PVEK	Manage Course Program

You can use this transaction to create and maintain course programs. You can also create a new course program by copying an existing course program into the new program. The system will assign a new course program number and you can make the required changes to create a new course program.

LSO_RHXKBED0	Course Demand

This report displays the number of planned and required course dates by course type. You can generate the report for a calendar year or for individual quarters. The report can also be generated by location and language delivered.

LSO_RHXKBRO0	Course Brochure

This report generates a brochure for the specified course type/group, language, and the reporting period. You will be able to download the brochure to a Word file. In the selection screen, if you check the Create Table of Contents option, the table of contents will be created by the system. The brochure will contain listing of course types with page numbers.

LSO_RHXKBRO1	Course Dates

For the specified reporting period, this report generates a listing of the course dates scheduled per course type, location where the course is being held, delivery method, and language delivered.

LSO_RHXKBRO2	Course Prices

For the specified reporting period, this report generates a listing of internal and external course prices per course type. The delivery method and the currency are displayed as well. The internal and external prices should be maintained in infotype 1021 for the specific course types.

LSO_RHXKURS2	Participation Statistics

For the specified reporting period, this report generates a listing of the number of bookings and number on the waitlist per course type. The course dates and the delivery method are displayed as well. You can also report on course types that are in "Planned" status and not yet firmly booked.

LSO_RHXKURS3	Participation and Sales Statistics

For the specified reporting period, this report generates a listing of number of bookings, sales statistics and allocation data per course type.

LSO_RHXKVOR0	Participation Prerequisites

For the specified reporting period, this report generates a listing of prerequisites required to attend the specific course type.

LSO_RHXMARP0	Material Requirements per Course

This report generates a listing of materials required per course type. Through this report, you can generate a material reservation for materials that are in stock. For non-stock materials, you can generate a purchase requisition.

LSO_RHXORES1	Resources not yet Assigned per Course

This report lists all the resources that are required but not reserved for the course. The course dates, total number of hours for the course, and the delivery method are listed as well.

LSO_RHXQANF0	Prerequisites Matchup

Using this report, you can perform qualifications matchup between a participant's qualifications and the prerequisites required to participate in a course.

LSO_RHXRESO0	Resource Reservation Statistics

This report lists the resources (and resource type) and the courses for which these resources are reserved. The reservation dates and the total number of hours for which the resource is reserved are displayed as well.

LSO_RHXSTOR0	Cancellations per Course

This report lists the course and the name of the participants who cancelled the course. The cancellation reason and the cancellation fee (where levied) are displayed as well.

LSO_RHXSTOR1	Cancellations per Participant

This report displays the names of participants and the courses cancelled by them. The cancellation fee (where levied) and the cancellation reason are displayed as well.

LSO_RHXTEILA	Attendance List

This report generates the check attendance sheet, listing the course name, name of the participant, and a column for marking the participant's signature.

LSO_RHXTEILN	Participant List

This report lists the external and internal participants in the courses. The course details are displayed as well. In the selection screen, if you checkmark the option FORMAT AS ATTENDANCE LIST, the report will display a column for the participants signature. The report format will be similar to the Attendance List (transaction LSO_RHXTEILA) report.

LSO_RHXTHIST	Participants Training History

This report displays all the training courses a participant has attended or is booked to attend. The course details are displayed as well.

LSO_RHXUMBU0	Participants for Rebooking

This report lists all the participants and the course they were registered to attend but did not attend, either because the course reached maximum capacity or the course was cancelled. Such registrants are put on the waiting list for the specific course.

LSO_ RHXVORM0	Prebookings per Course Type

For the specified reporting period, the report lists the course type and the prebookings that were made per course type.

LSO_ RHXVORM1	Prebookings per Participant

You can use this transaction to generate a report that lists prebookings per attendee.

LSO_TAC_ ITEMSTAT	Results Overview: Item Statistics

You can use this transaction to execute a report that displays the item statistics for a specified test. The report output is displayed in the following structure: test object, section, learning objective, and individual items. These contain details that are customized in the authoring environment. The report provides details such as number of results evaluated, mean value at each of the level, maximum possible score at the level of the item, and total score achieved by the participants at the level of the item.

LSO_TAC_ PART_ RESULT	Results Overview: Participant

You can use this transaction to execute a report that provides the course results of a specified participant. The report will provide details such as the course participation document, the participants score at the level of test and learning objective, maximum possible score at the level of the test and learning objective, and the passing score at the level of test and learning objective, etc.

LSO_TAC_ TRAIN_ RESULT	Results Overview: Course

For the specified course type, you can use this report to generate a listing of all course results. The report provides information such as course participation document, cut-off value for passing, maximum score possible, participants' scores, etc. In the initial screen, the course type (object ID) is a required field, and you can also enter the reporting period for which you want to execute this report.

OOER	Create External Instructor

You can use this transaction to create an external instructor and the required relationships. If you have an existing Instructor object, you can use that as a reference and create a New Instructor object. You should maintain relationships 050 (Is the Instructor for) and A003 (Belongs to) to complete the creation of the external instructor.

PVD0	Course Type

You can use this transaction to create course types. In the data screen, enter the abbreviation and the short text of the course type. If any resources are required for this course type, you should maintain the relationship Requires Resource Type, while creating the course type.

PVG0	Create/Change Resource

You can use this transaction to create and maintain resources that are required to conduct and deliver the courses.

PVG1	Create/Change Room

You can use this transaction to create and maintain the resource room required for the courses. While creating the resource, you can also maintain the required relationships. The relationships that are to be maintained include Belongs to Location, Is a Specialization of Resource Type, Is Equipped with Resource Type, Cost Center Assignment, Capacity, Address, and Further Information.

PVH1	Create/Change Instructor

You can use this transaction to create and maintain instructors. These instructors are external instructors and are maintained in your SAP ECC HCM system. The instructors you create here are assigned to the object type External Person (H).

PVL0	Course Group

You can use this transaction to create a course group. If you are maintaining a course group hierarchy, you need to create the relationship Belongs To Course Group, and assign it to a higher course group. You can assign Course Types to Course Groups. The Course Group hierarchy is maintained top-down.

PVR0	Create/Change Resource Type

You can use this transaction to create and maintain different resource types. Resource types are a grouping of similar types of resources. The different resource types maintained in Learning Solutions are Room, Instructor, Material, and Other Resources.

11.8 Travel Management

ACTEXP_ APPR_LITE	Approve Trips and Time Sheets

You can use this transaction to approve times in CATS and for Travel Management. To use this transaction for approvals, the data for times and travel management must be in the same system. You cannot use this transaction for approvals in a distributed environment.

PR_CHECK	Check Customizing Settings

You can use this transaction to validate and check the customizing settings you have created in Travel Management. The report checks the settings in Travel Planning, Travel Expenses, and Geocoding functions. The transaction executes the report RPR_CUSTOMIZING_CHECK.

PR00	Travel Expenses

You can use this transaction to display the SAP Travel & Expenses application menu. The SAP Menu tree structure displays the transactions that are related to Travel & Expenses.

PR01	Maintain Trip Data

This transaction is obsolete and is no longer being used. This transaction is replaced by transactions PR05/TRIP. Refer to SAP Note 801559—Transaction PR01: Maintain Trip Data (Old) for details.

PR02	Travel Calendar

You can use this transaction to create, edit and maintain the domestic travel plans of an employee. Enter the time period for which you wish to maintain the travel plans. By default, the current month is displayed.

PR03	Trip Advances

You can use this transaction to record any reimbursable amounts that were given to the employee as travel expenses. The system will reduce the travel expenses calculated for the entire trip by the advance amount. Trip advances will record information on the amount that was given as trip advance, the currency, the date of entry, the local currency, and the currency exchange rate. All trip advances are also assigned a cash indicator.

PR04   Edit Weekly Reports

You can use this transaction to create and maintain weekly reports. The weekly reports are displayed as week-by-week calendars. The weekly reports can be used to enter individual receipts. The weekly reports can be customized to meet the specific requirements of your enterprise. During customizing, you will be required to define travel expense types and customize the feature TRVPA.

PR05   Travel Expense Manager

You can use this transaction to enter per-diems and individual receipts for international and domestic trips. You can use the travel manager to maintain expenses for any trips that were recorded using travel expense manager, travel advances or travel calendar. You can also maintain trips that were already transferred to accounting, payroll accounting, or data medium exchange. In the travel expense manager, you can only maintain one trip at a time.

PR10   Number Ranges for Trip Numbers

You can use this transaction to maintain number ranges for Travel Management. In the PR10 screen, enter the personnel area for which you are maintaining the travel management related number range. You can click the INTERVALS button to display the number range being used and the current number available for usage.

PR11   Days Carried FI/CO: Travel Expenses Posting Documents

You can use this transaction to create and maintain number ranges for assignment to trip transfer documents.

PR12   HR PAY: Accounting Analyses

You can use this transaction to create and maintain number ranges for assignment to posting runs.

PRAA   Automatic Vendor Maintenance

This transaction executes the report RPRAPA00 (Create/Change/Block Vendor Master Records from HR Master Records). You can use this transaction (or the report) to maintain vendor master records for an employee. The program will use the following HR Master Data infotypes: 0000 (Actions), 0001 (Org. Assignment), 0002 (Personal Data), 0006 Subtype 1 (Permanent Residence), and 0009 (Bank Details). The link between the employee's HR master record and the corresponding vendor master record is created by entering the employee's personnel number in the company code segment of the vendor master record.

PRAP   Approval of Trips

Approval of Trips is normally used by the department that tracks travel expenses. You can use this transaction to maintain and display all trips that need to be checked and approved. You can use this transaction to approve, display, make changes, simulate or put trips on hold. You can also access Approval of Trips by executing the report RPR_APPROVE_TRAVEL_EXPENSES.

PRCC   Import Credit Card Files

You can use this transaction to import credit card transactions into SAP for use in travel costs. The credit card transaction file will be in a format that is decided with the credit card provider. The data file will contain details like the employee's name, the credit card number of the employee, and the various expenses in the proper transaction currency.

PRCCD	Display Credit Card Receipts

You can use this transaction to evaluate credit card expenses of your employees. In the selection screen, you can select whether the data evaluation is for a single employee or for a group of employees. You can further restrict the data selection by entering data for the other selection criteria such as the receipt information.

PRCCE	Process Incorrect Transactions

The credit card transactions that are delivered by credit card companies need to be transferred to SAP for processing by SAP Travel Management. During the transfer, there might be transactions that cannot be processed further; such transactions are stored in SAP correction table PTRV_CCCC. You can use this transaction to display all credit card transactions that were not assigned and need to be corrected. You can view the record and make corrections to the master data or to the credit card file.

PRCCF	Generate File with Corrected Transactions

This transaction executes the report RPRCCC_CREATE_CORRECTION_FILE (Create File with Corrected Credit Card Transactions). After you have corrected the credit card transactions (using transaction PRCCE), you can create a new file in CCD format for the corrected credit card transactions, using this transaction. The records that are included in the new file are deleted from correction table PTRV_CCCC.

PRCO	Copy Trip Provision Variant

This transaction corresponds to the customizing step DEFINE/DELETE/RESTORE TRIP PROVISION VARIANTS. In this transaction, you can create new trip provision variants, delete unneeded trip provision variants, copy trip provision variants, and restore trip provision variants. SAP recommends that you define a trip provision variant for each trip provision for a country or for the industry you are involved in.

PRCU	Check Printing

You can use this transaction to print pre-numbered checks or, if you use non-numbered checks, you can assign a number from the pre-defined number range. The system then assigns the check number to SAP payment document number or to the settlement result. During check printing, you can also print payment advice notes and payment summary.

PRD1	Payment Medium <Country of Selection> – Transfers/Bank Direct Debits in ACH Format

You can use this transaction to create the file with funds transfer data details. The generated file can be downloaded into a DME (Data Medium Exchange) and sent to an ACH operator for further processing. You can also print the DME cover sheet and forms that state the specific payment advice and payment summaries.

PRDE	Delete Trip Prov. Variant

You can use this transaction to delete a trip provision variant in the current client. In the standard delivered, the system deletes the trip provision variants from all associated tables.

PRDH	Employees with Exceeded Trip Days

This transaction executes the report RPRDUR00 (Determination of Employees with Exceeded Trip Days). In the selection screen, you have to enter values for REPORTING ANALYSIS PERIOD, INTERVAL DURATION, DAY LIMIT, NO DISTINCTION: DOM./INTERNAT,

DISTINCTION: DOMESTIC/INTERNAT, CONSIDER 1ST LETTER OF LOC, TRIPS and WEEKLY REPORTS. The report displays all employees who have spent more than the value entered in the DAY LIMIT field, within value entered in the INTERVAL DURATION field, during the reporting analysis period.

This report is particularly useful to identify employees who were to be paid different reimbursement rates. This situation might arise due to local laws; for example, in Germany, a double residence triggers this type of payment.

PRDX	Data Medium Exchange: Travel Expenses (USA)

You can use this transaction to create a dataset from travel expenses that are to be transferred. The programs Payment Medium (RFFOUS_T) and Check Printing (RFFOUS_C) use this data as input for further processing. You can also use the report RPRDTAU0 to execute this transaction. As prerequisite, the employee address and the bank details must be created and maintained in HR Master Data. You must also have completed the travel expenses settlement. In the initial screen, you will be required to select the country grouping for which you wish to execute this transaction.

PREC	Settle Trips

For a specific accounting or payroll period, the application determines the amount required to be reimbursed based on the trip data that are entered. You can customize the feature TRVCT to set the accounting rules for trips settlements as required by your organizational policy. You can also process Trips Settlement by executing the report RPRTEC00.

PREP	Import Program for Per-Diems

Most often, organizations based in the US follow the per-diem rates determined by the US government agency the Per Diem, Travel and Transportation Allowance Committee. You can download the per-diem rates from this agency's Website (available as a zip file), unzip the file and save it to your local drive. You can use this transaction to import the per-diem file and update the customizing tables. This process is efficient since you do not need to maintain the tables manually. This transaction is similar to the customizing activity IMPORT US PER DIEMS/FLAT RATES FROM INTERNET.

PREX	Create Expense Report

You can use this transaction to create a travel expense report for an employee (under a specific trip schema). This transaction is similar to the TRIP (Travel Manager) transaction, which also enables you to create a travel expense report.

PRF0	Standard Travel Expense Form

You can use this transaction to print a report that will display details of the trip expenses for a single trip (for the specified accounting period).

PRF1	Summarized Form 1

This transaction executes the report RPRTEF01 (Summarized Form 1 for Travel Expenses). The report displays all trips that were accounted during the specific accounting period that you entered in the selection screen. The report is useful to display trip expense category details and expense types for the specified accounting period.

PRF2 Summarized Form 2

Transaction PRF2 produces a report similar to that generated by transaction PRF1 (Summarized Form 1). The report generated by transaction PRF2 has a line length of 132 characters: this enables you to display additional details, like number of miles travelled, trip advances, and any additional amounts for each trip.

PRFI Posting to Financial Accounting

This transaction executes the report RPRFIN00_40 (Create Posting Run). For the specified payroll period, you can use this transaction to select and transfer trips to accounting. The program also checks the posting ability of the selected trips, replaces any CO objects with errors, and creates the trip source document under a posting run number.

PRMC Travel Expenses: Feature TRVCT

You can use this transaction to display and maintain the travel expenses feature TRVCT (Travel Control for Travel Expense Accounting). You can use this feature TRVCT to assign a trip provision variant to the employees, based on the enterprise structure.

PRMD Maintain HR Master Data

You can use this transaction to maintain HR Master Data for employees that are related to travel management. You can maintain infotypes related to bank details, travel privileges and cost distribution.

PRMF Travel Expenses: Feature TRVFD

You can use this transaction to maintain the feature TRVFD (Travel Fields) for Field Control via T706Z.

PRML Change Country Grouping

When you log into SAP for first time and execute any transactions related the Payment via Data Medium Exchange, a country grouping screen is displayed. You will be required to select a country. The country you selected will be used by the system automatically to display the relevant and country specific screens. If you are required to change the country grouping, you can use this transaction to select a different country grouping.

PRMM Personnel Actions

You can use this transaction to execute Personnel Actions related to Travel Management, which include Travel Expenses (mini-master), Org. Re-assignment (TE mini-master), Mini-maestro TV (ALTA).

PRMO Travel Expenses: Feature TRVCO

You can use this transaction to maintain the feature TRVCO—Dynamic Screen Layout of the Account Assignment Block.

PRMP Travel Expenses: Feature TRVPA

You can use this transaction to maintain the feature TRVPA (Travel Parameters) for Trip Costs Parameters.

PRPL Create Travel Plan

You can use this transaction to create travel plans. This transaction is similar to the TRIP (Travel Manager) transaction.

PRPY	Transfer to an External Payroll

You can use this transaction to transfer travel expenses accounting results from Travel Management logical system to HCM Payroll logical system. You need to execute this program only if Travel Management and HCM Payroll are in different logical systems.

PRRQ	Create Travel Request

You can use this transaction to create travel requests. This transaction is similar to the TRIP (Travel Manager) transaction.

PRRW	Post Accounting Data

After you have created the posting run using transaction PRFI (Posting to Financial Accounting), you can use this transaction to validate the posting run, reject the posting run, delete the rejected posting run, or post the posting run. You can also use this transaction to display the trip source document created in the posting run.

PRRL	Reset Status

You can use this transaction to reset the status of trips. Any trip with status "Trip Approved, Accounted" will be reset to status "Trip Approved, To Be Accounted" and the posting status will be set to "Not Posted." As a prerequisite, the trip status must be in "Trip Approved, Accounted"; the posting can be in any status.

PRST	Period Statistics

This transaction executes the report RPRSTA01 (Travel Expense Reporting by Period). The report displays a statistical overview of the trip expenses for the specified reporting period. In the PERIOD MODIFIER field, you can enter the parameter that will sub-divide the results into the specified periods. Only trips that are paid and that are within the specified reporting period are selected for the report. In the selection screen, if you select the parameter ALLOW RECEIPT DETAIL DISPLAY, you will be able to drill down to individual receipts in the displayed report.

PRTC	Display Imported Documents

This transaction executes the program RPCL-STTC – Overview of Existing Credit Card Documents (Document Buffer). The report displays the contents of the cluster TC on PCL1 (Credit Card Document Buffer) for individual employees.

PRTE	Trip Details

You can use this transaction to display the entire travel and expense details of an employee(s). In the selection criteria, if you select the option OVERVIEW OF TRIPS, the report will display a list of all trips, sorted by employee personnel number. You can select a specific trip from the list, which will branch to another selection screen, where you can select what trip details you want to be displayed. If the OVERVIEW OF TRIPS option is not selected, the report will display all details related to the trip.

PRTS	Overview of Trips

This transaction is obsolete and SAP recommends you use transaction PRTE (Trip Details).

PRUL	Travel Expenses Per Diems: Update from File

Whenever there is a statutory change in travel expense per-diems, SAP releases the new per-diem rates in SAP Service Marketplace. You can use this transaction to import into SAP the files containing the changed per-diem rates. As a prerequisite, you should have downloaded the files from service market-place and saved them to your local drive. The current files are available in SAP Service Marketplace and you can download them from *http://service.sap.com/tm-downloads*.

PRVT	VAT Recovery

For the specified trip duration, this report displays a list of all receipts that were incurred during international trips. The organization can use this report to claim a refund of the paid VAT tax. You can further shortlist the selection based on country, currency and travel expense type.

PTRV_ PAYMENT_ HISTORY	Travel Expenses Payment History

You can use this transaction to generate a report that will display the trip header data and the trip data. You can also get details about the FI posting, including the posting date, payment date, amount paid, currency of payment, and the document number. You use this report to give the employee an overview of payments for the recent trips and to evaluate the recent payments.

PTRV_ QUERY	Travel Management Queries

You can also use this transaction to access delivered SAP Query infosets related to travel management.

S_AHR_ 61000596	Specify Attributes for Trip Rules – Flight

Use this transaction to assign trip routes and flight service providers to the trip rules. You can assign different trip routes and airline companies to a trip rule. This enables you to follow your corporate travel policy, by assigning different priorities to different flight availability results.

S_AHR_ 61000601	Define Class Rules – Flight

Use this transaction to define class rules for flights for your corporation. These define the flight classes that employees are eligible to book for their flights, depending on the travel duration and the employee sub-group they belong to.

S_AHR_ 61000608	Define Trip Rules – Hotel

Use this transaction to define hotel-specific trip rules for your corporation. You can add more details to the defined trip rules in the customizing steps HOTEL CLASS RULES. SAP recommends the delivered trip rule GENERIC be retained and not be deleted.

S_AHR_ 61000649	Specify Attributes for Trip Rules – Hotel

Use this transaction to assign hotel chains to the defined hotel-specific trip rules. The assignment is dependent on the hotel chain and the geographic location of the trip destination.

S_AHR_ 61000654	Define Priorities

Use this transaction to define travel priorities for your corporation. These priorities control compliance with the customized trip rules when travel services are booked. If a travel service is not assigned a priority, the system defaults it to priority 9. It is a suggested best practice to assign a meaningful name to priority 9.

S_AHR_ 61000671	Price and Availability Strategies

Use this transaction to define the strategies for the different travel services (Hotel/Flight/ Car Rental and Rail). The values you enter in this customizing activity are used to control the price and availability queries. It is a prerequisite that you have completed DEFINE GROUPINGS FOR TRAVEL PLANNING CONTROL prior to this customizing activity.

S_AHR_61000677	Define Class Rules – Hotel

Use this transaction to define hotel services class rules for your corporation.

S_AHR_61000679	Specify Attributes for Class Rules – Hotel

Use this transaction to define class rules for hotel services for your corporation. These rules define the hotel classes that employees are eligible to book, depending on the travel duration and the employee sub-group they belong to.

S_AHR_61000681	Define Trip Rules – Car Rental

Use this transaction to define car rental-specific trip rules for your corporation. You can add more details to the defined trip rules in the customizing steps CAR RENTAL CLASS RULES. SAP recommends the delivered trip rule GENERIC be retained and not be deleted. If you delete the trip rule GENERIC, then only car rentals that have been assigned a priority can be found by the application.

S_AHR_61000683	Specify Attributes for Trip Rules – Car Rental

Use this transaction to assign car rental companies to the defined car rental-specific trip rules. The assignment is dependent on the car rental company and the geographic location of the destination.

S_AHR_61000685	Define Class Rules – Car Rental

Use this transaction to define class rules for car rentals for your corporation.

S_AHR_61000687	Specify Attributes for Class Rules – Car Rental

Use this transaction to assign car rental class rules to car rental types depending on the duration of the car rental.

S_AHR_61000689	Define Trip Activity Types

Use this transaction to define trip activity types for your corporation. Trip activity types are used as base criteria for definition of trip rules. During customization these activity types are assigned to trip rules.

S_AHR_61000691	Define Travel Profiles

Use this transaction to define travel profiles for your corporation. These travel profiles are assigned to the trip rules. You can also travel profile to an employee in infotype 0470 (Travel Profile)

S_AHR_61006686	Define Trip Rules – Flight

Use this transaction to create flight-specific trip rules for your corporation.

S_AHR_61006688	Specify Attributes for Class Rules – Flight

Use this transaction to assign the flight class rules to the specific cabin class and flight schema. Prior to this customizing step, it is a prerequisite that you have completed the customizing step DEFINE CLASS RULES FOR FLIGHTS.

S_AHR_ 61006705	Assign Trip and Class Rules

Use this transaction to assign the services related trip rules to the defined travel profiles. You can then assign the travel profiles to infotype 0470 (Travel Profile) to individual employees. This will help you enforce your corporate level travel policy at the time of travel booking.

S_AHR_ 61006706	Enterprise – Specific Methods of Payment

Use this transaction to assign the payment method to the defined payment method group. If you are using the employee's personal credit card (payment method "P"), you can store the credit card details in infotype 0105 (Communication), subtype 0011

S_AHR_ 61012509	Assign Profile/Hotel Catalog Item

Use this transaction to assign travel profiles to the individual hotel properties in the hotel catalog. When you assign the hotel property to a travel profile, you also specify the trip activity type, the validity period, the hotel class and the priority rule.

S_AHR_ 61016279	Hierarchical Overview of Flights by Airline

This report displays the number of flights per airline. When you expand the report display, the personnel number of the employee on the specific flight is displayed. You can get details about the employee by clicking the personnel number

S_AHR_ 61016283	Business Volume with Hotel Chains, Hierarchical

The report is displayed in a ranking list showing total business volume by hotel chain. You can select a hotel chain, click the EXPAND button, and get details/business volume of the individual bookings.

S_AHR_ 61016286	Business Volume with Car Rental Companies

You can execute this transaction to get details about total business volume by car rental company.

S_AHR_ 61016287	Business Volume by Rental Location

You can execute this transaction to get details about total business volume by car rental location.

S_AHR_ 61016401	General Trip Data/ Trip Totals

This report displays trip data and trip totals per individual trip for an employee. In the displayed list, if you click the personnel number, the employee details/org. assignments are displayed in a dialog box. If you click the trip number, you can branch to trip, trip receipts, cost assignment and trip block list.

S_AHR_ 61016402	Trip Receipts

This report displays the trip data, trip totals and trip receipts per individual trip that the employee has completed. If you click the personnel number, the employee name and the org. assignment are displayed. If you click the trip number, you can branch to trip, cost assignment and trip block list.

S_ALN_ 01000812	Define Class Rules – Rail

Use this transaction to define class rules for rail for your corporation.

S_ALN_ 01000813	Specify Attributes for Class Rules – Rail

Use this transaction to assign rail class rules to rail class types depending on the duration of the rail travel. It is a prerequisite that class rules for rail are defined prior to this customizing activity.

S_ALN_ 01000814	Assign Class Rules – Rail

Use this transaction to assign rail related class rules to the defined travel profiles. These travel profiles can be assigned to employees in infotype 0470 (Travel Profile). This will help you enforce your corporate level travel policy at the time of rail travel booking.

TP01	Planning Manager

You can use this transaction to create and maintain travel plans. Using the Planning Manager you can also make online bookings of hotels, flights, car rentals, approve a travel plan, and maintain your HR Master Data.

TP31	Queries for Travel Planning

You can use this transaction to create, maintain, and execute SAP Queries that are based on travel management related infosets.

TPMD	Maintain (Travel Planning)

You can use this transaction to maintain travel management related HR Master Data for an employee. For example, you can maintain the following infotypes: Travel Profile, Flight Preference, Hotel Preference, Rental Car Pref-erence, Train Preference, Customer Program and Travel Privileges.

TPMM	Personnel Actions (Travel Planning)

You can use this transaction to execute the personnel action Trip Planning (mini-master).

TPMS	Display (Travel Planning)

You can use this transaction to display the travel-related HR Master Data of an employee.

TRIP	Travel Manager

The Travel Manager is a simple user interface where an employee can create and maintain travel request, travel plans and travel expenses. The travel manager also displays the list of open trips for the particular employee. Against each trip, the trip data and follow-on activities, if any, are also displayed. If you have a group of employees whose travels are required to be maintained, you can click the CHANGE PERSONNEL NUMBER button to toggle between personnel numbers.

11.9 Performance Management

OOHAP_ BASIC	Basic Appraisal Template Settings

You can use this transaction to create new columns, roles, substatus (that can be used in the appraisal process), push buttons, value lists and access to new BAdi registration (through the enhancement areas). OOHAP_BASIC is one of the two most frequently used transactions during customizing of the SAP HCM Performance Management.

OOHAP_CAT_GROUP	Category Group Settings

This transaction is to be used only for transport of the category groups, to correct critical errors and to create new category groups. You can also create and maintain category groups by executing transaction PHAP_CATALOG_PA. All the functionalities that are available in transaction OOHAP_CAT_GROUP can be accessed through transaction PHAP_CATALOG_PA.

OOHAP_CATEGORY	Appraisal Category Settings

This transaction is to be used only for transport of a category, to correct critical errors and to create new categories. You can also create and maintain a category by executing transaction PHAP_CATALOG_PA. SAP strongly recommends that you create and maintain category groups/category through transaction PHAP_CATALOG_PA in order to avoid inconsistencies.

OOHAP_SETTINGS_PA	PA: Settings

You use this transaction to maintain the switch settings for the parameter HAP00/REPLA. If the switch is blank, SAP will use the old Appraisal Systems component. If you maintain switch A, X, or T, then SAP will use the Object Settings and Appraisals component. If you want the HCM Performance Management system to be integrated into SAP SEM, you can maintain the RFC connection using the parameter HAP00/RFCSE. You can also maintain the switch settings through the IMG customizing step EDIT BASIC SETTINGS. Refer to SAP Note 1171576 for more details about the individual switch values A, X, and T.

OOHAP_VALUE_TYPE	Standard Value Lists

You can use this transaction to create and maintain new scales. You can also create new scales through the IMG customizing step EDIT SCALES. Many customers have a need to create specific types of scales they frequently use them to rate objectives and assess employees.

PHAP_ADMIN_PA	PA: Administrator – Appr. Document

You can use this transaction to perform appraisals document related administrator functions. For example, using this transaction you can lock/unlock, prepare and delete appraisal documents. Another potential use of this transaction is to find the status of the appraisal document of the employees in your organization.

PHAP_CATALOG_PA	PA: Catalog for Appraisal Templates

You can use this transaction for customizing the appraisal templates. You can use this transaction to create the category, appraisal template (VA object), criteria (VB object), and criterion (VC object). Other functionalities are available: download/upload category, download/upload template, change the status of the appraisal template (release or cancel), do a consistency check, translate the appraisal template, preview the appraisal template, etc. PHAP_CATALOG_PA is possibly the most important transaction in HCM Performance Management. Familiarize yourself will all the functionalities available in this transaction to gain a good understanding of and competency in HCM Performance Management.

PHAP_ CHANGE_PA	PA: Change Appraisal Document

You can use this transaction to make changes to an existing appraisal document. For example, you can use this transaction to add new objectives or delete objectives.

PHAP_ CREATE_PA	PA: Create Appraisal Document

You can use this transaction to create new appraisal documents for your employees. When you execute the transaction, select the appraisal template with which you are planning to create the document. The status of the document is now "In Preparation." Enter the name of the manager and employee and click the SET OBJECTIVES button. The document creation is completed (the objectives are displayed) and the status is changed to "In Preparation."

PHAP_ PMP_ TIMELINE	Maintain Process Timeline

This transaction is similar to the customizing step CONFIGURE PERFORMANCE MANAGEMENT PROCESS and is used only for the PRE-DEFINED PERFORMANCE MANAGEMENT PROCESS. Using this transaction you can define the time schedule and the description of each process step in the appraisal cycle. This enables the process to run in sequence and the relevant due dates are displayed to the user in the user-interface. You can also define the goal distribution in percentages for the employees completed appraisals.

PHAP_ PREPARE_PA	PA: Prepare Appraisal Document

You can use this transaction to create appraisal documents. The creation process is wizard driven and in the first screen you are provided with different options for how you can create the document. At each step, a description is provided, detailing what steps need to be completed.

PHAP_ SEARCH_PA	PA: Evaluate Appraisal Document

You can use this transaction to generate reports based on the appraisal template. In the selection screen, enter the required details and click the EXECUTE button to generate the report. You can also export the results into a local file.

PHAP_ START_BSP	Generate Internet Addresses

This transaction can be used only for Business Server Pages (BSP) based UI. You can use this transaction to generate the URL, which can be deployed into an iView or can be used to display the UI, where you can create the appraisal documents for your employees.

11.10 Succession Management

HRTMC_ CATALOG_ TMC	TMC Catalog for Appraisal Forms

You can use this transaction to transport the assessment forms that you created in the customizing activity DEFINE TEMPLATES FOR TALENT ASSESSMENT. To transport the form, in the APPRAISAL TEMPLATE CATALOG screen, select the category group or category or the form that you want to transport. Click the right-mouse button and select TRANSPORT. Specify the transport request to create the transport. You can also execute the customizing activity TRANSPORT FORMS in the IMG to transport the assessment forms.

HRTMC_ CONF_ ASSESS	Start WD Application

You can use this transaction to create the forms required for talent assessment. When creating the forms, you need to specify the scales that will be used for the assessment. You can create forms for the following processes: Performance Management, Development Plan, Potential, Risks, Derailers, Competencies, and Nominations to Talent Groups. You can also execute the customizing activity DEFINE FORMS FOR TALENT ASSESSMENT in the IMG to create the required forms.

HRTMC_ PPOC	Create Succession Planning and Org.

If the organizational management is configured and available, you can use this transaction to create the job architecture and make organizational arrangements for Succession Planning. For example, you can assign the talent management specialist to an organizational unit and define the area of responsibility. The application uses the relationship Is Responsible for/Is in Area of Responsibility of (741) between the talent management specialist position and the organization unit that he or she is assigned to (responsible for).

HRTMC_ PPOM	Change Succession Planning and Org.

You can use this transaction to edit and maintain the different objects types in SAP HCM Talent Management.

HRTMC_ PPOS	Display Succession Planning and Org.

You can use this transaction to display the different object types and the basic data in SAP HCM Talent Management.

HRTMC_ SET_KEY	Determine Key Positions

This transaction executes the report RPTMC_SET_KEY_INDICATION to indicate or delimit jobs or positions as key jobs or key positions. The report will use the business logic in the BAdI HRTMC_CALCULATE_KEY_INDICATION (Calculation of Key Indication of Jobs and Positions) to specify the key indication. In the standard, the BAdI HRTMC_CALCULATE_KEY_INDICATION (Calculation of Key Indication of Jobs and Positions) is not activated. You need to activate the BAdI and include your custom business logic. The report RPTMC_SET_KEY_INDICATION will then call this BAdI to indicate jobs or positions as key jobs or key positions.

SLG1	Application Log – Display Logs

You can use this transaction to display transaction logs for the different activities in the SAP system. The log can used to analyze and determine the causes of error when a transaction or report fails. You can also use the log to check whether a particular report or process is executed successfully. You can restrict the log display by entering the relevant search filter in the selection screen; for example, you can display logs for a particular user or a transaction code. The log display can also be restricted to a specified time period.

11.11 Payroll

Payroll processing involves maintenance of country-specific master data. In this chapter, we discuss transactions that are specific to US payroll. Where required, we also discuss the transactions related to international payroll.

It is important to note that SAP requires all US payroll customers to use the BSI TaxFactory version 9.0 by September 1, 2011.

SAP releases information regarding product rollout, support and documentation for US SAP ERP HCM at *http://service.sap.com/hrusa*. It is recommended that you bookmark this link and visit this site regularly for up-to-date information on the current tax year, including SAP Notes on relevant publications by the Internal Revenue Service (IRS) in the US.

FDTA	Data Medium Administration

You can use this transaction to manage the data media that you have created in the process step GENERATE PAYMENT MEDIUM. Based on the search filter entered in the selection screen, the system displays all the data media that were created and exist in the system. You can choose a specific data medium to get an overview or further information. This transaction supports the following functionalities:

1. Display data medium attributes

2. Delete a data media

3. Download one or more data media files to a hard drive or disk

4. Display the contents of a specific data media

5. Print the payment summary for a specific data media

6. Create a payment advice note for the specified data medium

HRCMP0042	Pay Scale Reclassification

You can use this transaction to create a pay scale reclassification for employees for the specified time period. The reclassification is done based on configuration settings in the process Pay Scale Reclassifications. The generated data are imported into infotype 0008 (Basic Pay) by batch input or by using transaction PA30 (Maintain HR Master Data). This transaction calls program RPIPSR00 and replaces program RPITUM00 executed by transaction PC00_M99_ITUM

HRWTT00MAIN	Wage Type Tool

You can use this transaction to configure wage types in the SAP Payroll system. Using this transaction you can create new wage types or edit/maintain an existing wage type. The wage types are active from the effective date specified in the screen.

P0000_M10_CL0_PBS	Generate Qualification Groups or Qualifications

You can use this report to transfer the classifications and codes configured in SAP HCM Personnel Administration to Qualification groups and Qualifications respectively, maintained in SAP HCM Personnel Development.

P0000_M10_CL1_PBS	Convert Certificate or License to Qualification

You can use this report to create Qualifications objects for the corresponding codes stored in infotype 0795 (Certification and Licensing) for a particular employee. It is a prerequisite that codes are maintained in infotype 0795 for the particular employee prior to executing this report.

P0000_M10_CL2_PBS	Out-of-Field Report

You can use this report to get a listing of employees who are working "out-of-field" (employees without the appropriate licensing or certification). It is a prerequisite that infotype 0795 (Certification and Licensing) and infotype 0796 (Duty Assignments) are maintained for the employees.

P0000_M10_CL3_PBS	Perform Certificates/Licenses Selection

Based on the selection criteria, this report will display a listing of employees who have or lack certification/licensing within specific areas. It is a prerequisite that infotype 0795 (Certification and Licensing) is maintained for the employees.

P0000_M10_CL4_PBS	Check Qualification and Certificate Consistency

This report checks the consistency of an employee's qualification in relation to the codes maintained in infotype 0795 (Certification and Licensing). Any inconsistencies in the qualifications are listed in the output.

P0000_M10_EEO_PBS	EEO-4 and EEO-5 Reporting

This report generates the EEO-4 and EEO-5 forms, which are required to be filed with the Equal Employment Opportunity Commission. It is a prerequisite that EEO-related data, such as ethnicity, gender and job category, are maintained for the employees. If the EEO-related data are not maintained for an employee, that employee will not be processed for reporting purposes.

P0000_M10_ORM_PBS	Form 1042-S Printing

This report generates a form with the details required for Form 1042-S (Foreign Person's US Source Income Subject to Withholding) tax filing. The tax year and tax payer identification number are mandatory fields in the selection screen. It is a prerequisite that configuration is completed for Non-Resident Alien Payroll in the IMG.

P0000_M10_SBT_PBS	Savings Bonds Purchase

This report generates a file in ASCII format with a listing of successfully processed employees, related to savings bond purchase. This ASCII file can be used for compliance filing with the Federal Reserve Bank. It is a prerequisite that company name, company ID, location ID and company address are maintained in the system. The Federal Reserve Bank should have provided your organization the servicing FRB District Designator. This information should also be maintained in the SAP system.

P0000_M10_SPT_PBS	Substantial Presence Test

You can use this report to determine the taxation status of non-US citizens who live and work in the US in a temporary engagement. The report will read the residence field, maintained in infotype 0094 (Residence Status), to determine whether the person is qualified to undergo the substantial presence test and enjoy the tax advantages provided to non-resident aliens. For those employees who are required to undergo the SPT, it is a prerequisite that infotype 0094 (Residence Status) is maintained. The RESIDENCE STATUS field is set to value "A." The report will include only personnel who have IT0094 maintained only if the value of the RESIDENCE STATUS field is "A."

P0000_M10_SVB_PBS	Display Savings Bonds Purchases

For the specified evaluation period, the report evaluates the payroll results and displays the number of savings bonds purchased and their total cost. The bond owners and their beneficiaries are displayed as well. For an employee to be enrolled in the savings bonds purchase program, infotype 103 (Bond Purchases) and infotype 104 (Bond Denominations) should be maintained in the HR Master Data for the employee.

PC_PAYRESULT	Display Payroll Results

You can use this transaction to display and get an overview of the payroll results for specified employee(s) and for a specified payroll run. The Payroll Results table shows the results of the payroll calculations that generated the earning statements and warrants for the specified payroll run. You need to execute this transaction if an employee has warrant issues or requires adjustments. It is a prerequisite that you execute this transaction only after the payroll is completed and results are stored for the required payroll period. Transaction PC00_M99_CLSTR and Transaction S_AHR_61018754 provide the exact same functionality.

PC00	Run Payroll

You can use this transaction to display an area menu related to HCM Payroll. The SAP Easy Access menu tree structure displays the transactions that are related to payroll configuration for all countries.

PC00_M07_STDR	Short-Term/Long-Term Disability Monitoring Report

You can use this transaction to generate a listing of employees who are on short-term disability leave and who may transition into long-term disability leave. Based on the selection criteria, the report extracts data stored in infotype 0021 (Absences). Using the report, you can also get an overview of employees whose short-term disability leave will soon expire. It is a prerequisite that short-term/long-term disability plans are configured prior to executing this report.

PC00_M10_CALC	Payroll Driver (USA)

You can use this transaction to do full payroll runs for the payroll period specified in the selection screen. You can store the results of the payroll run for a later review. The payroll driver will process the statements in the payroll schema specified in the selection screen sequentially, as well as interpret the control tables. The payroll driver interprets and executes the schema in table T52C0 (T52C1) and the existing payroll rules existing in table T52C5. You can also access the payroll driver (US) by executing the report RPCALCU0.

PC00_M10_CALC_SIMU	Simulation Payroll Accounting (USA)

You can use this transaction to simulate a payroll run. This generates a "mock" payroll, which aids in identifying payroll errors, if any. If there are payroll errors, then you should analyze, correct the errors and run the payroll simulation again for the rejected personnel number. This will ensure that payroll errors are corrected. Payroll Simulation does not change the status of the payroll area in the control record. There is a limit on the number of times a specified payroll area can be run for the same payroll period. Hence, it is a suggested best practice to run the payroll in simulation mode until the payroll corrections are completed.

PC00_M10_CDTB	Per Payroll Period – Advance

You can use this transaction to process advance payments. The wage types for advance payments are stored and processed in these infotypes: 0011 (External Bank Transfers), 0014 (Recurring Payments/Deductions), and 0015 (Additional Payments). This transaction generates payment data, which are further processed in Accounting when making advance payments. This transaction is for US payroll only. It is a prerequisite that you have not completed payroll for the payroll period for which you are making these advance payments. Customizing of advance payments should be done such that advance payments are made prior to the payroll run for that period; payroll treats advance payments as already paid.

PC00_M10_CDTC	Payroll Transfer Prelim. Program DTA – USA

This program extracts the payment data from the payroll results and from table BT, which contains the payment information. These payment data are used by the payment medium programs in accounting to create payment mediums. The payment data will be further processed by subsequent programs. You can also use transaction PC00_M10_CDTC (DME Preliminary program) if you want to process payroll within one pay period for qualified advance payment.

PC00_M10_CDTE	Payroll Transfer – Test Transfer

You can use this transaction to create prenotifications in ACH format so that a bank transfer can be facilitated. You use prenotifications to prepare data medium exchange with banks as well to validate bank details for bank transfers.

PC00_M10_CEDT	Payroll Remuneration Statement

You can use this transaction to display or print a payroll remuneration statement. The remuneration statement is a reprint of the stub portion of an employee's pay advice. In the selection screen, if you select the option CHECK ESS, the remuneration statement is not printed for employees who have set the indicator "ESS—do not print" in infotype 0655 (ESS Settings: Remuneration Statement). For those employees, the remuneration statement is available only in the ESS.

PC00_M10_CLAIMS	Claims Processing

You can use this transaction to analyze and investigate the circumstances that created a specific claim. Using this report, you can get details regarding wage type amounts, component breakdown—original period amounts including pre-tax deductions, post-tax deductions, component breakdown—deltas including overpaid wages and overpaid taxes. With these details, the administrator can determine what amounts need to be paid by the employee or can be forgiven. The difference between what taxes were taken and what taxes should have been taken can be determined as well.

It is a suggested best practice to use the Payroll Reconciliation report (PC00_M10_REC) to get an overview and listing of claims for a particular time period. Later you can execute transaction PC00_M10_CLAIMS to determine the reasons for a particular claim.

PC00_M10_CLJN	Payroll Journal

You can use this transaction to display and get an overview of detailed payroll data for the selected employee(s). It is a prerequisite the payroll run should be completed for the selected time period. You can use the payroll journal to identify any errors in the payroll results. You can also structure how you want the payroll journal to be displayed. Transaction S_ALR_87014259 provides the exact same functionality.

PC00_M10_CLMR	US Overpayment Recovery

You can use this transaction to review existing claims that have been generated for employees. You can also execute this transaction to review overpayment details for employees as well as to create employee records in infotype 0909 (US Overpayment Recovery). The records are maintained in infotype 0909 to specify the amount that should be recovered from the employee's payroll during subsequent payroll processing. US Overpayment Recovery is an additional step in payroll processing. You should execute this report after the payroll run has been released for corrections.

PC00_M10_CPL3U0	Garnishment Statistics

For the selected payroll period and area, you can use this transaction to generate and display garnishment statistics. From the output, you can select the line that contains garnishments to get details about the garnishment. In the selection screen, you have the option to select what garnishment status needs to be included in the output list.

PC00_M10_CPRS	PY Reconciliation Report (Scheduler)

You can use this program for the flow control of parallel and distributed reporting. If there are a large number of records to process for payroll reconciliation, it is a suggested best practice to use this splitter program.

PC00_M10_FFOC	Payroll Transfer – Check Printing

You can use this transaction to print prenumbered checks or non-prenumbered checks whose numbers are assigned from a specified number range. You can link these check numbers to the SAP payment document number or to the settlement result. You can also print payment advice notes and payment summaries in the same program run. Transaction PRCU provides the exact same functionality.

PC00_M10_FFOT	Create DME (USA)

You can use this transaction to generate a file containing funds transfer data. This file can be downloaded onto a disk or any other DME and sent to an ACH operator for processing. The payment advice, the DME accompanying sheet, and payment summaries can also be printed during the program run. Transaction PRD1 provides the exact same functionality.

PC00_M10_HRF	Wage Statements with HR Forms

You can use this transaction to print wage statements or remuneration statements on an HR Form for the selected employee(s). In the selection screen, enter the name of the form that you want to print.

PC00_M10_IPIT0	Garnishment – Active->Inactive

You can use this transaction to set the status of a garnishment as "Inactive" or "Released." Only garnishments that have status "Active" can be set to status "Inactive." Garnishments that have status "Active" or "Inactive" can be set to status "Released."

PC00_M10_ IPIT1	Garnishment – Pending->Active

You can use this transaction to change the status of a garnishment from "Pending" to "Active." In the field ACTIVATE WITH BEGIN DATE displayed in the selection screen, you can specify the date on which the status of the selected garnishments needs to be set. If this field is empty, the current date will be chosen as the date of activation. In the field CATEGORY TO BE INCLUDED displayed in the selection screen, you can also select what categories of garnishments need to be included in the selection. Only garnishments with status "Pending" or "Active" and belonging to the garnishment category specified in the selection screen are selected and displayed as output. In the selection screen, if you checkmark the option RUN AS BATCH PROCESSING, a batch input session is created for processing.

PC00_M10_ IPIT2	Garnishment – Delimit

You can use this transaction to delimit a garnishment. In the selection screen, in the field DELIMIT WITH END DATE you can specify on which date the garnishment needs to be delimited. If this field is empty, the current date is taken as the delimitation date. In the field STATUS displayed in the selection screen, you can also select what categories of garnishments need to be included in the selection. Only garnishments that meet the selection criteria are included in the selection. In the selection screen, if you checkmark the option RUN AS BATCH PROCESSING, a batch input session is created for processing.

PC00_M10_ REC	Payroll Reconciliation Report

For the selected time period or payroll period, you can use the Payroll Reconciliation

report to reconcile the payroll results with the tax reporter output and with postings to accounting (FI). By cross-validating with these outputs, you can identify if there are any discrepancies and resolve them.

PC00_M10_ RFFOAVIS	Print Zero Net Advices

You can use this transaction to create notifications for customers and vendors that their payables and receivables balance to zero.

PC00_M10_ UAUTU1	Display Tax Authorities

You can use this transaction to display tax authorities stored in table T5UTZ (Tax Authorities). The results are sorted by authority, state, tax level or county. Transaction S_AHR_61018778 provides the exact same functionality.

PC00_M10_ UBSIU7	Compare BSI Mapping Table with BSI Tax Authority Table

You can use this transaction to compare the entries in table BTXAUTH (standard tax authorities delivered by BSI) with entries in table BTXTAXC (authorities loaded by the customer).

PC00_M99_ ABKRS	Set Payroll Area

You can use this transaction to set the payroll area for payroll processing. This payroll area is used for further payroll processing, for example, payroll release.

PC00_M99_ CALC	Payroll Driver (International)

You can use this transaction, to process international payroll.

PC00_M99_CDTA	Preliminary Program – Data Medium Exchange for Several Payment Runs

This transaction evaluates the payroll results and creates payment data. (Creating payment data is the first step in the wage and salary payment process.) It is a prerequisite that the payroll run has ended for the specified payroll period. Prior to running this program, you should have also completed the following settings: set up the payment method, set up house bank and house bank account, define the sending bank, and where required define the paying company code, and check text keys for payment transactions. You can also use transaction PC00_M99_CDTA to perform qualified advance payment processing.

PC00_M99_CIPC	Check Completeness of Posting

You can use this transaction to display and get an overview of payroll results that were not posted to accounting. In production environment, there should not be any payroll results that are not posted.

PC00_M99_CIPE	Create Posting Run

You can use this transaction to evaluate payroll results and create summarized documents for posting to Accounting (SAP-FI). You should execute this transaction after every payroll run.

PC00_M99_CKTO	Payroll Account (International)

You can use this transaction to create an international payroll account. In this report, it is possible to print several periods at once. You can also create a special column to display the total or average of each wage type.

PC00_M99_CLGA00	Wage Type Statement (International)

For the specified payroll area, time period, employee(s), this transaction displays the wage type distributions based on the payroll data. You also get an overview of the values assigned to these wage types. The displayed results can be sorted based on sort criteria such as organizational assignment or employee name.

PC00_M99_CLGV00	Wage Type Distribution (International)

You can use this transaction to display lists of wage types for multiple payroll periods without considering retroactive accounting differences. The generated list provides an overview of the values assigned to these wage types. In the selection screen, you can specify the selection criteria for the generated list. The sorting criteria can also be specified in the selection screen.

PC00_M99_CLSTPC	Display Cluster PC – Personal Calendar and Cover Table

For the specified calendar year, you can use this transaction to display a cluster PC for an employee or group of employees.

PC00_M99_CLSTR	Display Payroll Results

See transaction PC_PAYRESULT for details.

PC00_M99_CMLI0	Cash Breakdown List Payment (International)

For the specified payroll area, payroll period, or employee(s), this transaction generates the cash breakdown list. If the company code is from a different country, the program will automatically assign the relevant currency.

It is a prerequisite that the notes and coins available in each currency are stored in table 520M.

PC00_M99_ CPRC	Payroll Calendar (International)

You can use this transaction to execute the following:

1. For the specified date, you can schedule jobs related to payroll accounting.
2. For the specified date, you can view jobs that have been scheduled.

Prior to executing this transaction, it is a prerequisite that you have completed the configuration for scheduling setup.

PC00_M99_ CWTR	Wage Type Reporter

You can use this transaction to evaluate the wage types contained in the payroll results for the selected payroll period. Only data from the tables RT (Results Table) and WPBP (Work Place Basic Pay) are evaluated. You can execute this report after the payroll cycle is exited. Transaction S_PH9_46000172 provides the exact same functionality.

PC00_M99_ DKON	Assign Wage Types – Display G/L Accounts

You can use this transaction to get an overview and display the listing of wage types assigned to G/L accounts. The selection can be restricted to criteria such as country grouping, particular wage types, company code and business processes. It is also required that you specify the key date since wage types are time-dependent.

PC00_M99_ DLGA20	Use of Wage Types in Payroll (International)

You can use this transaction to display and get an overview of wage type characteristics for all primary and secondary wage types used in your payroll system. The report displays the meaning of the wage type characteristics as well the personnel areas of the selected country grouping.

PC00_M99_ FPAYM	Create Payment Medium

You can use this transaction to create payments, which have payment methods assigned to a format. It is a prerequisite that payment programs configuration is completed prior to executing this transaction. In the payment programs configuration, you configure the payment methods and how payments are to be made. For example, payments can be made by bill of exchange or by a bank check. Currently, you can use this transaction only to create payment media without documents. You can create the associated payment advices by executing the report RFFOAVIS_FPAYM.

PC00_M99_ MOLGA	Set Personnel Country Grouping

You can use this transaction to set the country grouping for payroll processing, for an employee or group of employees.

PC00_M99_ PA03_CHECK	Check Results

You can use this transaction to set the payroll area status to "Check Payroll Results." In this status, the master data and the payroll area is locked for maintenance. This prevents a new payroll run from being executed.

PC00_M99_ PA03_CORR	Corrections

You can use this transaction to release the payroll area for corrections. Releasing the payroll area for corrections unlocks the HR Master Data; you can then make changes to the employee records to correct payroll errors. After you have completed the corrections, the payroll must be released and the payroll run started for the corrected employees only. You must repeat this process until no payroll errors exist. You can also use transaction PA03 (Maintain Control Record) to release payroll for corrections.

PC00_M99_ PA03_END	Exit Payroll

You can use this transaction to end the payroll for the current period of the payroll run. After doing this, all payroll corrections can be made for this payroll period only by retroactive accounting in the subsequent payroll periods.

PC00_M99_ PA03_RELEA	Release Payroll

You can use this transaction to release the payroll for the payroll period. This will set the payroll area status to "Released for Payroll" in the payroll control record. When the payroll area is in "Released for Payroll" status, master and time data are locked for any maintenance.

PC00_M99_ PAP	Area Menu – Subsequent Activities per Payroll Period

You can use this transaction to display an area menu related to subsequent activities in posting. The SAP Easy Access menu tree structure displays the transactions that are related to Posting to Accounting process, such as Create Posting Run and Generate Posting Run for Payments.

PC00_M99_ PPM	Generate Posting Run – Payments

You can use this transaction to automatically post payments to accounting.

PC00_M99_ TLEA	Annual Leave Listing (International)

You can use this transaction to display the leave overview for an employee or group of employees. The displayed output is dependent on the selection criteria. For example, you can display the total leave for an employee or display the report sorted by leave type. Transaction PC00_M99_TLEA reads the data maintained in infotype 0005 (Leave Entitlement). If employee leaves are maintained in infotype 2006 (Absence Quotas), then report RPTQTA10 (Display Absence Quota Information) needs to be executed.

PC00_M99_ TLEA30	Annual Leave Update (International)

For a given time period, you can use this transaction to create leave entitlements (infotype 0005) for an employee or group of employees. The leave type and amount of entitlements are determined by the configuration setting you have specified. If required, you can create the leave entitlements as a batch input.

PC00_M99_ U510	Pay Scale Increase (International)

You can use this transaction to make pay scale changes. In the selection screen, you can determine whether pay scale changes should be based on percentage rate or a constant base amount. In the selection screen, you can specify the rounding amount, rounding type (up/down) as well. All pay scale changes are made to table T510 (Pay Scale Groups) and are automatically written to a transport request.

PC00_M99_ UDIR	Restructure Payroll Directory

If the payroll directory is destroyed or is inconsistent, you can use this transaction to re-create the payroll directory. In the selection screen, if you select the option DETAILED LOG, the following will be displayed:

1. The new payroll directory.

2. Comparison of data (if you have selected the option COMPARE DIRECTORY).

3. Payroll results structure (if you have selected the option payroll results structure).

PC00_M99_ URMC	Run Remittance Completeness Check

You can use this transaction for each payroll area to get a listing of personnel numbers with incomplete third-party remittances. The selection screen provides three options to check remittance completeness:

1. Employees and payroll results not yet evaluated.

2. All payee items that have been evaluated but not posted.

3. All posting runs in transaction PCP0 that are not released yet.

Refer to SAP Note 734483—MSC: Remittance Completeness Check for more details about this transaction.

PC00_M99_ URMD	Undo Third-Party Remittance Runs

You can use this transaction to undo or delete all remittance documents produced by evaluation runs, posting runs, acknowledgement runs, and all third-party remittance runs. You should execute this report whenever you evaluate and discover that an evaluation run has written incorrect data to the tables. Prior to executing in production mode, it is a suggested best practice to execute in test mode, which will display which data will be deleted in a productive run.

PC00_M99_ URME	Run Remittance Evaluation

You can use this transaction to provide an overview and update the third-party remittance tables in the SAP system. The third-party remittance process handles the posting and payment information for third parties such as garnishment recipients, benefits providers, and tax authorities.

PC00_M99_ URMP	Create Third-Party Remittance Posting Run

You can use this transaction to extract remittance items from third-party remittance tables and create a posting run. The posting run provides an overview of financial posting information. You can review and examine the remittance documents, release and post it to FI. It is recommended that you run this report daily.

PC00_M99_ URMR	Third-Party Remittance Reconciliation

You can use this transaction to get an overview of all third-party remittances that have been evaluated, posted, or paid. The generated list also provides information such as receipt of posting, payee item details, acknowledgement and payment of posting. The generated list is dependent on the data entered in the selection screen.

PC00_M99_ URMU	Store Third-Party Remittance Evaluation Run

The program RPCALC collects data pertaining to third-party remittance from an existing payroll run and creates two temporary sequential (TemSe) objects. The TemSe objects contain:

1. Cumulated remittance: sum total of all remittance data

2. Individual remittance: contains detailed, employee related remittance data

You can use this transaction to update remittance tables with data from these two TemSe files. You must select both files for a successful execution of the transaction.

PC00_M99_ URMW	Third-Party Check Processing Classes

This program verifies that wage types have been assigned the correct processing class type in processing class 78. If there is an incorrect assignment, the program will correct the error by assigning the correct processing class type or it will prompt you to make the correction. It is a prerequisite that you have completed the configuration to set up HR creditors for regular remittance and tax remittance prior to running this report. If you execute this transaction as a test run, a log of which wage types are required to be changed will be displayed.

PC00_MNA_ CC_ADM	Cost Center Report – Administrator

You can use this report to display the costs incurred for each employee, per wage component, per posting period. By default, the report output is sorted by Cost Center, employee, cost element, wage component, and posting date. Using this report, you can get an overview of charges incurred on a Cost Center, as well facilitate cost planning. To execute this report, infotype 105, subtype 0001 should be set up for the user who will be executing this report. This will enable the Cost Center manager to access the information. The feature 10CCM must be configured for each Cost Center manager. A similar report is available for Cost Center managers. Payroll posting must be completed for the selection period prior to executing this report. It is a suggested best practice to run this report regularly to balance FI postings with the Payroll Reconciliation report (PC00_M10_REC).

PC10	Payroll Menu USA

You can use this transaction to display an area menu related to HCM Payroll (US). The SAP Easy Access menu tree structure displays the transactions that are related to US Payroll Configuration.

PCP0	Edit Posting Runs

You can use this transaction to verify the correctness of payroll, payments, and third-party remittance documents and also to ensure that these are posted correctly. The status of the documents will be "Created." It is a prerequisite that Create Posting Run (PC00_M99_CIPE), Generate Posting Run-Payments (PC00_M99_PPM), and Run Remittance Evaluation (PC00_M99_URME) are completed prior to executing this transaction. It is a suggested best practice to execute this transaction daily.

PDF7	Delete Form in Customer Client

You can use this transaction to delete a form from a customer client. Using this transaction you can only maintain one form at a time.

PDF8	Copy Form from SAP Client

You can use this transaction to copy forms from client 000 to customer client.

PDF9	Copy Forms within Customer Client

You can use this transaction to copy a form within customer client.

PDSY	HR Documentation Maintenance

You can use this transaction to display and (where required) maintain documentation on an HR object in a contextual environment. For example, you can maintain documentation on a personnel calculation rule, function, or an operation. In an SAP system, no object should exist without a corresponding documentation and no documentation can exist if the corresponding object does not exist.

PE01	HR – Maintain Payroll Schemas

You can use this transaction to create, maintain, and display the payroll schemas. The payroll schema consists of processing steps that are executed in a specific order. In the schema directory, you can list and get an overview of all the schemas in the system. You can restrict the selection based on the entries in the selection screen. The SAP-delivered US schema is U000.

PE02	HR – Maintain Calculation Rules

You can use this transaction to create, maintain, and display payroll calculation rules. These rules link the employee and the employee sub-grouping to a set of wage types and wage type rules, which aids in payroll processing.

PE51	HR Form Editor

You can use this transaction to design and create HR Forms. These forms are process-based and can be used in self-services applications. You can also use or edit delivered forms that are available. You can use the HR Form Editor to design forms that are related to payroll, for example, wage type statements or remuneration statements.

PEST	Maintenance of Process Model

You can use this transaction to create and maintain different process models that are required for off-cycle subsequent processing. Some of the process models that are required for subsequent processing are off-cycle payroll runs, replace payments, reverse payments, etc. It is a suggested best practice that you copy SAP-delivered process models into customer space and customize them to meet your requirements.

PRCU	Payroll Transfer – Check Printing

See transaction PC00_M10_FFOC for details.

PRD1	Create DME (USA)

See transaction PC00_M10_FFOT for details.

PU01   Delete Current Payroll Result

You can use this transaction to delete the payroll result of an employee. (You can delete the payroll result of one employee only.)

PU19   Tax Reporter

You can use this transaction to generate, in the prescribed format, payroll tax and other reports that are required for government filing. Using Tax Reporter, the following reports can be generated: Form W-2 (Wage and Tax Statement), Form W2-C, 1099-R, 1099-RC, Form 940 (Employer's Annual Federal Unemployment Tax Return), Form 941 (Employer's Quarterly Federal Tax Return), Form 941C, multiple worksite reports (required for the US Bureau of Labor Statistics), and unemployment insurance reports for all states in the US.

PU30   Wage Type Maintenance

For the selected country grouping, you can use this transaction to create customer wage types by copying a model wage type. You can also use this transaction to delimit or delete wage types or to do a completeness check of the wage types in your system. SAP recommends that you do not delete model wage types. When you copy a model wage type to a customer wage type, the system will also copy the documentation of the model wage type. You can edit and maintain the copied documentation by using transaction PDSY (HR Documentation Maintenance).

PU98   Assign Wage Types to
             Wage Type Groups

The customer wage types that you created using transaction PU30 (Wage Type Maintenance) get assigned to the same wage type group as the model wage type, by default. You can use this transaction to assign customer wage types to wage type groups. You can

also use this transaction to delete wage type groups assignments of customer wage types, display all wage types that are not assigned, and display wage type groups containing the assignments. A wage type can be assigned to one or more wage type groups at the same time.

PUFK   Form Manager

You can use this transaction to edit and maintain several forms at once.

PUOC_10   Off-Cycle Workbench (USA)

This transaction provides functionalities for off-cycle payroll processing. For example, using this transaction, you can generate an off-cycle check for one or several employee(s). There is simulation available that you can use to perform a test run.

PUOCBA   Off-Cycle Batch –
               Subsequent Activity

You can use this transaction to obtain a listing that shows what processes the system will use for subsequent processing of off-cycle payroll, payment replacement, or reversals. If an employee's check is cancelled but is getting processed as void, refer to SAP Note 160515 – OCP: Off-Cycle Cancellations, Reversals Versus Voids for details on how to mitigate this error.

PUST   HR Process Workbench

You can use this transaction to perform the following tasks: create processes required for payroll processing based on specific process models; execute the processes immediately or schedule it for later processing or based on an event; repeat the processes or the individual process steps again; send email notifications to the concerned team about the status of the process execution; check the status of the process execution and correct errors where required; complete and delete the processes where required.

S_AHR_61016142	Tax Infotype Summary

For the specified employee and reporting period, this report provides a summary of all tax infotypes and related data. A checkmark is highlighted against each infotype for which a record is maintained for the specified time period.

S_AHR_61016146	Garnishment Details Report

For the selected payroll period and area, you can use this report to generate a list of employees whose wages are garnished. In the output, garnishment-related details are also displayed for the selected employees. The report uses the payroll results as its basis.

S_AHR_61016148	Workers Compensation Report

You can use this report to calculate the workers compensation (WC) wages and premiums. The report calculates the WC wages and premiums per pay date; hence, the reporting period in the selection screen should cover at least one pay date. It is a prerequisite that you have completed the configuration for workers compensation.

S_AHR_61018754	Display Payroll Results

See transaction PC_PAYRESULT for details.

S_AHR_61018777	Taxability Models/Tax Types by Tax Authority

You can use this report to get an expanded listing of taxability model for each tax authority. As displayed in the selection screen, you can get an output in any one of these three types:

▶ A – displays a list of tax types per tax authority.

▶ B – displays a list of all tax authorities without a tax model.

▶ C – displays a list of tax models that are used by an authority but not defined in table T5UTM.

In the selection screen, you can select the report type that you want to use for the list output.

S_AHR_61018778	Display Tax Authorities

See PC00_M10_UAUTU1.

S_ALR_87014136	Paydays on Holidays or Weekends

For the calendar year specified in the selection screen, the report creates a list of all paydays. If the payday falls on a weekend or a holiday, it is flagged in the payday list as Sa, Su, or Hol. It is a prerequisite that paydays are defined and set up in table T549S.

S_ALR_87014137	Payday Calendar

You can use this report to create a payday calendar for the calendar year specified in the selection screen.

S_ALR_87014259	Payroll Journal

See transaction PC00_M10_CLJN for details.

S_PH9_46000172	Wage Type Reporter

See transaction PC00_M99_CWTR for details.

S_PH9_ 46000232	Tip Income and Allocated Tips Report

You can use this report to print and submit Form 8027—Employer's Annual Information Return of Tip Income and Allocated Tips. It is a prerequisite that you have completed the configuration in the IMG for Define establishments for tip processing. The settings you make in the IMG are reflected in the output of Form 8027.

S_PH9_ 46000233	Pensionable Earning and Hours Report

The report evaluates the payroll results to calculate and determine: Pensionable earnings and hours, Social Security wages, Social Security taxes, employee pre-tax contribution, employee post-tax contribution, and employer contribution. The results are written to table T7USBENPE (Pensionable Earnings and Hours). It is a prerequisite that you have configured and set up a gross compensation model for pensionable earnings and a gross compensation model for pensionable hours.

S_PH9_ 46000360	Exemption Expiration Report

For the selected reporting period, this report provides a listing of employees whose tax exemptions are due to expire soon. This report is important since many countries and states do not allow automatic renewal of employees' tax exemptions. Employees' tax exemptions are maintained in infotype 0210 (W-4 Withholding Info).

S_PH9_ 46000361	W-4 Withholding Allowance Report

This report evaluates an employee's infotype 0210 (W-4 Withholding Info) and provides a listing where employees have claimed more allowances than allowed by that tax authority; more allowances than the values maintained in infotype 0161 (IRS Mandates) for that tax authority; and have a filing status different from the filing status maintained in infotype 0161 (IRS Mandates).

11.12 Others

HRUSER	Set Up and Maintain ESS Users

You can use this transaction to set up and maintain authorizations for your employees who will be provided access to the ESS. All activities that are executed using this transaction are recorded in a log, which can be displayed and reset, when required.

LPD_CUST	Launchpad Customizing

You can use this transaction to make configuration settings for the ESS launchpad. The settings can be made by an administrator for all users or by a user. Settings made by a user are specific to that user only.

POWL_ CAT	Maintain POWL Categories

You can use this transaction to create default categories. These categories will be used to assign default queries.

POWL_ QUERY	Maintain POWL Query Definition

You can use this transaction to create default queries or worklists. Using this transaction, you can also create layout variants.

POWL_ QUERYR	Maintain POWL Query Role Assignment

You can use this transaction to make queries (created using transaction POWL_QUERY) active for a user group or for an entire application. Using this transaction, you can also assign categories (created using transaction POWL_CAT) or organize the sequence of queries.

POWL_ QUERYU	Maintain POWL Query User Assignment

You can use this transaction to make queries active for a specific user.

POWL_ TYPE	Maintain POWL Type Definition

You can use this transaction to register the newly created POWL feeder classes. You will be required to create a type ID and fill in all necessary data.

PU22	HR Archiving

You can use this transaction to create archiving groups. After you have created the archiving group, you can use the functions available in the menu for further archive processing.

SIMG_ SPORT	IMG Business/ Functional Packages

You can use this transaction to access the business and functional packages that are related to MSS configuration.

SOTR_ EDIT	OTR: Maintain Initial Screen

You can use this transaction to create OTR texts. OTR texts created using this transaction are shorter than 255 characters. These OTR texts are displayed in the user interface and can be re-used multiple times.

12   Basis System

AL03	Operating System Alert Monitor

This transaction is obsolete. Refer to SAP Note 953552 – CCMS: Obsolete Transactions Deleted for more details. The functionality offered by this transaction is replaced by CCMS: Monitoring Architecture and by transaction RZ20.

AL05	Monitor Current Workload

See transaction RZ20 for details.

AL08	Users Logged On

You can use this transaction to get a listing of all users who are currently logged into the SAP landscape. The SAP active instance, the client, the user name, the terminal and the transaction (currently being executed) are displayed as well.

AL11	Display SAP Directories

You can use this transaction to display all directories in the SAP landscape. You can use the report to view and browse the directory structure. In the screen (where the report is rendered), you can click the CONFIGURE button to maintain the individual directories.

AL12	Display Table Buffer (Exp. Session)

You can use this transaction to get an overview of the buffers in an instance (the instance you are working on). The different buffers in the instance, the size of the buffers, the free bytes that are available, and the efficiency are displayed in the report. In the screen (where the

report is rendered), you can click the REFRESH button to get an updated display of results. Every application server has buffers allocated to it. You can change the size of the buffers for performance optimization.

AL13	Display Shared Memory (Expert Mode)

You can use this transaction to provide a display of the shared memory segments. The report displays the shared memory size, the address range of the memory segment, and the name of the shared memory. The date and time when the report is generated is displayed in the report title.

AL15	Customize SAPOSCOL Destination

You can use this transaction to manage existing logical destinations that call up RFCOSCOL. You can access transaction SM59 – RFC Destinations (Display/Maintain) from AL15 landing screen. In the AL15 screen, click the button NEW RFC DESTINATION; this will take you to the SM59 landing screen. From transaction SM59 landing screen, you can test the connection to RFCOSCOL.

AL19	Remote File System Monitor

This transaction is obsolete. Refer to SAP Note 953552 – CCMS: Obsolete Transactions Deleted for more details.

ALRTCATDEF	Editing Alert Categories

You can use this transaction to configure alert processing. Using this transaction, you can create long and short text, alert priority, optional subsequent actions, etc. for the alert. To make custom settings for alert processing (for all categories), in the ALERT CATEGORIES DISPLAY (CENTRAL ALERT SERVER) screen, choose SETTINGS • CONFIGURATION from the menu. This will take you to the DISPLAY VIEW ALERTS: CONFIGURATION: DETAILS screen, where you can make the required settings for:

► Inbound Processing – The user will be able to confirm alerts by SMS or email.
► Status Handling with Mails – The user can specify which statuses are to be reported.
► Logging – The user can create a log containing additional information while processing alerts. You can view this log using transaction SLG1 (object ALERT).

It is a prerequisite that the required authorizations are assigned to the user who is creating and maintaining alerts/alert categories.

ALRTMON	Alert Monitor

You can use this transaction to monitor the alerts that belong to the alert category MPA_TEMPLATE. You can enter the time period for which you want to monitor the alerts in the selection screen.

ALRTPROC	Process Alerts

Administrators are frequently flooded with alerts or messages about a failed job. You are also required to confirm such alerts. You can use this transaction to process such types of alerts.

BALE	Area Menu for Administration

You can use this transaction to display an area menu related to ALE Administration. The SAP Easy Access menu tree structure displays the transactions that are related to ALE Administration.

BD22	Delete Change Pointers

You can use this transaction to delete change pointers from database tables. In the selection screen, you can select to delete OBSOLETE CHANGE POINTERS (change pointers that are created in the specified date range), or PROCESSED CHANGE POINTERS (change pointers that have been processed in the specified date range).

BD54	Maintaining Logical Systems

You can use this transaction to create and maintain logical systems in the ECC. While creating, you enter the name of the logical system and a short text.

BD87	Status Monitor for ALE Messages

You can use this transaction to re-process a failed IDoc. In the selection screen, you can select an IDoc by using the IDoc number, the error number, the message type, etc. You can use transaction BD87 to re-process inbound IDocs only, and you cannot re-process a successful IDoc. The system retains the IDoc number, even after re-processing by transaction BD87.

BDLS	Convert Logical System Names

You can use this transaction to convert the logical system name to a new name. The logical system name should exist and be maintained to perform the conversion. If you are performing a logical system conversion, then all IDocs need to be processed too (because the logical system name can be included in the IDoc data record). To perform the conversion, you need to be assigned the authorization object B_ALE_LSYS. SAP recommends not making the system name conversion by directly changing the name in the tables. Doing so may lead to inconsistencies.

CMOD Enhancements

You can use this transaction to create projects and to activate/deactivate enhancements. Every enhancement is attached to a project (an enhancement can be assigned to one and only one project) and you can use CMOD to group those enhancements. Using CMOD, you can display and get an overview of all enhancements and function exits contained in an activated project.

DB01 Analyze Exclusive
  Lockwaits

You can use this transaction to monitor database locks that are created during a read/write or delete on the database table. With this monitoring, you can identify the deadlocks and mitigate them. Refer to SAP Note 806342 – FAQ: Analyzing Exclusive Database Locks on SQL Server, for more details about database locks and lockwaits.

DB02 Tables and Indexes
  Monitor

You can use this transaction to analyze and monitor database objects such as tables and indexes. Using this transaction, you can collect statistics such as database growth and size of the table spaces, check for missing indexes and size of the indexes, and look for space critical objects. This transaction is being replaced by transaction DBACOCKPIT.

DB03 Parameter Changes
  in Database

You can use this transaction to display and maintain the active database parameters. Using this transaction, you can check the status and the validity of these parameters. You will be able to display the history of these parameters as well. The functionality of transaction DB03 is similar to transaction DB26.

DB05 Analysis of a Table
  According to Index

You can use this transaction to determine whether adding another column(s) to the index will improve the selectivity of the index. You can also determine what sequence of fields provides the best selectivity. Transaction DB05 reads the full table to perform the analysis. If the table is large, then a full table read will be expensive.

DB11 Create Database
  Connection

Usually, database connections are created during installation. When required, you can create new database connections or maintain existing connections. You can use this transaction to create a new database connection. For creating a new database connection, you will be required to enter the name of the database connection, database connection information, and the user data.

DB12 DBA Backup Logs

This transaction is primarily used if you are using MS-SQL*Server as the database. You can use this transaction to collect and get an overview of information that is required to monitor database backups. This is an important transaction for database administrators (DBAs) who are responsible for database backups. For non MS-SQL*Server databases, you can use transaction DB12_MSS, which performs the same function.

DB13 DBA Planning Calendar

You can use this transaction to plan and schedule backups. Using this transaction, you can view the tasks scheduled for the day or for a specific date. You can also view the job log and action logs and get an overview of the status of the job or any other statistics.

DB14	Display DBA Operation Logs

Many Basis administrators use BRTOOLS for their daily DBA activities. These BRTOOLS create a daily log file, which records the activities and their status (succeed, warnings, failed). You can use transaction DB14 to access those logs. In the log, you can highlight particular records and get a detailed overview.

DB15	Data Archiving – Database Tables

You can use this transaction to schedule data archiving, using one of the following:

► Find archiving objects that will delete records from the specified database table.

► Display database space information for those tables that were included in archiving.

► Use the archiving object and branch to archive administration to schedule a data archive.

► List tables that were accessed when using a specific archiving object. You can delete data from these tables after archiving them to a file. You can list all tables that were accessed, including tables whose data were archived.

DB24	Administrative Database Operations

This transaction is obsolete and is no longer supported by SAP.

DB26	DB Profile: Monitor and Configuration

You can use this transaction to change and maintain the Oracle database parameters. Using this transaction, you can also check the status and validity of the Oracle database parameters, as well display its history. This transaction provides similar functionality as transaction DB03

DBACOCKPIT	Start DBA Cockpit

You can use this transaction to monitor and perform database administration. This transaction is platform independent (i.e., you can administer any database technology), and the user interface provides options to perform any aspect of database administration. You can refer to SAP Note 1072066 – DBA Cockpit: New Function for DB Monitoring for details about the transaction DBACOCKPIT. The transaction DBACOCKPIT replaces individual monitors like ST04 (DB Performance Monitor) and DB02 (Tables and Indexes Monitor).

DBCO	Database Connection Maintenance

You can use this transaction to maintain the systems table DBCON. SAP maintains information about the additional non-standard database connections in this table. You can use this transaction to create new information or maintain/delete existing information.

FILE	Cross-Client File Names/Paths

You can use this transaction to define a logical path name and cross-client logical file name. Using transaction SF01 (Client-Specific File Name), you can create a client-specific logical file name. The client-specific logical file name overrides the cross-client logical file name. Hence, in any client, it is essential that you delete any client-specific logical file names, which are not required. You can call transactions FILE and SF01 directly from transaction SARA (Archive Administration). In the initial screen of SARA, click the button Customizing. A dialog box is displayed where you can select the options Cross-Client File Names/Paths or Client-Specific File Names.

ICON	Display Icons

You can use this transaction to maintain and display a list of all icons in the SAP system. You can get a list of icons in the SAP system by executing the program SHOWICON using transaction SE38 or SA38.

LICENSE_ ADMIN	License Administration Workbench (LAW)

You can use this transaction to collect and consolidate license relevant measurement data, such as the number of users and number of engines being used. These data are collected from the component systems as well the central system from where LAW is run. These data are an important component of the license audit process.

LSMW	Legacy System Migration Workbench

LSMW is a cross-platform component of the SAP system. You can use LSMW for data migration from legacy/non-SAP systems to an SAP system. LSMW can be used to read data from spreadsheets, sequential files, etc., convert data from source to the target format, and import data into the SAP system.

OS01	LAN Check with Ping

You can use this transaction to conduct a performance check of the network connections to the different hosts in the network. The SAP program PING is used to determine the minimum/maximum/average transfer time for data packets and number of lost PING data packets.

OS06N	Operating System Activity Monitor

You can use this transaction to display OS data for the application server of the current SAP system. This transaction provides functionality similar to transaction ST06N.

OS07	Remote Operating System Activity Monitoring

This transaction provides functionality similar to transaction ST06. Refer to transaction ST06 for details. SAP recommends that you use transaction OS07N for remote operating system activity monitoring, rather than transaction OS07.

OS07N	Remote Operating System Activity Monitoring

This transaction is used for operating system monitoring. Compared to other operating system monitoring transactions such as ST06 or OS07, this transaction provides better usability, offers flexible options to collect history data, and displays data accurately in virtual OS environments.

Refer to SAP Note 1084019 – OS07N New Operating System Monitor for details about transaction OS07N. SAP recommends using transaction OS07N if you experience problems with transactions ST06 or OS07. Refer to SAP Note 994025 – Virtualized OS Environments in the Operating System Monitor for details about transactions OS06N, OS07N and ST06N.

OSS1	Logon to SAPNet

You can use this transaction to download the required SAP Notes from the SAP Service Marketplace. This transaction can be used for SAP support connection as well. This transaction is obsolete and is no longer supported by SAP. It is recommended that you use SAP Solution Manager to perform these functionalities.

OY19	Customizing Cross-System Viewer

See transaction SCU0 for details.

PFCG	Role Maintenance

You can use this transaction to create and maintain authorizations, roles and profiles in the SAP systems. Refer to SAP Note 113290 – PFCG: Merge Process when Maintaining Authorization Data for details about maintenance of authorization data using transaction PFCG.

It is a suggested best practice that you do not use transaction SU02: Maintain Authorization Profiles to manually edit or maintain profiles. SAP recommends that you use transaction PFCG for profile generation and administration. Similarly, it is a suggested best practice not to use transaction SU03: Maintain Authorizations for manual authorization administration. SAP recommends that you use transaction PFCG for all authorization administration.

PFUD	User Master Data Reconciliation

You can use this transaction to perform user master comparison for selected roles. (You can enter the roles in the selection screen.) In the selection screen, if you select the option DISPLAY LOG, the errors and warnings are displayed in a dialog box after the report is executed.

RZ01	Job Scheduling Monitor

This transaction is obsolete and is no longer supported as of Basis Release 7.20. Refer to SAP Note 1257300 – RZ01: Job Scheduling Monitor is no Longer Available for details.

RZ02	Network Graphics for SAP Instances

This transaction is obsolete. Refer to SAP Note – 953552 CCMS: Obsolete Transactions Deleted for details.

RZ03	Presentation, Control SAP Instances

You can use this transaction to start the control panel. The control panel provides you with an overview of systems activity in your landscape. Using this transaction, you can get an overview of the application server name, server services, statuses, and active operation type. You can sort the results by server name or by status (active/inactive).

RZ04	Maintain SAP Instances

You can use this transaction to maintain instance definition. You are required to maintain instance definition if a new server is added, if the server name is changed, or if the profiles are changed. (Profiles are files that contain instance configuration information.) It is a prerequisite that you have the required authorization to maintain instances.

RZ06	Alerts Thresholds Maintenance

This transaction is obsolete. Refer to SAP Note 953552 – CCMS: Obsolete Transactions Deleted for details.

RZ08	SAP Alert Monitor

This transaction is obsolete. Refer to SAP Note 953552 – CCMS: Obsolete Transactions Deleted for details.

RZ10	Maintain Profile Parameters

You can use this transaction to create and copy profiles. Profiles can be created either as BASIC MAINTENANCE or as EXTENDED

MAINTENANCE. Profiles are operating system files and contain instance setup information. To create and maintain profiles, you should have the authorization object S_RZL_ADM (Computing Center Management System Administration) assigned to your authorization profile.

RZ11   Maintain Profile Parameters

You can use this transaction to enter the profile parameter attributes and the parameter documentation. You must create and maintain parameter documentation for each profile parameter.

RZ12   Maintain RFC Server Group Assignment

You can use this transaction to create and maintain RFC Server Groups. The CCMS: RFC SERVER GROUP MAINTENANCE screen displays the name of the existing RFC Group (displayed as LOGON GROUP), the list of servers in the SAP system (displayed as INSTANCE), and the current status of the server. To define a new RFC group, in the menu select EDIT • CREATE ASSIGNMENT. By defining RFC groups, you can specify which servers can be used by parallel processed jobs. This aids in optimizing SAP systems resources usage.

RZ15   Read XMI Log

You can use this transaction to display and get an overview of the XMI log files maintained in the SAP systems. Based on the search filter entered in the selection screen, the XMI log files are displayed in the report output.

RZ20   CCMS Monitoring

You can use this transaction to start the alert monitor. Normally, the alert monitor monitors the system where you start it. To monitor multiple and remote systems, you need to identify one system as the central monitoring system. You then add the other systems to the alert monitor in the central monitoring system. As per SAP Note 626771 – CCMS Performance Menu: Obsolete Menu Entry, transaction AL05 (Monitor current workload) is obsolete and is replaced by transaction RZ20.

RZ21   CCMS Monitoring Arch. Customizing

You can use this transaction to configure a Central Monitoring System (CEN). In CEN, you can use this transaction to create the CSMREG user, activate background dispatching, activate central system dispatching, and create CSMCONF file for agents.

RZ23N   Central Performance History (CPH)

You can use this transaction to save the performance values of the monitored systems and to display them as reports (at a later date) or for comparisons with the earlier saved data. Using this transaction, you can create the report definitions, schedule the reports as jobs, select the performance attributes that need to be saved in the CPH, and define how long the performance values need to be saved in CPH. It is a suggested best practice that CPH exist only in the central monitoring system. Transaction RZ23 (Central Performance History Reports) is obsolete and is replaced by RZ23N.

RZ70   SLD Administration

You can use this transaction for local administration of the SLD directory. The following functions can be performed:

1. You can register a technical system in the SLD.

2. Using the RFC connection, an ABAP-based SLD data supplier, you can send data about

an ABAP system to the SLD bridge by means of a SAP gateway.

3. You can schedule a data supplier as a periodic batch job and set a time interval to collect data about the current system.

The default time interval for data collection is 720 minutes. (You can see this default setting in the RZ70 screen.) With this setting, the data will be updated in the SLD twice every day.

SA38   ABAP Reporting

You can use this transaction to run (execute) programs or reports in SAP. Using this transaction, you can also execute a program in the background. To be able to access and execute this transaction, you need to have the authorization object S_PROGRAM assigned to the user.

SAINT   Add-On Installation Tool

You can use this transaction to install and upgrade add-ons or install a preconfigured system (SAP Best Practices applications) directly from the SAP system. This is very helpful because you are not required to restart the system or access the operating system to install the add-ons. The SAINT user interface is available in English or German only.

SALE   Display ALE Customizing

You can use this transaction to display the IMG customizing steps related to the IDoc interface and ALE.

SARA   Archive Administration

You can use this transaction to initiate the archiving of data. Once the archiving is completed, an archiving file will be created; you can also delete the archived data from the database in one step. SAP systems also create a log describing the reasons that some of the objects were not archived. The system logs provide detailed information about the archiving session.

SARI   Archive Information System

You can use this transaction to retrieve previously archived files. SARI is an SAP tool that facilitates access to the previously archived data in SAP.

SCAT   Computer Aided Test Tool

You can use this transaction to record a test script in SAP. You can also use this transaction to execute test cases remotely by specifying a valid RFC destination. To execute test cases in the remote system, you need to have the authorization object S_DEVELOP assigned to your profile.

SCC1   Client Copy – Special Selections

You can use this transaction to transport change requests from one client to another in the same server. You are not required to release the transport request.

SCC3   Client Copy Log

You can use this transaction to perform an analysis of the client copy and transport log. The transaction displays the jobs that are completed or currently being processed. Double-click a specific job to see more details about the job. After a successful client copy, if you see the error: "tp status incorrect/ unknown" on the SCC3 landing screen, refer to SAP Note 624069 – CC-Info: tp Status Incorrect/Unknown for more details.

SCC4   Client Administration

You can use this transaction to create new clients in your landscape, and/or to maintain clients that exist in your landscape. You need to have required authorization to create new clients.

SCC5	Delete Client

You can use this transaction to delete a client in your landscape. To delete a client, you need to have authorization object S_CLNT_IMP assigned to you.

SCC7	Post-Client Import Methods

After a client import, you should perform post processing activities in the target client. The post processing activities are performed to adapt the runtime environment to the current state of data. It is a suggested best practice to execute transaction SCC7 in the target client. (You can also execute transaction SCC7 by remotely logging in from the source client.)

SCC8	Client Export

You can use this transaction to transport clients between systems. You can create up to three transport requests. The output will contain the names of the transports that are to be imported. In transaction SCC8, the data export is asynchronous. Therefore, you should not perform any other client copy until the export is completed. Using transaction SE01 (Transport Organizer—Extended View), you can check the status of the client export.

SCC9	Remote Client Copy

Copying a client between two different systems is known as remote client copy. You can use a remote client copy to transfer customizing and other data between two systems. In a remote client copy, the data are transferred directly by an RFC interface; hence, it is a good idea to test the RFC connections prior to initiating the copy. If you have issues with transaction SCC9, refer to SAP Note 557132

– CC-Topic: Remote Client Copy. The note describes the prerequisites and how to use the remote client copy.

SCCL	Local Client Copy

You can execute this transaction in the target client to transport user master records and authorization profiles from other clients. In preparation for the client copy, in the source client you need to perform the following: all users (except system administrators) need to be locked, and all background jobs that were released need to be cancelled.

SCMA	Schedule Manager – Scheduler

You can use this transaction to schedule an entire task list for processing, in the scheduler. The tasks in the task plan appear in the calendar with details about when they are scheduled for processing. You can refer to SAP Note 451999 – Schedule Manager: Overview of New Functions for details about the functionalities in Schedule Manager.

SCMP	View/Table Comparison

You can use this transaction to compare a table between two different clients. This transaction is particularly useful to confirm whether all the transports made from one client to another are complete and whether the clients are now identical. You can filter the results based on your selection criteria.

SCON	SAPConnect Administration

You can use this transaction to configure and maintain communication types, conversion rules, protocols, etc. These configurations ensure communications between the SAP system and outside systems, such as telefax. The transaction can also be used for administration purposes such as maintaining inbound distribution, scheduling send processes, etc.

SCOT SAPConnect Administration

Refer to transaction SCON for details.

SCU0 Customizing Cross-System Viewer

You can use this transaction to compare system settings, IMG/customizing settings between two clients. The selection page has a number of options that you can use to build your selection criteria. Transaction OY19 provides the same functionality. Refer to SAP Note 18611 – Table Evaluation (OY19, RSTBSERV): Quest. Problem for details about transaction SCU0 and OY19. The SAP Note explains common problems with the table compare function.

SCU3 Table History

You can use this transaction to display and view existing logs for tables and customizing objects. It is a suggested best practice to activate the logging of changes to table data for those tables that are identified as critical for audits. The downside is that if logging is activated, there is a cost: it will slow down system performance. You can execute report RSTBHIST to display a list of tables where logging is activated. Refer to SAP Note 1916 – Logging Table Changes in R/3 for details about logging table changes.

SCUA Central User Administration

You can use this transaction to create Central User Administration. When you create CUA, the partner profiles are created automatically, the appropriate ALE model is created, and text comparison is started. You can use Central User Administration to create and maintain user master records centrally in one system. This provides an overview of all user data in the landscape in one central system. Any change to the user master record is distributed to the child systems.

SCUG Transfer Users

This is a useful transaction if you are using Central User Administration (CUA). If a new SAP system is added to the distribution model, you can use this transaction to transfer the user master records in the new system to the central system. You can use transaction SCUL to view and validate the distribution of the users after the transfer.

SCUL Central User Administration Log

You can use this transaction to display the distribution logs for the Central User Administration. When a company address or the user master data are changed in the CUA central system, the change is replicated and distributed to the child systems attached to the central system. The log gives an overview of the status of the IDoc distribution; the log output displays whether the change to the user data or company address has been successfully distributed to the child systems.

SCUM Central User Administration

This is a useful transaction if you are using central user administration (CUA). You can use the distribution parameters available in this transaction to get an overview of where the user master record and its individual parts are maintained. If you are using CUA, refer to these SAP Notes: 159885 – CUA: Collective note for Central User Administration, 313945 – CUA: Incorrect Logon Locks not Globally Reversible, and 862937 – SCUM: Initial Password Can Be Changed Everywhere.

SDBE Explain an SQL Statement

You can use this transaction to get details about the cost and resources used to execute an SQL statement. These details provide an overview of the performance of the SQL statement and are very helpful to fine tune and improve the performance of the SQL statement.

SDCCN   Service Data Control Center

You can use this transaction to support the preparation and delivery of SAP service sessions, such as GoingLive and SAP EarlyWatch Alert (EWA). In this transaction, non-ABAP systems are also supported. The new Service Data Control Center (SDCCN) supersedes the old Service Data Control Center (SDCC). If you are using the old Service Data Control Center (SDCC), it must be deactivated prior to activating the new Service Data Control Center (SDCCN). Refer to SAP Note 792941 – Maintenance of Transaction SDCC or SDCCN for details on how to maintain SDCCN (or SDCC) for your basis release.

SE01   Transport Organizer (Extended View)

You can use this transaction to start the transport organizer, where you can perform the following activities that are available in the various tab pages: display requests and tasks (DISPLAY); display, edit and maintain transports (TRANSPORTS); display and edit piece lists (PIECE LISTS); display all client transports (CLIENT); display, edit and maintain delivery transports (DELIVERY TRANSP.). You need the required authorization to execute transaction SE01.

SE03   Transport Organizer Tools

This transaction provides tools that you can use with Transport Organizer. The tools are organized under the following groupings: OBJECTS IN REQUESTS, OBJECTS, OBJECT DIRECTORY, and REQUESTS/TASKS.

SE06   Set Up Transport Organizer

You need to execute this transaction once in every newly installed SAP system. You can use SE06 to perform the following functionalities: Generate basic settings of the Change and Transport Organizer; close other requests and tasks; set the SYSTEM CHANGE option.

SE07   TMS Import Monitor

You can use this transaction to check the status of imports into one or more systems in the landscape. The status information displayed in the import monitor is read from the status information stored by the transport control program tp. Each system displays two pieces of information:

▶ Scheduling Job: This displays details such as name of the request, the user who scheduled this request, target client for client-specific imports, date and time of the job schedule.

▶ Execution: This displays the date, time and status of the import, and system message generated by the transport control program.

SE09   Transport Organizer

You can use this transaction to start the Workbench Organizer. You can use the workbench organizer to track changes to ABAP workbench objects. You can also access the Transport Organizer (transaction SE09) from transaction SE01 (Transport Organizer Extended View) by clicking the TRANSPORTS tab. At first glance, transactions SE09 and SE10 appear to be the same and call the same program RDDM0001. However, a closer look at the program reveals a different logic for each of the transactions.

SE10   Transport Organizer

You can use transaction SE10 to track customizing changes and to display customizing requests in the system. At first glance, transactions SE09 and SE10 appear to be the same and call the same program RDDM0001. However, a closer look at the program reveals a different logic for each of the transactions.

SE11   ABAP Dictionary Maintenance

You can use this transaction to view the ABAP dictionary of objects such as database tables, data types, search help, etc. You can also maintain the ABAP dictionary of the objects or create new objects.

SE12   ABAP Dictionary Display

You can use this transaction to display the ABAP dictionary of objects such as database tables, data types, search help, etc. Transaction SE12 can be used for display only.

SE14   Utilities for Dictionary Tables

You can use this transaction to edit all objects derived from the ABAP dictionary objects. In the database utility initial screen, enter the object name and select the relevant object type, to navigate to the relevant maintenance screen; for example, selecting TABLE as the object type will navigate you to the database table's maintenance screen. To be able to use this transaction, you need to be assigned authorization to the authorization object S_DDIC_OBJ.

SE15   ABAP/4 Repository Information System

You can use this transaction to open up the repository information browser. Using the browser, you can browse all repository objects, including the data dictionary, pro-

grams, classes, Web Dynpros, BSP library, etc. that currently exist in the system.

SE16/ SE16N   Data Browser

You can use this transaction to view the contents of a table. The limitation is that with this transaction you cannot change or add new fields to the existing table structure. Hence, you can use this transaction for display only. You can also use transaction SE16N – General Table Display to display the contents of a table. SE16N is the most recent version of transaction SE16 (Data Browser). It provides a number of improvements and enhanced functionality compared to transaction SE16. For example, in SE16N, ALV functionality is delivered as standard. If you have any performance issues while using transaction SE16N, refer to SAP Note 1004869 – Performance Problems in Transaction SE16N.

SE17   General Table Display

You can use this transaction to display the data in a specified table. In the DISPLAY TABLE selection screen, you can select which columns of the table are to be displayed in the output; the sort order of the output can be specified as well.

SE38   ABAP Editor

You can use this transaction to view the source code, attributes, variants, or documentation of the program. Using the ABAP Editor, you can also develop and debug programs in the SAP system. You can also use this transaction to execute a program or a report. It is a suggested best practice to restrict access to the ABAP Editor in the production environment.

SE63   Translation – Initial Screen

You can use this transaction to perform the translation of texts in R/3 enterprise objects,

OTR objects, and non-ABAP objects. You can also translate multiple objects via a worklist. From the initial screen of transaction SE63, you can access statistics, proposal pool, translation environment, and the translation planner. It is a prerequisite that, prior to executing the translation, you have defined the translator settings to meet your requirements; for example, make sure the source and target languages are correct.

SE80	Object Navigator

You can use this transaction to access the ABAP Development Workbench. You can use SE80, as a single integrated interface to access ABAP Editor, ABAP Dictionary, Menu Painter, Screen Painter, Function Builder, and Class Builder. In SE80, you can also choose one of the following browsers: MIME Repository, Test Repository, Repository Browser, Repository Information System, Tag Library, and Transport Organizer. It is a suggested best practice to restrict access to less frequently used browsers. To restrict access and selection, click UTILITIES (displayed in the task bar), select SETTINGS • WORKBENCH (GENERAL). Here you can select/deselect browsers that you would like to access.

SE93	Maintain Transaction Codes

You can use this transaction to create customer specific transaction codes. You can use these custom transaction codes to call a custom report or to support business requirements that are not available in delivered transaction codes. It is essential that you assign required authorizations to these custom transaction codes.

SF01	Client-Specific File Names

You can use this transaction to define a client-specific logical file name and logical path. You can use transaction FILE: Cross-Client File Names/Paths to define a cross-client

specific logical file name and path. Refer to SAP Note 40582 – Create New File Names via Transaction SF01 for details on how logical file names/paths are created and maintained. A client-specific definition always overrides a cross-client specific definition. Hence, it is important that you delete any unrequired client-specific definitions in every client in the system.

SF07	File Name Analysis

You can use this transaction to display and get an overview of the path name, file name definitions and their specifications for the respective syntax groups.

SFT2	Maintain Public Holiday Calendar

You can use this transaction to display a list of public holidays, holiday calendar or factory calendar. The holiday and the factory calendar are identified in the system, by a two-character calendar ID. The calendar hierarchy is Public Holidays, which is defined and combined into Public Holiday Calendars. A holiday calendar is included in every factory calendar.

SFW5	Switch Framework Customizing

You can use this transaction to activate and switch on the SAP delivered business functions. Using this transaction, you can display the activation logs or create a transport request with the current settings as well. When new business functions are made available by SAP (for example, during new enhancement pack releases), you can use this transaction to activate those business functions.

SGEN	SAP Load Generator

You can use this transaction to generate the ABAP loads of programs, function groups, classes, etc. You can also use this transaction to generate BSP applications of selected software components. The selection screen provides a number of options to select for a generation task. The report RSGENINVLAS can be periodically scheduled for an automatic regeneration of invalidated loads. Refer to SAP Note 438038 – Automatic Regeneration of Invalidated Loads for details on how to schedule the report RSGENINVLAS.

SHDB	Batch Input Transaction Recorder

You can use this transaction to record a series of transactions and their screens. The recording is later stored in the database under a twelve-digit name. The initial screen of the transaction recorder displays a list of available recordings. You can use these recordings to create batch input sessions, data transfer programs that use batch input, test data, and function modules. Each of these options is available as a menu option in the task bar.

SICF	HTTP Service Hierarchy Maintenance

You can use this transaction to maintain HTTP Services for HTTP communication in the SAP system. The communication is enabled using the Internet Communication Manager (ICM) and Internet Communication Framework (ICF). In the SAP system, every service has a list of HTTP request handlers, which are implemented as ABAP object classes. If a string containing a service or an alias for the service is defined in the URL of the calling request, the HTTP request handler for this service is called. These HTTP request handlers generate the required responses, which are sent to the client.

SICK	Installation Check

You can use this transaction to detect and identify any inconsistencies in the SAP system. After the install, when you log on to the system for the first time, you need to execute this transaction manually. After the first logon, this transaction is called automatically every time you start the server. The installation check determines whether the release number and character set mentioned in the SAP kernel match the data stored in the database system. Transaction SM28 provides the same functionality.

SIGS	IGS Administration

You can use this transaction for IGS administration. Executing this transaction displays the administration page of IGS. The administration page displays the static charts for the number of calls for each registered interpreter, as well the min/max/avg processing time for a chart per interpreter. From the administration page, you can also read the IGS log files of the multiplexer, and each registered portwatcher.

This transaction implements the report GRAPHICS_IGS_ADMIN. Hence it is not required that you use transaction SA38 or SE38 to implement this report. As a prerequisite to using transaction SIGS, you should have installed support package SAPKB70011. You are also required to implement SAP Note 988677 – New Transaction SIGS.

SLAW	License Administration Workbench

See transaction LICENSE_ADMIN for details.

SLDAPICUST	SLD API Customizing

You can use this transaction in the business system to define the SLD access data. The access data consists of the host and port of the SLD. The user ID and password are mentioned as well in the SLD access data.

SLDB	Logical Databases (Tree Structure)

You can use this transaction to display the logical databases in your system. Using any of the options available in the initial screen, you can get details such as the structure of the logical database or the database program of the logical database. If you have the right authorizations, you will be able to create new logical databases and maintain logical databases.

SLDCHECK	Test SLD Connection

You can use this transaction to test whether the System Landscape Directory (SLD) exists and to test the connection to the SLD.

SLICENSE	Administer SAP Licenses

You can use this transaction to manage the licenses of your SAP system. Using this transaction, you can display and get an overview of all the installed licenses, install a new SAP license or delete an installed license, and determine the hardware key of any host in the SAP system. You need to be assigned the authorization object (S_ADMI_FCD=SLIC) to be able to use this transaction.

SLIN	ABAP – Extended Program Check

You can use this transaction to perform an extended check on ABAP programs. In the initial screen, you can select the checks that are listed in the CHECKS group box; the transaction will execute those selected checks on the ABAP program. If you execute the optional STANDARD CHECK, the program will report those errors that are identified as critical.

SM01	Lock Transactions

You can use this transaction to lock or unlock transaction code(s) for general usage. This transaction should be available and used only by Basis administrators to avoid user misuse and inconsistencies.

SM02	System Messages

You can use this transaction to create system messages and broadcast it to users system-wide. In the SYSTEM MESSAGE CREATE screen, you can specify the client/server to which the message is to be sent. If these fields are blank or if you enter * (wildcard), the message will be broadcast to all users logged into the system. You can also specify the expiration date of this message.

SM04	User List

You can use this transaction to generate a list of users who are currently logged into the system. The terminal name and the transaction the user is currently executing are displayed as well. You can get the name of the server from the status bar displayed at the bottom of the screen.

SM12	Display and Delete Locks

You can use this transaction for lock management. Using this transaction, you can perform the following: display lock entries, based on the selection criteria; manually delete those locks that cannot be released; test the locks for any errors; monitor the locks that are set in the system.

Unless required, it is a suggested best practice never to delete locks manually. Unreleased locks are a pointer to a configuration or a development issue. When the issue is resolved, the locks will be released automatically.

SM13   Administrate Update Records

You can use this transaction for update management. Using this transaction, you can display update requests, change the status of update requests, delete update requests, display statistics about update requests, and debug any issues pertaining to update requests.

SM14   Update Program Administration

You can use this transaction to perform the following activities: control the update and display the update records; configure and maintain the update servers in the system; configure and maintain update server groups (Note: Servers can be assigned to a group); monitor and maintain the profile parameters that pertain to updates. You can access transaction SM14 from transaction SM13. In the initial screen, click the ADMINISTRATION button displayed in the UPDATE SYSTEM group to access the UPDATE PROGRAM ADMINISTRATION screen.

SM18   Reorganize Security Audit Log

You can use this transaction to delete old security audit logs.

SM19   Security Audit Configuration

You can use this transaction to define the activities that you wish to log in filters and in the security audit logs. Some of the activities and information that can be recorded are successful and unsuccessful logon (dialog/ RFC) attempts, any changes to the user master records, monitoring of activities being performed by a remote support user, etc.

SM20   Analysis of Security Audit Log

You can use this transaction to read the security audit log. The security audit log maintains a log of those activities that were specified for audit. These logs are accessed by auditors, who need to get a detailed overview of what is being executed in the SAP system. The information that is captured in the audit log can be displayed as an audit analysis report for easy reading and evaluation.

SM21   Online System Log Analysis

SAP logs all system errors, warnings, process messages and users who were locked out in a log file. You can use this transaction to display the entries and messages that are captured in the system log. In the selection screen, you can enter the selection criteria and results are displayed based on the entered selection.

SM28   Installation Check

See transaction SICK for details.

SM29   Model Transfer for Tables

Using the specified command file, the system copies the customizing settings from client zero to your client.

SM30   Call View Maintenance

You can use this transaction (also referred to as Extended Table Maintenance), to display and view entries in database tables. In SM30 initial screen, you have the option of three modes: DISPLAY (you can only display the table entries); CHANGE (you can change, delete, copy existing entries or create new entries); TRANSPORT (you can include entries from database tables in transport request).

Refer to SAP Note 28504 – Table Maintenance in R/3 (SM31, SM30) for details about this transaction.

SM31	Call View Maintenance

This transaction is obsolete. Refer to SAP Note 28504 – Table Maintenance in R/3 (SM31, SM30), for details about this transaction.

SM35	Batch Input Monitoring

You can use this transaction to get an overview of batch input sessions. In the selection criteria group, enter the selections, and the details are displayed in the table below. From the displayed results, highlight and double-click a record for further details and analysis. You can also use this transaction to explicitly start a batch input session.

SM35P	Batch Input – Log Monitoring

You can use this transaction to display and get an overview of batch input session logs. A detailed log of each batch input session that is processed is maintained. The log contains progress messages and error messages (if any) from the transactions that are processed. A session log is maintained only if the session is processed with KEEP option, if the session is aborted, or if an error is generated.

SM36	Schedule Background Job

You can use this transaction to define and schedule background jobs. If you are not familiar with transaction SM36, you can click the JOB WIZARD button (displayed in the toolbar) to schedule a background job. The job wizard will guide you through a step-by-step process to schedule a background job. You can also use transaction SM36WIZ to call the Job Wizard.

SM36WIZ	Job Definition Wizard

You can use this transaction to call the Job Wizard for scheduling background jobs.

SM37	Overview of Job Selection

You can use this transaction to perform a variety of functions related to monitoring and maintaining jobs. Using this transaction, you can perform the following functions: define jobs, schedule, reschedule, edit jobs and job steps, debug an active job, cancel/delete jobs, compare the specifications of several jobs, review job logs, release or cancel the release of jobs. This transaction replaces the obsolete transaction SM39.

SM38	Queue Maintenance Transaction

In SAP, ABAP function modules act as an interface for asynchronous data transfer. Prior to the transfer, the data are stored temporarily in the database in queues. You can use this transaction to administer and maintain queues and the queue processing logs.

SM39	Job Analysis

This transaction is obsolete and being replaced by SM37 (Overview of Job Selection).

SM49	Execute External OS Commands

You can use this transaction to execute external commands. For each external command, the system contains information about the OS command, the pre-defined parameters, and whether additional parameters are permitted to be used. The administrators can use this transaction to maintain a list of allowed external OS commands. You need to assign authorization object S_LOG_COM to users to be able to execute external commands. Refer to SAP Note 677435 – Overview: External Programs and External Commands to get more details about executing external commands.

SM50 Work Process Overview

You can use this transaction to get the current statuses of the work processes in the server you are currently logged onto. You can use this information to determine whether the server is working to full capacity, whether fine tuning is required, or whether you are required to perform any trouble shooting activities.

SM51 List of SAP Systems

You can use this transaction to get a list of application servers that are registered with the SAP Message Server. From the displayed results, select a record and click the specific button (displayed in the tool bar) to branch to SM50 – Work Process Overview, SM04 – User List, or SM21 – Online System Log Analysis to gather more details about the specific server.

SM54 TXCOM Maintenance

You can use this transaction to configure CPIC destinations for Secure Network Communications (SNC) protection. It is a prerequisite that SNC is activated on the application server and CPIC destination is identified. You can also execute transaction SM30 (Call View Maintenance) to configure CPIC destinations for SNC.

SM55 THOST Maintenance

In SAP, host names are only 8 characters long. You can use this transaction to assign an internal SAP short name (a short alias) to a host with a very long name. You can enter this short alias in the destination host name field. Refer to SAP Note 10743: Host Name Longer than 8 Characters for more details on how to use transaction SM55.

SM56 Number Range Buffer

You can use this transaction to administer the number range buffer. In the initial screen of SM56 (Number Range Buffer), you can see the statistics related to number range buffer. It is a prerequisite that you have activated buffering in the main memory for a number range object.

SM59 RFC Destinations (Display/Maintain)

You can use this transaction to define and establish a HTTP connection from an SAP system to an HTTP server. Using this transaction, you can establish an HTTP connection to an external server (connection type G), as well an HTTP connection to an ABAP system (connection type H).

SM61 Backgroup Control Objects Monitor

You can use this transaction to create server groups. These server groups can be used to run jobs in the background. Such a distribution of jobs maximizes optimal usage of server resources and greatly aids in load balancing.

SM62 Event History and Background Events

You can use this transaction to create and maintain an event. An event by itself does not do any processing. Using the jobs that were defined in transaction SM36, you can specify the newly created event as a "start condition." You can use transaction SM64: Manage Background Processing Events to manually trigger an event in your SAP system.

SM63	Display/Maintain Operating Mode Sets

You can use this transaction to maintain which operation mode should be defined for a specific time slot in a 24-hour time period (Time slots are usually defined in 1-hour cycles). You can specify operation mode sets as:

▶ NORMAL OPERATION: In this option, you can define your normal daily operation modes.
▶ EXCEPTION OPERATION: In this option, you can define a specific one-time operation mode.

The system will switch to the exception operation for the specific time slot, one time only. After the execution of the exception operation, the system will switch back to normal operation.

SM64	Manage Background Processing Events

You can use this transaction to manually trigger an event in your SAP system.

SM65	Background Processing Analysis Tools

You can use this transaction to check and validate the consistency of the background processes. The initial screen displays the selections for the simple test. To execute an expert mode test, select GO TO • ADDITIONAL TESTS from the menu bar; the selection screen for an expert mode test is displayed. Make sure there are no background jobs running when you are executing the transaction SM65. The transaction locks the table TBTCO during execution and unlocks it when the analysis is complete.

SM66	Systemwide Work Process Overview

You can use this transaction to get an overview of work process load and view what may be causing the performance degradation. Using this transaction, you can view and monitor the work process load on all active instances in the system, identify locks in the database, identify which users are currently logged on and in which client, and view any report that is currently being executed.

SM69	Execute External OS Commands

See transaction SM49 for details.

SMGW	Gateway Monitor

You can use this transaction to monitor the gateway from the SAP system. You can use this transaction to analyze and administer the gateway. A number of functions for gateway monitoring are available in the menu. For example, you can increase the trace level of the gateway trace by following the menu path GO TO • TRACE • GATEWAY • INCREASE LEVEL. Every instance of an SAP system has a gateway. This gateway enables communication between work processes and external programs. The gateway also enables communication between work processes from different instances of SAP systems. You can also run the gateway monitor at the OS level and outside the SAP system.

SMICM	ICM Monitor

You can use this transaction to monitor and administrate the Internet Communication Manager (ICM). ICM is used to send and receive HTTP requests to and from the Internet. From the menu on the initial screen, the following functions are available: monitor the state of ICM, monitor and administrate the ICM server cache, display and change services, and administrate ICM.

SMLG   CCMS: Maintain Logon Groups

You can use this transaction for the following functionalities: to create a logon group or add an instance to a logon group, to delete a logon group or delete an instance from a logon group, to change properties of a logon group or an instance in the logon group. The logon group SPACE is SAP-reserved; hence, do not use it to name a customer logon group.

SMLT   Language Management

You can use this transaction for language management and to import additional language packages into the SAP system. By default, English and German are installed in all new SAP systems and are not required to be imported again. You can use transaction SMLT_EX – Language Export to create language packages. The transaction is wizard driven and takes you through the selection screens, which facilitates ease of user inputs.

SMMS   Message Server Monitor

Message servers are an important component of SAP SLD. The task of the message server is to inform all the instances in a SAP system about the existence of other instances. Other clients communicate with the message server to get information about load balancing. You can use this transaction to monitor and administrate the message server. You can access all the functions available to monitor the message server from the menu option GO TO.

SMOD   SAP Enhancement Management

You can use this transaction to maintain the enhancements. In SMOD you can see a list of objects contained in an enhancement.

SMQ1   qRFC Monitor (Outbound Queue)

qRFC denotes Queued Remote Function Call. Remote Function Call is an interface that manages the task of applications communicating with one another. This communication can be between internal applications or an SAP application communicating with a third party vendor application.

You can use this transaction to get an overview and monitor the status of the LUW (Logical Unit of Work) in the outbound queue. You can restart any hanging queues manually. In the selection screen, you can select the option WAITING QUEUES ONLY if you want to display those queues that have errors.

SMQ2   qRFC Monitor (Inbound Queue)

You can use this transaction to monitor the status of the LUWs in the inbound queue. It is assumed that qRFC with an inbound queue always means that an outbound queue exists in the client system.

SMQ3   qRFC Monitor (Saved E-Queue)

You can use this transaction to monitor the status of LUWs in the saved inbound queue.

SMQE   qRFC Administration

You can use this transaction for qRFC administration, as well for registering/de-registering events. A host of functionalities are available in the menu. For example, you can access the qRFC Monitor (Outbound Queue) by following the menu path GO TO • MONITOR • OUTBOUND QUEUE.

SMQR	Registration of inbound Queues

Use this transaction to register an inbound queue.

SMQS	Registration of Destinations

You can use this transaction to register, deregister, and exclude destinations. You also have the option to REGISTER WITHOUT ACTIVATION. In this option, the queue is not triggered immediately by the outbound scheduler. The other available functionalities in this transaction are TRFC Monitor to activate the tRFC monitor and QRFC Monitor to activate the qRFC monitor.

SMT1	Trusted Systems (Display <-> Maint.)

In SAP, you can establish trusted relationships between systems. In a trusted relationship, no passwords are required, and SSO is possible. To enable the trusted relationships, you need to register the calling SAP system in the called SAP system as a trusted system. The trusted relationship is valid in one direction only. You can use this transaction to register the calling system in the called system as a trusted system.

SMX	Display Own Jobs

You can use this transaction to display your own jobs. When you execute this transaction, all active, completed, and cancelled jobs are displayed. Refer to SAP Note 846002 – Changes in transaction SMX for details about this transaction. You can use transaction SMXX – Display Own Jobs for a display only of all your own background jobs. The user will not be allowed to carry out any other functions or processes. Refer to SAP Note 912117 – New transaction SMXX (display all own jobs) for more details about this new transaction.

SNOTE	Note Assistant

You can use this transaction to implement SAP Notes. In the initial screen you will see a worklist that contains SAP Notes assigned to you as a user, all SAP Notes that are inconsistent (includes SAP Notes that are assigned to other users), and new SAP Notes to be processed.

SNRO	Number Range Objects

You can use this transaction to create and maintain a number range object. A number range object must be maintained to enable number ranges to be used. You can also use this transaction for number range buffering.

SNUM	Number Range Objects

See transaction SNRO for details.

SP00	Spool and Related Areas

You can use this transaction to display an area menu related to spool. The SAP Easy Access menu tree structure displays the transactions that are related to spool and related areas.

SP01	Output Controller

You can use this transaction to display and access reports (or other outputs) located in your SAP spool. The reports remain in the spool for seven days, after which it will be automatically deleted by the system.

SP02	Display Spool Requests

You can use this transaction to display and get an overview of spool requests. In the displayed list, if you click the DOCUMENT icon (displayed in the column TYPE), the document is displayed. You can also print directly from the spool list.

SP11   TemSe Directory

Objects that are not stored permanently in the system are stored in the TemSe. For example, the spool system stores the output data temporarily in TemSe. You can use this transaction to display the TemSe objects.

SP12   TemSe Administration

You can use this transaction to manage and administer TemSe objects. Using this transaction, you can administer the character set buffer used by the spool system, as well.

SPAD   Spool Administration

This transaction is intended for administrators only or for users with administration authorization. You can use this transaction for defining output devices in the SAP system, for analyzing printing problems, and for maintaining and administering the spool database. Refer to SAP Note 1036961 – Device Type Selection Wizard in Transaction SPAD for details about output device creation and the selection wizard, available in transaction SPAD.

SPAM   Support Package Manager

You can use this transaction to import SAP Support Packages into your SAP system. SAP releases support packages regularly and are made available in the SAP Service Marketplace (*http://service.sap.com/patches*).

SPAU   Display Modified DE Objects

You can use this transaction to process objects that require adjustment after an upgrade or an import. In the selection screen, you can enter the selection criteria and the overview screen displays all objects that have been modified. Transactions SPAU and SPDD provide similar functionalities.

SPDD   Display Modified DDIC Objects

During an upgrade, objects that were modified by the customer are overwritten by the delivered objects. You can use this transaction to adjust modifications to the objects during an upgrade. All objects that were modified with the Modification Assistant are displayed with a green or yellow traffic light. All objects that were modified without a Modification Assistant are displayed with a yellow or red traffic light. Transactions SPDD and SPAU provide similar functionalities.

SPRO   Customizing – Edit Project

You can use this transaction to access the SAP Reference IMG (Implementation Guide). In the IMG, you can access the standard settings and configure them for specific customer requirements.

SPRO_ADMIN   Customizing – Project Management

You can use this transaction to create and maintain customizing projects. You can define the project scope by manual selection of nodes in the reference IMG, selecting the required countries and application components. You can later generate a project IMG based on these selections. The initial screen of SPRO_ADMIN will display the existing customizing projects. To use transaction SPRO_ADMIN to create a customizing project, you need to be assigned the authorizing object S_PROJECT.

SPROXY   Enterprise Repository Browser

You can use this transaction to create and maintain proxies for all object types that you have modeled in the enterprise services repository. Using the enterprise repository browser, you can check, regenerate, and activate proxies. You can also use the enterprise repository browser to display and view the structure of the objects in the enterprise services repository.

SQ01	SAP Query – Maintain Queries

You can use this transaction to create, change, display and execute queries for a specific user group. Using SQ01, you can get a listing of existing queries in the system. The query table in the initial screen will display details such as name of the query, short text, the infoset based on which this query was created, the name of the logical database, and the short text of the infoset.

SQ02	SAP Query – Maintain Infoset

You can use this transaction to create, change, and display infosets. Using this transaction, you can also assign infosets to user groups. The initial screen will display details such as name of the infoset, short text of the infoset, data source, the author of the infoset, and the time stamp.

SQ03	SAP Query – Maintain User Groups

You can use this transaction to create, change, and display user groups. Using this transaction, you can also assign infosets and users to user groups. From the initial screen, you will be able to initiate transports of queries, infosets, and user groups.

SQVI	Quickviewer

You can use this transaction to create one-off reports or user-specific query reports. The query reports developed using the SAP Quickviewer tool cannot be exchanged between clients or between SAP systems. The query reports developed using the SAP Quickviewer are user dependent; hence,

these queries do not require assignment to user groups.

SRMO	SAP Retrieval – Monitor

You can use this transaction to display the RETRIEVAL: SEARCH SERVER RELATION MONITOR. You can use the transaction to change or delete settings for:

▶ Search Server Relation (SSR): SSR contains information about which search engine and which RFC destination the service uses. It is a prerequisite that SSR must be defined for an index category to be created.

▶ RFC destinations

▶ Index category: this is relevant only if TREX is implemented outside the portal.

SAP recommends using the Search Server Relation Monitor if there are problems with an index category or if you want to delete an index category. You can use transaction SRMO to perform a TREX RFC setup test between TREX and application server.

SSAA	System Administration Assistant

You can use this transaction to get an overview of the most important and most frequent system administration tasks in a single location. You get an overview in a hierarchical tree structure, where the tasks are grouped into logical areas and sorted according to periodicity. At the end of the structure, the tasks and the related documentation are displayed. For SAP NetWeaver 7.0 and later releases, SAP recommends using SAP Solution Manager as a replacement for transaction SSAA.

ST01	System Trace

You can use this transaction to record the system activities of your SAP system. The system trace is normally used when an authorization trace is to be used. Using ST01, you can monitor the following components: Authorization Checks, Kernel Functions, General Kernel, DB Access (SQL Trace), Table Buffer Trace, RFC Calls, Lock Operations. You can also use transaction ST05: Performance Analysis to monitor the following components: DB Access (SQL Trace), Table Buffer Trace, RFC Calls, Lock Operations.

| ST02 | Setups/Tune Buffers |

You can use this transaction to get an overview of the current and maximum memory usage for a SAP instance where the user is logged on. The table displays the values for the various SAP memory types, such as SAP Roll Area, SAP Extended Memory and Private Memory. The table also displays the amount of space used in memory and on disk; information about buffer used for the instance where the user is currently logged on; buffer-related information such as hit ratio, buffer quality, allocated size, free space, number of directories, swapping,and database accesses.

| ST03 | Workload and Performance Statistics |

You can use this transaction to view and analyze data from the SAP Kernel. The transaction displays data such as distribution of response times, table accesses, memory usage for each user or transaction, workload related data, etc. You can use these data to analyze the performance of the SAP system or to compare performances of individual instances over a defined period of time. Using these data, you can determine the reasons for the performance downgrade.

| ST03N | Workload Monitor |

You can use this transaction to analyze statistical data from the SAP Kernel. This transaction completely replaces transaction ST03.

| ST03G | Global Workload Statistics |

Using ST03G, you can display and get an overview of statistical records for the entire landscape, for both ABAP and non-ABAP systems. Using these data, you can analyze and determine the workload of the monitored systems in greater detail. Transaction ST03G is similar in operation to transaction ST03 and uses the functions of ST03 when you analyze the workload of ABAP systems.

| ST04 | DB Performance Monitor |

You can use this transaction to monitor the performance of the database. Using this transaction, you can check and monitor important indicators, such as database size, database buffer, database indexes, table scans, redo log buffer, etc. You can execute transaction ST04 from any application server in the SAP landscape. You can use transaction ST04RFC – SAP Remote DB Monitor for SQL Server for remote database monitoring of SQL*Server database. Refer to SAP Note 530317 – Sql Server 2000 Profiler Trace for details on how to start a SQL profiler trace. You can use transaction ST04_MSS – ST04 for MS-SQL*Server to monitor a SQL Server database from a non-SQL Server SAP Application Server. Using this transaction, you can display and get an overview of the parameters and performance indicators in SQL Server for further analysis. This transaction is being replaced by transaction DBACOCKPIT.

| ST05 | Performance Analysis |

Use this transactions to monitor the following components: DB Access (SQL Trace), Table Buffer Trace, RFC Calls, Lock Operations.

| ST06/ ST06N | Operating System Monitor |

You can use this transaction to display the following details: memory requirements, swap space, CPU, disk with highest response time, etc. for the operating system of your SAP system. ST06N is the new operating system monitor. This transaction completely replaces transaction ST06 and is available as of Basis release 7.0

| ST07 | Application Monitor |

You can use this transaction to get details about the number of users currently logged into the individual SAP application modules. Using the options available in the menu bar, you can get additional details such as SAP buffer, DB accesses, DB memory, response time, etc. In the application monitor, the data are grouped according to the SAP application components. From the initial view, you can drill down to get a more detailed view of the modules and also determine which modules or transactions are using the most system resources.

When you click the HISTORY option, if no data are displayed, it may be because the program RSAMON40 has not been started yet. It is a suggested best practice to run the program RSAMON40 on a regular basis or schedule it as a background job. The program RSAMON40 generates snapshots of the data displayed in the application monitor and saves them to the database.

| ST10 | Table Call Statistics |

You can use this transaction to display details such as the number of table changes, direct reads, sequential reads, number of rows affected, etc. at the table level. You can display the data as daily, weekly, or monthly summaries.

| ST11 | Display Developer Traces |

You can use this transaction to display trace files from within the SAP system. You can also display trace files at the operating system

level by accessing the work directory of the specific SAP application server. It is a suggested best practice to display trace file from within the SAP system. You can download trace files to your local drive by executing the report RSMON000_DOWNLOAD_TRACES.

| ST12 | Single Transaction Analysis |

Transaction ST12 combines ABAP and SQL trace into a single transaction with major functional enhancements for ABAP tracing. ST12 is similar to a combination of ABAP and SQL trace, transactions SE30 (ABAP Objects Runtime Analysis) and ST05 (Performance Analysis). Refer to SAP Note 755977 – ST12 "ABAP Trace for SAP EarlyWatch/GoingLive" for more details and documentation about transaction ST12.

| ST13 | Analysis & Monitoring Tool Collection |

Transaction ST13 maintains a list of analysis/service tools and is a launch pad for these tools. In the initial screen, in the field TOOL NAME, if you click [F4] a dialog box with a list of Analysis/Service tools is displayed. Selecting any of these tools will take you to that particular transaction.

| ST14 | Application Analysis |

You use this transaction primarily during SAP GoingLive session. Batch jobs collect performance-relevant data, such as document statistics and customizing settings. These analysis results can be viewed as a tree and downloaded into a service session for further analysis. Refer to SAP Note 69455 – Service Tools for Applications ST-A/PI (ST14, RTC-CTOOL, ST12) for details and documentation about transactions ST13 and ST14.

ST20	Screen Trace

This transaction provides a graphical navigation tool to analyze screen trace files. The trace files can be loaded directly from the application server or from the local presentation server.

ST22	ABAP Dump Analysis

You can use this transaction to analyze runtime errors. In the selection screen, enter the criteria and execute the selection. In the LIST OF SELECTED RUNTIME ERRORS screen, highlight and double-click the specific runtime error that you wish to analyze. In the RUNTIME ERROR LONG TEXT screen, different options are available for you to identify and debug the cause of runtime error.

STAD	Statistics Displays for All Systems/Business Transaction Analysis

You can use this transaction to display and get an overview of all the statistics of a specific user (or users) and clients on selected application servers. These statistical data are related to user transactions, background processing, or are application-specific.

STCTRL_ COPY	Copy Table Control User Settings

You can use this transaction to copy display variants for other users by using an existing variant as a template. Where required, you can make copies between different clients. By default, you make copies only in the current client.

STF3	Maintain Factory Calendar

See transaction SFT2 for details.

STMS	Transport Management System (TMS)

You can use this transaction to organize, perform, and monitor transports between SAP systems. Using this transaction, you can perform the following functions: configure transport routes using a graphical editor, display import queues, import requests, perform transport workflow, and perform TMS quality assurance. You can use the following transactions to access the TMS: STMS_QUEUES (TMS Import Overview), STMS_IMPORT (TMS Import Queue), STMS_INBOX (TMS Worklist), STMS_QA (TMS Quality Assurance), STMS_DOM (TMS System Overview), STMS_PATH (TMS Transport Routes), STMS_ALERT (TMS Alert Monitor), STMS_TCRI (Display/Maintain Table TMSTCRI), and STMS_FSYS (Maintain TMS System Lists).

STMS_ MONI	TMS Import Monitor

See transaction SE07 for details.

STUN	Menu Performance Monitor

You can use this transaction to display the transactions related to performance monitoring as a tree structure in the SAP Easy Access. This transaction is not available in versions SAP R/3 4.6x. SAP Note 948066 – Performance Analysis: Transactions to Use is an important SAP Note that you may wish to refer to, to gather details on what transactions are available and can be used to analyze performance problems in SAP systems.

SU0	Maintain Own Fixed User Values

A user can use this transaction to set up details such as default printer, personal time zone, date format, time format, decimal notation, etc. The values that the user sets up here will be set as default every time the user logs into the SAP system.

SU01 — User Maintenance

You can use this transaction to create, maintain, and administer users and user master records. You can also create a new user by copying an existing user. When you create a new user by the copy method, you can select the parts that need to be inherited. Other user administration tasks that can be performed are managing users, user groups, and roles; locking/unlocking users; password maintenance.

SU01D — User Display

You can use this transaction to display user master records. This is a display-only transaction and no changes can be made to the user master records.

SU05_OLD — Maintain Internet Users

This transaction is obsolete and is no longer supported. Refer to SAP Note 593439 – SU05 "Maintain Internet Users" – No Further Development for details.

SU1 — Maintain Own User Address

A user can use this transaction to set up and maintain personal addresses (except e-mail). These include details such as title, academic title, language, phone numbers, etc. It is a suggested best practice that a user's e-mail address can be changed only by the system administrator.

SU10 — User Mass Maintenance

You can use this transaction for mass user administration. You can use this transaction to create multiple or mass number of users (user IDs and passwords) in one step. You can select the users either by address data or authorization data. You can also use this transaction for user maintenance of multiple users in one go.

SU22 — Authorizations Object Usage in Transactions

You can use this transaction to maintain the assignment of authorization objects to the applications (manually assign the authorization object or delete the assignment). Using this transaction, you can also maintain the default values of the assigned authorization objects. The data built here form the basis of role authorization creation by transaction PFCG. In the initial screen, the field TYPE OF APPLICATION has a DDL with the different types of application: transaction, RFC function module, TADIR service, and external service.

SU3 — Maintain Users Own Data

You can use this transaction to set up and maintain personal data. These include address (can be maintained by transaction SU1), defaults (can be maintained by transaction SU0), and parameters (can be maintained by transaction SU2).

SU53 — Evaluate Authorization Check

You can use this transaction to get an overview of the access-denied errors and to perform authorization error analysis. The output will display the last failed authorization check, the user's authorizations, and the failed HR authorization check.

SU56 — Analyze User Buffer

You can use this transaction to get a list of authorization objects assigned to a user. This transaction displays the authorization objects for the user who is executing this transaction. Details such as server name, server instance, client, and the number of authorizations assigned to the user are also displayed. This is a very useful transaction that helps a user to verify what authorizations are assigned to him or her.

SUIM	User Information System

This is a very useful transaction to display and get an overview of authorization profiles of a user. A number of options are available in the user information system menu tree for querying and displaying the users who are granted a particular authorization, etc.

SUPC	Role Profiles

You can use this transaction to generate profiles for activity groups who do not yet have a current profile. If you have created an activity group for a future need, you can use this transaction to create an authorization profile for that activity group.

SWDD	Workflow Builder

You can use this transaction to call the Workflow Builder. The Workflow Builder is the main tool to create, process, and display workflow definitions. Using this transaction, you can also test the workflow definitions and generate executable versions.

SWDD_ CONFIG	Workflow Configuration

You can use this transaction to configure a workflow. By configuring a workflow, you can define values for every step of the workflow definition. These values are evaluated at runtime and take precedence over the values in the workflow definition.

SWDM	Business Workflow Explorer

You can use this transaction to display and get an overview of all tasks for the specified search range. In the Business Workflow Explorer, you can create new tasks/workflows; you can also process the tasks that are displayed.

SWEL	Display Event Trace

You can use the event trace to check for any errors that might be generated in event-driven workflows.

SWU3	Automatic Workflow Customizing

You can use this transaction to execute all activities that pertain to technical basic settings. You can execute START VERIFICATION WORKFLOW to start a workflow that will test the workflow environment. You can execute CHECK EVENT LINKAGES to conduct a validation check of existing event linkages.

SXDA	Data Transfer Workbench

You can use this transaction for an initial automatic transfer of data into the SAP system. This ensures that data are transferred efficiently and that the transferred data are consistent. The data load file needs to be in SAP format and is loaded into the SAP system using a BAPI interface, as a batch input, or by direct input. The data transfer workbench also provides tools for analyzing the required SAP structures. You can also use this transaction to create, maintain, and administer data transfer projects.

SXMB_ ADMIN	Integration Engine – All Functions

You can use this transaction to display a menu tree combining the transactions for monitoring, configuration, and administration of XML messages.

SXMB_IFR	Start Integration Builder

You can use the Integration Builder to define all objects for the integration repository either during the design time or during the configuration time.

SYSADM_ TASK	System Administration – Task List

You can use this transaction to get a listing of all periodic administrative tasks. The initial screen displays the basic list, and the task list is sorted alphabetically by system name. The legend for the status information:

▶ A red light means the task has not been executed on time.

▶ A green light means the task has been executed on time.

▶ A gray light means the system cannot be accessed remotely.

▶ A yellow light means the remote connection to the system is currently broken and there are no status updates for the tasks in this system.

You can access the task list by executing the report RSSAA_WORKPLACE. The output of this report will display a reduced list only.

TAANA	Table Analysis

You can use this transaction to analyze how table entries are distributed across specific fields. To perform a table analysis, you always require an analysis variant (use transaction TAANA_AV – Table Analysis: Analysis Variants). You can also use this transaction to display, delete and re-organize table analysis; create ad hoc analysis variants; create virtual fields (use transaction TAANA_VF – Table Analysis: Virtual Fields). If you wish to analyze multiple tables in a single step, you can execute the program TAAN_PROCESS_MULTIPLE using transaction SA38.

You can display the results of the analysis in transaction TAANA.

TREXADMIN	TREX Administration Tool

You can use this transaction to administer TREX, the delivered search engine for SAP systems. Using this transaction, you can display information about the TREX component, monitor TREX, administer the queues and indexes.

UCCHECK	Unicode Syntax Check

You can use this transaction to check a program set for syntax errors in a Unicode environment. By using this transaction, you can bypass the requirement to set the attribute UNICODE CHECKS ACTIVE for every program. In the output list, if any errors are displayed, you can navigate directly to the specific program and correct the errors. Using this transaction, you can create transport requests as well.

USMM	Customer Measurement

You can use this transaction to exclusively determine the number of users and the utilized units of SAP products. The results of the system measures are consolidated in the License Administration Workbench (transaction SLAW) and the consolidated measurement results are transferred to SAP.

WE02	Display IDoc

You can use this transaction to view and monitor IDocs. The selection screen has a variety of options that you can use to restrict the selection. For example, you can use the IDoc number or basic type to display a list of IDocs. You can access WE02 from area access menu WEDI. There is little or no difference between transaction WE02 and transaction WE05. Both are attached to the program RSEIDOC2.

WE05 | IDoc Lists

See transaction WE02 for details.

WE06 | Active IDoc Monitoring

You can use this transaction to monitor inbound and outbound processing of IDocs. Reports and graphic displays are available, which aids in IDoc monitoring. For example, you can run the active monitoring report on a regular basis, and if too many incorrect IDocs are found, a predefined recipient will automatically receive a workflow notification about the status.

WE07 | IDoc Statistics

You can use this transaction to display and get an overview of IDoc statistics. For example, in the selection screen, if you choose the option ERROR HISTORY, this transaction will display all IDocs (inbound and outbound) that are currently in Error Status, IDocs whose errors are resolved, and IDocs that are marked for deletion.

WE19 | Test Tool

You can use this transaction to generate an IDoc manually, without restriction to any specific port type. This is particularly useful for testing new IDoc types. You can also use an old IDoc as a template and edit the IDoc (by adding segments or changing data) to meet your requirements. You can use this IDoc for inbound or outbound processing.

WE20 | Partner Profiles

You can use this transaction to create partner profiles for partners with whom you wish to communicate via IDocs. Using this transaction, you can create profiles for inbound and outbound partners.

WE21 | Port Definition

Ports are essential for communicating via IDocs. You can use this transaction to create and maintain port definition for any of the delivered and supported port types: file interface, CPI-C connection to the R/2 system, ABAP programming interface, and port type XML (XML file and XML HTTP).

WE46 | Error and Status Processing

You can use this transaction to assign processors by workflow tasks, to process errors, and to provide status inputs.

WE47 | Status Maintenance

You can use this transaction to maintain the status at which process codes are active. For example, you can maintain certain IDoc statuses as archivable. Using this transaction, select the status code from the displayed list and maintain the archivability. The status values for inbound IDocs are maintained between status codes 50-99. The status values for outbound IDocs are maintained between status codes 01-49.

WEDI | EDI Basis

You can use this transaction to display an area menu related to EDI and IDoc. The SAP Easy Access menu tree structure displays the transactions related to EDI.

The Authors

Venki Krishnamoorthy is an author, speaker, and SAP ERP HCM talent management solutions subject matter expert. He is currently an SAP ERP HCM functional consultant with SAP America. Venki Krishnamoorthy has over 10 years of experience as a functional lead and project manager/program manager in the HCM space. Besides implementing SAP HCM solutions, he has implemented and acted as a trusted advisor on SAP ERP HCM talent management implementations including E-Recruiting, HCM Performance Management, Succession Planning, SAP Talent Visualization by Nakisa, and Employee Self-Service and Manager Self-Services. You can reach him via email at *venki.krish@ymail.com*.

Martin Murray joined the computer industry upon his graduation from Middlesex University in 1986. In 1991, he began working with SAP R/2 in the materials management area for a London-based multinational beverage company, and in 1994, he moved to the United States to work as an SAP R/3 consultant. Since then, he has been implementing the Materials Management (SAP MM) and Warehouse Management (SAP WM) functionality in projects throughout the world. He is employed by IBM Global Business Services.

Martin is the author of the best-selling book *Materials Management with SAP ERP: Functionality and Technical Configuration (3rd Edition)*, as well as *SAP Warehouse Management, Discover Logistics with SAP ERP, Maximize Your Warehouse Operations with SAP ERP* and *Understanding the SAP Logistics Information System*.

Norman Reynolds is an information technology professional with a passion for process improvement. Expert in SAP functionality, tools, and management techniques required to create first-class process designs quickly and consistently, Norman specializes in helping companies develop practical solutions to resolve the difficult business process issues that come with complex organizations. In 1994, he began working with SAP R/2 in the finance area for a London-based multinational oil company, and in 1996, he moved to the United States to work as an SAP R/3 consultant. Since then, he has been implementing SAP Finance, Controlling, and Sales and Distribution functionality throughout the world. He is an Independent SAP Certified Consultant and can be reached via email at *nreynoldsatlanta@ yahoo.com*.

Index

B

D

E

I

L

M

O

P

Q

S

V

W

X

Y

Z

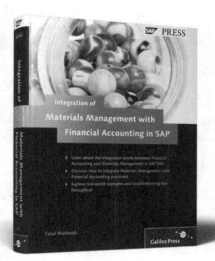

Gives a detailed overview of the finance integration points in materials management

Teaches how to integrate MM with the Financial Accounting and Controlling components of SAP ERP Financials

Provides best practices and real-world examples of various logistics business transactions

Faisal Mahboob

Integration of Materials Management with Financial Accounting in SAP

If you work with Materials Management and SAP ERP Financials, this book teaches you about the intersection points between them. It explains how to configure the system effectively to streamline your business processes and continually improve your procurement processes. You'll learn about account and controlling postings, and their impact on MM functional design and configuration. With the practical examples, troubleshooting techniques, and step-by-step instructions, this is the must-have guide you need to master MM and FI integration.

429 pp., 2010, 79,95 Euro / US$ 79.95
ISBN 978-1-59229-337-7

>> www.sap-press.com